CENGAGE

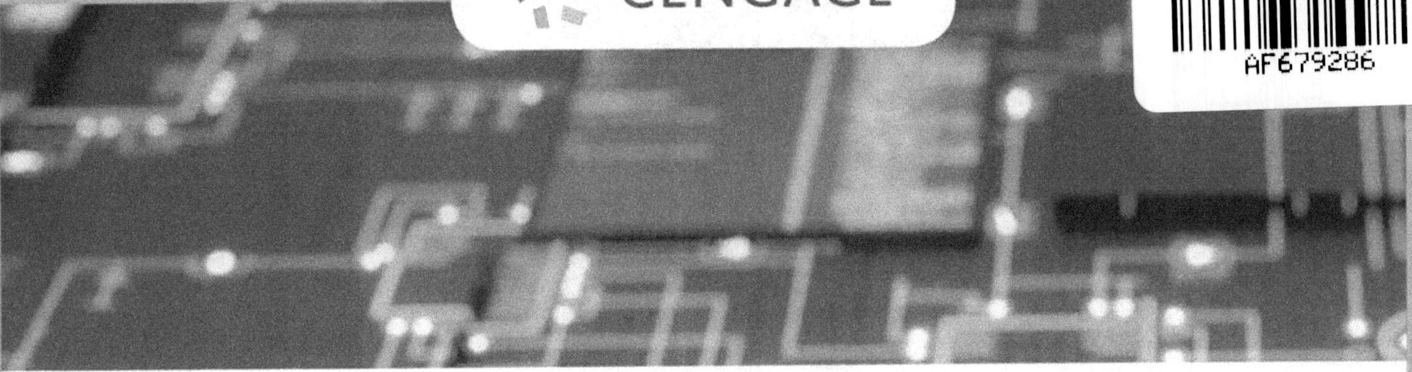

FIFTH EDITION

Legal and Ethical Aspects of

HEALTH INFORMATION MANAGEMENT

Dana C. McWay, JD, RHIA, FAHIMA

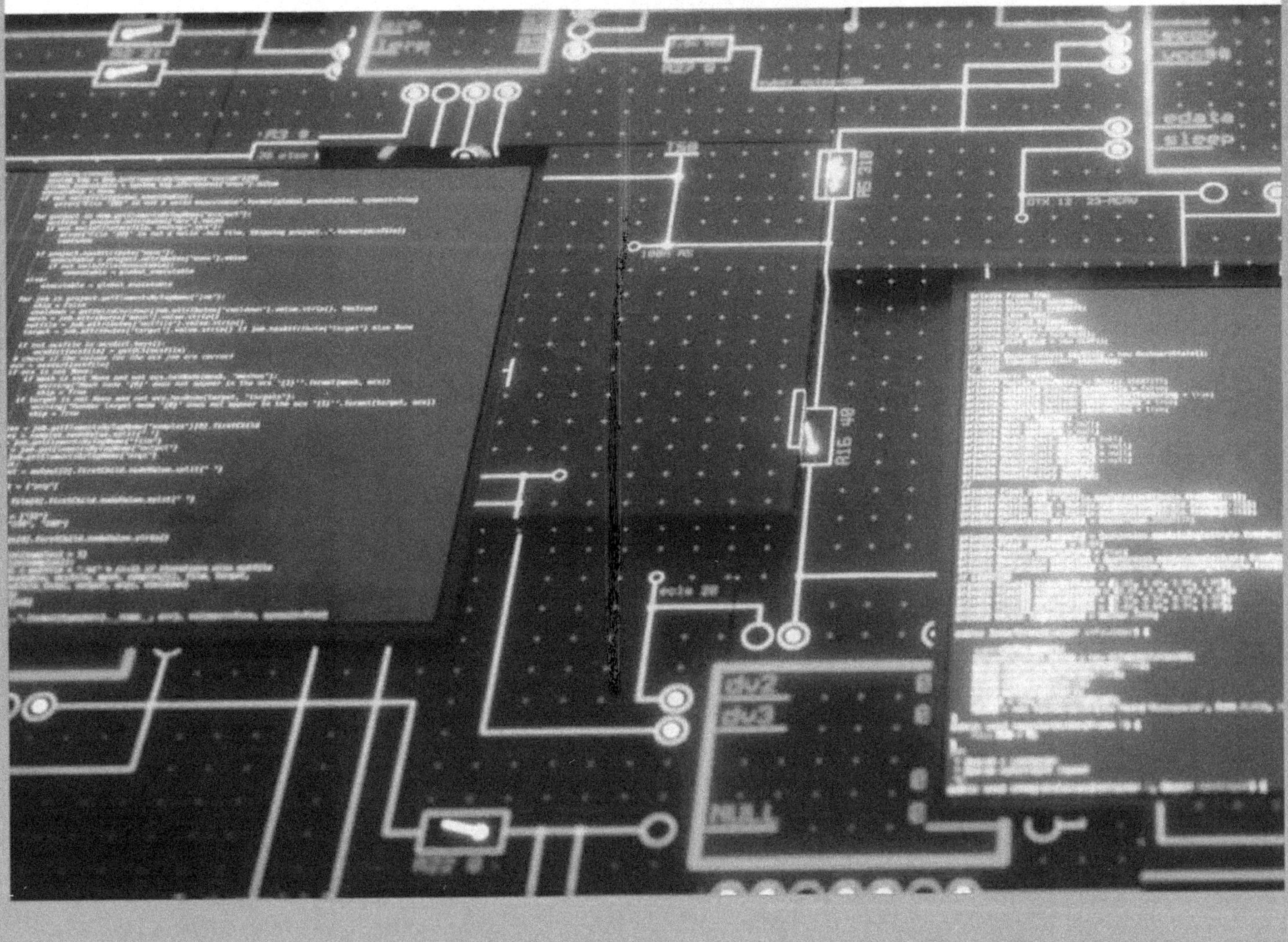

FIFTH EDITION

Legal and Ethical Aspects of HEALTH INFORMATION MANAGEMENT

Dana C. McWay, JD, RHIA, FAHIMA

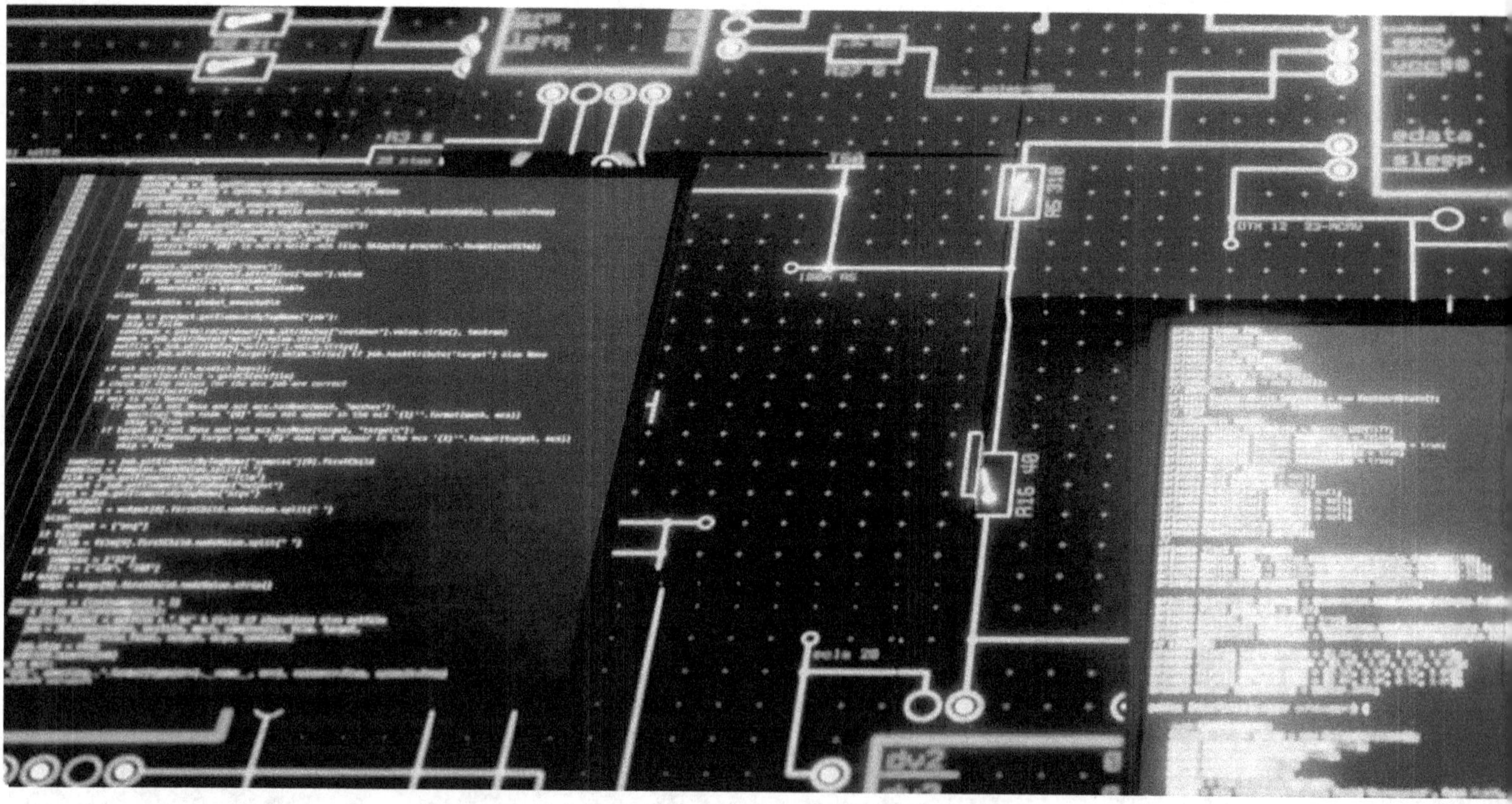

CENGAGE

Australia • Brazil • Mexico • Singapore • United Kingdom • United States

CENGAGE

***Legal and Ethical Aspects of Health Information Management*, Fifth Edition**
Dana C. McWay JD, RHIA, FAHIMA

SVP, Higher Education & Skills Product: Erin Joyner

Product Director: Matthew Seeley

Product Manager: Lauren Whalen

Product Assistant: Dallas Wilkes

Director, Learning Design: Rebecca von Gillern

Senior Manager, Learning Design: Leigh Hefferon

Learning Designer: Debbie Bordeaux

Marketing Director: Sean Chamberland

Marketing Manager: Jonathan Sheehan

Director, Content Creation: Juliet Steiner

Content Creation Manager: Stacey Lamodi

Senior Content Manager: Thomas Heffernan

Digital Delivery Lead: David O'Conner

Design Director: Jack Pendleton

Senior Designer: Angela Sheehan

Cover image: iStockPhoto.com/matejmo

For product information and technology assistance, contact us at **Cengage Customer & Sales Support, 1-800-354-9706** or **support.cengage.com.**

For permission to use material from this text or product, submit all requests online at **www.cengage.com/permissions.**

Library of Congress Control Number: 2019912839

ISBN: 978-0-357-36154-2

Cengage
200 Pier 4 Boulevard
Boston, MA 02210
USA

Cengage is a leading provider of customized learning solutions with employees residing in nearly 40 different countries and sales in more than 125 countries around the world. Find your local representative at **www.cengage.com.**

Cengage products are represented in Canada by Nelson Education, Ltd.

To learn more about Cengage platforms and services, register or access your online learning solution, or purchase materials for your course, visit **www.cengage.com.**

Notice to the Reader

Publisher does not warrant or guarantee any of the products described herein or perform any independent analysis in connection with any of the product information contained herein. Publisher does not assume, and expressly disclaims, any obligation to obtain and include information other than that provided to it by the manufacturer. The reader is expressly warned to consider and adopt all safety precautions that might be indicated by the activities described herein and to avoid all potential hazards. By following the instructions contained herein, the reader willingly assumes all risks in connection with such instructions. The publisher makes no representations or warranties of any kind, including but not limited to, the warranties of fitness for particular purpose or merchantability, nor are any such representations implied with respect to the material set forth herein, and the publisher takes no responsibility with respect to such material. The publisher shall not be liable for any special, consequential, or exemplary damages resulting, in whole or part, from the readers' use of, or reliance upon, this material.

Printed in the United States of America
Print Number: 01 Print Year: 2019

BRIEF CONTENTS

CONTENTS

Dedicated to
Patrick, Conor, William, and Ryan for their patience and encouragement throughout the development and revision of this text.

PREFACE

INTRODUCTION

The fifth edition of this text addresses numerous changes in the law and in society since the time the fourth edition was developed. Revised chapter content and learning objectives meet CAHIIM curriculum standards and competencies for accreditation and are designed to keep the learner abreast of the latest trends in health care. Throughout the text, provisions relating to protection of data and confidentiality concerns are integrated. The chapter on Information Technology is substantially revised, with additional focus placed on future legal and ethical trends in health IT. Changes in regulations relating to long-term care, home health care, research, patient rights, and substance abuse are included.

The success of the third and fourth editions validated the approach of expanding the text to incorporate both legal and ethical aspects of health information management. Woven throughout the text is a thorough updating of the law plus changes in rules of procedure, evidence, and the HIPAA standards. Newer concepts have been either added or expanded upon, including discussion of social media and its various applications to health information management. This provides the reader and instructor with the opportunity to focus solely on law, solely on ethics, or on both law and ethics. This text incorporates the model curriculum of the American Health Information Management Association (AHIMA) for both the health information administrator and health information technician programs, effective with the 2018 revisions. Although differences exist in the curricula between the programs, it is my belief that the content of this text is applicable to students in both groups because it is written with multiple levels of detail. Instructors may determine the emphasis level of each chapter as it is taught during the semester.

ORGANIZATION OF THE TEXTBOOK

While each chapter is designed to stand alone, it is grouped with related chapters to form a unit of study. Four units of study are found in this text.

Part 1 serves as an introduction to the study of law in general. The unit comprises four chapters, beginning with a discussion of the workings of the American legal system. This chapter is followed by a discussion of court systems and legal procedures, including e-discovery, and a chapter addressing judicial process of health information, including discovery requests. The fourth chapter addresses principles of liability, including intentional and nonintentional torts and defenses to lawsuits.

Part 2 serves as an overview of ethics and includes three chapters. The unit begins with a study of ethical standards, outlining concepts and theories basic to an understanding of ethics. Building on this basic understanding, the next chapter addresses decision making and challenges from an ethical perspective. Specialized bioethical issues are the focus of the third chapter, with each life stage forming the framework in which to examine ethical issues.

Part 3 summarizes both legal and ethical issues central to health information management: control and use of patient-specific health information. Four chapters comprise the unit. The first chapter addresses patient record requirements, including use, content, retention, and destruction requirements. Confidentiality and informed consent are addressed in the next chapter, with emphasis on both theory and application. Issues related to access to health information, including ownership of health information and management of the various parties requesting access to that information, form the basis of the next chapter. A discussion of specialized patient records completes the unit, with expanded focus given to genetic information.

Part 4 is composed of four chapters and addresses specialized areas of concern in health information management. The first chapter discusses the concepts of risk, quality, and utilization management, addressing general principles, trends, and application. Information systems forms the next chapter, with focus given to the legal health record, HIPAA regulations, and future legal and ethical trends in health IT. A discussion of health care fraud and abuse follows, including an overview of applicable laws and the necessity for compliance programs. The last chapter provides an understanding of the role of law and ethics in the workplace, including employee rights, discrimination, and workplace protections.

Three things set this text apart from others in the field. First, the text is authored by only one person, allowing for a consistent voice and tone across chapters. It also means that one chapter will not contradict the content of another chapter within the same book and that the difficulty level will not vary from one chapter to the next. Second, this text provides a thorough grounding in ethics, both as to theory and its application to the health information management discipline. This grounding in ethics is addressed throughout the text. Third, the text integrates into each chapter, as applicable, four legal areas that are significant to health information management: the Health Insurance Portability and Accountability Act (HIPAA), electronic health records (EHRs), the Genetic Information Nondiscrimination Act (GINA), and the American Recovery and Reinvestment Act (ARRA). This approach is taken so that while the student is learning the substantive matter, he or she can also understand the interplay between these areas and the substantive matter. Special boxes in the text highlight the interplay of ethics and these special areas with the subject matter of the chapter.

FEATURES OF THE TEXTBOOK

Each textbook chapter contains the following elements:

- **Learning Objectives** and **Key Concepts** identify and organize learning expectations for each chapter.
- **Critical Thinking exercises** pose questions designed to stretch the reader's analytical skills.
- **Text Alerts** highlight issues related to important HIPAA, Genetic Information Nondiscrimination Act (GINA), American Recovery and Reinvestment Act (ARRA), electronic health record (EHR) information, and ethics.
- **Case Studies** apply concepts learned to real-world situations.
- **Review Questions** test comprehension of the chapter material.
- **Enrichment Activities** assist critical thinking about chapter content.
- End-of-chapter **Notes** provide source references so you can explore topics further and expand your knowledge of industry standards, guidelines, and practices.

- The **Appendix** includes:
    - A table of cases
    - A list of common acronyms
    - The Patient Care Partnership
    - Selected Laws Affecting HIM

New to the Fifth Edition

- Revised chapter content and learning objectives meet CAHIIM standards and competencies for accreditation and reflect the latest trends in health care.
- Feature boxes calling for the use of critical thinking skills to answer questions that cause the reader to apply the text material in a related, but somewhat different, manner. Suggested answers to each critical thinking exercise are provided in the Instructor Manual for use in stimulating class discussion.
- Substantial revision to Chapter 13, Information Systems, including the section on electronic health records, and inclusion of new materials focusing on future legal and ethical trends in health IT. These materials are designed to prepare students with a solid foundation to address the rapid changes happening in the health IT context.
- New material on confidentiality in the research and HIV contexts. Confidentiality is a cornerstone tenet of health care, and understanding the nuances present in selected contexts prepares the student for later practice.
- New material on the use of Psychiatric Advance Directives. These forms augment Durable Powers of Attorney for Healthcare and are being presented in health care facilities. Students need to understand how these forms affect the health record.
- New materials explaining the European General Data Protection Regulation and the California Consumer Privacy Act. These two developments pose significant impacts for HIM and will influence future statutory and regulatory changes.
- Updated material concerning substance abuse records—this sensitive HIM area carries significant risk for error, and instruction on the proper care of these records is important to ensure compliance with federal and state statutes and regulations.
- Expansion of existing materials on data privacy and protection, substance abuse, HIV, patient rights, confidentiality, licensing and certification, credentialing, use of copy and paste practice, e-discovery and metadata, enterprise risk management, and informed consent.
- Up-to-date information regarding the latest health care legislation, including coverage of the 21st Century Cures Act, and the latest federal health care regulations, including those covering long-term care, home health care, research, and substance abuse.

SUPPLEMENTS

The following supplements have been developed to accompany this textbook to assist with learning content covered in *Legal and Ethical Aspects of Health Information Management*, Fifth Edition.

Student Online Companion

A website has been created for this textbook to provide a space for updates and additional information related to textbook content. To access student resources located at the online companion site, please visit login.cengage.com

Instructor Resources at the Instructor Companion Site

Features of the instructor's companion site include the following:

- The Instructor's Manual in Adobe's PDF format, which contains answers for all chapter activities, case studies, critical thinking exercises, and review questions. It also includes a curriculum crosswalk, identifying the competencies and curriculum guidance applicable for health information management baccalaureate and associate degree programs.
- Cengage Learning Testing Powered by Cognero, a flexible, online system that allows you to
  - author, edit, and manage test bank content from multiple Cengage Learning solutions;
  - create multiple test versions in an instant; and
  - deliver tests from your LMS, your classroom, or wherever you want.
- Customizable instructor support slide presentations in PowerPoint® format, which focus on key points for each chapter.

MindTap

New: McWay's *Legal and Ethical Aspects of Health Information Management*, Fifth Edition, on MindTap is the first of its kind in an entirely new category: the Personal Learning Experience (PLE). This personalized program of digital products and services uses interactivity and customization to engage students, while offering instructors a wide range of choice in content, platforms, devices, and learning tools. MindTap is device agnostic, meaning that it will work with any platform or learning management system and will be accessible anytime, anywhere: on desktops, laptops, tablets, mobile phones, and other Internet-enabled devices.

This MindTap includes the following:

- An interactive eBook with highlighting, note-taking (integrated with Evernote), and more
- Flashcards for practicing chapter terms
- Computer-graded activities and exercises:
  - Self-check and application activities integrated with the ebook
  - Additional computer-graded activities and exercises
- Easy submission tools for instructor-graded exercises

ABOUT THE AUTHOR

Dana C. McWay, JD, RHIA, FAHIMA, is a lawyer as well as a health information management professional. With training and experience in both disciplines, experience as a member of the Institutional Review Board at Washington University Medical School from 1991 to present, and experience in converting a paper-based record management system to an electronic record management system, she brings wide-ranging experience to this textbook.

Ms. McWay serves as the Clerk of Court for the U.S. Bankruptcy Court for the Eastern District of Missouri, an executive position responsible for all operational, administrative, financial, and technological matters of the court. In this capacity, she organized the court's conversion to an electronic case filing system, resulting in widespread acceptance by end users. This success led to her appointment as a member and, later, as the chair of the Case Management/Electronic Case Filing (CM/ECF) Working Group, an entity within the federal judiciary responsible for providing guidance and assistance in all phases of the development of bankruptcy CM/ECF software releases. She previously served as the chair of the Clerk's Office Functional Requirements Group for the Next Generation Bankruptcy CM/ECF Project, a project designed as the successor to the current CM/ECF system. She serves on numerous national committees and working groups within the judiciary, including those involved in identifying the impact of new legislation upon judicial operations and those involved in advising on the education and training needs of court staff. Prior to this position, she worked as the Chief Deputy Clerk of Court for the U.S. Court of Appeals for the Eighth Circuit, responsible for daily operations of the court.

Ms. McWay began her legal career as a judicial law clerk to the Honorable Myron H. Bright of the U.S. Court of Appeals for the Eighth Circuit. She then became an associate with the law firm of Peper, Martin, Jensen, Maichel, & Hetlage, a multispecialty firm located in St. Louis, Missouri. Ms. McWay's legal practice encompassed a variety of health law topics, including contracts, medical records, and physician practice issues. She is admitted to practice in both Illinois and Missouri. She has received national recognition from the National Bar Foundation, a component of the American Bar Association, for creating the "Kids in Court Program," now operated by the Bar Association of Metropolitan St. Louis, which was cited as one of the five most outstanding children's legal education programs for 1995.

Prior to her legal career, Ms. McWay worked in health information management as a director as well as assistant director of medical records in a large teaching hospital and a for-profit psychiatric and substance abuse facility. She continues to participate in the HIM profession, having served as a project manager for the Missouri Health Information Management Association (MOHIMA) and as a member of MOHIMA's Legislative Committee. On the national level, she served as a director on the Board of Directors of the American Health Information Management Association. Her past AHIMA activities include serving as the chair and a member of AHIMA's Professional Ethics Committee, a faculty member for continuing education seminars, a peer reviewer of AHIMA book proposals and texts, a contributing author to AHIMA's HIM Practice Standards, and a member of both the Committee for Professional Development and the Triumph Awards Committee. She serves as a professional practice experience site coordinator for health information management students and has served as a member of the Advisory Board of the Health Information Management program at Saint Louis University. She has served as an adjunct faculty in the Master's of Health Informatics programs at Saint Louis University and Logan University; at the Law School of Saint Louis University; and in the PreLaw Studies program at Saint Louis University.

Ms. McWay is an author as well as an editor. Her textbook *Today's Health Information Management: An Integrated Approach*, second edition, provides a comprehensive discussion of the principles and practices of health information management in a user-friendly manner. With the Peper, Martin law firm, she revised *The Legal Manual to Medical Record Practice in Missouri* in 1991. She has authored numerous other publications and served as coeditor of several online continuing education modules presented by the American Health Information Management Association. She has also presented numerous seminars, serving as faculty and panel presenter. She has served as a guest lecturer at several regional colleges and universities, focusing on the intersection of legal issues and health care practices. She currently serves on the advisory boards of two Health Information Management academic programs.

Ms. McWay is a *magna cum laude* graduate of the Saint Louis University School of Allied Health Professions, with a degree in medical record administration, and a *cum laude* graduate of the Saint Louis University School of Law, awarded the Order of the Woolsack upon graduation. While in law school, Ms. McWay served as the health law editor of the *Saint Louis University Law Journal* and as a faculty research fellow. She is a recipient of the Alumni Merit Award from Saint Louis University and a Triumph Award (the Legacy Award) from the American Health Information Management Association for the first edition of the textbook *Legal Aspects of Health Information Management*. She has received the Missouri Health Information Management Association's Distinguished Member and Outstanding Volunteer Awards. She is the recipient of the Director's Award for Outstanding Leadership to the federal judiciary and the Director's Award for Excellence in Operations—Mission Requirements.

ACKNOWLEDGMENTS

Many persons have played a role in the creation and revision of this textbook, including family, friends, and colleagues. A special thank you is warranted for my family who showed patience, understanding, and support for the long hours spent on this new edition of my first textbook. I express my appreciation to my parents for their guidance and support over a lifetime. My editor for this project, Thomas Heffernan, and former editor, Lauren Whalen, guided me through the transition of this text to a fifth edition, and I am grateful for their assistance. Debbie Bordeaux assisted me with refining the many learning objectives and review questions, and I am grateful for her insight. My appreciation is extended to the reviewers of my manuscript. Your comments aided in strengthening this text.

Dana C. McWay, JD, RHIA, FAHIMA

Reviewers

The author and publisher would like to recognize the following reviewers for their invaluable feedback on this product:

Irma Rodriguez M.Ed, RHIA, CCS
Program Chair of the Health and Medical Administrative Services
South Texas College
McAllen, TX

Erica Wilson, MS, MHA, RHIA, CPC
Program Chair
Southern Regional Technical College
Thomasville, Georgia

Karen N. Williams, MHIM, RHIA, CPHQ, CHTS-TR
Professor, Program Director,
Health Information Technology Program
Del Mar College
Corpus Christi, Texas

Annette Bigalk, RHIA
HIT Program Chair
Arapahoe Community College
Littleton, Colorado

Marie T. Conde, MPA, RHIA, CCS
Program Director and Instructor, Health Information Technology Program
City College of San Francisco
San Francisco, California

Carolyn Eberly, RHIT
Allied Health Instructor
Kaplan College
Hagerstown, Maryland

Lissa Jarr, RHIT
Instructor
Indian Hills Community College
Ottumwa, Iowa

Kathleen M. Olewinski, MS, RHIA, NHA, FACHE
Program Director
Bryant & Stratton College
Milwaukee, Wisconsin

ABOUT LEGAL CITATIONS

A legal citation identifies a legal authority or reference work, such as a constitution, statute, court decision, administrative rule, or treatise. Legal citations are used throughout this work to (1) identify the source of a quotation, (2) identify an authority referred to in the text, or (3) support the propositions stated. Legal citations are found in both the body of the text and the endnotes.

The learner may be interested in legal citations for more than one reason: to identify legal authority that is binding on the health care provider or to learn how to obtain full copies of a citation to read as a supplement to the text. For most citations other than statutory provisions and court decisions, the legal citation is self-explanatory. Some explanation is warranted for understanding how to read citations of statutes and court decisions.

Both federal and state statutes are published in either official or unofficial codes. For federal statutes, the official code is the *United States Code* (U.S.C.); unofficial codes include the *United States Code Annotated* (U.S.C.A.) and the *United States Code Service* (U.S.C.S.). Every effort has been made in this book to cite federal statutes published in the official code. A typical federal statutory citation cites first to the title number, next to the abbreviation of the official code, third to the numbered section or paragraph, and finally to the year that appears on the spine of the volume cited. Where statutory material can be found in a supplement to the official code, it is identified as a supplement with the year of the supplement identified. For example, the citation 42 U.S.C. §11101 (1988 & Supp. V 1993) shows that the particular statute may be found in title 42 of the *United States Code* as section number 11101 in both the volume published in 1988 and the fifth supplement to that volume published in 1993.

Similarly, state statutes are published in either official or unofficial codes and generally follow the same practice as federal statutes. For example, the citation FLA. STAT. ANN. §395.0197 (West 1993) shows that the particular statute may be found in the unofficial code *Florida Statutes Annotated* at section 395.0197 published by the West Publishing Company in 1993. Multiple state statutory citations are listed in alphabetical, rather than year, order, using standard abbreviations.

Court decisions are cited according to a similar approach. The name of the case and the numbers, letters, and years following it are referred to as the citation for the decision. For example, the citation *Warwick v. Bliss*, 195 N.W. 502 (S.D. 1923) shows that the case involving those named parties may be found in volume 195 of the *NorthWestern Reporter* on page 502. The initials and year in parentheses refer to the identity of the court that issued the decision, in this case the Supreme Court of the State of South Dakota, and the year the decision was issued.

The same case may show more than one citation, indicating that a decision has been issued in the same case by different courts. If the first citation is followed by the abbreviations *aff'd*, *rev'd*, or *cert. denied*, the citation indicates the subsequent history of the case, namely, that a higher court has reviewed the decision of the lower court. For example, the citation *Johnson v. Misericordia Community Hospital*, 294 N.W.2d 501 (Wis. Ct. App. 1980) *aff'd*, 301 N.W.2d 156 (Wis. 1981) shows that the case involving those named parties appears in two different reporters. First, the case may be found in volume 294 of the *NorthWestern Reporter*, second series, on page 501, and was issued by the Wisconsin Court of Appeals in 1980. Second, the case was affirmed by the Wisconsin Supreme Court in 1981 and can be found in volume 301 of the *NorthWestern Reporter*, second series, on page 156.

The legal citations listed in this book are cited according to the standards of the book *A Uniform System of Citation*, Fifteenth Edition, commonly referred to as *The Blue Book*, a joint publication of the Columbia Law Review Association, the Harvard Law Review Association, the University of Pennsylvania Law Review, and the Yale Law Journal.

ABOUT LEGAL RESEARCH

To the uninitiated, legal research can be bewildering, overwhelming, or intimidating. Entire books have been devoted to the subject, making the topic difficult to summarize easily. Nonetheless, a basic review of legal research methods is provided so that the learner may research an area of law covered in this book or review the exact wording of a constitutional provision, statute, or administrative regulation.

Before beginning any research project, the learner must first obtain an understanding of the sources of law in order to know where to look. The sources of law are explained in detail in Chapter 1, and a brief description is provided here. The sources of law are divided into two categories: primary sources and secondary sources. Primary sources are *the law themselves*, including constitutions, statutes, court decisions, and administrative decisions and regulations. They are located in official and unofficial codes in the case of constitutions, statutes, and administrative regulations and in case digests when looking for court cases or administrative decisions. Case digests are grouped by cases issued by federal courts, state courts, or courts found in a particular region of the United States. Citations to these primary sources are explained in the "About Legal Citations" section. Secondary sources are the writings or commentaries *about the law*, including legal encyclopedias, articles found in professional journals, and legal treatises. This book is an example of a secondary source.

With so many sources to choose from, how does the learner find the answer? There are several techniques to choose from, all of which apply to the traditional method of using books for research or through the newer method of using computer-based legal databases. The learner should choose from the following techniques when beginning legal research:

1. *Generalized approach.* This approach is most applicable when the learner has little or no general knowledge about the problem or area that is the subject of research. It begins with a review of secondary source materials, such as legal encyclopedias or articles in professional journals. These materials often have a table of contents or indexes to guide further research, leading to review of topics of interest. Many of these topics of interest list citations, footnotes, or references to primary source material, which will further aid the learner's research.
2. *Known authority approach.* This approach is most applicable when the learner knows the citation to the constitutional provision, statute, case, or administrative decision or regulation (the "authority"). It begins with a review of primary source materials to locate the citation of the authority in question and follows with a review of that authority.
3. *Descriptive word or fact word approach.* This approach is most applicable when the learner knows general information about the subject matter but does not have a specific citation to the relevant primary authority. After choosing a descriptive or fact word, the learner should look into the index to a set of official or unofficial codes to find constitutions, statutes, and administrative regulations or to the applicable case digest to find a court case or administrative decision.
4. *Known topic approach.* This approach is most applicable when the learner knows the area of law involved but not the specific legal authority. For constitutions, statutes, and administrative regulations, the learner should look into the subject matter grouping within the official and unofficial codes. For court cases or administrative decisions, look into the topic and subtopic sections of the applicable case digest.

Once the learner has found the authority being researched, the research activity is not over. Rather, the learner must continue the research to check the current status (i.e., validity) of the authority. The easiest, most thorough, and most complete method to check the status of the authority in question is through the use of a computer-based legal database. A search begins for references to the citation by typing the authority's citation into the database. The learner should review the listed references to evaluate their effect, if any, on the citation in question.

Alternatively, nonelectronic methods of checking the current status of an authority are available. Many hardbound volumes contain so-called pocket parts, which are paperbound pamphlets inserted into a slot in the cover of the hardbound volume. The pocket parts follow the same format as the hardbound volume to which they correspond and report any additions to or decisions for the main text. Supplements to hardbound volumes follow the same principles. The learner should review the references to the citation to evaluate their effect, if any, on the citation in question.

Another method is to trace the subsequent work of a legal authority through a citator publication; the best known is *Shepard's Citations*. The entries contained in *Shepard's* list authorities (e.g., other cases, journal articles, and attorney general opinions) that have cited the legal authority that is the subject of the research. Detailed instruction on the use of a citator publication such as *Shepard's* is beyond the scope of this book.

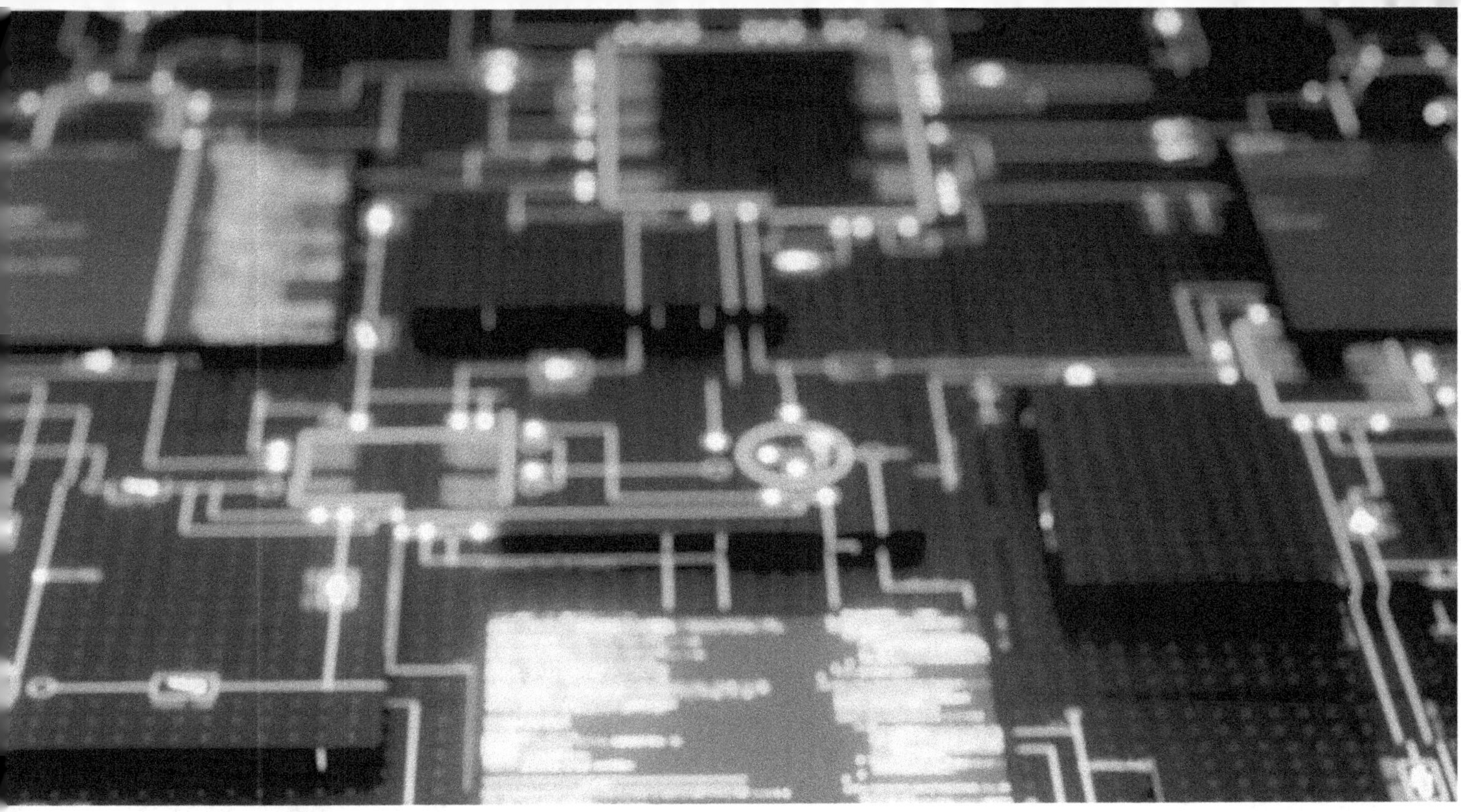

PART

1 STUDY OF THE LAW IN GENERAL

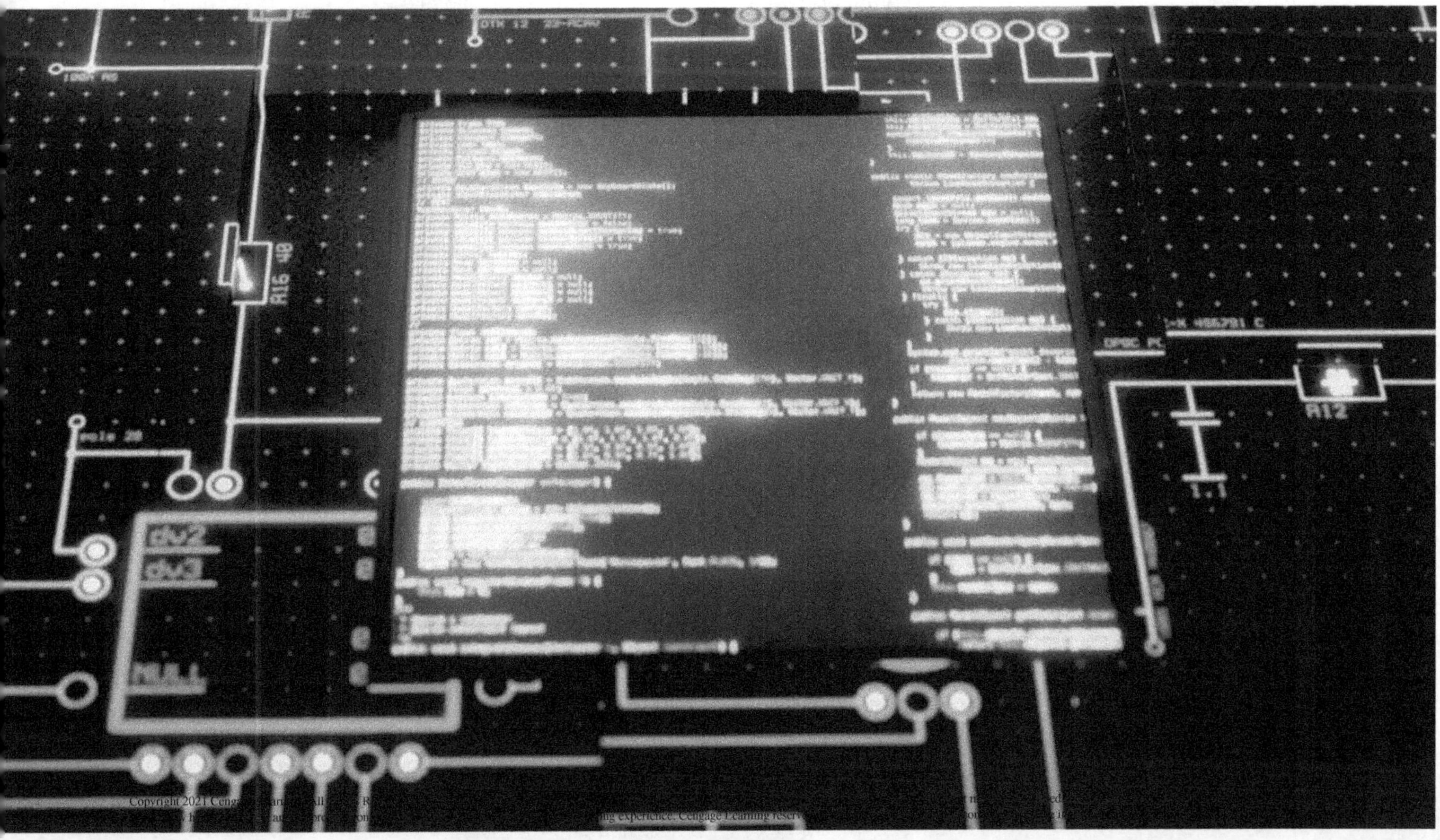

CHAPTER 1

WORKINGS OF THE AMERICAN LEGAL SYSTEM

LEARNING OBJECTIVES

After reading this chapter, the learner should be able to:

1. Differentiate between public and private law.
2. Compare and contrast contract and tort law.
3. Compose a scenario that illustrates the difference between the substantive and procedural aspects of criminal law.
4. Explain the differences between various sources of law.
5. Compare and contrast licensure and certification.
6. Describe the roles of each branch of government in creating, administering, and enforcing law.
7. Explain the process of how a bill becomes a law.
8. Describe quasi-legal requirements to which health care organizations are subject.

KEY CONCEPTS

Adjudication
Certification
Civil law
Common law
Conflict of laws
Constitution
Contract law
Criminal law
Deeming authority
Electronic case filing systems
Executive branch
Felonies
Injunction
Intellectual property
Judicial branch
Law
Legislative branch
Licensure
Misdemeanors
Ordinances
Pleadings
Private law
Procedural law
Public law
Res judicata
Separation of powers
Stare decisis
Statutes
Substantive law
Tort law
Words of authority

INTRODUCTION

As health care becomes more complex, the interplay between the law and health care increases. Government regulation of the health care field continues almost without pause, while lawsuits against health care providers appear to increase. The interplay of these forces significantly affects the ability to manage patient-specific health information. Thus, those who are concerned with protecting health information must possess a fundamental understanding of the law. This chapter provides that understanding through a discussion of the differences between public law and private law, the sources of law, the branches of government and their respective roles, and quasi-legal requirements to which health care organizations are subject.

PRIVATE AND PUBLIC LAW

In the most general sense, **law** is defined as a system of principles and processes devised by organized society to deal with disputes and problems without resorting to the use of force. Law establishes certain standards for human behavior. When those standards are not met, conflict emerges. Individuals and governments then look to the law to resolve the conflicts and enforce the established standards.

Conflicts between private parties constitute **private law**; by contrast, conflicts between the government and private parties constitute **public law**. It is not always easy to make a distinction between these two types of law because in certain instances behavior that deviates from the established standard violates both public and private law. For example, an assault and battery violates both private and public law. Although no clear distinction is possible, understanding the differences between public and private law will assist in understanding the American legal system. The distinctions between public and private law are illustrated in Figure 1.1.

Private Law

Private law consists of the body of rules and principles that governs the rights and duties between private parties. Private law is sometimes referred to as civil law because it is concerned with private rights and remedies. **Civil law** is more properly defined, however, as that part of the law that does not include criminal law. Table 1.1 provides more details differentiating between civil and criminal law cases.

Generally, lawsuits brought between private parties fall into one of two categories: contract law or tort law. **Contract law** is concerned with an agreement between two or more parties that creates some type of obligation to act (do something) or refrain from acting (not do something) in exchange for some type of consideration. Table 1.2 lists the elements of a contract. Contracts may be oral or written agreements and should abide by applicable federal and state statutes and regulations. When a party fails to fulfill the terms of the contractual agreement, a breach of contract occurs and the aggrieved party may sue to force performance of the terms of the contract or seek compensation.

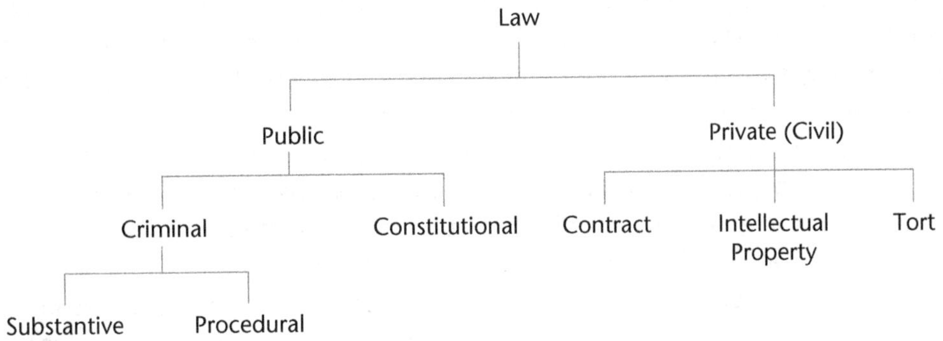

Figure 1.1 Distinctions between Public Law and Private Law

Table 1.1 Differences between Civil and Criminal Law Cases

Civil Law	Criminal Law
1. Both parties may be anybody, including governments, corporations, and individual persons.	1. The plaintiff is always the state or federal government.
2. The loser in a civil case cannot be imprisoned, even if she cannot pay the damages assessed by the court.	2. Punishment may be a fine and/or imprisonment.
3. Civil law is established through both state and federal statutes and court decisions.	3. State or federal statutes always establish criminal law.
4. In some state court systems, a majority vote of the jury is required to win a decision. Some state court systems require a unanimous jury decision. Federal courts require a unanimous jury decision.	4. The jury decision in a criminal trial must be unanimous.
5. The burden of proof is "preponderance of the evidence," which is defined as "more likely than not."	5. The burden of proof is "beyond a reasonable doubt."
6. Either party may appeal in a civil case.	6. Only the defendant may appeal a guilty verdict in a criminal case.
7. The plaintiff and the defendant may both be found partially right and partially at fault.	7. The defendant is either guilty or not guilty; there is no partial fault.

Table 1.2 Elements of a Contract

- Meeting of the minds—at least two persons or entities must reach an agreement.
- Offer—one or more parties promise to do something (obligation) or not do something (refrain) and communicate that offer to the other party.
- Acceptance—the other party agrees to the promise.
- Consideration—what one party to a contract receives from the other party in return for performing the contractual obligations.

An example of a lawsuit involving breach of contract is *Mordecai v. Blue Cross/Blue Shield of Alabama*.[1] In *Mordecai*, the patient sued her insurance company after it denied payment for the majority of her claim for medical expenses. The court held that the patient could proceed against the insurance company for breach of contract on the issue of whether the insurer correctly determined that the patient's care was not medically necessary.

Claims of breach of contract were also at the heart of *Prevost v. Coffee County Hospital Authority*.[2] In *Prevost*, the hospital sued a doctor for breach of contract, seeking to recover a loan it made to induce the doctor to open a medical practice at the hospital. The doctor counterclaimed, asserting that the hospital failed to comply with the terms of the contract by not purchasing certain medical equipment to facilitate his practice or reimbursing him for expenses in renovating his office space. A jury found that each side breached the contract and awarded damages to each. Other examples of activities covered by contract law include the sale of goods, the employment of others, the furnishing of services, the loaning of money, and the contract between hospitals and physicians for clinical privileges.

Tort law encompasses the rights and duties that exist between parties that are independent of a contract. When one party claims that the wrongful conduct of the other party has caused harm, the aggrieved party may seek compensation. An example of a lawsuit involving tort law is *John Roe v. Jane Doe*.[3] In *Roe*, the court held a physician liable for negligence and breach of confidentiality after the physician improperly disclosed her patient's HIV status. Other examples of activities covered by tort law include medical malpractice, defamation, and invasion of privacy. Additional discussion of tort law can be found in Chapter 4, Principles of Liability.

While most legal issues in the health care field involve either contract or tort law, one emerging area of law is that of **intellectual property**. Ordinarily associated with patents and trademarks, intellectual property law involves the question of legal rights to processes and products of technology, in particular, the concrete application of a principle or idea. Intellectual property law is used in the health information management field as the basis for the legal rights to the software used to control and store information in the patient's electronic health record.

EHR

The legal rights to the software used in electronic health records arise from intellectual property law.

Public Law

Public law is the body of rules and principles that governs the rights and duties between government and a private party or between two parts or agencies of government. Public law defines appropriate behavior between citizens, organizations, and government.

One very large segment of public law is **criminal law**. The essence of criminal law is to declare certain conduct as injurious to the public order and to provide specified punishment for those found to have engaged in such conduct. Criminal law can be divided into two subcategories: **substantive law** and **procedural law**. Substantive criminal law defines specific offenses, general principles of liability, and specific punishment. Examples of specific offenses are **felonies**, crimes of a grave or serious nature punishable by a term of imprisonment exceeding one year, and **misdemeanors**, crimes of a less serious nature punishable by fine or a term of imprisonment of less than one year. Criminal procedure focuses on the steps through which a criminal case passes, from the initial investigation of a crime through trial and sentence and the eventual release of the criminal offender.

A second large segment of public law consists of constitutional provisions, statutes, and regulations that govern society by requiring governmental entities and private parties to follow certain courses of action. Although some government regulations contain criminal penalties, their purpose is not to punish offenders but to secure compliance with the goals of the law.

To further understand the contrast between private and public law, their sources must be examined. The primary source of private law is decisions of the courts, which may be subsequently modified by statute or regulation. The primary sources of public law are written constitutions, statutes, regulations, and decisions from both judicial and administrative bodies. The interplay of these sources within private and public law provides the starting basis for understanding the legal aspects of health information.

CRITICAL THINKING Differentiating between private and public law is not always easy. Would you agree that the following statements properly differentiate between the two types of law?

1. Private law applies to issues that affect individuals and groups of people or organizations, whereas public law applies to issues that affect society as a whole.
2. Private law applies to verbal contracts, whereas public law applies to written contracts.
3. Private law applies to criminal matters, whereas public law applies to governmental matters.

SOURCES OF LAW

Because private and public law originate from a variety of sources, there is no one document or place to turn to find the rules governing health information. Even if such a document or place existed, its value would be questionable because law is not constant; rather, it is constantly changing. Accordingly, it is important to understand that all of the following sources of law may affect the management of health information.

Constitution

A **constitution** is the fundamental law of a nation or state and may be written or unwritten.[4] A constitution establishes the basic principles to which the nation or state must conform, organizes the branches of government, and limits the functions of its different departments.

A constitution familiar to most Americans is the Constitution of the United States, which has as its basic premise the ensuring of each person's rights to life, liberty, and religious freedom. As illustrated in Figure 1.2, the main body of the U.S. Constitution establishes and defines the three branches of government: (1) the **legislative branch**, (2) the **executive branch**, and (3) the **judicial branch**. Following the main body of the Constitution are twenty-seven amendments that have been ratified by at least three-fourths of the states in existence at the time of their ratification. The first ten amendments are referred to as the Bill of Rights and include the rights to freedom of speech and religion, freedom from unreasonable search and seizure, freedom to bear arms, freedom to be protected against self-incrimination, freedom to demand a jury trial, and freedom to be afforded due process of law. A listing of the Bill of Rights is provided in Table 1.3.

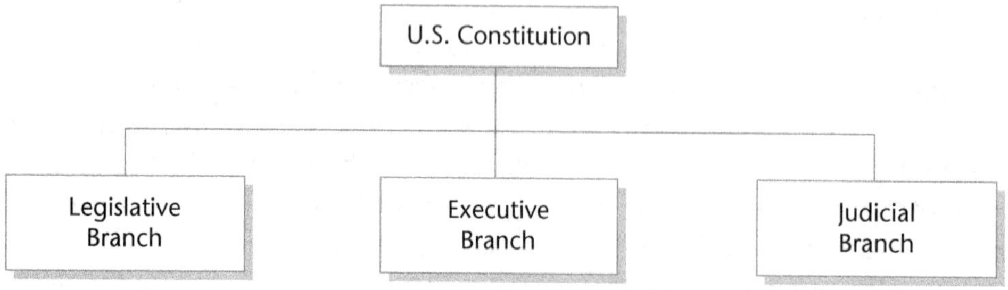

Figure 1.2 Branches of the Federal Government

Table 1.3 The Bill of Rights

Amendment I
Congress shall make no law respecting an establishment of religion, or prohibiting the free exercise thereof; or abridging the freedom of speech, or of the press; or the right of the people peaceably to assemble, and to petition the Government for a redress of grievances.

Amendment II
A well regulated militia, being necessary to the security of a free State, the right of the people to keep and bear arms, shall not be infringed.

Amendment III
No Soldier shall, in time of peace be quartered in any house, without the consent of the owner, nor in time of war, but in a manner to be prescribed by law.

Amendment IV
The right of the people to be secure in their persons, houses, papers, and effects, against unreasonable searches and seizures, shall not be violated, and no warrants shall issue, but upon probable cause, supported by oath or affirmation, and particularly describing the place to be searched, and the persons or things to be seized.

Amendment V
No person shall be held to answer for a capital, or otherwise infamous crime, unless on a presentment or indictment of a Grand Jury, except in cases arising in the land or naval forces, or in the militia, when in actual service in time of war or public danger; nor shall any person be subject for the same offense to be twice put in jeopardy of life or limb; nor shall be compelled in any criminal case to be a witness against himself, nor be deprived of life, liberty, or property, without due process of law; nor shall private property be taken for public use, without just compensation.

Amendment VI
In all criminal prosecutions, the accused shall enjoy the right to a speedy and public trial, by an impartial jury of the State and district wherein the crime shall have been committed, which district shall have been previously ascertained by law, and to be informed of the nature and cause of the accusation; to be confronted with the witnesses against him; to have compulsory process for obtaining witnesses in his favor, and to have the assistance of counsel for his defense.

Amendment VII
In Suits at common law, where the value in controversy shall exceed twenty dollars, the right of a trial by jury shall be preserved, and no fact tried by a jury, shall be otherwise reexamined in any Court of the United States, than according to the rules of the common law.

Amendment VIII
Excessive bail shall not be required, nor excessive fines imposed, nor cruel and unusual punishments inflicted.

Amendment IX
The enumeration in the Constitution, of certain rights, shall not be construed to deny or disparage others retained by the people.

Amendment X
The powers not delegated to the United States by the Constitution, nor prohibited by it to the States, are reserved to the States respectively, or to the people.

In addition to the U.S. Constitution, each state has its own constitution. These state constitutions provide the fundamental laws for each state but are subordinate to the U.S. Constitution. A state constitution typically contains not only language similar to the U.S. Constitution but also language that is unique to that state. Sometimes, state constitutions provide even broader rights and protections than the U.S. Constitution. For example, one state's courts have interpreted their state's constitutional provision guaranteeing the right to privacy to include a patient's right to die and right to refuse treatment—matters that the U.S. Constitution does not expressly address.[5]

Statutes

A second source of law flows from federal and state legislatures. The laws written by these legislatures are called **statutes** and become effective after being signed by the president, in the case of federal statutes, or by the governor, in the case of state statutes. As a general rule, statutes passed at the federal level address matters of national concern; statutes passed at the state level address matters of particular interest to the individual state.

HIPAA/ARRA

Both the Health Insurance Portability and Accountability Act (HIPAA) and the American Recovery and Reinvestment Act (ARRA) address the privacy and security of health records.

Multiple statutes written at the same level can address the same subject matter. For example, the Health Insurance Portability and Accountability Act (HIPAA) addresses issues of privacy and security of protected health information of individual patients. Provisions of the American Recovery and Reinvestment Act of 2009 (ARRA) also address the same subject matter. Because Congress passed ARRA after passing HIPAA, any conflicting provisions between the two statutes will be governed by the provisions of ARRA. The two statutes can be reconciled because of a provision in ARRA that states any HIPAA statutory provision or regulation remains in effect to the extent that it is consistent with ARRA.[6] Any regulations issued after passage of ARRA may contain language and guidance that reconcile the two statutes.

ARRA

Provisions of the American Recovery and Reinvestment Act demonstrate the interplay of federal and state law.

On occasion, federal statutes will address matters of state law. Under ARRA, provisions include financial incentives in the form of grants to states to promote adoption of health information technology and dissemination of best practices information concerning electronic health records. Further provisions establish or expand health informatics education programs and the integration of certified electronic health record technology in the clinical education of health professionals.[7]

Statutes written in one state can differ greatly from statutes written in other states on the same topic. For example, one state's statute may directly address a patient's access to her own health record, whereas the neighboring state's statute governing access to patient records may be silent on the issue of direct patient access. For more information concerning the patient's right of access to health information, see Chapter 10, Access to Health Information.

Where the statutes of different states are inconsistent in deciding how to resolve a particular dispute, a conflict of laws has arisen. A **conflict of laws** refers to an inconsistency between different jurisdictions over the same issue in a legal action. For example, a contract requirement to submit a dispute to arbitration may be effective in the state in which the parties resided at the time of entering the contract but may not be effective in a neighboring state if one of the parties moves to that neighboring state and the contract terms do not specifically comply with the neighboring state's laws governing arbitration requirements. In this instance, a conflict of laws has occurred.

Lawyers frequently avoid the potential for conflicts of law in contracts by including a provision specifying which state's law will govern in the event of a conflict. In a court case, the judge will decide which state's laws will govern in the event of a conflict.

Similarly, one state's response to a perceived problem may result in statutes that are imitated by other states. For example, several states have responded to allegations of high photocopying charges for copies of health records by passing statutes that place caps on the amount the health care provider may charge for these copies. Other states have followed suit and adopted statutes that vary in detail (e.g., the cap amount) but address similar results (e.g., the need for a cap). More information concerning the reasonableness of photocopying fees is provided in Chapter 10, Access to Health Information.

In addition to these legislative bodies, legislatures on the local level, such as city councils or boards of aldermen, may pass laws regulating matters not already covered by federal or state law. City councils or boards of aldermen may also pass laws to supplement federal or state laws. Frequently, laws passed at the local level are called **ordinances**. Areas typically not governed by federal or state law but by ordinances include zoning, building, and public safety. Areas where ordinances supplement federal or state law include content requirements for health records.

To understand statutes and ordinances, one must be familiar with certain verbs that hold legal meaning. Referred to as **words of authority**, these verbs set forth duties, rights, prohibitions, and responsibilities in statutes and ordinances. The most commonly used words of authority for statutes and ordinances are listed in Table 1.4. These words of authority may also be found in rules and regulations and share the same meaning as used in statutes and ordinances.

CRITICAL THINKING

Rights and duties can vary based on the specific language of a statute, rule, or regulation. Consider the impact of changing the word *must* to *may* in the following sentence:

A covered entity must train all members of its workforce on the policies and procedures with respect to protected health information.

Table 1.4 Words of Authority

Word	Meaning
Shall	Has a duty to
Must	Is required to
Must Not	Is required not to; is disallowed from
Is Entitled to	Has a right to
Will	Expresses a future contingency
May	Has discretion to; is permitted to
May Not	Is not permitted to; is disallowed from
Should	Denotes a directory provision

Source: B. Garner, *A Dictionary of Modern Legal Usage*, 2d ed. (1995).

Administrative Decisions and Regulations

A third source of law comes from the decisions and regulations of administrative agencies. Common at both the federal and state levels, administrative agencies are governmental bodies charged by the legislature with administering and implementing particular legislation. The legislature delegates to the agency the power to promulgate rules, adopt regulations, and decide how the statutes, rules, and regulations apply to particular situations.

When promulgating rules, adopting regulations, and making decisions, agencies must follow certain procedures contained in administrative procedure acts. Administrative procedure acts exist at both the federal and state levels. Under these acts, agencies may not make certain decisions until after they (1) have given advance notice, (2) allowed affected parties an opportunity to present arguments for or against the proposed action, and (3) provided a public record for their action.

The second part of the process is commonly known as providing a notice and comment period. Proposed rules and regulations on the federal level are first published in the *Federal Register*. After the time for notice and comment has expired, the agency determines what comments it will incorporate in its final rules and regulations. These final rules and regulations are then published in the *Code of Federal Regulations*, commonly referred to as the *CFR*, and have the force of law.

HIPAA

HIPAA regulations were created pursuant to an administrative procedure act and were subject to multiple notice and comment periods.

A recent example of a federal agency following the requirements of an administrative procedure act is the final privacy rule issued pursuant to the Health Insurance Portability and Accountability Act (HIPAA). HIPAA required Congress to take action to establish privacy standards within a prescribed time frame; if it did not take action, the U.S. Department of Health and Human Services (HHS) was required to establish privacy standards. After Congress failed to act within the requisite time period, HHS published a proposed rule in the *Federal Register* concerning privacy standards and received widespread commentary. After determining what comments to incorporate, HHS issued the revised rule in the *Federal Register.* This rule would have become effective in the ordinary course with publication in the *CFR*, but because a new presidential administration was taking office, the effective date of the rule was delayed by several months. Eventually, the rule was incorporated into the *CFR*, meaning that it received the force of law.

In addition to these federal publications, many states issue comparable publications. For example, the state of Missouri initially publishes proposed rules and regulations in the *Missouri Register*. After the expiration of the notice and comment period, the final rules and regulations are published in that state's *Code of State Regulations* (*CSR*). In addition, Missouri's *CSR* includes references to cases that have interpreted the individual rule or regulation. These case references are termed *annotations*.

Administrative rules and regulations are valid only to the extent that they fall within the scope of the authority granted to the agency by the legislature. Legislatures are limited by both the U.S. Constitution and state constitutions in delegating authority to governmental agencies; they cannot abdicate their responsibilities and delegate too extensively. To accommodate those limits, legislatures generally identify the specialized subject matter and empower the agency to develop rules and regulations within that specialized subject matter.

In addition to rule-making authority, legislatures at both the federal and state levels often grant agencies quasi-judicial powers. These powers include the authority to make decisions concerning certain defined matters and provide hearings for parties dissatisfied with the agency's decision. For example, the Centers for Medicare and Medicaid Services (CMS), formerly known as the Health Care Financing Administration (HCFA), of the Department of Health and Human Services (HHS) administers the Medicare program for the federal government. CMS determines the amount of reimbursement to be paid to health care providers who participate in the Medicare program. Dissatisfied providers may request a hearing before the Provider Reimbursement Review Board. If still dissatisfied, the provider can pursue an appeal of the board's decision within the HHS. Then, if the provider is dissatisfied with the agency's final decision, the provider can request judicial review—that is, review of the final agency decision by a U.S. district court. Decisions of administrative agencies, such as those of the HHS, are published chronologically in sets of administrative reports.

Administrative decisions and regulations are not limited to the federal level; many administrative bodies also operate at the state and local levels, sometimes addressing the very same substantive matter. For example, both a state and a municipal board of health may exist in a community and address the spread of communicable diseases, a matter addressed at the federal level by the Centers for Disease Control and Prevention in the HHS. At each of these three levels, the respective administrative body possesses power to issue decisions and regulations concerning communicable diseases. Other examples of the administrative bodies at the state and local levels that issue decisions and regulations in the health care field include licensing boards, coroners, and medical examiners. These decisions and regulations are published by their respective administrative body, with many decisions and regulations now accessible via the Internet.

Licensure and Certification

Various administrative bodies across the United States engage in work to license and certify health care professionals. **Licensure** involves the process by which an authorized authority, often at the state level, grants permission to a qualified individual to perform certain activities that would otherwise be considered as illegal absent a license. In the health care field, boards, agencies, or departments at the state level are granted authority pursuant to state statutes to determine the level of competence and standards to be met before a health care professional earns the legal right to practice a health care profession and use a specific health care title. Licensing laws serve to limit and control who is admitted to practice in a given profession. These same laws serve to protect the public from being treated by unqualified practitioners.

Licensing boards act in several ways. They issue regulations establishing standards of practice, determine the minimum educational and experience requirements and competency levels of applicants, and collect licensing fees. Licensing boards may suspend or revoke a health care professional's license if the board determines that the professional has acted beyond an inappropriate manner. These actions may include obtaining a license through fraud, acting beyond the scope of the professional's license, committing malpractice, or engaging in conduct that is immoral, dishonorable, or illegal.

By contrast, certification generally does not involve a governmental entity. **Certification** refers to recognition by a professional association that an individual possesses the knowledge, experience, and expertise of the standards set by the professional association. The concept is that the certification serves to attest that an individual is qualified to perform a task or job. Certifications are generally undertaken voluntarily and are very common in the health care field.

Some similarities exist between licensure and certification. Both exist as means to protect the public from unqualified individuals practicing in a field that requires specific knowledge and expertise. Both require individuals to maintain their competence, demonstrating that competence by earning credits through continuing education courses. While both limit and control who can practice in a given field, licensure provides a stronger means by which to do so because licensing boards are created by statute, whereas certification comes from professional associations not backed by law.

Judicial Decisions

A fourth source of law is the decisions of courts, sometimes referred to as common law. **Common law** is formed when a court, attempting to resolve a dispute, renders a decision. In reaching this decision, courts may interpret relevant constitutional provisions, federal or state statutes, regulations, and/or previous court decisions. The resulting court decision establishes a precedent that may be relied on in future court cases involving similar issues. This reliance on precedent is referred to as ***stare decisis***, a Latin term meaning "to let the decision stand."

Stare decisis applies to all courts within the same geographic area and within the same jurisdiction. *Stare decisis* operates in a pyramid-type fashion. Courts at the top of the pyramid issue decisions on particular topics. All lower courts within the pyramid that have the same geographic area and jurisdiction are then bound to follow the decisions issued by the court above it in the pyramid.

An example of this pyramid structure is the federal court system. At the top of the pyramid is the U.S. Supreme Court, the highest court in the land. Immediately below are the U.S. Courts of Appeals. These courts of appeal, called circuit courts of appeal, are divided into geographic areas and are numbered one through eleven, except for one named court of appeal, the U.S. Court of Appeals for the District of Columbia. Additionally, one court of appeal is not defined by its geography but by the type of cases it can hear. This court is the U.S. Court of Appeals for the Federal Circuit, which hears, among other subjects, cases involving patent appeals from all over the United States. The geographic breakdown of the thirteen circuit courts of appeal is illustrated in Figure 1.3.

Finally, the lower level of the pyramid includes the trial courts, called U.S. District Courts. Each state has at least one federal trial court and, depending on the size and population of the state, may have more. Each state also has at least one U.S. Bankruptcy Court and, depending on the size and population of the state, may have more.

Under *stare decisis*, U.S. District Courts and U.S. Bankruptcy Courts are bound by decisions of both the U.S. Supreme Court and the U.S. Court of Appeal that is located in their geographic area. However, the doctrine of *stare decisis* does not operate in the reverse direction. For example, the courts of appeal are not bound by trial court decisions but only by decisions of the U.S. Supreme Court and prior decisions of that particular court of appeal. In turn, the U.S. Supreme Court is not bound by decisions of either the trial court or the court of appeal but only by its own previous decisions. If certain circumstances exist, such as significantly changed conditions, the U.S. Supreme Court may decide to overrule its precedent and not follow the doctrine of *stare decisis*.

In addition to *stare decisis*, courts are also subject to the doctrine of **res judicata**, which literally means "a thing or matter settled by judgment." Whenever a court with jurisdiction over the lawsuit renders a final decision on the merits, the parties to the lawsuit are forever barred from bringing a subsequent action raising the same claim or demand. *Res judicata* applies only after all avenues of appeal have been exhausted. It differs from *stare decisis* in that *res judicata* applies only to the parties and issues involved in a particular lawsuit; by contrast, *stare decisis* applies to future decisions involving different parties with similar issues.

Unlike constitutions and statutes, many court decisions are not made available to the general public for review. Cases settled either before or during trial generally do not involve published

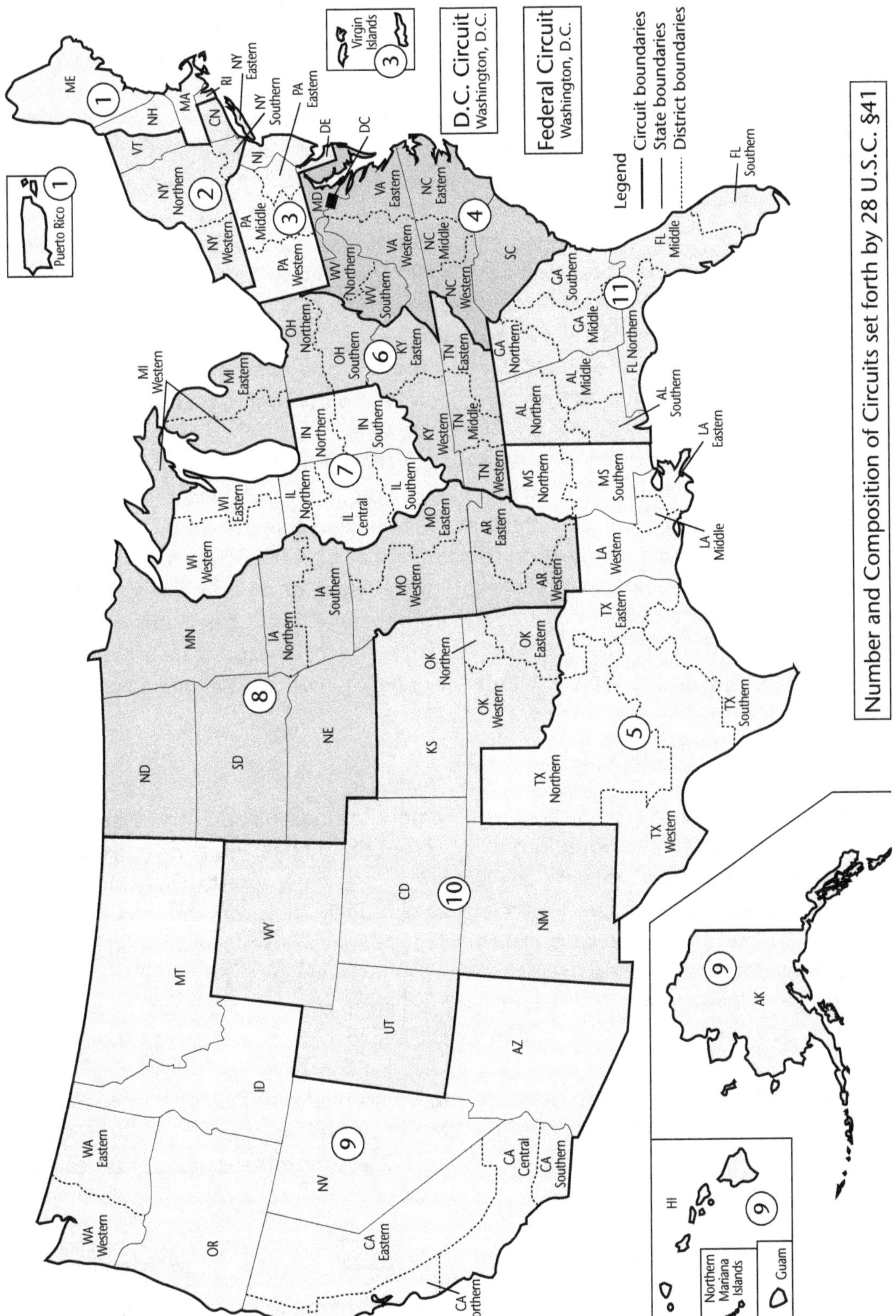

Figure 1.3 Geographical Boundaries of U.S. Courts of Appeal and U.S. District Courts
Source: Administrative Office of the U.S. Courts (2019).

decisions; many times a written trial court decision is made available only to the parties involved in the case. If one of the parties later appeals the trial court's decision, the appellate court may publish its decision, therefore making it available for review.

The process of making court decisions more widely available has been aided by the advent of **electronic case filing systems**. Common in the federal court system and increasingly found at the state and local levels, these systems consist of a component for case management (e.g., a database of cases and parties), plus electronic creation and storage of pleadings and testimony (e.g., digital images and audio recordings). These systems are similar to electronic health record systems in the health care environment (e.g., one for every legal case vs. one for every patient) but differ in the sense that virtually all record content in a court proceeding is available to the public. Only if a specific order is issued, **pleadings** or testimony are kept private (under seal). These systems typically are accessible to the general public via the Internet, though sometimes for a fee. These systems allow searches by the case file number, the name of a party to a case, and sometimes by a party's Social Security number.

Despite the fact that not all court decisions are published, numerous cases are available for study. By reviewing cases with similar circumstances, an idea can be obtained of how a court may view a new controversy involving similar circumstances. In making this determination, it is important to remember that the doctrine of *stare decisis* applies at both the state and federal levels. In the state systems, *stare decisis* applies so that the decisions in one particular state have binding precedence only over future decisions of courts in that same state; decisions of other states regarding similar circumstances have only persuasive value. For this reason, cases involving similar circumstances but involving courts in different states may result in opposite conclusions.

BRANCHES OF GOVERNMENT

In the federal and state systems, the powers of government are described in the system's respective constitution. These powers are divided into three distinct branches: legislative, executive, and judicial (Figure 1.4). As their names indicate, the legislative branch enacts the laws, the executive branch enforces and administers the laws, and the judicial branch interprets the laws. Each branch exercises those powers that belong to its branch and refrains from exercising those powers that properly belong to the other branches, except in instances in which the constitution expressly directs or permits. This division of power was designed so that no one branch of government would dominate the other two. This system of checks and balances is referred to as the **separation of powers**.

Although the three branches of government maintain a separation of powers, they do interact in certain areas. For example, the president of the United States may see the need for particular legislation to advance her agenda and may therefore ask a member of Congress to act as a

	Legislative Branch	***Executive Branch***	***Judicial Branch***
Government of the United States (federal government)	United States Congress	President of the United States	Federal courts
State governments	State legislatures	Governors	State courts

Figure 1.4 The Division of Governmental Power

sponsor of the particular bill the president has drafted. Additionally, the names of individuals nominated by the president for appointment to the federal judiciary must be submitted to the Senate for its approval (the advise and consent process). And while Congress and the president may not change any decision reached by the U.S. Supreme Court in a specific controversy, Congress may pass new or revised legislation to replace the law previously held unconstitutional. In addition, the amendment process to the U.S. Constitution can serve as a mechanism to offset or override a U.S. Supreme Court decision.

> **HIPAA**
>
> All three branches of government play a role in HIPAA: Congress creates a statute, the executive branch enforces it, and the judicial branch resolves litigation relating to it.

One recent example of interaction between the three branches of government involved the Health Insurance Portability and Accountability Act (HIPAA). Congress passed HIPAA in part to battle perceived health care fraud and abuse. HIPAA established or strengthened five programs to assist with fraud enforcement, all to be administered by the executive branch. HIPAA also empowered executive branch agencies to promulgate rules and regulations concerning the confidentiality, privacy, and security of health information. The judicial branch of government, in turn, works to resolve the litigation brought by law enforcement agencies of the executive branch concerning fraud and abuse and the appeals from administrative bodies deciding issues related to confidentiality, privacy, and security of health information. These resolutions may result in **injunctions**, fines, and jail time.

> **HIPAA/GINA**
>
> The terms of the Genetic Information Nondiscrimination Act (GINA) specifically address the application of the statute to the HIPAA Privacy Rule.

A second example of interaction between the three branches of government is the Genetic Information Nondiscrimination Act (GINA). Congress passed GINA in 2008 to address perceived areas of discrimination in employment and insurance relating to the use of genetic information. The statutory terms of GINA provide the executive branch with the authority to issue rules and regulations, with one term of the statute specifically instructing the Secretary of the Department of Health and Human Services to revise the HIPAA privacy regulations to encompass and address genetic information.[8] The judicial branch, in turn, possesses authority to resolve disputes brought pursuant to GINA.

> **ARRA**
>
> Provisions of the American Recovery and Reinvestment Act of 2009 require the executive branch to report to Congress on compliance with the act.

A third example of interaction between the branches of government is the terms of the American Recovery and Reinvestment Act of 2009 (ARRA). ARRA requires the Secretary of Health and Human Services to report to Congress concerning violations of confidentiality and security of protected health information. Details of what must be contained in this report are listed in Table 1.5. ARRA also tasks the General Accounting Office with reporting to Congress best practices related to disclosure

Table 1.5 Elements of a Compliance Report

A compliance report relating to privacy and security of health information must contain:
The number of complaints
The number of such complaints resolved informally, a summary of those resolved complaints, and the number of covered entities receiving technical assistance to achieve compliance
The number of such complaints that have resulted in imposition of civil monetary penalties or through monetary settlements
The number of compliance reviews conducted and the outcome of each such review The number of subpoenas or inquiries issued
The plan of the Secretary of HHS for improving compliance with and enforcement of such provisions for the following year
The number of audits performed and a summary of audit findings

Source: 42 U.S.C. § 17954(a) (2019).

of protected health information, including those of states and other entities; the success of those practices as they relate to quality of care; and the use of electronic informed consent for disclosing protected health information for treatment, payment, and health care operations.[9]

Legislative Branch

The legislative branch functions to enact laws. The legislature determines the need for new laws and changes in existing laws. At the federal level and in almost all states, the legislature is bicameral, consisting of two houses: one upper house (called the Senate) and one lower house (called the House of Representatives or Assembly). At the federal level, the Senate and the House of Representatives are collectively referred to as the Congress.

Legislative proposals are called bills. Bills are shepherded through the legislature by means of a committee system. When a particular bill is introduced into one of the houses, it is assigned or referred for study to a committee with prescribed areas of concern or interest. To assist their study of a bill, committees may conduct investigations and hold hearings, inviting interested persons to present their views. Some bills "die in committee," meaning they never reach the full legislative body. If a bill does emerge from committee, it is subject to further consideration and debate and, eventually, approved or rejected by one of the houses.

Before a bill can be sent to the chief executive for signature, both houses must pass identical versions of the bill or resolve their differences by way of a joint conference committee. If the joint conference committee approach is used, the bill must be resubmitted to both houses for vote before being forwarded to the chief executive for signature.

Executive Branch

The executive branch functions to enforce and administer the laws. The executive branch is organized on a departmental basis, with each department assigned a particular responsibility. The departments are subdivided into administrative agencies, each with defined powers to administer and implement particular legislation.

Health care providers deal most frequently with the executive branch. Although each agency by definition is assigned a particular area of responsibility, health care organizations are subject to the rules and regulations of multiple agencies at both the federal and state levels. For example, at the federal level, the Department of Health and Human Services regulates Medicare payments to health care providers, and the Department of Labor regulates the hours and wages of employees of these same providers. At the state level, various licensing boards issue licenses to practice medicine, nursing, and pharmacy and other professions and to operate hospitals and nursing homes.

The role of the executive branch is not limited to the action of administrative agencies; the chief executive plays a large role in this branch of government. For instance, it is only after the chief executive approves a particular bill by signing it that the bill becomes law. If, however, this chief executive disapproves of the bill, she may veto the bill, effectively killing the legislation unless the legislature successfully overrides the veto through the voting process.

Moreover, the chief executive can issue executive orders. These orders interpret, implement, or give administrative effect to a provision of the constitution or law. Executive orders have the effect of law after being published in the *Federal Register*, in the case of the federal system, or in a comparable publication at the state level.

Judicial Branch

The judicial branch functions to interpret the law through the **adjudication** and resolution of disputes. In situations where the parties cannot resolve their dispute among themselves, they may resort to a lawsuit, asking the court to resolve their dispute.

In order to resolve a particular dispute, a court looks to the relevant statutes, constitutional provisions, and administrative rules and regulations and applies them where appropriate to the facts of the case. The court also applies the doctrines of *stare decisis* and *res judicata* where necessary.

Where the circumstances of the case warrant, a court will examine the specific law or regulation to determine whether it conforms to or violates the U.S. Constitution. Where the law violates the terms of the U.S. Constitution, the court will declare that law, or portion thereof, invalid. The power of the courts to pass on the constitutionality of an act of Congress was decided in the landmark U.S. Supreme Court case of *Marbury v. Madison*.[10] The configuration of the judicial branch is explained in detail in Chapter 2, Court Systems and Legal Procedures.

QUASI-LEGAL REQUIREMENTS

In addition to the many requirements imposed directly by law, health care organizations are subject to a multitude of additional requirements: ethical, accreditation, and licensure. To add a further layer of requirements, health care institutions frequently develop their own policies, procedures, and medical staff bylaws in response to state licensing requirements, accrediting standards, and/or the recommendations of professional associations. While these additional requirements are not laws in and of themselves, they greatly influence the operation of health care organizations. Furthermore, health care organizations can be held responsible for failing to meet these requirements. For these reasons, they are referred to as quasi-legal requirements.

The prevalence of these requirements across the United States is great. For example, a requirement that hospitals follow their own medical staff bylaws and regulations or be subject to judicial oversight applies across most of the United States.[11] Where a hospital's bylaws provide a physician with certain rights, such as those to notice, an opportunity to be heard, and appellate procedures before terminating medical staff privileges, the hospital must follow those bylaws. In all but the states of Iowa, Oklahoma, and South Carolina, the failure to do so can result in judicial review and enforcement of the terms of the bylaws.[12]

In the legal context, quasi-legal requirements are most often used to establish the standard of care in a medical malpractice lawsuit or a licensing hearing. As discussed in Chapter 4, Principles of Liability, if the standard of care established under the quasi-legal requirements is higher than the minimally acceptable standard found in a statute, it is the higher standard against which the health care organization will be measured.

Quasi-legal requirements can also be seen in the context of accrediting standards used in replacement for compliance with regulations. For example, the U.S. Department of Health and Human Services has granted deeming authority to the Joint Commission and the American Osteopathic Association to conduct accreditation surveys. **Deeming authority** means that compliance with the requirements and standards of either or both accrediting organizations may substitute for compliance with the *Medicare Conditions of Participation for Hospitals* published by CMS. In a legal action, a party may submit evidence of compliance with accrediting standards of either or both organizations in lieu of evidence of compliance with the *Medicare Conditions of Participation.*

CONCLUSION

In large measure, the sources of law define the government's authority to control the activities of individuals and organizations. By understanding these sources of law and the separate branches of government, those involved in protecting health information should be better equipped to deal with the government's regulation of the health care industry. And as the branches of government pose even further regulation, the health information professional may be able to influence the direction of this further regulation.

CASE STUDY A

You are the director of health information services for a medium-sized health care facility. Like many of your peers, you have contracted with an outside copying service to handle all requests for release of patient health information at your facility. You have learned that a lobbying organization for trial attorneys in your state is promoting legislation to place a cap on photocopying costs, which is significantly below the actual cost incurred as part of the contract. Discuss the roles each branch of government will play in considering this legislation and how you and your professional organization may act to influence this process.

CASE STUDY B

Michelle Sargol offers to pay $9,000 for a particular car located on John Weber's car lot. Weber accepts Sargol's offer and promises to transfer title next week, at which time Sargol will pay for the car. The next day, Laura Kavanaugh visits the car lot and offers to pay Weber $10,000 for the same car. Can Weber accept Kavanaugh's offer? What area of law is involved?

REVIEW QUESTIONS

1. Why should a health information professional possess a fundamental understanding of the law?
2. How does contract law differ from tort law?
3. How do substantive law and procedural law differ?
4. Does a single document or source of law exist where an individual can find all of the rules governing health information? Why or why not?
5. How does the content of state constitutions compare with the content of the U.S. Constitution?
6. What are the three levels at which statutes governing health information are found?
7. Describe the difference between licensure and certification of a health care professional.
8. Explain the concepts of *stare decisis* and *res judicata*.
9. When does an executive order have the effect of law?
10. What must both houses in the legislature do before a bill is sent to the chief executive for signature?
11. What is the function of the judicial branch of government?

ENRICHMENT ACTIVITY

Through the use of the Internet, identify bills pending in your state legislature that deal with health care issues. Contact by written mail, e-mail, or telephone the office of the sponsoring state legislator of one of the bills. Identify yourself as a student, indicate your course of study, and request to interview the legislator about the sponsored bill. Ask about the origins of the bill, the amount of support or opposition the bill has garnered, and the chances for successful passage and signature by the governor. Report your results to your instructor and/or discuss them with your classmates.

NOTES

1. 474 So.2d 95 (Ala. 1985).
2. 453 S.E.2d 760 (Ga. Ct. App. 1995).
3. 599 N.Y.S.2d 350 (N.Y. App. Div. 1993).
4. In the United States, constitutions at the federal and state levels are written. By contrast, Great Britain's constitution is unwritten.
5. *See Bartling v. Superior Court,* 163 Cal. App. 3d 186, 195 (1984).
6. 42 U.S.C. § 17951 (2019).
7. 42 U.S.C. §300jj-36 (2019).
8. Genetic Information Nondiscrimination Act of 2008, 42 U.S.C. § 1320d-9 (2019).
9. 42 U.S.C. § 17932(i) (2019).
10. 5 U.S. 137 (1803).
11. *Clemens v. Fairview Med. Ctr. Inc.,* 449 So.2d 788 (Ala. 1984); *Kiester v. Humana Hops. Alaska, Inc.,* 843 P.2d 1219, 1222 (Alaska 1992); *Bock v. John C. Lincoln Hosp.,* 702 P.2d 253 (Ariz. Ct. App. 1985); *Baptist Health v. Murphy,* 226 S.W.3d 800 (Ark. 2006); *Miller v. Eisenhower Med. Ctr., 6124 P.2d 258 (Cal. 1980); Hawkins v. Kinsie, 540 P.2d 345 (Colo. Ct. App. 1975); Gianetti v. Norwalk Hosp., 557 A.2d 1249 (Conn. 1989); Dworkin v. St. Francis Hosp., Inc.,* 537 A.2d 302, 306 (Del. Super. Ct. 1986); *Lake Hosp. & Clinic, Inc. v. Silversmith,* 551 So.2d 538 (Fla. Dist. Ct. App. 1989); *Satilla Health Servs. Inc. v. Bell,* 633 S.E.2d 575, 580 (Ga. Ct. App. 2006); *Robles v. Humana Hosp. of Cartersville,* 785 F. Supp. 989, 1001 (N.D. Ga. 1992); *Silver v. Castle Mem'l Hosp.,* 497 P.2d 564 (Haw. 1972); *Miller v. St. Alphonsus Reg'l Med. Ctr., Inc.,* 87 P.3d 934, 943–44 (Idaho 1994); *Adkins v. Sarah Bush Lincoln Health Ctr.,* 544 N.E.2d 733 (Ill. 1989); *Pepple v. Parkview Mem'l Hosp., Inc.,* 536 N.E.2d 274, 276 (Ind. 1989); *Dutta v. St. Francis Reg'l Med. Ctr. Inc.,* 867 P.2d 1057 (Kan. 1994); *McElhinney v. William Booth Mem'l Hosp.,* 544 S.W.2d 216, 218 (Ky. 1976); *Smith v. Our Lady of the Lake Hosp., Inc.,* 639 So.2d 730, 756 (La. 1994); *Bartley v. E. Maine Med. Ctr.,* 617 A.2d 1020 (Me. 1992); *Sadler v. Dimensions Healthcare Corp.,* 836 A.2d 655 (Md. 2003); *St. Louis v. Bay State Med. Ctr., Inc.,* 568 N.E.2d 1181, 1187088 (Mass. App. Ct. 1991); *Feyz v. Mercy Mem'l Hosp.,* 719 N.W.2d 1 (Mich. 2006); *Campbell v. St. Mary's Hosp.,* 252 N.W.2d 581 (Minn. 1977); *Wong v. Garden Park Cmty. Hosp., Inc.,* 565 So.2d 550 (Miss. 1990); *Egan v. St. Anthony's Med. Ctr.,* S.W.3d, 2008 WL 307689 (Mo. 2008); *N. Valley Hosp., Inc. v. Kauffman,* 544 P.2d 1219, 1224 (Mont. 1976); *Babcock v. Saint Francis Med. Ctr.,* 543 N.W.2d 749 (Neb. Ct. App. 1996); *Clark v. Columbia/HCA Info. Servs., Inc.,* 25 P.3d 215 (Nev. 2001); *Bricker v. Sceva Speare Mem'l Hosp.,* 281 A.2d. 589 I (N.H. 1971); *Greisman v. Newcomb Hosp.,* 192 A.2d 817 (N.J. 1963); *Clough v. Adventist Health Sys., Inc.,* 780 P.2d 627 (N.M. 1989); *Mason v. Cent. Suffolk Hosp.,* 819 N.E.2d 1029, 1031 (N.Y. 2004); *Lohrmann v. Iredell Mem'l Hosp., Inc.,* 620 S.E.2d 258, 262 (N.C. Ct. App. 2005); *Van Valkenburg v. Paracelsus Healthcare Corp.,* 606 N.W.2d 908, 917–18 (N.D. 2000); *Bouquett v. St. Elizabeth Corp.,* 538 N.E.2d 113 (Ohio 1989); *Straube v. Emanuel Lutheran Charity Bd.* 600 P.2d 381, 386 (Or. 1979); *Lyons v. St. Vincent Health Ctr.,* 731 A.2d 206, 211 (Pa. Commw. Ct. 1999); *Hagan v. Osteopathic Gen. Hosp.,* 232 A.2d 596, 600 (R.I. 1967); *Mahan v. Avera St. Luke's,* 621 N.W.2d 156 (S.D. 2001); *Lewisburg Cmty. Hosp. v. Alfredson,* 805 S.W.2d 756, 759 (Tenn. 1991); *E. Tex. Med. Ctr., Cancer Inst. v. Anderson,* 991 S.W.2d 55 (Tex. App. 1998); *Brinton v. IHC Hosps., Inc.,* 973 P.2d 956 (Utah 1998); *Woodard v. Porter Hosp., Inc.,* 217 A.2d 37 (Vt. 1966); *Med. Ctr., Hosps., v. Terzis,* 367 S.E.2d 728, 230 (Va. 1988); *Rao v. Auburn Gen. Hosp.,* 573 P.2d 834 (Wash. Ct. App. 1978); *Mahmoodian v. United Hosp. Ctr. Inc.,* 404 S.E.2d 750, 755 (W.Va. 1991); *Seitzinger v. Cmty. Health Network,* 676 N.W.2d 426 (Wis. 2004); *Garrison v. Bd. of Trs. of Mem'l Hosp. of Laramie County,* 795 P.2d 190, 193 (Wyo. 1990); *Balkissoon v. Capitol Hill Hosp.,* 558 A.2d 304, 307 (D.C. 1989).
12. *See Natale v. Sisters of Mercy,* 52 N.W.2d 701, 710 (Iowa 1952); *Metcalf v. Coleman,* 71 P.3d 53, 56 (Okla. Civ. App. 2003); *Wood v. Hilton Head Hosp., Inc.,* 356 S.E.2d 841, 8942 (S.C. 1987).

CHAPTER 2

COURT SYSTEMS AND LEGAL PROCEDURES

LEARNING OBJECTIVES

After reading this chapter, the learner should be able to:

1. Compare and contrast subject matter jurisdiction between the federal and state court systems.
2. Differentiate between subject matter jurisdiction and personal jurisdiction.
3. Explain the basic differences between a trial and an appeal.
4. Identify the steps in a civil lawsuit.
5. Distinguish among the different forms of discovery.
6. Explain the uniqueness of e-discovery and electronically stored information.
7. Describe the concept of metadata.
8. Describe the roles of the judge and the jury during a trial.
9. Compare and contrast an order of garnishment and writ of execution.
10. Differentiate between the types of alternative dispute resolution.

KEY CONCEPTS

Alternative dispute resolution
Appeal
Arbitration
Audit trail
Certiorari
Complaint
Counterclaim
Court structures
Defendant
Deponent
Deposition
Discovery
Diversity jurisdiction
E-discovery
Electronically stored information
Federal question jurisdiction
Interrogatories
Jurisdiction
Jury instructions
Legal process
Litigation hold
Mediation
Mental examinations
Metadata
Negotiation and settlement
Notice of preservation
Order of garnishment
Order of preservation
Plaintiff
Personal jurisdiction
Pretrial conference
Production of documents and things
Request for admission
Rules
Satisfying the judgment
Service of process
Spoliation
Subject matter jurisdiction
Subpoena duces tecum
Summons
Trial
Verdict
Writ of execution

INTRODUCTION

It is truly an American phenomenon that a primary method of resolving disputes in the United States is through the court system. Although alternative methods of dispute resolution increasingly are being used, filing a lawsuit has become the way many Americans deal with resolving their disputes. Understanding the court systems and the legal procedures employed to process cases through these systems will assist the health information manager in understanding the use of health information in a legal action.

COURT SYSTEMS

Federal and state courts are similar in certain respects but differ in others. Both the federal and state court systems employ a multitier structure: trial courts, intermediate courts of appeal, and a supreme court. They differ, however, on what matters can be brought before them.

Jurisdiction

Jurisdiction is the authority by which courts and judicial officers may hear and decide a case. Jurisdiction encompasses authority not only over the parties involved, called **personal jurisdiction**, but also authority over the question at issue, called subject matter jurisdiction. This distinction is illustrated in Figure 2.1. The scope and extent of subject matter jurisdiction vary between federal and state courts, with subject matter jurisdiction in the federal courts being more limited in nature than subject matter jurisdiction in state courts. The contrast between jurisdictions is illustrated in Figure 2.2.

Figure 2.1 Types of Jurisdictions

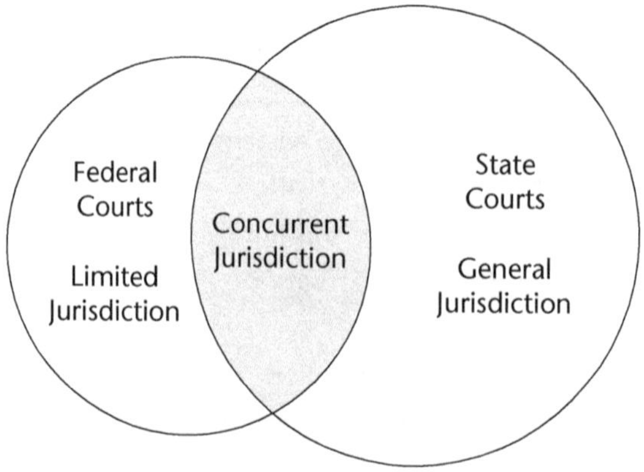

Figure 2.2 Jurisdictional Contrasts between Courts

Subject matter jurisdiction in federal court is limited by both the U.S. Constitution and statute. As a general rule, cases may be brought to federal court if they meet the requirement of either federal question jurisdiction or diversity jurisdiction. **Federal question jurisdiction** refers to cases that call into question or involve a U.S. constitutional principle, treaty, federal statute, or federal rule or regulation. It also involves those cases that would traditionally be considered state cases but occur on federal land. For example, negligence occurring at a military base hospital or theft of property at a national park would fall within federal question jurisdiction.

Additional cases may be brought to federal court under the theory of **diversity jurisdiction**: the case in question involves parties who are citizens of different states and the amount in controversy is over $75,000. Both points must exist in order to meet the requirements of diversity jurisdiction. In diversity cases, the federal courts apply the substantive law of the particular state in which the federal court is located to resolve the dispute. Procedural matters in diversity cases are governed by federal common law and the pertinent rules of court, such as the Federal Rules of Civil Procedure.

By contrast, state courts usually maintain courts of general jurisdiction, meaning that the subject matter is not limited. Within a particular state system, the state courts may be subdivided into special courts dealing with limited subjects, such as probate court, juvenile court, or small claims court. Lawsuits that cannot be brought before the state's specialized courts will be brought in the court of general jurisdiction.

In some instances, federal courts have exclusive jurisdiction over a certain subject matter; therefore, a lawsuit covering that subject matter may be brought only in federal court. For example, judicial review of a decision by the Provider Reimbursement Review Board can occur only in a U.S. District Court, and matters relating to bankruptcy can only be heard in U.S. Bankruptcy Courts, which have exclusive jurisdiction over these matters.

In other instances, jurisdiction is concurrent between the federal and state courts. Where concurrent jurisdiction exists, the party bringing the lawsuit may go to either federal or state court and thus must choose between the two court systems. For example, a medical malpractice action involving a citizen of one state (the patient) and a citizen of a second state (the health care provider) could be brought either in a federal court using diversity jurisdiction, if the jurisdictional amount is also met, or in a state court of general jurisdiction. The decision over which court to choose rests on many factors, including how long it will take before obtaining a trial date in a certain court and whether certain procedural rules are more advantageous to one side over another.

Many persons find it difficult to understand the differences between federal and state courts. Table 2.1 provides a comparison between these two types of courts. Table 2.2 provides examples of jurisdiction in federal court and state court and when that jurisdiction is concurrent.

In addition to subject matter jurisdiction, courts must have personal jurisdiction in order to issue a valid judgment. Personal jurisdiction refers to the authority of a court over the person as opposed to authority over the person's property. When a plaintiff files a lawsuit, the plaintiff voluntarily submits to the personal jurisdiction of the court. Personal jurisdiction over the defendant depends on a number of factors, mainly whether the defendant was properly served with the summons and complaint.

Court Structure

As stated in Chapter 1, Workings of the American Legal System, both the federal and state court systems operate within a multitier structure. An organizational chart illustrating these

Table 2.1 Comparison of Court Systems

<table>
<tr><th></th><th>Federal Courts</th><th>State Courts</th></tr>
<tr><td>Structure</td><td><ul><li>Article III of the Constitution invests the judicial power of the United States in the federal court system. Article III, Section 1, specifically creates the U.S. Supreme Court and gives Congress the authority to create the lower federal courts.</li><li>Congress has used this power to establish the 13 U.S. Courts of Appeals, the 94 U.S. District Courts, the 94 U.S. Bankruptcy Courts, the U.S. Court of Federal Claims, and the U.S. Court of International Trade. U.S. Bankruptcy Courts handle bankruptcy matters. Magistrate judges handle some district court matters.</li><li>Parties dissatisfied with a decision of a U.S. District Court, the U.S. Court of Claims, and/or the U.S. Court of International Trade may appeal to a U.S. Court of Appeals.</li><li>A party may ask the U.S. Supreme Court to review a decision of a U.S. Court of Appeals, but the Supreme Court is the final arbiter of federal constitutional questions. In some cases it is a court of general jurisdiction.</li></ul></td><td><ul><li>The U.S. Constitution and laws of each state establish the judiciary. A court of last resort, often known as a supreme court, is usually the highest court. Some states also have an intermediate court of appeals. Below these appeals courts are the state trial courts. Some are referred to as circuit or district courts.</li><li>States also usually have courts that handle specific legal matters, e.g., probate court (wills and estates), juvenile court, family court, etc.</li><li>Parties dissatisfied with the decision of the trial court may take their case to the intermediate court of appeals.</li><li>Parties have the option to ask the highest state court to hear the case.</li><li>Only certain cases are eligible for review by the U.S. Supreme Court.</li></ul></td></tr>
<tr><td>Selection of Judges</td><td>Article II, Section 2, of the U.S. Constitution states that federal judges are to be nominated by the president and confirmed by the Senate. They hold office during good behavior, typically for life. Through congressional impeachment proceedings, federal judges may be removed from office for misbehavior.</td><td>State court judges are selected in a variety of ways, including election, appointment for a given number of years, and combinations of these methods, e.g., appointment followed by election.</td></tr>
<tr><td>Types of Cases Heard</td><td>Cases that deal with the constitutionality of a law, the laws and treaties of the United States, ambassadors and public ministers, disputes between two or more states, admiralty law, and bankruptcy are heard by the federal courts.</td><td>Most criminal cases, probate, most contract cases, tort cases (personal injuries), family law (marriages, divorces, adoptions), etc. are heard by state courts. State courts are the final arbiters of their own laws and constitutions. Their interpretation of federal law of the U.S. Constitution may be appealed to the U.S. Supreme Court. The U.S. Supreme Court may choose to hear or not hear such cases.</td></tr>
</table>

Source: Administrative Office of the U.S. Courts (2019).

Table 2.2 Jurisdictional Examples

State Courts	Federal Courts	State or Federal Courts
• Crimes under state legislation • State constitutional issues and cases involving state laws or regulations • Family law issues • Real property issues • Landlord and tenant disputes • Most private contract disputes (except those resolved under bankruptcy law) • Most issues involving the regulation of trades and professions • Most professional malpractice issues • Most issues involving the internal governance of business associations such as partnerships and corporations • Most personal injury lawsuits • Most workers' injury claims • Probate and inheritance matters • Most traffic violations and registration of motor vehicles	• Crimes under statutes enacted by Congress • Most cases involving federal laws or regulations (e.g., tax, Social Security, broadcasting, civil rights) • Matters involving interstate commerce, including airline and railroad regulation • Cases involving securities and commodities regulations, including takeover of publicly held corporations • Admiralty cases • International trade law matters • Patent, copyright, and other intellectual property issues • Cases involving rights under treaties, foreign states, and foreign nationals • State law disputes when diversity of citizenship exists • Bankruptcy matters • Disputes between states • Habeas corpus actions • Traffic violations and other misdemeanors occurring on certain federal property	• Crimes punishable under both federal or state law • Federal constitutional issues • Certain civil rights claims • Class-action cases • Environmental regulations • Certain disputes involving federal law

Source: Administrative Office of the U.S. Courts (2019).

court structures is provided in Figure 2.3. At the bottom tier is the trial court. Above trial courts are intermediate courts of appeal, and above these courts are the highest courts, supreme courts. In the federal court system, all three levels exist. Each of the fifty states has at least a trial court and a supreme court. In some states, however, no intermediate courts of appeal exist; therefore, cases moving through the court system in those states may go directly from a trial court to the supreme court of the state.

Trial courts conduct trials in civil and criminal matters and supervise the discovery process that occurs before trial. In a trial, the judge and jury listen to the testimony of witnesses and view exhibits in an attempt to reach a verdict. The names of trial courts vary within the fifty states; trial courts in the federal system are called district courts.

It is the nature of a trial that one party must lose, either in whole or in part. The losing party at trial may then decide to appeal. If so, the lawsuit moves to the intermediate appellate court.

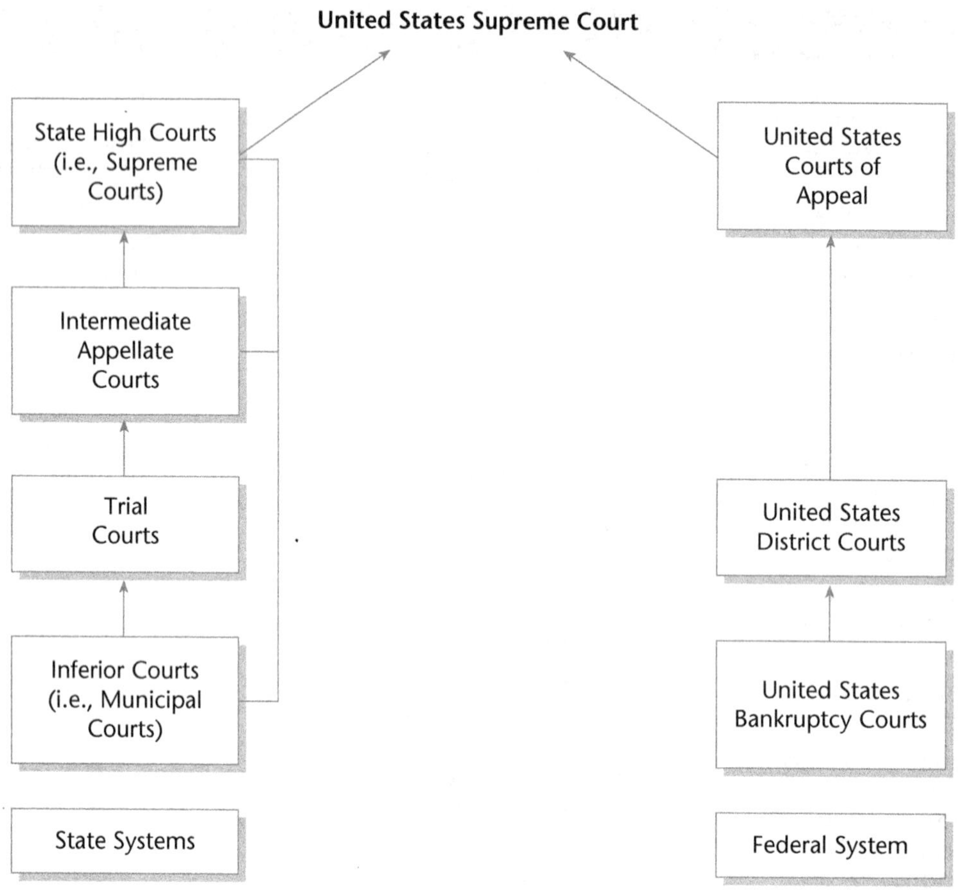

Figure 2.3 Structure of Court Systems

Appellate courts differ dramatically from trial courts in that the appellate court looks to the record of events at trial to determine, if error in law or procedure occurred, which would warrant reversal or modification of the result reached at trial. In an appellate court, there is no testimony of witnesses or introduction of exhibits. In short, there is not another trial. Cases proceed on the basis of the parties' written briefs; the only "live" portion of an appeal consists of the oral argument the parties present to the court after the briefs are filed. Appellate courts in the state systems are generally referred to as courts of appeal for that particular state—for example, the Missouri Court of Appeals. Appellate courts in the federal system are divided by geographic region and are referred to as circuit courts of appeal (see Chapter 1, Workings of the American Legal System).

The highest level of court is the supreme court. Each of the fifty states and the federal government has a court of last resort called a supreme court, with one exception. In New York State, the court of last resort is called the court of appeals, whereas the trial court is termed the supreme court.

These supreme courts, except in New York State, hear appeals from the intermediate appellate courts. Under very limited exceptions, a case may be brought directly in the supreme court without first having been heard in a trial or intermediate appellate court.

The U.S. Supreme Court hears appeals brought from the various federal circuit courts of appeal and the highest state courts in cases involving the U.S. Constitution, federal statutes, treaties, or rules and regulations. The U.S. Supreme Court decides which cases to hear by granting a writ of certiorari. Each year, litigants in thousands of cases apply for writs of **certiorari**; the U.S. Supreme Court grants only approximately 150 of these writs per year. Similarly, state supreme courts maintain guidelines concerning the type and number of cases they can decide per year.

Court Rules

One feature common to every court in America is the existence of court rules. **Rules** are the principles established by authorities that prescribe or direct certain action or forbearance from action. In the context of the judiciary, rules are used to implement statutory requirements, establish uniform procedures, and guide attorneys and parties to a case regarding how proceedings will be conducted. Legislatures authorize courts to issue rules of procedure, just as legislatures authorize administrative agencies to promulgate rules and regulations for their areas of expertise. Rules issued by courts that are not inconsistent with an action of a legislature have the force of law and are binding on the court, its personnel, and parties to a case.

Rules issued at the federal level are mirrored by rules issued by courts at the state level and, in some instances, by courts at the municipal level. Because of this mirroring approach, the discussion of rules in this text focuses on the federal rules. The U.S. Supreme Court, pursuant to a grant of authority from Congress, promulgates rules in all areas of federal court proceedings. The federal rules govern procedure, practice, and evidence in the federal courts. The most well-known federal rules are the Rules of Civil Procedure, the Rules of Criminal Procedure, and the Rules of Evidence. As their names suggest, the Civil Procedure Rules govern civil cases, the Criminal Procedure Rules govern criminal cases, and the Evidence Rules govern admission or exclusion of evidence in both civil and criminal cases.

EHR

Rules governing procedure and evidence govern both paper-based and electronic health records.

The Civil Procedure Rules and the Evidence Rules are of most interest to health information management professionals because they govern the admissibility of the health record into evidence. The Civil Procedure Rules of relevance to HIM are listed in Table 2.3 and are discussed in further detail in this chapter. The Evidence Rules are divided into eleven articles, which are listed in Table 2.4. Of particular importance to HIM professionals are Article V governing privileges (e.g., attorney–client privilege), Article VII governing opinions and expert testimony (e.g., expert testimony used in a medical malpractice case), Article VIII governing hearsay (e.g., introduction of the health record as evidence), Article IX governing authentication and identification (e.g., data compilations admitted as evidence), and Article X governing contents of writings, recordings,

Table 2.3 The Federal Rules of Civil Procedure—Selected Rules

- Rule 16 (pretrial conferences)
- Rule 26 (duty of disclosure and depositions)
- Rule 33 (interrogatories)
- Rule 34 (production of documents, including business records)
- Rule 35 (physical or mental examinations)
- Rule 36 (requests for admissions)
- Rule 45 (subpoena)

Table 2.4 The Federal Rules of Evidence

- Article I—General Provisions
- Article II—Judicial Notice
- Article III—Presumptions in Civil Actions and Proceedings
- Article IV—Relevancy and Its Limits
- Article V—Privileges
- Article VI—Witnesses
- Article VII—Opinions and Expert Testimony
- Article VIII—Hearsay
- Article IX—Authentication and Identifications
- Article X—Contents of Writings, Recordings, and Photographs
- Article XI—Miscellaneous Rules

and photographs (e.g., allowing an exact duplicate copy to serve as evidence in replacement of the original). Additional information concerning these matters is addressed in Chapter 3, Judicial Process of Health Information; Chapter 12, Risk Management, Quality Management, and Utilization Management; and Chapter 13, Information Systems.

LEGAL PROCESS

As stated in Chapter 1, Workings of the American Legal System, the law is divided into two general areas: criminal law and civil law. The stages through which a lawsuit passes are referred to as **legal process**. Because the civil lawsuit has traditionally played a large role in health care, its steps are described in this section and are illustrated in Figure 2.4.

The characteristics of a civil lawsuit vary somewhat from state to state because of the differences in each state's procedural rules. The following description is modeled on the Federal Rules of Civil Procedure, which is the pattern more than half of the states have used to develop their own procedural rules. For simplicity, all references are made to persons, not organizations or corporations.

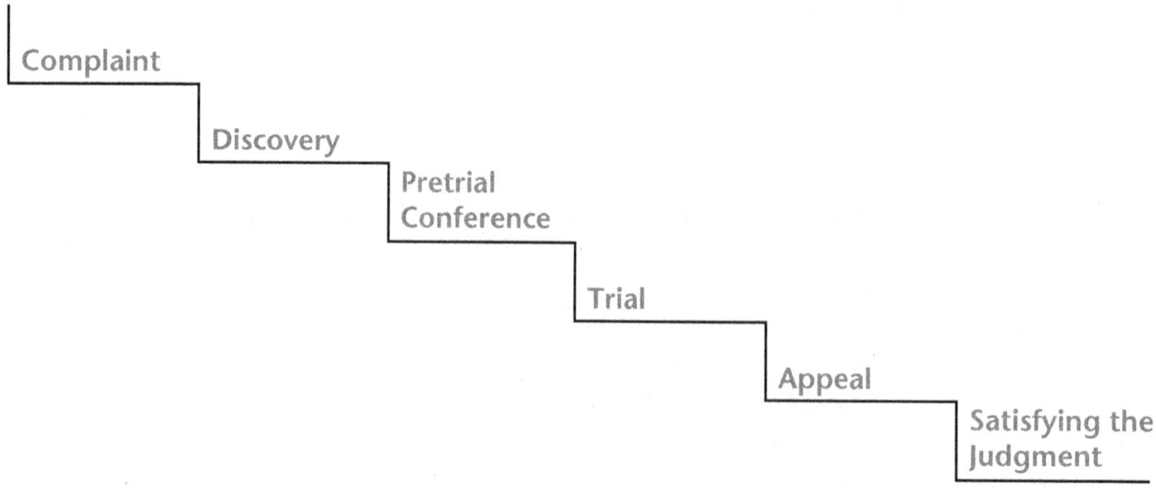

Figure 2.4 Steps in a Civil Lawsuit

Beginning the Lawsuit

The person who initiates the lawsuit is called the **plaintiff**. The person sued by the plaintiff is called the **defendant**. Additional parties may also be present, depending on the complexity of the lawsuit. Where appropriate, these additional parties are identified in this discussion. They are also identified in Figure 2.5.

The first step of every lawsuit is the filing of the plaintiff's complaint. The **complaint** is a written document that describes (1) the grounds of jurisdiction of the court, (2) the plaintiff's claim in a short and plain statement, and (3) the demand for relief to which the plaintiff feels he is entitled—for example, damages. After filing the complaint with the court clerk, the plaintiff or his attorney receives a summons from the clerk that must be personally delivered to the defendant along with a copy of the complaint. A **summons** is a document used to start a civil action and acquire jurisdiction over a defendant. An example of a summons in a civil action is provided in Figure 2.6. The delivery of the summons and complaint is referred to as **service of process**.

After receiving the complaint, the defendant must file a written response, called an answer. In the answer, the defendant admits or denies the contents of the complaint and raises any affirmative defenses, such as contributory negligence. The defendant may also include in the answer a **counterclaim**, which is a claim presented by the defendant against the plaintiff. For example, a physician sued in a medical malpractice action may decide to raise as a counterclaim against his former patient a claim of malicious prosecution.

Furthermore, the defendant may decide to pursue a claim against someone who was not originally part of the lawsuit but is liable for all or part of the plaintiff's claim. In that case, the defendant is referred to as a third-party plaintiff in addition to being the defendant. In this situation, the person being sued by the defendant is called a third-party defendant.

The defendant has only a limited time frame in which to file an answer, generally twenty days after service of process. If the defendant fails to file an answer, the court may decide the case against the defendant by entering a default judgment. The rules on answering the complaint also apply to third-party defendants who must file an answer or risk a default judgment.

In addition to the answer, a defendant may file any of a number of motions in the hope that the case can be decided without going to trial. For example, the plaintiff can file a motion to dismiss the case or a motion for summary judgment, citing specific reasons such as failure to state a claim or that no disputed facts exist and no reasonable jury could find in the plaintiff's favor. If the motion is granted, the lawsuit in the trial court stops, and the only action the losing party can then take is to pursue an appeal.

Discovery

Once the complaint and answer stage of the lawsuit is complete, the parties and their lawyers start an investigative process, gathering information related to the lawsuit. This investigative process is

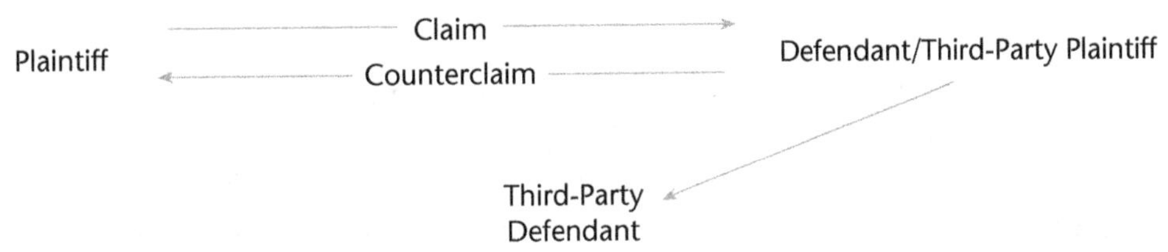

Figure 2.5 Parties to a Lawsuit

AO 440 (Rev. 06/12) Summons in a Civil Action

UNITED STATES DISTRICT COURT
for the
__________ District of __________

____
Plaintiff(s)
v.) Civil Action No.
____
Defendant(s)

SUMMONS IN A CIVIL ACTION

To: *(Defendant's name and address)*

A lawsuit has been filed against you.

Within 21 days after service of this summons on you (not counting the day you received it) — or 60 days if you are the United States or a United States agency, or an officer or employee of the United States described in Fed. R. Civ. P. 12 (a)(2) or (3) — you must serve on the plaintiff an answer to the attached complaint or a motion under Rule 12 of the Federal Rules of Civil Procedure. The answer or motion must be served on the plaintiff or plaintiff's attorney, whose name and address are:

If you fail to respond, judgment by default will be entered against you for the relief demanded in the complaint. You also must file your answer or motion with the court.

CLERK OF COURT

Date: ______________ ______________________________
Signature of Clerk or Deputy Clerk

Figure 2.6 Summons in a Civil Action
Source: Courtesy of www.uscourts.gov.

called discovery and often serves to unearth facts and documents previously unknown to at least one party to the lawsuit. **Discovery** can be defined as those devices or tools used by one side to obtain facts and information about the case from the other side in order to prepare for trial.

As a general rule, a party may obtain information that is pertinent to an issue in the case, no matter how slight the connection may be between the issue and the information obtained. Examples of information sometimes sought in a lawsuit are seen in Table 2.5. The exception to the general rule is if the information is legally protected from discovery, such as by the attorney–client privilege addressed in more detail in Chapter 3, Judicial Process of Health Information. Types of discovery include depositions, written **interrogatories**, production of documents or things, physical and **mental examinations**, and requests for admissions (Table 2.6). The parties may use any or

AO 440 (Rev. 06/12) Summons in a Civil Action (Page 2)

Civil Action No.

PROOF OF SERVICE

(This section should not be filed with the court unless required by Fed. R. Civ. P. 4 (l))

This summons for *(name of individual and title, if any)* ______________________

was received by me on *(date)* ______________ .

☐ I personally served the summons on the individual at *(place)* ______________________

______________________ on *(date)* ______________ ; or

☐ I left the summons at the individual's residence or usual place of abode with *(name)* ______________

______________________ , a person of suitable age and discretion who resides there,

on *(date)* ______________ , and mailed a copy to the individual's last known address; or

☐ I served the summons on *(name of individual)* ______________________ , who is

designated by law to accept service of process on behalf of *(name of organization)* ______________

______________________ on *(date)* ______________ ; or

☐ I returned the summons unexecuted because ______________________ ; or

☐ Other *(specify)*:

My fees are $ ________ for travel and $ ________ for services, for a total of $ 0.00 .

I declare under penalty of perjury that this information is true.

Date: ______________

____
Server's signature

____
Printed name and title

____
Server's address

Additional information regarding attempted service, etc:

Figure 2.6 Continued

Table 2.5 Information Often Sought through the Discovery Process

1. The personal, educational, and professional background of a witness
2. Documents relating to the dispute
3. Whatever a witness or party saw, heard, or did in connection with the dispute
4. Whatever anyone said at a particular time and place
5. The identity of anyone who may know something about the dispute or about the injuries or money losses suffered by either party
6. If the lawsuit involves a business, detailed information concerning how the business is run

Table 2.6 Methods of Discovery

Defined	Method
Deposition	Testimony given under oath outside the courtroom pursuant to a subpoena
Interrogatories	Written questions presented to a party or witness designed to gather information
Production of Documents	Inspection and/or copying of documents or other physical evidence upon written request
Physical/Mental Examination	Ordered by the court upon a party's request with good cause shown
Requests for Admissions	Written questions presented to a party designed to obtain admission of a certain fact

all of these forms of discovery. The delay between the commencement of a lawsuit and a trial date is usually explained by the quantity and complexity of the discovery in a case and the volume of cases before the court.

CRITICAL THINKING

Discovery can be a wide-ranging process and encompass almost anything pertinent to a lawsuit. Using Table 2.5 as a guide, determine what type of information might be sought as part of the discovery process in the following situations:

1. A car accident
2. A business dispute
3. An employment dispute
4. Injury caused by a dangerous product

E-Discovery

When discovery seeks information stored electronically in any medium, including business records such as the patient's electronic health record, it is referred to as **e-discovery**. The Federal Rules of Civil Procedure govern all forms of discovery conducted in proceedings filed in federal court. These rules were revised in 2006 to recognize the existence of electronically stored information (ESI) and to address how that information may be produced in response to discovery requests.[1] **Electronically stored information** refers to a distinct category of information that includes e-mails, Web pages, word processing files, and databases stored in the memory of computers (laptops, desktops, and mainframes), magnetic disks (such as computer hard drives and floppy disks), optical discs (such as DVDs and CDs), flash memory (such as thumb or flash drives), and backup media. ESI differs from conventional, paper-based information in distinct ways, as shown in Table 2.7.

The uniqueness of ESI has raised significant issues that are generally not seen when conventional, paper-based information is disclosed as part of the discovery process. Among these issues are the form or format in which ESI must be produced, the concept of undue burden, the existence of metadata, the need to preserve ESI, the possibility of waiver of privilege and work–product protection, and questions related to spoliation. See Table 2.8.

Table 2.7 How ESI Differs from Paper Information

1. Volume—use of electronic programs, databases, and devices is routine in the workplace (e.g., e-mail traffic of one employee in a year may easily number in the tens of thousands), resulting in a large number of potentially relevant documents to review.
2. Variety of Sources—one electronic document may reside in multiple places, (e.g., on the hard drive of the document's creator, reviewer, and recipient; on an organization's server; on laptops and home computers; and on backup tapes).
3. Dynamic Quality—the ability to change or mutate data (e.g., computer systems that automatically recycle and reuse memory space and thereby alter potentially relevant information without the knowledge of the program operator).
4. Hidden Information—metadata and embedded data.
5. Reliance upon Systems—complex ESI may only be comprehensible and usable if not separated from the system that created it.
6. Deletion—ESI may be recovered from multiple sources (e.g., hard drives, archival media, backup tapes for disaster recovery purposes, etc.) even if deleted from the medium in which it was originally stored.

Table 2.8 Significant ESI-Related Issues

1. Form or Format of Production—in what manner should ESI be produced?
2. Undue Burden—to what extent does complying with the e-discovery request result in excessive costs or inordinate time-consuming activity?
3. Metadata—will ESI be inadvertently produced to the detriment of a party?
4. Preservation—do routine computer operations need to be changed so that ESI is not inadvertently destroyed?
5. Waiver—will privilege or work–product protection be waived if ESI is produced?
6. Spoliation—if ESI is modified or destroyed, will sanctions be imposed?

The issue of form production centers on the form or format in which ESI will be produced. For example, ESI produced as a TIFF or PDF file is essentially a photograph of a digital document, whereas the same ESI produced as a file in native format shows the information in the manner in which it was created and used in the ordinary course of business operations. The difference between these examples illustrates how the choice of form or format raises many implications. For example, the format chosen by a party may influence the ability of the opposing side to easily search information electronically, to see relevant and sensitive information, and to use that information easily later at trial.

As a routine matter, procedural rules guide the parties on how to designate the form or format in which ESI will be produced. Where parties do not comply with those rules, courts will become involved. Two significant cases concerning form of production are *Hagenbuch v. 3B6 Sistemi Elettronici Industriali S.R.L.*[2] and *Williams v. Sprint/United Management Co.*[3] In *Hagenbuch*, the defendant had produced ESI as a TIFF image instead of in native format. The court held that doing so was insufficient to accomplish discovery and ordered the defendant to reproduce the same ESI in its original format. In *Williams*, the defendant produced ESI as a spreadsheet in static format. The court held that doing so was insufficient because the lack of mathematical formulas, the presence of text exceeding cell size, and the elimination of metadata impaired the discovery process. The court ordered the defendant to produce the same ESI as a spreadsheet in native format.

A second issue significant to parties to litigation is undue burden. The undue burden concept allows the individual or organization from whom the information is sought (the responding party) to indicate that complying with the discovery request will constitute an undue burden or cost because the information is stored in sources that are not reasonably accessible. Although it is generally true that electronic storage systems make it easier to locate and retrieve information, the volume of information to be searched, the age of the technology in which the information is stored, and the need to review all the information produced to determine if it is subject to privilege may cause the responding party to incur substantial burdens or costs. For example, information stored in a legacy system that can be used only by superseded systems may require the responding party to convert the information into a more usable form at considerable expense and effort. Figure 2.7 illustrates the undue burden associated with discovery of ESI.

Merely responding that the information sought will not be produced because of unreasonable burden or cost is not sufficient to excuse compliance with an e-discovery request. The responding party must show, rather, that the burdens and costs to search for, retrieve, and produce the responsive information that is found cannot be justified in the circumstances of the case. The requesting party may reply that its need for discovery outweighs the burdens and costs of locating, retrieving, and producing the electronically stored information. At this point, the parties may either negotiate between themselves to share the cost or ask the judge assigned to the case to determine what amount or type of electronically stored information must be produced in response to the e-discovery request.

A third important concept concerning e-discovery is metadata. Sometimes referred to as "data about data," **metadata** refers to unseen or hidden information in common computer files, which can indicate when a document was created, viewed, or revised and can contain edits, notes,

Figure 2.7 The Undue Burden Concept

or other private data. For example, word processing files may retain in electronic form a number of editorial comments, draft language, or deleted matter that are not otherwise apparent to the reader of the word processing document produced in hard copy or as a screen image. Metadata involving e-mail can indicate the history of transmission. In the context of spreadsheets, metadata includes embedded information, such as computational formulas. In the context of the electronic health record (EHR), metadata can identify who has reviewed, manipulated, or otherwise accessed the patient's record.

Metadata poses a problem when it is accidentally or unintentionally released. The metadata describing the history, tracking, or management of an electronic file can pose substantial risks to the party responding to a request to produce documents if the party is not aware of the presence of metadata when producing ESI pursuant to an e-discovery request. For example, an earlier draft version of a now-completed document may have contained a phrase that is considered favorable to the opposing party, but during the editing process, that same phrase had been omitted. If that document is disclosed in response to an e-discovery request in an electronic form that allows access to both the earlier and current versions, the opposing side would learn both variations and have an insight into the views and strategy of the responding party. For these reasons, it is incumbent upon health care organizations and those who manage information and data to establish and maintain policies and procedures that govern production of discovery materials, whether in paper or electronic form.

Releasing metadata may be appropriate in certain circumstances. For example, in *Miller v. Sauberman*,[4] a former patient sued a nursing home and his physician for medical malpractice after undergoing multiple surgeries to correct problems caused by bedsores he suffered from while at the nursing home. The former patient received a copy of his electronic health record (EHR) before filing his lawsuit and additional copies of the same record after filing his lawsuit. These records contained conflicting entries for the same items on the same days, particularly the entries related to the bedsores. Because the defendants did not provide a credible explanation for the different and conflicting versions of the patient's electronic health record, the court ordered the defendants to produce metadata to determine if the electronic health record was altered and, if so, when and by whom.

Possessing an understanding of the concept of metadata is important to health information managers who respond to requests for audit trails of EHRs. Such an understanding allows the manager to ensure metadata is properly produced as part of the audit trail. An **audit trail** is a record or catalog showing a sequence of user activity of a computer system, including who accessed what data, when such access occurred, and whether and what changes were made. Creating and reviewing audit trails are requirements of the Security Rule of the Health Insurance Portability and Accountability Act (HIPAA). More information about the Security Rule can be found in Chapter 13, Information Systems.

The duty to preserve ESI is a fourth significant issue. Preservation of ESI, while easy in theory, is difficult in practice. By its nature, ESI is dynamic and changeable. Routine computer operations critical to a party's activities plus limitations on memory for electronic storage may require parties to overwrite data. E-mails may be regularly deleted or backup tapes may be recycled as part of a party's regular business practices. For these reasons, the need to preserve information is always balanced against the need to continue routine computer operations critical to a party's business activities.

Parties accomplish this balancing act in one of two ways: issuing a litigation hold or obtaining a preservation order. A **litigation hold** refers to the actions of a party who possesses data to make efforts to prevent routine destruction and preserve ESI that may be discoverable, even before the time when a lawsuit is filed. This duty is independent of whether a party has had a lawsuit filed against it and arises when a party becomes aware that he possesses evidence that could be relevant to potential litigation. The opposing party may trigger this duty by advising that he may intend to file a lawsuit or by sending a **notice of preservation**, a letter notifying an adversary of the need to preserve relevant electronic evidence, even if paper copies are available. An **order of preservation** is a court order requiring a party to preserve electronic and other evidence, regardless of the party's need to engage in routine deletion or destruction practices and procedures. An order of preservation is of a temporary nature, meaning that at some future date, the order will be lifted and the opposing party may resume ordinary computer deletion and destruction practices and procedures. Often, case management plans issued as a part of routine scheduling by a court will incorporate agreements or orders related to preservation of data in pending litigation.

A fifth significant issue is the risk that producing ESI will result in a waiver of the protections afforded by the attorney–client privilege or the work–product privilege. The sheer volume of ESI can be enormous, making review of every piece of ESI before production both expensive and time-consuming. Extreme care is required to ensure that privileged communications or work product are not inadvertently disclosed because once disclosed, the protections previously available are waived. To avoid this problem, parties sometimes enter into agreements stating that inadvertent disclosure of privileged ESI does not waive either privilege before disclosing ESI to the opposing side. If the parties cannot reach agreement by themselves, they may seek a court order specifically stating that inadvertently disclosed privileged ESI must remain confidential.

Spoliation is another significant issue related to e-discovery. **Spoliation** refers to the wrongful destruction or material alteration of evidence or the failure to preserve property or data for another's use as evidence in pending or reasonably foreseeable litigation. In many respects, it is the opposite of preservation. The central question of spoliation is whether the party who destroyed or altered the evidence had reason to know not to do so. For example, had the party received a notice of preservation or had reason to anticipate that litigation was probable or likely, not just possible? The *Zubulake v. UBS Warburg, LLC* case is instructive on this point. After Ms. Zubulake filed her gender discrimination charge, the defendant UBS Warburg deleted certain e-mails from its live e-mail system and then later failed to preserve backup tapes that contained the e-mails in question. The court found the actions to delete relevant e-mails and not preserve the backup tapes to be violations of discovery and imposed sanctions. Eventually, a jury awarded Ms. Zubulake $9.1 million in compensatory damages and $20.1 million in punitive damages.[5]

The more recent case of *Apple, Inc. v. Samsung Electronics Co. Ltd.* illustrates both the spoliation and litigation hold concepts. In this case, Apple had sued Samsung for patent infringement and sought copies of e-mails and documents as part of e-discovery. The court found that Samsung was unable to produce the e-mails and documents because it failed in its duty to preserve relevant emails and comments. Specifically, Samsung failed to disable the "auto-delete" feature on its in-house e-mail system that automatically deleted all e-mails after fourteen days absent affirmative action by the custodian of records. Further, Samsung distributed its litigation hold instructions to a small fraction of the affected employees and made no effort to reinforce those instructions or check for compliance by those employees. After expanding its litigation hold notices to additional employees, Samsung failed to monitor its employees' preservation efforts in any way while leaving the e-mail auto-delete function operational. The court held that Samsung's actions constituted spoliation and allowed an instruction to the jury that it could infer from Samsung's failure to preserve the e-mails and documents that the lost evidence would have been used at trials and would have been favorable to Apple.[6]

Under the Federal Rules, a responding party should produce ESI that is relevant, not privileged, and reasonably accessible, subject to any limitations ordinarily present in discovery. State and local courts also promulgate rules covering discovery, and many of these courts have adopted e-discovery rules modeled upon the Federal Rules. Further, the National Conference of Commissioners on Uniform State Laws has issued model rules on discovery of ESI, with the hope of accelerating their adoption at the state level.

Experience during the first two decades of e-discovery has shown that courts are quite involved in the management of e-discovery requests. Parties often dispute many areas of discovery, including its scope, the obligation of parties to preserve information, whether certain information is privileged, and how information should be produced. Where ESI is concerned, courts often take a proactive approach and direct lawyers and parties to identify at the earliest stages of litigation any potential problems in the discovery of ESI and propose resolutions to those problems. Where the parties are unable to negotiate a satisfactory resolution among themselves to ESI issues, they seek the court's guidance on how to proceed.

EHR

E-discovery impacts the electronic health record in a variety of ways, including litigation holds and notices of preservation.

The impact of e-discovery upon the HIM profession and the health care industry is significant. In particular, litigation holds and notices of preservation are seen more frequently with regard to electronic health records. For this reason, it is incumbent upon health care organizations and those who manage information and data to establish and maintain policies and procedures that govern production of discovery materials, whether in paper or electronic form, in order to minimize and avoid such problems. Issues related to litigation holds or notices of preservation such as identifying potential litigation cases, what to hold or preserve, how to monitor the hold or preservation, and how to produce an electronic health record that has been the subject of a hold or preservation should all be addressed. Such policies and procedures should be developed by health information management professionals in concert with legal counsel, information technology professionals, risk management staff, and senior organizational management. In turn, these policies and procedures should be communicated to all members of the health care organization who possess responsibility concerning e-discovery.

CRITICAL THINKING

Responding to e-discovery requests in the health care context may depend on gathering data from multiple components of a health care institution. Examine what difficulties could be present if all aspects of a patient's care encounter in a hospital are created and stored by different departments electronically as opposed to held centrally in the patient's electronic health record. Examples to consider include the following:

1. Radiology imaging systems
2. Fetal monitor data
3. Patient registration systems

Depositions

A **deposition** is a discovery device provided for in Federal Rule of Civil Procedure 26 in which one party subpoenas a witness to appear at a given time and place to testify under oath. The person answering the questions is called the **deponent**. Depositions take place outside the courtroom, frequently in a lawyer's office, in the presence of counsel for both sides and a court reporter who administers the oath and transcribes the testimony word for word. Depositions can include both written and oral questions, with the questions presented in the same manner as during trial, with direct examination and cross-examination of the deponent. Counsel can object to any of the questions asked of the deponent. Although depositions are relatively expensive, they are considered by many to be the most effective way of obtaining a hostile individual's knowledge of the facts.

The main purpose of a deposition is to uncover details of the case. Depositions are also submitted as evidence at trial if the deponent is unavailable or to contradict a deponent's testimony if an inconsistent statement is given.

In the e-discovery context, depositions are often used as a means to obtain preliminary information about ESI so that later requests for ESI can be specifically tailored to the facts of the case. Depositions seeking preliminary information about ESI are often made of technical staff knowledgeable about computer networks and electronic information storage. Specific issues probed in these depositions may concern the architecture of computer networks, the maintenance practices and procedures of those networks, the types of hardware and software used by the party, the specific location of files, the party's retention policies and practices, and steps that may have been taken to preserve ESI in connection with the case. Depositions of nontechnical staff regarding ESI often address what data that staff stores in computers and other devices and how that staff organizes and stores the data. At times, the deposition of nontechnical staff in this manner may reveal sources and locations of ESI that even technical staffs are unaware exist—for example, personal digital assistants or flash memory.

Written Interrogatories

Written interrogatories are governed by Federal Rule of Civil Procedure 33 and are a far less expensive method to uncover details of a case. This discovery device consists of one party submitting written questions about the case to another party or witness. The questions are answered separately in writing, with the person answering the questions signing a sworn statement that the answers are true. The party or witness may object to answering the question, stating the reason for the objection in writing. The party must answer the interrogatories generally within thirty days from the time they are sent.

In the e-discovery context, interrogatories may be used to gather information about the sources of electronic information systems used by an opposing party, plus any retention and destruction policies and practices it maintains. Alternatively, interrogatories may focus on identifying key staff members, such as network administrators, or where and how ESI is handled, including whether responsibility for operating e-mail systems and computer archives is outsourced. Gathering information in this way helps parties to understand the context of how to use ESI in a specific lawsuit and often leads to further discovery requests, such as for **production of documents and things**.

Production of Documents and Things

This discovery device is governed by Federal Rule of Civil Procedure 34 and permits one side to inspect and copy documents and things that are not already in that side's physical possession. In this instance, a written request is served on the other side, identifying the item and category along with a reasonable time, place, and manner in which to inspect and copy the document or thing. A party receiving the request must respond in writing, generally within thirty days, either stating that inspection and copying will be permitted as requested or that the party has an objection to the request.

This discovery tool is subject to wide variation. In some cases, a written request for documents may only require the respondent to photocopy documents and send them to the requestor. A complete and valid release of information submitted to a health care provider asking for photocopies of a health record would be an example of this type of request. By contrast, a request accompanied by a **subpoena duces tecum**, a formal request to produce a record made pursuant to Federal Rule of Civil Procedure 45, would require a person who possesses the document in question to produce the document at a certain time and place pursuant to the authority of the court supervising the lawsuit, unless the subpoena duces tecum indicates that personal delivery is not required and mailing of the document will suffice. In either instance, the health information manager will produce the health record pursuant to valid request or subpoena by using the certification process, a matter discussed in more detail in Chapter 3, Judicial Process of Health Information.

In the e-discovery context, one issue often raised is the form or format in which the documents and things must be produced. The variety of forms and formats available may impact many areas, including how easily the information can be electronically searched, whether relevant information is obscured or sensitive information is revealed, and how the information can be used in later stages of litigation. Courts have addressed this issue by applying the cost-shifting analysis of the undue burden concept, relying on two seminal cases for guidance: *Rowe Entertainment, Inc. v. William Morris Agency, Inc.*[7] and *Zubulake v. UBS Warburg LLC.*[8] In *Rowe*, a racial discrimination case, and *Zubulake*, a gender discrimination case, the defendants objected to producing e-mail information that only existed on backup tapes and other archival media, citing invasion of the privacy of nonparties and the unlikelihood of finding relevant information. The court in each case directed the defendants to produce the e-mails, determining that they were relevant to the case and did not unnecessarily invade the privacy of nonparties. After applying the cost-shifting analysis, each court shifted only a portion of the cost of producing the e-mails to the plaintiffs, ordering the defendants to bear the remaining costs.

Physical or Mental Examination

When the physical or mental condition of the plaintiff is at issue in the case, the defendant may ask the court to order the plaintiff to submit to a physical or mental examination by a physician. The request is made pursuant to Federal Rule of Civil Procedure 35 and must be supported by a demonstration of good cause to order the examination. A notice is given to the person to be examined of the time, place, manner, conditions, and scope of the examination along with the name of the physician who will conduct the examination. The physician then prepares a detailed written report of his findings, the results of all tests, diagnoses, and conclusions. The report is made available to the party examined at that party's request.

Requests for Admission

Requests for admission are governed by Federal Rule of Civil Procedure 36 and are similar to written interrogatories in that one party asks the other side a series of written questions. They differ from written interrogatories in that these questions are not designed to gather information; rather, the questions are designed so that the other side will admit certain facts. A party must respond in writing to a **request for admission** within thirty days or else the subject matter of the request for admission will be deemed admitted.

Many routine and mundane matters are the subject of requests for admission—for example, the date, day of the week, and time of occurrence of a particular event. Conversely, disputed matters may be the subject of a request for admission. In those instances, the party responding to the request may object to the question or deny the fact that is central to the question. Any matter that is admitted pursuant to a request for admission is conclusively established for purposes of that lawsuit only. Under certain circumstances, the trial court may later permit withdrawal or amendment of the admission.

Once admitted, the parties do not need to resort to presenting unnecessary proof at trial concerning the subject matter of the admission. Admissions save each side both time and expenses.

Pretrial Conference

Many trial courts have local rules that require the parties to meet with the trial judge before a trial date is set and discuss the status and issues of the case. This activity is referred to as a **pretrial conference** and is governed by Federal Rule of Civil Procedure 16. At the pretrial conference, the trial judge rules on any outstanding motions, resolves certain discovery disputes, helps the parties further define the issues, and discusses the possibility of settlement. If the case is not settled at that time, the trial judge sets the court date and enters a pretrial order that controls the course of the trial.

In the e-discovery context, the judge will address any outstanding issues relating to ESI at the pretrial conference stage. Often, judges will issue a scheduling order that includes provisions for any further disclosure or discovery of ESI and for any agreements the parties may have negotiated for asserting claims of privilege or protection of trial-preparation material after production.

Trial

A **trial** is a hearing or determination by a court of the issues existing between the parties to an action. Cases that proceed to trial will be decided by either a trial judge or a jury. Certain categories of cases are not entitled to jury trials—for example, divorce and adoption proceedings. In those instances, the trial judge will make decisions about the disputed facts in the case. Where the case is tried before a jury, the jury will decide the disputed facts in the case.

After choosing a jury, each side's counsel presents an opening statement to the jury. The opening statement is an outline or summary of the case and the evidence that each side anticipates will be presented to the jury during the course of the trial. The opening statement gives a general picture of the facts so that the jury will be able to understand the evidence as it is presented. The plaintiff's attorney presents his opening statement first. The defendant's attorney immediately follows unless he defers until after the plaintiff rests his case.

The next step is the presentation of the plaintiff's case. The plaintiff's lawyer may call witnesses to explain the facts of the case. The plaintiff's lawyer engages the witness in a question-and-answer dialogue, which is called direct examination. After direct examination is completed, the defendant's lawyer has the right to question the same witness. This is referred to as cross-examination.

During either direct or cross-examination, the lawyer who is not questioning the witness may choose to object to a question asked or the answer given if the lawyer believes that either is outside the bounds of admissible evidence. The lawyer voices the objection to the trial judge, giving reasons that the question or answer is improper. The trial judge allows the opposing counsel to respond to the objection. The trial judge then decides whether to allow the evidence to be considered by the jury. This decision is based on many factors, including trustworthiness of the witness, relevance of the evidence, and prior appellate decisions concerning that particular form of evidence. The trial judge announces his decision by saying that the objection is sustained or overruled, and the case proceeds.

After the plaintiff has called all witnesses and introduced the remaining evidence, such as exhibits, he rests his case. At that time, the defendant can ask the court to rule in the defendant's favor because the plaintiff has failed to prove his case. This request is called a motion for directed verdict. If the trial judge grants the motion, the lawsuit stops; if denied, the trial proceeds with the defendant presenting his case. The same procedures used in the plaintiff's case, direct and cross-examination, are followed in the defendant's case for each of the defendant's witnesses.

After both sides have "rested," either side may renew the request for a directed verdict. If granted, the lawsuit is over; if denied, the case is ready for closing statements. Similar to opening statements, a closing statement summarizes the evidence that has been presented during the trial and highlights the weaknesses of the other side's case. As a general rule, the plaintiff first presents the closing statement; the defendant then replies with a closing statement, with the plaintiff being allowed to rebut the defendant's closing statement. This scenario may differ, however, if any party elects not to present a closing statement.

Closing statements often include references to a witness's credibility. The lawyer will explain to the jury why a particular witness should be believed and another witness not believed. Decisions concerning credibility are among the most difficult decisions a jury must make. Credibility decisions call into play the jury's understanding of the witness's intelligence, knowledge of the circumstances in question, reputation for telling the truth, and impartiality to the matter at issue in the case.

Following closing statements, the trial judge will provide directions to the jury concerning the law that applies to the case. These directions are called **jury instructions**. The jury uses these instructions to reach its ultimate decision in the case, which is called the **verdict**.

After the jury returns the verdict, the losing party can ask the trial judge to overturn the verdict by filing a motion for judgment notwithstanding the jury's verdict. The losing party can also seek a new trial by submitting a list of errors to the trial judge that the party believes caused him to lose. The trial judge may grant either of these posttrial motions if the jury verdict is against the weight of the evidence submitted at trial. Whatever the trial court's decision on these posttrial motions, the trial court eventually enters a judgment indicating who won and who lost in the case.

As this discussion illustrates, distinct roles exist for both the trial judge and the jury. The trial judge determines the admissibility of the evidence, instructs the jury on the applicable law, and can remove a case from the jury by granting a directed verdict, a motion notwithstanding the verdict, or a motion for new trial. It is the role of the jury to decide the facts in the case and reach the ultimate decision of whether the plaintiff has proved his case. Simply stated, it is the trial judge who decides questions of law and the jury that decides questions of fact.

Appeal

Once all posttrial motions are decided and judgment is entered, the losing party in the trial court may pursue an appeal. On **appeal**, a case may be affirmed, modified, or reversed. Furthermore, a new trial may be ordered. The written opinion issued by the appellate court provides reasons for the decision made by that court. Any party losing on appeal from a decision of an intermediate appellate court may then choose to pursue an appeal with that state's court of last resort or with the U.S. Supreme Court, as discussed earlier in this chapter.

On appeal, the order of each party's name may be reversed from how they were listed in the trial court. For example, the title of the case at trial may have been *Mary Smith v. John Doe*, with the plaintiff being Mary Smith and the defendant being John Doe. If John Doe loses and takes the appeal, the order of the parties is frequently switched to show who is the party initiating the appeal—for example, *John Doe v. Mary Smith*. If Mary Smith loses and takes the appeal, the order of the names will usually remain the same. Although this is a fairly minor point, it can cause some confusion.

Satisfying the Judgment

After all appeals have been exhausted, the winning party must still collect the amount of the judgment if a money award has been made. This process is frequently referred to as **satisfying the judgment**.

Among the most common ways to satisfy a judgment is to obtain a **writ of execution** or an **order of garnishment**. A writ of execution, the most common method used in the federal court system, is a written document that orders the sheriff or other local official to take the property of the losing party and sell it to satisfy the judgment. An order of garnishment is an order directed to a third person to whom the losing party is indebted that orders payment of the debt directly to the winning party in the lawsuit. Garnishment is frequently used to obtain a portion of the losing party's wages. In this situation, the employer of the losing party is directed to pay a certain percentage of the losing party's wages to the winning party.

ALTERNATIVE DISPUTE RESOLUTION

Alternative methods of dispute resolution are increasing in popularity in the United States. Commonly referred to as **alternative dispute resolution** (ADR), these methods seek to resolve conflicts and disagreements to the satisfaction of all parties without using the court system. ADR arose as a result of dissatisfaction with the existing legal system and its costs to litigants in terms of time, stress, and fees. ADR has steadily grown in popularity because it involves decision making in an expedited and economically feasible manner. Although most often used in the business world, ADR is now seen more frequently in the health care field. The similarities and differences of three forms of ADR are listed in Table 2.9.

Table 2.9 Similarities and Differences in ADR

	Mediation	Arbitration	Negotiation and Settlement
Actors	Neutral third party called mediator involved; often one **without** expertise in the subject of the lawsuit	Neutral third party called arbitrator involved; often one **with** expertise in the subject of the lawsuit	No third parties, only litigants and their attorneys involved
Control	Voluntary process	Often a mandatory process	Voluntary process
Resolution	Parties reach mutually acceptable resolution	Arbitrator makes decision	Parties reach mutually acceptable resolution
Binding Nature	Resolution binding on both sides of lawsuit	Decision binding on both sides of lawsuits; those unhappy may appeal to court	Resolution binding on both sides of lawsuit

The most frequently used form of ADR in the United States is mediation. In **mediation**, a neutral third party assists both sides of a dispute in resolving their differences and reducing their resolution to writing. Unlike a court decision imposed on the parties to a lawsuit, mediation allows the parties themselves to reach a decision that binds all sides to the controversy. After learning the positions of the respective sides, the third-party mediator tries to reach some form of common ground. That common ground is then agreed to by both sides, and the mediator reduces the agreement to writing. Because the mediator is seeking active involvement of the parties in reaching common ground, it is not necessary that the mediator be an expert in the field in which the dispute arises. Mediation is popular because it allows the parties to remain in control of their destiny; the mediator cannot force a decision upon the parties. Its popularity also stems from the fact that it is generally voluntary, not mandatory, and is a private process with no documents filed in the public record.

A second form of ADR is arbitration. Like mediation, **arbitration** uses a neutral third party to hear both sides of a dispute and render a written decision, called an award. The neutral third party is called an arbitrator. Unlike mediation, the arbitrator's award is not based on the parties' agreement; rather, the arbitrator's award is imposed on the parties after consideration of each side's position. Depending on the situation, the arbitrator's award may be binding on the parties. A party unhappy with the arbitrator's award may seek to appeal it by bringing a lawsuit in a court of general jurisdiction to overturn the award.

One advantage to the use of arbitration is that the arbitrator is frequently an expert or at least knowledgeable about the field in which the dispute arises. This knowledge often gives confidence to the parties that the decision to be reached is solidly grounded not only on the facts but also on the business practices in the field in which the dispute arises. Parties may agree to keep the written arbitration award confidential. If, however, a party wanted to warn others of the danger posed by whatever is the subject of the arbitration, a confidential award will not suffice. Additionally, it can be hard to predict the outcome of an arbitration award, leaving parties with a feeling of uncertainty until an award is reached. Finally, many parties do not willingly enter into the arbitration process but must do so as a condition of receiving services where the contract contains a clause mandating arbitration in the event of a dispute.

A third method of ADR is negotiation and settlement. Like arbitration and mediation, negotiation and settlement seeks to resolve a dispute. **Negotiation and settlement** differs in that no neutral third party is used. The parties (or their representative) must work with each other (the negotiation) in order to succeed in reaching resolution of the dispute (the settlement). A written document memorializing the settlement is then drafted and signed by all the parties involved. Settlement agreements often contain a release of claims, meaning that the parties agree to give up any rights to otherwise pursue the claims listed in the release.

Negotiation and settlement is frequently used where there is minimum animosity between the parties. It is also pursued as an avenue to defray costs, as no neutral third party is involved who must be paid by the parties for the time expended in the mediation or arbitration. Negotiation and settlement is also attractive because the parties themselves control the process.

CRITICAL THINKING

Pursuing a lawsuit is a frequently used mechanism to resolve a dispute. Consider whether an individual would reap advantages by employing any of the alternative dispute resolution (ADR) techniques discussed in this chapter in lieu of pursuing a lawsuit.

All three forms of ADR are used throughout the United States. Depending on the situation, more than one form of ADR may be used if the first form of ADR does not result in a successful outcome. For example, the parties may try negotiation and settlement but reach a stalemate. They may then proceed with either mediation or arbitration to resolve their differences. These forms of ADR may be used even after the parties have resorted to a lawsuit to resolve their differences.

CONCLUSION

Each lawsuit filed in the United States differs in some respect from every other lawsuit. Lawsuits may vary not only by the type of law involved and the facts underlying the case but also by the jurisdiction of the court in which they are filed and the types of discovery devices used. Furthermore, Americans are increasingly using alternative forms of dispute resolution to address their legal issues. A thorough understanding of these variations will assist health information managers in complying with the requirements of the legal process.

CASE STUDY

You are the in-house counsel at General Hospital. You have been contacted by an attorney for a former patient of the hospital whose inpatient hospitalization resulted in some harm to the patient. That harm was memorialized in an incident report prepared by hospital staff. Your review of the incident report indicates that the harm described by the attorney is consistent with the harm described in the incident report. Based on your conversations with the attorney, you believe a lawsuit is imminent. Because you believe it is in the best interests of all concerned to avoid the cost of litigation, you wish to consider methods of alternative dispute resolution. Discuss the relative advantages and disadvantages of each method.

REVIEW QUESTIONS

1. Why should a health information manager need to understand the court system and legal procedures?
2. Give examples of federal question jurisdiction and diversity jurisdiction.
3. Does each state have trial courts, intermediate courts of appeal, and supreme courts?
4. What is meant by the term *legal process*?
5. What are the steps in a civil lawsuit?
6. What are the elements of a complaint?
7. Name the methods of discovery discussed in this chapter.
8. What do the terms *metadata*, *spoliation*, and *litigation hold* mean?

9. Why should those who manage health information and data establish and maintain policies and procedures that govern production of metadata in electronic form?
10. What are the similarities and differences between opening and closing statements at trial?
11. Does the judge or the jury decide what evidence can be admitted?
12. What is a garnishment typically used for?
13. How did alternative dispute resolution become a popular alternative to litigation?

ENRICHMENT ACTIVITY

Contact the Clerk of Court's office of your local trial court or court of appeals to learn the date of a scheduled trial or scheduled oral argument on appeal. Attend and observe the trial or oral argument. Discuss your observations with your class and/or instructor.

NOTES

1. Federal Rules of Civil Procedure 16 (pretrial conferences), 26 (duty of disclosure), 33 (interrogatories), 34 (production of documents, including business records), 37 (failure to disclose/sanctions), 45 (subpoena), and form 35 (report of planned meeting) (2019).
2. 2006 WL 665005 (N.D. IL March 8, 2006).
3. 230 F.R.D. 640 (D. Kan. 2005).
4. No. 805270/16, 2018 NY Slip Op 33142(U), (S.Ct. N.Y. Dec. 4, 2018).
5. *Zubulake* V, 229 F.R.D. 422 (S.D. N.Y. 2004) and *Zubulake VII*, 382 F. Supp. 2d 536 (S.D. N.Y. 2005).
6. *Apple, Inc. v. Samsung Electronics Co. Ltd.*, 11-1846, Docket entry #895 (N.D.Cal. July 25, 2012).
7. 205 F.R.D. 421 (S.D. N.Y), *aff'd* 53 Fed. R. Serv. 3d 296 (S.D. N.Y. 2002).
8. 217 F.R.D. 309 (S.D. N.Y 2003).

CHAPTER 3

JUDICIAL PROCESS OF HEALTH INFORMATION

LEARNING OBJECTIVES

After reading this chapter, the learner should be able to:

1. Define the following legal terms associated with the role of a health record in a lawsuit: evidence, admissible, and hearsay.
2. Explain why health records are considered hearsay evidence.
3. Explain how the health information professional establishes the foundation and trustworthiness requirements for admitting the health record into evidence.
4. List the questions typically asked of the health information professional when establishing the foundation and trustworthiness requirements.
5. Discuss the different forms of privileges.
6. Explain the use and application of the physician–patient privilege.
7. Discuss the differences among a subpoena, a subpoena ad testificandum, and a subpoena duces tecum.
8. Compare and contrast a court order authorizing disclosure of health information with a subpoena.
9. Describe e-discovery in the context of requests for production of documents and things.
10. Compare and contrast the three recommended responses of a health information professional to the presentation of a subpoena.
11. Assess the steps to take when presented with an invalid subpoena duces tecum.

KEY CONCEPTS

Admissible
Attorney–client privilege
Business record exception
Certification process
Court order
E-discovery
Electronically stored information
Evidence
Exigent circumstances
Foundation
Hearsay
Hearsay rule
Litigation response plan
Motion to quash
No-knock warrant
Physician–patient privilege
Plain view doctrine
Privilege
Probable cause
Show cause order
Subpoena
Subpoena ad testificandum
Subpoena duces tecum
Trustworthiness requirements
Warrant
Work–product privilege

INTRODUCTION

Health information contained in the health record serves a variety of clinical and nonclinical purposes: supporting direct patient care, quality improvement activities, public health monitoring, and billing and reimbursement, to name a few. One of the most important purposes of health information contained in the health record is as the legal document recording a particular episode of a patient's care. As such, it serves as the backbone of virtually every professional liability action and is used to establish whether the applicable standard of care was met. Other civil actions also require the admission of the health record as evidence, including credentialing and disciplinary proceedings of physicians and other health care professionals. Furthermore, criminal actions may require admission of the health record to establish the cause of the victim's death, an insanity defense, or a party's physical condition—for example, blood alcohol content. These uses are illustrated in Table 3.1.

Because of the myriad of legal protections to which health information is subject, disclosure of health information contained in the health record may only be made pursuant to legal authority. Generally stated, health information may be disclosed only on the patient's written consent, pursuant to statutory requirements or on proper legal process. This chapter addresses those instances where disclosure is made pursuant to legal process. Those persons interested in protecting health information must understand those instances where disclosure pursuant to legal process is appropriate or inappropriate so that they may properly respond to legal process.

HEALTH RECORDS AS EVIDENCE

As noted, the health record serves as the legal document of a particular episode of patient care. To understand the role the health record plays in a lawsuit, the learner must first become familiar with several legal terms that are covered in this chapter.

Lawsuits use health records as evidence to support or discredit a party's claim. **Evidence** is defined as testimony, writings, material objects, or other things presented to prove or disprove a fact. In the context of health information, health records may be used as evidence in civil or criminal court actions or in administrative agency proceedings.

Before a party may use the health record as evidence to support or discredit a claim, she must determine whether the evidence is **admissible**. To be admissible, the evidence must be both pertinent and proper. What is considered pertinent and proper for use by a jury and/or a judge in reaching a decision is governed by rules of evidence. In the context of health records, the applicable rule of evidence is the hearsay rule.

Table 3.1 Legal Uses for the Health Record

- To establish the applicable standard of care
- As evidence in civil actions
- As evidence involving the credentialing process
- For disciplinary proceedings of health care professionals
- To establish the cause of death
- To determine blood alcohol content
- To support an insanity defense
- As proof of a party's physical condition

Hearsay

Hearsay is defined as out-of-court statements that are offered to prove the truth of the matter asserted. Health records are considered hearsay evidence because the health care providers making the statements, that is, the entries into the record, do not do so in court under oath. The complexity of bringing to court the multitude of health care providers who made entries into a particular health record and the cost associated with doing so make it inevitable that very few health care providers will actually serve as witnesses in court with regard to a particular health record. If not present in the courtroom, the witnesses cannot be subject to cross-examination. Accordingly, the majority, if not all, of the entries made in the health record are not subject to cross-examination and are considered hearsay evidence.

Because health records are considered hearsay evidence, they are subject to the **hearsay rule**, which prohibits their admission into evidence, absent an exception to the rule. The most commonly used exceptions to the rule are the **business record exception**,[1] a subset of that exception specifically governing health records,[2] or an exception governing public or official documents.[3]

Under each of these exceptions, the party seeking to admit the health record must meet the **foundation** and **trustworthiness requirements** of the exception. A foundation is made by establishing that the record was (1) made and kept in the ordinary course of business, (2) at or near the time the event was recorded, and (3) by a person with knowledge of the acts, events, conditions, opinions, or diagnoses appearing in it.[4] After meeting these requirements, the party seeking to introduce the record must establish the accuracy and trustworthiness of the health record. The party accomplishes these tasks by presenting the custodian of records as a witness to explain record-keeping procedures.

The health information professional, acting as custodian of the record, must be able to testify as to both the foundation and trustworthiness requirements of the business record exception. To assist in establishing the foundation, the health information professional must possess knowledge of the requirements to create and maintain a health record issued by governmental entities, accrediting agencies, and internal policies and procedures of the health care provider, along with knowledge of the manner in which data are recorded. To assist in establishing trustworthiness, the health information professional must possess knowledge of internal policies and procedures, governing access to the health record, and quality control techniques, such as approved methods to make corrections to and use abbreviations in the record. If electronic health records are involved, additional steps are necessary to establish the foundation and trustworthiness requirements. For more information concerning EHR in general, see Chapter 13, Information Systems.

In a typical situation, the health information professional testifies either at a deposition or at trial. In both situations, the health information professional is placed under oath and answers a series of questions designed to establish the foundation and trustworthiness requirements. If the health information professional is presented with a subpoena duces tecum, the health information professional will present and deliver the original or a copy of the health record to the requesting party, in the case of a deposition, or to the court, in the case of trial. A sample listing of questions typically presented to the health information professional acting as custodian of records is provided in Table 3.2.

Table 3.2 Sample Questions Presented to the Custodian of Records

1. State your full name and business address.
2. Are you the custodian of records for [name of health care provider]?
3. In answering these questions, have you made a full and complete search of [name of health care provider]'s records for patient [name of patient]?
4. Have you presented today a true, complete, and accurate copy of all [name of health care provider]'s records for patient [name of patient]?
5. If not, please state as accurately as possible all such documents that are not presented today and the reason(s) therefore.
6. Are all entries contained in the records presented today made by [name of health care provider] or her employees in the ordinary course of business?
7. If not, please identify which document or entry presented today is not made in the ordinary course of [name of health care provider]'s business.
8. What procedures are taken to ensure the accuracy of the records you have presented today?

Privilege

In addition to overcoming the hearsay rule, a party wishing to admit the health record as evidence must overcome application of the privilege doctrine. A **privilege** is the legal right to keep certain information confidential and protect it from subpoena, discovery, or introduction into evidence at trial. A privilege will be considered waived if the confidentiality is breached through either carelessness or deliberate disclosure by the party holding the privilege.[5]

In the context of health information contained in the health record, the most frequently used privilege is the **physician–patient privilege**. The physician–patient privilege is created by statute and is used to prevent the forced disclosure of, or testimony about, information obtained by the health care provider during the course of treatment.[6] The privilege exists to encourage the patient's disclosure of relevant information to the health care provider, no matter if that information is of an embarrassing or a humiliating nature. The privilege is generally held to rest with the patient but may be asserted on the patient's behalf by the health care provider to prevent forced disclosure.

The privilege frequently applies in situations in which the health care provider is a party to a lawsuit. It generally does not apply in criminal actions, will contests, and physician licensure proceedings. Whether the health care provider should assert the physician–patient privilege is a question to be answered with the assistance of legal counsel.

Other privileges, such as the attorney–client and attorney work–product privileges, are also used in the context of health information. An **attorney–client privilege** refers to the legal protection of communications between a client and her attorney, made in confidence for the purpose of obtaining legal advice. A **work–product privilege**, sometimes referred to as the work–product doctrine, refers to materials prepared in anticipation of litigation that may be shielded from discovery. Unlike the attorney–client privilege, the work referred to under the work–product privilege is not limited to an attorney's communications but can include tangible materials prepared by persons other than the attorney. For more information concerning the application of these privileges to incident report situations, see Chapter 12, Risk Management and Quality Management.

CRITICAL THINKING

This discussion illustrates the concept that certain confidential information will be protected from being disclosed without a party's consent. Examples include the physician–patient and attorney–client privileges. Should other confidential conversations be protected from disclosure? Consider the merits of shielding the following conversation topics from disclosure in a lawsuit:

1. Health or body issues
2. Religious or spiritual beliefs
3. Sexuality, sexual partners, or sexual practices
4. Immediate family relationships

Exclusions

Similar to the concept of privilege, exclusions operate to prevent admission of evidence in a court case. One such exclusion is the apology of the health care provider for any unanticipated outcome of the delivery of medical care. Such apologies may be contained in the health record or may be separated entirely from the health record. In either instance, the laws of several states may shield the apology from admission into evidence in a medical malpractice case. These laws fall into two categories: those offering a full apology (both an expression of sympathy and admission of responsibility) and those offering a partial apology (an expression of sympathy alone). For purposes of understanding the role of apologies in litigation, the concept is that an offer of an apology given in a timely manner will decrease the number of medical malpractice lawsuits.

Sometimes referred to as "I'm Sorry Statutes," laws in several states exclude from evidence an apology expressed by a health care provider that contains a full admission of fault, not just an expression of sympathy. For example, Colorado excludes apologies to the patient, or the patient's relatives or representatives, concerning an unanticipated outcome of medical care.[7] Oregon law excludes any apology or expression of regret from admission of liability for any purpose, not just those arising from the delivery of health care.[8] Several other states have followed suit, protecting health care providers from seeing their apologies admitted as evidence in a civil suit.[9]

Some state laws stop short of protecting complete apologies; rather, state law extends protection to statements that express sympathy but do not admit responsibility. These laws focus on statements, writings, or benevolent gestures that express sympathy to the patient or patient's family and exclude them from admission as evidence. If these excluded statements are coupled with admissions of responsibility, however, only the expression of sympathy will be excluded—the admission of responsibility will be admitted.[10]

RESPONSES TO LEGAL PROCESS

The general rule of ownership of health information states that the health care provider owns the medium in which health information is stored, the health record, with limited property interests possessed by the patient. From this rule flows the principle that the record must remain within the provider's control and safekeeping and may be removed only in accordance with proper legal process. Subpoenas, court orders, discovery requests, and warrants constitute proper legal process.

When faced with a subpoena, a court order, a discovery request, or a warrant, the health information professional is placed in the difficult position of how to respond. Should she release the requested records, refuse to release the requested records, or excise those portions of the records that the health information professional determines are protected and release the remainder? If the health information professional fails to respond to the subpoena, court order, discovery request, or warrant, she exposes the health care provider to potential contempt of court charges. If the health information professional improperly releases the records, she may subject the health care provider to liability for breach of confidentiality. Only upon a determination that a valid subpoena, court order, discovery request, or warrant has been presented and that a valid legal defense against disclosure does not exist should the health information professional release the requested records. The next section addresses subpoenas, court orders, discovery requests, and warrants and the methods used to respond to them.

Subpoenas

The most common legal process a health care provider will encounter is being served with a subpoena. A **subpoena** is a command issued by a court or other authorized official to appear and/or present certain documents and other things. A subpoena commanding the appearance of a witness to give testimony is called a **subpoena ad testificandum**.[11] A subpoena commanding the production of books, documents, and other things is called a **subpoena duces tecum**.[12] A subpoena duces tecum is often used in the context of health information management, commanding the custodian of the records to produce a particular record at trial or deposition and provide testimony as to the authenticity of the record produced. An example of a subpoena duces tecum in a civil case brought in federal court is illustrated in Figure 3.1.

Certain elements are common to all valid subpoenas and are listed in Table 3.3. Subpoenas may vary in certain respects, depending on whether the subpoena was issued by a federal or state court. For example, a subpoena issued by a federal court may be issued only by the clerk of the federal court under seal of the court.[13] By contrast, subpoenas issued by a state court are issued pursuant to state rules, which may allow noncourt officials to issue subpoenas, such as a notary public or someone appointed by the state court to take testimony.[14] Subpoenas also differ concerning provisions of advance notice. In the federal court, no provision exists requiring advance notice for a subpoena in connection with discovery[15]; in the state court, advance notice for a discovery subpoena may be required.[16] Finally, subpoenas may differ as to witness fees, with fees given in federal court often greater than those given in state court actions.[17] Health information professionals dealing with subpoenas should become familiar with the requirements of a valid subpoena for their particular jurisdiction.

Court Orders

In addition to subpoenas, health information professionals may be presented with court orders authorizing disclosure of patient-specific health information. A **court order** differs from a subpoena in that the court order authorizes disclosure that would otherwise be prohibited by statute and regulation. A subpoena cannot authorize disclosure that would otherwise be prohibited by statute and regulation; a subpoena is subject to any and all legal defenses created by statute, regulation, and common law. The method used to apply for a court order authorizing disclosure is subject to regulation and rules of court and may vary by jurisdiction.

In certain situations, such as where the treatment of substance abuse is present, disclosure of portions of the health record or the record in whole is mandated only upon presentation of both

AO 88 (Rev. 02/14) Subpoena to Appear and Testify at a Hearing or Trial in a Civil Action

UNITED STATES DISTRICT COURT
for the
_________ District of _________

_______________________________)
Plaintiff)
v.) Civil Action No.
_______________________________)
Defendant)

SUBPOENA TO APPEAR AND TESTIFY
AT A HEARING OR TRIAL IN A CIVIL ACTION

To:

____
(Name of person to whom this subpoena is directed)

YOU ARE COMMANDED to appear in the United States district court at the time, date, and place set forth below to testify at a hearing or trial in this civil action. When you arrive, you must remain at the court until the judge or a court officer allows you to leave.

Place:	Courtroom No.:
	Date and Time:

You must also bring with you the following documents, electronically stored information, or objects *(leave blank if not applicable)*:

The following provisions of Fed. R. Civ. P. 45 are attached – Rule 45(c), relating to the place of compliance; Rule 45(d), relating to your protection as a person subject to a subpoena; and Rule 45(e) and (g), relating to your duty to respond to this subpoena and the potential consequences of not doing so.

Date: ___________

CLERK OF COURT

OR

_______________________________ _______________________________
Signature of Clerk or Deputy Clerk *Attorney's signature*

The name, address, e-mail address, and telephone number of the attorney representing *(name of party)* ___________
_______________________________ , who issues or requests this subpoena, are:

Notice to the person who issues or requests this subpoena
If this subpoena commands the production of documents, electronically stored information, or tangible things before trial, a notice and a copy of the subpoena must be served on each party in this case before it is served on the person to whom it is directed. Fed. R. Civ. P. 45(a)(4).

Figure 3.1 Subpoena in a Civil Case: A U.S. Government Document
Source: Courtesy of www.uscourts.gov.

a subpoena duces tecum and a court order.[18] The components of a court order authorizing disclosure in such a situation are illustrated in Table 3.4.

A variation of a court order is a show cause order. A **show cause order** is a court decree directing a person or organization to appear in court and explain why the court should not take a proposed action. If the person or organization fails to appear or sufficiently persuade the court to take no action, the court will take the action originally proposed. In the health information context, show cause orders may be issued in the event of no response to the subpoena or court order originally issued.

AO 88 (Rev. 02/14) Subpoena to Appear and Testify at a Hearing or Trial in a Civil Action (page 2)

Civil Action No.

PROOF OF SERVICE

(This section should not be filed with the court unless required by Fed. R. Civ. P. 45.)

I received this subpoena for *(name of individual and title, if any)* ______________________

on *(date)* ______________ .

❒ I served the subpoena by delivering a copy to the named person as follows: ______________

______________________________ on *(date)* ______________ ; or

❒ I returned the subpoena unexecuted because: ______________________________ .

Unless the subpoena was issued on behalf of the United States, or one of its officers or agents, I have also tendered to the witness the fees for one day's attendance, and the mileage allowed by law, in the amount of

$ ______________ .

My fees are $ __________ for travel and $ __________ for services, for a total of $ 0.00 .

I declare under penalty of perjury that this information is true.

Date: ______________

____
Server's signature

____
Printed name and title

____
Server's address

Additional information regarding attempted service, etc.:

Figure 3.1 Continued

Table 3.3 Common Elements of a Valid Subpoena

1. Name of court where lawsuit is brought
2. Names of the parties to the lawsuit
3. Docket number of the case
4. Date, time, and place of the requested appearance
5. Specific documents to be produced if a subpoena duces tecum is involved
6. Name and telephone number of attorney who requested the subpoena
7. Signature, stamp, or seal of the official empowered to issue the subpoena
8. Witness fees, where provided by law

Discovery Requests

In addition to requests for health information made through subpoenas and court orders, the discovery process will involve the health information professional in responding to requests for health information. Discovery requests include those methods described in Table 3.5, which are discussed in more detail in Chapter 2, Court Systems and Legal Procedures. Of particular interest to health

Table 3.4 Components of a Valid Court Order Authorizing Disclosure

1. Name of court issuing order authorizing disclosure
2. Names of the parties to the lawsuit
3. Docket number of the case
4. Limitations for disclosure of only those components of the patient's records that are essential to fulfill the objective of the order
5. Limitations for disclosure to those persons whose need for information is the basis for the order
6. Any other limitations on disclosure that serve to protect the patient, the physician–patient relationship, and/or the treatment given, such as sealing the court proceeding from public scrutiny
7. Signature of judge authorizing disclosure

Table 3.5 Methods of Discovery

Method	Defined	Federal Rule of Civil Procedure
Deposition	Testimony given under oath outside the courtroom pursuant to a subpoena	26
Interrogatories	Written questions presented to a party or witness designed to gather information	33
Production of Documents and Things	Inspection and/or copying of documents or other physical evidence upon written request	34
Physical/Mental Examination	Ordered by the court upon a party's request with good cause shown	35
Requests for Admissions	Written questions presented to a party designed to obtain admission of a certain fact	36

information professionals is the request for production of documents and things, a standard practice of discovery. This request requires inspection and/or copying of documents or other physical evidence upon written request.

The request for production of documents and things has long been present in the world of paper-based health records. A party receiving the request must respond in writing, generally within thirty days, either stating that inspection and copying will be permitted as requested or that the party has an objection to the request. In some cases, a request for documents may only require the respondent to photocopy documents and send them to the requestor. A complete and valid release of information submitted to a health care provider asking for photocopies of a health record would be an example of this request. New complexity has emerged in light of the transition to the use of electronic health records in health care.

The Federal Rules of Civil Procedure govern all forms of discovery conducted in proceedings filed in federal court. In 2006, the federal judiciary revised the Rules of Civil Procedure to specifically address discovery and production of electronically stored information (ESI). **Electronically stored information** refers to a distinct category of information that includes e-mails, Web pages, word processing files, and databases stored in the memory of computers (laptops, desktops, and mainframes), magnetic disks (such as computer hard drives and floppy disks), optical discs (such as DVDs and CDs), flash memory (such as thumb or flash drives), and backup media. The discovery process involving ESI is commonly referred to as **e-discovery**.

> **EHR**
> E-discovery impacts the electronic health record (EHR), particularly related to preserving data and records.

The uniqueness of ESI has raised significant issues that are generally not present when conventional, paper-based information is disclosed as part of the discovery process. Many of those differences are discussed in detail in the discovery section of Chapter 2, Court Systems and Legal Procedures. For purposes of this chapter, the discussion centers on the duty to preserve ESI and prevent spoliation.

The duty to preserve ESI, while easy in theory, is difficult in practice. By its nature, ESI is dynamic and changeable. Routine computer operations critical to a party's activities, plus limitations on memory for electronic storage, may require parties to overwrite data. E-mails may be regularly deleted or backup tapes may be recycled as part of a party's regular business practices. Destruction of data and records may be performed in the ordinary course of business. For these reasons, the need to preserve information is always balanced against the need to continue routine computer operations critical to a party's business activities. Additional concerns related to the duty to preserve ESI, including litigation holds and preservation notices and orders, are addressed in Chapter 2, Court Systems and Legal Procedures.

Warrants

On rare occasions, health information professionals will be faced with a demand for property and/or information by a law enforcement officer seeking to execute a warrant. A **warrant** refers to a court's prior permission for the police to search and seize property and/or information. Law enforcement officers seeking a warrant must provide to a judge detailed characteristics of the property and/or information they seek and the reasons supporting their request. Warrants are issued if the detailed characteristics and reasons indicate **probable cause**, a belief based on specific facts that a crime has been or is about to be committed.

Warrants must be executed or carried out within a specified time period. As a general rule, law enforcement officers must announce themselves as police officers and execute the warrant during the daytime unless the warrant specifically allows other arrangements. Law enforcement officers must inventory and describe in writing all the items they seize and usually provide a receipt to the suspect.

Special circumstances may permit the police to execute a warrant without announcing their presence in advance. This is referred to as a **no-knock warrant** and applies to situations where the evidence is likely to be destroyed or the police administering the warrant likely will be in danger.

The law permits searches without a warrant under time-sensitive or emergency conditions, referred to as **exigent circumstances**. For example, if police officers believe evidence will be destroyed if the officers wait for the court to issue a warrant, then they may act without one. Similarly, the **plain view doctrine** permits searches without a warrant if the suspect leaves an item where it is openly visible in an area where officers are authorized to be; the officers are not required to wait for the court to issue a warrant before acting to seize the evidence.

Response Methods

Before ever being presented with a subpoena, a court order, or a discovery request, the health information professional should have in place a **litigation response plan**, a tool consisting of policies and procedures that address how to respond to legal process requests. This plan should be developed with the advice of the health care provider's legal counsel and should address the division of labor between the health information professional, counsel, and other members of the health care team. Where the requests for discovery and instances of subpoenas are minimal, it may be appropriate for the health information professional to consult with or forward to counsel all discovery requests and subpoenas received. Where instances of discovery requests and subpoenas are not minimal, involvement of counsel each time may be cost-prohibitive and impractical; in those cases, the health information professional could handle all discovery requests and subpoenas and refer to counsel only those that present problems.

Where e-discovery is concerned, it is helpful to create a litigation response team. The team should consist of the health care provider's legal counsel, senior management of the health care organization, health information management professionals, and information technology professionals. Table 3.6 outlines the responsibilities of litigation response team members.

As an initial matter, the health information professional should not automatically assume that every discovery request or subpoena presented requires the release of the information requested. If such an assumption is made and the information released is subject to a valid legal defense such as the physician–patient privilege, the health information professional subjects the health care provider to potential liability for improper release of records. The health information professional should first determine whether subpoenas issued in her particular jurisdiction also require valid written consent given by the patient before release is made.[19]

One case illustrating the peril of releasing health information without a valid written consent accompanying the subpoena is *Hageman v. Southwest Gen. Health Ctr.*[20] In *Hageman*, a patient undergoing both a divorce and psychiatric treatment was charged with assaulting his wife. The patient learned that his psychiatrist had released the patient's health record in response to a subpoena from his wife's divorce attorney despite not having received the patient's signed written

Table 3.6 Litigation Response Team

Team Members	Responsibilities
Legal Counsel	Serves as team leader and oversee e-discovery process
Senior Management/ Health Care Provider/ Governing Board	Defines and delineates measures to take in identifying, preserving, searching, retrieving, and producing relevant electronically stored and other information
Health Information Management Professional	Serves as custodian of the record for legal purposes; advises and serves as resource about forms, format, use, storage, retention, and destruction of data and records; produces data and records in response to discovery requests; testifies concerning foundation and trustworthiness requirements
Information Technology Professional	Serves as resource concerning management, storage, retention, and destruction of data and records in an electronic environment; identifies costs, location, and related issues concerning production of electronically stored information

consent to release his health record. The contents of the health record so alarmed the divorce attorney who had subpoenaed the record that she provided a copy of the record to the prosecutor of the criminal assault case. After the patient's acquittal in the criminal case, he sued his wife's divorce attorney for invasion of privacy. The court found in his favor, ruling that his right to keep his health information confidential had been violated. The court found that the waiver of confidentiality that applied through the use of a subpoena applied only to the specific case in which it is sought; here, the divorce case. Hence, releasing the record to a third party, the prosecutor violated the requirement of confidentiality of health records.

The health information professional should also determine whether the information requested involves treatment for substance abuse, mental health, genetic testing information, or AIDS—all areas subject to strict confidentiality protections. One case illustrating the difficulties of responding to a subpoena for health information subject to strict confidentiality protections is *John Roe v. Jane Doe.*[21] In *Roe*, a physician received both a subpoena and a signed release of information authorizing release of information regarding the patient's workers' compensation claim. The physician complied with the subpoena by forwarding the patient's entire health record to the requesting attorney.

In the patient's subsequent lawsuit for breach of confidentiality, the court held that the physician improperly disclosed her patient's HIV status and was liable for punitive damages. Specifically, the court noted that the signed release of information that accompanied the subpoena was not sufficient under New York law to permit disclosure of HIV information. Only a signed release of information that specifically authorized release of HIV information and use of a form developed or approved by the State of New York would have permitted such disclosure. For more details concerning disclosure of HIV information, see Chapter 11, Specialized Patient Records.

If after determining that the information requested cannot be released because of the confidentiality restrictions listed previously or because of the potential for another valid legal defense, the health information professional has several choices of how to respond. First, she may refer these problematic discovery requests and subpoenas to the health care provider's legal counsel for assistance. If the health care provider has been named a party in the lawsuit, prompt referral of the discovery request or subpoena to counsel is always in order. The counsel, in turn, has several choices, including: (1) responding by letter to the requesting attorney informing her of the health care provider's refusal to release the requested information; (2) filing with the court a motion to quash the discovery request or subpoena; or (3) where appropriate, advising the health information professional to release the requested information in whole or in part. If the court denies counsel's motion to excuse compliance with the discovery request or to quash the subpoena, it will issue a court order authorizing release of the requested information.

A second option is for the health information professional to contact the requesting attorney and make a noncommittal response acknowledging the confidentiality restrictions under which the health care provider operates. The health information professional should then forward to the requesting attorney a predrafted release form to be signed by the patient that complies with all applicable confidentiality restrictions. Upon receipt of this completed release form, the health information professional may then release the requested information.

A third available option is to excise those portions of the health record that the health information professional determines are protected and release the remainder. When exercising this option, the health information professional is advised to inform requesting counsel that she complied with the discovery request or subpoena in part and that the nonreleased information is subject to confidentiality protections barring release without a court order or a valid consent given by the patient.

CRITICAL THINKING

The discussion to this point in the chapter presumes that a subpoena issued to a health information manager is about a patient who was treated by the health care provider and therefore a health record can be produced. What if the health care provider never treated the patient, but the health information manager receives a subpoena that presumes the patient had been treated by the health care provider and the subpoena seeks a copy of the patient's health record? What should the health information manager do in this situation?

At times, the health information professional may find that responding to a subpoena would be unduly burdensome, unreasonable, oppressive, or may call for privileged documents. In those instances, the health information professional may consult legal counsel to determine if a motion to quash is in order. A **motion to quash** is an approved method to challenge the validity of a subpoena duces tecum. The motion requests a court to examine the subpoena to determine whether the person who is the subject of the subpoena, here the health information professional, must produce the documents in question or can legally withhold some or all of the documents sought by the subpoena. Evidentiary hearings are routinely held on motions that seek to quash production of documents sought in the discovery process.

If the health information professional determines that all legal requirements are met and a health record may be disclosed pursuant to a legally valid request, the professional engages in the **certification process**. In certifying a record, the professional verifies that the copy she provides pursuant to the request is an exact duplicate of the original. The method of doing this varies by state law. At minimum, most states require a written certification letter signed by the custodian of the record stating that the copy is an exact duplicate of the original. Some states add an additional requirement that the custodian's signature on the certification letter be accompanied by the signature of a witness or a notary public. As a matter of practice, health information professionals typically number the pages of the copy supplied to the requestor in a consecutive manner, both for easy reference and to indicate that a formal process has been followed. Some health information professionals also include a reference in the certification letter that confidential health information has been disclosed pursuant to legal process and should not be redisclosed without written patient authorization. Where sensitive information is involved, such as that involving substance abuse, mental health, or HIV/AIDS, health information professionals will routinely include the language of the federal regulations prohibiting redisclosure in their certification letters. For additional information concerning disclosure of sensitive health information, see Chapter 11, Specialized Patient Records.

At no time should the health information professional ignore the discovery request or the subpoena. Substantial penalties exist for failing to respond to discovery or failing to obey a subpoena, including fines and contempt of court proceedings.[22] If the health information professional questions the validity of the discovery request or the subpoena or whether it should be honored, consultation with the health care provider's counsel to determine how to proceed is in order.

CONCLUSION

In the course of any given day, a health information professional may be presented with a request for discovery, a court order authorizing disclosure of health information, a subpoena requesting health information, a warrant seeking to seize property or information, or a combination of these. In order to respond to these situations, the health information professional must possess knowledge of the similarities and differences between these types of legal process and the role a health record plays in a lawsuit. Armed with this knowledge, the health information professional can develop policies and procedures that both protect the health care provider and comply with applicable legal requirements.

CASE STUDY

You supervise the correspondence unit of the health information services department of a medical center. Today, you received a subpoena duces tecum from an attorney, demanding either the originals or copies of all health records concerning Mary Smith, who allegedly is or was a patient of the medical center. The subpoena lacks sufficient information for you to determine whether Mary Smith is or was a patient in your facility. The subpoena is not accompanied by a valid authorization to release information for Mary Smith, as required in your state. How should you respond to the subpoena?

REVIEW QUESTIONS

1. What are the legal uses of the health record?
2. Are the entries made in the health record ordinarily subject to cross-examination? Why or why not?
3. How is a foundation established to admit a health record into evidence?
4. How is trustworthiness established to admit a health record into evidence?
5. What questions are typically presented to the custodian of records in order to introduce a health record into evidence?
6. What legal processes may be used to remove the health record from the health care provider's safekeeping?
7. What are the different forms of privilege?
8. Why is the physician–patient privilege useful?
9. What are exclusions?
10. Compare and contrast a subpoena, a subpoena ad testificandum, and a subpoena duces tecum.
11. How are court orders different from subpoenas?

12. Should the health information professional assume that each subpoena presented requires the release of the information requested? Why or why not?
13. Why is it difficult to preserve ESI?
14. What is a litigation plan?
15. A health information professional has three options to respond to a subpoena. Name these three options.
16. How should the health information professional handle an invalid subpoena duces tecum?

ENRICHMENT ACTIVITY

Engage in a role-playing activity with another student. One student should act as a health information professional and the other as an attorney. The attorney should present the health information professional with a series of questions designed to establish the foundation and trustworthiness requirements in order to admit a health record into evidence.

NOTES

1. *See, e.g.*, Federal Business Records Act, 28 U.S.C. § 1732(a) (2019) (general business record exception); Fed. R. Evid. 803(6) (general business record exception); Ark. R. Evid. 803(6); Cal. Evid. Code § 1271 (West 2019); Del. R. Evid. 803(6); Fla. Stat. Ann. § 90.803(6) (West 2019); Iowa Code Ann. § 622.28 (West 2019); Kan. Stat. Ann. § 60-460(m) (2019); Mass. Gen. Laws Ann. ch. 233, § 78 (West 2019); N.J. R. Evid. 803(c) (6); R.I. R. Evid. 803(6).
2. *See, e.g.*, Ga. Code Ann. § 24-7-8 (Michie 2019); 725 ILCS 5/115-5.1 (Smith-Hurd 2019); Ind. Code Ann. § 34-43-1-4 (West 2019); Nev. Rev. Stat. § 51.135(2) (2019).
3. *See, e.g.*, Ark. R. Evid. 803(8); Del. R. Evid. 803(8); Fla. Stat. Ann. § 90.803(8) (West 2019); Haw. R. Evid. 803(b) (8); Kan. Stat. Ann. § 60-460(o) (2019); N.J. R. Evid. 803(c) (8); R.I. R. Evid. 803(8).
4. Fed. R. Evid. 803(6).
5. Charles A. Wright & Kenneth W. Graham, Jr., Federal Practice and Procedure: Evidence § 93 (1980).
6. *See, e.g.*, Ark. Code Ann. § 16-41-101 (Michie 2019); Cal. Evid. Code §§ 990-995 (West 2019); Ga. Code Ann. § 24-9-40 (Michie 2019); Kan. Stat. Ann. § 60-427 (2019); Mich. Comp. Laws Ann. § 600.2157 (West 2019); Miss. Code Ann. § 13-1-21 (2019); Neb. Rev. Stat. § 27-504 (2019); N.J. Stat. Ann. §§ 2A:84A-22.1 to :84A-22.2 (West 2019); Ohio Rev. Code Ann. § 2317.02(B) (1) (Baldwin 2019); Okla. Stat. Ann. tit. 12, § 2503 (West 2019); S.D. Codified Laws Ann. §§ 19-13-6 to -8 (2019); Wis. Stat. Ann. § 905.04 (West 2019).
7. Colo. Rev. Stat. § 13-25-135 (2019) (defining an unanticipated outcome as one that differs from an expected result).
8. Or. Rev. Stat. § 677.082 (2019) (extending protection for any apology or expression of regret).
9. Ariz. Rev. Stat. § 184 (2019); Conn. G. Stat. § 275 (2019); Ga. Code Ann. § 24-3-37.1 (2019); Md. Code Ann. § 10-920(b)(1) (2019); Mont. Code Ann. § 26-1-814(1) (2019); Okla. Stat. Ann. Tit. 63, § 1-1708.1H9 (West 2019); Wyo. Stat. Ann. § 1-1-30 (2019).
10. Cal. Evid. Code § 1160(a) (2019); Fla. Stat. ch. 90.4026(2) (2019); Mo Rev. Stat. § 538.229 (2019); Tex. Civ. Prac. & Rem. Code Ann. § 18.061 (2019); Wash. Rev. Code § 5.66.010(1) (2019).
11. Black's Law Dictionary 1654 (10th Ed. 2014).
12. *Id.*
13. Fed. R. Civ. P. 45(a).

14. *See, e.g.*, Ala. R. Civ. P. 45(a); Ky. R. Civ. P. 45.01; Mo. Sup. Ct. R. 57.09(b) Tenn. R. Civ. P. 45.01; Vt. R. Civ. P. 45(a).

15. Fed. R. Civ. P. 45(a).

16. *See, e.g.*, Mo. Sup. Ct. R. 30 (providing three days' notice).

17. *Compare*, 28 U.S.C. § 1821 (2019); Fed. R. Civ. P. 45(c) (offering $40 per day including travel time) with Ark. R. Civ. P. 45(d) (offering $30 per day) and Mo. Rev. Stat. § 491.280.1 (2019); (offering $25 per day plus a mileage allowance).

18. 42 C.F.R. § 2.61(a-b) (2019).

19. Such is the case in Ohio, where information subject to the physician–patient privilege may not be released pursuant to a subpoena without presentation of a valid consent given by the patient. *Pacheco v. Ortiz*, 463 N.E.2d 670, 671 (Cuyahoga Cty. 1983); *see also*, *Henry v. Lewis*, 102 A.D. 2d 430 (N.Y. App. Div. 1984); *People v. Bickham*, 431 N.E.2d 365 (Ill. 1982).

20. 2008 WL 2715717 (Ohio July 9, 2008).

21. 599 N.Y.S.2d 350 (N.Y. App. Div. 1993).

22. *See, e.g.*, Ark. R. Civ. P. 45(g); Del. R. Civ. Proc. 45(f); Haw. R. Civ. Proc. 45(f); Mo. Rev. Stat. § 491.140-.200 (2019); Mo. S. Ct. R. 57.09(e).

CHAPTER

4

PRINCIPLES OF LIABILITY

LEARNING OBJECTIVES

After reading this chapter, the learner should be able to:

1. Describe the physician–patient relationship.
2. Describe the hospital–patient relationship.
3. Describe the hospital–physician relationship.
4. Define medical malpractice.
5. Define negligence.
6. Identify the elements of a negligence claim.
7. Define the meaning of standard of care.
8. Explain the role of standard of care in medical malpractice cases.
9. List the methods a plaintiff may use to establish the standard of care in a medical malpractice case.
10. Distinguish among the three types of damages.
11. Analyze the difference between negligence and *res ipsa loquitur*.
12. Compare and contrast vicarious liability, corporate negligence, and failure to warn.
13. Explain the difference between assault and battery.
14. Explain the differences between each of the following intentional torts: defamation, invasion of privacy, and medical abandonment.
15. Explain the difference between a claim for nonperformance and improper performance.
16. Identify how social media can implicate liability.
17. Identify the defenses commonly raised in lawsuits involving health care providers.
18. Differentiate between contributory and comparative negligence.

KEY CONCEPTS

Actual damages
Assault
Assumption of risk
Battery
Breach of confidentiality
Breach of contract
Breach of duty of care
Causation
Charitable immunity
Comparative negligence
Compensatory damages
Contributory negligence
Corporate negligence
Credentialing process
Damages
Defamation
Duty of care
Encryption
Exemplary damages
Expert witness
Failure to warn

False arrest	Intentional torts	Physician–patient relationship
False imprisonment	Invasion of privacy	Protected health information (PHI)
Good Samaritan statutes	Libel	Punitive damages
Governmental immunity	Malpractice	*Res ipsa loquitur*
Health care relationships	Medical abandonment	Slander
Hospital–patient relationship	Medical malpractice	Standard of care
Hospital–physician relationship	Medical staff privileges	Statute of limitation
Improper disclosure	Negligence	Tort
Intentional infliction of emotional distress	Nominal damages	Vicarious liability
	Nonintentional torts	

INTRODUCTION

Liability for injury is feared by many health care providers. Injury may encompass not only physical damage but also damage to a party's rights, reputation, or property. Improper disclosure of health information is an injury for which a party is entitled to bring a lawsuit. Accordingly, individuals engaged in protecting health information must understand the principles of liability.

To understand the principles of liability, the nature of the relationships from which liability can arise must be understood. The legal theories underlying lawsuits in the health care field and the type of defenses raised in many of these lawsuits can then be studied.

HEALTH CARE RELATIONSHIPS

Before an individual can bring a lawsuit to establish some form of liability against a health care provider, the individual must have established a relationship with that provider. Without this relationship, the parties to a lawsuit are basically strangers who have no obligation to each other that could serve as the basis for a malpractice lawsuit.[1] Although many variations of **health care relationships** exist between provider and patient, this section addresses those relationships most common to a lawsuit in the health care field, as illustrated in Figure 4.1. Furthermore, this section addresses a relationship that does not directly involve patient care, the physician–hospital relationship, because this relationship increasingly serves as the subject of lawsuits.

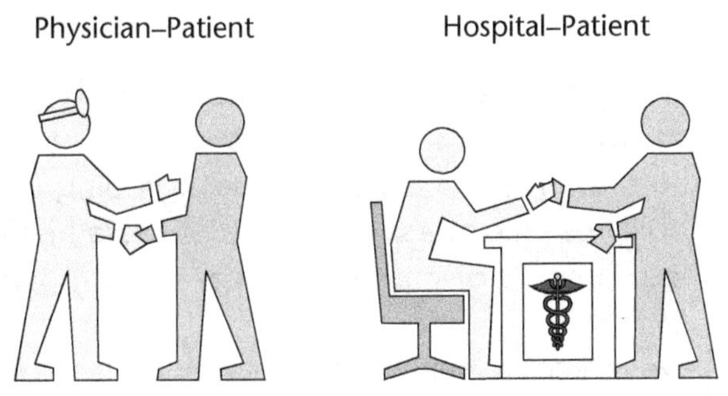

Figure 4.1 Health Care Relationships

Physician–Patient Relationships

Physician–patient relationships have traditionally served as the cornerstone of health care in the United States. Originally viewed as existing only between the physician and patient, the large role played by other health care providers in the health care field and the liability questions arising from those relationships have caused the relationship to evolve in terms beyond physicians. Many of the basic principles of the physician–patient relationship apply not only to physicians but also by analogy to other types of health care providers, such as nurses and physical therapists. An understanding of the basic principles of the physician–patient relationship will assist the student in making these analogies to situations involving other health care providers.

The **physician–patient relationship** begins when the patient requests treatment and the physician agrees to render that treatment. This relationship is a contractual one because it involves both an offer (the request for treatment) and an acceptance (the agreement to render the treatment). This contractual relationship can exist as either an express contract or an implied contract.

In an express contract, the terms, rights, and responsibilities of the parties are agreed on either orally or in writing. For example, an express contract is established when a physician and a patient agree, in advance of any treatment, on the amount the patient must pay and what treatment or result the physician will render for that payment. By contrast, an implied contract exists when the conduct of the parties and the circumstances of the situation create a tacit understanding that an agreement has been reached. In this instance, details of the contract are not reached in advance of treatment. For example, an implied contract is created when a physician treats the patient prior to an agreement on the terms for payment and treatment.

A physician–patient relationship may also be formed if the physician engages in providing medical advice to individuals who see the physician's expertise through social media, such as blogs. If the physician has never before met the specific individual to whom he has just provided medical advice, he may have accidentally established a physician–provider relationship. (More information regarding social media and liability can be found later in this chapter.)

Once the physician–patient relationship is established, it continues until such time that it has been properly terminated or the patient no longer requires treatment. Terminating this relationship can be accomplished in a number of ways: (1) the physician may withdraw from the contract, (2) the patient may dismiss the physician, or (3) the physician and patient may mutually agree to end the relationship. If the physician decides to withdraw from the contract, he must give the patient reasonable notice so that the patient may obtain alternative treatment. Most often, termination is due to the fact that the patient is either cured or has died. The relationship may also terminate as a result of the patient's failure to comply with the physician's orders.

Hospital–Patient Relationships

Many of the same concepts addressed in the physician–patient relationship also apply to the **hospital–patient relationship**. The relationship begins when the patient is voluntarily admitted to the hospital. At the time of admission, the patient signs certain forms, agreeing to pay for the treatment that will be rendered. This act establishes an express contract to receive health care. The hospital–patient relationship ends when the patient is discharged or leaves the hospital against medical advice.

As a general rule, a hospital does not have a responsibility to treat every patient who arrives at its door. The exception to this rule is an emergency-care situation. Under various provisions of federal and state law, along with the standards of the Joint Commission, formerly known as the Joint Commission on Accreditation of Healthcare Organizations (JCAHO), the general rule has been modified so that hospitals must have, at minimum, a procedure for assessing whether an ill or an injured person who appears at the hospital's door can be treated at that hospital or transferred to another facility for treatment.

Under the Emergency Medical Treatment and Active Labor Act (EMTALA)[2] of the Consolidated Omnibus Budget Reconciliation Act of 1985, hospitals and physicians who participate in the Medicare program must follow certain guidelines for the treatment and transfer of all patients, regardless of whether a particular patient who appears for care is eligible for Medicare. Commonly referred to as the "antidumping law," EMTALA requires a hospital or physician to treat a patient who is in active labor or in an emergency medical condition until the condition is stabilized. Once the condition is stabilized, the hospital and physician have the following three choices: (1) continue to treat the patient, (2) transfer the patient, or (3) discharge the patient.

An example of a physician's failure to comply with EMTALA is illustrated in *Burditt v. U.S. Department of Health and Human Services*.[3] In *Burditt*, a pregnant woman in active labor with dangerously high blood pressure presented at the hospital's emergency room. The patient had not received prenatal care and did not have the means for payment of her medical treatment. The on-call obstetrician initially refused to treat her but, when pressured by the hospital staff, arranged for her transfer to a hospital 170 miles away. Despite repeated attempts by hospital staff to challenge the obstetrician's transfer order, the patient began transfer by ambulance to the designated facility. Within forty miles of the original hospital, the patient delivered her child. When the nurse accompanying the patient in the ambulance notified the obstetrician of the birth, he ordered her to continue the transfer to the second hospital. The nurse instead returned the patient to the original hospital, where the obstetrician directed the patient's discharge. At that point, the hospital arranged for the patient's treatment with a second obstetrician. The court held that the obstetrician's conduct in ordering the patient's transfer violated EMTALA and supported imposition of a $20,000 fine.

The requirement under EMTALA and similar state laws to treat emergency-care patients necessarily influences the hospital's ability to decide whether to create a hospital–patient relationship. As these laws illustrate, the law may create a duty to treat the patient, which, in turn, forms the basis for the hospital–patient relationship. A branch of this duty creates the possibility of liability.

Hospital–Physician Relationships

Unlike the relationships previously discussed, this relationship is not based on direct patient care. Rather, it is based on the contract between hospital and physician that allows the physician to bring patients to the hospital to receive health care. In this relationship, the hospital furnishes and coordinates patient care along with the physician.

The **hospital–physician relationship** begins with the credentialing process. Merely being licensed as a physician is not sufficient to become a member of a hospital's medical staff. The **credentialing process** involves examination by the hospital's governing board of the physician's background, experience, and licensure against established criteria. If the established criteria are met, the physician is admitted to the medical staff. This activity is important because it ensures the physician has received proper education, training, and licensing to provide safe care. The process also serves to ensure that the physician is who he says he is and not someone providing false credentials or a false identity. The process serves to verify the professional scope of practice to allow health record documentation privileges, including role-based access to data. Finally, the process serves as a way to hold all physicians to the same standards. Entities that provide primary source verification of health care provider credentials are listed in Table 4.1.

Table 4.1 Credentialing Entities

Names	Areas of Focus
National Practitioner Data Bank	Nationwide program addressing medical malpractice claims, complaints, license suspensions/revocations, or other issues
American Board of Medical Specialties	Board certifications
American Nurses Credentialing Center	Board certifications
American Association of Nurse Practitioners	Board certifications
Student Clearing House	Verification of education
Office of Inspector General, DHHS	Sanctions and exclusions
System for Award Management	Sanctions and exclusions
Federation of State Medical Boards	License verification

Once admitted to the medical staff, the governing board determines the scope and limit—that is, **medical staff privileges**—of the physician's practice in the hospital. In determining medical staff privileges, the board again reviews the physician's background, experience, and licensure against criteria established by the medical departments or specialties of the hospital. The physician then may exercise only those privileges that have been granted or be subject to a charge of practicing beyond the scope of his privileges.

Medical staff admission and privileges may be curtailed or terminated for a variety of reasons, among them the failure to meet applicable quality of care standards or misconduct by the physician. Depending on the circumstances, the physician may have a right to a formal hearing to challenge the action taken against him. The Health Care Quality Improvement Act of 1986 allows hospitals to summarily suspend or restrict medical privileges to avoid imminent danger to patients, provided that the procedures specified by the act are followed. Further discussion on the act is provided in Chapter 12, Risk Management, Quality Management, and Utilization Management.

In sum, hospitals have a duty to ensure that their medical staffs are competent. Failure to perform this duty may result in a finding of direct liability to the patient. Such liability is discussed later in this chapter in the section on corporate negligence.

THEORIES OF LIABILITY

The theories of liability underlying lawsuits in the health care field can be divided into three areas: breach of contract, intentional torts, and nonintentional torts. **Intentional torts** are torts committed by persons with the intent to do something wrong. **Nonintentional torts**, by contrast, are torts committed by persons who lack the intent to do something wrong. Table 4.2 lists the theories of liability of intentional and nonintentional torts. A fuller description of contract and tort law is provided in Chapter 1, Workings of the American Legal System. The majority of medical malpractice lawsuits filed in the United States involve nonintentional torts.

Nonintentional Torts

Negligence and Medical Malpractice

Because of its frequent use in medical malpractice lawsuits, negligence has become almost synonymous with medical malpractice, although they are separate legal terms. Negligence is the most frequently used theory of liability, but it is only one of many theories that may support a medical malpractice claim.

Negligence refers to someone failing to do something that a reasonably prudent person would do in a similar situation or, alternatively, doing something that a reasonably prudent person would *not* do in a similar situation. **Malpractice**, on the other hand, refers to professional misconduct. This misconduct involves a professional who fails to follow a standard of care prevalent for his profession that results in harm to another person. In **medical malpractice**, this misconduct generally involves the failing of a physician to follow a standard of care, which results in harm to the patient.

Medical malpractice actions are not limited to physicians and may be brought against other health care providers and institutions. Underlying any medical malpractice action is, of course, the existence of a relationship between the patient and the health care provider or institution.

To succeed in a negligence claim for medical malpractice, the plaintiff (the patient) must prove the following four elements: (1) a duty of care is owed to the patient, (2) a breach of this duty of care, (3) a causal connection between the breach of duty and the patient's injury, and (4) damages. If all four elements are not proved, the plaintiff will lose the case. Figure 4.2 illustrates this interrelationship. The following discussion defines each of these elements and describes how they fit in a medical malpractice lawsuit.

Duty of Care

A **duty of care** is an obligation, to which the law gives recognition and effect, to conform to a particular standard of conduct toward another. That is, this duty of care requires a person to behave in a particular way, with the risk that if he does not do so, he will become subject to liability for any harm sustained by another because of his actions. For example, an automobile driver has a duty to drive in a safe manner and may become liable for damages resulting from an accident if he fails to do what a reasonably prudent automobile driver would do.

As the example illustrates, the duty of care is measured under the reasonably prudent person standard. The mythical reasonably prudent person is someone with average intelligence and

Table 4.2 Theories of Liability

Intentional Torts	Nonintentional Torts
Assault and battery	Negligence
Defamation	*Res ipsa loquitur*
Invasion of privacy	Vicarious liability
Medical abandonment	Corporate negligence
False imprisonment	Failure to warn
False arrest	Breach of confidentiality
Intentional infliction of emotional distress	

Duty of Care
+
Breach of Duty of Care
+
Causation
+
Damages
―――――――
Negligence

Figure 4.2 Elements of a Negligence Claim

experience. This standard is applied when negligence is alleged against someone who is not a professional. Where negligence is alleged against the professional, however, a different standard of care is involved: that of a reasonably prudent professional.

Breach of Duty of Care

The basis of every negligence claim in a medical malpractice case is the allegation of a **breach of duty of care**, meaning that the medical professional failed to maintain a certain standard of care. This **standard of care** is the level of care a reasonably prudent professional would have rendered in the same or similar circumstances. Like the reasonably prudent person, the reasonably prudent professional is someone with average intelligence and comparable training and experience.

During a medical malpractice trial, the plaintiff attempts to show that the defendant, the medical professional, deviated from the appropriate standard of care. To do this, the plaintiff must first establish what standards were appropriate at the time the care was received. This procedure can be accomplished in several ways.

First, the plaintiff may introduce into evidence the general standards contained in state laws and regulations governing the pertinent profession, such as nursing practice acts. If the state law and/or regulation was designed to protect a class of persons from certain types of harm and the law was violated, a court and jury will find the medical professional liable.

Second, general standards of care can be found in written materials from various sources. For example, a professional association or accrediting organization may have published general standards for the profession or the institution it accredits. Furthermore, certain textbooks provide guidelines that illustrate the appropriate standard of care.

A health care facility's internal policies and procedures, including medical staff bylaws and manuals, are a third way to establish the standard of care. As a general rule, an institution's policies and procedures are more specific than the standards found in textbooks. In some instances, an institution's policies and procedures may establish a higher standard of care than the minimally acceptable standard found in textbooks. If a higher standard is established by an institution's policies and/or procedures, it is the higher standard of care against which the institution will be measured.

Fourth, a plaintiff uses expert testimony to establish a breach of the standard of care. An **expert witness** is a person who is permitted to testify at trial because of special knowledge or proficiency in a particular field relevant to the case. Under this scenario, the plaintiff contacts a medical professional who is proficient in the same area of practice as the defendant. After reviewing the facts of the plaintiff's case, the medical professional, referred to as the expert witness, testifies in court, describing what he believes to be the appropriate standard of care and comparing that standard to the care the defendant provided to the plaintiff.

When trying to establish the standard of care, the plaintiff is not limited to using only one of these methods. And, of course, courts and juries may use ordinary common sense when establishing an appropriate standard of care. If the very nature of the act committed by the medical professional indicates improper treatment and malpractice, such as amputating the wrong limb, expert testimony would not be necessary and the court and jury could rely on ordinary experience and knowledge to determine the standard of care. For example, the patient was not required to use the testimony of an expert in *Larrimore v. Homeopathic Hospital Association*[4] to establish a failure to meet the standard of care. In *Larrimore*, a nurse injected the patient with a medication rather than administering it orally, despite the patient's protest that the physician had prescribed oral administration of the medicine in question. The court held the jury members could rely on their own common sense to conclude that the nurse's failure to follow the doctor's written instructions constituted a breach of the standard of care.

At one time, courts looked to the locality where the care was rendered to determine the standard of care. Commonly referred to as the locality rule, the standard of care under this rule is measured in a given situation solely against the practice of other medical professionals in the same locality. The locality rule was formulated at a time of great variance between the knowledge and skill of medical professionals in rural and urban areas. Due to improved transportation and communication systems, the trend since the 1970s has been away from a locality-based standard of care toward a national standard of care that exists in every state in the country. Whether the state in which a lawsuit is brought uses the locality rule or a national standard of care is determined by that state's rules of evidence and its case law.

Causation

Once the patient has demonstrated that the medical professional breached the standard of care owed to him, he must then establish that it was this breach that caused the injury. The breach of duty must constitute the proximate cause of his injury, meaning the primary or moving cause without which the injury would not have occurred.

Proving the causal connection, sometimes referred to as **causation**, can be difficult. In some cases, all or part of an injury is not the direct result of the medical professional's negligence but is the indirect result of an intervening force. Under these circumstances, the test to determine proximate cause is foreseeability: if the reasonably prudent medical professional had anticipated that the intervening force would occur, then the injury is considered foreseeable and the medical professional will be held liable.

Damages

After establishing the causal link between the breach of duty and the injury, the patient is entitled to damages. **Damages** may be of three types: (1) nominal, (2) actual, or (3) punitive.

Nominal damages are awarded for the vindication of a right in which minimal injury can be proved. These damages constitute a *very small* amount of money, for example $1, and are awarded as a recognition of a technical invasion of a person's rights. Where other types of damages are proved, nominal damages are not awarded. An example in which nominal damages can be awarded is discussed in the section of this chapter dealing with assault and battery.

Actual damages, sometimes referred to as **compensatory damages**, are awarded to "make the plaintiff whole" and restore him to his position before the injury. These damages compensate for actual loss and include, but are not limited to, the value of past and future medical expenses and past and future loss of income.

Punitive damages, sometimes referred to as **exemplary damages**, are awarded above and beyond actual damages. These damages are awarded when there is proof of outrageous, malicious, or intentional conduct. The theory behind punitive damages is a public policy consideration: by punishing wrongdoers or making an example of them, others will be deterred from future outrageous, malicious, or intentional conduct. Punitive damages are not often awarded in medical malpractice cases because most of these cases are based on a negligence theory involving deviation from the standard of care, as opposed to intentional tort theories involving conduct that is outrageous, malicious, or intentional.

Res Ipsa Loquitur

In addition to the traditional negligence theory just described, a second negligence theory, ***res ipsa loquitur***, can serve as the basis for a medical malpractice action. In the most fundamental sense, *res ipsa loquitur* means "the thing speaks for itself."[5] This theory is not widely used and applies only when a plaintiff cannot prove negligence with the direct evidence available. Figure 4.3 illustrates the concept of *res ipsa loquitur*.

Using this theory, the patient attempts to convince the jury that the injury would not have happened except as a consequence of negligence, therefore creating a presumption of negligence that the medical professional must rebut. Underlying this theory is the belief that the medical professional has better access to evidence of what happened than does the patient.

To succeed on this claim, the patient must prove the following elements: (1) the injury is of such a character that it would not ordinarily occur without someone's negligence, (2) the medical professional had exclusive control and management over the instrument or cause of the accident, and (3) the injury could not have occurred as a result of any action by the patient. In some states, the patient must also prove that the medical professional had superior knowledge of the course of the accident.

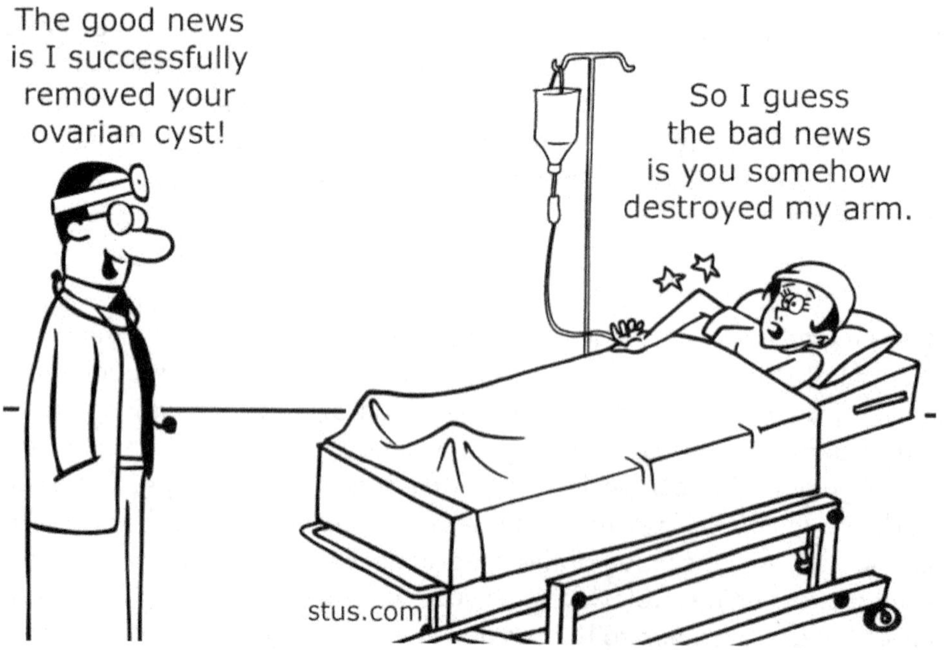

Figure 4.3 Res Ipsa Loquitur Theory. *Image © Stu Rees, www.stus.com*

The doctrine of *res ipsa loquitur*, by its definition, can apply in only limited situations. For example, the doctrine may be used in instances in which the patient is undergoing surgery and emerges from the anesthetic with a foreign object inside his body, such as a sponge. Applying the elements listed previously, the patient would be able to prove his claim because (1) the foreign object would not ordinarily be present in the patient following surgery but for the medical professional's negligence, (2) the medical professional had exclusive control and management over the operation, and (3) the patient did not contribute in any way to leaving a foreign object inside his body.

At one time, res *ipsa loquitur* could not be applied in a lawsuit if the patient sued more than one defendant. The case of *Ybarra v. Spangard*[6] changed this rule. In *Ybarra*, the court reasoned that any one of the medical professionals involved in the surgery to remove the appendix (i.e., the surgeon, the anesthesiologist, the consulting physician, and hospital employees) could have been responsible for the patient's subsequent paralysis in his right shoulder. The court ruled that the patient was not required to show which medical professional was responsible for his injury because the patient did not have access to direct evidence proving which medical professional was responsible. The court allowed the patient to use *res ipsa loquitur* to create a presumption of negligence that any of the medical professionals involved in the surgery could have been responsible for the injury and then allowed the medical professionals the opportunity to rebut the presumption and individually prove their innocence.

Patients may also rely upon expert testimony to establish their claim of *res ipsa loquitur*. In *Sides v. St. Anthony's Medical Center*,[7] the patient contracted an *E. coli* infection after undergoing a lumbar laminectomy with spinal fusion. Applying the elements to the facts of the case, the court held that expert testimony could be used as evidence to show that an infection such as the patient's does not occur in the absence of negligence. More than half of the states follow the approach of allowing expert testimony to establish a claim of *res ipsa loquitur*.[8]

Vicarious Liability

The doctrine of **vicarious liability**, also referred to as *respondeat superior*, makes a health care organization, such as a hospital, responsible for the negligent acts of its employees committed within the course and scope of their employment. Underlying the doctrine is the common law concept that a master is subject to liability for the torts of his servants if the servants were acting within the scope of their duties. Moreover, the reasoning holds that if an individual will be held responsible for the consequences of his own actions, so should employers be held responsible for the consequences of the acts of their agents and employees who act within the scope of their employment.

Vicarious liability is a derivative concept. If a jury determines that the employee is not liable, liability cannot be imposed on the employer under this theory. That is to say that the employer can be found liable under other theories, but the vicarious liability theory will not apply.

Whether an employment relationship exists may vary from case to case. To determine the existence of this relationship, courts look to a number of factors, including (1) who selected the employee, (2) who pays the employee, (3) who has power to fire the employee, and (4) who has power to control the details of the employee's work.

Among these factors, control is the most important. If the employer has control over the employee's work, an employment relationship will generally be found. In the health care field, hospitals have generally been found vicariously liable for the negligent conduct of nurses, interns, residents, and technicians due to the level of control hospitals generally have over these employees. For example, the hospital in *Bernardi v. Community Hospital Association*[9] was found negligent under the doctrine of *respondeat superior* when a nurse improperly injected a patient with medication, causing the patient to lose normal use of her right foot. The court ruled that the nurse was acting within the scope of her employment of the hospital, and therefore, the hospital was responsible for her negligent acts.

By contrast, hospitals have generally not been found vicariously liable for the negligent conduct of physicians because the physicians are typically classified as independent contractors. Courts frequently classify the physician as an independent contractor because of the high degree of skill, learning, and judgment the physician exhibits, which the hospital is incapable of controlling. If, however, the physician is an employee of the hospital, the classification of independent contractor generally does not apply, and vicarious liability can be used.

Corporate Negligence

Unlike vicarious liability, **corporate negligence** recognizes that a health care organization, such as a hospital, owes a duty directly to a patient with regard to care and treatment. The doctrine has been defined as "the failure of a hospital, entrusted with the task of providing the accommodations necessary to carry out its purpose, to follow the established standard of conduct to which it should conform."[10] This duty cannot be delegated, and because it is not centered on the physician–hospital relationship, it is separate and distinct from the doctrine of vicarious liability.

The doctrine of corporate negligence was first applied in the landmark case of *Darling v. Charleston Community Memorial Hospital.*[11] In *Darling*, a college football player broke his leg during a game and was treated at the emergency room of the hospital. The on-call doctor, who had no orthopedic training, improperly applied a cast to the leg, which impaired blood circulation. Despite the patient's complaints, the cast remained on for fourteen days. After the patient was transferred to another hospital, his new physician removed the cast, discovered accumulated dead tissue, and subsequently amputated the leg.

In the player's lawsuit against the first hospital, the court found the first hospital liable under the theory of corporate negligence, reasoning that the hospital had a duty to require that the patient be examined by members of the hospital staff who were skilled in the particular treatment required under the circumstances. The hospital's failure to provide this examination, along with its failure to review the treatment the patient received, as well as not requiring consultants to be called in, was a breach of its direct duty to the patient.

The doctrine of corporate negligence also encompasses the hospital's duty to adhere to its own bylaws and the applicable state statute governing the credentials process. In *Johnson v. Misericordia Community Hospital,*[12] the hospital failed to investigate the qualifications of the physician who was accused of negligence. By granting staff privileges without doing this investigation, the court determined that the hospital created a foreseeable and unreasonable risk that unqualified physicians might be appointed and harm to patients would result. For that reason, the doctrine of corporate negligence applied.

Failure to Warn

Failure to warn, sometimes referred to as failure to protect, is a negligence theory that applies to a psychotherapist's failure to take steps to protect an innocent third party from a dangerous patient. First developed in the case of *Tarasoff v. Regents of University of California,*[13] the theory holds that when a psychotherapist determines that his patient presents a serious danger of violence to a third person, he incurs a duty to use reasonable care to protect the third person from this danger.

After determining that such a danger exists, the psychotherapist must then determine what steps to take to protect the intended victim. These steps may include warning the victim directly, warning others who can apprise the victim of the danger, notifying the police, or taking other steps that are reasonable under the circumstances.

> **ETHICS**
> The duty to warn is both an ethical and legal duty.

In addition to being a legal duty, the duty to warn is an ethical duty. For example, the ethics code of the American Psychological Association provides that despite the general duty of confidentiality, a psychologist may reveal patient confidences if not doing so would pose a clear danger to the patient or others.[14] This provision illustrates how a professional association's own guidelines and requirements can be used to establish a standard of care.

Failure to warn is only one of a variety of possible theories that could support a lawsuit involving a patient's danger to a third party. Among other theories are the failure to adequately diagnose the patient, the failure to treat the patient so that the patient's violent tendencies could be brought under control, and the failure to commit the individual to a mental institution for care.

Breach of Confidentiality

The physician–patient and hospital–patient relationships both share a duty to maintain patient confidentiality. A nonintentional tort, the **breach of confidentiality**, has been recognized under the law for some time. With the passage of the Health Information Technology for Economic and Clinical Health Act of 2009 (HITECH Act), a part of the American Recovery and Reinvestment Act (ARRA), this **tort** has been redefined as "the unauthorized, acquisition, access, use or disclosure of protected health information which compromises the security or privacy of such information, except where an unauthorized person to whom such information is disclosed would not reasonably have been able to retain such information."[15]

In the event of a breach of confidentiality, either by the health care provider or by a business associate of the health care provider, the provider or business associate must provide notice to the patient of the breach. Such notice must be given within sixty days after discovery of the breach, with limited exceptions beyond that time in instances where patient contact data are insufficient to provide notice within the time frame. The content of the notice is listed in Table 4.3.

Additionally, the health care provider must notify the Secretary of Health and Human Services of the breach. The notification should take place immediately if more than 500 residents of a state or jurisdiction have been affected or on an annual basis if the number of individuals affected is less than 500. If the breach involves more than 500 residents, the health care provider must also notify prominent media outlets serving the state or jurisdiction. The Secretary of Health and Human Services, in turn, must compile an annual report to Congress summarizing the breaches over a calendar year. Using calendar years 2013 and 2014 as examples, the Secretary's summary indicates that "breaches involving 500 or more individuals affected more than 29 million individuals."[16] The Secretary identified six general causes of incidents: (1) theft; (2) loss; (3) unauthorized access/disclosure; (4) improper disposal; (5) hacking/IT incident; and (6) unknown/other (capturing breaches attributable to other causes or breaches where the cause is unknown).[17] The report further identifies remedial actions taken by health care providers, the most common of which include revising policies and procedures, improving physical security, providing additional training to workforce members, adopting **encryption** technologies, revising business associate contracts, performing new risk assessments, imposing sanctions on employees for violating policies and procedures, and providing free credit report monitoring to impacted individuals.[18]

Table 4.3 Content of Notice of Breach of Confidentiality

CONTENT OF NOTIFICATION—Regardless of the method by which notice is provided to individuals under this section, notice of a breach shall include, to the extent possible, the following:

(1) A brief description of what happened, including the date of the breach and the date of the discovery of the breach, if known.
(2) A description of the types of unsecured protected health information that were involved in the breach (such as full name, social security number, date of birth, home address, account number, or disability code).
(3) The steps individuals should take to protect themselves from potential harm resulting from the breach.
(4) A brief description of what the covered entity involved is doing to investigate the breach, to mitigate losses, and to protect against any further breaches.
(5) Contact procedures for individuals to ask questions or learn additional information, which shall include a toll-free telephone number, an e-mail address, Web site, or postal address.

Source: 42 U.S.C. § 17932(f) (2019).

Since the breach notification requirement became effective in 2009, a total of 1187 large breaches of **protected health information (PHI)** affecting over 41.2 individuals have been reported to the Secretary.[19] In 2014 alone, over 21 million patient health records were breached.[20] The two largest breaches in 2014 involved the cyberattacks against hospital networks with the next largest breach involving the failure of a business associate to safeguard PHI.[21] It is unclear whether these trends will continue unchanged or if increased awareness of the dangers posed by these breaches will reduce the number and scope of breaches in the future.

The breach of confidentiality is sometimes referred to as improper or wrongful disclosure of individually identifiable health information. In addition to the civil liability provisions of the HITECH Act, the Health Insurance Portability and Accountability Act (HIPAA) addresses wrongful disclosure in statutory provisions specifying that knowing disclosure of individually identifiable health information to another person in violation of the HIPAA provision is a federal offense.[22] This offense is subject to punishment of fines, imprisonment, or both, and the level of fine or imprisonment gradually increases if the offense is committed under false pretenses or with the intent to steal, transfer, or use the information for commercial advantage, personal gain, or malicious harm.

HIPAA

Federal law addresses wrongful disclosure of health information by making it a crime to do so in knowing violation of HIPAA.

A case illustrating a breach of confidentiality is *Biddle v. Warren General Hospital*.[23] In *Biddle*, the hospital had forwarded to a law firm all patient registration forms for a two-year period without first obtaining patient consent. The hospital's legal counsel, in turn, contacted selected patients concerning the patient's potential eligibility for disability payments. A group of patients sued the hospital for breach of confidentiality. The court held that because patient consent was required before the hospital could release this information; the hospital was liable for breach of confidentiality. Similar cases in other jurisdictions have reached the same result.[24]

Intentional Torts

Assault and Battery

Although frequently referred to in connection with each other, assault and battery are two separate torts. An **assault** occurs when an individual is placed in reasonable anticipation of being touched in such a way that is insulting, provoking, or will cause the individual physical harm. An assault is a threat that does not involve physical contact. By contrast, a **battery** consists of physical contact involving injury or offense. In assault and battery, the individual does not give permission or authority for either act.

In addition to being considered a tort, assault and battery is considered a crime, punishable under the criminal law. A medical professional, like any other person, may be accused of the crime of assault and battery. It is infrequent, however, that a medical professional is accused of assault and battery in a civil matter. When that occurs, it is usually an accusation of technical battery.

Technical battery occurs when a medical professional, in the course of treatment, exceeds the consent given by the patient. In so doing, the medical professional does not necessarily intend a wrongful act and most likely sincerely hopes to aid the patient. Nonetheless, the medical professional does not have the patient's permission to act beyond that to which the patient originally consented. Unless an emergency is present, the patient may recover damages for the technical battery. If, however, the patient benefited from the technical battery, the patient may recover only nominal damages.

For example, a claim of battery succeeded in a case where the patient consented to exploratory surgery but instead received a mastectomy.[25] Similarly, a battery claim has succeeded where there has been an obvious mistake, such as operating on the wrong ear.[26]

Defamation

Defamation consists of the wrongful injuring of another person's reputation. Defamation may expose the other person to ridicule, contempt, or hatred and tends to diminish the esteem, respect, goodwill, or confidence in which the other person is held.

Defamation expressed in print, writing, pictures, or signs is referred to as **libel**; defamation expressed by oral expressions or transitory gestures is referred to as **slander**. In both libel and slander, the defamatory statement must be "published," meaning that the defamatory statement must be made to a third party and not just to the patient.

As a general rule, truth of the statement at issue is an absolute defense in a defamation lawsuit. This defense can be applied in cases against health care institutions alleging wrongful release of health records because the contents of a health record are generally considered true.

Where the defense of truth does not apply, because some or all of the statement at issue is false, health care providers may be able to use the defenses of absolute privilege and qualified privilege. Under absolute privilege, publications made as part of judicial, legislative, and/or administrative proceedings are protected in a subsequent defamation lawsuit. For example, a health care provider who releases information pursuant to lawful judicial process, for example, a lawful subpoena, and then is sued for defamation, is protected from liability.

Similarly, qualified privilege may be used as a defense if the statement was made in good faith, without malice, under a reasonable belief to be true, by someone with an interest or legal duty to disclose the statement to another with a corresponding duty or interest. For example, a health care provider who possesses a duty to inform another of his possibility of contracting a contagious disease from the physician's patient, and does so in good faith, without malice and reasonably believing the diagnosis to be true, can avail himself of the defense even if he later learns he was mistaken concerning the contagious disease.

Invasion of Privacy

Invasion of privacy involves the dissemination of information about another person's private, personal matters. To charge invasion of privacy, the plaintiff must show any one of the following: (1) an unwarranted appropriation or exploitation of an individual's personality; (2) a publication of an individual's private affairs, which would cause embarrassment; (3) a wrongful intrusion upon an individual's private concerns or activities; or (4) some form of publicity that paints the individual in a false light.

Invasion of privacy lawsuits in the health care field can arise in a number of ways, including using a patient's likeness for commercial purposes without the patient's consent. For example, using "before" and "after" photographs of a surgery patient for purposes of medical instruction would constitute an invasion of privacy if the patient had not given consent.

Similarly, a charge of invasion of privacy can be brought if there has been **improper disclosure** of a patient's health information given in the course of treatment. For further information discussing this topic, see Chapter 9, Confidentiality and Informed Consent; Chapter 10, Access to Health Information; and Chapter 11, Specialized Patient Records.

Medical Abandonment

Medical abandonment generally means the unilateral severing, by the physician, of the physician–patient relationship without giving the patient reasonable notice at a time when there is a necessity for continuing care. To prove medical abandonment, the patient must establish the following elements: (1) the existence of a physician–patient relationship and (2) that the abandonment is the proximate cause of the injury for which the patient is suing. Unless the injury is an obvious result of the abandonment, the patient must use an expert witness to establish proximate cause between the abandonment and the injury. If there is abandonment but no injury, the physician will not be held liable.

Courts have found physicians liable for abandonment in a number of instances: for intentionally leaving their patients alone at a critical time[27] and for failing to be available because of the needs of other patients,[28] vacation,[29] or the physician's erroneous belief that the patient had recovered and no longer needed treatment.[30] Conversely, courts have found physicians not liable for abandonment in cases in which the patient does not need immediate treatment and the physician gives the patient a list of qualified substitute physicians. Courts have been split concerning whether a physician can be liable for failing to be available because of personal illness.[31]

Although the tort of medical abandonment is nearly one hundred years old, changes in the economics of health care provide new opportunities for its use. With the advent of health maintenance organizations, preferred provider organizations, and Medicare's Prospective Payment System, critics have charged that economic issues and pressures, rather than medical reasons, have caused the premature discharge of patients. These critics charge that hospitals and physicians may succumb to the temptation to discharge a patient prematurely, rather than extend the hospital stay or transfer the patient to another institution, in order to obtain full diagnostic-related group (DRG) reimbursement. This premature discharge raises the possibility of a medical abandonment claim if there is not adequate follow-up treatment for the patient.

With the advent of the use of social media, a new theory of medical abandonment has arisen. Patients have complained that their health care provider abandoned them because the provider did not respond to requests for medical advice or care made through blogs, e-mails, or other forms of social media. If the health care provider had previously established a provider–patient relationship and then failed to continue this relationship within the social media context, the patient's claim of abandonment is strengthened.

False Imprisonment

The tort of **false imprisonment** involves the intentional detention or restraint of someone against his will without legal justification. Such detention or restraint must be intentional, meaning that the person imposing confinement does so willfully. False imprisonment is sometimes confused with the tort of false arrest. While both torts involve detention or restraint of a person against his will, the tort of **false arrest** also involves the intent to make an arrest or actually making an arrest. A person can be falsely imprisoned without also being falsely arrested; however, any person falsely arrested is also falsely imprisoned.

The case of *McGlone v. Landreth*[32] illustrates both false arrest and false imprisonment. McGlone took a taxicab home from the bus station and felt that the driver charged an inflated price. McGlone asked for a reduced fee. The cabdriver disagreed, refused to let McGlone out of the cab, and drove her back to the bus station. At the bus station, city police arrested McGlone based on the allegations of the taxicab driver. McGlone sued the taxicab company and the driver for false imprisonment and false arrest. McGlone succeeded on both counts. The driver's actions in refusing to let her leave the taxicab and transporting her back to the station constituted false imprisonment, and the driver's efforts to have the city police arrest McGlone based on her refusal to pay him constituted false arrest.

Intentional Infliction of Emotional Distress

Intentional infliction of emotional distress refers to (1) a defendant's conduct that is so extreme and outrageous that it causes the plaintiff to experience severe emotional distress and (2) the defendant engaged in the conduct with the intent to cause the emotional distress. Cases measure whether conduct meets this definition by determining whether the conduct was so extreme in degree and so outrageous in character that it falls beyond all possible bounds of decency and cannot be considered tolerable in a civilized community. Merely expressing disagreement in an inconsiderate or unkind manner is not sufficient to meet the definition. A brief, isolated instance of a supervisor losing his temper with an employee, even where the use of profanity is involved, does not meet the definition.[33]

Additionally, the distress suffered must be of the kind that a reasonable person would not be expected to endure it. In some states, the distress must be severe enough to require medical attention and be medically significant. For example, a plaintiff who suffered from nausea and loss of sleep would not meet the definition of emotional distress.[34]

Breach of Contract

Breach of contract claims generally involve express contracts and the failure to perform these contracts. In express contracts, the parties have agreed in advance upon a specific treatment or the physician may have guaranteed a certain cure or result. If the physician fails to perform the particular act promised, the patient may sue under the theory of nonperformance.

Physicians who fail to perform as specifically promised have been found liable in court. For example, the physician in *Brooks v. Robinson*[35] expressly agreed to treat the patient for tuberculosis but took no action whatsoever. Similarly, in *Foran v. Carangelo*,[36] the physician agreed to perform a hysterectomy but did not do so. In both instances, the basis of the patient's successful lawsuit was nonperformance.

A claim for nonperformance should not be confused with a claim for improper performance. In a lawsuit for improper performance, the physician begins to take whatever action he and the patient agreed on but performs it improperly. For example, the physician in *Horowitz v. Bogart*[37] agreed to remove the patient's ulcer but instead removed the patient's appendix. In such an instance, the lawsuit is not for breach of contract but for negligence or battery.

Social Media

Participating on social media platforms is among the more recent activities in which health care providers engage. While social media promises benefits to providers and patients, it also presents risks of liability. Examples of social media platforms include, but are not limited to, wikis, online forums and message boards, social networking sites, video- and image-sharing sites, blogs, and chat rooms.

Health care providers often use social media as a means to communicate with the general public and patients, informing them of general health care information and the health care services offered by the provider. While this information can benefit the public and patients, it can also open the health care provider to legal claims. For example, a health care provider who has never met or treated a specific individual may accidentally establish a provider–patient relationship by providing a patient-specific response or advice to a request made through a wiki, online forum or message board, social networking site, video- or image-sharing site, blog, or chat room. Any establishment of the provider–patient relationship results in levels of professional responsibility by the provider and failure to exercise that professional responsibility may lead to liability.

A second area of liability concern rests with the unauthorized practice of the health care provider's profession. Most health care professions are regulated at the state level through the issue of licenses that allow practice specific to that state. A health care provider's use of social media may not be limited to patients residing in the same state in which the provider is licensed. If the health care provider establishes a provider–patient relationship with a patient who resides in a state in which the provider is not licensed, the provider is subject to a claim of unauthorized practice of the provider's profession.

Liability also involves the potential for malpractice claims. A provider can be subject to claims of professional misconduct if his use of social media did not include a thorough understanding of the patient's condition or need for treatment. Responses to requests for advice, care, or treatment without this thorough understanding may harm the patient, resulting in a malpractice claim.

CRITICAL THINKING

Social media can be used to improve customer service.

1. How might the use of social media benefit *patients* in the health care context?
2. How might the use of social media with patients benefit the *health care provider*?
3. Are there any ethical and/or legal downsides for the patient and/or the health care provider in the use of social media to improve customer service?

Liability also involves concerns relating to the privacy and security of protected health information. For example, a provider may respond through a social media platform to a patient's inquiry with patient-specific protected health information. If the patient has not assented through a patient authorization, there may be a privacy breach. Similarly, if the response is not sent in a secured fashion, such as through the use of privacy settings or encryption, there may be a security breach.

Health care providers can work to mitigate the risks presented by the use of social media. As a threshold issue, providers should weigh the benefits and costs of communicating with patients through social media and proceed only if the benefits outweigh the costs. To the extent possible, providers should obtain patient authorization when communication is necessary and include disclaimers in communications and postings. Providers can limit the audience who views patient-specific protected health information by using privacy settings on sites, secure servers, and encryption methods. Providers should be prepared in the event of a privacy or security breach by knowing how to comply with notification regulations and how to address patient concerns. Finally, providers should understand that communications between patients and providers through social media may be subject to discovery rules and record retention regulations and may be considered part of the legal health record.

DEFENSES AND LIMITATIONS ON LIABILITY

In virtually every lawsuit, the defendant must decide which defenses to present to the charges leveled against him. In addition to disputing the merits of the lawsuit, the defendant may choose to raise defenses that shield him from liability or reduce his level of liability, regardless of whether the defenses address the merits of the lawsuit. Defenses commonly raised in lawsuits involving health care providers are addressed in the following sections.

Statutes of Limitations

A **statute of limitation** is a law that sets forth a fixed time period in which a lawsuit must be brought. If a lawsuit is not brought within the time frame specified in the applicable statute of limitations, the lawsuit is barred, and the court must dismiss the case.

Statutes of limitations are designed for two purposes: (1) to force those persons considering a lawsuit to bring the lawsuit at a time when memories are intact and evidence is available and therefore not "sit on their rights" and (2) to allow potential defendants a time frame from which to know that a lawsuit can no longer be maintained against them.

Statutes of limitations are technical in nature, as illustrated by the fact that the time period of each statute of limitations varies between the types of lawsuit—that is, contract or tort—and between each state's laws. Statutes in virtually every state provide a fixed time frame in which to bring medical malpractice lawsuits and other personal injury lawsuits.

In certain instances, specific statutes or court decisions have extended the time period of the general statute of limitation. For example, the time frame in which to bring a lawsuit is generally measured from the time the injury occurred. If, however, the injury involves a foreign object left in the body following surgery, the limitations period begins to run when the injured person discovers or should have discovered the injury.

Extensions of the statute of limitations period also apply to minors or persons under some type of legal disability. The extension of the statute of limitations period in these instances is referred to as tolling the statute of limitations. For example, a particular state's law may extend the period of time to a certain number of years after the minor reaches the age of majority to bring a lawsuit. This extension is granted so that the minor is not penalized for the failure of his parent to bring a lawsuit on his behalf.

For a variety of reasons, parents do not bring lawsuits on behalf of their injured children, including reasons of unwillingness or financial inability. For public policy considerations, the law allows children whose rights were not vindicated by their parents to bring lawsuits to vindicate their rights once they reach the age of majority. For this same reason, this extension concept applies to an injured person who is under some form of legal disability, such as being adjudged insane. Once the period of legal disability is removed, the time period of the statute of limitations begins to run.

Illinois law provides a perfect illustration of these concepts. The statute of limitation governing malpractice actions against physicians, dentists, registered nurses, or hospitals in Illinois provides a two-year time period in which to bring a breach of contract or tort lawsuit.[38] The two-year time period is measured from the time of injury or death, or the time the patient should have known or received notice of the injury or death, whichever occurred first. The statute provides that in no event can a lawsuit be brought more than four years from the date of injury or death at issue.

If, however, the person entitled to bring the lawsuit is a minor at the time of the injury, the statute provides an eight-year period to bring the lawsuit, measured from the date of injury. The statute further provides that in no event can the lawsuit be brought after the minor reaches twenty-two years old. Furthermore, if the person entitled to bring the lawsuit is under a legal disability, the time period does not begin to run until the disability is removed.

Charitable Immunity

At one time, a majority of the states permitted the use of the **charitable immunity** defense. In this defense, a charitable institution such as a hospital could be shielded from liability for any torts committed on its property or by its employees. The defense was permitted so that assets intended for charitable purposes would not be used for "improper" reasons, such as paying damage awards. The doctrine originated in England and was adopted in the United States in the late nineteenth century.[39]

The doctrine of charitable immunity was followed until the case of *Bing v. Thunig*.[40] In *Bing*, New York's highest court expressly overruled applying the doctrine to shield charitable hospitals from liability and proceeded to apply the doctrine of *respondeat superior*. The court in *Bing* reasoned that charitable institutions should be forced to compensate persons for the injuries the institutions caused, just as any other business organization would be required to compensate for injuries caused by the business organization. After the *Bing* case, virtually every state either limited or abolished the doctrine of charitable immunity.

Governmental Immunity

Governmental immunity precludes a plaintiff from asserting a meritorious lawsuit against a governmental entity unless the governmental entity consents to the lawsuit. The doctrine has its origin in the English common law concept that the king could do no wrong; therefore, he and his subordinates could not be sued. As developed in the United States, federal and state governments were immune from lawsuits arising out of the negligence of their officers, agents, and employees, *unless* the federal or state government expressly consented to the lawsuit.

Most jurisdictions have abandoned this doctrine in favor of permitting tort lawsuits with certain limitations and restrictions. For example, the government of the United States may not be sued without its consent. With the passage of the Federal Tort Claims Act in 1946, the U.S. government's immunity from tort liability was largely abolished and certain conditions for suits and claims against the U.S. government were established.

Among those conditions was the requirement that the government employee being sued had to be acting within the scope of his employment. Whether a government employee, such as an employee of a veterans' hospital, is acting within the scope of his employment depends on the facts of the particular case.

Conversely, certain restrictions on lawsuits against the United States do remain. The U.S. government is protected from liability for the traditional category of intentional torts and from claims brought against employees who exercise due care in executing a statute or regulation. Finally, the U.S. government is protected from claims brought against its employees based on the performance of, or failure to perform, a discretionary duty. States that have passed laws abandoning the doctrine of governmental immunity have done so with similar conditions and restrictions.

Good Samaritan Statutes

Several states, seeking to encourage physicians, other rescuers, and even private citizens to provide emergency treatment, have passed what are referred to as **Good Samaritan statutes**. As a general rule, these statutes protect physicians, other rescuers, and private citizens from civil liability as a result of their acts or omissions in rendering emergency care.[41] If, however, the rescuer acts in a willful, wanton, or reckless manner in providing emergency treatment, he cannot avail himself of the Good Samaritan statute as a defense.

Generally, the statutes are not designed to protect health care providers who routinely treat patients in immediate need of emergency care, such as emergency room physicians. Rather, the statutes address those health care providers who render emergency care in a nontraditional setting, such as at an automobile accident on the side of the road. If the nontraditional setting is present, the health care provider may raise the Good Samaritan defense.

Contributory and Comparative Negligence

Contributory negligence and comparative negligence, although often used interchangeably, are separate legal concepts used to limit a defendant's liability. **Contributory negligence** means conduct of the plaintiff that contributes in part to the injury the plaintiff received. In some states, a finding of contributory negligence on the plaintiff's part is sufficient to bar any form of recovery. Therefore, even if the plaintiff proves every element of a negligence claim against a defendant, he still will lose if the defendant proves that the plaintiff contributed to his own injuries.

Comparative negligence, on the other hand, builds on the concept of contributory negligence but is not as harsh in the result. Rather than bar recovery, proof that the plaintiff contributed to his own injuries only serves to reduce the amount of damages the plaintiff can recover.

Under comparative negligence principles, negligence is measured in terms of percentages. The percentage that can be attributed to the plaintiff will then be reduced proportionally from the overall award of damages. In some states, if the plaintiff's percentage of fault outweighs the defendant's percentage of fault, the plaintiff can recover nothing. The same situation in another state, however, may merely reduce the damage award. Similarly, some states permit recovery when the plaintiff and defendant are equally at fault; other states do not permit any form of recovery in such a situation.

Under both contributory and comparative negligence theories, the negligence of the defendant is not in doubt; it has already been proved by the plaintiff. The basic difference between the two concepts is that comparative negligence attempts to compensate the plaintiff for some portion of his injury, no matter how small, whereas contributory negligence serves to bar completely a damage award for injury.

In the health care setting, documentation in the health record may be the only successful way to support either of these defenses. For example, nurses' notes documenting the instructions given to a patient and the patient's multiple refusals to follow those instructions would support a defense that the patient's own actions caused, or contributed to, his complications.

Such documentation was used in *Seymour v. Victory Memorial Hospital*[42] to support a contributory negligence defense. In *Seymour*, the patient was instructed not to smoke unless someone was with her and to call the nurses' station when she wanted to smoke. The patient bought cigarettes from a volunteer cart, smoked alone, dropped a match, and burned herself. She then sued the hospital, raising claims of both negligence and *res ipsa loquitur*. The court ruled that the hospital was not liable because the patient knew the smoking procedures and was aware of the danger if she did not follow the procedures. The patient's action in obtaining the cigarette without calling the nurse amounted to contributory negligence.

Assumption of Risk

Assumption of risk, like contributory and comparative negligence, is a method used to limit liability either completely or in part. Under this doctrine, a plaintiff who voluntarily exposes himself to a known and appreciated danger may not recover damages caused by incurring that risk. In order to prevail in this defense, the defendant must prove that the plaintiff knew about the risk, assumed the risk voluntarily, and was not coerced. If all elements are proved, the defendant cannot be held liable for negligence.

Apologies

In light of the length and cost of litigation, many in the health care community have sought to reduce both the length and cost of litigation, or avoid litigation entirely, by focusing on admitting mistakes that caused injury to patients. This effort has culminated in the passage of laws in several states that permit a health care provider to apologize to patients and their families for their mistakes without fearing that their apology will be used against them in court as an admission of their liability. These laws fall into two categories: those offering a full apology (both an expression of sympathy and admission of responsibility) and those offering a partial apology (an expression of sympathy alone). Specific information about these laws and their effect on admission of evidence can be found in Chapter 3, Judicial Process of Health Information. For purposes of understanding the role of apologies in litigation, the hope is that such apologies will decrease the number of medical malpractice lawsuits.

CONCLUSION

In order to manage health information wisely, the differences and similarities between the principles listed in this chapter must be understood. Each main section builds on its predecessor: understanding health care relationships provides the basis for understanding the types of lawsuits that may be brought and the defenses that may be raised. Understanding these principles should assist the health information professional in recognizing potential legal situations.

Furthermore, those involved with managing health information must be aware that the principles of liability differ depending on which jurisdiction applies to a particular case. Learning the particular statutory, common law, and administrative requirements of that jurisdiction in order to make prudent decisions concerning health information is extremely important.

Finally, adopting a constant learning approach to the principles of liability is essential because the law is constantly changing. Keeping abreast of changes in the law at all levels, particularly statutory and common law changes, must be a goal of health information professionals.

CASE STUDY

A surgeon performs elective surgery on John Smith. Smith later complains to his surgeon about pain resulting from the surgery. His surgeon dismisses his complaints as not credible and eventually withdraws from the case. Smith is then treated by another surgeon, who determines that Smith developed complications from surgery and that the delay in treatment has made the complications worse. Smith sees an attorney about a possible lawsuit against the first surgeon.

Describe the theories that could support a lawsuit under these circumstances.

REVIEW QUESTIONS

1. How do the principles of liability influence the health information professional's role in protecting health information?
2. When do the physician–patient and hospital–patient relationships begin?
3. How does the hospital–physician relationship differ from the physician–patient and hospital–patient relationships?
4. What are the requirements of the Emergency Medical Treatment and Active Labor Act that hospitals must meet?
5. What are medical staff privileges, and how are they determined?
6. Compare and contrast negligence and medical malpractice.
7. What are the elements of a negligence claim?
8. What is meant by the term standard of care?
9. What are the different methods one can use to establish the standard of care?
10. What is the role of an expert witness in a negligence claim?
11. What are the purposes of nominal damages, actual damages, and punitive damages?
12. How does the principle of *res ipsa loquitur* fit into the context of negligence?
13. How does vicarious liability differ from corporate negligence?
14. What is the failure to warn theory, and how may it be exercised in the context of a dangerous patient?

15. How does assault differ from battery?
16. What are the differences between defamation, invasion of privacy, and medical abandonment?
17. How does a claim for nonperformance of a contract differ from a claim of improper performance of a contract?
18. How can the use of social media in health care present risks of liability?
19. Compare and contrast the defenses commonly raised in lawsuits involving health care providers.
20. How does comparative negligence differ from contributory negligence?

ENRICHMENT ACTIVITY

Construct a series of flowcharts. Each flowchart should illustrate a health care relationship, a type of lawsuit, and a defense that may be raised. Compare the differences between the flowcharts and determine whether any of the elements in your flowcharts can be interchanged with another element.

ENRICHMENT ACTIVITY

Visit the website of the Federation of State Medical Boards (https://www.fmsb.org). At the bottom of the page under information for consumers, click the link titled Learn about a Physician. Search the DocInfo.org function for a physician you know or have heard of to learn: (a) if the physician is licensed; (b) where the physician went to medical school; and (c) whether the physician has been disciplined by a licensing board. After completing this exercise, determine the value this type of information provided to you and what value it may provide in the credentialing process.

NOTES

1. Louis Goldstein & Miles Zaremski, Medical and Hospital Negligence, Volume 1, § 6:01 (1990 & Supp. 1992).
2. 42 U.S.C. §§ 1395 et seq. (2019).
3. 934 F.2d 1362 (5th Cir. 1991).
4. 181 A.2d 573 (Del. 1952).
5. Black's Law Dictionary 1173 (8th ed. 2004).
6. 154 P.2d 687 (Cal. 1944).
7. 258 S.W.3d 811 (Mo. 2008).

8. *McWain v. Tucson Gen. Hosp.* 670 P.2d 1180 (Ariz. Ct. App. 1983); *Schmidt v. Gibbs*, 807 S.W.2d 928 (Ark. 1991); *Kerr v. Bock*, 486 P.2d 684 (Cal. 1971); *Holmes v. Gamble*, 624 P.2d 905 (Colo. App. 1980); *Gilliam v. Thomas*, 1997 WL 746384 (Conn. Super. Ct. Nov. 20, 1997); *Walker v. Rumer*, 381 N.E.2d 689 (Ill. 1978); *Vogler v. Dominguez*, 624 N.E.2d 56 (Ind. Ct. App. 1993); *Kennis v. Mercy Hosp. Med. Ctr.*, 491 N.W.2d 161 (Iowa 1992); *Green v. Owensboro Med. Health Sys. Inc.*, 231 S.W.3d 781 (Ky. App. 2007); *Cangelosi v. Our Lady of the Lake Reg'l Med. Ctr.* 564 So.2d 654 (La. 1990); *Enrich v. Windmere Corp.*, 616 N.E.2d 1081 (1993); *Jones v. Porretta*, 405 N.W.2d 863 (Mich. 1987); *Keys v. Guthmann*, 676 N.W.2d 354 (Neb. 2004); *Buckelew v. Grossbard*, 435 A.2d 1150 (N.J. 1981); *Mireles v. Broderick*, 872 P.2d 863 (N.M. 1994); *States v. Lourdes Hosp.*, 792 N.E.2d 151 (N.Y. 2003); *Morgan v. Children's Hosp.*, 480 N.E.2d 464 (Ohio 1985); *Sisson v. Elkins*, 801 P.2d 722 (Okla. 1990); *Brannon v. Wood*, 444 P.2d 558 (Or. 1968); *Jones v. Harrisburg Polyclinic Hosp.*, 437 A.2d 1134 (Pa. 1981); *Wilkinson v. Vesey*, 295 A.2d 676 (R.I. 1972); *Van Zee v. Sioux Valley Hosp.*, 315 N.W.2d 489 (S.D. 1982); *Seavers v. Methodist Med. Center of Oak Ridge*, 9 S.W.3d 86 (Tenn. 1999); *King v. Searle Pharm.*, 832 P.2d 858 (Utah 1992); *Connors v. Univ. Assoc. in Obstetrics & Gynecology, Inc.*, 4 F.3d 123 (2d Cir. 1993); *Pederson v. Dumouchel*, 431 P.2d 973 (Wa. 1967); *Hoven v. Kelble*, 256 N.W.2d 379 (Wis. 1977); *Harris v. Cafritz Mem'l Hosp.*, 364 A.2d 135 (D.C. 1976).

9. 443 P.2d 708 (Colo. 1968).

10. *Johnson v. Misericordia Community Hospital*, 294 N.W.2d 501, 506 (Wis. Ct. App. 1980), *aff'd*, 301 N.W.2d 156 (Wis. 1981).

11. 211 N.E.2d 253 (Ill. 1965).

12. *Supra* note 10.

13. 529 P.2d 553 (Cal. 1974), *reargued*, 551 P.2d 334 (Cal. 1976).

14. American Psychological Association, Ethical Principles of Psychologists and Code of Conduct, Ethical Section 4, Principle 8 (2013).

15. 42 U.S.C. § 17831 (A)(1) (2019).

16. Annual Report to Congress on Breaches of Unsecured Protected Health Information for Calendar Years 2013 and 2014. Available at https://www.hhs.gov/sites/default/files/rtc-breach-20132014.pdf. (Last accessed February 28, 2019.)

17. Ibid.

18. Ibid.

19. Ibid.

20. Ibid.

21. Ibid.

22. 42 U.S.C. § 1320d-6 (2019).

23. *Biddle v. Warren Gen. Hosp.*, 715 N.E.2d 518 (Ohio 1999).

24. *Horne v. Patton*, 287 So.2d 824 (1973); *Mrozinski v. Pogue*, 423 S.E.2d 405 (Ga. App. 1992); *Saur v. Probes*, 476 N.W.2d 496 (Mich. App. 1991); *Stempler v. Speidell*, 495 A.2d 857 (N.J. 1985); *Crocker v. Synpol, Inc.*, 732 S.W.2d 429 (Tex. App. 1987).

25. *Corn v. French*, 289 P.2d 173 (Nev. 1955).

26. *Mohr v. Williams*, 104 N.W. 12 (Minn. 1905).

27. *Johnson v. Vaughn*, 370 S.W.2d 591 (Ky. Ct. App. 1963).

28. *Katsetos v. Nolan*, 368 A.2d 172 (Conn. 1976).

29. *Vann v. Harden*, 47 S.E.2d 314 (Va. 1948).

30. *Mucci v. Houghton*, 57 N.W. 305 (Iowa 1894).

31. *Dashiell v. Griffith*, 35 A. 1094 (Md. 1896) (finding the physician liable); *Warwick v. Bliss*, 195 N.W. 502 (S.D. 1923) (finding the physician not liable).

32. 195 P.2d 268 (Okla. 1948) (overruled in part on other grounds by *Parker v. Washington*, 421 P.2d 861 (Okla. 1966).

33. *White v. Monsanto Co.*, 585 S.2d 1205 (La. 1991).

34. *Rooney v. National Super Markets, Inc.*, 668 S.W.2d 649 (Mo. Ct. App. 1984).

35. 163 So.2d 186 (La. Ct. App. 1964).

36. 216 A.2d 638 (Conn. 1966).

37. 217 N.Y.S. 881 (N.Y. 1926).

38. 735 ILCS § 5/13-212 (2019).

39. *McDonald v. Massachusetts General Hosp., 120 Mass. 432 (Mass. 1876).*

40. 143 N.E.2d 3 (N.Y. 1957).

41. *See, e.g.*, Conn. Gen. Stat. § 52-557b (2019); Fla. Stat. Ann. § 768.13 (2019); Miss. Code Ann. § 73-25-37 (2019); Mont. Code Ann. § 41-1-405 (2019).

42. 376 N.E.2d 754 (Ill. 1978).

PART

2 AN OVERVIEW OF ETHICS

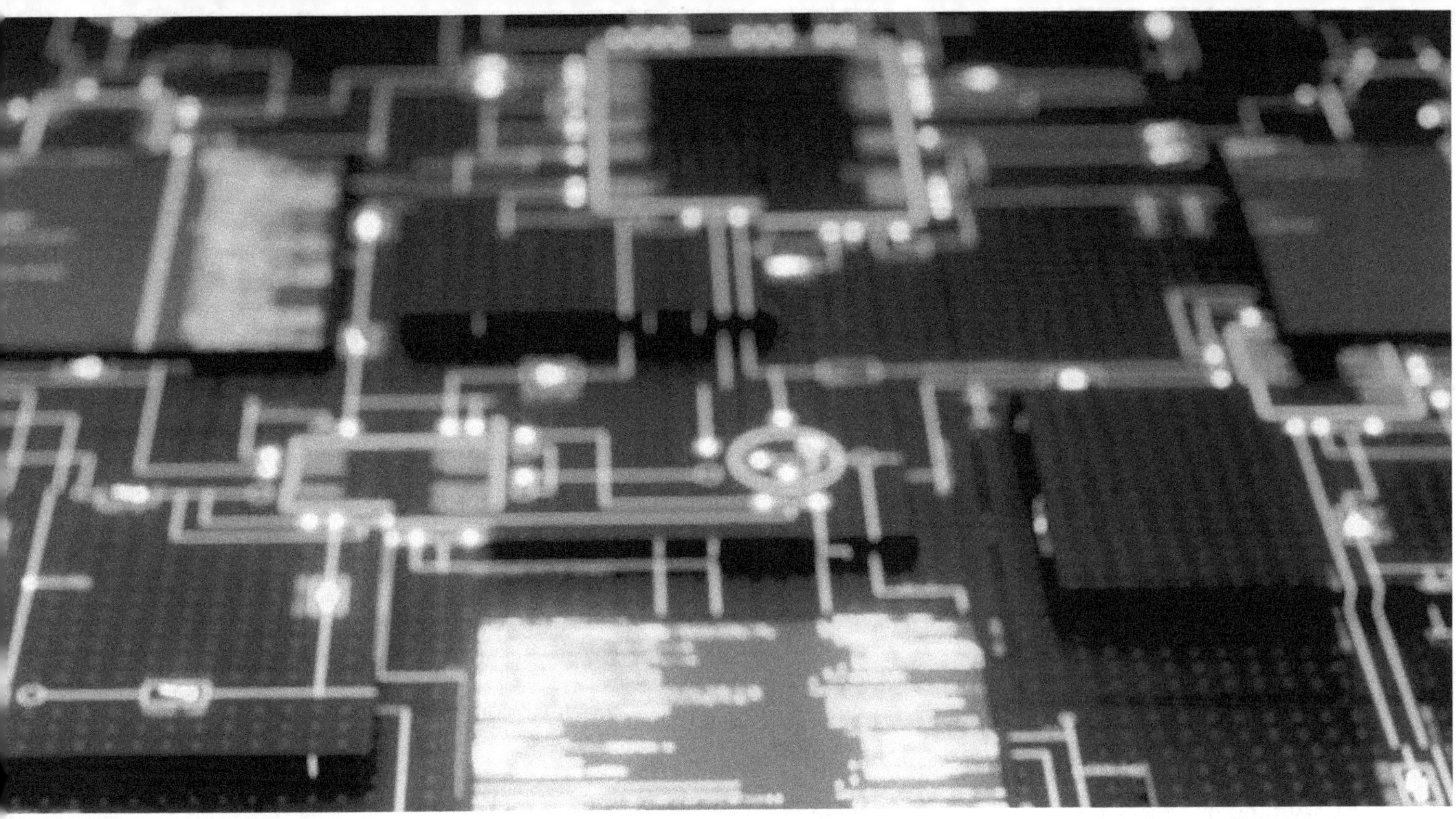

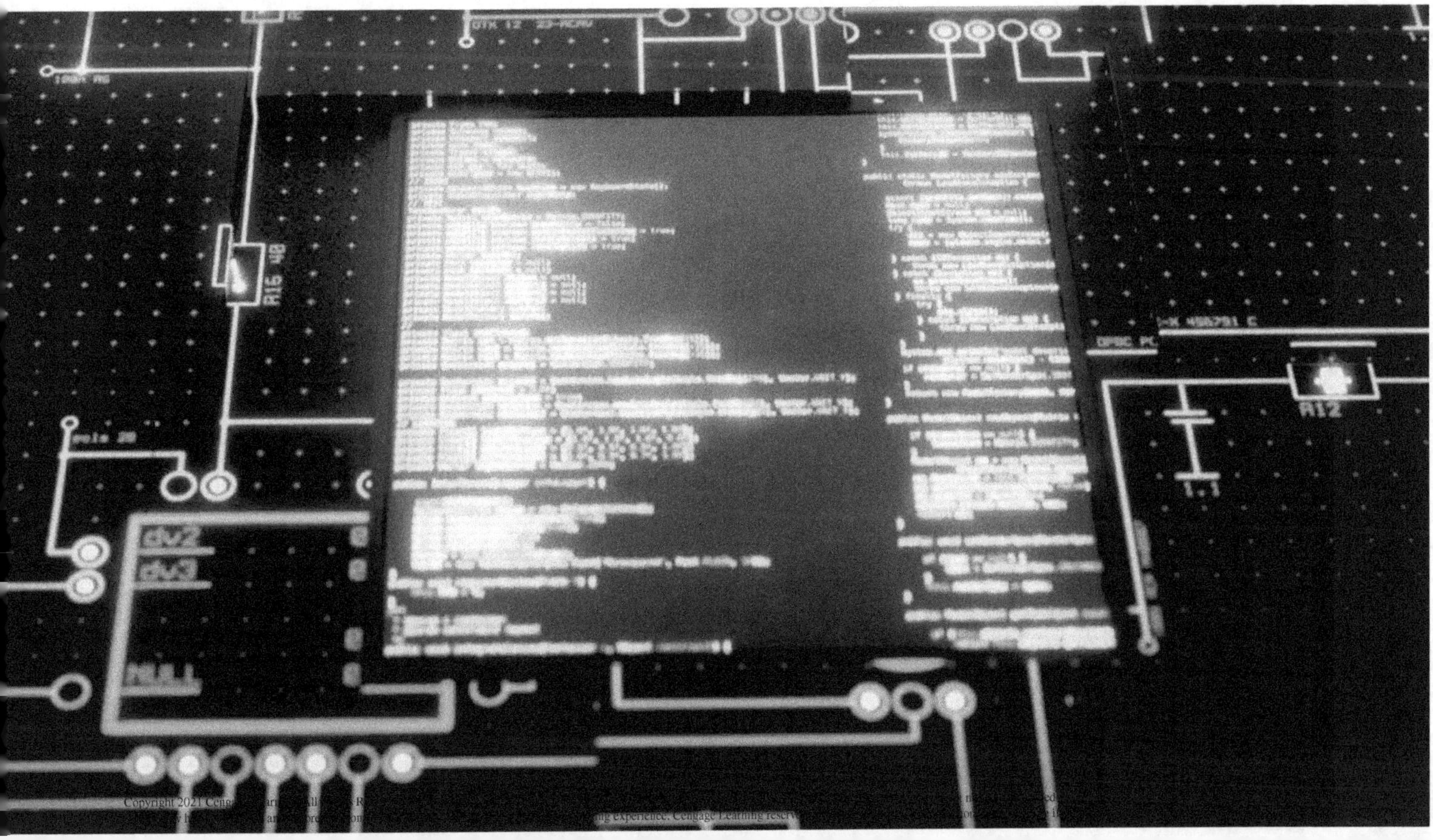

CHAPTER

5 ETHICAL STANDARDS

LEARNING OBJECTIVES

After reading this chapter, the learner should be able to:

1. Differentiate between ethics, morals, values, etiquette, and law.
2. Describe ethical concepts and their applications to the health care field.
3. Explain ethical theories.

KEY CONCEPTS

Autonomy
Beneficence
Best-interest standard
Categorical imperative
Comparative justice
Confidentiality
Cost–benefit analysis
Deontology
Distributive justice
Double-effect principle
Ethical concepts
Ethical theories
Ethics
Etiquette
Fidelity
Incompetent
Justice
Law
Morals
Nonmaleficence
Patient rights
Placebos
Privacy
Rights
Utilitarianism
Values
Veracity

INTRODUCTION

Reaching decisions that are ethically sound is simultaneously among the most challenging and the most routine activities of life. So pervasive is ethics in daily life that many people are not even aware that ethical components are present in many of the decisions they reach daily. Some of these decisions are made quite easily, such as deciding whether to abide by the customs of an organization to which a person has belonged for a long time, while others are reached only after experiencing considerable anxiety, such as determining whether a conflict of interest exists. Possessing literacy in the field of ethics can assist the learner with navigating through many difficult situations in life. Understanding what constitutes ethics requires learning about various models, concepts, and theories. This understanding assists the learner to identify ethical challenges and determine how to resolve the dilemmas posed in varying situations.[1]

ETHICAL MODELS

Ethics is the formal study of moral choices that conform to standards of conduct. Derived from the Greek word *ethos*, ethics is sometimes referred to as listening to one's conscience or making judgments between right and wrong. Ethics is sometimes confused with other areas of study, such as morals, values, etiquette, and law. The differences between these areas are made clear by the definitions contained in Table 5.1.

Morals, from the Latin word *mores*, are the principles or fundamental standards of "right" conduct that an individual internalizes. Right moral conduct is often based on traditional religious teachings and personal moral choices. Morals and ethics are related in that ethics puts personal moral principles and standards into practice in the manner of making judgments with clarity and consistency.

Etiquette is a separate area of study that bears a relationship with ethics. **Etiquette** refers to how human beings relate to one another under certain circumstances. In other words, etiquette is a social code of customs and rituals. Examples include courtesy, politeness, and proper dress. While part of everyday life, etiquette is often associated with ceremonial behavior, such as the president's inauguration ceremony or a wedding ceremony. In some areas, etiquette is highly developed, as in the etiquette expressed through customs and rituals that each branch of the armed forces observes.

Law, by contrast, is a body of rules of action or conduct prescribed by a controlling authority that has binding legal force. Laws are created as a means to control behavior and protect the public from danger. Law and ethics are closely related. Many times, law only expresses the minimum level of one's expectations of right and wrong, leaving ethics to fill the void. In these instances, behavior that would be considered legally acceptable may not be considered ethically acceptable. Consider the situation of a person who could save a drowning man but fails to make an attempt. Failing to make an attempt to save a drowning man may be legally correct if the law does not

Table 5.1 Ethical Comparison

	Ethics	Morals	Etiquette	Law	Values
Definition	The formal study of moral choices that conform to standards of conduct	The principles or fundamental standards of "right" conduct that an individual internalizes	The principles of how human beings relate to one another under certain circumstances	A body of rules of action or conduct prescribed by a controlling authority that has a binding legal force	Concepts that give meaning to an individual's life and serve as the framework for decision making
Basis	Philosophy	Traditional religious beliefs and personal choices	Society	Controlling authority, for example, legislature	Society, religion, and family
Short Statement	Judgments of right and wrong	Right-conduct standards	Social code	Rules with legal force	Life's meaning

require a person to make such an attempt but may be ethically incorrect, and the person may be considered personally irresponsible for failing to make such an attempt.

Distinguishing between legal and ethical issues has been problematic for many. Ordinarily, one looks to ethics (1) when there is no obvious right or wrong, (2) when the enforcement of law does not appear to bring about justice, (3) when right behavior appears to bring about a wrong effect, or (4) when personal sacrifice is the consequence of following ideals. One can also distinguish between legal and ethical issues by looking to consequences. Breaking the law results in penalties enforced by the law; breaking ethical codes results in the disapproval of at least one segment of society, such as professionals in an organization. Finally, one can distinguish between law and ethics by looking at whether the focus of a choice is external or internal. Because law by definition involves some form of controlling authority (e.g., legislature or city council), the focus of the choice is external. Because ethics involves listening to one's conscience, the focus of the choice is internal.

All four concepts—ethics, morals, etiquette, and law—are based on values. **Values** are the concepts that give meaning to an individual's life and serve as the framework for decision making. Hard work, honesty, sincerity, genuineness, and cleanliness are all examples of values. Values are based on societal norms, religion, and family orientation and assist in the decision-making processes of everyday life.

Often, values are so interwoven into everyday life that people do not think of them until a conflict arises. This conflict may arise when something goes wrong or when a difficult decision must be made or from contact with other persons who do not share the same values. For example, the societies of two different countries may place different values on the role of women in the workplace or their role in the political setting. These different values would result in a values conflict. Once the conflict is identified, one engages in the values clarification process. This process requires a person to become more conscious of what she considers worthy and name those values. By becoming more aware and understanding of values, the person is better equipped to make choices.

Ethical Concepts

Because ethics often touches upon an individual's principles of living, ethics is best understood by learning it at the abstract level and then applying it to a personal level. Multiple approaches to ethical reasoning have been developed over the centuries, and many of those approaches are outlined in this chapter for reference.

Abstract ideas or thoughts that deal with ethics are referred to as **ethical concepts**. These ideas and thoughts serve as part of the values that undergird the decision-making process. Included are the concepts of autonomy, beneficence/nonmaleficence, best-interest standard, fidelity, justice, rights, and veracity. Table 5.2 provides a quick reference for each concept. No importance should be attached to the order in which these concepts are presented in this text, as alphabetical order is used solely for the sake of simplicity.

Autonomy

Readily understood by many, **autonomy** refers to independence, self-determination, or freedom. The word derives from two Greek words: *autos*, meaning self, and *nomos*, meaning governance. Respect for the individual and an expectation that an individual will make decisions in accordance with the individual's plan of choice are hallmarks of autonomy. Three main elements comprise autonomy: the ability to decide, the power to actualize or implement a decision, and a respect for the autonomy of others. Each must be present for autonomy to exist. For example, receipt of adequate information and the ability to understand information address

Table 5.2 Ethical Concepts

	Definition	Example
Autonomy	Independence, self-determination, or freedom	Informed consent
Beneficence	Kindness, mercy, and charity	Hippocratic Oath
Nonmaleficence	Prohibition against doing harm	Hippocratic Oath
Best-Interest Standard	Process of determining what is in the best interest of another who cannot determine it herself	Decision making for impaired persons
Fidelity	Faithfulness, loyalty, and devotion to one's obligations	Operating within acceptable practice constraints
Justice	Fairness to all people	Access to health care services
Rights	A just claim or entitlement that others must respect	Confidentiality and privacy
Veracity	Habitual truthfulness and honesty	Patient–provider relationship

the element of ability to decide, whereas treating others as unique and equal addresses the element of respect for the autonomy of others.

Within the health care field, autonomy is embedded in the concept of informed consent. The concept requires health care providers to disclose to patients adequate information in a manner the patient can understand. Armed with this information, the competent patient determines whether and what actions to take or forgo in relation to medical care. This type of decision making—often in the form of granting permission to the health care provider to take action that will benefit the patient—is voluntary, demonstrating that the power rests with the patient and not with the health care provider.

While autonomy is often viewed as freedom or individualism, some restrictions on autonomy do exist. Society recognizes that one individual's actions may interfere with another person's rights, health, or well-being. The ethical dilemma arises from the extent to which autonomy is curbed. For example, an individual has the right to scream "Fire!" even where no fire exists. If the screaming is done in a crowded theater, however, other individuals are impacted, resulting in possible panic or injury in exiting the theater. Accordingly, society has balanced these interests by discouraging an individual from falsely screaming "Fire!" and roundly criticizing those who do so. A second example is the smoking debate. This debate pits the individual's freedom to smoke against the dangers secondhand smoke poses to the rest of the society. Society as a body attempts to balance these interests by carefully weighing individual freedoms against the common good of the community. As these examples demonstrate, autonomy is not an absolute but rather a freedom that is subject to some level of restriction.

Beneficence and Nonmaleficence

Two interlocking concepts in ethics are beneficence and nonmaleficence. **Beneficence** means the qualities of kindness, mercy, and charity. As seen in the ethical context, beneficence refers to the obligation to do good in all circumstances. **Nonmaleficence** means the prohibition against doing harm. As seen in the ethical context, nonmaleficence refers to the obligation to prevent evil or harm. The two concepts can be seen as opposites of each other: beneficence from a positive perspective (e.g., promoting good) and nonmaleficence from a negative perspective (e.g., refraining from inflicting harm).

A prime example that illustrates both concepts is the Hippocratic Oath, shown in Figure 5.1. This oath contains multiple examples of beneficence, stating in part that the physician will apply "measures to benefit the sick," creating an obligation to promote the health and welfare of the patient above other considerations. The oath contains multiple examples of nonmaleficence, stating in part that the physician will keep the patient "from harm and injustice" and will refrain from "all intentional injustice." In essence, the oath stresses the physician's obligation to maximize the good for the patient (beneficence) and minimize the harm to the patient (nonmaleficence).

In the health care field, one's professional duty is impacted by these two concepts. Improving, not worsening, the patient's health is the expectation of providing health care services. Unfortunately, the delivery of health care services may result in the patient's health worsening—for example, nosocomial infections, adverse drug reactions, and side effects of cancer treatments and other serious diseases may occur. Reconciling the existence of unfortunate events and outcomes with these two concepts can be accomplished by applying the double-effect principle. The **double-effect principle** refers to the principle that recognizes that ethical choices may result in untoward outcomes. One may proceed with an ethical choice presenting a double effect if the untoward outcome is not the intended outcome but a secondary outcome and is outweighed by

I swear by Apollo Physician and Asclepias and Hygieia and Panaceia and all the gods and goddesses, making them my witness, that I will fulfill according to my ability and judgment this oath and this covenant:

I will apply dietetic measures for the benefit of the sick according to my ability and judgment; I will keep them from harm and injustice.

I will neither give a deadly drug to anybody if asked for it, nor will I make a suggestion to this effect. Similarly, I will not give to a woman an abortive remedy. In purity and holiness I will guard my life and art.

I will not use the knife, not even on sufferers from stone, but will withdraw in favor of such men as are engaged in this work.

Whatever house I may visit, I will come for the benefit of the sick, remaining free of intentional injustices, of all mischief and in particular of sexual relations with both female and male persons, be they free or slaves.

What I may see or hear in the course of the treatment or even outside of the treatment in regard to the life of men, in which on no account one must noise abroad, I will keep to myself holding such things shameful to be spoken about.

If I fulfill this oath and do not violate it, may it be granted to me to enjoy life and art, being honored with fame among all men for all time to come; if I transgress it and swear falsely, may the opposite of all this be my lot.

Figure 5.1 Hippocratic Oath
Source: Courtesy of the United States National Library of Medicine, National Institutes of Health (www.nlm.nih.gov).

the intended positive or neutral outcome (harm vs. benefits analysis). Because health care providers do not intend harm in cases where nosocomial infections and adverse drug reactions occur and the patient has consented to the treatment resulting in side effects after gaining a thorough understanding of the associated risks and benefits, the health care provider will be considered to have acted ethically.

Best-Interest Standard

Determining what is in the best interest of an individual when the individual cannot make such a decision alone is the essence of the **best-interest standard**. The ability to make a decision is generally determined by competency. For example, severely mentally retarded individuals are generally considered persons who cannot meet the criteria of competence as a matter of law. Additionally, the best-interest standard often applies to persons who once met the competency standard but are now considered **incompetent** due to illness or injury. When using this standard, the decision maker considers whether and how the individual will benefit or be harmed, examining mental, physical, and fiscal risks and whether the individual ever expressed an opinion on the subject at issue. The focus rests more on concepts such as beneficence and nonmaleficence than autonomy.

Within the health care field, the best-interest standard is most often seen when a decision must be made about the direction of a patient's health care treatment and the patient is unable to provide informed consent. In such instances, health care providers look to past evidence of the patient's expressed wishes—such as a living will or power of attorney for health care—for guidance. Absent such documents, health care providers may look to family members and guardians for guidance. If these steps do not determine the direction of treatment, the health care provider may turn to the judicial system.

Many famous cases involving the health care treatment of incompetent patients have emerged in the last half century, such as those involving Karen Ann Quinlan, Nancy Cruzan, and Terry Schiavo. Some of these cases arose because of the application of technology to health care, resulting in prolonged life for the patient. Because questions of life and death are so often at stake in these cases, they are fraught with emotion. While judges frequently apply the best-interest standard in these cases, many persons have disputed the results. It appears unlikely that these cases will dwindle in the near future, since medical technology continues to make new advances not previously anticipated. Additional information about these cases can be found in Chapter 9, Confidentiality and Informed Consent.

Fidelity

Similar to autonomy in understanding by the general public is the concept of fidelity. **Fidelity** means faithfulness, loyalty, and devotion to one's obligations or duties. Fidelity is most often seen in the context of agreements and commitments between individuals. This concept undergirds much of the discussion on accountability, because accountability is often measured by the level to which a person adheres to her responsibilities and obligations.

CRITICAL THINKING

Adhering to responsibilities and obligations is the hallmark of accountability and engenders trusting relationships. Think of examples of how accountability might contribute to a well-functioning health care setting.

Fidelity is sometimes addressed in the health care field in terms of the role each health care professional plays. In the modern health care world, multiple professionals attend to a patient's care. Each professional operates within the constraints of acceptable practice, some of which are imposed by law and some of which are imposed by custom. Working within these constraints requires the health care professional to exercise fidelity to her role in treating the patient. For example, delivering and explaining a diagnosis to a patient for the first time is generally seen as the responsibility of the physician and not of the allied health professional.

Justice

Justice refers to the obligation to be fair to all people. Justice encompasses several ideas, including fairness, honesty, and impartiality. Although justice requires that no person would be favored over another, it does not require that all persons be treated the same. Opinions vary considerably over the concept of justice—what one person considers to be fair may conflict with the opinion of others. This same disagreement exists to a lesser extent over the ideas of impartiality and entitlement.

The concept of justice can be subdivided into two parts: comparative justice and distributive justice. **Comparative justice** refers to balancing the competing interests of individuals and groups against one another, with no independent standard used to make this comparison. This concept posits that because the needs or interests of some individuals or groups are greater than the needs or interests of other individuals or groups, it is acceptable for the individual or group with the greater need or interest to receive more resources than those with the lesser need or interest. For example, an individual who is close to death and in need of an organ transplant would be considered more needy than a person who is diagnosed with the same disease who is not close to death absent an organ transplant. **Distributive justice** refers to the fair distribution of burdens and benefits using an independent standard. This concept posits that all persons have an equal opportunity to resources and requires that those in a position of authority provide the service that is due to others. For example, distributive justice applied in the legal sense is shown by the rule that all are innocent until proven guilty.

In the health care context, distributive justice often applies to questions raised about access to scarce resources, requiring health care providers and health plans to provide an individual recipient with the care and service she is due. The concept encompasses six criteria to define just distribution where resources are limited: need, equity, contribution, ability to pay, effort, and merit, as shown in Figure 5.2. Need refers to required, not elective, procedures. Equity refers to trying to distribute equally to all in need. Contribution refers to what a person might be expected to contribute to society at a future date. Ability refers to the power to pay and is considered part of distributive justice in the sense that needed services may be rendered to one who cannot afford to pay for those services. Effort refers to the willingness to comply or not comply with instruction (medical advice). Merit refers to the potential for benefit after the initial investment of limited resources. Considering all six criteria together can assist in solving problems associated with providing fair distribution of benefits and burdens to all patients.

Distributive justice is sometimes considered as an issue related to the financial controls imposed by prospective payment systems and health maintenance organizations (HMOs). Prospective payment systems establish limits on the amount a health care provider may be reimbursed for rendering care. HMOs establish gatekeeping procedures that may limit access to specialty care. Both systems reward health care providers monetarily for maintaining lower costs and penalize those providers who do not keep costs within preestablished limits. With regard to ethics, placing such monetary rewards and penalties before health care providers may impact both the quantity and quality of patient care.

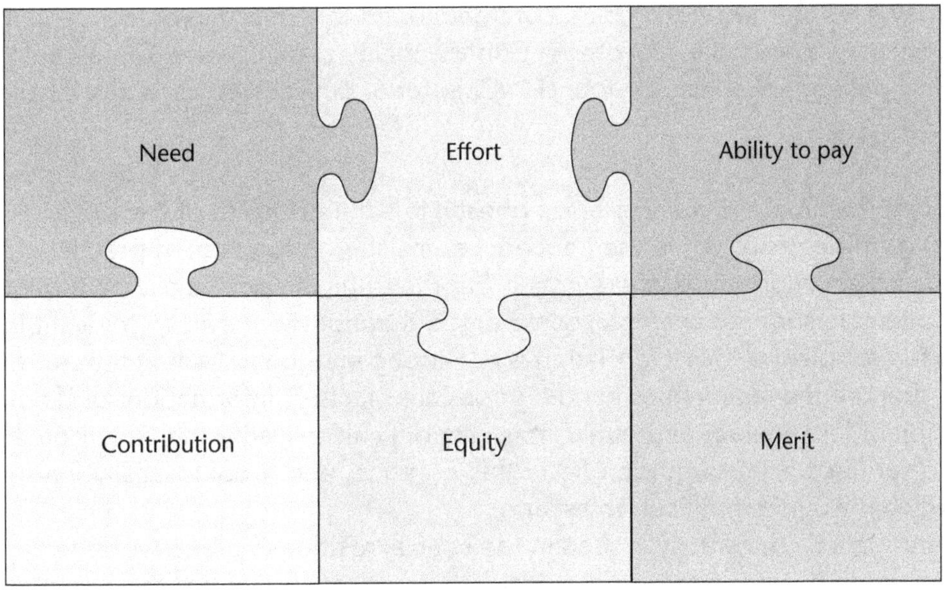

Figure 5.2 Access and Distributive Justice

Rights

Rights refer to a just claim or entitlement, whether based on law, ethics, or morality, that others are obliged to respect. The concept of rights derives from the concept of justice in the sense that both involve obligations. Rights, however, do not always encompass the ideas of fairness, honesty, and impartiality. The rights concept also relates to the autonomy concept in that both encompass the idea of self-determination. The rights concept considers actions as they relate to affirming or violating basic human rights.

Rights can vary according to the moral values of a given culture. What may be considered a right in one culture may not be considered a right in another culture. For example, societal norms in the Western tradition view circumcision of female children as a form of mutilation, thereby recognizing a right to be free from female circumcision. Some non-Western cultures view this in an exactly opposite light, seeing the lack of female circumcision as an insult to womanhood, thereby making the right to female circumcision a right to be upheld and enforced. Because the values underpinning the societal norms in each culture vary greatly across the globe, it is difficult to argue that all rights must be applied to all cultures. This difficulty is one impediment to international organizations—they must clearly identify and agree upon the rights and values they cherish before they can identify the aims they seek to accomplish.

Within the health care context, **patient rights** are often the focus of discussion. The term patient rights refers to the recognition that the patient is entitled to determine for himself or herself the extent to which he or she will receive or forego care and treatment. Patient rights are often addressed in terms of confidentiality and privacy. **Confidentiality** refers to the obligation of the health care provider to maintain patient information in a manner that will not permit dissemination beyond the health care provider. **Privacy** refers to the right to be left alone or the right to control personal information. Both of these rights have legal and ethical bases, as they can be enforced through penalties (law) and disapproval by one's peers (ethics). Both confidentiality and privacy are referred to in many ethics codes. In practice, these rights grant patients control over how sensitive information is shared and place restrictions on health care providers on what to do with the information they have learned in the course of treatment. More information concerning confidentiality and privacy may be found in Chapter 9, Confidentiality and Informed Consent. More information concerning patient rights may be found in Chapter 6, Ethical Decisions and Challenges.

Veracity

Veracity refers to habitual truthfulness and honesty; it is the opposite of the practice of intentionally deceiving or misleading. While the concept seems straightforward, in practice the concept is less clear because situations arise where not telling the truth can potentially be argued as justified to protect another person. For example, some argue that not disclosing all relevant information is acceptable if the recipient of this information is not strong enough to handle the truth, if more time is needed to prepare the recipient to handle unpleasant facts or information, or if doing so would make the recipient less anxious and afraid. It is very difficult to justify such an approach, however, because no clear lines exist to guide one in this practice, and it could easily lead to a slippery slope from which it would be difficult to escape.

In the health care field, veracity is seen in the special relationship between the patient and the health care provider. It is important to the patient's care that she inform the health care provider of all relevant information pertaining to her health; failure to do so may result in misdiagnosis or improper treatment. Similarly, veracity requires the health care provider to disclose factual information to the patient so that she can exercise her autonomy and determine the course of her care. Failure to do so can lead to a lack of trust between not only the patient and her health care provider but also between the health care provider and others (e.g., family members and other health care staff) who would then view the health care provider as unreliable at best and deceitful at worst.

CRITICAL THINKING

It is important for a patient to share pertinent information with a health care provider to avoid a misdiagnosis or improper treatment. Why would patients be reluctant to share pertinent information with their health care provider?

Veracity also plays a role in medical research; the research subject must be informed of all information pertaining to the research and its potential effect upon her health. Some medical research involves the use of **placebos**, medically inert substances that are used as a control in testing the effectiveness of another medicated substance. In essence, the placebo is a form of deception since the research subject does not know whether she has received the real medication or the placebo when participating in the research trial. Researchers justify the use of placebos by seeking informed consent from the research subject. The consent process requires informing the research subject that placebos will be used but that the patient will not know whether she is receiving the placebo or the real medication during the course of research participation. Only upon receipt of this informed consent may the researcher ethically proceed with the medical research. Additional information concerning research may be found in Chapter 10, Access to Health Information.

Ethical Theories

Ethical theories refer to systematic statements or plans of principles used to deal with ethical dilemmas. These theories exist so that individuals, organizations, and groups can act consistently

Table 5.3 Ethical Theories

	Utilitarianism	Deontology
Definition	Promote greatest balance of good over harm for everyone	Moral rules and unchanging principles derived from reason and applied universally
Short Statement	Advancing the public good	Categorical imperative
Application	Cost–benefit analysis	Research involving human subjects
Strength	Group benefit valued	Universality of rules and principles
Weakness	End justifies means	Overly rigid

and coherently when making ethical decisions. These theories contrast with ethical concepts, which do not rise to the level of a systematic statement or plan. Two main ethical theories exist: utilitarianism and deontology. Similar to ethical concepts, no hierarchy of importance is attached to these theories; each theory has its own strengths and weaknesses. Table 5.3 contrasts utilitarianism with deontology.

Utilitarianism

Utilitarianism, sometimes referred to as consequentialism, proposes that everyone, including persons, organizations, and society in general, should make choices that promote the greatest balance of good over harm for everyone. Under this theory, society promotes conditions that would allow an individual to seek the greatest amount of happiness or benefits. Developed by Jeremy Bentham and John Stuart Mill, utilitarianism posits that an act is right when it is useful in bringing about a desirable or good end. Utilitarianism encourages consideration of the effects of actions on everyone involved in a situation, not merely the effects upon one individual. Western society has interwoven this theory and its values together with regard to work ethic and the behavioralistic approach to education, philosophy, and life.

In application, utilitarianism is often used when preparing cost–benefit analyses. In a **cost–benefit analysis**, all possible options are considered, the utility or value of each option is determined, and the option that poses the highest total utility is chosen. Net benefits are compared against costs to reach a decision. The option that offers society the best benefits at the least cost or offers businesses the greatest return for the lowest costs is seen as the logical choice. Said simply, the analysis examines the positive outcomes (the benefits) against the negative outcomes (the costs) to reach a decision.

Utilitarianism has been used to justify the capitation approach of managed care organizations in the health care field. Under capitation, a fixed amount per member per month is paid to a contracted provider for health care services, regardless of the quantity or nature of the services rendered by the contracted provider. Under such an arrangement, the managed care organization asserts that it has provided the greatest good for the greatest number of members, a central tenet of utilitarianism.

Weaknesses are present with utilitarianism. Some have interpreted this theory to support the principle of the end justifying the means. Using this interpretation, even immoral acts can be justified if substantial benefits will be afforded to a majority of persons, even though the minority may face unbearable costs. As such, a decision that results in violating others' rights or creates an injustice is exonerated. Another weakness is the difficulty present in identifying and measuring all of the possible benefits that may result from a decision since this involves looking to the future and making, at best, informed predictions.

Deontology

Deontology, sometimes referred to as formalism or duty orientation, asserts that ethical decision making is based on moral rules and unchanging principles that are derived from reason and can be applied universally. These universal rules and principles must be considered separately from the consequences or the facts of a particular situation. By looking to the intrinsic nature of an act to determine its basic rightness or wrongness, the consequences of the act are considered irrelevant. Although a positive result is always helpful, the deontologist would not consider advancing the public good as an adequate basis for ethics—what is considered the public good is ever evolving and not considered an unchanging principle.

Developed by philosopher Immanuel Kant, the fundamental principle of deontology is called the **categorical imperative**, which means a command derived from a principle that does not allow exceptions. The categorical imperative requires application of unconditional commands in a similar manner in all situations without exception. For example, the deontologist who considers life to be sacred could never justify killing, no matter what factual circumstance might have led to a killing, such as self-defense. The duty to protect life remains the universal command.

In application, deontology would require one to compare possible solutions to an ethical dilemma against universal rules and principles to determine which solution should be chosen. Where the possible solutions both comply and conflict with the universal rules and principles, those that pose a conflict are discarded from consideration as unacceptable and the remaining compliant solutions are ranked according to their acceptability with universal rules and principles. The compliant solution that ranks highest in acceptability is the logical choice.

Deontology has been used in the health care field in the context of research involving human subjects. All research projects involving human subjects are subject to both ethical and legal restrictions, including making sure that the subject fully understands the study's purposes and what is expected of the subject, resulting in informed consent. From an ethical perspective, the subject must be treated as one who possesses freedom of choice and not as a means to the end of implementing a research protocol. From the viewpoint of deontology, no subject could be coerced or tricked into participating in the research project because the value placed on freedom of choice is an unchanging principle.

Similar to other ethical theories, deontology poses some weaknesses. Because it does not consider the variety of real-life situations that create ethical dilemmas and allows no exceptions, it is often considered overly rigid. Additionally, the disregard for consequences derived from actions may lead to absurd results, such as when one obeys the letter of the law to such an extent that it conflicts with the spirit of the law. Furthermore, some disagree that people's motivations are derived from universal values but argue that they actually derive from changing values instead.

CONCLUSION

The study of ethics has been present throughout centuries, as ethics assists individuals in reaching moral choices that conform to standards of conduct. Multiple approaches to ethical reasoning exist, each of which apply to the health care field. The awareness gained from this chapter should assist the decision maker in identifying the ethical concepts and theories she relies upon to reach a decision.

CASE STUDY

You are a health information manager in a hospital setting. Your facility has purchased an electronic health record (EHR) system. During the testing period, you and your staff discover that the EHR system does not comply with applicable federal privacy and security standards. Pressure is mounting to deploy the system in the near future. What ethical issues should you consider? How should you proceed?

REVIEW QUESTIONS

1. How can one distinguish between legal and ethical issues?
2. What are the concepts of ethics, morals, etiquette, and law based on?
3. Is it ever appropriate to curb a person's autonomy?
4. What is the double-effect principle?
5. When is the best-interest standard most frequently used?
6. How does comparative justice differ from distributive justice?
7. Are all rights recognized universally across the globe?
8. How does a cost–benefit analysis work?
9. What is the categorical imperative?

ENRICHMENT ACTIVITY

Review each of the ethical concepts and theories addressed in this chapter. Decide which concept or theory best fits with your personal point of view. Examine how you have used that concept or theory in the past, and decide how you will use it in the future.

NOTES

1. This chapter is based in large measure on Chapter 4, Ethical Standards, in my text *Today's Health Information Management: An Integrated Approach*, 2nd ed. (Cengage Learning, 2014).

CHAPTER 6

ETHICAL DECISIONS AND CHALLENGES

LEARNING OBJECTIVES

After reading this chapter, the learner should be able to:

1. Explain the ethical decision-making process.
2. Describe the factors that influence the decision-making process.
3. Define codes of ethics.
4. Discuss the importance of codes of ethics.
5. Identify ethical challenges in general.
6. Discuss ethical challenges present in supervision.
7. Discuss ethical challenges present in the field of health care.
8. Discuss ethical challenges present in the specialized area of health information management.

KEY CONCEPTS

Codes of ethics	Disparagement	Impaired colleagues
Conflict of interest	Ethical challenges	Paternalism
Copy and paste	Ethics committees	Patient rights

INTRODUCTION

While many individuals study ethics from a theoretical perspective alone, great value can be gained when individuals apply ethics to the situations that confront them. The number and types of challenges confronting the health information management profession are almost limitless. Personnel matters, conflicts of interest, the pressure on health care providers to remain fiscally solvent, the connection between coding and reimbursement, and the protection of sensitive information all pose ethical issues for the health information management professional to resolve.

Recognizing ethical challenges and learning how to address them through the decision-making process is the focus of this chapter. A discussion of the factors influencing the ethical decision-making process begins the chapter, followed by a discussion of the process itself. Ethical challenges are presented to demonstrate the application of ethical reasoning and decision making on a personal level and as a health information manager. The purpose of these discussions is to frame ethical issues so that learners recognize them in their personal and professional lives and also understand them when they are discussed in society at large. In turn, the learner may apply critical thinking skills to situations at work and in everyday life and reach ethical resolutions.[1]

ETHICAL DECISION MAKING

Each person will face many ethical dilemmas throughout life and will be forced to reach a decision about these dilemmas. Some of these decisions will be made on an individual level, affecting professional or personal life, while others will be made on an organizational or group level, affecting many others. The quality of the ethical decision reached may vary greatly, depending in large measure on the factors that influence the individual and the process he chooses to follow. No one universal "right" answer exists that can be applied to every situation. The decisions reached at one stage in life may be challenged later in life by new problems and realities that confront the decision maker. Accordingly, the decision maker must examine what factors influence his decision making and what process he will follow if he is to be well equipped for future decision making.

Influencing Factors

Numerous factors influence the ethical decision-making process. Whereas one person may rely on a particular ethical concept or theory to reach a decision, another person may rely on religious beliefs. Still others may rely on personal experiences or may look to a professional code of ethics to guide them. Whether an individual relies on one factor or a combination of factors, it is important to recognize that the individual does not operate in a vacuum when reaching a decision. Many factors influence the decision-making process, including those discussed here.

ETHICS

Ethical codes of professional associations define the ethical and moral standards of the profession.

Codes of Ethics

One of the most significant features of professional associations is their codes of ethics. **Codes of ethics** are written lists of a profession's values and standards of conduct. Codes of ethics are important because they identify for the broader community what the professional association defines as the basic ethical and moral standards to which its members must adhere. These ethical and moral standards are to be used by the profession's membership as the guiding principles governing their conduct.

Codes of ethics embody many concepts. One is that the members of the profession differentiate themselves from the broader group of occupations and technical careers that exist in the working world. These ethics codes also show that the professional is an autonomous, responsible decision maker, not someone who just follows orders. A related concept is that the professional possesses a loyalty to both the client/patient and to fellow members of the profession. Within this concept is an implied promise that the practitioner who is governed by an ethical code will not pursue his own interests at the expense of a client or patient. Balanced with this promise is the professional's loyalty to fellow members of the profession, which manifests in both positive ways (prohibitions on disparagement of colleagues) and negative ways (reporting professional misconduct). Where the professional must choose between his loyalty to a client or patient and his loyalty to other members of his profession, codes of ethics elevate the client or patient above the interests of fellow professionals.

Codes of ethics are living documents in the sense that they are open to change over time. Initially, some ethics codes operated more as statements that limited competition, promoted a profession's particular image, or imposed restrictions on members rather than as statements of ethical and moral standards. While the restrictions element persists in some ethics codes—for example, restrictions on advertising—these codes have evolved over time as professions have developed. Ethics codes are now seen as statements of ethical and moral principles that govern the conduct of a given profession's members.

Virtually every professional association has promulgated an ethics code, as have many firms, businesses, and organizations. A prominent example is the ethics code of the American Osteopathic Association, shown in Figure 6.1. The principles articulated in this document address many salient points of a physician's everyday life, such as the obligations to provide competent medical service, safeguard patient confidences, and study and advance scientific knowledge. These principles also address the balance the physician must make as a professional. For example, the physician is obliged to recognize the patient's right to "complete freedom to choose his/her physician," while not refusing "to accept patients because of the patient's race, creed, color, sex, national origin, or handicap."[2]

Similar to other professions, ethics has been a cornerstone of the health information management profession since its beginning. The most recently revised Code of Ethics promulgated by the American Health Information Management Association (AHIMA) is shown in Figure 6.2. This Code not only guides the health information professional in his obligations to himself but also guides the professional in his obligation to the patient, other members of the health care team, his employer, his peers, his professional association, and the public. Examples of the ethics codes from other professions can be found at the Web site addresses listed at the end of this chapter.

The effectiveness of ethics codes is diminished when the codes are not widely communicated. It is insufficient to merely publish a code of ethics; the profession, firm, business, or organization that adheres to a code of ethics should communicate it widely to its members, staff, and customers. One of the most effective means of communicating an ethics code is by professional education. This may be accomplished through staff training involving both discussion of the applicable ethics codes and their application to the workplace. In some organizations, this training is more focused on making staff aware of ethical aspects of their business lives and the consequences of unethical behavior than on the wording of the ethics code itself. Still other training programs use a case-by-case analysis approach with active discussion and interaction by participants. Both of these approaches stress the need for each participant to think for himself rather than merely repeat the themes of the organization's ethics code.

Codes of ethics—like all forms of communication—are more effective if they are enforced than if they are merely statements posted on a wall. One of the most effective means to enforce an ethics code is to use an ethics committee. **Ethics committees** are groups formed within an organization to establish new and evaluate existing ethics codes and corporate policies and to address ethical issues that arise in the workplace. The functions of ethics committees may vary among organizations, with some committees focusing on communicating information, while others focus on classifying and interpreting ethical issues, and still others focus on compliance with the organization's ethics code. Regardless of the extent of their function, ethics committees contribute to the discussion and debate of ethical issues in their organizations.

Within the health care setting, ethics committees often perform philosophical and practical functions. One of these functions is to establish institutional policy concerning bioethical issues, including the removal of life support systems, the treatment of seriously ill newborns, and procedures governing organ procurement. Additional details concerning bioethical issues addressed by institutional policies can be found in Chapter 7, Bioethics Issues. These committees may also establish policies that deal with the intersection of financial and health care matters. These include questions associated with

Code of Ethics

The AOA has formulated this Code to guide its member physicians in their professional lives. The standards presented are designed to address the osteopathic and allopathic physician's ethical and professional responsibilities to patients, to society, to the AOA, to others involved in health care and to self.

Further, the AOA has adopted the position that physicians should play a major role in the development and instruction of medical ethics.

Section 1. The physician shall keep in confidence whatever she/he may learn about a patient in the discharge of professional duties. Information shall be divulged by the physician when required by law or when authorized by the patient.

Section 2. The physician shall give a candid account of the patient's condition to the patient or to those responsible for the patient's care.

Section 3. A physician-patient relationship must be founded on mutual trust, cooperation, and respect. The patient, therefore, must have complete freedom to choose her/his physician. The physician must have complete freedom to choose patients whom she/he will serve. However, the physician should not refuse to accept patients for reasons of discrimination, including, but not limited to, the patient's race, creed, color, sex, national origin, sexual orientation, gender identity, or disability. In emergencies, a physician should make her/his services available. View further interpretation.

Section 4. A physician is never justified in abandoning a patient. The physician shall give due notice to a patient or to those responsible for the patient's care when she/he withdraws from the case so that another physician may be engaged.

Section 5. A physician should make a reasonable effort to partner with patients to promote their health and shall practice in accordance with the body of systematized and scientific knowledge related to the healing arts. A physician shall maintain competence in such systematized and scientific knowledge through study and clinical applications.

Section 6. The osteopathic medical profession has an obligation to society to maintain its high standards and, therefore, to continuously regulate itself. A substantial part of such regulation is due to the efforts and influence of the recognized local, state and national associations representing the osteopathic medical profession. A physician should maintain membership in and actively support such associations and abide by their rules and regulations.

Section 7. Under the law a physician may advertise, but no physician shall advertise or solicit patients directly or indirectly through the use of matters or activities which are false or misleading. View further interpretation.

Section 8. A physician shall not hold forth or indicate possession of any degree recognized as the basis for licensure to practice the healing arts unless she/he is actually licensed on the basis of that degree in the state or other jurisdiction in which she/he practices. A physician shall designate her/his osteopathic or allopathic credentials in all professional uses of her/his name. Indications of specialty practice, membership in professional societies, and related matters shall be governed by rules promulgated by the American Osteopathic Association. View further interpretation.

Section 9. A physician should not hesitate to seek consultation whenever she/he believes it is in the best interest of the patient.

Section 10. In any dispute between or among physicians involving ethical or organizational matters, the matter in controversy should first be referred to the appropriate arbitrating bodies of the profession.

Section 11. In any dispute between or among physicians regarding the diagnosis and treatment of a patient, the attending physician has the responsibility for final decisions, consistent with any applicable hospital rules or regulations.

Section 12. Any fee charged by a physician shall compensate the physician for services actually rendered. There shall be no division of professional fees for referrals of patients.

Section 13. A physician shall respect the law. When necessary a physician shall attempt to help to formulate the law by all proper means in order to improve patient care and public health.

Section 14. In addition to adhering to the foregoing ethical standards, a physician shall recognize a responsibility to participate in community activities and services.

Figure 6.1 American Osteopathic Association Code of Ethics
Source: Reprinted with the consent of the American Osteopathic Association, https://osteopathic.org/about/leadership/aoa-governance-documents/code-of-ethics/.

Section 15. It is considered sexual misconduct for a physician to have sexual contact with any patient with whom a physician-patient relationship currently exists.

Section 16. Sexual harassment by a physician is considered unethical. Sexual harassment is defined as physical or verbal intimation of a sexual nature involving a colleague or subordinate in the workplace or academic setting, when such conduct creates an unreasonable, intimidating, hostile or offensive workplace or academic setting.

Section 17. From time to time, industry may provide some AOA members with gifts as an inducement to use their products or services. Members who use these products and services as a result of these gifts, rather than simply for the betterment of their patients and the improvement of the care rendered in their practices, shall be considered to have acted in an unethical manner. View further interpretation.

Section 18. A physician shall not intentionally misrepresent himself/herself or his/her research work in any way.

Section 19. When participating in research, a physician shall follow the current laws, regulations and standards of the United States or, if the research is conducted outside the United States, the laws, regulations and standards applicable to research in the nation where the research is conducted. This standard shall apply for physician involvement in research at any level and degree of responsibility, including, but not limited to, research, design, funding, participation either as examining and/or treating provider, supervision of other staff in their research, analysis of data and publication of results in any form for any purpose.

Figure 6.1 Continued

AHIMA CODE OF ETHICS

Preamble

The ethical obligations of the health information management (HIM) professional include the safeguarding of privacy and security of health information; appropriate disclosure of health information; development, use, and maintenance of health information systems and health information; and ensuring the accessibility and integrity of health information.

Healthcare consumers are increasingly concerned about security and the potential loss of privacy and the inability to control how their personal health information is used and disclosed. Core health information issues include what information should be collected, how the information should be managed, who should have access to the information, under what conditions the information should be disclosed, how the information is retained, when it is no longer needed, and how is it disposed of in a confidential manner. All of the core health information issues are addressed in compliance with state and federal regulations, and employer policies and procedures.

Ethical obligations are central to the professional's responsibility, regardless of the employment site or the method of collection, storage, and security of health information. In addition, sensitive information (e.g., genetic, adoption, substance use, sexual health, and behavioral information) requires special attention to prevent misuse. In the world of business and interactions with consumers, expertise in the protection of information is required.

Purpose of the American Health Information Management Association Code of Ethics

The HIM professional has an obligation to demonstrate actions that reflect values. The American Health Information Management Association (AHIMA) Code of Ethics sets forth these principles. (See also AHIMA Mission, Vision, Values) The code is relevant to all AHIMA members, non-members with the Commission on Certification for Health Informatics and Information Management (CCHIIM) certifications, and students enrolled in a formal certificate or degree granting program directly relevant to AHIMA's Purpose regardless of their professional functions, the settings in which they work, or the populations they serve. These purposes strengthen the HIM professional's efforts to improve overall quality of healthcare.

Figure 6.2 AHIMA Code of Ethics

Source: Revised & adopted by AHIMA House of Delegates – (April 19, 2019). Permission to reprint granted by AHIMA. Copyright © by the American Health Information Management Association. All rights reserved. No part of this may be reproduced, reprinted, stored in a retrieval system, or transmitted in any form or by any means, electronic, photocopying, recording or otherwise, without the prior written permission of the association.

The AHIMA Code of Ethics serves six purposes:

- Promotes high standards of HIM practice.
- Summarizes broad ethical principles that reflect the profession's core values.
- Establishes a set of ethical principles to be used to guide decision-making and actions.
- Establishes a framework for professional behavior and responsibilities when professional obligations conflict or ethical uncertainties arise.
- Provides ethical principles by which the general public can hold the HIM professional accountable.
- Mentors practitioners new to the field to HIM's mission, values, and ethical principles.

The code includes principles that are enforceable and aspirational. The extent to which each principle is enforceable is a matter of professional judgment to be exercised by those responsible for reviewing alleged violations of ethical principles.

Principles

The following principles are based on the core values of the American Health Information Management Association and apply to all AHIMA members, non-members CCHIIM certifications, and students.

1. Advocate, uphold, and defend the consumer's right to privacy and the doctrine of confidentiality in the use and disclosure of information.
2. Put service and the health and welfare of persons before self-interest and conduct oneself in the practice of the profession so as to bring honor to oneself, their peers, and to the health information management profession.
3. Preserve, protect, and secure personal health information in any form or medium and hold in the highest regard health information and other information of a confidential nature obtained in an official capacity, taking into account the applicable statutes and regulations.
4. Refuse to participate in or conceal unethical practices or procedures and report such practices.
5. Use technology, data, and information resources in the way they are intended to be used.
6. Advocate for appropriate uses of information resources across the healthcare ecosystem.
7. Recruit and mentor students, peers and colleagues to develop and strengthen professional workforce.
8. Represent the profession to the public in a positive manner.
9. Advance health information management knowledge and practice through continuing education, research, publications, and presentations.
10. Perform honorably health information management association responsibilities, either appointed or elected, and preserve the confidentiality of any privileged information made known in any official capacity.
11. State truthfully and accurately one's credentials, professional education, and experiences.
12. Facilitate interdisciplinary collaboration in situations supporting ethical health information principles.
13. Respect the inherent dignity and worth of every person.

Figure 6.2 Continued

treating the uninsured or medically indigent or the premature discharge of patients under DRG regulations. The ethics committee may also serve a consultative function, addressing questions related to the ethical use of new treatments or medical devices or other emerging ethics areas.

Patient Rights

One of the most significant developments of the last half century has been the recognition that patients are not merely passive participants in the delivery of health care but play an integral role in their own treatment. Whereas this concept may seem elementary to many who read this book, recognition of this concept has not been the hallmark of medical care until recently.

The extent to which the patient has played a role in his own health care and treatment has varied over time. Patients have always played some role in their treatment, initially with the decision to even seek care and later with the decision to comply with the advice of a treating physician. This participation has been limited to some extent by the way in which the health care delivery system in the United States operates. In many respects, the patient cannot enter a health care institution for treatment without the express approval of a physician, save for emergency medical care. Although the patient could for many years control who became his health care provider, some patients have seen this control limited by the advent of health maintenance organizations (HMOs) and preferred provider organizations (PPOs) that require the patient to select a health care provider from a preapproved list.

Payment for health care services also may limit the patient's participation, since third-party payers generally control funding, not the patient. This control over who gets paid, how much they will be paid, and when payments will be made often influences the level of service a patient may receive. For example, the patient may forego elective surgery that could result in a positive outcome for the patient if the third-party payer determines that it will not cover the costs of the surgery.

Though the patient's role in health care has varied, a general recognition that a patient possesses certain health care rights emerged simultaneously with two developments: the rise of the consumer culture and a movement away from paternalism in health care. These two developments derived from several circumstances, including increased levels of education among the U.S. population, dissatisfaction with the way things were run, and inaction or lax oversight by regulatory agencies. Consumers began to focus on health care, demanding higher-quality care and a larger say in its delivery. They rejected the prevailing principle of paternalism that had been a part of the ethical model followed by health care professionals for centuries. Under **paternalism**, the health care professional acted in the role of a father to his children, deciding what was best for the patient's welfare without first being required to consult with the patient. Utilizing this principle, the physician alone would determine the treatment for a patient with a certain disease, presenting only the preferred treatment to the patient and omitting disclosure of any other possible treatment alternatives. Paternalism serves to limit the patient's autonomy intentionally. As consumers, and to some extent health care professionals, became more dissatisfied with this approach, they began to demand consultation before the professional took action. All of these demands, in combination, directly affected the patient's health care role, developing into the concept of patient rights.

Patient rights are essentially the recognition that the patient is entitled to determine for himself the extent to which he will receive or forgo care and treatment. One aspect of this recognition began to occur in the form of provisions found in the ethics codes of professional associations during the 1950s. Wider recognition did not occur until the 1970s with the advent of the American Hospital Association's publication of the *Patient's Bill of Rights*. This document initially served to express to the patient the existence of such rights as privacy, confidentiality, and informed consent. In later revisions, provisions were added concerning the health care provider's responsibilities to the patient, such as the expectation that a hospital will reasonably respond to the patient's request for appropriate and medically indicated care and services. In its current iteration, this document is referred to as the *Patient Care Partnership*, emphasizing the collaborative nature of health care in the twenty-first century. This document, continuing to emphasize patient rights, also explains what a patient may expect during his hospital stay and how he can express any concerns over his care.

Although patient rights have generally been viewed from an ethical context, they also can be viewed from a legal context. Some states have formalized the concept of patient rights into statutory provisions. Furthermore, the U.S. Congress has repeatedly attempted to pass a statute incorporating the full concept of patient rights into federal law. By taking such action, these legislative bodies attempt to change the consequences for failing to honor patient rights from one of an ethical breach with limited opportunities for redress to one of a legal breach that can result in penalties enforced by law.

One of the most successful efforts in moving the concept of patient rights from an ethical basis to a legal basis is the federal Patient Self-Determination Act (PSDA). The goal of Congress in passing the PSDA is "to ensure that a patient's rights to self-determination in health-care decisions be communicated and protected."[3] The PSDA obligates health care providers who are Medicare or Medicaid certified to inform their patients of the status of state law governing a patient's rights to make advance directives for accepting or refusing health care services and the health care provider's written policies concerning implementation of the patient's rights. By placing this obligation on health care providers, the law recognizes that it is the patient's right to determine the extent of the health care services he will receive, not the exclusive right of the health care provider. Additional information concerning the PSDA can be found in Chapter 9, Confidentiality and Informed Consent.

HIPAA

New rights are granted to patients pursuant to HIPAA.

A second example of granting patient rights at the federal level is the Privacy Rule issued pursuant to the Health Insurance Portability and Accountability Act of 1996 (HIPAA). In addition to offering confidentiality protections to patient information, this rule enumerates several rights to patients pertinent to their health information. These rights include, but are not limited to, the right to be informed of the uses and disclosures of this information, the right to restrict uses or disclosures of this information, the right to amend this information, and the right to inspect and copy this information. A full list of these rights can be found in Table 6.1.

ARRA

The American Recovery and Reinvestment Act reinforces patients' rights of access to their own information when the health record is in electronic format.

Table 6.1 Patient Rights under HIPAA

- To access, inspect, and maintain a copy of his protected health information
- To be notified of the information privacy practices a health care entity follows
- To limit the use or disclosure of protected health information, including for marketing purposes
- To request that the health care provider take reasonable steps to ensure that communications with the patient are confidential
- To request an accounting of all disclosure of protected health information
- To file a formal complaint concerning the privacy practices of the health care entity

With passage of the American Recovery and Reinvestment Act of 2009 (ARRA), Congress has reinforced patient rights. ARRA states that patients have the right to obtain a copy of their protected health information in an electronic format if care was received from a covered entity that uses or maintains an electronic health record. ARRA further states that at the patient's direction, the covered entity must transmit a copy of this information to an entity or a person so designated by the patient, provided such designation is clear, conspicuous, and specific.[4] Patient rights concerning health information are also the subject of a patient's rights document published by the American Health Information Management Association (AHIMA), available on the AHIMA website listed at the end of this chapter.

The federal government has also taken action by modifying the Medicare Conditions of Participation for home health agencies to further safeguard patient rights. The new regulation requires home health agencies to inform patients and their representatives of the patient's rights, both verbally and in writing in the patient's preferred language, during the initial evaluation visit. These rights include not only the rights to be treated with respect and free from abuse and discrimination but also the right to participate in patient care assessments, be informed about their rights in the admission, transfer, and discharge processes, and how to make complaints when necessary.[5]

In summary, the concept of patient rights influences ethical decision making in the sense that health care providers must consider the patient's rights as one element in the decision-making process. By recognizing these rights, the health care provider sees the patient as a stakeholder whose values are important. Accordingly, the patient's interests must be weighed heavily in each and every decision.

Other Factors

Whereas codes of ethics and the concept of patient rights are significant factors in the decision-making process, a variety of other factors also play a role. The extent to which an individual considers these factors depends heavily upon the value the decision maker places on them.

ETHICS Various factors play a significant role in resolving ethical dilemmas.

For generations, religious beliefs and philosophical views have served as the centerpiece for the values cherished by many. Some ethical dilemmas are seen through these frameworks. While some individuals adhere firmly to their religious beliefs and philosophical views when facing ethical dilemmas, others rely on their religious beliefs and philosophical views less strictly, using them as one of the many bases from which to reach a decision. Decisions reached through these frameworks can be based on both moral beliefs and ethical reasoning.

Advances in science and technology also play a role in ethical decision making. New medical devices, surgical techniques, treatment modalities, and pharmaceutical creations have not only enhanced the quality and length of life but they have also created some new ethical dilemmas. Examples include determining who should receive these new technologies when they are scarce in number, whether embryonic stem cells should be used for research, and whether animal tissues should be used for transplantation purposes in lieu of human tissues. These and other ethical dilemmas will continue to challenge health care providers into the near future.

Legal factors also influence ethical decision making. As explained in Chapter 5, Ethical Standards, legal and ethical issues are often closely related. Ethical questions may spur subsequent legal action. For example, the civil rights movement in the 1960s progressed mainly as a challenge to values and beliefs that were seen as unethical in modern society. Some of the solutions identified by this movement were later transformed into legal protections. Even when the law addresses an ethical concern, it may not do so fully but merely serve as a bare minimum, leaving ethics to fill the void. For example, abortion is legal in the United States but many persons strongly oppose it, including some health care providers. The ethical issue for them is whether to participate in the procedure in any respect. What these examples illustrate is that the law will not serve as a deciding factor in all instances but rather serves as one of the factors on which to base an ethical decision.

Ethical Decision-Making Process

Just as ethical challenges come in many forms, solving these ethical challenges may take many forms as well. Decisions may be reached individually or as a group or may be the result of consensus building or negotiation. These decisions do not stand alone, since decisions made in one aspect of an ethical situation may affect other aspects of the same problem. Figure 6.3 provides an example of the relationships between different aspects of a fictional ethical problem.

Though the literature addressing ethics identifies several approaches to problem solving, in essence, these approaches can all be addressed as part of a multistep process. The steps in this process are listed in Table 6.2. Included in the initial steps are defining the ethical issue clearly and determining the facts. The defining step involves identifying and clarifying the problem presented and examining what values are in conflict. Determining the facts can be accomplished by gathering data. Data gathering can occur by speaking with others who may have information about the situation or by reviewing relevant records. Once the problem is clearly defined and data are gathered, one must determine who has a stake in making this decision. At times, the person faced with making the ethical decision is not the same as the person or party who is the victim of the problem. There might be more parties with interests who should be taken into consideration than may be immediately obvious, warranting a wider approach to identifying stakeholders. Additionally, the relationships between stakeholders should be explored, as should potential biases or other motivations.

The information gleaned at each of these prior steps leads to a determination of the options available to the decision maker. These options should be examined thoroughly, looking at both the short- and long-term outcomes each option will reach and their impact upon each person or group involved. Each option can be compared against an ethical theory for guidance in decision making. For example, which option presents the greatest good for the greatest number (utilitarianism),

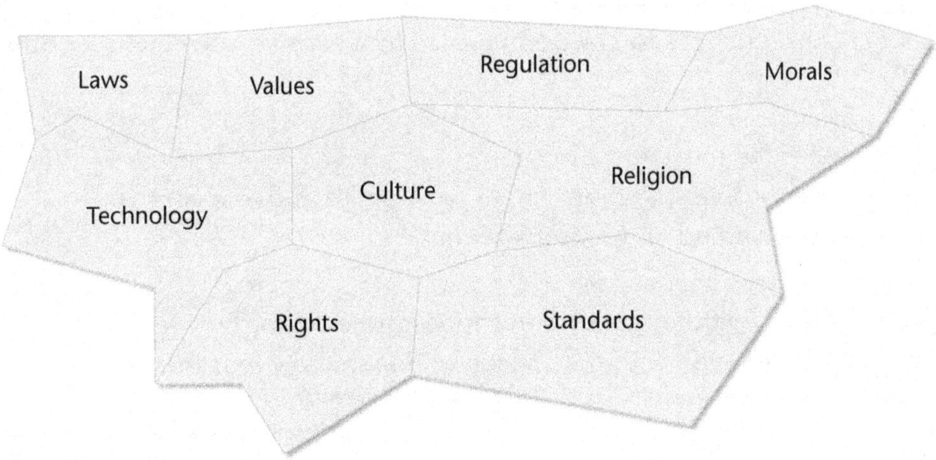

Figure 6.3 Different Aspects of Ethical Problems

Table 6.2 Steps in Ethical Decision Making

1. Clearly define the issue.
2. Determine the facts of the situation.
3. Determine who the stakeholders are, the values at stake, and the obligations and interests of each stakeholder.
4. Determine what options are available and evaluate them.
5. Decide what should be done.
6. Justify the decision made by identifying reasons that support the decision.
7. Implement the decision.
8. Evaluate the outcome of the decision.
9. Examine how to prevent the issue from recurring.

Source: Information adapted from Harman, L. (2001). Ethical challenges in the management of health information. *Journal of AHIMA*, 72(3), 27–30; and Navron, F. (2001). Crossing the spectrum: Steps for making ethical decisions. *Journal of AHIMA*, 72(3), 31–36.

which option supports doing one's duty (deontology), and which option promotes the rights and dignity of all persons (social equality and justice)? By linking an ethical theory with each option, the decision maker clarifies the basis supporting each one.

After weighing each option, the decision maker must reach a decision and act upon it. Choosing the course of action is not always easy and sometimes is fraught with difficulty. Some guidance for choosing the course of action is provided in the list of questions found in Table 6.3. Once the

Table 6.3 Guidance Questions for Ethical Decision Making

Analogous Situations:

- Do analogous situations exist?
- How are they similar to or different from the present situation?
- What course of action was chosen?
- What was the outcome?

Legal Implications:

- Does any option violate the law, a clear moral rule, or a provision of an ethics code?
- Are there legal consequences to any option, such as an arrest, conviction, or other punishment?

Sensibility:

- Which option makes the most sense?
- Can you justify it as sensible to others whom you admire and respect?
- Will the chosen option stand up to media scrutiny?

Feelings:

- Can you sleep at night without guilt when choosing the option?
- Are you comfortable enough with the chosen option in the event that friends, relatives, coworkers, supervisors, and the community become aware of it?
- How would you feel if the Golden Rule applied and you were the subject or victim of the ethical problem at issue?
- Does the decision reflect accurately the type of person or organization you are or want to be?

decision is implemented, the decision maker must evaluate the outcome, comparing the actual outcome against the predicted outcome. When the actual outcome is unforeseen, the decision maker can evaluate what he may have missed in the data-gathering and option-generation stages and learn from this for future reference. If steps can be taken to prevent the ethical problem from recurring, the decision maker should engage in these actions. The decision maker may wish to record the entire situation for use in the future as part of an educational program or dissemination to a wider audience.

In summary, the complexity of the ethical decision-making process shown in this section demonstrates the difficulty with which individuals and organizations are faced. Some of the approaches addressed may resonate with the learner's personal experiences or may be entirely new. By examining the factors that influence decision making and understanding the steps of the process, the decision maker is better positioned to reach decisions that are ethically sound.

ETHICAL CHALLENGES

Ethical challenges are situations in which no clear-cut "right" answer exists, and an individual is required to make a choice between two or more equally unfavorable alternatives or between a neutral alternative and a tempting but unfavorable alternative. The choice may center on a conflict between the individual rights of two separate people, on a conflict between the obligations of one person and the rights of another person, or some combination of these. Honest differences of opinion between sincere and virtuous persons may lead to frustration over how to make the right choice. Perfect solutions may not exist for every ethical dilemma, and the person who has made a choice may have to defend his decision later to others.

Ethical challenges primarily center upon the relationship an individual has with another, whether the other is a person, a firm or an organization, a specific community, or society as a whole. When a person engages in activities beyond his own self and establishes relationships with a larger group, he accepts broader obligations to that group. When these relationships and obligations clash, ethical challenges often result.

CRITICAL THINKING

Sometimes an ethical problem that seems apparent to one person is not as apparent to another person. Even persons who consider themselves conscientious and responsible can behave unethically on occasion. Why might so-called "good people" behave unethically?

Generalized Challenges

Although some ethical challenges also present legal implications, the focus of this discussion rests solely on the ethical aspect of a problem. Ethical challenges may arise in home, school, or work environments, with a seemingly endless variety of challenges emerging on a regular basis. This discussion focuses on the work environment, since employees who practice ethical behaviors in their home or school environment may be influenced by those in their organization who are unethical, by the values of the organization itself, the so-called "corporate culture," or by opportunities to take advantage of others for personal gain—and may therefore face ethical challenges. This discussion illustrates challenges as they relate to the work environment, but one can apply many of the areas addressed in this section to the home as well as school environment.

One of the most significant ethical challenges that may be encountered in any endeavor is the conflict of interest. A **conflict of interest** is the clash between an individual's selfish interests and his obligation to an organization or group. Such conflicts exist when the individual uses his position in or with an organization or group to promote his own interests or those with whom he is closely aligned at the expense of the best interests of the organization or group. Conflicts of interest are sometimes addressed by company policy, such as a prohibition on secondary employment with a competitor.

Conflicts of interest may be either potential or actual. Potential conflicts are those conflicts that give the appearance of harm or impropriety without resulting in the harm or impropriety itself. Actual conflicts are those conflicts that go beyond appearance but actually involve the impropriety and harm. For example, a strong-minded purchasing agent who maintains independent judgment but accepts favors from a vendor may still act in the best interests of the organization if he makes purchasing decisions based on the merits of the bids received. Although he has not actually harmed the organization, he has placed himself in a position of being perceived as not acting in the best interests of the organization and therefore has a potential conflict of interest. If that same purchasing agent allowed the favors to influence his decision making and chose not on merit but based on the receipt of favors, he would be engaged in an actual conflict of interest.

A second ethical concern is the issue of substance abuse in the workplace. Those colleagues who can no longer function appropriately in the workplace due to substance abuse such as alcohol or drugs are often referred to as **impaired colleagues**. Impaired colleagues may impede business performance, pose safety risks to both their organization and fellow workers, and engage in unethical and illegal conduct such as embezzling to support a drug habit. No easy answers exist for how to deal with such a situation. One perspective is to adopt a no-tolerance policy that advocates employment termination for those found guilty of substance abuse. A second perspective is to view the substance abuse as a disease, warranting an opportunity to attend a rehabilitation program and, upon successful completion, reinstatement of a job. Both opposing perspectives are supported by different values, and neither perspective is necessarily right or wrong.

A third ethical challenge involves **disparagement**, which means the belittling or criticizing of the skills, knowledge, or qualifications of another professional. The concept of disparagement is included in the codes of ethics of some professions; engaging in disparagement is considered by many to be professional misconduct. This concept does not mean that a professional cannot attempt to affect positive change through the presentation and discussion of problems. What it does mean, however, is that the nature of a presentation or discussion should not be tainted with personal attacks upon other professionals but should focus on the merits of an issue instead. By exercising such care, the professional increases the possibility of persuading others of the correctness of his position.

CRITICAL THINKING

Consider an incident of professional misconduct involving the delivery of substandard patient care. Can someone do the right thing by reporting the incident but avoid disparaging (speaking ill of another professional) those involved when relating that same incident?

Whereas each of the conflicts just addressed may not occur with frequency, other ethical challenges seem to arise on an almost daily basis. It seems that questions concerning truth telling abound in the workplace, with some instances that are more severe than others. For example, personal memos and daily conversations with coworkers may involve shading of the truth or lack of full disclosure. Some advertising messages may cross the boundary of puffery into outright deceptive communications. Some businesses may not meet their obligations to disclose to government entities all of the information required by statute, reasoning that the less information given the better, in light of competitive pressures. Some government entities may not disclose all of the information requested by reporters or members of the public, citing concerns of national defense or security. Some employees may copy another employee's work, such as a planning document, add a quick change of name, and submit it as their own. Whether these practices are seen as lying, lack of full disclosure, or plagiarism, such practices lead to the erosion of trust in the workplace, a matter of vital importance to organizations that rely on honesty and dependability to conduct ordinary business exchanges.

The Role of Ethics in Supervision

Any manager must recognize that ethical issues extend beyond concerns for his own personal conduct and into supervision. The supervisor plays three direct ethical roles in an organization: serving as a role model, encouraging ethical behavior, and monitoring employee conduct. Figure 6.4 illustrates the relationships of these three roles. These three roles require increased accountability from supervisors, causing them to be more alert to ethical issues than they otherwise might be.

Serving as a role model requires the supervisor to engage in ethical behaviors that can be emulated by others. One such behavior is setting a good example. For example, the supervisor who can confront problems in a constructive and ethical manner signals to employees that their future problems will be handled that way. The supervisor who refrains from actions that could be construed as conflicts of interest or unethical conduct influences others to follow this example when making ethical decisions.

Another role model behavior involves accepting responsibility for mistakes. This requires the supervisor to admit a mistake has occurred and assume responsibility for the predicament.

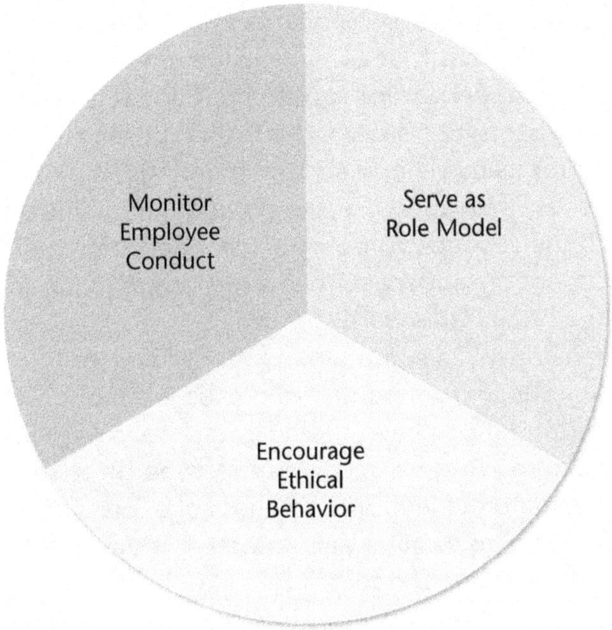

Figure 6.4 Supervisor's Ethical Roles

This action communicates to others that the supervisor is ethical and honest and seeks some form of resolution to a problem. It also may reduce anxiety within the organization because others view the action as meaning that by admitting his own limitations, the supervisor is signaling staff that he may also be accepting of others' mistakes.

Though role modeling can be an effective means of influencing staff behavior, supervisors also play a separate ethical role in organizations: encouraging staff to engage in ethical behavior through supervisory actions. These two roles differ in that role modeling does not require the supervisor to interact with staff and is therefore a more passive behavior, whereas encouragement involves interaction between supervisor and staff, making this an active behavior. These encouragement actions can take several forms. First and foremost are the organization's ethical standards or codes of ethics. Communicating these policies and procedures clearly and frequently and enforcing them fairly can lead to improved ethical behavior throughout the organization. Second, ethical content can be inserted into policies and procedures used every day by staff. By not limiting ethical content to the organization's standards or codes of ethics, the organization and its supervisors send the message that ethical behavior is part of every department and function.

In addition to encouraging ethical behavior through policies and procedures, supervisors may influence such behavior using rewards and punishment. Rewards in this context refers to both providing respect and praise for those acting ethically and making certain that unethical behavior is not inadvertently rewarded by the organization through approval and increased status. Specifying the boundaries for and ensuring punishment of unethical behavior may influence those who are supervised and reduce the opportunity for such behaviors to occur in the future.

Although role modeling and encouragement may influence staff to behave in an ethical manner, staff may not consistently do so. For that reason, a third supervisory function exists: monitoring employee conduct. This monitoring function is analogous to the monitoring function the supervisor engages in to determine whether an employee meets productivity and performance standards, only it involves ethics. The supervisor may monitor employee conduct in multiple ways, including reviewing compliance with organizational policies and procedures. Policies that address an employee's outside interests, such as prohibitions on a second job, may require the supervisor to both address the matter before it becomes a problem and to address it in the event that a problem is presented to the supervisor for resolution. For example, the supervisor may follow a procedure to address the organization's second-job prohibition policy during the new employee's entrance interview or at regularly scheduled staff meetings as a means to preventing a future problem. If a problem emerges, the supervisor should engage in an extensive examination of the facts before taking action. If the second job poses a potential conflict of interest with the employee's position in the organization, the supervisor has a responsibility to address the matter with the employee and to enforce the organization's policy.

When the management hierarchy in some organizations involves multiple levels of supervision, the behaviors of both the line supervisor and the employee are monitored by a higher-level supervisor. For example, many organizations have promulgated policies that consider it inappropriate for supervisors to receive expensive gifts from an employee on a birthday or holiday. Because most people can easily understand the inappropriateness of expensive gift giving to supervisors, it is easy for higher-level supervisors to monitor and enforce this type of ethical policy.

Another way to monitor employee conduct is to make the matter of ethics an explicit part of an employee's performance evaluation. Whether it falls within the category of judgment or business ethics, a portion of the evaluation can address whether and how the employee applies ethical standards in the workplace. Elements of ethics that can be evaluated include whether the employee treats others with respect, keeps commitments, inspires the trust of others, works with integrity, models ethical behavior, and upholds the values of the organization. Each of these elements can be rated and explained to the employee as part of the performance evaluation. Specific deviations from the organization's ethical expectations can be addressed, with goals set for future performance.

Other methods can be used to monitor the ethical behavior of employees as well. These include employing a well-developed structure that provides a system of checks and balances. These checks and balances serve as both a means to detect noncompliance with the organization's ethical standards and a way to limit the opportunity for an employee to act unethically.

In summary, the three direct ethical roles require supervisors to engage in behaviors that focus beyond themselves. These behaviors vary in the amount of interaction required with others and the level of complexity. Some supervisory issues require little more than common sense to address, whereas other issues require extensive examination and counseling. Because of the wide range of ethical issues that may occur in the work environment, it is necessary for supervisors to be aware of the roles they play and their influence upon others in the workplace.

Health Care Challenges

Ethical challenges can be found in numerous places and in differing situations within the general health care field. The ethical challenges addressed in this section illustrate areas that are of importance and have been the subject of considerable discussion during the last twenty years.

Conflicts of interest exist in the health care field, just as they do in the business arena. For example, physicians who engage in joint venturing or self-referral practices raise the question of a conflict of interest. Under these scenarios, the physician invests financially in a health care facility but does not provide direct medical service at that facility. The health care facility might offer a broad range of activities or services, such as physical therapy, diagnostic imaging, ambulatory surgery care, and durable medical equipment. The physician then refers his patient to the health care facility in which he has the financial interest, and the insurance company or government payer is billed for the activities or services rendered at the facility. Such referrals have drawn considerable criticism as, at minimum, ethically suspect and have resulted in states passing laws and professional groups such as the American Medical Association adopting policies against these practices.[6] Over time, this position has evolved. The AMA's current position allows the physician ownership in facilities, products, or equipment when the financial interest is disclosed to the patient and the physician is directly providing care or services.[7]

Conflicts of interest are also present if the health care practitioner engages in sexual relations with a patient. The nature of the practitioner–patient relationship is one of inequality; the practitioner is in a position of advantage over the patient in terms of knowledge, power, and status. At the same time, the patient may be vulnerable, especially when he has experienced intense pressures or traumatic life events. In view of this inequality, true consent cannot be forthcoming from the patient, and the sexual relationship will be viewed at best as ethically inappropriate.

Substance abuse issues are also present in the health care context and are particularly troubling because of the increased risk to patient safety. Under the ethical concept of nonmaleficence, health care workers must consider how, not whether, to address situations involving substance abuse. Whether addressing the situation requires informing management personnel, confronting an impaired colleague directly, or intervening with a group, it is important that fellow health care workers understand the obligations, policies, and practices articulated by their professional associations and their employers before taking action. Within many health care contexts, the impaired colleague will be treated like a patient who needs effective assistance and guidance to a treatment program. Such a humane approach may permit the impaired colleague to salvage his practice.

Another organizational policy may prohibit an employee from using nonpublic health information for private financial gain. Again, the supervisor may need to conduct an extensive examination of the facts of the situation before making a conclusion and decision that the policy has been violated.

The financing of health care influences ethics. For example, third-party payers may affect the clinical decisions of some physicians by authorizing inpatient stays for a shorter time frame than the physician thinks is medically prudent, thereby exposing the patient to the potential discharge from the hospital in a seriously ill condition. The ethical dilemma is whether the physician should place the well-being of the patient first by only discharging the patient when he is clinically ready, thereby forcing the hospital or patient to bear the expense of prolonged treatment or discharge the patient earlier than desired in order to financially benefit the hospital, not jeopardize the physician's place on the hospital staff, and not place a financial burden on the patient. Ethical challenges also exist in areas such as research involving human subjects, the allocation of organs for transplant, withholding or withdrawing life support, and employee health and safety on the job. Further information concerning ethical issues involving human subject research is found in Chapter 10, Access to Health Information; information concerning bioethical issues such as organ transplant and life support is found in Chapter 7, Bioethics Issues; and information concerning ethics and employee health and safety is found in Chapter 15, Law and Ethics in the Workplace.

ETHICS

The practice of copy and paste of patient information in the EHR implicates the ethical concept of nonmaleficence, the prohibition against doing harm.

Ethical challenges can also occur in the context of the patient's electronic health record (EHR). While EHRs may assist in the delivery of patient care and exchange of information, the health care provider's duty is to create an accurate record of patient care. The temptation to **copy and paste**, the practice of duplicating information within the same patient record or moving it across multiple records, is great as it is seen as a way to improve efficiency and increase time spent with patient. The ethical challenge is that engaging in this practice presents risks of harm to the patient, the exact opposite of the ethical concept of nonmaleficence. Ethical challenges posed by the use of EHRs have prompted some health care professional associations to amend their ethics guidance, as seen by the example in Table 6.4.

Health Information Management Challenges

As the health information management field has evolved, new ethical challenges have emerged. These challenges have generally arisen from (1) changes in the health care environment, such as the development of managed care, (2) requirements for documentation and access to and release of information, (3) developments in technology, including the ease of sharing information electronically, and (4) changes in reimbursement systems and their attendant coding systems.

In the specialized area of health information management, ethical challenges also arise. The most frequent ethical challenges center on the coding–reimbursement connection; quality review; information security; data resource management; and the protection of sensitive information, including genetic, drug and alcohol abuse, mental health, and sexual abuse information.

Table 6.4 Ethical Guidance on Use of Electronic Health Records by Physicians

1. Physician entries in health records must contain accurate and complete information about all communications, including those done in-person and by telephone, letter, or electronic means.
2. Ethically and legally, patients have the right to know what information is contained in their health records and the physician must release this information.
3. While the health care provider may legally own the health record, the information contained within the record is the property of the patient.
4. EHRs should facilitate patient care, align with physician ethical duties, and support clinical reasoning. Accordingly, the copy and paste practice should be used carefully and only to produce an accurate health record.
5. If a physician dies or leaves a group practice, patients must be notified and health records forwarded according to patient instructions.

Source: Sulmasy, L. S., Bledsoe, T. A., ACP Ethics, Professionalism and Human Rights Committee. (2019). American College of Physicians Ethics Manual, 7th ed. *Annals of Internal Medicine*, 170, S1–S32. doi:10.7326/M18-2160

Of these, the most substantial numbers of recent ethical challenges have focused on the coding–reimbursement connection and protection of sensitive information.

Those health information management professionals assigning diagnostic and procedural codes have seen an increased focus on third-party payer reimbursement as the means for a health care facility to remain financially viable. Most, if not all, reimbursement mechanisms tie the coded diagnosis and procedure to the amount reimbursed to the health care facility. Along with the growing complexity of coding and reimbursement guidelines, some coders face the dilemma of whether to focus on the accuracy of coding versus coding to obtain a better reimbursement for the health care facility. When assigning codes for reimbursement, the individual coder may be pressured by a health care institution into relying on inaccurate, incomplete, or misleading information, or information without a sound clinical basis or documentation, in order to obtain the maximum reimbursement for the health care facility. AHIMA provides Standards for Ethical Coding to guide coding professionals in ethical gray areas, such as this example.[8]

As a result of the increased demand for patient information, health information management professionals have seen a growing challenge for access to sensitive patient information. It has long been a core ethical obligation of a health information management professional to protect patient privacy and confidential communication. Consider the instance of admission of a celebrity patient to an acute care hospital. Inquiries from the press or hospital staff for detailed health status information about the celebrity patient are inappropriate since neither group has an inherent right to this information without the patient's consent. With the advent of computers, the temptation is present to satisfy curiosity by gaining access to the celebrity's health information in a seemingly anonymous fashion. Such temptations should be tempered by the existence of audit trails, which allow the hospital the ability to determine how frequently the celebrity patient's health information is accessed and by whom. If inappropriate access is found, the hospital can take appropriate disciplinary action.

Other ethical examples in the health information management field may include pressure by a health care facility to obtain fully accredited status from an accrediting organization by "fudging" statistics that would indicate that the health information management department meets the required percentage of completed charts. Or a physician may complete progress notes long after seeing a patient and ask that the health information manager indicate that he has completed those notes in a contemporaneous fashion. Other examples include failure to disclose conflicts of interest and incorrectly representing one's professional credentials.

In addition to ethical challenges internal to the health care organization, health information managers may face ethical challenges from third parties. Some third parties seek inappropriate access to genetic, adoption, or behavioral health information. Others, such as commercial vendors, may seek to be paid for work not performed. For example, the health information manager may audit invoices submitted by an outside vendor providing transcription services and discover that the vendor has submitted an inaccurate invoice with a discrepancy between billed and actual line counts. If the manager determines that the discrepancy is not an error but an inflated line count, the manager may consider revising the transcription contract to require greater invoice detail and include penalty clauses for any future discrepancies.

In working through the decision-making process of such situations, the health information manager should use the steps listed in Table 6.2. Additional steps include turning to colleagues for a so-called reality check to determine if the ethical dilemma is legitimate or based on misperception. Assuming that a colleague confirms that the dilemma is legitimate, the manager should document the situation, including underlying facts and times, dates, and places of conversation about the matter. Where possible, the manager should address the issue through the organizational hierarchy and, if necessary, through the organization's ethics committee. If it remains unresolved, the manager can seek expert advice from a local health information management chapter or the American Health Information Management Association. In the end, the manager must determine a personal course of action.

CONCLUSION

Codes of ethics, patient rights, religious beliefs, and scientific advances all play a role in influencing ethical decision making. Understanding these influences and the complexity of the ethical decision-making process will assist the learner when faced with ethical challenges. The number and type of ethical challenges present in the workplace, particularly relating to supervision and health information management, require the health information manager to reach decisions that are ethically sound. Recognizing ethical challenges is made easier through the concepts and applications illustrated in this chapter.

CASE STUDY A

You are a supervisor in the Health Information Services Department of a facility with a policy prohibiting secondary employment with a competitor. One of the employees you supervise is a coder who has just begun the process of repaying his student loan debt. The coder has decided that he needs a second job to help defray expenses. He has been offered a position as a coder for one eight-hour shift per weekend at a doctor's office. This doctor is a member of your facility's medical staff. Because you addressed the issue of secondary employment in the coder's entrance interview, he comes to you now seeking advice. How do you respond?

CASE STUDY B

Read the fictional case of the Killer Robot at www.onlineethics.com/CMS/computers/compcases/killerrobot.aspx. The case involves the accidental death of a human being by a robot due to faulty programming code. Read through the articles listed in the Table of Contents to learn about the various factors that contributed to the accident and answer the following questions:

1. Responsibility for an act is rarely defined clearly and is often difficult to trace to one or two people or causes. In this fictional case, it appears a large number of people share responsibility for the accident. Identify all of the people you think were at least partially responsible for the death of Bart Mathews and explain why you think so.
2. Imagine you are the leader of a task force assigned to correct the problems uncovered by this accident. Using the steps found in Table 6.2 Steps in Ethical Decision Making, develop a list of the six most significant actions to take to avoid future problems.

Source: Adapted from Reynolds, G. (2015). *Ethics in Information Technology* (p. 286). Cengage Learning, Boston, MA.

REVIEW QUESTIONS

1. Compare the steps typically taken in the ethical decision-making process shown in Table 6.2 with the additional steps listed in the last section of the chapter.
2. State what is meant by the phrase "code of ethics."
3. Why are codes of ethics important?
4. What role do patient rights play in ethical decision making?
5. Are ethical challenges ever clear-cut?
6. Name the three direct ethical roles that supervisors play in organizations.
7. Can methods used to finance health care influence ethics?
8. What are the most frequent ethical challenges in health information management?
9. How can health information professionals experience ethical challenges when dealing with third parties?

ENRICHMENT ACTIVITY

Consider an ethical decision that you have made within the last three years. Examine how you reached this decision and compare that process against the ethical decision-making model discussed in this chapter. In light of the materials addressed in this chapter and your personal experiences since the decision was made, determine whether you would make the same decision today. If not, examine how and why your decision would be different.

WEBSITES ADDRESSING CODES OF ETHICS

American Academy of Professional Coders, http://www.aapc.com

American Association of Medical Assistants, http://www.aama-ntl.org

Association for Healthcare Documentation Integrity (AHDI), http://www.ahdionline.org

American Dental Hygienists Association, http://www.adha.org

American Health Information Management Association, http://www.ahima.org

American Medical Association, http://www.ama-assn.org

American Nurses Association, http://www.nursingworld.org

American Occupational Therapy Association, http://www.aota.org

American Osteopathic Association, http://www.osteopathic.org

American Pharmacists Association, http://www.aphanet.org

American Physical Therapy Association, http://www.apta.org

American Society of Radiologic Technologists, http://www.asrt.org

NOTES

1. This chapter is based in large measure on Chapter 4, Ethical Standards, in my text *Today's Health Information Management: An Integrated Approach*, 2nd ed. (Delmar Cengage Learning, 2014).

2. American Osteopathic Association. (2016). *American Osteopathic Association Code of Ethics.* Chicago: Author.

3. 42 U.S.C. § 1396a(w)(1)A)(i) (2019).

4. 42 U.S.C. § 17935(e) (2019).

5. 42 C.F.R. § 484.50 (2019).

6. N.J.STAT.ANN. § 45:9–22.5 (2019) (prohibiting doctors from referring patients to an entity in which they have a financial interest, with limited exceptions) (commonly referred to as the Codey Act). See also American Association of Respiratory Care prohibition on referral arrangements involving home care providers.

7. American Medical Association, Opinions of the Council on Ethical and Judicial Affairs, Opinion E8.132 Referral of Patients: Disclosure of Limitations (revised Nov. 2007) (physicians must disclose financial incentives related to diagnostic and therapeutic alternatives offered to patients).

8. AHIMA Standards of Ethical Coding, http://www.ahima.org. See also Health Care Compliance Association, http://www.hcca-info.org.

CHAPTER

7

BIOETHICS ISSUES

LEARNING OBJECTIVES

After reading this chapter, the learner should be able to:

1. Restate the dilemmas posed by bioethical issues.
2. Compare and contrast the ethical issues related to the beginning of life.
3. Explain the role of confidentiality with regard to HIV/AIDS.
4. Explain the role of confidentiality with regard to genetic science.
5. Discuss the ethical issues related to organ transplantation.
6. Differentiate between the ethical issues related to death and dying.

KEY CONCEPTS

Abortion
Active euthanasia
Advance directives
Allografts
Artificial insemination
Autografts
Bioethics
Contraception
Durable power of attorney for health care
Eugenics
Euthanasia
Family planning
Gene therapy
Genetic screening
Heterografts
Homografts
Human Genome Project
In vitro fertilization
Living will
Organ transplantation
Passive euthanasia
Perinatal ethics
Prenatal surgery
Prenatal testing
Stem cell research
Sterilization
Surrogate mother
Withdrawing treatment
Withholding treatment
Xenografts

INTRODUCTION

It is virtually impossible for an individual to function in the modern health care world unaware of bioethical issues. Without such knowledge, the health care provider cannot protect both patients and providers adequately. **Bioethics** is the study of ethical issues that result from technologic and scientific advances, especially in biology and medicine. As science and technology advance, the number and complexity of bioethical issues seem to increase. At times, science and technology have progressed at such a fast pace that society in general and governmental entities in particular have not been prepared to address the public policy questions that accompany the ethical dilemmas created. Many of the bioethical dilemmas that society has faced during the last half century are listed in Table 7.1 and are discussed in detail in this chapter.[1]

Table 7.1 Current Bioethics Issues

Relating to the Beginning of Life:
- Family planning (controlling the size of one's family or spacing births within that family)
- Abortion (termination of pregnancy before the viability of the fetus)
- Perinatal ethics (ethical questions involved in or occurring during the period closely surrounding birth)
- Eugenics (the effort to improve the human species through control of hereditary factors in mating)

Relating to Sustaining and Improving Quality of Life:
- HIV/AIDS (confidentiality and duty to treat patients)
- Organ transplantation (form of surgery wherein one body part [tissue or organ] is transferred from one site to another or from one individual to another)
- Genetic science (use of genetics in the Human Genome Project, gene therapy, and stem cell research)

Relating to Death and Dying:
- Planning for the end of life (planning in advance for the level of medical care a person will receive at the end of life)
- Euthanasia (the act or practice of causing death painlessly, with the aim to end suffering)
- Withholding/Withdrawing life support (the decision of the patient, her family, or legal guardian to refrain from giving permission for treatment or care)

RELATED TO THE BEGINNING OF LIFE

A multitude of ethical issues surrounds the beginning of life: family planning, abortion, perinatal ethics, and eugenics. Many of these issues elicit strong emotional reactions because they ask us to question our fundamental beliefs and values about reproduction and the relationships associated with it. This questioning is not only performed on a personal level but also on a societal level, resulting in extensive debate and efforts toward political and social control. Each of these issues has an ethical component, as shown in Table 7.2.

Family Planning

Family planning refers to the behavior associated with controlling the size of one's family or spacing the births within that family. Family planning can encompass a wide range of behaviors, including controlling family size through methods of contraception and increasing family size through adoption or infertility treatment.

The term most commonly associated with the phrase "family planning" is *contraception*. **Contraception**, sometimes referred to as birth control, refers to efforts to prevent or interfere with conception or impregnation through voluntary or artificial means. The ethical issues surrounding contraception are numerous and are often closely tied to the moral beliefs and values held by various religious groups. Some view contraception as evil because it interferes with the purpose of sexual activity, which they consider a means to create life. Some view contraception as wrong only when it requires the use of artificial birth-control methods. Others are strong advocates of contraception, citing the need to control population growth because of its impact on physical resources.

Table 7.2 Ethical Issues Relating to the Beginning of Life

Ethical Issue		Ethical Component
Family planning	Contraception	Autonomy Best-interest standard Paternalism Right to personal liberty
	Adoption/Infertility Treatment	Autonomy Beneficence/Nonmaleficence Justice Right to personal liberty
Abortion		Autonomy Rights to personal liberty
Perinatal ethics		Autonomy Rights to personal liberty
Eugenics		Autonomy Justice Nonmaleficence Right to reproduce

Still others advocate the use of contraception methods as a means to provide a woman with the ability to control both her own body and the course of her life.

Among the most problematic ethical areas, dealing with contraception is the question of minors. Whereas much discussion focuses on those adults who employ contraception methods, the ethical question regarding whether minors can consent to employing these same contraception methods has created considerable anxiety. In instances of medical care not related to reproduction, consent must be obtained from the parent or legal guardian before care is rendered to a minor. This consent is required because both the law and society in general recognize that the concept of the best-interest standard and the principle of paternalism apply to these situations. Where reproductive issues are involved, the best-interest standard and paternalism are not recognized strongly because a different concept comes into play: the concept that a minor possess a "right" to control her reproduction. This rights concept conflicts directly with the best-interest standard and paternalism. In most states, the legislatures have solved this conflict by granting minors who are mature and able to give informed consent the legal right to obtain contraceptive care and treatment without the consent of a parent or legal guardian. Often this legal right extends to care and treatment of other areas surrounding reproduction, such as pregnancy care and treatment for sexually transmitted diseases. Although the questions surrounding these matters may be addressed by law, they still remain ethical questions that cause considerable debate.

Increasing family size through adoption or infertility treatment raises serious ethical questions that are also emotionally charged. Ethical questions relating to adoption include the extent to which identity and genetic information about the birth parents should be disclosed. If an adoption does not succeed, can the adoptive parents return the child? If so, what criteria should be applied to allow the adoptive parents to do so? Several ethical questions were initially raised during the development of infertility treatment, such as whether scientific procedures should be employed to separate reproduction from the act of sexual intercourse. Although the question of whether to use scientific procedures is no longer as prominent, related questions remain, such as: What scientific procedures can be employed that will be considered responsible ethical conduct? Does responsible conduct include **artificial insemination**, the planting of sperm into a woman's body to facilitate conception? Does responsible ethical conduct include fertilization of human gametes outside the human body in a test tube or other artificial environment, called **in vitro fertilization**? Should those gametes be implanted in only the donor, or can another woman act as a surrogate to bring a baby to term? Can a **surrogate mother**, defined as one who agrees to bear a child conceived through artificial means and relinquish it upon its birth to others for rearing, change her mind and retain the baby? What should happen to embryos if they are no longer wanted by the donors or the donors are no longer living? What genetic information should be provided about the donors to any adoptive parents? For each of these questions, concepts of autonomy, beneficence/nonmaleficence, justice, and rights must be considered.

Abortion

Although abortion is sometimes considered a form of family planning because it acts to reduce family size, it is addressed separately here because of the unparalleled attention it has received. **Abortion** refers to the termination of pregnancy before the viability of the fetus. Several forms of abortion exist, including those due to natural causes (referred to as spontaneous abortion or miscarriage), those performed for medical reasons (therapeutic abortions), and those performed for personal reasons (elective abortion). Those abortions that are classified as therapeutic and elective are the focus of ethical concerns.

Stripped to its essentials, the abortion debate revolves around the definition of human life and when a fertilized egg should be considered a human being worthy of protection. Ideas about the definition of human life and related questions have been hotly contested for generations. On one side, some view human life as beginning at the moment of conception, making the fetus a human being worthy of protection. These views rest on the moral beliefs and values held by various religious groups. Seen from this viewpoint, abortion amounts to murder and therefore should be stopped. Others believe that human life does not begin at conception and that the fetus is not considered a human being until its birth or until the age of viability, the earliest age a baby can survive outside the womb. These views not only rest on the moral beliefs and values held by various religious groups but also on the concept of autonomy and the right to personal liberty inherent in an individual's control over her own body and course of life. In between these two views lie several variations. Some believe that abortion constitutes murder but feel that the value placed on personal liberty is such that only the individual facing the crisis may decide whether to proceed with an abortion. Some view abortion as wrong but find that other considerations, such as a rape leading to conception, outweigh the wrongness, justifying an abortion to proceed. Others do not view abortion itself as wrong but believe it is misused and treated as merely another form of birth control.

These ethical views have spilled over into both the political and legal arenas. The U.S. Supreme Court, in the case of *Roe v. Wade*,[2] decided the abortion question from a rights perspective by recognizing that state laws restricting abortion could impair a woman's personal liberty and her right to privacy. The court addressed the protection question by splitting pregnancy into three trimesters, allowing abortion to proceed freely in the first trimester, allowing states to issue some restrictions related to maternal health in the second trimester, and allowing states to severely restrict or ban abortion outright in the third trimester. Numerous battles have been fought in subsequent years over how to interpret, expand, or restrict the rights articulated in this case, on both a political and legal basis.

The abortion issue has been further complicated by additional issues. What is the male's role with regard to abortion? How should informed consent be handled, particularly where minors are concerned? Should fetal tissue from an abortion be used for stem cell research or some therapeutic purpose? What role should politicians play in this debate of an intensely personal subject? These and other questions indicate that the abortion debate will continue for some time.

Perinatal Ethics

Some of the same concerns voiced over abortion are also present in the discussion regarding **perinatal ethics**, the ethical questions involved in or occurring during the period closely surrounding birth. These ethical questions center on prenatal testing, genetic screening, and prenatal surgery.

Prenatal testing refers to those tests performed after conception but before birth that are designed to detect fetal abnormalities. These tests include amniocentesis, chronic villus sampling (CVS), and sonograms or other technological forms of viewing the fetus in utero. Each of these tests poses risks, and the first two are not generally employed without an indication or suspicion of a medical disorder. Some question whether or how often the tests should be employed, since the results may force the patient into a difficult ethical decision over whether to proceed with the pregnancy or with an abortion. Some see this as an issue of autonomy and personal liberty, similar to what is articulated concerning abortion, since many of these tests are performed in the early stages of pregnancy when the right to an abortion is protected by law. Others view this type of testing as unreliable because false positives can be reported, requiring retesting for confirmation and causing stress and anxiety for those involved.

Prenatal testing is interrelated with the practice of genetic screening. In **genetic screening**, a person's genetic makeup is tested to reveal a predisposition to certain diseases or other abnormalities. These predispositions or abnormalities may affect the subject of these tests or a child borne of that subject. Viewpoints differ concerning the ethics of genetic screening, ranging from the autonomy/personal liberty view to concerns that genetic screening promotes abortion. In between these views exist concerns for the guilt that may be placed on the person carrying the defective gene and the stress that the results may place on a marriage bond.

Fetal abnormalities can be corrected in some instances through prenatal surgery. **Prenatal surgery** refers to surgery conducted upon the fetus prior to birth. The level of risk associated with these surgeries varies, with some performed so rarely that they are considered experimental in nature. Some see the risk level as too high to condone prenatal surgery, arguing that life with an abnormality is just as valuable as life without an abnormality. Others weigh the risks and determine that the opportunity to correct an abnormality will result in an enhanced life for the fetus, thereby justifying the surgery. Still others view prenatal surgery not as a scientific advancement but as a chance for a human being to "play God." As these views illustrate, the ethics issues surrounding prenatal surgery are fraught with both reason and emotion.

Eugenics

Eugenics refers to the effort to improve the human species through control of hereditary factors in mating. Essentially, eugenics is a breeding practice aimed at producing superior offspring. Although it was not given the name "eugenics" until more recent history, the idea of eugenics has been advocated since the days of ancient Greece.[3] Eugenics has been advocated by some scientists during different time periods, worldwide, but its most famous application was in Nazi Germany in twentieth-century Europe.

Eugenics has been applied in modern history using two methods: encouragement of reproduction by those groups deemed desirable and sterilization of those persons who some authority group has decided should not reproduce. The first method is not really one of science but one of persuasive rhetoric. Those persons deemed superior by some controlling authority were persuaded or pressured to reproduce, and those deemed inferior were pressured or persuaded to refrain from reproducing. The second method, however, requires the use of science. **Sterilization** refers to the actions taken to make an individual incapable of reproducing, whether by removing the reproductive organs or by preventing them from functioning effectively. Utilizing eugenics principles, if those persons who should not reproduce did not voluntarily agree to sterilization, forced sterilization should occur.

The ethical issues related to eugenics are many. The idea that some forms of human life are inferior to others, whether judged by race, sex, creed, or some other criteria, affronts the concept of justice, in which no person is favored over another. The concept of autonomy becomes involved, since decisions to reproduce are considered highly personal and not to be decided by others. Nonmaleficence is also an issue, because the individual undergoing a forced sterilization views the procedure as harm done to her and nonmaleficence tries to do no harm. Finally, the concept of rights comes into play, since individuals frequently view reproduction as one of the basic rights belonging to human beings. These objections, combined with the repugnance engendered by Nazi Germany's application of eugenics, have led eugenics into disrepute.

RELATED TO SUSTAINING OR IMPROVING THE QUALITY OF LIFE

Ethical issues related to sustaining or improving the quality of life are fraught with great emotion, because they challenge the belief systems and values held dear by many. What is considered an improvement to the quality of life may differ based on the perspectives brought to the discussion. Many of the ethical issues surrounding the question of quality of life are listed in Table 7.3.

HIV/AIDS

Human immunodeficiency virus (HIV) and acquired immunodeficiency syndrome (AIDS) are among the most significant health threats worldwide. In some areas of the world, these health threats have spread so rapidly and become so prevalent as to constitute an epidemic. Known causes of HIV and AIDS include intravenous drug use and the sharing of contaminated needles, tainted blood supply used for transfusion purposes, sexual intercourse, and direct mucous-to-mucous contact. Because no vaccine or cure has been discovered, most medical efforts have focused on containing the spread of infection.

Table 7.3 Ethical Issues Relating to Sustaining or Improving Life

Ethical Issue	Ethical Component
HIV/AIDS	Autonomy Double-effect principle Justice Right to confidentiality
Organ transplantation	Best-interest standard Justice
Genetic science	Justice Right to confidentiality Right to privacy Veracity

Several methods to contain the spread of infection have been employed, including clean needle exchange programs for IV drug users, extensive screening of blood supplies, sexual abstinence programs, and the use of condoms during sexual intercourse. All of these methods have raised ethical issues, because they implicate the concepts of autonomy, justice, rights, and the double-effect principle. For example, the creation of clean needle exchange programs for IV drug users implicates their autonomy and arguably supports their choice to continue using illegal drugs. This, in turn, raises the double-effect principle: does the intended outcome (reducing the spread of HIV/AIDS) outweigh the secondary outcome (continuing to engage in illegal activity)? Alternatively, the action of screening blood supplies implicates the principle of distributive justice if all blood supplies are screened (equal review). This principle is not implicated where the screening of only a sampling of blood supplies is performed.

Entangled with any discussion of HIV/AIDS are questions related to confidentiality. As one would expect, those who are afflicted with the disease view confidentiality as extremely important; many have suffered from stigmatization or outright discrimination as a result of unauthorized disclosure. Balanced against this are the legitimate policy concerns of health authorities that need to know the extent of the disease's existence in their community and the health care resources needed to combat it. Many health authorities have resolved their policy concerns by implementing testing policies (voluntary, mandatory, confidential, and anonymous) and requiring health care providers to report test results on a mandatory basis without revealing the subject's identity.

The confidentiality question relates to both the patient who suffers from HIV/AIDS and to the health care provider who is afflicted. Without a legal reporting requirement, health care providers may not disclose a patient's HIV/AIDS status to third persons without consent. This prohibition against disclosure may even continue after the patient's death, as identified in the ethical guidelines of the American Medical Association.[4] Furthermore, ethical guidelines frequently require the HIV/AIDS-infected health care provider to disclose her status to those patients upon whom invasive procedures are performed so that they are aware of the risks posed by the health care provider.[5] These ethical precautions rest on the concepts of beneficence and nonmaleficence as well as the patient's autonomy as the ultimate decision maker in her own care.

Although confidentiality is a central concern for HIV/AIDS patients, a separate issue also exists: the health care provider's duty to treat the afflicted patient. It is difficult for some health care providers to separate the patient suffering from HIV/AIDS from the high-risk behavior that may have caused the disease. As a result of the disapproval of these high-risk behaviors and the statistically small, but real, risk of contracting the disease from the patient, these health care providers are reluctant to treat patients suffering from HIV/AIDS. Professional associations have responded to the concern by incorporating provisions into their ethics codes that identify a duty to provide care commensurate with the scope of practice. They have also published universal precautions guidelines for use in creating a barrier to infection, thereby reducing risk to the health care provider.

Organ Transplantation

One of the most effective developments in improving the quality of life in the twentieth century has been organ transplantation. **Organ transplantation** is a form of surgery wherein one body part (tissue or organ) is transferred from one site to another or from one individual to another. Transplants using one's own body parts are called **autografts**. Transplants using a donor's body part are called **allografts** or **homografts**. Transplants involving animal tissue, cells, or organs into human bodies are called **xenografts** or **heterografts**. By receiving a transplant, the patient's quality of life can improve, since the healthy tissue or organ substitutes for the diseased or failing tissue or organ.

The number of tissue/organs available has never met or exceeded the demand. Government entities and professional associations have engaged in various efforts to increase the number of organs available, including instituting publicity campaigns, making tissue/organ donor cards readily available, and providing space on driver's licenses where individuals can authorize permission for organ donation. Although these efforts are laudable, demand still outstrips supply, creating competition for the limited number of tissue/organs available.

How to address the scarcity of these tissue/organs and how to allocate those that are available are difficult ethical questions that involve the concepts of the best-interest standard and justice. Society, worldwide, generally abhors the concept of dealing in human organs for profit, and many nations have codified this concept into law. They instead rely upon educational efforts to persuade individuals to donate tissue/organs. Some nations, such as the United States, support this effort by promulgating regulations that require hospitals that receive federal government funds to ensure they have in place policies requesting permission from the next of kin for the removal of organs after death. In such instances, the next of kin relies upon the best-interest standard to decide whether to grant permission to remove the organs. Other efforts include publicity campaigns and outreach efforts at the community level designed to decrease barriers to donations.

Once the tissue/organ becomes available, allocating it among the many who are in need becomes very difficult. Should all persons in need of an organ be treated equally (distributive justice), or should the needs of some—for example, the very young, those closest to death, and so on—be placed before the needs of others (comparative justice)? To assist with this dilemma, the federal government funds an organization called the United Network for Organ Sharing, which serves as a clearinghouse for organ procurement and matching. Using the criteria of medical acceptability, the organization looks for compatibility in the tissue and blood type between the donor and the recipient.

One answer to the overall scarcity is the use of nonhuman tissue and organs. These nonhuman tissue and organs may be created artificially in a medical laboratory or they may come from animals. Neither artificially created tissue nor animal tissue and organs have proved to be effective for long-term use, but they have provided humans with additional time to locate a suitable donation of human tissue or organ. Some of the work and research involved in these efforts has led to the development of artificial joints, valves, and other prostheses that have proved to be successful for long-term care.

Genetic Science

Much of the progress in medicine during the past century has been due to scientific advancements and the application of technology to the health care setting. Future progress in medicine appears to focus on genetic science and its application in the health care setting. Several efforts in genetics are in progress, including the Human Genome Project, gene therapy, and stem cell research.

The **Human Genome Project** (HGP) is an enterprise designed to map the genes found in human DNA and determine the sequences of the chemical base pairs that make up human DNA. These genes comprise the forty-six human chromosomes, which considered together are called the human genome. By obtaining knowledge of the genome, scientists hope to discover new ways to diagnose, treat, and someday prevent diseases and disorders affecting humankind. Some find this effort to obtain such knowledge laudable; others view it with reluctance because of concerns over application of this knowledge; and still others view it as immoral because they think it indicates hubris and an attempt to equate oneself with God. Of particular ethical concern is the application of this knowledge, because issues of justice, fairness, privacy, and confidentiality of genetic information are all present. Ethicists are also concerned over philosophical implications such as the role of free will versus genetic determination in human development. Many of these issues are yet to be fully explored and will remain with us for some time.

GINA

The Genetic Information Nondiscrimination Act (GINA) addresses confidentiality of genetic information.

As sometimes happens with ethical disputes, laws are passed to address a discrete portion of the ethical dispute. In 2008, the United States Congress followed this approach by passing the Genetic Information Nondiscrimination Act (GINA), which addresses the ethical issue of confidentiality of genetic information. GINA provides protection of genetic information in the contexts of insurance and employment, prohibiting the use of genetic information as a condition of eligibility for health insurance and prohibiting employment discrimination based on genetic information. The Department of Health and Human Services enforces Title I of GINA addressing discrimination in health coverage; the Equal Employment Opportunity Commission (EEOC) enforces Title II of GINA addressing discrimination in employment. Much of the regulations that have been issued concerning GINA come from the EEOC and govern employment discrimination.[6] GINA does not protect people from all forms of discrimination that may result from knowledge of genetic information. Employers with fewer than fifteen employees are not bound by GINA's provisions nor are those entities that write life insurance, disability insurance, and long-term care insurance policies. Various states have subsequently provided protections against genetic discrimination beyond what is specified by GINA. Additional information on state law measures are found in Chapter 11, Specialized Patient Records.

> **CRITICAL THINKING**
>
> A female patient undergoes genetic testing that shows she has an increased risk of getting breast cancer. Can a life insurer use this information to determine whether to write a policy for this woman? Can an employer who learns of this information use it to determine whether to hire this woman?

One application currently being explored is gene therapy. **Gene therapy**, sometimes referred to as genetic engineering, involves genetically altering organisms for various purposes. For example, one purpose may be to supply the missing portion of a length of DNA that is the cause of a disorder such as sickle cell anemia or cystic fibrosis. Today's exploration involves experimentation on mice or other animals, not human beings. Many of these experiments have not been successful; science is still trying to better understand gene functionality and determine a mechanism for inserting the altered gene into the animal's body. Although these therapies show some promise, ethical questions surround them. Will altered genes help or harm humans or other living beings? Can scientists be trusted to act responsibly in these experiments? Will veracity be sacrificed for the sake of medical progress? These and other concerns will need to be addressed fully for society to accept gene therapy efforts.

Another area engendering considerable debate is stem cell research. **Stem cell research** is the careful, systematic study and investigation of a special kind of cell not committed to conduct a specific function that has the capability to renew itself and differentiate into specialized cells. These cells are not committed to differentiating into specialized cells until they receive a signal to do so. Because of the wide variety of specialized cells that can be generated and used for replacement, scientists view stem cell research as a promising area for medical advancement. Stem cells may be derived from adult stem cells or early human embryos. Adult stem cells may replicate and differentiate into specialized cells, but they are considered rare and difficult to identify. Early human embryos also replicate and differentiate but are less rare and much easier to identify. Because of this, the scientific community generally utilizes embryonic stem cells in research.

This reliance on embryonic stem cells has fueled national debates in the United States and elsewhere. Some of the debates are similar to those conducted over the subject of abortion. For those who view human life as beginning at conception, these embryonic stem cells are human life and cannot be the subject of research and experimentation under any circumstances. They argue that research should continue only with adult stem cells or with existing stems cells drawn from embryos previously destroyed. Others view these same embryonic stem cells as devoid of human life, thereby justifying research and experimentation. Some view embryonic stem cells as potentially human but not yet human, thereby justifying research because of its potential to reap life-saving benefits. Others are concerned with the financing of this research, arguing that public funds cannot be used to support such a divisive area of research. Individuals and groups on all sides of this issue have spent a considerable amount of time and money lobbying politicians to achieve their respective goals, and the debate does not appear to be ending anytime soon.

RELATED TO DEATH AND DYING

Whereas each of the bioethical issues previously addressed engenders heated debate, ethical issues related to death and dying are especially problematic because death and dying are not abstract concepts but real events with which virtually all persons are familiar. Accordingly, strong emotions accompany the issues of planning for the end of life, euthanasia, and withholding or withdrawing life support. The ethical components of these issues are listed in Table 7.4.

Table 7.4 Ethical Issues Relating to Death and Dying

Ethical Issue	Ethical Component
Planning for the end of life	Autonomy Best-interest standard
Euthanasia	Double-effect principle Nonmaleficence
Withdrawing/Withholding treatment	Autonomy Best-interest standard Right to die Right to personal liberty

Planning for End of Life

Issues of death and dying have always been present in society, but the increase in educational levels and advancements in medical science and technology have caused more individuals to contemplate the meaning of the term *quality of life* as it applies to the ends of their own lives. Employing the ethical concept of autonomy, some plan in advance what level of medical care they wish to receive or forgo at the end of life.

Facilitating these planning efforts are various documents that can provide guidance to family members and health care providers in the event that the patient is unable to communicate her wishes at the time a decision must be reached. Combined together under the term **advance directives**, these written instructions describe the kind of health care the patient wishes to have or not have if she becomes incapacitated. Advance directives are based on the substantive legal rights found in state law but are also recognized at the federal level through the Patient Self-Determination Act (PSDA). Additional information concerning the PSDA can be found in Chapter 6, Ethical Decisions and Challenges, and Chapter 9, Confidentiality and Informed Consent.

Two types of advance directives are used in the health care setting: living wills and powers of attorney for health care. A **living will** is a document, executed while a patient is competent, that provides direction as to medical care the patient should receive in the event she is incapacitated or unable to make personal decisions. Living wills are analogous to blueprints or maps of the patient's wishes. The value of a living will is that it specifies the patient's wishes, thereby lessening the decision-making burden on family members and health care providers concerning what actions they should or should not take with regard to the patient's care. A living will provides a measure of assurance to family members and health care providers that if they follow the terms specified in the living will, they will act in compliance with the patient's wishes.

A second form of advance directive is a **durable power of attorney for health care**. This document allows a competent individual to name someone else to exercise health-related decisions on her behalf in the event that the individual becomes incapacitated or unable to make decisions. Under a durable power of attorney for health care, the person empowered to act by proxy may or may not know the patient's wishes; the document may merely name the person empowered to act by proxy or it may include details of the patient's wishes. The level of detail contained in a durable power of attorney for health care depends upon the patient's preference. Where details are not specified and provided by the patient, it is then left to the named individual to exercise the best-interest standard when reaching decisions on behalf of the patient.

CRITICAL THINKING

The types of advance directives discussed in the text, living wills and powers of attorney for health care, have existed for a number of years and are readily available through health care providers, at law offices, and on the Internet. Studies have consistently shown, however, that only about one-third of those studied have completed an advanced directive. Can you identify reasons why individuals would be reluctant to create a living will and/or power of attorney for health care?

Euthanasia

The term **euthanasia** refers to the act or practice of causing death painlessly, with the aim to end suffering. Euthanasia derives from the Greek words *eu*, meaning good, and *thanatos*, meaning death. Euthanasia practices are divided into two categories: passive and active.

Passive euthanasia, also called negative euthanasia, involves the practice in which no heroic measures are taken to preserve life. Passive euthanasia is recognized in the health care setting with the use of Do Not Resuscitate (DNR) or "no-code" orders. These orders essentially instruct the health care provider not to engage in extraordinary measures or otherwise attempt to revive those persons whose vital processes have ceased to function on their own. Several difficulties arise with this concept. As part of their training, health care providers learn how to save or improve patients' lives. Asking them to forgo action at the end of a patient's life seems contradictory to this training, implicating the ethical concept of nonmaleficence. Definitions of extraordinary measures also differ between health care professionals, causing confusion during application to a specific situation. Additionally, the patient's decision regarding end of life may not have taken into consideration when the DNR or no-code orders should be implemented.

Active euthanasia, also called positive euthanasia, involves the practice of actions that speed the process of dying. Within the health care setting, active euthanasia occurs in situations where the provider prescribes, supplies, or administers an agent that results in death. Such a situation occurs most frequently when the patient has suffered excruciating pain from a terminal illness or from a disease for which no cure or hope for improvement exists. Active euthanasia may not be limited to health care providers, as recent high-profile situations involving close family members who facilitated the death of a loved one have been publicized. These so-called "mercy killings" by close family members have been received by the public with varying degrees of sentiment, ranging from acceptance to outrage. The variation in sentiment generally correlates with the facts of the particular situation.

The practice of euthanasia raises a variety of ethical issues. Some view euthanasia from a deontological approach, seeing it as an outgrowth of patient autonomy in those situations where the patient has made her wishes known. Some view the idea of mercy killings with a utilitarian approach, seeing it as a compassionate and concerned answer for those who are painfully or terminally ill. Some employ the double-effect principle, citing instances where the administration of strong narcotics to a terminally ill patient to relieve pain (the intended outcome) can be justified, even if such administration hastens death (the untoward outcome). Religious beliefs also play a role, with the sanctity of life principle operating to either support or condemn euthanasia.

Some consider Judeo-Christian principles to tolerate passive euthanasia because absence of actions permits death, whereas those same principles are employed to condemn active euthanasia because overt acts cause the patient's death. Some reject euthanasia principles entirely, applying the slippery slope argument that allowing passive euthanasia will lead to active euthanasia in the future. Regardless of the ethical approach that is used, the public debate over euthanasia does not appear to be over.

Withholding/Withdrawing Treatment

Closely related to passive euthanasia is the concept of withholding or refusing treatment. **Withholding treatment** refers to the decision of the patient, her family, or her legal guardian to refrain from giving permission for treatment or care. Both euthanasia and withholding treatment may result in the death of the patient, but they differ in the sense that withholding treatment does not always include activities that would be considered heroic measures. Activities that may be withheld or refused may serve to improve the quality of patient's life but not hasten or result in her death.

Withdrawing treatment refers to the decision of the patient, her family, or her legal guardian to discontinue activities or remove forms of patient care. Decisions to withdraw treatment frequently, but not always, result in the patient's death. Used in the context of discontinuing treatment that results in death, this concept is sometimes referred to as the "right to die." Arguments supporting the right to die address many fears, including the patient's fear of loss of control over her life, fear of degradation or lack of dignity in death, and fear of a prolonged death due to medical interventions.

Withholding or withdrawing treatment is based upon several ethical concepts. Where the patient is lucid and of sound mind, concepts of autonomy and the right to personal liberty are present. Where the patient is incapacitated, incompetent, or otherwise unable to convey her wishes, the best-interest standard applies. Many people support these concepts as a general rule but differ with regard to their application, particularly as the application relates to vulnerable persons such as children or the mentally impaired. When dealing with those populations, health care providers may look to the ethical guidelines of their professional associations or to the judicial system for guidance in how to proceed with the patient's care. This last approach particularly applies to questions of withdrawal of treatment for incapacitated patients when family members disagree over whether or what support measures may be withdrawn.

CONCLUSION

By understanding the various problems associated with bioethics issues, the learner is better positioned to address both personal and public policy questions that may arise during her lifetime. The decision-making process is particularly important in bioethical issues, as concerns of life and death are present.

CASE STUDY

You have been approached by an elderly relative who trusts your judgment. Your relative seeks information about her options in planning for future medical care in the event she is unable to communicate her wishes or otherwise direct her care. How should you respond? What options should you provide?

REVIEW QUESTIONS

1. Why should health care providers be aware of bioethical issues?
2. Name the ethical concepts at issue concerning the access of minors to contraception.
3. What ethical concerns are expressed about prenatal ethics?
4. What ethical concepts underlie the ethical precautions used in not disclosing HIV/AIDS status on a routine basis?
5. In what contexts does GINA provide protection of genetic information?
6. What ethical concepts are used to address the scarcity of organs to be used in human transplants?
7. What does the term *advance directives* mean? Provide examples.

ENRICHMENT ACTIVITY

Identify one bioethics issue in your lifetime that engendered sufficient media attention to warrant political involvement. Discuss with a small group the parameters of that bioethics issue and what role politics played in shaping the issue's outcome.

NOTES

1. This chapter is based in large measure on Chapter 4, Ethical Standards, in my text *Today's Health Information Management: An Integrated Approach*, 2nd ed. (Delmar Cengage Learning, 2014).

2. 410 U.S. 113 (1973).

3. Plato referred to the practice of infanticide for the disabled or diseased newborn in his work, THE REPUBLIC, Book V, 460C (380 B.C.), as cited in EDGE, R. S. & GROVES, J. R., THE ETHICS OF HEALTH CARE (2006).

4. American Medical Association Council on Ethical and Judicial Affairs, *Confidentiality of Human Immunodeficiency Virus Status on Autopsy Reports*. (1992).

5. Centers for Disease Control and Prevention, *Recommendations for Preventing Transmission of Human Immunodeficiency Virus and Hepatitis B Virus to Patients During Exposure Prone Invasive Procedures* (retrieved March 16, 2019), http://www.cdc.gov/mmwR/preview/mmwrhtml/00014845.htm.

6. 29 C.F.R. § 1635 (2019).

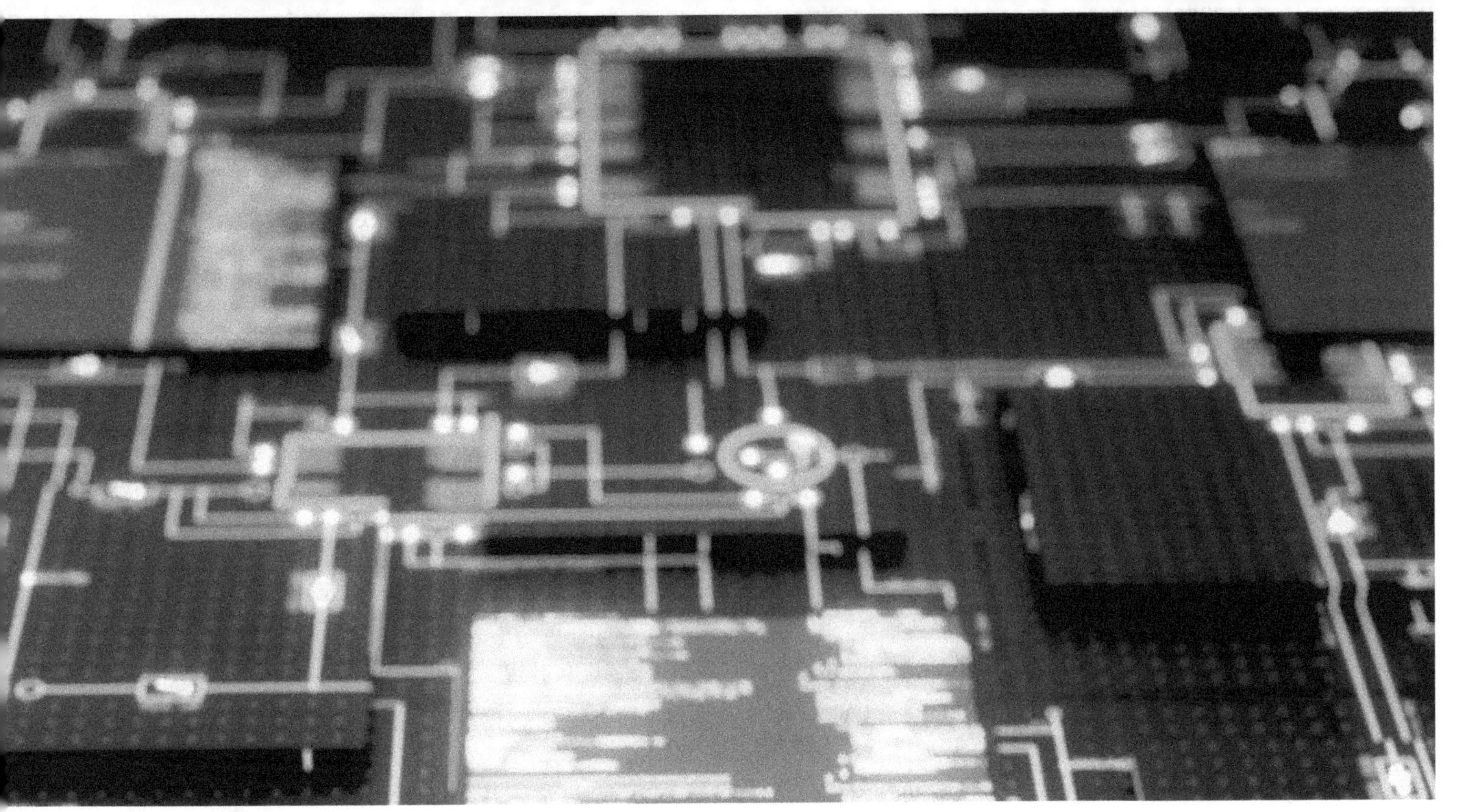

PART

3

LEGAL AND ETHICAL ISSUES CENTRAL TO HEALTH INFORMATION MANAGEMENT

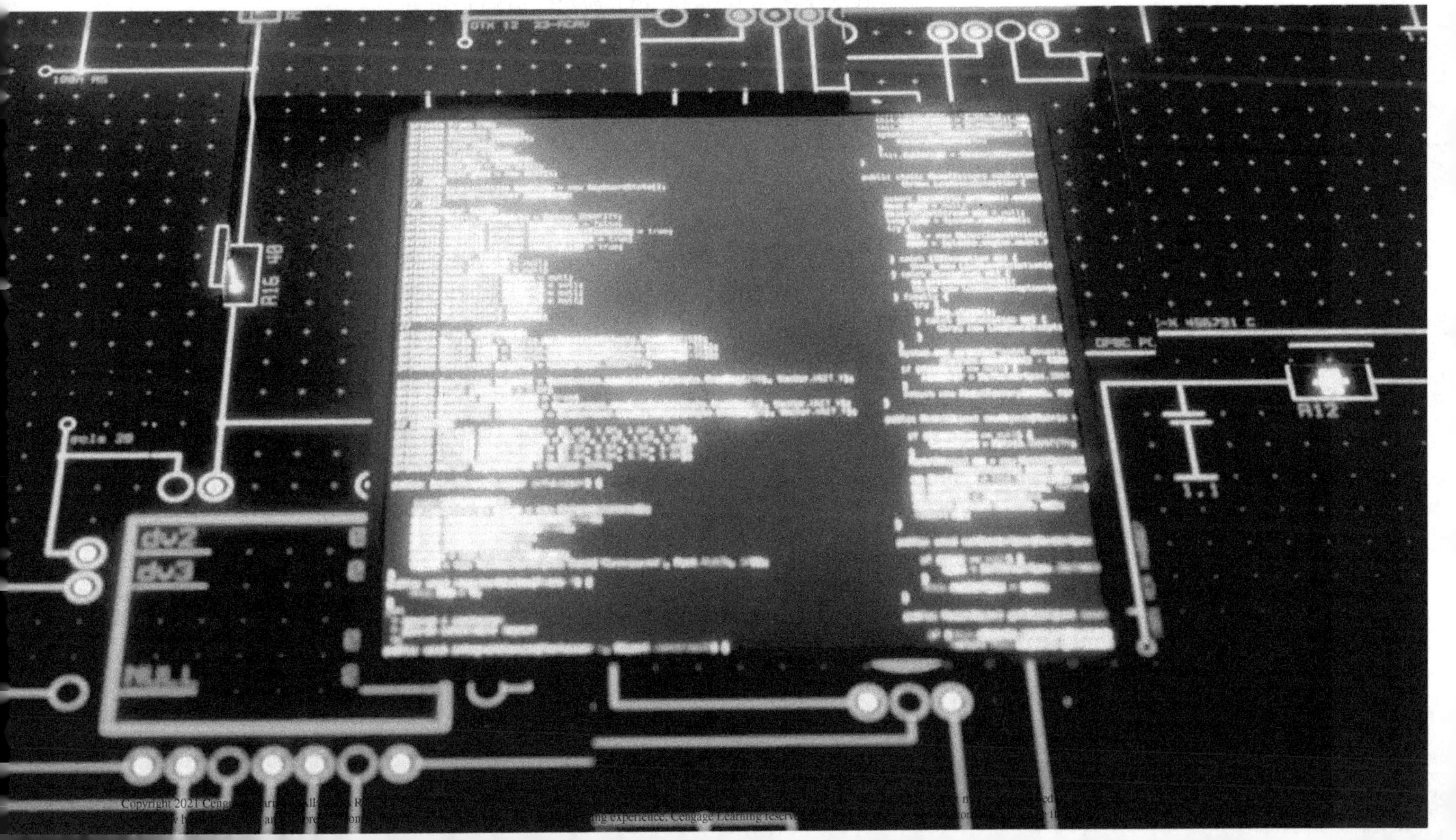

CHAPTER 8

PATIENT RECORD REQUIREMENTS

LEARNING OBJECTIVES

After reading this chapter, the learner should be able to:

1. Summarize the multiple functions and uses of a health record.
2. Identify the sources of law governing the content of the health record.
3. Explain how the sources of law influence the content of the health record.
4. Distinguish between authorship and authentication.
5. Differentiate between proper and improper methods for a health provider to correct the health record.
6. Compare and contrast the procedures used to comply with or refuse a patient's request to correct the record.
7. Identify the factors influencing a record retention policy.
8. Explain what role a statute of limitations plays in a record retention policy.
9. Compare and contrast record destruction done in the ordinary course with that done due to closure.
10. Identify the importance of keeping permanent evidence of a record's destruction in the ordinary course.
11. Identify the special procedures involved with the destruction of alcohol and drug abuse records upon a program's closure.

KEY CONCEPTS

Authentication
Authorship
Certificate of destruction
Copy and paste
Corrections to the record
Deeming authority
Electronic health record
Electronic signature
Enterprise content and record management
Health record
Health record content
Hybrid records
Legal health record
Medical advice
Record destruction policies
Record retention policies
Record retention schedule
Statute of limitations

INTRODUCTION

The health information contained in a paper health record, an electronic health record, an abstract of patient-specific information, or some other format plays a primary role in the delivery of health care. In addition to its role in direct patient care, health information maintained in these formats serves as the health care provider's legal record of patient care. As such, it is subject to stringent legal requirements.

While technology has advanced quite rapidly, advances in the law concerning technology have not been as rapid. Despite new methods of storing health information, legal requirements governing such information sometimes reference only one format, the paper health record, while at other times they reference multiple formats: paper, electronic, and abstracted information. For purposes of clarity, this chapter refers to both the traditional concept of a health record and other record formats in explaining the legal requirements governing the content, retention, and destruction of health information.

To understand the legal requirements governing the health record, those interested in protecting health information should first recognize its function and uses. Functions and uses, in turn, are affected by statutory, regulatory, accrediting, and institutional requirements. By understanding these concepts, effective policies governing **health record content** (the characteristics essential to constitute an adequate health record), retention, and destruction can be created.

FUNCTION AND USE OF THE HEALTH RECORD

The multiple functions and uses of the health record have resulted in its having various names: medical record, hospital chart, outpatient record, clinical record, **electronic health record** (EHR), computerized patient record, and other such descriptors. Generally defined, a **health record** is a document that contains a complete and accurate description of a patient's history, condition, diagnostic and therapeutic treatment, and the results of treatment. The health record includes detailed personal, medical, financial, and social data about the patient.[1] Figure 8.1 categorizes these data by their sensitivity and need for confidentiality. Because extensive literature already exists that addresses these types of data, more detail will not be given here.

The health record serves both clinical and nonclinical uses, as shown in Figure 8.2. In the most basic sense, the health record serves as the chronological document of clinical care rendered to the patient. Created contemporaneously with the clinical care rendered, it provides a method for various medical disciplines to communicate about the patient's illness and course of treatment

Figure 8.1 Patient Data Categories

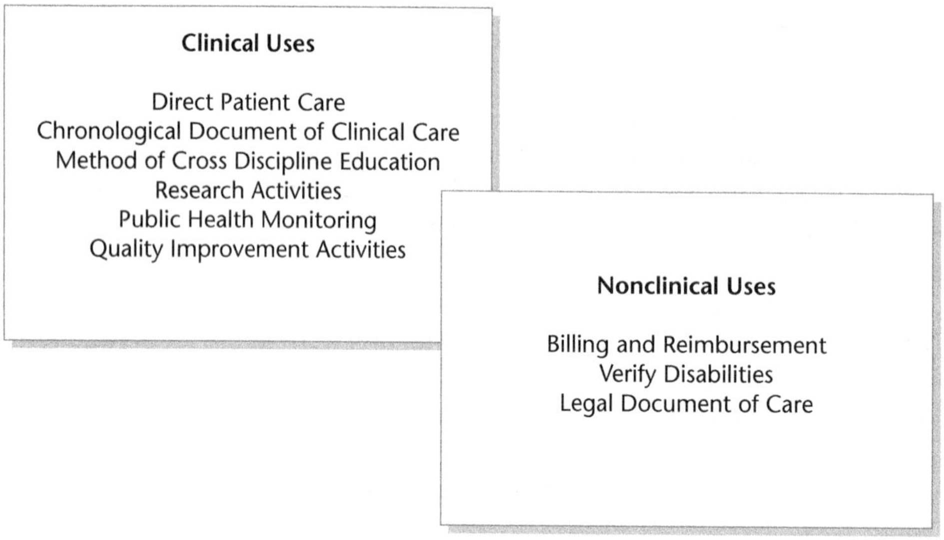

Figure 8.2 Uses of Health Records

during a particular episode of care. Further, it supplies information to caregivers involved in a patient's subsequent episode of care.

In addition to direct patient care, health records serve other clinical purposes. Through concurrent and retrospective analysis, health records are relied on by the medical, nursing, and scientific communities as a primary source of information for research. By identifying specific incidences of disease, health records assist the public health community's efforts to control disease and monitor the overall health status of a population. Furthermore, health records assist in quality improvement activities because they provide a source from which to evaluate the adequacy and appropriateness of patient care.

In addition to clinical uses, health records serve other secondary purposes. Health care providers rely on health records to support the billing of insurance and benefits claims of individual patients to whom they have provided care. Third-party payers rely on health records to make payments on claims to health care providers and to monitor the appropriateness of care and services rendered to the patient. Employers rely on health records to document the extent of an employee's disability.

Finally, health records serve as legal documents: the record of a particular episode of a patient's care. The backbone of virtually every professional liability action, health records are used to prove what did or did not happen in a particular case and to establish whether the applicable standard of care was met. Because memories fade and persons who participated in direct patient care are not always available at the time of trial, the health record serves as the most frequently used method to reconstruct an episode of patient care.

The health record as a legal document has traditionally been viewed as being paper-based. With the advent of digital imaging, some health care providers created **hybrid records**, a health record that is partly paper-based and partly electronic. As technology has improved, some health care providers and organizations moved to an entirely electronic health record. Regardless of the medium in which data resides, the concept of a **legal health record** focuses on its definition: the business record generated at or by the health care provider or organization that addresses the patient's episode of care that was delivered by the provider or organization. The transition from the paper world to the electronic world has generated additional complexity as to what is considered the legal health record, especially in light of the lack of clarity in statutes, regulations, and standards addressing electronically stored information (ESI). Additional information about the interplay of the legal health record and the electronic health record is contained in Chapter 13, Information Systems. Throughout the discussion of this chapter, principles and concepts are introduced that apply to both paper-based and electronic health records. Where differentiation between them is warranted, specific material is presented.

LEGAL REQUIREMENTS FOR HEALTH RECORD CONTENT

In the light of the many uses of health records, it is incumbent on health information professionals to design and manage systems that ensure accurate and complete health records. Before doing so, health information professionals must become aware of the legal requirements governing the content of a health record.

Content of the Health Record

Unfortunately, no one source of law definitively addresses the legal requirements governing the content of health records. Rather, a myriad of sources supply these requirements: statutory, regulatory, accrediting, institutional, and professional guidelines. Although each source is separate, they must all be reviewed together to obtain an understanding of the legal requirements governing health records. See Figure 8.3.

Statutory Provisions

First and foremost in any review of the legal requirements governing health records are statutory provisions. Although very few statutes address the contents of health records specifically, statutory provisions should be reviewed first because of the critical role they play in the legal system.

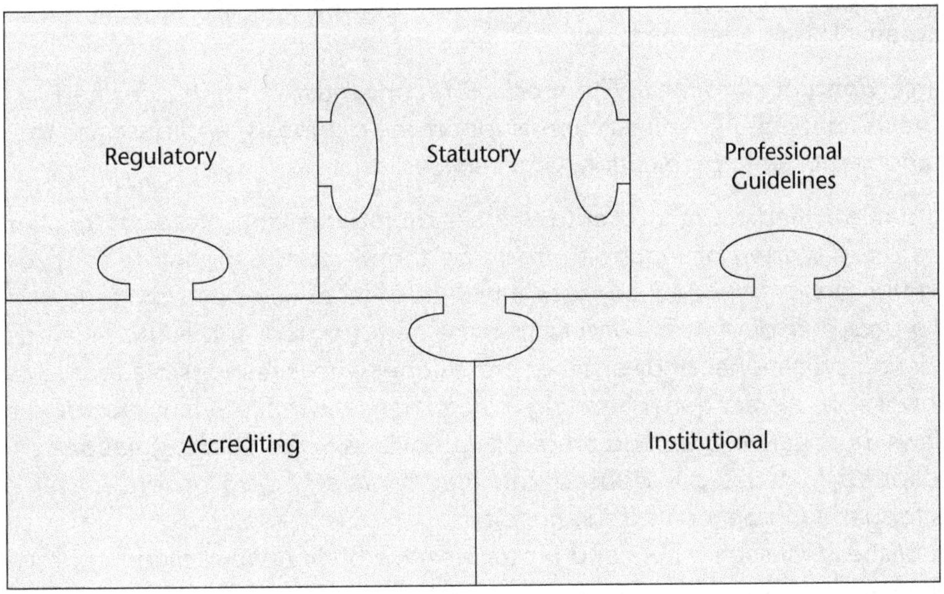

Figure 8.3 Interrelationship of Legal Requirements Governing Content of the Health Record

As explained in Chapter 1, statutory provisions can be federal or state laws or municipal codes. Unfortunately, no one federal law addresses the legal requirements governing all patient records. Rather, a small patchwork of federal and state laws on this subject exists. For example, the section of federal law that establishes the Conditions of Participation in federal reimbursement programs such as Medicare defines a hospital, in part, as an institution that "maintains clinical records on all patients."[2] That same section does not, however, define what a clinical record must contain.

Similarly, states that have passed statutes referring to health records generally limit the statute to the requirement that the health care provider merely create a health record.[3] If the content of the health record is defined by statute, the definition is often provided in the context of hospital licensing. For example, a portion of the Tennessee law that licenses health facilities, referred to as the Medical Records Act of 1974, defines the content of a health record. It provides:

> *(5) (A) "Hospital records" means those medical histories, records, reports, summaries, diagnoses, prognoses, records of treatment and medication ordered and given, entries, X rays, radiology interpretations, and other written, electronic, or graphic data prepared, kept, made or maintained in hospitals that pertain to hospital confinements or hospital services rendered to patients admitted to hospitals or receiving emergency room or outpatient care.*[4]

Regulations

Closely related to statutory provisions are regulations promulgated by executive-branch agencies. Frequently, statutory provisions delegate certain powers to the executive-branch agency responsible for licensing a health care facility, such as the power to promulgate and enforce rules and regulations governing the health care facility's health records.

Found at both the federal and state levels, these regulations vary between (1) general statements that a health record be maintained, (2) broad listings of content requirements, and (3) specific, detailed provisions governing content.

An example of specific, detailed provisions at the federal level include a regulation promulgated by the Department of Health and Human Services as a Condition of Participation in the Medicare program. This regulation states:

> *c) Standard: Content of record. The medical record must contain information to justify admission and continued hospitalization, support the diagnosis, and describe the patient's progress and response to medications and services.*
>
> *(1) All patient medical record entries must be legible, complete, dated, timed, and authenticated in written or electronic form by the person responsible for providing or evaluating the service provided, consistent with hospital policies and procedures.*
>
> *(2) All orders, including verbal orders, must be dated, timed, and authenticated promptly by the ordering practitioner or by another practitioner who is responsible for the care of the patient only if such a practitioner is acting in accordance with State law, including scope-of-practice laws, hospital policies, and medical staff bylaws, rules, and regulations.*
>
> *(3) Hospitals may use pre-printed and electronic standing orders, order sets, and protocols for patient orders only if the hospital:*
>
> *(i) Establishes that such orders and protocols have been reviewed and approved by the medical staff and the hospital's nursing and pharmacy leadership;*
>
> *(ii) Demonstrates that such orders and protocols are consistent with nationally recognized and evidence-based guidelines;*

(iii) Ensures that the periodic and regular review of such orders and protocols is conducted by the medical staff and the hospital's nursing and pharmacy leadership to determine the continuing usefulness and safety of the orders and protocols; and

(iv) Ensures that such orders and protocols are dated, timed, and authenticated promptly in the patient's medical record by the ordering practitioner or by another practitioner responsible for the care of the patient only if such a practitioner is acting in accordance with State law, including scope-of-practice laws, hospital policies, and medical staff bylaws, rules, and regulations.

(4) All records must document the following, as appropriate:

(i) Evidence of—

(A) A medical history and physical examination completed and documented no more than 30 days before or 24 hours after admission or registration, but prior to surgery or a procedure requiring anesthesia services. The medical history and physical examination must be placed in the patient's medical record within 24 hours after admission or registration, but prior to surgery or a procedure requiring anesthesia services.

(B) An updated examination of the patient, including any changes in the patient's condition, when the medical history and physical examination are completed within 30 days before admission or registration. Documentation of the updated examination must be placed in the patient's medical record within 24 hours after admission or registration, but prior to surgery or a procedure requiring anesthesia services.

(ii) Admitting diagnosis.

(iii) Results of all consultative evaluations of the patient and appropriate findings by clinical and other staff involved in the care of the patient.

(iv) Documentation of complications, hospital acquired infections, and unfavorable reactions to drugs and anesthesia.

(v) Properly executed informed consent forms for procedures and treatments specified by the medical staff, or by Federal or State law if applicable, to require written patient consent.

(vi) All practitioners' orders, nursing notes, reports of treatment, medication records, radiology, and laboratory reports, and vital signs and other information necessary to monitor the patient's condition.

(vii) Discharge summary with outcome of hospitalization, disposition of case, and provisions for follow-up care.

(viii) Final diagnosis with completion of medical records within 30 days following discharge.[5]

In place of specific regulations, some states have adopted as their own all or portions of the requirements of the Medicare Conditions of Participation.[6] Finally, at least two states have adopted the accreditation standards of the Joint Commission (JC), formerly known as the Joint Commission on Accreditation of Healthcare Organizations (JCAHO), as the governing regulations.[7]

Accrediting Standards

Although accrediting standards do not have the force of law standing alone, they are frequently used to establish the standard of care in negligence actions against health care providers. As stated previously, at least two states have adopted accrediting standards as their governing regulations. Thus, health care providers must pay close attention to these standards of accreditation. For further information concerning the standard of care in negligence actions, see Chapter 4, Principles of Liability.

Two widely recognized voluntary accrediting bodies in health care are the JC and the American Osteopathic Association's (AOA) Healthcare Facilities Accreditation Program (HFAP). A newer organization, Det Norske Veritas (DNV) Healthcare, has recently entered the accrediting market in the United States. All three bodies have been granted deeming authority by CMS to conduct accreditation surveys. **Deeming authority** means that compliance with the requirements and standards of both accrediting organizations may substitute for compliance with the federal government's Medicare Conditions of Participation for Hospitals published by CMS. Accreditation by any of these organizations often enhances a health care facility's public image, competitiveness, and ability to borrow money or float bond issues. Each of the accrediting organizations has issued standards requiring hospitals to maintain health records for each patient and describe in detail the contents of the health record.[8] Additional accrediting bodies exist, often covering specialized areas of health care. A listing of accrediting bodies is found in Table 8.1.

Institutional Standards

Where no specific statute or regulation specifically addresses the existence or content of a health record, health care institutions may wish to create their own standards or adopt the standards issued by an accrediting agency. These institutional standards may be either broad statements or

Table 8.1 Accrediting Bodies

Name	Bodies Accredited
Joint Commission	Hospitals, behavioral health facilities, critical access hospitals, long-term care facilities, home care facilities, transplant centers, ambulatory care centers, clinical laboratories, and disease-specific care programs
American Osteopathic Association's Healthcare Facilities Accreditation Program	Hospitals, behavioral health facilities, critical access hospitals, primary stroke centers, substance abuse centers, rehabilitation facilities, and ambulatory care centers
DNV Healthcare	Hospitals
National Committee for Quality Assurance (NCQA)	Managed care organizations
Commission on Accreditation of Rehabilitation Facilities (CARF)	Programs and services in medical rehabilitation, assisted living, behavioral health, adult day care, and employment and community services
Community Health Accreditation Program (CHAP)	Home care organizations
Accreditation Association for Ambulatory Healthcare (AAAHC)	Ambulatory care centers, community health centers, health plans/QHPs, office-based surgery centers
National Commission on Correctional Health Care (NCCHC)	Correctional institutions
American Correctional Association	Correctional institutions
College of American Pathologists (ACP)	Clinical laboratories

detailed listings or fall somewhere in between. They serve as a guide to health record content for that institution.

Similar to accrediting standards, institutional standards do not carry the force of law. Nevertheless, they are useful to establishing the standard of care in a negligence action. And, as indicated in Chapter 4, Principles of Liability, if the institutional standards are higher than the minimally acceptable standard found in a statute or textbook, it is the higher standard against which the institution will be measured.

Professional Guidelines

In addition to the sources listed previously, allied health professional organizations publish guidelines that address the existence and content of health records. For example, the American Health Information Management Association publishes position statements and practice briefs regarding health record content.[9] Although these health care associations are not providing legal advice when publishing these guidelines and position statements, the documents address sensitive legal issues related to health records. As such, they assist health information managers to ensure accurate and complete health records.

Timely and Complete Health Records

As described earlier, a health record serves multiple functions and uses. It is axiomatic that a timely and complete health record is essential to achieving these purposes.

Authentication and Timeliness

All entries in the health record must be authored and authenticated. **Authorship** identifies the health care provider who has made the entry, either in writing, by dictation, by keyboard, or by keyless data entry. **Authentication** confirms the content of the entry, either by written signature, initials, or computer-generated signature code. This confirmation implies that the entry as recorded is accurate.

> **EHR**
>
> The flexibility available in the functionality of electronic health records has underscored the need to strictly enforce authorship principles.

The concept of authorship has become more complicated with the advent of the electronic health record. Unless designed to prevent an occurrence, the ability to copy and paste portions of the health record exists in an EHR. **Copy and paste** refers to the practice of duplicating information within the same patient record or moving it across multiple records. Such actions may result in a host of problems, including misidentifying who is making an entry, placing portions of one person's health record in another person's health record, mistakenly adding services on dates when services were not rendered, and inadvertently repeating entries that are no longer accurate. These and other problems listed in Table 8.2 can seriously compromise the integrity of the record. To reduce this risk, health care providers and organizations should create policies to address the use of the copy and paste functions and train their staff accordingly. Internal auditing of the use of copy and paste functions can identify issues of compliance with these policies and whether modification or additional training is warranted. To the extent, the software program supporting the EHR can do so, the ability to copy and paste can be eliminated from EHR functionality.

Table 8.2 Risks posed by use of copy and paste practice

1. Copying and pasting inaccurate or outdated information
2. Redundant information in the EHR, which makes it difficult to identify the current information
3. Inability to identify the author or intent of the documentation
4. Inability to identify when the documentation was first created
5. Propagation of false information
6. Internally inconsistent progress notes
7. Unnecessarily lengthy progress notes

Source: Preventing copy-and-paste errors in EHRs, *Joint Commission Quick Safety Advisory,* Issue 10 (Feb. 2015).

In some localities, the licensing authority may consider authentication to include the use of a rubber stamp signature by the medical staff member the signature represents. In such an instance, the licensing authority may require the health care institution to maintain in its administrative offices a signed statement that the medical staff member whose signature stamp is involved is the only one who has the stamp and the only one authorized to use it. Duplication and delegation of the stamp by others would be strictly prohibited[10] and, if allowed, would defeat the concept of verifying the accuracy of the entry in the health record. Although a state or local licensing authority may permit the use of a signature stamp, the Centers for Medicare and Medicaid Services (CMS) no longer accepts the use of these stamps in health record documentation. CMS accepts physician signatures that are handwritten, electronic, or facsimiles of original written or electronic signatures. Because CMS manages regulations for both the Medicare and Medicaid programs, this decision affects virtually all health care organizations that are reimbursed by these programs.

Because accuracy of the health record is paramount, authentication principles dictate that only the author of the entry may authenticate the entry. For example, it would not be legally sound for a physician within a group practice to sign for another physician within that same practice unless specific accreditation standards or regulations allowed for this action. This is because the proper foundation for admitting health records into evidence requires that the record be made by a person with knowledge of the acts, events, conditions, opinions, or diagnoses appearing within it. Presumably the physician who signs an entry that he did not author cannot have the requisite knowledge of the acts, events, conditions, opinions, or diagnoses in question—in other words, the physician would not have firsthand knowledge of what transpired to support the entry in the health record. Allowing a physician to sign for another physician therefore raises a question concerning the reliability and integrity of the health record.

As an ordinary matter, health care providers who make an entry in the health record must do so contemporaneously with the actual occurrence of the event.[11] Timeliness matters for both paper-based and electronic health records, with the date and time entered manually for paper-based records and entered automatically in the electronic health record. This need for timeliness is not only critical to delivering quality patient care; it is required as a condition of both licensing and accreditation.

Completeness

Completeness of a health record is a matter addressed by state laws, federal and state regulations, and accrediting standards, as well as a matter of common sense.[12] Without a complete health record, the health care provider's ability to render quality patient care and conduct research and education is impaired. In addition, the health care provider's ability to present a defense in a lawsuit is called into question.

The impact of an incomplete record on a medical malpractice lawsuit is illustrated by *Ravenis v. Detroit General Hospital.*[13] In *Ravenis*, two patients who received cornea transplants from a cadaver subsequently developed ophthalmitis and eventually lost their sight. In the lawsuit the patients brought against the hospital, the evidence indicated that the results of lab tests that had been performed on the deceased and that revealed an acute infection were not made a part of the record at the time the decision to harvest the organs was made. Because the hospital failed to maintain complete records showing the medical history of the eye donor, the jury found the hospital liable for medical malpractice.

Completeness of a health record is measured against the requirements governing health record content examined earlier in this chapter. An incomplete record may be discovered during concurrent or postdischarge review by the health information management department. A health care provider's immediate attention to the deficiencies identified in such a review support a conclusion that the health care provider is documenting the actual treatment rendered rather than making belated entries to support a defense in a lawsuit.

For considerable time, courts have held the opinion that if an event or aspect of patient care was not recorded in the health record, it is appropriate to conclude that it did not occur. This is sometimes phrased as "If it wasn't charted, it didn't happen" or "not documented, not done." The impact of the absence of proper documentation in the health record on the health care provider's defense in a negligence lawsuit is illustrated by *Collins v. Westlake Community Hospital.*[14]

In *Collins*, the plaintiff alleged that the nursing staff's failure to observe and record the condition of his leg while it was in a cast culminated in amputation of the leg. The court examined the plaintiff's health record and noted that no entries were made in the nurses' notes during a critical seven-hour time period, despite a physician's order directing the nursing staff to "watch condition of toes." Testimony by the nurse on duty that a nurse does not always record her observations on the chart every time the patient is checked and that she usually records only abnormal findings, did not overcome the inference that no observations were actually made of the patient.

By contrast, the absence of documentation of patient care was overcome in the case of *Hurlock v. Park Lane Medical Center.*[15] In *Hurlock*, the attending physician had ordered the nursing staff to turn a paraplegic patient every two hours to avoid development of decubitus ulcers. The patient developed decubitus ulcers at multiple sites, which eventually contributed to amputation of her leg.

The health record introduced at trial indicated that the nurses' notes contained only eighteen entries concerning turning the patient. Had the order to turn the patient been complied with and properly documented, the patient's health record should have included 117 such entries in the nurses' notes. This absence of documentation allowed the jury to infer that the nurses had not turned the patient as ordered by the physician. The jury's verdict in the patient's favor was later overturned on appeal because the court determined that the patient had failed to prove definitively that the nurses were negligent.

Although both *Collins* and *Hurlock* resulted in different outcomes, they illustrate the necessity for a complete health record reflecting the patient care rendered, even routine care.

In the twenty-first century, a different concern regarding completeness has emerged: the need to memorialize in the health record the care rendered by health care providers delivered through the electronic means of e-mail, text messaging, and social media. Many health care providers communicate with patients through e-mail, secured text messaging, blogs, wikis, online forums, and video- and/or image-sharing sites, to name only a few examples.

The type of information exchanged through these means determines whether the information should be memorialized as part of the health record. Where the information exchanged constitutes medical information of a general nature, which is not specific to a particular patient's situation and is accessible to many persons in relatively public forums, this information will not require entry into the patient's record. By contrast, information that constitutes **medical advice**, the provision of a professional's opinion about what action an individual should or should not take with regard to their health, will likely require entry into the patient's health record. It is this personalization of content relating to a specific patient's health and course of treatment and care that is the key to deciding whether to include the information in the health record. The fact that this information is exchanged electronically makes it fall into the category of electronic protected health information under HIPAA.[16] Additionally, other statutes, regulations, accrediting and institutional standards may require this information to be placed in an existing patient's health record or require the creation of a health record for a new patient. It is this inclusion in the patient's record that satisfies the requirement for completeness found in the varying statutory, administrative, and institutional provisions governing patient health records.

Corrections to the Record by the Care Provider No matter how careful the health care provider is, at times, details of patient care may be incorrectly recorded. Perhaps the patient information is recorded in the wrong patient's health record or words are misspelled. When these mistakes occur, it is appropriate for the person who made the original entry to make **corrections to the record**.

The proper method to correct a paper-based health record is to draw a single line through the entry and write "error" next to it, along with the date, time, and initials of the person making the correction. The line should be drawn so that whatever was written can be read. Under no circumstances should the original entry be obliterated or covered with correction fluid. Where appropriate, the reason for the correction should be noted, for example, "wrong patient record." Finally, only the individual who made the mistaken entry should correct the entry.

The same principles apply to correction of information stored in an electronic health record. The difference is in the method of making that correction. Typically, the correction is made by way of an addendum to the electronic record. Unlike the paper-based record, the original document in the electronic record is left in an unaltered state. A new document showing the correction is created and added to the electronic record, with a computer code attribute used to reference the original document to the addendum. An **electronic signature** is required to authenticate the addendum. Tracking mechanisms such as a flag or notation may be employed as another way to indicate a correction. Specific guidelines for the correction of electronic health record entries have been issued by standards organizations.[17]

In either a paper-based or electronic health record, data should not be deleted because health care providers may have relied upon certain data in their decision-making process when rendering care. Deletion of this same data would not allow subsequent reviewers of the record to learn to what extent the decision made was based upon the deleted data. Deleting data compromises the integrity of the record and impacts the trustworthiness of the record for evidentiary purposes. Only in the rarest circumstances should deletion of data be permitted, and when permitted, a means to recover the deleted data should be available in the event recovery is necessary. Additional information concerning the record as evidence can be found in Chapter 3, Judicial Process of Health Information.

CRITICAL THINKING

As the text indicates, deleting data in the context of an electronic health record generally means "hiding" data that can later be retrieved as opposed to removing it entirely. Can you think of any instance where data entered into a health record might be considered a mistake that would be a candidate for deletion?

A case illustrating the wrong way to correct the record is *Ahrens v. Katz.*[18] In *Ahrens*, a portion of the nurses' notes had been covered up with correction fluid. To determine what was recorded under the correction fluid, the court allowed x-rays to be taken of notes in question. Testimony at trial indicated that the use of correction fluid to make corrections to the record was not in accordance with correct nursing practices.

A case illustrating the principle that the only individual who should correct the record is the one who made the mistaken entry is *Henry by Henry v. St. John's Hospital.*[19] In *Henry*, a child was born with cerebral palsy, allegedly because of the use of an inappropriate amount of anesthetic. At trial, it became clear that the physician who had administered the anesthetic had corrected the entries made by a nurse concerning the amount of anesthetic given. The court noted that a physician would not ordinarily write on, or correct, nursing notes. Because the physician had altered the entry of another health professional, it created an inference that she was attempting to conceal information and was therefore liable for negligence.

Corrections to the Record by the Patient Although health care providers typically are the individuals who discover the need to correct the record, this is not always the case. For example, the patient who has received a copy of his health record may discover some inaccuracy or incompleteness and may decide to correct the record accordingly. Such correction by the patient is a matter governed by both federal and state law.

HIPAA

The Privacy Rule grants rights to patients to amend their health record.

Federal standards for the privacy of patient-specific health information issued pursuant to the Health Insurance Portability and Accountability Act, also known as the HIPAA Privacy Rule, dictate that an individual possesses a right to have a covered entity[20] amend patient-specific health information or a record about the individual contained in a designated record set for as long as the patient-specific health information is maintained in that record set.[21] If the covered entity grants the amendment request in whole or in part, it must insert or provide a link to the amendment, inform the requestor it has accepted the amendment, and make reasonable efforts to inform other persons identified by the requestor as having previously received patient-specific health information. The covered entity may deny the request for amendment for a limited number of reasons but in doing so must give written notice to the requestor.

The HIPAA Privacy Rule sets a floor requirement for health care providers to respond to patient requests to correct the record. Similar requirements exist at the state level. Where state law requirements are more stringent than those outlined under the federal standards, health care providers must comply with both sets of requirements.

One state statute illustrating the proper method for the patient to correct the record is that of Washington State. Under Washington law, a patient who determines that his record is inaccurate or incomplete may request in writing that the health care provider correct or amend the record.[22] The health care provider then has a limited time frame in which to make the correction or amendment and inform the patient of the action. The procedure to make the correction or amendment involves adding the amending information to the record and marking the challenged entries as corrected or amended entries. The health care provider then must indicate where in the record the corrected or amended information is located.

If the health care provider refuses to make the requested correction or amendment, the health care provider must inform the patient in writing of that decision and of the patient's right to add a statement of disagreement. Upon receipt of a concise statement of the correction or amendment requested and the reasons, the health care provider must file the statement as part of the patient's health record, mark the challenged entry as inaccurate or incomplete according to the patient, and note where in the record the corrected information is located.

The health care provider who fails to comply with these requirements may be subject to liability. State law may permit the patient to bring a lawsuit against the health care provider or facility for noncompliance and receive actual damages along with attorney's fees and costs.[23] Such potential for liability should cause all interested in protecting health information to examine their policies governing patient correction to the health record for compliance with their own state's laws.

RETENTION REQUIREMENTS

Retention of health information has long been influenced by both external and internal forces. Certain statutes and regulations provide specific requirements on record retention. The ability of a health care provider to meet the needs of continuing patient care, education, research, and defense of professional liability actions influences how long health information will be retained. Furthermore, storage constraints, new technology, and fiscal concerns play a role in reaching a decision on this issue. See Figure 8.4.

The health information manager must be able to reconcile these forces when creating effective **record retention policies**. Record retention policies are the general principles determining the length of time health data, and the health records in which those data are stored, must be maintained by the health care provider. For example, should a health information manager choose a form of document imaging rather than retain records in their paper form? If so, what form is cost-effective? Or if electronic health records are the norm, when should the health information manager consider transferring these records to an archival database? Decisions reached on questions like these result in establishment of a **record retention schedule**, a document that details what data will be retained, the retention period, and the manner in which the data will be stored. Data storage choices include paper files, microfilm/microfiche, magnetic tape, optical discs, and electronic systems, including archiving systems. Whatever the choices made, the organization's record retention policy and retention schedule must necessarily addresses legal requirements in addition to institutional needs.

CRITICAL THINKING

As your family and friends learn you are studying health information, some have asked you whether health records ever go away. How would you answer that question?

Statutory and Regulatory Requirements

Health Care Provider's Ability to:
Render continuing patient care
Conduct education and research
Defend a professional liability action

Storage Constraints

New Technology

Fiscal Concerns

Figure 8.4 Forces Influencing Retention of Health Information

Statutes and Regulations

Statutes on the state level and regulations on both the state and federal levels address retention requirements. For example, some state statutes establish specific time frames for which to retain the health record following the death or discharge of a patient.[24] These time frames may differ if the patient is an adult or minor or has a mental disability.[25]

More often, it is regulations rather than statutes that provide the specific time frames. On the federal level, the Conditions of Participation in the Medicare program require hospitals to maintain health records for the period of the state's applicable **statute of limitations** or, if there is no applicable statute, for five years after discharge.[26] For more information concerning statutes of limitation, see Chapter 4, Principles of Liability.

Finally, statutes of limitation in contract and tort actions also influence retention decisions because the ability to defend a lawsuit successfully depends in part on the availability of the health record. An example of the unavailability of a health record to defend a lawsuit is illustrated by *Bondu v. Gurvich*.[27] In *Bondu*, Mrs. Bondu's husband died of a heart attack during the administration of anesthesia as part of heart surgery. When she sought copies of her husband's health record as part of the evidence to support her medical malpractice lawsuit, she discovered that the hospital had either lost or destroyed it.

In addition to suing the hospital and the physicians for medical malpractice, Mrs. Bondu sued the hospital for negligent loss of records. Not only did the court find that state statutes required the hospital to maintain patient records, the court found that state regulations required the hospital to maintain medical and surgical treatment notes and reports as part of the content of the health record. The hospital's inability to produce the records caused a shift in the burden of proof to the hospital to prove that it was not negligent. With this significant change in burden of proof, the court let both claims proceed to trial.

An additional area that deserves attention is the retention of health care business records. These business records may include books of accounts, vouchers, canceled checks, personnel and payroll documents, sales records, compliance documents, and correspondence, to name only some of the many business records in existence in health care organizations today. Retention requirements for these types of records are based on statutes and regulations at both the federal and state levels. As with health data, business record retention policies must encompass all forms of media in which the business record is created or stored, including paper and electronic records.

HIPAA

Although it is typically thought of as addressing individually identifiable patient data, HIPAA also addresses business records, specifying retention periods for those records.

One of the regulations that health care organizations must consider when developing a business record retention policy deals with the HIPAA requirement that covered entities must retain records showing HIPAA compliance for a period of six years.[28] Such records include those documents that demonstrate the integrity and effectiveness of the compliance program and may include audit and monitoring results, internal investigations, hotline reports, documentation of employee training, the original details of the compliance program plus any modifications, and self-disclosures.

Other External Forces

Beyond these strictly legal considerations, other external forces may guide health information managers in developing a retention policy. For example, the health information manager may look to professional organizations for guidance. Along this line, the American Health Information Management Association (AHIMA) recommends a ten-year retention period on adult patient records, measured from the date of the patient's last encounter.[29] Furthermore, AHIMA recognizes that records of minor patients pose special concerns and therefore recommends retaining records until the patient reaches the age of majority plus the statute of limitations period governing medical malpractice lawsuits.

Similarly, the American Hospital Association (AHA) suggests a ten-year retention period for clinical records, again measured from the date of the patient's last encounter.[30] The AHA's policy permits storage of inactive records, either in the hospital or off-site if permitted by law or the appropriate licensing body.

EHR

Record retention issues relating to electronic health records raise concerns about discovery costs.

Another external force that should be considered in a retention discussion is new technology. The increased use of electronic health records has caused many in the health care field to reconsider policies related to record retention. In contrast to paper-based records, EHRs offer the advantage of not requiring as much physical storage space. Guidelines that address creating, identifying, retaining, retrieving, and destroying electronic data are listed in Figure 8.5. Because of the storage space advantage, many health care providers are tempted to retain electronically stored information (ESI) longer than required by statute or regulation. The difficulty that arises from taking such an approach is that unwarranted retention of ESI can result in massive amounts of information that must be searched and produced in response to discovery requests. In turn, the health care provider incurs significant expenses in complying with these discovery requests. Accordingly, retention policies governing EHRs should address what information should be retained and for how long, just as policies governing paper-based records do. For more information concerning electronic health records, review Chapter 13, Electronic Health Records.

One emerging development to combat the potential for increased costs associated with the legal discovery process of EHRs is **enterprise content and record management** (ECRM). ECRM

1. **An organization should have reasonable policies and procedures for managing its information and records.**
   a. Information and records management is important in the electronic age.
   b. The hallmark of an organization's information and records management policies should be reasonableness.
   c. Defensible policies need not mandate the retention of all information and documents.
2. **An organization's information and records management policies and procedures should be realistic, practical and tailored to the circumstances of the organization.**
   a. No single standard or model can fully meet an organization's unique needs.
   b. Information and records management requires practical, flexible and scalable solutions that address the differences in an organization's business needs, operations, IT infrastructure and regulatory and legal responsibilities.
   c. An organization must assess its legal requirements for retention and destruction in developing an information and records management policy.
   d. An organization should assess the operational and strategic value of its information and records in developing an information and records management program.
   e. A business continuation or disaster recovery plan has different purposes from those of an information and records management program.
3. **An organization need not retain all electronic information ever generated or received.**
   a. Destruction is an acceptable stage in the information life cycle; an organization may destroy or delete electronic information when there is no continuing value or need to retain it.
   b. Systematic deletion of electronic information is not synonymous with evidence spoliation.
   c. Absent a legal requirement to the contrary, organizations may adopt programs that routinely delete certain recorded communications, such as electronic mail, instant messaging, text messaging and voice-mail.
   d. Absent a legal requirement to the contrary, organizations may recycle or destroy hardware or media that contain data retained for business continuation or disaster recovery purposes.
   e. Absent a legal requirement to the contrary, organizations may systematically delete or destroy residual, shadowed or deleted data.
   f. Absent a legal requirement to the contrary, organizations are not required to preserve metadata.
4. **An organization adopting an information and records management policy should also develop procedures that address the creation, identification, retention, retrieval and ultimate disposition or destruction of information and records.**
   a. Information and records management policies must be put into practice.
   b. Information and records management policies and practices should be documented.
   c. An organization should define roles and responsibilities for program direction and administration within its information and records management policies.
   d. An organization should guide employees regarding how to identify and maintain information that has a business purpose or is required to be maintained by law or regulation.
   e. An organization may choose to define separately the roles and responsibilities of content and technology custodians for electronic records management.
   f. An organization should consider the impact of technology (including potential benefits) on the creation, retention and destruction of information and records.
   g. An organization should recognize the importance of employee education concerning its information and records management program, policies and procedures.
   h. An organization should consider conducting periodic compliance reviews of its information and records management policies and procedures, and responding to the findings of those reviews as appropriate.
   i. Policies and procedures regarding electronic management and retention should be coordinated and/or integrated with the organization's policies regarding the use of property and information, including applicable privacy rights or obligations.
   j. Policies and procedures should be revised as necessary in response to changes in workforce or organizational structure, business practices, legal or regulatory requirements and technology.
5. **An organization's policies and procedures must mandate the suspension of ordinary destruction practices and procedures as necessary to comply with preservation obligations related to actual or reasonably anticipated litigation, government investigation or audit.**
   a. An organization must recognize that suspending the normal disposition of electronic information and records may be necessary in certain circumstances.

Figure 8.5 The Sedona Guidelines for Managing Information and Records in the Electronic Age
Source: Reprinted with the permission of The Sedona Conference® (www.thesedonaconference.org).

b. An organization's information and records management program should anticipate circumstances that will trigger the suspension of normal destruction procedures.
c. An organization should indentify persons with authority to suspend normal destruction procedures and impose a legal hold.
d. An organization's information and records management procedures should recognize and may describe the process for suspending normal records and information destruction and indentify the individuals responsible for implementing a legal hold.
e. Legal holds and procedures should be appropriately tailored to the circumstances.
f. Effectively communicating notice of a legal hold should be an essential component of an organization's information and records management program.
g. Documenting the steps taken to implement a legal hold may be beneficial.
h. If an organization takes reasonable steps to implement a legal hold, it should not be held responsible for the acts of an individual acting outside the scope of authority and/or in a manner inconsistent with the legal hold notice.
i. Legal holds are exceptions to ordinary retention practices and when the exigency underlying the hold no longer exists (*i.e.*, there is no continuing duty to preserve the information), organizations are free to lift the legal hold.

Figure 8.5 Continued

addresses both electronic records management principles (all of the digital and analog records) and enterprise content management principles (the technology, tools, and methods to capture, store, deliver, and preserve content across an enterprise). ECRM encompasses both traditional health record management plus management of newer clinical content (e.g., e-mail, voice, text, and speech files) and nonclinical content (e.g., financial and administrative data). By viewing all data and records from an enterprise perspective, retention of data and records is managed systematically, and the potential increases for a more streamlined process of responding to e-discovery requests.

Bases for Decision

As this discussion demonstrates, there is no answer to the question of how long health records should be retained. Under the reasoning of the *Bondu* case, it is clear that institutions should strive to retain their records for a minimum of the period specified under statute and regulation. Retaining health records beyond that period should be decided based on medical and administrative needs, along with fiscal, technological, and storage constraints.

RECORD DESTRUCTION

Each institution that retains health records faces the prospect of destroying those records at some future date. When that time arrives, the institution should have in place a policy governing destruction. Destruction of health records occurs in any of three instances as outlined in Figure 8.6 and as described in the following paragraphs.

Destruction in Ordinary Course

Record destruction policies should address, at minimum, the controlling statute and/or regulation. These controlling statutes and regulations may specify or recommend the method of destruction, for example, shredding, burning, or recycling.[31] Some laws may also require the hospital to create an abstract of patient data before destroying the patient's record.[32] Other state laws may require the facility to notify the patient or the licensing authority before destroying the patient's record.[33]

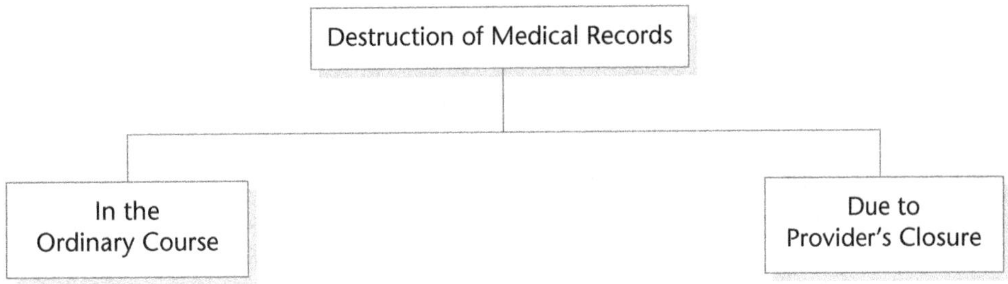

Figure 8.6 Instances of Destruction of Health Records

> **HIPAA**
>
> The Security Rule's requirement for effective information security policies encompasses the concept of handling data destruction.

One controlling regulation is the HIPAA Security Rule. This rule establishes a requirement for effective information security policies.[34] Because information security policies provide answers to the "who, what, where, when, why, and how" questions of information security, they cover the issue of destruction of protected health information. As a general rule, data are only destroyed after the retention period has expired, using only those methods specified in an information security policy. With regard to data stored in paper-based records, such methods may include dissolving the records in acid or burning, pulverizing, or shredding the records with the result that the data is unreadable, indecipherable, or otherwise cannot be reconstructed prior to being placed in a dumpster or other trash receptacle. With regard to data stored in electronic media, such methods may include clearing (using software or hardware products to overwrite media with nonsensitive data), purging (magnetic degaussing), and destruction of media (disintegration, pulverization, melting, incinerating, or shredding).[35]

The obligation to destroy protected health information properly applies not only to patient records but also to media such as computers, photocopy machines, facsimile machines, smartphones, and tablet devices if they contain protected health information (PHI). Before this hardware is disposed of or reused, any PHI should be removed from the hardware in one or more of the manners listed above for destruction of PHI in electronic record form.[36]

No matter what method is selected, the paramount concern should be one of keeping the contents of the record confidential, as required by the HIPAA Privacy Rule. Failure to maintain confidentiality can result in civil fines and punishments. The *CVS Pharmacy* case illustrates this peril. In *CVS*, pharmacy employees in several different locations disposed of old prescription data, including prescription bottles with labels, by tossing them in the dumpster. After media reports surfaced that protected health information (PHI) subject to HIPAA protection was easily available to any person willing to dive into a trash dumpster to retrieve the information, the Office of Civil Rights of the U.S. Department of Health and Human Services joined forces with the Federal Trade Commission to investigate. The investigation determined that *CVS* had failed to implement adequate policies and procedures governing disposal of PHI, failed to adequately train its staff on proper disposal methods, and failed to maintain and implement a sanctions policy for staff who failed to dispose of PHI properly. In addition to a multimillion-dollar fine, *CVS* was directed to correct its failings, institute internal monitoring, engage a third-party assessor to conduct compliance assessments, and submit compliance reports for a three-year period.[37]

Institutions may attempt to protect the confidentiality of PHI by destroying the records internally or by using a commercial contractor that is subject to stringent restrictions. If a commercial contractor is involved, the institution should include restrictions in the written contract that specify the method of destruction, the safeguards to be employed, the indemnification provided in the event of an unauthorized disclosure, and the certification procedure indicating that the records received were properly destroyed.[38]

Whether destroyed internally or externally, the institution should retain permanent evidence of the record's destruction in the ordinary course of business. This permanent evidence would most likely be a **certificate of destruction** (COD), a document that shows what data and records were destroyed, who destroyed those data and records, and the method used for that destruction. Such certificates are particularly important if the destruction is performed by a third party pursuant to an outsourcing contract, because the health care organization possesses a duty to ensure that the contracting agent follows the instructions outlined in the contract's terms for handling and processing data and records. These certificates also serve the purpose of defending a health care provider in an investigation before a governmental agency or in a medical malpractice lawsuit in which the absence of a health record is an issue.

Failure to retain a certificate of destruction of health records opens the health care provider to a charge that an individual record was destroyed for suspicious reasons, such as to gain advantage in a lawsuit. Just such a claim was made in *Carr v. St. Paul Fire & Marine Insurance.*[39] In *Carr*, the hospital briefly treated the patient in the emergency department and then sent him home. Shortly after returning home from the emergency department, the patient died. Because the hospital could not produce the emergency department record upon request or show that it had been destroyed in the ordinary course of business, it was accused of destroying the patient's record contrary to acceptable hospital practice. This claim went to trial, and the jury was allowed to infer that the destroyed record may have shown evidence of a medical emergency necessitating further care than that provided by the hospital staff.

As the *Carr* case illustrates, destruction of records in other than the ordinary course of business may result in civil liability. Criminal liability may also apply if the destruction is for the purpose of concealing responsibility for a patient's illness, injury, or death.[40] Finally, health care providers should not destroy records currently involved in litigation, audits, or investigations, even if the retention period would otherwise have ended, because of the possibility of civil or criminal penalties. Such concerns are particularly acute when the health care provider is the subject of litigation because a litigation hold will become effective, causing any destruction of health data or records to be considered suspicious activity or spoliation of evidence.

Destruction Due to Ownership Change

Destruction of health data and records may also occur because of a change in ownership of a health care provider or organization. Contrary to the reality of decades past, many providers and organizations of the twenty-first century participate in numerous ownership arrangements. These arrangements frequently specify that health data and records are considered the property and assets of the owners and are subject to the contractual terms upon which the owners have agreed. When one of the owners dies, retires, or otherwise ceases to participate in ownership by leaving the practice or organization, the terms of the contractual agreement will address what happens to the health data and records the departing owner created, including whether the data or records will be destroyed.

ETHICS

Professional associations often offer guidance concerning the ethical duty of the health care provider who dies, retires, or otherwise ceases practice.

In addition to the contractual terms, health care providers are also guided by the licensing authorities and the ethical principles of their respective profession. For example, state licensing authorities may specify that the health care provider offer the patient the opportunity to receive either the original or copies of the health record before it is destroyed. Similarly, the American Medical Association provides guidance through its Code of Ethics and interprets opinions to the effect that the physician must inform the patient about the change in practice status and offer the patient the opportunity to forward his health records to the physician's new place of practice.[41]

HIPAA

Ownership change meets the definition of health care operations under HIPAA.

Where health data and records are transferred rather than destroyed due to an ownership change, health care providers and organizations can be guided by the HIPAA Privacy Rule. This rule addresses the sale, transfer, merger, or consolidation of all or part of a covered entity with another covered entity and defines it as part of the business management and general administrative activities of the covered entity. As such, the patient's authorization is not required before the data and records are transferred from one covered entity to another.[42]

Destruction Due to Closure

Destruction of the health record may be necessary after a health care institution closes or a medical practice dissolves. Health care providers generally are liable for accidental or incidental disclosure of health information at such a time.

State laws and regulations vary on how a health care provider should handle this situation. Some states recommend that the health care provider transfer health records to another health care provider, while other states recommend delivery of health records to the state licensing authority for storage.[43] Some states require the health care provider to notify the appropriate licensing authority before taking action.[44]

Additionally, if the health care provider offered alcohol and/or drug abuse services, the health information manager should examine federal regulations governing these areas to determine how to proceed. These regulations require health care providers to obtain the patient's written authorization before transferring records to an acquiring program or any other program named in the authorization. If transfer has not been authorized and records must be retained for a period specified by law, the records must be placed in a sealed envelope or other container and labeled as follows:

> *Record of [insert name of program] required to be maintained under [insert citation to statute, regulation, court order or other legal authority requiring that records be kept] until a date not later than [insert appropriate date].*[45]

These sealed records must be held confidential under the procedures outlined in the regulations until the end of the retention period. At that time, the records may be destroyed.

Further information concerning the special handling of alcohol/drug abuse records is discussed in Chapter 11, Specialized Patient Records.

If the health care provider closes due to filing for bankruptcy protection under Chapter 7 (Liquidation), Chapter 9 (Adjustment of Debts of a Municipality), or Chapter 11 (Reorganization), federal laws and rules provide guidance concerning how to handle the situation. The Bankruptcy Abuse Prevention and Consumer Protection Act of 2005 (BAPCPA) and Federal Rules of Bankruptcy Procedure inform the case trustee, a person appointed by the court to make administrative decisions on behalf of the bankrupt health care provider, of what actions to take and how to reconcile those actions with other federal and state laws and regulations.[46] The provisions specifically direct the trustee to notify patients to claim their health records, and if not claimed within the requisite time frame, to request a federal agency to accept the patient records. If the federal agency declines to accept the records, the trustee shall destroy the patient records. These and other situations present complexities for the health care provider and the health information manager to address when considering data and record destruction due to closure.

CONCLUSION

The legal requirements governing the content, retention, and destruction of health information most closely resemble a patchwork quilt: various federal and state laws and regulations address issues central to these health information matters. No single reliable scheme exists that addresses all of the issues contained in this chapter.

Until one such scheme exists, health information managers must review and understand those legal requirements that apply to their particular situation. A review of the legal requirements should begin with the applicable statutes and regulations. The review should also include quasi-legal requirements such as accrediting and institutional standards and professional guidelines. Health information managers must then incorporate these legal and quasi-legal requirements into policy, balancing these factors against the functions and uses of health information and practical concerns, such as storage constraints. Striking such a balance should lead to policies that are not only legally sound but realistic and practical.

CASE STUDY

You are the director of health information at a large medical center that offers inpatient, outpatient, and emergency care at several sites in one state. Your medical center has announced that it will acquire a facility offering similar services in a neighboring state. The laws and regulations governing the retention and destruction of health records differ between these states. Discuss how the lack of a consistent set of laws and regulations on these two matters affects the institution you serve, and outline the steps you will take to deal with the situation.

REVIEW QUESTIONS

1. Compare and contrast the clinical uses of a health record with the secondary purposes of a health record.
2. How does a health record serve as a legal document?
3. Name the five sources that serve as legal requirement for health record content.
4. Does one need to look to both federal and state regulations to determine standards for health record content?
5. Is it legally proper for a physician in a group practice to sign medical entries made by another physician in the same practice? Why or why not?
6. How can an electronic health record be corrected?
7. Explain the concept of an amendment to the record under the HIPAA Privacy Rule.
8. What legal requirements apply to a record retention policy?
9. What is a certificate of destruction?
10. Why is a certificate of destruction important?
11. Will civil or criminal liability apply to a health care institution that destroys a record in other than the ordinary course? Why?
12. Do federal regulations decide how records involving treatment of alcohol and/or drug abuse should be handled when a health care facility closes?

ENRICHMENT ACTIVITY

Review the record retention requirements for the Medicare Conditions of Participation and the statutes and regulations for your state. Develop a record retention policy for a fictional hospital that complies with those requirements. With the applications of new technologies to health information management, can you see any inadequacies in those requirements?

ENRICHMENT ACTIVITY

Discuss with a fellow student the functions and uses of a health record. With the permission of the administration of a local health care facility, jointly survey members of the facility staff to determine their awareness of the functions and uses of a health record. Do not limit your survey to health information department staff. Categorize your results by department. Share those results with the facility's administration and health information department manager. Present recommendations, if survey results so indicate, to educate facility staff as to the functions and uses of the health record. If it is impractical to survey a local health care facility, arrange with the permission of your faculty advisor or department chair to survey other students at your educational institution to determine their awareness of the functions and uses of a health record. Share those results with your instructor, and brainstorm what efforts you can make to raise awareness of the functions and uses of the health record among the student population.

NOTES

1. For example, Missouri regulations specify the contents of a health record in the hospital context to include a unique identifying record number; pertinent identifying and personal data; history of present illness or complaint; past history; family history; physical examination; provisional admitting diagnosis; medical staff orders; progress notes; nurses' notes; discharge summary; final diagnosis and evidence of informed consent. Where applicable, medical records shall contain reports such as clinical laboratory, x-ray, consultation, electrocardiogram, surgical procedures, therapy, anesthesia, pathology, autopsy, and any other reports pertinent to the patient's care. Mo. Code Regs. tit. 19, § 30-20.094 (9) (2019).

2. 42 U.S.C. § 1395x(e) (2) (2019).

3. *See, e.g.*, N.J. Rev. Stat. Ann. § 26:8-5 (2019) (requiring institutions treating disease to "make a complete medical record covering the period of such person's confinement ..."); N.Y. Pub. Health Law § 4165 (Consol. 2019) (requiring health care providers to "make, at the time of their admittance, a record of all the personal and statistical particulars relative to the patients and inmates in their institutions ...").

4. Tenn. Code Ann. § 68-11-302 (2019).

5. 42 C.F.R. § 482.24 (2019).

6. *See, e.g.*, Mass. Regs. Code tit. 105, § 130.200 (2019); Mont. Admin. R. 37.106.704 (2019).

7. Alaska Stat. § 18.20.080 (2019); N.H. Rev. Stat. § 151:5-b (2019).

8. Joint Commission, Comprehensive Accreditation Manual for Hospitals, Management of Information, IM 6.10 (2003) (these characteristics include not only those items specified in the Medicare Conditions of Participation, but also include items such as evidence of known advance directives, patient-generated information [e.g., information entered into the record over the Web or in previsit computer systems], and details of emergency, operative, and anesthetic care); DNV Healthcare's NIAHO Accreditation Requirements, Medical Record Service §26, MR 2, 5, & 7 (2019).

9. The American Health Information Management Association, http://www.ahima.org.

10. *See, e.g.*, Mo. Code Regs. tit. 19, § 30-20.11(5) (2019).

11. *See, e.g.*, Miss. Code Ann. § 41-9-63 (2019); Mo. Code Regs. tit. 19, § 30-20.094(2) (2019); Joint Commission, Comprehensive Accreditation Manual for Hospitals, Management of Information IM 6.10 (2003); DNV Healthcare's NIAHO Accreditation Requirements, Medical Record Service §26, MR 5 (2014).

12. *See, e.g.*, 42 C.F.R. § 405.1722(c) (2019) (Medicare Conditions of Participation); Joint Commission, Comprehensive Accreditation Manual for Hospitals, Management of Information, IM 6.10-.60 (2003); DNV Healthcare's NIAHO Accreditation Requirements, Medical Record Service §26, MR 2 (2019).

13. 234 N.W.2d 411 (Mich. Ct. App. 1976).

14. 312 N.E.2d 614 (Ill. 1974).

15. 709 S.W.2d 872 (Mo. Ct. App. 1986).

16. 45 CFR § 164.105(a)(2)(i)(D) (2019).

17. Health Level Seven, EHR-S Records Management and Evidentiary Support (RM-ES) functional profile, http://www.HL7.org.

18. 595 F. Supp 1108 (N.D. Ga. 1984).

19. 512 N.E.2d 1042, 1044 (Ill. App. 1987).

20. *Covered entity* refers to health plans, health care clearinghouses, and health care providers who submit certain transactions electronically. 42 U.S.C. § 1320d (2019).

21. 45 C.F.R. § 164.526 (2019).

22. The Uniform Health Care Information Act, Wash. Rev. Code Ann. § 70.02.100,110 (West 2019).

23. Wash. Rev. Code Ann. § 70.02.170 (West 2019).

24. *See, e.g.,* Alaska Stat. § 18.20.085 (2019) (seven years); Haw. Rev. Stat. § 622-58 (2019) (seven years); Mass. Gen. Laws Ann. ch. 111, § 70 (2019) (thirty years); N.J. Rev. Stat. Ann. § 26:8-5 (2019) (ten years for the entire record; twenty years for the discharge summary); Or. Admin. R. 333-700-0090 (2019) (seven years); Tenn. Code Ann. § 68-11-305 (2019) (ten years).

25. *See* Miss. Code Ann. § 41-9-69 (2019); (retain for a period of minority plus seven years, not to exceed twenty-eight years); Tenn. Code Ann. § 68-11-305 (2019); (retain for a period of minority or mental disability, plus one year or ten years following discharge, whichever is longer).

26. 42 C.F.R. § 405.1722(d) (2019).

27. 473 So.2d 1307 (Fla. Dist. Ct. App. 1984).

28. 45 C.F.R. §§ 164.316(b) & 164.530(j)(2) (2019).

29. American Health Information Management Association, Practice Brief: Retention and Destruction of Health Information (Updated 2013).

30. American Hospital Ass'n, Statement on Preservation of Medical Records.

31. *See* 45 C.F.R. §164.530(c) (shredding or recycling) (2019); Tenn. Code Ann. § 68-11-305(c) (1) (2019) (shredding or burning).

32. *See* Miss. Code Ann. § 41-9-75 (2019); Tenn. Code Ann. § 68-11-306 (2019).

33. *See, e.g.,* Md. Health-Gen. Code Ann. § 4-403(c) (2019) (if health care provider dies, administrator of estate must send notice of destruction, along with statement that patient may retrieve record within thirty days of destruction, by first-class mail to the patient's last known address); Or. Admin. R. 333-700-0090 (2019) (written approval of Health Division required before a renal dialysis facility may destroy patient records).

34. 45 C.F.R. § 164.302 et al. (2019).

35. 45 C.F.R. § 164.310(d)(2)(i) (2019).

36. 45 C.F.R. § 164.530(c) (2019).

37. https://www.hhs.gov/hipaa/for-professionals/compliance-enforcement/examples/cvs/index.html. (Last accessed July 27, 2019.)

38. Jonathan P. Tomes, *Healthcare Records: A Practical Legal Guide* (Kendall Hunt Publishing Co. for Healthcare Financial Management Association 1990).

39. 384 F. Supp. 821 (W.D. Ark. 1974).

40. Md. Health-Gen. Code Ann. § 4-401 (2019) (making concealment or destruction a misdemeanor offense); Mich. Comp. Laws § 750.492(a) (2019) (making such destruction of public records a felony offense).

41. American Medical Association (2005), *Opinion E-7.03: Records of Physicians upon Retirement or Departure from a Group*; available at http://www.ama-assn.org.

42. 45 C.F.R. §§ 164.501 &.506 (2019).

43. *See, e.g.,* Miss. Code Ann. § 41-9-79 (2019) (recommending transfer of record to other hospital; if none available, to licensing agency); Tenn. Code Ann. § 68-11-308 (2019) (requiring delivery of hospital records to Department of Health and Environment).

44. Alaska Stat. § 18.20.085(c) (2019) (requiring hospitals to make immediate arrangements to preserve records, subject to Department of Health and Social Services' approval); Haw. Rev. Stat. § 622-58(e) (2019) (same).

45. 42 C.F.R. Ch. 1, Part 2, § 2.19(b) (2019).

46. 11 U.S.C. § 351 (2019).

CHAPTER 9

CONFIDENTIALITY AND INFORMED CONSENT

LEARNING OBJECTIVES

After reading this chapter, the learner should be able to:

1. Explain the interrelationship between confidentiality and privacy.
2. Discuss the four sources of law on which the right of privacy is based.
3. Compare and contrast open record statutes and privacy statutes.
4. Explain the use and application of the physician–patient privilege.
5. Describe the types of restrictions that confidentiality statutes and ethical guidelines place on HIV/AIDS information.
6. Trace the historical development of the informed consent doctrine.
7. Explain the concept of substituted consent.
8. Discuss the application of substituted consent to minor patients.
9. Define the term advance directive.
10. List the obligations placed on health care providers by the Patient Self-Determination Act.
11. Distinguish between living wills and durable powers of attorney for health care.
12. Discuss the legal protections afforded to health care providers when treating patients in an emergency situation.
13. Compare and contrast the professional disclosure standard and the reasonable patient standard.

KEY CONCEPTS

Advance directives
Confidentiality
De-identified health information
Durable power of attorney
Emancipation
Ethical guidelines
Express consent
Implied consent
Informed consent
Living will
Open record statutes
Physician–patient privilege
Privacy
Privacy statutes
Professional disclosure standard
Psychiatric advance directive
Reasonable patient standard
Substituted consent
Tacit consent

INTRODUCTION

One striking development in the delivery of health care during the twentieth century concerned confidentiality. **Confidentiality** refers to the obligation of the health care provider to maintain patient information in a manner that will not permit dissemination beyond the health care provider. From its origin in professional practice to its development into legal protections, the concept of confidentiality has served to protect patient-specific health information from disclosure. Not only have those involved with direct patient care served to protect health information but health information managers have assumed responsibility for protecting confidential patient-specific health information. Actions by both groups to maintain confidentiality have become increasingly difficult, as demands for patient-specific information increase.

Demands for information arise not only from third-party payers and governmental entities, but also from patients themselves when deciding to consent to or forgo treatment. This demand for information has initiated a significant development in the relationship between law and medicine: the doctrine of **informed consent**.

To understand the responsibilities that confidentiality and informed consent place on health care providers, health information professionals must understand the historical development of each concept. From there, this chapter then examines the legal bases for confidentiality and the scope of the informed consent doctrine.

CONFIDENTIALITY

When addressing issues of confidentiality of patient-specific health information, the focus rests on the relationship between the patient and the health care provider. Through this relationship, the patient imparts to the health care provider information that will assist her in diagnosing and treating the patient's symptoms. This dialogue between the patient and health care provider is beneficial in two respects: the health care provider gathers the data needed to make informed diagnoses and treatment decisions, and the patient provides the necessary information without fear that it will be disseminated beyond the health care provider. (See Figure 9.1.)

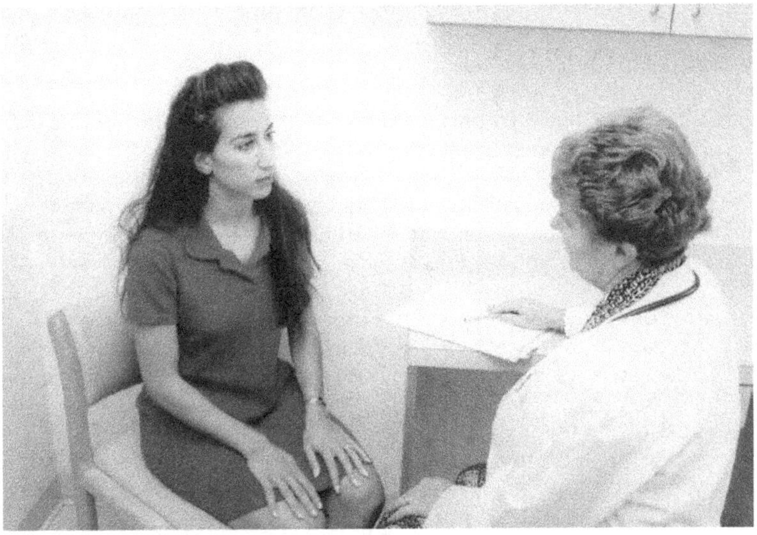

Figure 9.1 The Health Care Provider–Patient Relationship

The obligation of health care providers to maintain patient information in a confidential manner is as old as medicine itself. The Oath of Hippocrates, written centuries ago, states: "What I may see or hear in the course of the treatment or even outside the treatment in regard to the life of men, which on no account one must noise abroad, I will keep to myself holding such things shameful to be spoken about."[1] The Hippocratic Oath has served as the foundation of the current medical professions' guidelines on the confidentiality of health information.[2] (See Figure 9.2.) Over time, several alternatives to the Hippocratic Oath have emerged, each addressing the issue of holding patient information in confidence. Some of these alternative oaths are used in medical schools in lieu of the Hippocratic Oath.

With the development of the health care industry in the past century, particularly the significant changes in medical technology, the growth of government participation in health care, and the emergence of the central role of third-party payers, the amount and type of available patient-specific health information has greatly expanded. In the light of these developments, society has recognized the need for more than professionalism to protect patient-specific health information. Thus, a complex web has arisen of legal protections for patient-specific health information.

As a general matter, the underpinning to legal protections for patient-specific health information is the patient's right to **privacy**. This right to privacy is sometimes referred to as the right to be let alone and other times as the right to control personal information, depending on the source of law on which the right is based. The following sources form the foundation for rights to privacy: constitutional provisions, statutory provisions, common law provisions, and international provisions as illustrated in Figure 9.3.

> I swear by Apollo Physician and Asclepias and Hygieia and Panaceia and all the gods and goddesses, making them my witness, that I will fulfill according to my ability and judgment this oath and this covenant:
>
> I will apply dietetic measures for the benefit of the sick according to my ability and judgment; I will keep them from harm and injustice.
>
> I will neither give a deadly drug to anybody if asked for it, nor will I make a suggestion to this effect. Similarly, I will not give to a woman an abortive remedy. In purity and holiness I will guard my life and art.
>
> I will not use the knife, not even on sufferers from stone, but will withdraw in favor of such men as are engaged in this work.
>
> Whatever house I may visit, I will come for the benefit of the sick, remaining free of intentional injustices, of all mischief and in particular of sexual relations with both female and male persons, be they free or slaves.
>
> What I may see or hear in the course of the treatment or even outside of the treatment in regard to the life of men, in which on no account one must noise abroad, I will keep to myself holding such things shameful to be spoken about.
>
> If I fulfill this oath and do not violate it, may it be granted to me to enjoy life and art, being honored with fame among all men for all time to come; if I transgress it and swear falsely, may the opposite of all this be my lot.

Figure 9.2 Hippocratic Oath

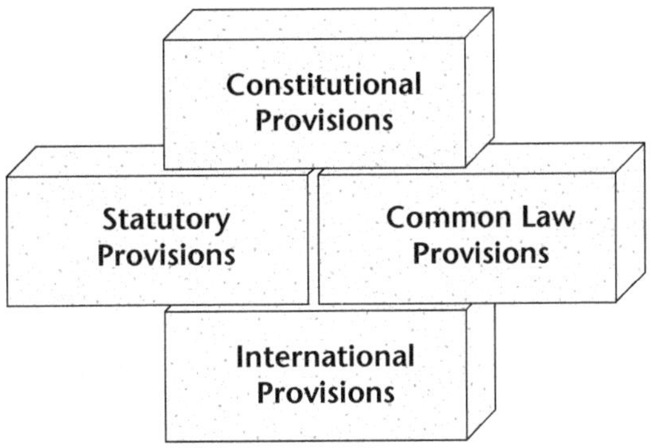

Figure 9.3 Foundation for the Rights to Privacy

Constitutional Basis

Any analysis of constitutional protections must begin with the constitution of the U.S. government. While the right to privacy is not explicitly listed in the U.S. Constitution, the U.S. Supreme Court has held that a fundamental right to privacy exists. Although the scope of the privacy right has never been clearly defined by the Supreme Court, the Court has applied it in the context of health information.

In *Whalen v. Roe*,[3] the Supreme Court examined the right to privacy in the context of New York State's effort to collect a computerized database concerning the use of certain drugs labeled as dangerous and likely to be abused. Under New York law, physicians were required to report to the state department of health the patient's name, age, and address, the names of the pharmacy and physician, and the dosage of the drug if one of the listed drugs was prescribed.

Several groups representing patients who had received the prescriptions and two physicians' associations challenged the law on grounds that it invaded the patients' privacy. In determining whether the reporting requirements amounted to a constitutional violation of the right to privacy, the Court applied a two-prong analysis relating to the patient's interests: (1) a nondisclosure prong that recognized the individual's interest in avoiding disclosure of personal matters and (2) an individual autonomy prong that recognized the individual's interest in independent decision making. The Court recognized that both patient interests existed and then balanced these interests against the state's interest in deterring drug abuse and the safeguards implemented to protect the information from subsequent disclosure. On balance, the Court concluded that the public's need for information outweighed the individual's privacy interests.

While specific to the facts of the case, the *Whalen* decision is significant for the fact that the Supreme Court recognized in it a right to informational privacy. The contours of this new right have never been fully explained, however, and are subject to further definition at the federal level. This right to privacy has also been recognized at the state level, with some states providing more explicit constitutional privacy protections than that of the federal government.[4]

Statutory Basis

At both the federal and state levels, the right to privacy has been recognized by the respective legislatures. The statutes created focus on the type of records involved, the limits placed on the use of the protected records, and whether the government or the private sector is involved.

Federal Level

Central to the federal government's efforts have been the Freedom of Information Act (FOIA)[5] and the Privacy Act of 1974.[6] Both laws apply to governmental record-keeping activities and do not focus on the activities of the private sector. The FOIA encourages access to government records and mandates disclosure upon request, absent an exception listed in the statute. By contrast, the Privacy Act presumes that certain information is confidential and may not be disclosed unless there is written consent of the individual.

In the health care arena, these provisions come into play in the context of data held by the Social Security Administration (SSA) and the Department of Health and Human Services (DHHS). Both executive branch agencies release information held by them for purposes of research and statistical studies. When releasing these data, the agencies abide by the statutory provisions listed earlier, including removing patient-identifying data.

Additional federal statutory confidentiality protections include the limited disclosure provisions governing drug and alcohol abuse treatment and participation in the Medicaid program.[7] These protections apply to health care providers in the private sector who accept federal funds. For more information concerning restrictions on drug and alcohol abuse treatment programs, see Chapter 11, Specialized Patient Records.

Confidentiality restrictions placed on health information are sometimes present in statutes that on their face do not appear to relate to patient care or health information management. For example, the Bankruptcy Abuse Prevention and Consumer Protection Act (BAPCPA) of 2005 addresses multiple changes in the activities involved in bankruptcy cases. One such change involves the authority of courts to appoint a patient care ombudsman for those health care businesses who file for bankruptcy protection. The ombudsman is subject to specific provisions under BAPCPA and the Federal Rules of Bankruptcy Procedure to maintain confidential patient information relating to the patient records of the health care business who is the subject of the bankruptcy.[8]

State Level

Confidentiality protections at the state level fall into three categories: open record statutes, physician–patient privileges statutes, and privacy statutes. **Open record statutes** generally apply to records held by a state agency and correspond with the principles of FOIA: a presumption of disclosure absent a statutory exemption.[9] The **physician–patient privilege** applies to the introduction of evidence at trial and is used to prevent the forced disclosure or testimony about information obtained by the health care provider during the course of treatment. The privilege exists to encourage the patient's disclosure of relevant information to the health care provider, no matter if that information is of an embarrassing or humiliating nature.[10] The privilege applies to both the governmental and private sectors and is generally held to rest with the patient but may be asserted on the patient's behalf by the health care provider to prevent forced disclosure.

Privacy statutes in most states generally correspond with the principles of the Privacy Act: a presumption of confidentiality, which may be rebutted with evidence of patient authorization to disclose information.[11] Privacy statutes at the state level may impose fines on health care facilities that breach confidentiality and allow fines to be assessed for each unauthorized access to confidential patient information.[12] Newly passed legislation in California, the Consumer Privacy Act of 2018, offers a wide array of protections to California residents and may become a model for other states. This act establishes a broad definition of personal information to include any "information that identifies, relates to, describes, is capable of being associated with, or could reasonably be linked directly or indirectly" with a person to be considered personal information worthy of legal protection.[13] This definition expands the concept of personal information warranting protection to include almost anything not already accessible to the public.

The significance of the Act is that the protections it affords apply to every California resident, regardless of whether (1) the citizen is acting in a traditional manner as a consumer or when acting as an employee, patient, tenant, or student; and (2) the geographic area in which the California resident receives care. This means that if a California resident is treated at a health care facility located in any other state in the United States and that health care facility suffers a data breach, California law will apply concerning the breach of that California resident's data.

The California Consumer Privacy Act grants an array of rights, including rights to be informed about what kinds of personal data companies have collected, why the data was collected, and to request deletion of personal information.[14] Significantly, the Act provides consumers with a right to statutory to damages, which means the California resident does not need to have suffered actual harm in the event of a data breach, merely that a data breach occurred, entitling her to statutory damages. [15]

Common Law Basis

Common law protections of health information essentially recognize the individual's right to bring a lawsuit for damages or injunctive relief against one who inappropriately obtains, discloses, or uses patient-specific health information. Examples of lawsuits of this type include actions for invasion of privacy, defamation, and breach of contract. Each of these lawsuits is described in detail in Chapter 4, Principles of Liability.

International Basis

Significant upgrades to data protection laws have taken place in the European Union (EU), the most significant of which is the General Data Protection Regulation (GDPR). Like the California Consumer Privacy Act, the GDPR expands the definition of what constitutes personal data that must be protected. The GDPR defines personal data as "any information relating to an identified or identifiable natural person" and mentions a wide array of factors, including the "physical, psychological, genetic, mental, economic, cultural, or social identity" of the person in question.[16] If an EU citizen interacted in anyway with a health care provider located in the United States, the provisions of the GDPR would apply, including the need to notify the patient of a data breach within seventy-two hours of its occurrence. While most U.S. health care providers do not treat EU citizens, some do and for those health care providers, the GDPR applies.

Confidentiality Application

Persons sometimes use the terms *confidentiality* and *privacy* loosely, interchanging them as though they possess the same meaning. As the definitions indicate, they are separate but related concepts. It is helpful to distinguish between these terms by referring to privacy as a right belongs to the patient and confidentiality as a duty belongs to the health care provider. Alternatively, one can view privacy as the patient looking inward, protecting information that belongs to her; one can view confidentiality as the outward-looking activity of the health care provider to not disseminate information that belongs to another, the patient.

The requirements of confidentiality apply only to certain patient-specific information. For example, information is considered confidential when the information is made available by the patient to the health care provider during the course of their confidential relationship (e.g., clinical or medical data). By contrast, information is nonconfidential when it is considered common knowledge, with no restrictions requested by the patient (e.g., demographic data). It is the sensitive nature of this confidential information that has been targeted under the law as requiring special protection.

HIPAA Information containing identifiers by which an individual can be recognized is considered protected health information (PHI).

To assist matters, the HIPAA Privacy Rule defines confidential health information as protected health information (PHI). The health information considered protected under HIPAA contains identifiers by which an individual can be recognized. These identifiers are listed in Table 9.1. Numerous restrictions are placed on individually identifiable health information under HIPAA. By contrast, the information that is stripped of all the identifiers listed in Table 9.1, plus any other information that could be used to identify an individual, is referred to as **de-identified health information**.

Confidentiality serves to protect patient-specific health information from disclosure. That protection applies whether health information concerns a living person or a deceased individual.[17] Not only must those persons involved with direct patient care act to protect health information but health information professionals must assume responsibility for protecting confidential patient-specific health information. This assumption exists because one of the primary ethical obligations of an HIM professional is to protect patient privacy and confidential information contained in the health record. Actions by both groups to maintain confidentiality have become increasingly difficult as demands for patient-specific information increase.

Table 9.1 Individual Identifiers under HIPAA
Name
All address information
Dates, including birth, death, admission, discharge, and any data indicating age
Telephone numbers
Fax numbers
E-mail addresses
Social security number
Health record number
Health plan beneficiary number
Account numbers
Certificate/license numbers
Vehicle identifiers
Device identifiers and serial numbers
URLs
IP addresses
Biometric identifiers
Facial photographs
Any other unique identifying number, characteristic, or code

Source: 45 C.F.R. § 164.514 (2019).

ETHICS

An HIM professional possesses an ethical obligation to protect patient privacy and the confidential information contained in the patient's health record.

In response to these increasing demands, the HIPAA Privacy Rule requires health care providers to issue a Notice of Privacy Practice to each patient. This notice informs the patient of the health care provider's duties concerning PHI, including how the provider may use and disclose PHI, with whom PHI will be shared, and the safeguards in place for the PHI. The notice also informs the patient of her rights under HIPAA, such as the right to an accounting of any disclosures of her PHI and the right to complain if she feels her privacy rights have been violated, along with the name and phone number of a contact person with whom she can lodge a complaint. Furthermore, the Privacy Rule requires the health care provider to inform the patient that disclosures, other than for treatment, payment, or operations, will only be made with the patient's consent. The Privacy Rule also requires the provider to make a good-faith effort to obtain the patient's acknowledgement that the notice has been received. Finally, the Privacy Rule requires the covered entity to post a complete copy of the notice in a clear and prominent location of its facility. An example of a Notice of Privacy Practices is included in Chapter 10, Access to Health Information, and the Appendix section of this textbook.

The HIPAA Privacy Rule does not stop with protection of the patient record per se but forms the basis for protections related to electronic health information exchanges. The Nationwide Privacy and Security Framework for Electronic Exchange of Individually Identifiable Health Information (Framework), issued by the U.S. Department of Health and Human Services, addresses privacy and security challenges related to these exchanges. The Framework is based in large measure on the HIPAA Privacy Rule. The eight principles comprising this Framework are listed in Table 9.2.

While HIPAA's expansive reach includes electronic health information exchange, limits do exist. For example, HIPAA does not address employment records kept by a covered entity in its capacity as an employer.[18] HIPAA also does not cover student health records; these types of educational records are covered by the privacy provisions of the Federal Educational Rights and Privacy Act (FERPA).[19]

EHR

The electronic health record poses new challenges to maintaining confidentiality and privacy of PHI.

HIPAA requirements, the implementation of the electronic health record, and the expansion of electronic health information exchange efforts have influenced health information professionals to expand their responsibilities for confidentiality and privacy in recent years. Instead of viewing the protection of health information as it relates to a set of paper-based patient records, health information managers now view privacy protection from an enterprise-wide perspective. Health information found in the electronic health record and other related databases requires the use of computer data security programs to address confidentiality and privacy concerns. These changes will continue to widen both the influence and responsibilities of health information professionals for years to come.

Table 9.2 Nationwide Privacy and Security Framework for Electronic Exchange of Individually Identifiable Health Information

Principle	Mediation
Individual Access	Individuals should be provided with a simple and timely means to access and obtain their individually identifiable health information in a readable form and format.
Correction	Individuals should be provided with a timely means to dispute the accuracy or integrity of their individually identifiable health information and to have erroneous information corrected or to have a dispute documented if their requests are denied.
Openness and Transparency	There should be openness and transparency about policies, procedures, and technologies that directly affect individuals and/or their individually identifiable health information.
Individual Choice	Individuals should be provided a reasonable opportunity and capability to make informed decisions about the collection, use, and disclosure of their individually identifiable health information.
Collection, Use, and Disclosure Limitation	Individually identifiable health information should be collected, used, and/or disclosed only to the extent necessary to accomplish a specified purpose(s) and never to discriminate inappropriately.
Data Quality and Integrity Principle	Persons and entities should take reasonable steps to ensure that individually identifiable health information is complete, accurate, and up-to-date to the extent necessary for the person's or entity's intended purposes and has not been altered or destroyed in an unauthorized manner.
Safeguards	Individually identifiable health information should be protected with reasonable administrative, technical, and physical safeguards to ensure its confidentiality, integrity, and availability to prevent unauthorized or inappropriate access, use, or disclosure.
Accountability	These principles should be implemented, and adherence assured, through appropriate monitoring, and other means and methods should be in place to report and mitigate nonadherence and breaches.

Source: U.S. Department of Health and Human Services, http://www.hhs.gov.

Confidentiality in the Research Context

Privacy and confidentiality are as important in the context of research involving human beings as it is in the delivery of direct patient care. In the research context, the application of these two concepts is a shared responsibility of the research team and the Institutional Review Board (IRB), the supervising body in institutions where research involving human subjects is conducted. It is the role of these two groups to ensure the provisions of the Common Rule are met by creating adequate provisions to protect the subject's privacy and maintain confidentiality of the data for the entire duration of the study and after the study is finished.[20] More information about the application of the Common Rule and IRBs is discussed in Chapter 10, Access to Health Information.

When considering the concept of privacy in the research context, the concern focuses on what control the human subject can exercise to decide access to not only their personal information but also to their body in the sense of collections of biological specimens. Examples of addressing privacy can include asking personal questions only in a private environment as opposed to a public setting; obtaining permission in advance before photographing or videotaping a human subject; and employing drapes or other barriers to permit a human subject to disrobe and not be seen without clothing.

> **CRITICAL THINKING**
>
> Privacy in the research context depends on the individual and can vary depending on gender, age, ethnicity, and ability. Examine the following situations to determine whether privacy would dictate the presence or absence of a parent:
> 1. when a young child participates in a research session with an investigator;
> 2. when a teenager participates in a research session with an investigator.

The issue of confidentiality is equally important in the research context and focuses on how private information provided by the human subject will be protected by the researcher. The private information that can identify the human subject may be printed information, electronic information, or visual information such as photographs. Confidentiality is concerned with the investigator's agreement with the human subject about how the participant's identifiable private information will be handled, disseminated, and managed. For example, will data be recorded anonymously, or coded with a master stored separately from the data, or with identifiers?

> **CRITICAL THINKING**
>
> Research protocols sometimes collect sensitive data, and participants may be reluctant to provide sensitive data without assurances confidentiality will be addressed. Examine whether the following situations require additional confidentiality safeguards:
> (1) genetic information;
> (2) discussion of risky or illegal behaviors;
> (3) treatments for sexual diseases; and
> (4) psychological or psychiatric diagnoses.

The nature of the research dictates the extent to which privacy and confidentiality safeguards are employed. As a general rule, the more sensitive the nature of the private identifiable information, the more review an IRB will give to a research protocol to ensure adequate protections are included. Examples of assessments that may be made by the IRB are seen in Table 9.3.

Confidentiality of HIV Information

Although all states consider health information confidential to some extent, the need to provide greater protection to health information concerning HIV status and AIDS has been legally recognized in the majority of states.[21] As a general rule, HIV/AIDS confidentiality statutes place restrictions on identifying both the patient tested and the test result. Disclosure of the patient's identity or the test result may be made only to the subject of the test or her legally authorized

Table 9.3 Typical IRB Assessments for Privacy and Confidentiality Safeguards

Privacy of the process and protection of collected data during recruitment and follow-up
Provisions to protect data and samples during use and subsequent storage
Identification of individuals or organization who may access identifiable information
Plans for de-identification and/or destruction of data or specimens, when appropriate

Source: 45 C.F.R. § 46.111 (2019) and 21 C.F.R.§ 56.111 (2019).

representative, a person designated in a legally effective release of information, the health care provider's staff directly involved in the patient's care, or the appropriate public health authority. In the case of mandatory testing by statute or court order, the relevant statute or court order will specify additional individuals who may receive the test results and/or the subject's identity.[22] Legal prohibitions exist against passing along or redisclosing information concerning an individual's HIV status to other parties, unless authorized by law.[23] Where improper or unauthorized disclosure of test results or the subject's identity occurs, the injured person may bring a civil suit for damages.[24]

One case illustrating these principles is *John Roe v. Jane Doe*.[25] In *Roe*, the patient informed his physician of his positive HIV status during an office visit for treatment of unrelated symptoms. He specifically asked and received assurances from his physician that his HIV status would be treated confidentially. Subsequently, his physician received a subpoena from the patient's employer along with a signed release of information authorizing release of information regarding the patient's workers' compensation claim. The physician complied with the subpoena by forwarding the patient's entire health record to the requesting attorney.

Roe then sued his physician for breach of confidentiality, negligence, and breach of contract. The court held that the physician improperly disclosed her patient's HIV status and was liable for punitive damages. Specifically, the court noted that the open-ended release of information form accompanying the subpoena was insufficient to permit disclosure of HIV information for two reasons: (1) New York law required that the release form specify authorization of the release of HIV information, which the form at issue did not address; and (2) New York law mandated use of a release of information form developed or approved by the commissioner of health, and the form at issue did not meet this requirement. The court also faulted the physician for releasing the patient's health records without including a statement prohibiting redisclosure of the patient's HIV information. As the *Roe* case demonstrates, a standard release of information may be insufficient to authorize release of HIV information.

As the *Roe* case indicates, physicians have been held liable for breaches of confidentiality and contract where they failed to comply with the applicable legal requirements restricting access to their patient's HIV information. Where the health care provider is the HIV-infected individual, the protections afforded by the legal restrictions on access to HIV information are not as clear. From one perspective, the health care provider is a patient who should be able to avail herself of all the confidentiality protections the law provides. From the opposite perspective, an HIV-infected health care provider may pose serious risks to any patient on whom she performs invasive procedures. For that reason, the patient is entitled to know the health care provider's HIV status. Such patient notification has been recommended by the Centers for Disease Control for a number of years.[26]

One case illustrating the first perspective is *Estate of Behringer v. Medical Center at Princeton*.[27] In *Behringer*, a physician sought medical treatment for pneumonia at the Princeton Medical Center. Between the time of admittance and discharge, his positive HIV status and subsequent diagnosis of AIDS was widely circulated among the medical center's staff. When he returned to his medical practice, he found that many of his patients had elected to see other physicians after learning through the medical community that he was HIV positive.

Behringer sued the medical center, raising a claim of breach of the duty to maintain the confidentiality of his diagnosis. The court found in his favor, noting that the medical center owed a duty to Behringer as a patient to take reasonable precautions to maintain the confidentiality of his diagnosis and that the duty was breached when the diagnosis became public knowledge.

In the *Behringer* case, the legal questions focused on the health care provider in his capacity as a patient seeking treatment. Where the HIV-infected health care provider is providing patient care as opposed to solely seeking treatment, the confidentiality protections afforded under the law are not as stringent. One case illustrating this concept is *In re: Milton Hershey Medical Center.*[28] In that case, a physician in a joint residency program between two medical centers was accidentally cut when operating on a patient. The resident voluntarily tested for HIV, with a positive result later confirmed by subsequent tests. The medical centers then petitioned a Pennsylvania court for permission to disclose information of the resident's positive HIV status to the patients who were potentially affected and to certain physicians on the medical staffs.

The court granted the medical centers' request, finding that the resident's interest in maintaining his privacy was outweighed by the interests of the medical centers in protecting the public's health and that of their patients in particular. The court ordered a very selective and limited disclosure of the resident's identity, using a pseudonym for disclosure to the patients and using the resident's real name for disclosure to only those physicians associated with his residency program. The court also narrowly tailored the information disclosed to the patients to include only the fact that the resident who participated in certain types of procedures was HIV positive and that the medical centers offered counseling and HIV testing.

As these cases demonstrate, the strict limits on disclosure of an individual's HIV status imposed by law may be enforced through lawsuits. Where the affected individual is the patient, the courts generally enforce the laws to benefit the patient's privacy interests. Where the affected individual is a health care provider, however, exceptions to these strict limits exist that may warrant disclosure despite the health care provider's opposition. In such a situation, courts generally perform a balancing test, weighing the privacy interests of the health care provider against the interests of the provider's patients and the public in general to know the risks to which they are subject. Where the health care provider's privacy interests are outweighed by the competing interests of patients and the public, courts will find that a compelling need exists that warrants disclosure of HIV information, however limited in scope.

ETHICS

Guidelines issued by professional associations can assist the health care provider in deciding a course of action when faced with an ethical issue.

In addition to legal restrictions, confidentiality protections may also be provided by **ethical guidelines**, which are standards of conduct issued by professional organizations to guide their members' future course of action. They are sometimes used to establish the standard of care in a negligence action. For example, the American Medical Association (AMA) determined more than two decades ago that the medical profession's obligation to maintain confidentiality of an individual's HIV status does not cease upon the death of the individual. In response to physicians' concerns that identification of a patient's cause of death as involving HIV or AIDS may result in adverse effects upon the character of the deceased patient or upon family members and friends, the AMA has promulgated ethical guidelines for use in determining when it is appropriate for a physician to include AIDS/HIV-related information in the autopsy report.[29] As discussed in earlier chapters, a professional association's guidelines may be used to establish the appropriate standard of care in a negligence action.

INFORMED CONSENT

Among the most significant developments in the relationship between law and medicine in the twentieth century is the doctrine of informed consent. From its origins in the right of privacy, this doctrine has developed into an integral part of the relationship between the health care provider and the patient. It has also served as the basis for federal regulations governing research involving human subjects and is reflected in consent forms used by health care providers before treatment is rendered.

Historical Development

Where the issue of consent originally came into play, courts in the early 1900s applied the theory of battery to lawsuits brought against health care providers.[30] As discussed in more detail in Chapter 4, Principles of Liability, battery constitutes the unauthorized touching of another. Initially, when a health care provider did not obtain the patient's consent before treating the patient and subsequently the health care provider touched the patient without authorization, the health care provider was liable for battery.

As the century progressed, the focus of lawsuits addressing the consent issue changed. No longer was the question whether the patient had consented to treatment; rather, the question became whether the patient truly understood the nature and effects of the treatment for which she had consented. Essentially, the question centered on the quality of the consent given by the patient: Did the patient have sufficient information from which to make an informed decision?

ETHICS

Autonomy is embedded in the concept of informed consent.

This questioning derives from the ethical concept of autonomy. The concept requires health care providers to disclose to patients adequate information in a manner the patient can understand. Armed with this information, the competent patient determines whether and what actions to take or forgo in relation to her medical care. This type of decision making—often in the form of granting permission to the health care provider to take action that will benefit the patient—is voluntary, demonstrating that the power rests with the patient and not with the health care provider.

As the focus changed, it became evident that the traditional battery theory would not suffice as a basis for these lawsuits. At the same time, courts across the country were abrogating the charitable immunity defense and refining the application of negligence principles to health care providers. It soon became apparent that negligence principles could be applied to the consent process. Thus developed the concept of a separate legal theory: the doctrine of informed consent.

By grounding the informed consent doctrine in negligence, courts necessarily placed the focus on the health care provider's duty of due care. As developed by the courts, the informed consent doctrine places a duty on the health care provider to not only obtain consent to treatment but also to disclose to the patient, in an adequate manner, the nature of the treatment or procedure, the risks involved, any available alternatives, and the benefits that could reasonably be expected as a result of the treatment or procedure. The health care provider's failure to discharge the duty to disclose sufficient information to the patient before treatment, accompanied by harm to the patient, resulted in a finding of liability for negligence.

> **EHR**
>
> Being able to show evidence of the informed consent process in an electronic health record is just as essential as it is in a paper-based record.

In addition to being a separate legal theory, informed consent is also a process. This process entails not only the discussion between health care provider and patient but physical evidence that this discussion took place and the results of that discussion (i.e., consenting to or forgoing treatment). Using a paper-based health record, this evidence consists of a paper form labeled as "Informed Consent." Using an electronic health record, this evidence can be shown through a digitized image of such a paper form or through an entry in the electronic health record that contains the essential elements of informed consent along with evidence of the patient's decision to consent to or forgo treatment or procedure.

Admission to a hospital to undergo an elective surgery involves multiple instances of obtaining informed consent. When the patient is admitted to the hospital, the patient signs a general consent that authorizes care of a generalized nature, such as receiving routine services by the health care staff. A separate informed consent is required before elective surgery takes place so that the risks specifically associated with the surgery are understood. If tissue or blood from the surgery will be retained by the hospital for future study and not disposed of in the ordinary course, a separate informed consent is required so the patient understands what will happen to the tissue or blood over time.

Scope of Informed Consent Doctrine

The scope of the informed consent doctrine can be measured in several ways: who may consent to treatment, how much information the health care provider must disclose to the patient, and what situations require informed consent. The scope of the informed consent doctrine is illustrated in Figure 9.4.

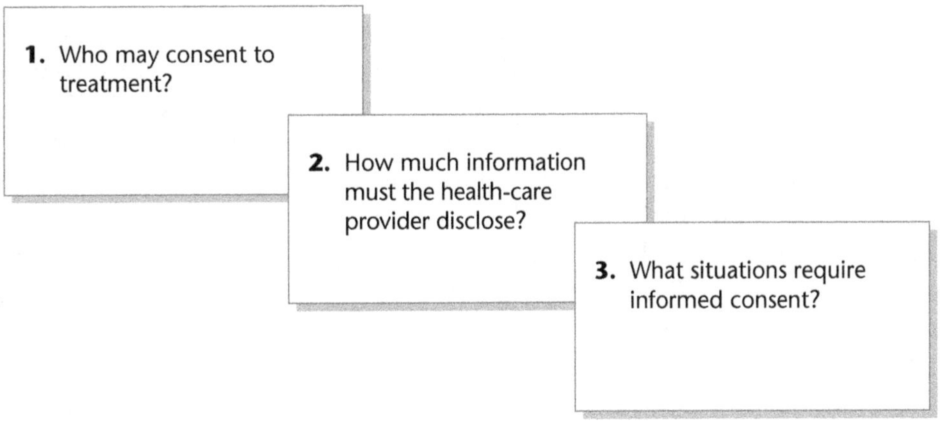

Figure 9.4 Scope of Informed Consent Doctrine

Who May Consent to Treatment?

As a general proposition, it is the patient and the patient alone who decides whether to consent to or forgo treatment. This general proposition assumes two things: that the patient is competent under the law to consent to treatment and that an emergency situation is not present. Adult patients are presumed competent absent an adjudication of incompetency by a court of law.

For those patients in whom legal competency is clearly an issue, for example, minors and comatose patients, the law provides that an authorized person may consent to or forgo treatment on the patient's behalf. Referred to as **substituted consent**, the process allows a health care provider to provide treatment to the patient when the patient cannot provide consent to treatment.

Minor Patients

In the minor context, substituted consent given by the parent or legal guardian will apply until the minor reaches the age of majority or becomes emancipated in the eyes of the law. Examples in which **emancipation** would provide legal authority for the minor to give consent include marriage,[31] childbirth,[32] or entry into the armed forces.[33] Where certain medical conditions are present, state law may provide for the minor's consent even if majority or emancipation requirements are not met. Examples of these special medical conditions include pregnancy, sexually transmitted diseases, and substance abuse.[34]

Legally Incompetent Patients

When speaking of legally incompetent patients, the focus rests on those patients who were either never competent or were once competent but subsequently became incompetent due to illness or accident. Often, consent issues in this context involve the question of whether the patient, or someone acting on the patient's behalf, has the right to refuse treatment with the result that the patient may die. Commonly referred to as the "right to die," this issue had been present in the health care community for many decades. It was not until the case of *Cruzan v. Director, Missouri Department of Health*[35] and responsive legislation that the country focused on the so-called "right to die" issue.

In *Cruzan*, the U.S. Supreme Court addressed whether life support could be withdrawn from Nancy Cruzan, a patient in a persistent vegetative state due to a car accident. The Court determined that Missouri's requirement of showing of clear and convincing evidence of Nancy's wishes indicating that she wished life support withdrawn before the health care provider withdrew treatment was not unconstitutional.

The national spotlight focusing on this one case eventually led to the passage of the Patient Self-Determination Act (PSDA).[36] The goal of the PSDA is "to ensure that a patient's rights to self-determination in health care decisions be communicated and protected."[37] It requires those health care providers who are Medicare or Medicaid certified[38] to inform their patients of the status of state law governing a patient's right to make advance directives for accepting or refusing health care services and the health care provider's written policies concerning implementation of the patients' rights. The text of the PSDA may be found in the online companion of this book.

Advance directives are defined as written instructions recognized under state law, such as living wills or durable powers of attorney for health care, that relate to the kind of health care the patient wishes to have or not have when incapacitated. A **living will** is a document, exercised while a patient is competent, that provides direction as to medical care in the event the patient becomes incapacitated or unable to make personal decisions. A **durable power of attorney** for health care is a document that allows a competent patient to name someone else to make health care decisions in the event the patient becomes incapacitated or unable to make personal decisions. In addition to informing the patient of the law and the provider's policy to implement it, PSDA requires the health care provider to ensure that the patient's health record reflects whether the patient has an advanced directive and, if so, what type. PSDA further requires the health care provider to avoid discrimination against patients on the basis of whether the patient has executed an advance directive.

Although PSDA places obligations on health care providers to educate and communicate with patients, staff, and the community, it does not create or modify any substantive legal rights. Each state possesses the authority to create or modify substantive legal rights concerning advance directives. In most states, the statutes addressing substantive legal rights grant permission to patients to use living wills, durable powers of attorney for health care, or both. A living will generally refers to a document that provides direction as to medical care in the event the patient is incapacitated or unable to make personal decisions.[39] By contrast, durable powers of attorney for health care allow a competent individual to name someone else to exercise health care–related decisions on her behalf, when certain conditions are met.[40] What is significant about the interplay between federal and state law in the context of advance directives is that state law addresses the patient's substantive rights, whereas federal law addresses the procedures by which those rights must be exercised when the patient receives treatment from a health care facility.

A variation of an advance directive is a **psychiatric advance directive** (PAD). A PAD is a legal document expressing a person's preference for future mental health treatment, which may include appointment of another person to interpret those preferences during a crisis. A patient creates a PAD when the patient is considered legally competent. The PAD is to be used at a future time when the patient's competency is in question due to the experience of an acute episode of psychiatric illness and the inability to make or communicate the patient's wishes for treatment. When the mental health crisis occurs, health care providers can consult the PAD in the patient's health record for direction. This variation in type of advance directive is recognized as a legally valid stand-alone document by half of the states; the remaining states either recognize that psychiatric decisions can be contained within traditional advance directives or may limit the decisions that can be made about mental health in a traditional advance directive.

Health information professionals should be aware not only of the PSDA but also of the fact that the U.S. Department of Health and Human Services has issued implementing regulations to PSDA, and that the Joint Commission and DNV Healthcare have issued standards that address advance directives.[41] Finally, health information professionals should realize that the substantive legal rights governing advance directives have fifty-one possible variations, covering each state and the District of Columbia.

Emergency Situations

As is self-evident, emergency situations pose difficult problems in obtaining the patient's informed consent. As a general proposition, an emergency situation is presented when the patient is unable to give consent, another person authorized to give consent on the patient's behalf is unavailable, and a delay in treatment would likely result in death or serious bodily harm to the patient.[42] Examples of emergency situations where informed consent may be difficult, if not impossible, to obtain include instances in which a person suffers sudden injury and any delay in treatment may result in increased risk to life or health and in which a patient who is undergoing treatment for a nonemergency condition experiences a worsening of the condition to the point that the patient's life is threatened.

State legislatures and courts have recognized that health care providers confronted with these situations risk potential liability and so have created legal protections for them. These legal protections are commonly referred to as Good Samaritan laws and serve to protect health care providers, other rescuers, and private citizens from liability for unauthorized treatment, as opposed to protection from rendering negligent treatment or intentional misconduct.[43] These laws are targeted at nontraditional settings in which health care is delivered, for example, by the side of the road after an automobile accident, as opposed to the treatment rendered by emergency room physicians. Good Samaritan statutes are addressed in more detail in Chapter 4, Principles of Liability.

Information To Be Disclosed

The extent to which information must be disclosed to the patient essentially rests with the question of whether the patient received sufficient information from which to make an informed decision. What constitutes sufficient disclosure is a matter of state law. Generally, sufficient disclosure includes information concerning the nature of the proposed procedure or treatment, the risks involved therein, any available alternatives, and the benefits that may be expected.[44] The states are split in their approach to measuring the duty of disclosure. Disclosure is measured under the law from two different perspectives: the health care provider's and the patient's.

Frequently referred to as the **professional disclosure standard**, this standard measures what a reasonable health care provider under the same or similar circumstances would disclose. Under this approach, expert testimony would be required to establish the parameters of the standard. Many states have adopted this standard, by statute[45] or case law.[46]

The second approach looks to the needs of the patient rather than the professional standards of the health care provider. Here, the **reasonable patient standard** measures what material information is necessary for an average, reasonable patient to reach a decision to consent to or forgo treatment. Because it is the patient's perspective that is measured, it is unnecessary to produce expert testimony concerning the standards of practice. Several states have adopted this standard, either by statute[47] or by case law.[48]

Situations Requiring Informed Consent

Absent an emergency situation, any treatment rendered by a health care provider involves consent of the patient, either implied or express.[49] **Implied or tacit consent** exists in situations in which a patient voluntarily submits to a procedure with apparent knowledge of that procedure and the procedure presents slight or no apparent risk, such as taking the patient's pulse or temperature. In these instances, the law presumes the patient has given consent.

By contrast, **express consent** of the patient, in the form of verbal or written informed consent, is necessary in cases where diagnostic or therapeutic procedures will be performed. Here, the risk of harm may or may not be readily apparent to the patient but is generally considered to be more than slight. Examples include invasive surgery, radiological therapy, or procedures that may change the body structure.

Similarly, express consent is ordinarily required in the research context. Patients who serve as subjects of research protocols are subject to risks as part of the research process, including risks unknown at the time the research is being conducted. Accordingly, the law requires patients to be informed fully of any risks and benefits associated with the research effort. A provision of the 21st Century Cures Act modifies the requirement of express consent for limited circumstances involving FDA research. The provision allows a waiver of informed consent if the research poses no more than minimal risk to the patient and other measures are in place to protect the patient's safety, rights, and welfare.[50]

Unfortunately, no one list exists that specifies those procedures requiring informed consent. Instead, health care providers must look to statutes, regulations, professional guidelines, and institutional requirements for guidance. And, when in doubt, health care providers are advised to take the cautious approach and obtain the patient's informed consent. In particular, health care providers should exercise caution with regard to experimental procedures that involve human subjects. Federal statutes governing experimental procedures involving human subjects specify strict requirements for informed consent. For further information about research involving human subjects, see Chapter 10, Access to Health Information.

CONCLUSION

Two of the most significant developments in the relationship between law and medicine during the twentieth century are the doctrines of confidentiality and informed consent. Just as confidentiality serves to protect information conveyed by the patient to her health care provider from inappropriate disclosure, informed consent serves to protect the patient from making decisions about treatment without first being provided the necessary information. Health information professionals must be aware of these legal protections that have become integrated into modern health care.

CASE STUDY

You are the director of health information services at a medium-size health care facility providing general, emergency, and pediatric care. Because of downsizing and consolidation of managerial functions, you are also responsible for staff education in your facility. Discuss how you would structure and present an inservice program to staff members of various departments that addresses confidentiality policies and procedures of your facility and the legal bases underlying these policies and procedures.

REVIEW QUESTIONS

1. Compare and contrast confidentiality and privacy.
2. What are open record statutes, and which federal law do they most closely follow?
3. What are privacy statutes, and which federal law do they most closely follow?
4. When does the physician–patient privilege apply, and what is its use?
5. Describe the difficulties faced by an HIV/AIDS patient whose infected status is disclosed without the patient's consent.
6. In what ways can the scope of the informed consent doctrine be measured?
7. What is meant by the phrase "substituted consent"?

8. How does the concept of emancipation of a minor affect substituted consent?
9. Define the terms *living will* and *durable power of attorney* for health care.
10. How does a psychiatric advance directive differ from a traditional advance directive?
11. What generally defines an emergency situation in the context of informed consent?
12. What perspectives are used to measure the professional disclosure standard and the reasonable person standard?

ENRICHMENT ACTIVITY

Imagine you are the director of health information management at a health care institution. Determine how your institution will address issues of patient confidentiality, including programs to educate staff on the issues of patient confidentiality. Contemplate the increased use of computerized databases and electronic means of communication and the impact these will have on the issue of patient confidentiality. Draft an outline of your institution's policy on patient confidentiality and plan for staff education.

ENRICHMENT ACTIVITY

Review the alternatives to the Hippocratic Oath found in the online companion website to this text. Search for provisions addressing confidentiality and privacy. Compare and contrast the substantive content of these alternative oaths to the Hippocratic Oath found in this text.

NOTES

1. L. Edelstein, The Hippocratic Oath: Text, Translation and Interpretation 3 (1943).

2. For example, the American Medical Association (AMA) has placed an ethical duty upon physicians to safeguard the communications made between physicians and patients and not disclose those communications absent patient consent. American Medical Ass'n, Current Opinions of the Judicial Council of the American Medical Association (1984).

3. 429 U.S. 589 (1977).

4. Alaska Const. art. I, § 22; Ariz. Const. art. II, § 8; Cal. Const. art. I, § 1; Fla. Const. art. I, § 23; Haw. Const. art. I, § 6; Ill. Const. art. I, § 6; La. Const. art. I, § 5; Mont. Const. art. II, § 10; S.C. Const. art. I, § 10; Wash. Const. art. I, § 7.

5. U.S.C. § 552 (2019). In addition, bills have been introduced into Congress to provide confidentiality protection at the federal level. S.R. 1360, 104th Cong., 2d Sess. (1995); H. R. 1057, 1941, 2404, 2455, 2470, 106th Cong., 1st Sess. (1999).

6. 5 U.S.C. § 552a (2019).

7. See Comprehensive Alcohol Abuse & Alcoholism Prevention, Treatment & Rehabilitation Act of 1970, 42 U.S.C. § 290ee (2019); Drug Abuse, Prevention, Treatment & Rehabilitation Act, 42 U.S.C. § 290dd (2019); Medicaid Program, 42 U.S.C. § 1396 (2019).

8. 11 U.S.C. § 333 (2019); Fed. R. Bank. P. 2015.1(b).

9. *See, e.g.*, Ark. Stat. Ann. §§ 25-19-101 to -107 (Michie 2019); Cal. Gov't Code §§ 9070-9079 (West 2019); Del. Code Ann. tit. 29, §§ 10001-10005 (2019); Ga. Code Ann. §§ 50-18-70 to -74 (2019); Iowa Code Ann. §§ 21.1 to .12 (West 2019); Ky. Rev. Stat. §§ 61.870 to .884 (Baldwin 2019); Mich. Comp. Laws Ann. §§ 15.231 to .246 (West 2019); N.Y. Pub. Off. Law §§ 84-90 (McKinney 2019).

10. *See, e.g.*, Ark. Code Ann. § 16-41-101, Rule 503 (Michie 2019); Cal. Evid. Code §§ 990-995 (West 2019); Del. R. Evid. 503; Ga. Code Ann. § 24-9-40 (2019); Haw. R. Evid. 504; Kan. Stat. Ann. § 60-427 (2019); Mich. Comp. Laws Ann. § 600.2157 (West 2019); Miss. Code Ann. § 13-1-21 (2019); Neb. Rev. Stat. § 27-504, Rule 504 (2019); N.J. Stat. Ann. §§ 2A:84A-22.1 to :84A-22.2 (West 2019); N.M. R. Evid. 11-504; N.Y. Civ. Prac. L. & R. 4504 (McKinney 2019); N.D. R. Evid. 503; Ohio Rev. Code Ann. § 2317.02(B) (1) (Baldwin 2019); Okla. Stat. Ann. tit. 12, § 2503 (West 2019); S.D. Codified Laws Ann. §§ 19-13-6 to -8 (2019); Vt. R. Evid. 503; Wis. Stat. Ann. § 905.04 (West 2019).

11. *See, e.g.*, Cal. Civ. Code §§ 1798.1 to .76 (West 2019); Conn. Gen. Stat. §§ 4-190 to 4-197 (2019); Ind. Code Ann. §§ 4-1-6-1 to -9 (Burns 2019); Mass. Ann. Laws ch. 66A, §§ 1-3 (Michie/Lawyers Co-op. 2019); Minn. Stat Ann. §§ 13.01 to .87 (West 2019); Ohio Rev. Code Ann. §§ 1347.01 to .99 (Baldwin 2019).

12. CAL. SB 541, AB 211 (2009).

13. California Consumer Privacy Act, Calif. Civil Code 1798.100 et seq. (2018). Available at https://leginfo.legislature.ca.gov/faces/billTextClient.xhtml?bill_id=201720180AB375.

14. Ibid.

15. Ibid.

16. European Union General Data Protection Regulation, Article 4 (2018). Available at https://eur-lex.europa.eu/legal-content/EN/TXT/?qid=1528874672298&uri=CELEX%3A32016R0679.

17. 45 C.F.R. § 164.502 (2019).

18. 45 C.F.R. § 160.103 (2019).

19. 20 U.S.C. § 1232g et seq. (2019).

20. 45 C.F.R. § 46.111 (2019) and 21 C.F.R. § 56.111 (2019).

21. Alaska Stat. § 40.25.120 (2019); D.C. Code Ann. § 7-131 (2019); N.C. Gen. Stat. § 130A-143 (2019); Utah Code Ann. § 26-6-27 (2019).

22. *See, e.g.*, Cal. Penal Code § 1524.1(g) (West 2019); Conn. Gen. Stat. Ann. § 19a-583(a) (10) (West 2019); Ga. Code Ann. § 24-9-47 (r & t) (2019); 410 ILCS 305/9(g) (2019); Me. Rev. Stat. Ann. tit. 5, § 19203(10) (West 2019).

23. See Ala. Code § 22-11A-54 (2019); Conn. Gen. Stat. Ann. § 19a-583(b) (West 2019); Ga. Code Ann. § 24-9-47(b) (2019); 410 ILCS 305/9 (2019); La. Rev. Stat. Ann. § 1300.14(A & D) (West 2019); Mo. Rev. Stat. § 191.656 (2019).

24. See Cal. Health & Safety Code § 120980 (West 2019); Mo. Rev. Stat. § 191.656(6) (2019).

25. 599 N.Y.S.2d 350 (N.Y. App. Div. 1993).

26. Centers for Disease Control, U.S. Department of Health and Human Services (1991, July 1), Recommendations for Preventing Transmission of Human Immunodeficiency Virus & Hepatitis B Virus to Patients during Exposure-Prone Invasive Procedures, at 5. Available at http://www.cdc.gov.

27. 592 A.2d 1251 (N.J. Super. Ct. Law Div. 1991).

28. 595 A.2d 1290 (Pa. Sup. Ct. 1991), *aff'd*, 634 A.2d 159 (Pa. 1993).

29. American Medical Association Council on Ethical & Judicial Affairs, Confidentiality of Human Immunodeficiency Virus Status on Autopsy Reports (1992). Available at http://www.ama-assn.org.

30. *See, e.g., Schloendorff v. Society of New York Hosp.*, 105 N.E. 92 (N.Y. 1914); *Rolater v. Strain, 137 P.96* (Okla. 1913); *Pratt v. Davis*, 79 N.E. 562 (Ill. 1906).

31. *See, e.g.*, Ala. Code § 22-8-5 (2019); Ariz. Rev. Stat. Ann. § 44-132 (2019); Colo. Rev. Stat. Ann. § 13-22-103 (West 2019); Ky. Rev. Stat. Ann. § 214.185(3) (Michie/Bobbs-Merrill 2019); MD. Health-Gen. Code Ann. § 2-301 (2019); Minn. Stat. Ann. § 144.342 (West 2019); Miss. Code Ann. § 93-1-5 (2019); Mont. Code Ann. § 41-4-402 (2019); N.J. Stat. Ann. § 9:17A-1 (West 2019); N.M. Stat. Ann. § 24-7A-2 (2019); N.Y. Pub. Health Law § 2504 (McKinney 2019); 35 PA. Cons. Stat. Ann. § 10101 (2019); S.C. Code Ann. § 20-7-270 (Law. Co-op. 2019); Va. Code Ann. § 54.1-2969 (Michie 2019).

32. *See, e.g.*, Ala. Code § 22-8-4 (2019); Ga. Code Ann. § 31-9-2 (Michie 2019); Ky. Rev. Stat. Ann. § 214.185(3) (Michie/Bobbs-Merrill 2019); Md. Health-Gen. Code Ann. § 2-301 (2019); Minn. Stat. Ann. § 144.342 (West 2019); Mont. Code Ann. § 41-1-402 (2019); N.Y. Pub. Health Law § 2504 (McKinney 2019).

33. *See, e.g.*, Ala. Code § 22-8-4 (2019); Mont. Code § 41-1-402 (2019).

34. *See, e.g.*, Ala. Code § 22-8-6 (2019) (all three medical conditions); Ark. Stat. Ann. § 20-9-602 (2019) (all three medical conditions); Ga. Code Ann. § 31-9-2 (2019) (pregnancy); Miss. Code Ann. § 41-41-3 (2019) (pregnancy); Mont. Code Ann. § 41-1-402 (2019) (all three medical conditions); Utah Code Ann. § 78-14-5 (2019) (pregnancy); Va. Code Ann. § 54.1-2969 (2019) (all three medical conditions).

35. 497 U.S. 261 (1990).

36. 42 U.S.C. § 1396a(w) (2019).

37. 42 U.S.C. § 1396a(w)(1)(A)(i) (2019).

38. The statute defines health care providers to include Medicare- or Medicaid-certified hospitals, skilled nursing facilities, home health agencies, hospices, and HMOs. 42 U.S.C. § 1396a (a) (57) (2019).

39. States with statutes authorizing living wills include: Ala. Code §§ 22-8A-1 to -10 (2019); Ariz. Rev. Stat. §§ 36-3261 to -3262 (2019); Colo. Rev. Stat. §§ 15-18-101 to -113 (2019); Del. Code Ann. tit. 16, §§ 2501-2509 (2019); Idaho Code §§ 39-4509 to -4515 (2019);

IOWA CODE ANN. §§ 144A.1 to 144A.11 (2019); KY. REV. STAT. ANN. § 311.621-643 (Baldwin 2019); LA. REV. STAT. ANN. §§ 40:1299.58.1 to 40:1229.58.10 (2019); MINN. STAT. § 145B.01 to 145B.17 (West 2019); NEV. REV. STAT. §§ 449.535 to 449.690 (2019); N.M. STAT. ANN. §§ 24-7A-1 to -18 (2019); OR. REV. STAT. §§ 127.505 to 127.660 (2019); S.C. CODE ANN. §§ 44-77-10 to 44-77-160 (2019) VT. STAT. ANN. tit. 18, §§ 5251-5262 (2019); W. VA. CODE §§ 16-30-1 to 16-30-13 (2019).

40. Examples of states with statutes allowing for durable powers of attorney for health care include: CAL. PROB. CODE §§ 4600 to 4806 (2019); COLO. REV. STAT. §§ 15-14-501 to -502 (2019); D.C. CODE ANN. §§ 21-2201 to -2213 (2019); GA. CODE §§ 31-36-1 to 31-36-13 (2019); KAN. STAT. ANN. § 58-625 to -632 (2019); ME. REV. STAT. ANN. tit. 18-A, § 5-501 to -506 (2019); MISS. CODE ANN. §§ 41-41-201 to 41-41-229 (2019); N.C. GEN. STAT. §§ 32A-8 to -27 (2019); OHIO REV. CODE ANN. §§ 1337.11 to 1337.17 (2019); R.I. GEN. LAWS § 23-4.10-1 to -12 (2019); S.D. CODIFIED LAWS ANN. §§ 59-7-2.1 to -8 (2019); WASH. REV. CODE ANN. § 11.94.010 to .070 (2019).

41. 42 C.F.R. §§ 417.436, 431.20, 434.28 (2019); THE JOINT COMMISSION, COMPREHENSIVE ACCREDITATION MANUAL, Patient Rights, RI1.2.5 (2004); DNV Healthcare's NIAHO Accreditation Requirements, Patient Rights, P.R. 2 (2012).

42. *See, e.g.*, ALA. CODE § 22-8-1 (2019); ARK. STAT. ANN. § 20-9-603 (2019); GA. CODE ANN. § 31-9-3 (2019); IDAHO CODE § 39-4507 (2019); NEV. REV. STAT. ANN. § 41A.120 (2019); PA. STAT. ANN. tit. 40, § 1301.103 (2019).

43. *See, e.g.*, CONN. GEN. STAT. § 52-557b (2019); FLA. STAT. ANN. § 768.13 (West 2019); MISS. CODE ANN. § 73-25-37 (2019); MONT. CODE ANN. § 41-1-405 (2019).

44. BARRY R. FURROW, ET AL., HEALTH LAW § 6-1 (1995).

45. *See, e.g.*, ALA. CODE § 6-5-484 (2019); ARK. STAT. ANN. § 16-114-206(b) (2019); ARIZ. REV. STAT. § 12-561, 563 (2019); DEL. CODE ANN. tit. 18, § 6852 (2019); FLA. STAT. ANN. § 766.103 (2019); IDAHO CODE § 39-4506 (2019); KY. REV. STAT. ANN. § 304.40-320 (Baldwin 2019); ME. REV. STAT. ANN. tit. 24, § 2905 (2019); NEB. REV. STAT. § 44-2816 (2019); NEV. REV. STAT. § 41A.100 (2019); N.H. REV. STAT. § 507-E:2.II (2019); N.C. GEN. STAT. § 90-21.13 (2019); TENN. CODE ANN. § 29-26-118 (2019); VT. STAT. ANN. tit. 12, § 1909 (2019).

46. *See, e.g.*, *Conrad v. Imatani*, 724 P.2d 89 (Colo. App. 1986); *Weekly v. Solomon*, 510 N.E.2d 142 (Ind. App. 1981); *Natanson v. Kline*, 350 P.2d 1093 (Kan. 1960); *Rice v. Jaskolski*, 313 N.W.2d 893 (Mich. 1981); *Baltzwell v. Baptist Med. Ctr.*, 718 S.W.2d 140 (Mo. 1986); *Collins v. Itoh*, 503 P.2d 36 (Mont. 1972); *Skripek v. Bergamo*, 491 A.2d 1336 (N.J. Super. 1985); *Hook v. Rothstein*, 316 S.E.2d 690 (S.C. App. 1984); *Bly v. Rhoads*, 222 S.E.2d 783 (Va. 1976).

47. *See, e.g.*, IOWA CODE ANN. § 147.137 (2019); TEX. REV. CIV. STAT. ANN. § 74.01 (2019); WASH. REV. CODE ANN. § 7.70.050(1) (2019).

48. *See, e.g.*, *Canterbury v. Spence*, 464 F.2d 772 (D.C. Cir. 1972); *Cobbs v. Grant*, 104 Cal. Rptr. 505 (Cal. 1972); *Sard v. Hardy*, 379 A.2d 1014 (Md. 1977); *Halley v. Birbiglia*, 458 N.E.2d 710 (Mass. 1983); *Kohoutek v. Hafner*, 383 N.W.2d 295 (Minn. 1985); *Scott v. Bradford*, 606 P.2d 554 (Okla. 1980); *Wilkinson v. Vesey*, 295 A.2d 676 (R.I. 1972); *Cross v. Trapp*, 294 S.E.2d 446 (W. Va. 1982).

49. BARRY R. FURROW, ET AL., HEALTH LAW § 6-9 (1995).

50. 21st Century Cures Act. 21 U.S.C. §355 (2019).

CHAPTER 10

ACCESS TO HEALTH INFORMATION

LEARNING OBJECTIVES

After reading this chapter, the learner should be able to:

1. Describe the continuum through which questions of health information ownership have passed.
2. Explain the concept of a notice of information practices.
3. Compare and contrast the terms *consent* and *authorization* with regard to a notice of information practices.
4. List the core elements of a valid release of information form.
5. Explain the principle of the minimum necessary standard.
6. Identify who is granted authority to release health information.
7. Describe the methods employed to disclose health information.
8. Explain the purpose of a redisclosure statement.
9. Compare and contrast the rights of access of patients and third parties to patient-specific health information.
10. Explain the concept of reasonable fees.
11. Discuss the challenges made to the concept of reasonable fees.
12. Explain the role that institutional review boards play in the access by researchers to health information involving human subjects.
13. Identify the duties and obligations of business associates to secure protected health information.
14. Describe the reasons for reporting public health threats.
15. Discuss the mechanism for reporting public health threats.
16. Compare the judicial approach with the legislative approach for access to adoption records.
17. Differentiate between the crimes of identity theft and medical identity theft.

KEY CONCEPTS

Accounting of disclosures
Adoption records
Authorization
Belmont Report
Breach
Business associate
Compound authorization
Consent
Continuum of ownership
De-identified data
Disclosure of information
Health record banks
Identifiable biospecimens
Identifiable private information
Identity theft
Institutional review board (IRB)
Limited data set
Medical identity theft
Minimum necessary standard
Notice of privacy practices
Personal health record
Preemption
Public health threats
Reasonable fee
Release of information

INTRODUCTION

Access to patient-specific health information is a complex issue governed by a variety of legal rules. Health care providers are charged under the law with the obligation to maintain patient-specific health information in a confidential manner. At the same time, health care providers are charged with the obligation to allow third parties and patients access to patient-specific health information, if appropriately requested. Understanding the balance between these obligations is essential to the health care provider's practice and compliance with the laws governing access.

The law particularly targets disclosure of patient-specific health information that is deemed confidential. Confidential information (e.g., clinical data) is distinguished from nonconfidential information by the fact that the information is made available by the patient to the health care provider during the course of their confidential relationship. By contrast, nonconfidential information (e.g., demographic data) is generally considered information that is a matter of common knowledge, with no restrictions requested by the patient. For purposes of this chapter, references to patient-specific health information are to confidential information.

Questions of access to and disclosure of patient-specific information frequently arise in the health care context. For that reason, the health information professional must understand the legal principles governing ownership and disclosure of health information, how disclosure principles differ with respect to who seeks access to health information, and when disclosure of health information is mandated by law. With that knowledge and understanding, the health information manager can develop and implement policies and procedures addressing access and disclosure of patient-specific information.

OWNERSHIP OF HEALTH INFORMATION

Who really owns health information? Is it the patient, the health care provider, or both? Or can health information be owned, as opposed to owning the medium in which information is stored, for example, the health record? At this time, the law is in transition, providing no certain answer to questions of ownership of health information and the media in which it is stored. To understand why generalizations exist rather than hard and fast rules, the continuum through which ownership questions have passed must be understood.

Traditionally, the law has focused on the medium used: the paper-based health record. Under the traditional approach, the health record was considered the sole property of the health care provider, and patient-specific health information was not considered separate from the medium used. Decisions on whether to allow access to the health record fell within the sole province of the health care provider. The health care provider reached decisions on access through the guidance of the provider's professional association. If the association's recommendation was to prohibit access to the patient and the health care provider did not believe otherwise, so be it.

As privacy rights were established and defined by courts and as consumer awareness blossomed, the concept of the patient possessing a right to his own health information contained in the health record developed. Although not always clearly defined and still focusing on the medium used, the patient's right of access to the health record and the health information contained in it could not be ignored by the health care provider.

Over time, the trend has moved away from focusing on the medium used and toward the protection of health information itself. The trend manifested in the regulations issued pursuant to the Health Insurance Portability and Accountability Act (HIPAA). The HIPAA Privacy Rule recognizes clearly that the patient possesses a right of access to his own information.[1]

HIPAA

The Privacy Rule establishes a patient's right of access to his own health information.

While HIPAA recognizes a patient's right of access, it does not go as far as specifying that the health care provider acts in a trust capacity for the patient. The idea of placing health information in a trust capacity is a trend of the future. Under this trend, the health care provider acts as trustee for the patient's benefit to create, receive, and protect patient-specific health information. Currently, the law has not caught up to this trend, leaving answers to questions of ownership of health information to fall somewhere in the middle of this continuum. (See Figure 10.1.)

While the law has not kept pace, the trend of placing health information in trust has come to reality in part with the introduction of **health record banks**, repositories of personal health records (PHRs) in electronic form operated by governmental or commercial entities who serve as trusted custodians of the data contained in the health record bank. Modeled upon a financial bank, health record banks can be thought of as involving both depositors and withdrawers of health information. Data is added by the patient, caregiver, and others to the PHR over the patient's lifetime. This data is fully accessible by the patient and available to others upon the patient's consent. An illustration of this model is shown in Figure 10.2. Several advantages of health record banks are listed

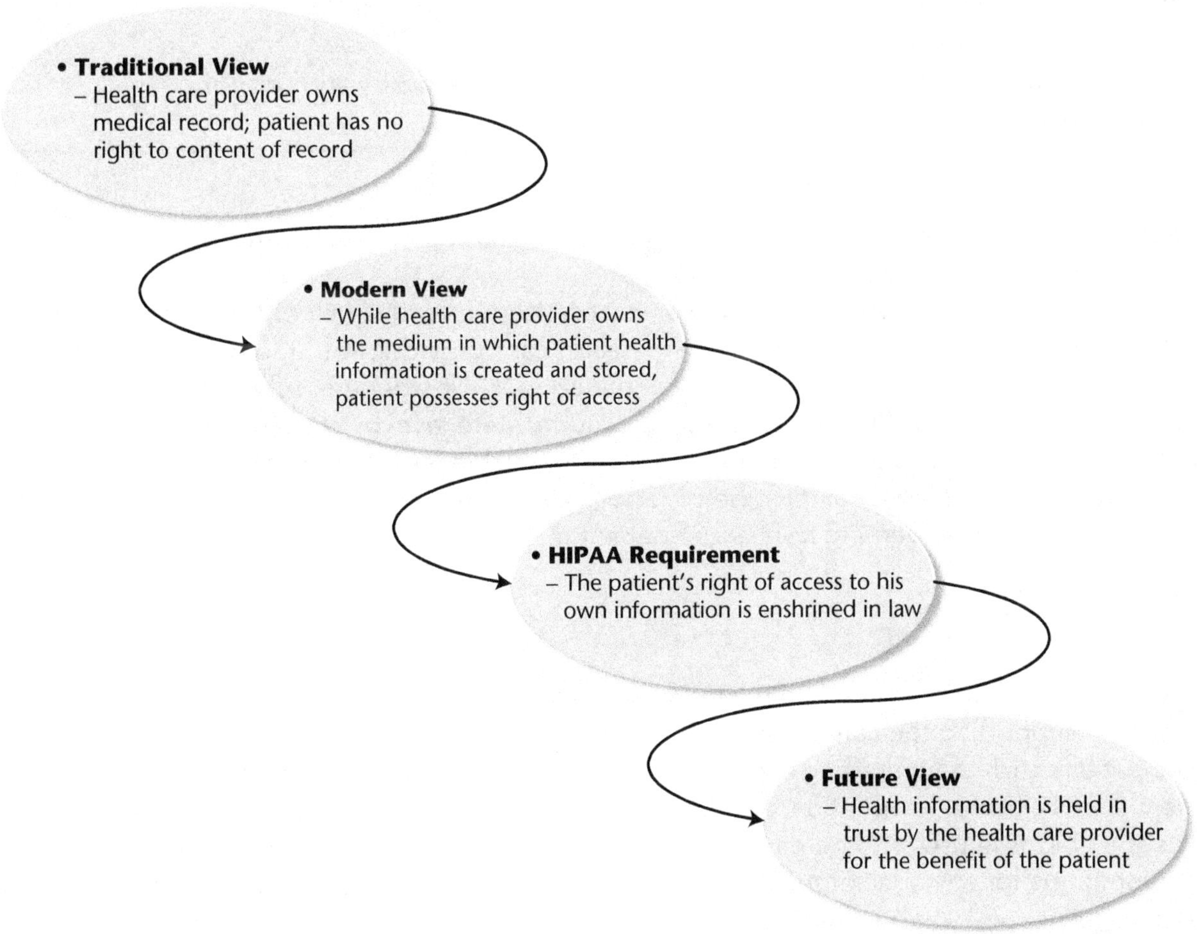

Figure 10.1 Ownership of Health Information: A Continuum

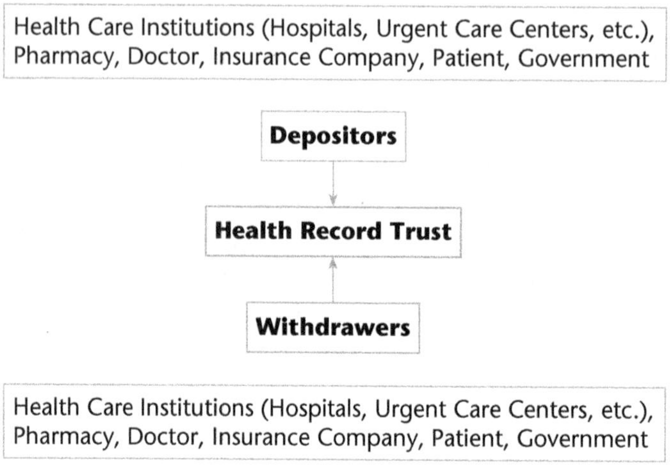

Figure 10.2 Health Record Banks

Table 10.1 Advantages of Health Record Banks
Eliminates fragmentation of medical data, today stored in many locations
May accelerate adoption of electronic health records
Patient control increased, as seen by
• Voluntary participation
• Use of privacy protection agreements to address confidentiality and privacy
• Penalties for violations of confidentiality

in Table 10.1. Bills promoting the legal recognition of health record banks have been introduced into Congress, with only mixed results.[2]

One general rule of ownership, however, is accepted in virtually all of the United States: the health record, as a medium, is owned by the health care provider, with the patient possessing a right or interest in the health information contained in it. This general rule is established at the federal level through the HIPAA Privacy Rule and at the state level by statute,[3] by licensing regulation,[4] and by judicial decision.[5] When determining ownership issues in any particular situation, the health information professional must be conscious of this rule and review state law for guidance, including regulations governing specialized patient records.

NOTICE OF USE AND DISCLOSURE

As described in Chapter 8, Patient Record Requirements, the health record serves multiple uses. In addition to supporting the care provided by health care professionals, uses traditionally unknown to the patient, such as fundraising and marketing, are involved. Federal standards for the privacy of patient-specific health information, also known as the HIPAA Privacy Rule, dictate that the patient be notified of these uses and be given the opportunity to consent, reject, or request restriction of this information for any or all of the many uses the health record serves. This notice requirement is commonly referred to as a **notice of privacy practices**.[6] The rule details both the content of the notice and the methods by which the patient is notified of the health care provider's information practices. A sample notice of information practices is illustrated in Figure 10.3.

Instruction A: Insert the covered entity's name

Instruction B: Insert the covered entity's address, web site and privacy official's phone, email address, and other contact information.

Your Information. Your Rights. Our Responsibilities.

This notice describes how medical information about you may be used and disclosed and how you can get access to this information.
Please review it carefully.

Your Rights

When it comes to your health information, you have certain rights. This section explains your rights and some of our responsibilities to help you.

Get an electronic or paper copy of your medical record	• You can ask to see or get an electronic or paper copy of your medical record and other health information we have about you. Ask us how to do this. • We will provide a copy or a summary of your health information, usually within 30 days of your request. We may charge a reasonable, cost-based fee.
Ask us to correct your medical record	• You can ask us to correct health information about you that you think is incorrect or incomplete. Ask us how to do this. • We may say "no" to your request, but we'll tell you why in writing within 60 days.
Request confidential communications	• You can ask us to contact you in a specific way (for example, home or office phone) or to send mail to a different address. • We will say "yes" to all reasonable requests.

continued on next page

Notice of Privacy Practices • Page 1

Figure 10.3 Sample Notice of Information Practices
Source: Courtesy of the US Department of Health & Human Services, www.hhs.gov.

HIPAA

The Privacy Rule sets a standard where the health care provider may seek the patient's consent before using protected health information to carry out treatment, payment, and health care operations.

Your Rights *continued*

Ask us to limit what we use or share	• You can ask us **not** to use or share certain health information for treatment, payment, or our operations.
	  • We are not required to agree to your request, and we may say "no" if it would affect your care.
	• If you pay for a service or health care item out-of-pocket in full, you can ask us not to share that information for the purpose of payment or our operations with your health insurer.
	  • We will say "yes" unless a law requires us to share that information.

Get a list of those with whom we've shared information	• You can ask for a list (accounting) of the times we've shared your health information for six years prior to the date you ask, who we shared it with, and why. • We will include all the disclosures except for those about treatment, payment, and health care operations, and certain other disclosures (such as any you asked us to make). We'll provide one accounting a year for free but will charge a reasonable, cost-based fee if you ask for another one within 12 months.
Get a copy of this privacy notice	• You can ask for a paper copy of this notice at any time, even if you have agreed to receive the notice electronically. We will provide you with a paper copy promptly.
Choose someone to act for you	• If you have given someone medical power of attorney or if someone is your legal guardian, that person can exercise your rights and make choices about your health information. • We will make sure the person has this authority and can act for you before we take any action.
File a complaint if you feel your rights are violated	• You can complain if you feel we have violated your rights by contacting us using the information on page 1. • You can file a complaint with the U.S. Department of Health and Human Services Office for Civil Rights by sending a letter to 200 Independence Avenue, S.W., Washington, D.C. 20201, calling 1-877-696-6775, or visiting **www.hhs.gov/ocr/privacy/hipaa/complaints/.** • We will not retaliate against you for filing a complaint.

Notice of Privacy Practices • Page 2

Figure 10.3 Continued

In addition to receiving a health care provider's notice of information practices, the Privacy Rule sets a standard where the health care provider may seek a general **consent** (agreement) from the patient to use or disclose patient-specific health information to carry out treatment, payment, and health care operations.[7] This consent is typically referred to as "Consent to the Use and Disclosure of Health Information for Treatment, Payment, or Health Care Operations." The Privacy Rule recognizes that patients may wish to restrict the uses and disclosures of their

Your Choices

For certain health information, you can tell us your choices about what we share. If you have a clear preference for how we share your information in the situations described below, talk to us. Tell us what you want us to do, and we will follow your instructions.

In these cases, you have both the right and choice to tell us to:	• Share information with your family, close friends, or others involved in your care • Share information in a disaster relief situation • Include your information in a hospital directory • Contact you for fundraising efforts *If you are not able to tell us your preference, for example if you are unconscious, we may go ahead and share your information if we believe it is in your best interest. We may also share your information when needed to lessen a serious and imminent threat to health or safety.*
In these cases we *never* share your information unless you give us written permission:	• Marketing purposes • Sale of your information • Most sharing of psychotherapy notes
In the case of fundraising:	• We may contact you for fundraising efforts, but you can tell us not to contact you again.

Our Uses and Disclosures

How do we typically use or share your health information? We typically use or share your health information in the following ways.

Treat you	• We can use your health information and share it with other professionals who are treating you.	Example: *A doctor treating you for an injury asks another doctor about your overall health condition.*
Run our organization	• We can use and share your health information to run our practice, improve your care, and contact you when necessary.	Example: *We use health information about you to manage your treatment and services.*
Bill for your services	• We can use and share your health information to bill and get payment from health plans or other entities.	Example: *We give information about you to your health insurance plan so it will pay for your services.*

continued on next page

Notice of Privacy Practices • Page 3

Figure 10.3 Continued

protected health information (PHI) and allows them to do so at the time of receipt of the consent document. The content requirements for a consent form in this context are illustrated in Figure 10.4.

How else can we use or share your health information? We are allowed or required to share your information in other ways – usually in ways that contribute to the public good, such as public health and research. We have to meet many conditions in the law before we can share your information for these purposes. For more information see: **www.hhs.gov/ocr/privacy/hipaa/understanding/consumers/index.html.**

Help with public health and safety issues	• We can share health information about you for certain situations such as: • Preventing disease • Helping with product recalls • Reporting adverse reactions to medications • Reporting suspected abuse, neglect, or domestic violence • Preventing or reducing a serious threat to anyone's health or safety
Do research	• We can use or share your information for health research.
Comply with the law	• We will share information about you if state or federal laws require it, including with the Department of Health and Human Services if it wants to see that we're complying with federal privacy law.
Respond to organ and tissue donation requests	• We can share health information about you with organ procurement organizations.
Work with a medical examiner or funeral director	• We can share health information with a coroner, medical examiner, or funeral director when an individual dies.
Address workers' compensation, law enforcement, and other government requests	• We can use or share health information about you: • For workers' compensation claims • For law enforcement purposes or with a law enforcement official • With health oversight agencies for activities authorized by law • For special government functions such as military, national security, and presidential protective services
Respond to lawsuits and legal actions	• We can share health information about you in response to a court or administrative order, or in response to a subpoena.

Instruction C: Insert any special notes that apply to your entity's practices such as "we do not create or manage a hospital directory" or "we do not create or maintain psychotherapy notes at this practice."

Instruction D: The Privacy Rule requires you to describe any state or other laws that require greater limits on disclosures. For example, "We will never share any substance abuse treatment records without your written permission." Insert this type of information here. If no laws with greater limits apply to your entity, no information needs to be added.

Instruction E: If your entity provides patients with access to their health information via the Blue Button protocol, you may want to insert a reference to it here.

To leave this section blank, add a word space to delete the instructions.

Notice of Privacy Practices • Page 4

Figure 10.3 Continued

ARRA

The American Recovery and Reinvestment Act of 2009 modifies the health care provider's ability to honor or not honor a patient's request to restrict disclosure of PHI.

Our Responsibilities

- We are required by law to maintain the privacy and security of your protected health information.
- We will let you know promptly if a breach occurs that may have compromised the privacy or security of your information.
- We must follow the duties and privacy practices described in this notice and give you a copy of it.
- We will not use or share your information other than as described here unless you tell us we can in writing. If you tell us we can, you may change your mind at any time. Let us know in writing if you change your mind.

For more information see: **www.hhs.gov/ocr/privacy/hipaa/understanding/consumers/noticepp.html.**

Changes to the Terms of This Notice

We can change the terms of this notice, and the changes will apply to all information we have about you. The new notice will be available upon request, in our office, and on our web site.

Instruction F: Insert Effective Date of Notice here.

This Notice of Privacy Practices applies to the following organizations.

Instruction G: If your entity is part of an OHCA (organized health care arrangement) that has agreed to a joint notice, use this space to inform your patients of how you share information within the OHCA (such as for treatment, payment, and operations related to the OHCA). Also, describe the other entities covered by this notice and their service locations. For example, "This notice applies to Grace Community Hospitals and Emergency Services Incorporated which operate the emergency services within all Grace hospitals in the greater Dayton area."

Instruction H: Insert name or title of the privacy official (or other privacy contact) and his/her email address and phone number.

Notice of Privacy Practices • Page 5

Figure 10.3 Continued

Previously, the Privacy Rule allowed covered entities to not honor the patient's request, making it possible for them to even condition treatment (in the case of a health care provider) or enrollment (in the case of a health plan) upon obtaining the patient's consent to use and disclose PHI. Provisions of the American Recovery and Reinvestment Act of 2009 (ARRA) changed that position. These provisions require a covered entity to comply with the requested restriction if:

(1) *"except as otherwise required by law, the disclosure is to a health plan for purposes of carrying out payment or health care operations (and is not for purposes of carrying out treatment); and*

(2) *the protected health information pertains solely to a health care item or service for which the health care provider involved has been paid out of pocket in full."*[8]

1. Consent must be in plain language;
2. Inform the individual that the information may be used and disclosed to carry out treatment, payment, or health care operations;
3. Refer the individual to the notice of information practices;
4. Inform the individual of the right to review the notice before signing the consent;
5. State that the notice may change and that the individual has a right to obtain a revised notice;
6. Inform the individual of the right to restrict use and disclosure of the information and the health care provider's option not to agree to the restriction;
7. State that the individual may revoke consent in writing except to the extent the health care provider has taken action in reliance thereon; and
8. Be signed by the individual and dated.

Figure 10.4 Content Requirements for Consent to Use and Disclose Patient-Specific Health Information to Carry Out Treatment and Payment of Health Care Operations

This means that the health care provider, and the health information professional by extension, may be required to sequester data for some situations (e.g., payment and operations) but not for others (e.g., treatment). Regulations issued by the Secretary of Health and Human Services provide further guidance concerning this issue.

Furthermore, the Privacy Rule requires that the health care provider obtain written **authorization** (permission) for specific disclosures not otherwise authorized by law.[9] Many of these specific disclosures are governed by the general principles of release of information addressed later in this chapter. The difference between the consent and the authorization rests with the type of use or disclosure in question.

The HIPAA Privacy Rule requires the health care provider to obtain the patient's consent before using or disclosing the health information to carry out treatment, payment, or health care operations. Some exceptions do exist to obtaining prior consent before using or disclosing the health information and are illustrated in Figure 10.5. The health care provider must document its attempts to obtain consent and the reasons that it was not obtained. Finally, the health care provider, and any business associate of the health care provider, must provide an **accounting of the disclosures** made upon request by the patient.[10]

In addition to the requirements of the HIPAA Privacy Rule, states have decided to take action. In the very recent past, Hawaii required health care providers to supply patients with a notice of confidentiality practices and authorizations in a manner similar to the HIPAA Privacy Rule. After determining that no widespread abuse of the privacy of health records existed in Hawaii, the state repealed its law and now relies solely on the HIPAA provisions.[11] Montana and Washington have adopted the Uniform Health-Care Information Act, specifying notice to the patient of confidentiality practices.[12] California passed the Consumer Privacy Act of 2018, which requires the health care provider to inform the patient about practices involving the collection of data, its use, and disclosure.[13] In the future, other states may enact even more stringent provisions addressing the same question. To the extent, health care providers treat patients from the European Union,

1. Disclosure to public health authorities as required by law (ex. reporting of communicable disease).
2. Disclosure to governmental authority to receive reports of abuse, neglect, or domestic violence.
3. Disclosure to a health oversight agency for oversight activities as required by law, including audits and inspections.
4. Disclosure to law enforcement agencies for limited purposes, such as reporting certain types of wounds or an individual's death, which may have resulted from criminal conduct.
5. Disclosure to coroners, medical examiners, and funeral directors as required by law and as necessary to carry out their duties with respect to a decedent.
6. Disclosure for research purposes, if stringent standards are met.
7. Disclosure to avert a serious threat to health and safety.
8. Disclosure for specialized governmental functions, such as for the conduct of lawful intelligence or the protection of the President.
9. Disclosure for workers' compensation.

Figure 10.5 Exceptions to Prior Consent

those providers will need to comply with the notice and use of data provisions of the General Data Protection Regulation.[14]

Both the federal and state governments may pass laws, rules, and regulations that address the same matter. In such instances, health information officers must determine how to reconcile federal and any state requirements. The first step in such a reconciliation process is to address the question of **preemption**. Under the preemption doctrine, certain matters are of such a national, as opposed to local, nature that federal laws preempt, or take precedence over, state laws. Accordingly, health information managers should examine carefully the content of the federal law, rule, or regulation in question to determine to what extent it addresses preemption.

Compliance with both the federal and state standards is the second step of reconciliation process. Two examples illustrate the preemption issue in the health information management context: provisions of the Health Insurance Portability and Accountability Act and the American Recovery and Reinvestment Act of 2009 (ARRA). The terms of the HIPAA Privacy Rule do not per se preempt the laws, rules, or regulations of the various states, except where the state laws, rules, or regulations are contrary to the HIPAA Privacy Rule.[15] Therefore, the HIPAA Privacy Rule provides a floor of protections, allowing a state to enact more stringent protections. Where the state provisions are more stringent than a standard requirement or implementation specification of the HIPAA Privacy Rule, the health care provider must comply with both the federal and state provisions. Similarly, the terms of ARRA address requirements for notification to individuals whenever a health care provider or a business associate discovers a breach of confidentiality of the patient's health information. These requirements address timeliness, method, and content of notification.[16] Many states also have laws addressing breaches and the timeliness, method, and content of notification of those breaches. Because ARRA does not preempt state law on these points, whichever provisions are more stringent will govern the actions of the health information manager.

An example where federal preemption does occur is with the changes to regulations of ARRA and the Clinical Laboratory Improvement Amendments (CLIA). In 2014, the Centers for Medicare and Medicaid Services amended the regulations of both laws to permit a patient, the patient's representative, or a person designated by the patient to access test reports belonging to the patient. Prior to that date, the Privacy Rule of the HITECH Act found within ARRA had exempted most lab test results from access by the patient. Such an approach was in alignment with a number of state laws that prohibited a laboratory from releasing a test report directly to the individual or prohibited the release without first obtaining the health care provider's consent. Those state laws are now contrary to the Privacy Rule mandating direct access by the individual and therefore preempted from enforcement.[17]

New provisions found in the HITECH-HIPAA Omnibus Final Rule add another layer of concern regarding the use of protected health information. The Omnibus Final Rule permits patients to sequester information from their health record if they pay for the related service out of pocket. The intent of this provision is to assist patients who have sought treatment for conditions the patients do not want their health plans to know about, such as mental health treatment or an HIV diagnosis. The provision must be stated in the health care provider's notice of privacy practices, and the health care provider must make efforts to separate any health information involving the patient's right to sequester from the rest of the patient's health record. This involves creating and using restriction functionality in electronic health records. Further, if the patient's health information is later released to a health plan pursuant to a valid release of information, the sequestered information is not subject to that release.[18]

ACCESS BY OR ON BEHALF OF THE PATIENT

Questions of access to health information by the patient or third parties on behalf of the patient are governed by a complex web of laws and regulations. To navigate through this web, health information professionals must understand the general principle of **disclosure of information**. From there, the health information professionals must understand the differences the law makes between access by the patient and access by third parties.

General Principles of Disclosure of Information

From the general ownership rule addressed earlier flow two additional principles: (1) records remain within the provider's control and safekeeping and may be removed only in accordance with a court order or subpoena, and (2) the provider may not disclose or withhold health information at will. Removal of records from the provider's control is addressed in Chapter 3, Judicial Process of Health Information; the disclosure or withholding of information is addressed in this chapter.

Before any health care provider or institution may disclose patient-specific health information, the law requires the express consent of the patient. Such express consent must be in writing or, where state law permits, via computer. Commonly referred to as the process for authorizing **release of information**, a valid release of information form provides health care providers and institutions with the authority to disclose patient-specific health information to persons not otherwise authorized to receive this information.

The minimum elements that must be present to constitute a valid release of information form are governed by both federal and state law. Health care providers may also be guided by professional guidelines, such as that of the American Health Information Management Association.[19]

Under the HIPAA Privacy Rule, a valid authorization must be in plain language and contain at least the following core elements: the individual's name; a specific and meaningful description of the information to be used or disclosed; the name or other specific identification of the person or class of persons authorized to make the disclosure; the name or other specific identification of the person to whom the disclosure is to be made; an expiration date or expiration event that relates to the individual or purpose of the use or disclosure; a statement of the individual's right to revoke the authorization in writing, exceptions to the right to revoke, together with how the individual may revoke the authorization; a statement that the information used or disclosed pursuant to the authorization may be subject to redisclosure and lose its protected status; the signature and date of the individual; and if the authorization is signed by a personal representative of the individual, a description of the representative's authority to act for the individual (see Figure 10.6).[20] A valid authorization may contain additional elements or information if clinical research is involved or as required by state law, provided that such additional elements or information are not inconsistent with the elements required under HIPAA.

Conversely, a release of information may be considered invalid if it contains any of the following defects: the expiration date has passed or the expiration event is known by the covered entity to have occurred; the authorization has not been filled out completely with respect to an element described in the core elements section; the authorization is known by the covered entity to have been revoked; the authorization lacks an element required in the core elements section; the authorization violates the compound authorization requirements; and/or any material information found in the authorization is known by the health care provider to be false (see Figure 10.7).[21] A **compound authorization** is defined as an authorization for use or disclosure of patient-specific health information that has been combined with any other document. Among the limited exceptions to the use of a compound authorization are permitting an authorization for use or disclosure of information created for research to be combined with one for treatment; the combination of

1. The individual's name and identifying information.
2. A specific and meaningful description of the information to be used or disclosed.
3. The name or other specific identification of the person or class of persons authorized to make the requested use or disclosure.
4. The name or other specific identification of the person or class of persons to whom the disclosure is to be made.
5. An expiration date or expiration event that relates to the individual or purpose of the use or disclosure.
6. A statement of the individual's right to revoke the authorization, the exceptions to the right to revoke, and a description of the individual may revoke the authorization.
7. A statement that the information used or disclosed is subject to redisclosure and may lose its protected status.
8. The signature and date of the individual.
9. If the authorization is signed by the individual's personal representative, a description of the representative's authority to act for the individual.

Figure 10.6 Core Elements of a Valid Release of Health Information Form

1. The expiration date has passed, or the expiration event is known by the health care provider to have occurred.
2. Authorization has not been filled out completely with respect to a core element.
3. Authorization is known by the health care provider to have been revoked.
4. Authorization lacks a core element.
5. Authorization contains a compound authorization violation.
6. Any material information contained in the authorization is known by the health care provider to be false.

Figure 10.7 Common Defects of an Invalid Release of Information Form

two or more authorizations for use or disclosure of psychotherapy notes; and where nonpsychotherapy notes are involved, a combination of authorizations as long as the health care provider has not conditioned the provision of treatment, payment, enrollment in a health plan, or eligibility for benefits on obtaining the authorization.[22]

HIPAA The Privacy Rule establishes the principle of the minimum necessary standard for release of protected health information.

What information may be released is also the subject of federal law. Introduced as part of the HIPAA Privacy Rule and reinforced with provisions of the American Recovery and Reinvestment Act of 2009 (ARRA), the principle of the **minimum necessary standard** governs the release of protected health information.[23] The principle of the minimum necessary standard under both HIPAA and ARRA requires the health care provider to make reasonable efforts to limit the patient-specific health information to a limited data set, a concept addressed later in this chapter, or to the minimum necessary to accomplish the intended purpose of such use, disclosure, or request, respectively. The health care provider must identify those who need access to the information to carry out their duties, what category of access is needed, and what conditions, if any, are appropriate to such access. As a logical extension, those persons in the workforce for identification purposes will include all classes of employees, volunteers, student interns, and others. Further, the health care provider is expected to develop and implement reasonable policies and procedures that limit the information released on a routine and recurring basis to the amount reasonably necessary to achieve the purpose of the disclosure. Where release is not routine or recurring, the health care provider is expected to develop criteria designed to reasonably limit the items of patient-specific health information disclosed such that the purpose for which disclosure is sought is accomplished and review requests for disclosure on an individual basis in accordance with the criteria established. The development of these criteria is aided by the ARRA regulations that provide guidance on what constitutes "minimum necessary" as it relates to HIPAA.

ARRA The American Recovery and Reinvestment Act (ARRA) limits the release of PHI to a limited data set or to the minimum necessary to accomplish the purpose of the use, disclosure, or request.

Who may grant authority to release health information is a matter governed by state law and regulation. Generally, the authority to release information rests with (1) the patient if the patient is a competent adult or emancipated minor; (2) a legal guardian or parent on behalf of a minor child; or (3) the executor or administrator of an estate if the patient is deceased.[24] The HITECH-HIPAA Omnibus Final Rule has clarified that a release of information is not required fifty years after the patient's death because the health information ceases to be protected after this length of time.[25] A covered entity may disclose to a family member, other relative, or a close personal friend of the deceased patient, or any other person identified by the deceased patient, the protected health information directly relevant to such person's involvement with the care or payment of care of the deceased patient prior to death, unless doing so is inconsistent with the patient's wishes expressed to the covered entity prior to death.[26]

The question of whether one is an emancipated minor is answered by the requirements of each state's laws and/or regulations. Common conditions of emancipation include evidence that the minor is married, on active duty with the U.S. armed forces, self-supporting and living away from home, or unmarried and pregnant.[27] Where the patient has been declared incompetent by a court of law or is otherwise unable to authorize disclosure (e.g., due to coma or critical condition), state law will provide the order of individuals who may serve to authorize disclosure.

Disclosure of protected health information to schools of immunization records is permitted under the HITECH-HIPAA Omnibus Final Rule as long as the protected health information disclosed is limited to proof of immunization. Such an approach is consistent with the minimum necessary provision addressed in other parts of the HIPAA Rule. Covered entities must receive oral agreement or written authorization from a parent, guardian, or person acting *in loco parentis* for the individual and must document the agreement obtained under this provision.[28]

Finally, the method of disclosure must be addressed. As a general matter, state law or regulation does not specify the method of disclosure. Rather, professional guidelines and institutional practices and procedures govern. The disclosure of health information is most frequently handled by mail but may also be accomplished through electronic transmittal, facsimile machine, or telephone where the mail method will not meet the need for urgent patient care. If handled in any of the last three ways, the health information professional should consider instituting additional safeguarding procedures. These safeguards could include encrypting data if public channels are used for electronic transmittal, creating documentation requirements for telephone disclosures, and following the guidelines of professional associations for faxing health information.[29]

One additional safeguard mandated in certain states is the inclusion of a redisclosure notice with the information sent.[30] This redisclosure notice is a statement placing the recipient on notice that the information received may be used only for the stated purpose, that the recipient is barred from redisclosing the information to third parties without the patient's authorization, and that the information should be destroyed after the stated purpose is fulfilled. An example of a redisclosure notice is shown in Figure 10.8. The inclusion of a redisclosure notice is mandated by the federal government when information relating to alcohol or drug abuse patients is released.[31]

By the Patient

Although it may seem a somewhat elementary concept that the health information contained in the health record belongs to the patient, and therefore the patient has a right to review and copy that information, that concept has only recently been established by the federal government pursuant to the HIPAA Privacy Rule. This rule grants an individual "a right of access to inspect and obtain a copy of protected health information about the individual in a designated record set, for

> Each disclosure made with the patient's written consent must be accompanied by the following written statement:
>
> This information has been disclosed to you from records protected by Federal confidentiality rules (42 CFR Part 2). The Federal rules prohibit you from making any further disclosure of this information unless further disclosure is expressly permitted by the written consent of the person to whom it pertains or as otherwise permitted by 42 CFR Part 2. A general authorization for the release of medical or other information is NOT sufficient for this purpose. The Federal rules restrict any use of the information to criminally investigate or prosecute any alcohol or drug abuse patient.

Figure 10.8 Notice to Accompany Disclosure of Information
Source: 42 C.F.R. § 2.32(a) (2019)

as long as the protected health information is maintained in the designated record set."[32] If a covered entity under HIPAA uses or maintains the patient's protected health information through an electronic health record, the American Recovery and Reinvestment Act of 2009 (ARRA) provides the patient with a right of access to his protected health information. The covered entity must provide the patient with access to the protected health information in the form and format requested by the patient, if it is readily producible, or if not, in a readable hard copy form or such other form or format agreed to by the patient and the covered entity. ARRA specifies that the patient may designate a third party to receive the information, provided the designation is clear, conspicuous, and specific. The covered entity may charge a fee for providing this service, subject to limitations.[33]

ARRA

The American Recovery and Reinvestment Act provides rights to patients to their information contained in an electronic health record.

While regulation at the federal level addresses the concept of patient access, not all states have a similar regulation or statute addressing this legal right. Because HIPAA establishes a "floor" of patient rights and not a ceiling, states are free to provide even further rights of access by the patient to his own health information. The extent of the patient's access to his own health information is similar to the **continuum of ownership** issue: ranging from those states that do not address patient access at all or allow the health care provider to determine the extent of access[34] to those that specifically grant patients access to their health records.[35] Because each state's law varies, health information managers developing policies on release of information directly to the patient must review not only the HIPAA Privacy Rule but also the applicable state law, particularly if the policy is to be developed for a hospital system spanning more than one state.

HIPAA

HIPAA provides a floor for the patient's right of access to his own health information; states have the flexibility to expand that right through statute or regulation.

Patients receiving care from health care facilities operated by the federal government, such as Veterans Administration hospitals and Indian Health Services clinics, have greater rights of access. The Federal Privacy Act governs patient care in those facilities and permits the patient the right of access to his own health information, to have a copy made of all or part of his record, and to correct or amend the record.[36] Unlike some federal statutes, the rights listed in the Federal Privacy

Act are limited to facilities operated by the federal government and do not apply to health care facilities that receive federal funds, such as Medicare reimbursement.

Although patients have gained greater rights of access to their health information, the rights of access are not absolute. Under certain circumstances, the health care provider may be justified in withholding access to health information from the patient. For example, if the health care provider determines that the release of information will have a detrimental effect on the patient, the provider may withhold the information from the patient but may be required to provide it to a third party authorized by the patient.[37] Where withholding of health information is justified, it frequently occurs in the context of mental health treatment.

In addition to reviewing state law, the health information professional should also examine the terms of the HIPAA Privacy Rule for guidance on the time and manner of access granted to patients to review their own health information. Specific provisions govern the time frame in which the provider must act on a request, the manner in which the patient may inspect or obtain a copy of the health information, and the method for review of a health care provider's denial of a request for access.[38]

One recent phenomenon affecting the patient's access to his own information is the advent of the **personal health record** (PHR). A PHR is a collection of a patient's important health information "that can be drawn from multiple sources and that is managed, shared, and controlled by or primarily for the individual."[39] Patients may keep their own personal health records or they may keep a personal health record for another person, such as a child or parent for whom the person has responsibility. This phenomenon has grown as a direct result of the right of access to the patient's own information recognized under HIPAA.

> **ARRA**
>
> The American Recovery and Reinvestment Act (ARRA) begins legal regulation of many forms of personal health records (PHRs).

The surge of interest in personal health records has drawn the attention of businesses that have developed and marketed technology directly for patient use. This has resulted in the creation and marketing of numerous types of PHRs in electronic form. As with most technology developments, this activity remained largely unregulated; the passage of the American Recovery and Reinvestment Act of 2009 (ARRA) brought PHRs within the context of regulation. ARRA contains provisions addressing vendors and others that offer PHRs to the public, applying reporting provisions upon those vendors. Specifically, ARRA imposes a requirement upon those vendors and others offering PHRs to notify the individual who is the subject of the PHR of any breach of confidentiality. ARRA also specifies that vendors and operators of PHRs are subject to Federal Trade Commission (FTC) regulations whenever HIPAA regulations do not apply.[40]

To Third Parties

As seen previously, a simple concept such as the patient being able to access his own health information does not translate into a legal right in every state. By contrast, third parties who may be perfect strangers to the patient have a right of access to the patient's health information, provided the patient has completed a valid release of information in their favor. And in certain instances, the third party may be able to access the information without patient authorization.

The extent of access and the need for patient authorization are defined by the identity of the third party seeking access. For example, if the party seeking access is the patient's attorney or insurance company, the health care provider may disclose patient-specific health information only with the patient's authorization. Similarly, patient authorization is generally necessary before disclosure may be made to a federal, state, or local government agency.

If the patient's employer seeks access, the patient's authorization is required, unless a workers' compensation claim is involved. Where workers' compensation claims are involved, state law may provide the employer with a right of access to the information without the patient's authorization.[41]

Another example of a third party requiring patient authorization is a member of the patient's family. Although the family member may believe he possesses an absolute right of access to the patient's health information by virtue of the family relationship, that is not the case under the law. A patient's friends and family may have access to a patient's protected health information under the HIPAA Privacy Rule if the patient agrees, or is given an opportunity to object but does not do so, or if the health care provider can reasonably infer from the circumstances that the patient would not object to the disclosure.[42] Covered entities must treat a patient's personal representative as the patient for access purposes, absent an indication that the personal representative lacks authority to act on behalf of the patient.

When the patient is an unemancipated minor, the parent, legal guardian, or person acting with parental rights may have access to PHI, unless the minor could lawfully obtain health care without parental consent (e.g., health care involving female reproductive rights); the covered entity must follow state law concerning disclosures. Under state law, a valid release of information form is required before the family member may legitimately gain access to the patient's health information.[43] An exception to this rule is where the family member has been appointed the patient's attorney in fact under a durable power of attorney for health care. In such an instance, the law generally allows the family member as attorney in fact to review the patient's health record.[44]

As indicated earlier, some third parties may be provided access to patient-specific health information without first obtaining the patient's authorization. For example, health care practitioners within the provider institution may be granted access on a need-to-know basis to perform their jobs with the patient. Similarly, surveyors with accrediting and licensing agencies may be granted access to the extent necessary to ensure compliance with standards or regulations for health information management. Additionally, a court may grant access to patient records in a lawsuit upon a finding of good cause.

ARRA

The American Recovery and Reinvestment Act prohibits health care providers from selling protected health information absent a patient's written consent.

Third parties seeking access to protected health information may offer to pay the health care provider for the information. Under provisions of the American Recovery and Reinvestment Act of 2009 (ARRA) and the HITECH-HIPAA Omnibus Final Rule, health care providers are prohibited from selling this information, absent an individual's written authorization to do so.[45] This provision eliminates the practice of aggregating patient data and selling it to third parties. Limited exceptions to this provision are listed in Table 10.2.

Reasonable Fees

With the demand for access to health information high, the cost to the health care provider to respond to such requests has increased proportionally in terms of both materials used and

Table 10.2 Exceptions to Prohibition on Selling Patient Health Information
Public health activities
Research activities
Patient treatment or payment
Sale, merger, or consolidation with another health care entity
Business associates pursuant to a written agreement

Source: 45 C.F.R. § 164.502 (2019).

employee time and labor. For many years, the law recognized that the health care provider should not bear these costs free of charge for those requesting information access. State law generally permits the health care provider to charge a reasonable fee for reproduction of the record.[46]

A **reasonable fee** is defined as a fee charged by the health care provider for the reproduction of the health record. On the federal level, rules enacted pursuant to the Health Insurance Portability and Accountability Act, including the HITECH-HIPAA Omnibus Final rule, clearly state that health care providers may impose a reasonable cost-based fee for reproducing the record.[47] Under the Privacy Rule, such fee may only include the cost of: (1) labor; (2) supplies; (3) postage, if mailed; and (4) preparation of a summary or explanation.[48]

Over time, the concept of charging a fee to the patient for access to the patient's own information has come under considerable criticism. Much of the criticism is supported by the discussion on ownership of health information discussed at the beginning of this chapter. The reasoning posits that if it is the patient's own data being held in trust by the health care provider, this data should be made available at no charge to the patient.

> **HIPAA**
>
> The Privacy Rule provides authority for health care providers to charge reasonable, cost-based fees for copies or a summary of PHI.

Where the patient's information is contained within an electronic health record, the provisions of the 21st Century Cures Act of 2016 seem to override provisions of the American Recovery and Reinvestment Act of 2009 (ARRA) and the HITECH-HIPAA Omnibus Final Rule that specified the fees to be charged by the health care entity when delivering the information to the patient in electronic format through a health information exchange. Previously, the health care entity's charge was limited to the entity's labor costs incurred in responding to the patient's request and the fee charged must have been both reasonable and cost-based. With this new legislation, patient access to their own health information may be at no charge to the patient if delivered pursuant to a health information exchange.[49] Implementing regulations to this provision are being developed at the time of publication of this textbook. Whether delivery of the same information in electronic form to those other than the patient can include a charge above that of labor costs appears unlikely.

The question regarding what is considered a reasonable fee has been flourishing as a matter of dispute. As health care providers have increased reproduction charges or have utilized correspondence services that set their own rates, the recipients of these charges have questioned whether the charge made is reasonable. Recipients have challenged "excessive" charges through two main approaches: filing lawsuits alleging that the charge was beyond the provider's actual costs or seeking legislative reform setting a price per page or price cap for reproduction. Both approaches have achieved mixed results, with more success achieved with legislation.[50]

Recipients who are attorneys have also sought to use the HIPAA provision concerning a patient's personal representative to reduce copy fee charges. Under HIPAA, an attorney who is a patient's personal representative in the sense of a health care power of attorney or who can otherwise legally act on the patient's behalf to make medical decisions can be charged a lesser fee than that charged to persons who are not the patient's personal representative, if state law allows for such reduced fees.[51] This approach is taken because the HIPAA regulation views the patient's personal representative as the patient himself for this purpose. Attorneys, insurers, or other third parties seeking health records who are not a personal representative within the meaning of the HIPAA regulation do not qualify for the copy fee reduction because they are not acting as the patient.

The increase in challenges to reasonable fees for reproduction has emerged as a trend throughout the United States. Health information managers involved with the process of releasing information should seriously review their policies and practices to determine whether the fee charged is reasonable or falls within the limits set by rule, statute, or case law.

ACCESS BY THE RESEARCHER

Central to the rapid advancement of health care is the role of medical research. Medical research studies have measured the impact, effectiveness, quality, outcome, and costs of occupational hazards, new pharmaceuticals, and the treatment methods of chronic diseases and infectious illnesses. The results of this research have led to improved understanding and improved possibilities for the management and prevention of disease and disability.

Considerable medical research involves the study of individuals rather than the study of health records for epidemiological purposes alone. As such, these studies are concurrent or prospective in nature, as opposed to retrospective.

The Ethical Perspective

A considerable volume of regulations exists at the federal level governing research of human subjects; this was not always the case. During the middle- and late-twentieth century in both Europe and the United States, medical experiments on human beings were conducted without regard to safeguarding patient health. Ranging from the medical experiments conducted by Nazis on concentration camp victims to Public Health Service experiments on African-American men concerning syphilis to the injection of dangerous substances into vulnerable members of the American population, numerous examples of atrocities committed in the name of science have occurred. Each of these studies, and others not listed here, brought to light ethical concerns over the proper manner in which to conduct research studies. As discussed in detail in Chapter 5, Ethical Standards, concepts such as autonomy, beneficence, justice, rights, and veracity are all central tenets of the health care world. When abusive research studies violated these concepts through such actions as withholding information from patients, employing coercive or deceptive tactics, or taking advantage of a vulnerable population, persons within and outside the health care world reacted with outrage. The world community responded with legal trials to punish wrongdoers (e.g., Nuremberg trials) and new guidelines for physician use when conducting research studies involving human subjects (e.g., Declaration of Helsinki).

ETHICS

Ethical concepts such as autonomy, beneficence, justice, rights, and veracity all play a role in research involving human subjects.

Whereas ethical concerns occupied the thoughts of many, others focused their concerns upon developing the means to establish and enforce ethical protections at a legal level. This effort evolved into regulations of the research study industry. In the 1970s, the U.S. Congress responded by passing the National Research Act, which authorized implementing regulations and the forming of a commission to identify basic ethical principles that underlie human research studies. Called the National Commission for the Protection of Human Subjects in Biomedical and Behavioral Research, and known as the National Commission, this new group published what many consider the landmark document in human subject research ethics: the **Belmont Report**.

The Belmont Report[52] asserted that three main principles form the ethical basis for all research involving human subjects: respect for persons, beneficence, and justice. Several requirements arose from each of these principles. For example, requirements for treating individuals as autonomous agents, obtaining informed consent, and respecting the privacy of research subjects derive from the principle of respect for persons. Requirements for studies to seek a balance between benefits and risks to the patient, along with a strong research design that maximizes benefits and reduces harms, derive from the beneficence principle. Requirements to select subjects equitably and avoid exploitation of vulnerable populations derive from the principle of justice. According to the authors of the Belmont Report, these three principles carry equal force and weight and are used to evaluate the ethical nature of any research study involving human subjects.

The Belmont Report also provides the ethical basis for the federal regulations that govern research involving human subjects. Known as the Common Rule, these regulations[53] govern how federal agencies, and institution to whom these agencies award grants, should conduct research involving human subjects. These regulations require: (1) review of all research involving human subjects by an institutional review board; (2) informed consent obtained from human research subjects; and (3) an assurance by the institution that it will comply with these federal regulations. The Office for Human Research Protections (OHRP), an agency within the U.S. Department of Health and Human Services (DHHS), administers these regulations.

The Regulatory Perspective

Because human subjects are involved, confidentiality of patient information becomes critical. At the same time, the success of research depends in large measure on the access to health information about these subjects. The balance that must be struck between these two competing interests has been answered on the federal level through the Department of Health and Human Services and the Food and Drug Administration (FDA), which promulgate regulations governing the participation of human subjects in clinical investigations. The Department of Health and Human Services supervises investigators who receive federal funds for research; the FDA supervises clinical trials of pharmaceuticals and related medical devices.

The regulations promulgated by each agency require investigators to obtain the approval of an **institutional review board (IRB)** before involving a human subject.[54] Typically associated with a university or academic medical center, the IRB is a group formally designated by an institution to safeguard the rights and welfare of human subjects by reviewing, approving, and monitoring medical research. The IRB relies on three ethical theories in its work: beneficence (do no harm, promote good); autonomy (respect for persons); and justice (fairness).

As part of the safeguards, the IRB requires the investigator to submit the research plan and informed consent form to the IRB for approval. The IRB reviews multiple elements of the research plan to determine if it meets regulatory standards and is ethically sound. Consideration is given to the study's design, to the risk/benefit ratio identified, how confidentiality will be maintained, and the methods for recruiting subjects and obtaining the subject's informed consent.[55] Confidentiality protections often include maintaining research data in a locked storage area, assigning security codes to data stored electronically, encrypting patient identifiable information, and identifying the patient in published articles by number or pseudonym only.

HIPAA

The Privacy Rule governs protected health information collected and used in the research environment.

Additional regulations have been introduced to the research environment as a result of HIPAA. The most significant regulation is the Privacy Rule, which protects individually identifiable health information (known as PHI) that has been electronically maintained or transmitted by a covered entity as well as such information when it takes any other form. Within the research context, IRBs have applied the HIPAA regulations in general, and the Privacy Rule in particular, to determine whether PHI can be used as the researcher suggests in the protocol, whether the patient has authorized such use, and whether a waiver of authorization is warranted under the protocol's circumstances. This examination by the IRB may result in changes made to submitted research protocols. HIPAA requirements are bolstered by the definitions found in the Common Rule for **identifiable private information** and **identifiable biospecimens**. In the context of research, identifiable private information is defined as the private information for which the identity of the human subject is or may readily be ascertained by the investigator or association with the information. In the same context, identifiable biospecimens means the biospecimens for which the identity of the human subject is or may be readily ascertained by the investigator or associated with the biospecimens.

HIPAA

The regulations offer two exceptions to IRB review: the use of deidentified data or a limited data set.

Furthermore, HIPAA offers two alternatives to researchers who are interested in collecting and using data about human subjects without undergoing the IRB's review of the protocol's provisions on the issues of use, authorization, and waiver. The first alternative, often referred to as the HIPAA safe harbor provision, allows use of **de-identified data**, which refers to data with all identifiers removed so that no one can reasonably identify the patient based on what remains. The second alternative allows researchers to utilize a **limited data set**, a form of data in which direct identifiers have been removed; other data—such as city, state, zip code, and dates of service, birth, or death—remain. A list of the direct identifiers that must be excluded or removed is given in Table 10.3. To employ limited data sets, researchers are required by HIPAA to enter into data use agreements with the covered entity that provides the limited data set.

GINA

Guidance on implementing the Genetic Information Nondiscrimination Act recommends changes to informed consent documents.

IRBs face another level of complexity with the passage of the Genetic Information Nondiscrimination Act of 2008 (GINA). Under GINA, an employer is prohibited from using genetic information for hiring, firing, or promotion decisions, and for any other decisions affecting terms of employment, regardless of where the information was obtained or collected. This means that if

Table 10.3 Limited Data Set Direct Identifiers
Name
Address
All elements of dates (except year) related to an individual
Telephone number
Fax number
E-mail address
Social Security number
Health record number
Health plan beneficiary number
Account number
Certificate/license numbers
Biometric identifiers, including finger and voice prints
Vehicle ID/license plate numbers
Internet protocol (IP) address numbers
Web universal resource locators (URLs)
Device identifiers and serial numbers
Full-face photographic images and comparable images

Source: 45 C.F.R. § 164.514(b) (2019).

the employer gained access to an employee's genetic information through the employee's participation in a research study, the employer is prohibited from considering this information. The Department of Health and Human Services has recommended to IRBs that they consider using the language contained in Figure 10.9 in informed consent documents used in research studies on human beings.

> A new Federal law, called the Genetic Information Nondiscrimination Act (GINA), generally makes it illegal for health insurance companies, group health plans, and most employers to discriminate against you based on your genetic information. This law generally will protect you in the following ways:
>
> - Health insurance companies and group health plans may not request your genetic information that we get from this research.
> - Health insurance companies and group health plans may not use your genetic information when making decisions regarding your eligibility or premiums.
> - Employers with 15 or more employees may not use your genetic information that we get from this research when making a decision to hire, promote, or fire you or when setting the terms of your employment.
>
> All health insurance companies and group health plans must follow this law by May 21, 2010. All employers with 15 or more employees must follow this law as of November 21, 2009. Be aware that this new Federal law does not protect you against genetic discrimination by companies that sell life insurance, disability insurance, or long-term care insurance.

Figure 10.9 Informed Consent Language Addressing Genetic Information Nondiscrimination Act (GINA)
Source: Courtesy of the U.S. Department of Health & Human Services, www.hhs.gov/ohrp.

Although the HIPAA and GINA regulations are the most recent effort to establish and enforce ethical protections at a legal level, they certainly will not be the last. Because of the ease with which data can be accessed in electronic form, regulators at the federal and state levels, along with professional associations and consumer watchdog groups, may take action in the future to strengthen ethical and legal protections even further. Such efforts have already been seen at the state level; legislatures have passed laws addressing requirements for informed consent and confidentiality protections as part of conducting the research process in their states.

Any health information professional whose institution is involved with medical research involving human subjects should ensure that all requests for access to health information from investigators have the prior approval of the IRB. A request for access to patient-specific health information for research purposes that has not been previously approved, by either an IRB if human subjects are involved or a health record committee if a retrospective review is called for, must be treated with great care. Unless patient consent has been given or patient identifying information has been removed or concealed, the health information professional should not grant the researcher access to the information sought. Furthermore, the health information professional should consider including, with *any* information released, a written statement prohibiting redisclosure without the institution's prior consent.

Health information professionals who work on the research study team as research analysts or in other capacities have a separate but complementary role to play from the traditional role of safeguarding access to data. These professionals work to ensure that the IRB's policies and decisions are applied to the research as it is conducted. This activity occurs at the beginning of the protocol with documentation that equitable recruiting standards are met and safeguards are being followed. It continues through the period of data creation into the periods of data maintenance and reporting. It involves ensuring that the informed consent presented to and signed by the human research subject is the same informed consent approved by the IRB. Woven throughout this activity is sensitivity to the application of proper data policies, standards, and procedures.

ACCESS BY THE BUSINESS ASSOCIATE

Virtually every health care provider has at one time or another contracted with a business associate to conduct its business. In the process of doing so, certain patient-specific health information may have been disclosed to the business associate. Until recently, access to and protection of this information by the business associate was subject only to the provisions contained in contractual agreements between the parties and not to statute, rule, or regulation. With the advent of the HIPAA Privacy Rule, passage of the American Recovery and Reinvestment Act of 2009 (ARRA), and the provisions of the HITECH-HIPAA Omnibus Final Rule reconciling provisions of HIPAA and ARRA, access to and protection of that information by the business associate has come under national regulation and statute.

CRITICAL THINKING

A health care organization possesses numerous patient records in paper format that have yet to be digitized. Some paper records are kept in an unlocked area, while others are kept on shelves in a locked area. A cleaning crew cleans both areas after hours. Each member of the crew has signed a confidentiality agreement. Is the signing of a confidentiality agreement acceptable to protect the information contained in the records held in an unlocked area or should the organization store all the records under lock and key?

Under HIPAA, a **business associate** is defined as one who performs or assists in performing a function or activity involving the use or disclosure of individually identifiable health information on behalf of a covered entity.[56] A business associate is not a member of the health care provider's workforce, such as an employee, trainee, or volunteer. Services provided by a business associate may be health related, including billing, claims processing, data analysis, utilization review, and quality assurance, or nonhealth related, including legal, actuarial, accounting, consulting, or management. Provisions of the Privacy Rule require that a health care provider may disclose patient-specific health information to a business associate only if the provider receives satisfactory assurance that the business associate will safeguard that information. This assurance must be manifested through a written agreement, with specific provisions required.

The written agreement must establish the permitted uses and disclosures of the patient-specific health information by the business associate and indicate that the business associate may not use or disclose the information other than as expressly permitted or required by the agreement. Additionally, the agreement should require the business associate to use appropriate safeguards to prevent unauthorized use of the information and a mechanism under which unauthorized use may be reported. The agreement should indicate that the business associate must make its practices, books, and records available to the Department of Health and Human Services (DHHS) to determine compliance with the privacy regulation and to provide an accounting of the uses and disclosures made since receipt of the information.

Provisions of the Omnibus Final Rule make it clear that subcontractors of business associates are also subject to the provisions of the Privacy Rule if they create, receive, maintain, or transmit protected health information on behalf of another business associate. Additionally, business associates are liable to their covered entity for the activities of their subcontractors who have entered into a business associate agreement with them.[57] Examples include e-prescribing gateways and personal health record vendors. Accordingly, the business associate agreement should bind any subcontractors or agents of the business associate to the same requirements and require the business associate to destroy or return the information at the termination of the agreement.[58]

HIPAA/ARRA

Both the American Recovery and Reinvestment Act and the Health Insurance Portability and Accountability Act place duties and obligations upon business associates to secure protected health information.

Under ARRA requirements, the health care provider has a duty to monitor the business associate's compliance with the terms of the agreement, particularly any HIPAA provisions. If the health care provider becomes aware that the business associate is not complying with HIPAA, the provider may direct the business associate to conform to HIPAA or may cancel the agreement between the parties. The health care provider's failure to monitor the business associate in this fashion may be in violation of both the Privacy Rule and ARRA if it knows of or reasonably should have known of material breaches by the business associate.[59] For that reason, health care providers would be wise to include audit provisions in the agreement.

ARRA expands this duty to monitor one step further: the business associate possesses the duty to respond to noncompliance by the health care provider. This means that if the business associate becomes aware of noncompliance by the health care provider, the business associate should seek to have the provider comply with HIPAA or cancel the agreement between the parties.[60] This expansion is referred to as a "two-way street" provision.

Table 10.4 Content of Notice of Breach of Confidentiality

CONTENT OF NOTIFICATION: Regardless of the method by which notice is provided to individuals under this section, notice of a breach shall include, to the extent possible, the following:

(1) A brief description of what happened, including the date of the breach and the date of the discovery of the breach, if known.

(2) A description of the types of unsecured protected health information that were involved in the breach (such as full name, Social Security number, date of birth, home address, account number, or disability code).

(3) The steps individuals should take to protect themselves from potential harm resulting from the breach.

(4) A brief description of what the covered entity involved is doing to investigate the breach, to mitigate losses, and to protect against any further breaches.

(5) Contact procedures for individuals to ask questions or learn additional information, which shall include a toll-free telephone number, an e-mail address, Web site, or postal address.

Source: 42 U.S.C. § 17932(f) (2019); 45 C.F.R. § 164.404(c) (2019).

Further, provisions of ARRA require the business associate to notify the health care provider of any breach of confidentiality involving the security or privacy of protected health information. Under the Omnibus Final Rule, a **breach** is defined as "the acquisition, access, use, or disclosure of protected health information in a manner ... which compromises the security or privacy of protected health information."[61] This definition applies to all breaches, whether occurring with a covered entity or a business associate. In the event the provider learns of a material breach or repeated breaches, it should take reasonable steps to cure or end the violations by the business associate, terminate the agreement, and/or report the violations to DHHS. Additionally, the provider and the business associate should coordinate notifying those patients affected by the breach of security within sixty days of the date of the breach, using the content of Table 10.4 in the notice, unless a low probability exists that PHI has been compromised. Where the breach affects more than 500 residents of a state or jurisdiction, notice must also be sent to prominent media outlets.[62]

Any health information professional whose institution is involved with business associates should ensure that the provisions of the written agreement comply with HIPAA's Privacy Rule and that the ARRA notice procedures are followed.

ACCESS PURSUANT TO REPORTING LAWS

Access to patient-specific health information may also be necessary to safeguard the public's health. In order to prevent and lessen the occurrence of threats to public health, such as communicable diseases, virtually all states require, by either statute or regulation, the reporting of certain patient-specific health information. Because local health care providers and institutions are in a position to observe patients posing public health threats, they are the most logical ones to initiate the chain of events that lead to control and prevention of these threats. For that reason, the law places a burden on health care providers and institutions to report public health threats.

Public health threats encompass a wide variety of health care problems that endanger the public health and must be reported to a public health agency. Common public health threats include communicable diseases (such as venereal diseases and AIDS),[63] child abuse,[64] injuries

Table 10.5 HIPAA Mandatory Disclosures
Circumstances under which protected health information may be disclosed without first obtaining the patient's authorization include, but are not limited to:
Emergencies concerning public health or safety.
Health oversight/Quality assurance reviews by authorized authorities.
Instances concerning victims of abuse, neglect, or domestic violence.
Reporting of adverse events, tracking of products, recalls of products, and postmarketing surveillance to entities subject to FDA regulation regarding FDA-regulated products or activities.
Law enforcement authorities for use in identifying or apprehending an escapee or violent criminal.
Judicial or administrative proceedings via court order.

Source: 45 C.F.R. § 164.512 (2019).

caused by deadly weapons,[65] fetal deaths,[66] and cancer.[67] Each state's law details its reporting requirements, including a listing of threats that must be reported, time frames within which to report the threat, and whether to disclose patient identity.

In practice, the health care provider or institution reports these threats to the state's department of health or similar agency, which collates the data and determines what action should be taken. Where injuries by deadly weapons are concerned, the health care provider or institution reports the incident to law enforcement personnel. Aggregate state data concerning communicable diseases are gathered by the U.S. Public Health Service, which collates and assesses the data on a national level. Working through the Centers for Disease Control, the Public Health Service publishes this information in the *Morbidity and Mortality Weekly Report*.

One requirement mandating disclosure of otherwise protected health information is the HIPAA Privacy Rule. This Rule mandates disclosure in certain circumstances, negating the need to obtain the patient's authorization before releasing information. Examples of those mandated disclosures are found in Table 10.5.

Every health information professional working with a health care provider or institution that deals with public health threats must determine what mechanism is in place to report these threats. Failure of the health care provider or institution to report public health threats may be an infraction of the law. The health information professional may wish to audit the patient's health record for the date and time that the health care provider reported the threat to determine if the reporting mechanism works properly.

ACCESS TO ADOPTION RECORDS

Adoption records are the health records of the individual placed for adoption. In virtually every state, adoption records are considered confidential, and disclosure of the information contained in them may only be made pursuant to legal procedures. At the core of the access to adoption records issue are two competing interests: (1) the interests of the biological parent(s) in placing a child for adoption, often with the promise of confidentiality, and (2) the interests of the adoptee for genetic information and to satisfy curiosity about his natural identity. These competing interests have clashed in recent years as more and more adoptees have sought access to their adoption records, including birth records (see Figure 10.10).

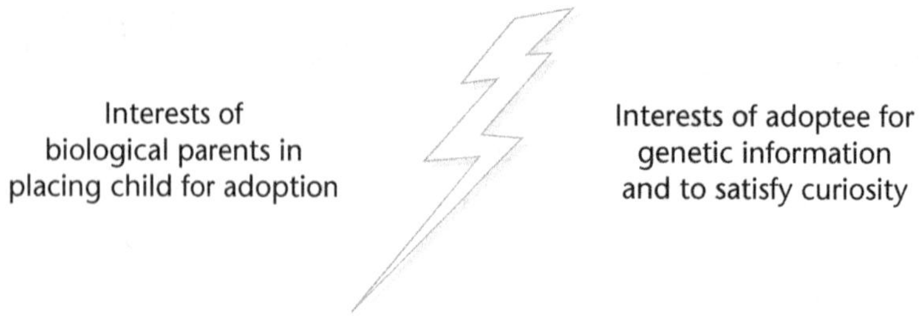

Figure 10.10 Access to Adoption Records: Clash of Competing Interests

The law governing access to adoption records is a mix of judicial decision and statute. For decades, courts have considered the requests of adoptees for access to their adoption records as potential impediments to the adoption process and so have discouraged granting access. Courts have erected barriers to access, such as requiring the adoptee to establish good cause for access and imposing notice and hearing requirements. Examples of good cause are specific with each court case and may include the need for genetic information to solve a medical condition or psychological trauma.[68] Notice and hearing requirements may include (1) conducting a search to determine if the biological parent(s) consents to the release of information, and (2) conducting a hearing to balance the interests of all parties.[69]

Because the barriers erected by courts are sometimes burdensome and difficult to overcome, adoptees have focused on state legislatures to obtain legal access to their adoption records. In some cases, legislatures have responded by easing the standards for access, by creating voluntary adoption registry services,[70] or by permitting independent searches for biological parents to solicit their consent for a meeting.[71] In the majority of states, the law still requires the adoptee to obtain a court order before permitting the health care provider or institution to disclose identifying information without the consent of the biological parent.

As a matter of practice, each health information professional should determine what laws apply to adoptees in their particular state and, in consultation with counsel, develop policies and procedures to address disclosure requests. If and when the health information professional receives a request by an adoptee for information relating to his biological parents, he will be better prepared to handle the request. As a general matter, where state law bars disclosure of the information sought, the health information professional is advised to refuse the request and refer the adoptee to the agency that handled the adoption or the appropriate court having jurisdiction over adoption proceedings. Where the request is accompanied by claims of an emergency nature, the health information professional should consult with counsel to determine how to assist the court in considering the request or whether to provide summary information from the record that does not include patient identification.

UNLAWFUL ACCESS

An assumption central to the discussion so far is that the demand for access to protected health information is made to the health information professional who, in turn, can decide how to address the request. Unfortunately, not all demands for access are legitimate but may be made pursuant to a crime. In criminal circumstances, the wrongdoer seeks access to health care data surreptitiously, by either concealing the true purpose of a request or not making a request at all. Accordingly, the health information professional is unaware of the improper attempt at access and is not in the position to refuse the request for data. This position raises new issues to resolve.

One such crime that has increased in the last decade is identity theft. **Identity theft** involves the knowing transfer or use, without lawful authority, of the identity of another person with the intent to commit, aid, or abet any unlawful activity that constitutes a violation of federal, state, or local law.[72] Identity theft knows no geographic, racial, gender, or age boundaries and is illegal at both federal and state law levels.[73] Personal data sought by identity thieves include names, addresses, Social Security numbers, bank or credit card numbers, and identities of minor children. Armed with this data, thieves may attempt to obtain money from bank accounts, charge to existing or open new credit card accounts, submit false insurance claims, obtain health care benefits, or damage another's credit rating by falsely filing for bankruptcy protection. Those who are victims of identity theft face an enormous challenge in clearing their name and recovering full possession of their identity.

Health information professionals can address the potential for identity theft of health information used to obtain or bill for medical services or medical goods (**medical identity theft**) by employing preventive measures. Such measures can include employing the technology available to safeguard electronic PHI, including passwords, access controls, encryption, firewalls, and electronic audits. Nontechnological safeguards—such as background checks for employees and business associates, redaction of portions of Social Security numbers or credit card account numbers, and restricted access to paper-based health records—may all be employed. Policies and procedures that address record retention, destruction, disposal, or reuse all should include provisions to restrict access to PHI to only those with a need to know. Review of these safeguards, policies, and procedures should occur on a routine basis, along with training for health care staff members.

Prevention measures are not only prudent actions, they are required by federal regulations. The Federal Trade Commission (FTC) has issued what are referred to as Red Flag Rules with which most health care organizations must comply. These Red Flag Rules require health care providers to develop sophisticated identify theft detection programs and train their staff in the use of these programs. Components of such a program are listed in Table 10.6. Additional information concerning the Red Flag Rules can be found in Chapter 14, Health Care Fraud and Abuse.

Even with preventive measures in place, identity theft may still occur. It is incumbent upon HIM professionals to develop a strategy to detect the occurrence of identity theft and respond to and address the occurrence once it is reported. Such a strategy is mandated by federal regulation.[74] This strategy should include the level of response deemed appropriate by the health care provider, the mechanism to investigate the report, and how notification to law enforcement or governmental agencies and the victim will occur. This notification step involves reconciling the HIPAA provision that allows release of evidence of criminal conduct to law enforcement authorities with state or local law that may require such release only on patient authorization or court order.[75] The strategy should also comply with the requirements of state law governing notification of security breaches involving personal information.[76] The strategy should also address the extent to which the health care provider may assist the identity theft victim with health care–related matters, such as billing or inaccurate entries in the health record, or non-health care–related matters, such as filing a police report or a fraud alert to a credit reporting agency. By having such a strategy in place, the health information professional is well positioned to assist the identity theft victim.

Table 10.6 Components of an Identity Theft Prevention and Disclosure Program

Component	Activity
Identify Relevant Red Flags	• Alerts, notifications, or warnings from a consumer reporting agency; • Suspicious documents; • Suspicious personally identifying information; • Suspicious activity relating to a covered account; • Notices from customers, victims of identity theft, law enforcement authorities, or other entities about possible identity theft in connection with covered accounts.
Detect Red Flags	Establish policies and procedures to detect red flags in day-to-day operations.
Prevent and Mitigate Identity Theft	Create appropriate responses to red flags.
Update Program Periodically	Consider new risks and trends when updating program on a regular basis.
Administer Program	• Obtain program approval from board of directors or designated senior employee; • Train staff; and • Monitor staff and service providers

Source: 16 C.F.R. Part 681 (2019).

CONCLUSION

Because the proper disclosure of health information is governed by complex legal requirements, requests for access to patient-specific health information should be handled only by those with proper training and supervision. Health information professionals responsible for disclosure of health information must develop, implement, and periodically revise training programs that incorporate the governing legal requirements. Such programs should address the principles raised in this chapter, particularly the differences the law makes between the categories of individuals seeking access to health information.

CASE STUDY A

You are the director of health information services at a tertiary-care hospital. You and the director of emergency room services are jointly responsible for reporting instances of communicable disease, child abuse, and cancer to the appropriate state authority. You have just completed an audit of your institution's reporting mechanism and discovered that the reporting requirements are not consistently met. The audit could not definitively establish whether the reporting never occurred or occurred but was not documented in the patient's health record. Discuss what legal issues are present and what approaches you should take to resolve this problem.

CASE STUDY B

You are the head of the health information management department at General Hospital. An FBI agent has arrived at your office with a search warrant in hand. He asks to speak with you about the hospital's health records. How should you respond?

REVIEW QUESTIONS

1. What is the difference between confidential and nonconfidential information for purposes of access to patient-specific health information?
2. To what extent do patients possess a right to the information contained in their health record? Explain your answer.
3. What purposes does a notice of privacy practices serve?
4. What is the difference between consent and authorization to use patient-specific health information?
5. What is the preemption doctrine, and how does it apply to patient-specific health information?
6. What are the minimum elements necessary to constitute a valid release of patient information?
7. What defects may invalidate a release of patient information form?
8. What is a compound authorization, and when is it permitted?
9. Describe the principle of the minimum necessary standard.
10. Who may grant authority to release information?
11. Identify three ways, excluding traditional mail, through which health information can be disclosed and the safeguards employed for each method.
12. What is a redisclosure notice, and when is its use mandated?
13. What limitations to the Federal Privacy Act exist in terms of a patient's access to his own health information?
14. How does a family member obtain access to a patient's health information?
15. Describe the concept of a reasonable fee to obtain a health record, and what costs may be included in the fee.
16. State the reasoning why a patient should not be charged a fee for access to his own health information.
17. How have those who were charged fees for access to health records challenged?
18. What is the name of the landmark document in the area of human research ethics?

19. What is an institutional review board (IRB) and what does it consider?
20. Define a business associate, and explain how the HIPAA final privacy rule applies to a business associate.
21. Why are local health care providers and institutions the logical entities to report public health threats?
22. How are public health threats reported?
23. Why do adoptees prefer using legislative rather than judicial means to obtain adoption records?
24. How does identity theft differ from medical identity theft?

ENRICHMENT ACTIVITY

Research the Internet for notices of privacy practices and policies, complete with forms, recommended for use by health care organizations. Are the components of the policies consistent with the final Privacy Rule enacted pursuant to HIPAA? If not, what components are missing or added? Evaluate whether the policies comply with HIPAA adequately.

ENRICHMENT ACTIVITY

Relying on the information contained in this chapter, develop a policy for a health care institution concerning release of patient-specific health information. What methods will you include to respond to requests for release of information? Will the methods differ based on who is making the request, what is being requested, or the urgency of the request?

ENRICHMENT ACTIVITY

Visit the health information management department in a local health care facility. Review the department's procedure manual concerning release of information to determine compliance with the concepts addressed in this chapter. Observe the activities involved in processing requests for release of information. Analyze whether the department staff comply with procedures listed in the manual.

ENRICHMENT ACTIVITY

Select one of the following Web links that address the protection of human subjects in research and complete the online training found there. You may have to create an account as a student to initiate the training. Upon completion of the training, print the completion certificate. Provide one copy of the certificate to your instructor and retain one copy for your professional portfolio. When you design your resume, make sure to include this certification among your list of accomplishments. https://phrptraining.com/#!/ or http://cme.cancer.gov/clinicaltrials/learning/humanparticipant-protections.asp. You may need to enroll/register to access these sites.

NOTES

1. 45 C.F.R. § 164.524 (2019).

2. The Independent Health Record Bank of 2006, S.B. 3454, 109th Cong. (2006); The Independent Health Record Trust Act of 2007. H.R. 2991, 110th Cong. (2007).

3. La. Rev. Stat. Ann. § 40:1299.96 (West 2019); Mass. Gen. L. ch. 111, § 70 (2019); Miss. Code Ann. § 41-9-65 (2019); Tenn. Code Ann. § 68-11-304 (2019).

4. Mo. Code Regs. tit. 19, § 30-20-084(1)(F) (2019).

5. *See, e.g., Pyramid Life Ins. Co. v. Masonic Hosp. Assoc., 191 F. Supp. 51 (W.D. Okla. 1961); Rabens v. Jackson Park Hosp. Found., 351 N.E.2d 276 (Ill. Ct. App. 1976).*

6. 45 C.F.R. § 164.520 (2019) states the general rule; 45 C.F.R. § 164.522 (2019) provides the standard for a patient to restrict use and disclosure of patient-specific health information.

7. 45 C.F.R. § 164.506 (2019).

8. Pub. L. 111-5, Title XIII, Subpart D, § 13405(a) (2019).

9. 45 C.F.R. § 164.508 (2019).

10. 45 C.F.R. § 164.528 (2019); 42. U.S.C. § 17935(c)(3) (2019).

11. 19 Haw. Rev. Stat. §§ 323C-1 to -54 (Repealed 2001).

12. Mont. Code Ann. §§ 50-16-501 to -542 (2019); Wash. Rev. Code Ann. §§ 70.02.005 to 904 (2019).

13. California Consumer Privacy Act of 2018, Civil Code 1798.100 et seq. (2018). Available at https://leginfo.legislature.ca.gov/faces/billTextClient.xhtml?bill_id=201720180AB375.

14. European Union General Data Protection Regulation, Article 4 (2018). Available at https://eur-lex.europa.eu/legal-content/EN/TXT/?qid=1528874672298&uri=CELEX%3A32016R0679.

15. 45 C.F.R. § 160.203 (2019).

16. 42 U.S.C. § 17932 (2019).

17. 42 C.F.R. § 493.1291(f) (2019), 45 C.F.R. § 164.524(a) (2019).

18. 45 C.F.R. § 164.522(a)(1)(vi)(A) (2019).

19. The American Health Information Management Association has published minimum requirements for an acceptable authorization for disclosure of health information. Release of Information Toolkit: A Practical Guide for Access, Use, and Disclosure of Protected Health Information (2013).

20. 45 C.F.R. § 164.508 (2019).

21. Ibid.

22. Ibid.

23. 45 C.F.R. § 165.514 (2019); U.S.C. § 17935(b) (2019).

24. *See, e.g.,* La. Rev. Stat. Ann. § 13:3715.1(B) (West 2019).

25. 45 C.F.R. § 164.502(f) (2019).

26. 45 C.F.R. § 164.510(b) (2019).

27. *See, e.g.,* Cal. Fam. Code § 7002 (West 2019); Conn. Gen. Stat. Ann. § 46 b-150b (West 2019); Mich. Comp. Laws Ann. § 722.4 (West 2019); Nev. Rev. Stat. § 129.080 (2019); Va. Code Ann. § 16.1-333 (Michie 2019).

28. 45 F.C.R. § 154.512(b)(6) (2019).

29. *See, e.g.,* Davis, Nancy, et al., Facsimile Transmission of Health Information (Updated) American Health Information Management Association, Practice Brief, Updated August 2006.

30. *See, e.g.,* Iowa Code Ann. § 228.5 (West 2019); N.Y. Pub. Health Law § 2785 (6) (b) (McKinney 2019).

31. 42 C.F.R. § 2.32 (2019).

32. 45 C.F.R. § 164.524 (2019). Exceptions to the right include information (1) found in psychotherapy notes; (2) compiled in reasonable anticipation of litigation; (3) maintained by a correctional institution or health care provider acting under the direction of a correctional institution; and (4) certain categories of research.

33. U.S.C. § 17935(e) (2019); 45 C.F.R. § 164.524 (2019).

34. Both Alabama and Kansas allow the hospital governing board to determine what access patients may have. R. Jones, Of Professional Interest: Medical Record Access Laws, 63 J. AMERICAN HEALTH INFORMATION MANAGEMENT ASSOC. 29 (1992).

35. Examples of states specifically permitting patients access to the health information contained in the record include: ALASKA STAT. § 18.23.005 (2019); CAL. HEALTH & SAFETY CODE § 123110 (West 2019); COLO. REV. STAT. ANN. §§ 25-1-801 & 802 (West 2019); CONN. GEN. STAT. ANN. § 4-104 (West 2019); FLA. STAT. ANN. § 455.241 (West 2019); HAW. REV. STAT. § 622-57 (2019); IND. CODE ANN. § 34-6-2-15 (Burns 2019); KY. REV. STAT. ANN. § 422.317 (Michie/Bobbs-Merrill 2019); LA. REV. STAT. ANN. § 40:1299.96 (West 2019); ME. REV. STAT. ANN. tit. 22 § 1711 (2019); MD. HEALTH-GEN. CODE ANN. § 4-304 (2019); MASS. GEN. LAWS ANN. ch. 112, § 12CC (West 2019); MINN. REV. STAT. ANN. § 144.292 (West 2019); MISS. CODE ANN. § 41-9-65 (2019); MONT. CODE ANN. § 50-16-541 (2019); NEV. REV. STAT. § 629.061 (2019); OHIO REV. CODE ANN. § 3701.74 (Baldwin 2019); OKLA. STAT. ANN. tit. 76, § 19 (West 2019); S.D. CODIFIED LAWS §§ 34-12-15 & 36-2-16 (2019); TENN. CODE ANN. § 68-11-304 (2019); WASH. REV. CODE ANN. § 70.02.080 (West 2014); W. VA. CODE § 16-29-1 (2019); WIS. STAT. ANN. § 146.83 (West 2019); WYO. STAT. § 35-2-611 (2019).

36. 5 U.S.C. § 552a (2019).

37. The federal government and several states sanction withholding health information in this manner, including: 45 C.F.R. § 164.520 (2019); HAW. REV. STAT. § 622-57 (2019); LA. REV. STAT. ANN. § 40:1299.96(d) (West 2019); ME. REV. STAT. ANN. tit. 22, § 1711 (West 2019); Md. HEALTH-GEN. CODE ANN. § 4-304 (2019); MASS. GEN. LAWS ANN. ch. 111, § 70 (West 2019); MINN. STAT. ANN. § 144.292 (West 2019); OHIO REV. CODE ANN. § 3701.74(c) (2019).

38. 45 C.F.R. § 164.524 (2019).

39. The American Recovery and Reinvestment Act of 2009, 42 U.S.C. §§ 17921, 17937(e)(11) (2019).

40. Id at § 17937(a-g) (2019).

41. *See, e.g.,* ALA. CODE § 25-5-77(b) (2019); FLA. STAT. ANN. § 440.13(1)(C) (West 2019); LA. REV. STAT. ANN. § 23:1127 (West 2019); MO. REV. STAT. §§ 287.140(7) & 287.210(4) (2019); NEB. REV. STAT. § 48-120(4) (2019); S.D. CODIFIED LAWS ANN. § 62-4-45 (2019).

42. 45 C.F.R. § 164.510 (2019).

43. *See, e.g.,* CAL. WELF. & INST. CODE § 4514.5 (West 2019); COLO. REV. STAT. ANN. § 25-3-109(12) (West 2019); *Cannell v. Medical & Surgical Clinic, S.C.,* 315 N.E.2d 278 (Ill. App. Ct. 1974).

44. *See, e.g.,* CAL. PROB. CODE § 4678 (West Supp. 2019); GA. CODE ANN. § 31-36-10 (2019); Ill. ANN. STAT. CH.. 755, para. 45/4-10 (2019); IND. CODE ANN. § 30-5-7-5 (West 2019); MO. REV. STAT. § 404.840(2) (2019); NEB. REV. STAT. § 30-3417(4) (2019); OR. REV. STAT. § 127.712 (2019).

45. 42 U.S.C. § 17935(d) (2019); 45 C.F.R. §§ 164.502(a) & .508(a) (2019).

46. *See, e.g.,* MINN. STAT. ANN. § 144.292 (West 2019) (allowing reasonable charge to patient); S.D. CODIFIED LAWS ANN. § 34-12-15 (2019) (allowing charge for actual reproduction and mailing expense); TENN. CODE ANN. § 68-11-304 (2019) (allowing charge for reasonable costs); WASH REV. CODE ANN. § 70.02.030 (2019) (allowing for reasonable charge).

47. 45 C.F.R. §§ 164.502(a) & .524 (2019).

48. Id.

49. 21st Century Cures Act. 42 U.S.C. § 17935(d) (2019).

50. *See, e.g.,* MD. HEALTH-GEN. CODE ANN. § 4-304 (2019) (allowing charge of no more than fifty cents per page); NEV. REV. STAT. § 629.061 (2019) (allowing charge of sixty cents per page for photocopies plus postage costs); WASH. REV. CODE ANN. § 70.02.010(38) (West 2019) (allowing charge not to exceed sixty-five cents per page for the first thirty pages and fifty cents per page thereafter).

51. 42 C.F.R. §§ 164.502(g); .524(c) (2019).

52. THE NATIONAL COMMISSION FOR THE PROTECTION OF HUMAN SUBJECTS OF BIOMEDICAL AND BEHAVIORAL RESEARCH (1978), THE BELMONT REPORT. Washington, DC: Department of Health, Education, and Welfare.

53. 45 C.F.R. Part 46.101 to .505 and 21 C.F.R. Part 56.11 (2019).

54. 45 C.F.R. § 46.101 (2019) (DHHS); 21 C.F.R. § 50.1 (2019) (FDA).

55. 45 C.F.R. § 46.116(a)(5) (2019) (DHHS); 21 C.F.R. § 50.25(a)(5) (2019) (FDA).

56. 42 C.F.R. § 164.103, .504 (2019).

57. 45 C.F.R. §§ 164.504(e) (2014), 164.314(a) (2019).

58. 42 C.F.R. § 164.506 (2019).

59. 42 C.F.R. § 164.506(e)(2)(iii) (2019); 42 U.S.C. § 17934(b) (2019).

60. Id.

61. 45 C.F.R. § 164.402 (2019).

62. 42 U.S.C. § 17932(d); (e)(2); (f)(1-5) (2019).

63. *See, e.g.,* IDAHO CODE § 39-609 (2019); KAN. STAT. ANN. § 65-6002 (2019); MO. CODE REGS. tit. 19, § 20-20.020 (2019); S.D. ADMIN. R. 44:20 (2019).

64. *See, e.g.,* CONN. GEN. STAT. ANN. § 17a-101 (West 2019); HAW. REV. STAT. § 350-1.1 (2019); MO. REV. STAT. § 210.110 (2019); R.I. GEN. LAWS § 40-11-3.1 (2019); S.D. CODIFIED LAWS ANN. § 26-8A-6 (2019).

65. MO. REV. STAT. § 578.350 (2019).

66. *See, e.g.,* MINN. STAT. ANN. § 144.222 (2019); S.D. CODIFIED LAWS ANN. § 34-25.-32. 2 (2019); TENN. CODE ANN. § 68-3-208 (2019); VA. CODE ANN. § 32.1-264 (Michie 2019).

67. *See, e.g.,* FLA. STAT. ANN. § 385.202 (West 2019); HAW. REV. STAT. § 324-21 (2019); MD. HEALTH GEN. CODE ANN. § 18-204 (2019); MO. REV. STAT. §§ 192.650-.657 (2019); NEB. REV. STAT. § 81-646 (2019); OHIO REV. CODE ANN. § 3701.262 (Baldwin 2019); VT. STAT. ANN. tit. 18, § 153 (2019). The Cancer Registry Amendment Act of 1992 authorized funding to states to enhance existing cancer registries, including establishing a computerized reporting and data processing system. 42 U.S.C. § 280e (2019).

68. Examples of good cause include: *Golan v. Louise Wise Services,* 507 N.E.2d 275 (N.Y. 1987) (for treatment of a medical problem); *In re: Wilson,* 544 N.Y.S.2d 886 (App. Div. 2d 1989) (for treatment of psychological trauma substantiated by health professionals).

69. *Application of Romano,* 438 N.Y.S.2d 967, 971-72 (N.Y. Surr. Ct. 1981).

70. Many states have enacted some form of voluntary adoption registry, including: ARK. STAT. ANN. §§ 9-9-501-508 (2019); FLA. STAT. ANN. § 63.165 (West 2019); IDAHO CODE § 39-259A (2019); IND. CODE § 31-19-18-2 (2019); ME. REV. STAT. ANN. tit. 22, § 2706-A (2019); MASS. GEN. LAWS ANN. ch. 210, § 5D (2019); MICH. COMP. LAWS § 710.68; NEV. REV. STAT. § 127.007 (2019); N.H. REV. STAT. ANN § 170-B:19 (2019).

71. ALA. CODE § 22-9A-12 (2019); MINN. STAT. ANN. § 259.47 (West 2019); MO. REV. STAT. § 453.121 (2019); N.D. CENT. CODE § 14-15-16 (2019); TENN. CODE ANN. § 36-1-141 (2019).

72. The Identity Theft and Assumption Deterrence Act of 1998, 18 U.S.C. § 1028 (2019). Some states with provisions addressing identity theft include: IA. STAT. ANN. § 554D.122 (2019); MINN. STAT. ANN. § 609.527 (2019); MO. REV. STAT. § 570.223.1 (2019); S.D. STAT. ANN. § 22.30A (2019).

73. Ibid. See also ARK. CODE ANN. 5-37-226 (2019); IA. STAT. ANN. § 554D.122 (2019); MINN. STAT. ANN. § 609.527 (2019); MO. REV. STAT. § 570.223.1 (2019); S.D. STAT. ANN. § 22.30A (2019).

74. Identity Theft Flags and Address Discrepancies under Fair and Accurate Credit Transactions Act of 2003, Final Rule, 16 C.F.R. Part 681 (2019) (requiring hospitals to create a plan to identify "red flags" that signal potential identity theft).

75. 45 C.F.R. § 164.512(f)(5) (2019).

76. Almost all states have laws requiring notification of security breaches involving personal information. ARIZ. REV. STAT. § 44-7501 (2019); ARK. CODE ANN. § 4-110-101 (2019); CAL. CIV. CODE §§ 56.06, 1785.11.2, 1798.29, 1789.82, & 1798.100 et seq. (2019); COLO. REV. STAT. § 6-1-716 (2019); CONN. GEN. STAT. § 36A-701(B) (2019); DEL. CODE tit. 6, § 128-101 (2019); FLA. STAT. ANN. § 817.5681 (2019); GA. CODE §§ 10-1-910, -911 (2019); HAW. REV. STAT. § 487N-2 (2019); IDAHO CODE § 28-51-104 to -107 (2019); ILL. COMP. STAT. § 530/1 (2019); IND. CODE § 24-4.9 (2019); IOWA CODE § 715c.1 (2019); KAN. STAT. ANN. § 50-7a01 (2019); LA. REV. STAT. ANN. § 51:3071 (2019); ME. REV. STAT. ANN. Tit 10, § 1347 (2019); MD. CODE ANN., COM. LAW § 14-3501 (2019); MASS. GEN. LAWS § 93H-1 (2019); MICH. COMP. LAWS § 445.72 (2019); MINN. STAT. §§ 325e.61, 325e.64 (2019); MONT. CODE § 30-14-1701 (2019); NEB. REV. STAT. §§ 87-801 to -807 (2019); NEV. REV. STAT. § 603a.010 (2019); N.H. REV. STAT. §§ 359-C:19 to -C:21 (2019); N.J. STAT. ANN. § 56:8-163 (2019); N.Y. GEN. BUS. LAW § 899-aa (2019); N.C. GEN. STAT. § 75-65 (2019); N.D. CENT. CODE § 51-30-01 (2019); OHIO REV. CODE §§ 1347.12. 1349.19, 1349.191, & 1349.192 (2019); OKLA STAT. § 74.3113.1 (2019); 73 PA. STAT. § 2303 (2019); R.I. GEN. LAWS § 11-49.2-1 (2019); TENN. CODE ANN. § 47-18-2107 (2019); TEX. BUS & COM. CODE § 48.001 (2019); UTAH CODE §§ 13-44-101, -102, -201, -202, -310 (2019); VT. STAT. tit 9 § 2430 (2019); WASH. REV. CODE § 19.255.010 (2019); W.V. CODE § 46a-2A-101 (2019); WIS. STAT. § 134.98 (2019); WYO. STAT. § 40-12-501 (2019).

CHAPTER 11 SPECIALIZED PATIENT RECORDS

LEARNING OBJECTIVES

After reading this chapter, the learner should be able to:

1. Summarize the difference between specialized patient records and general health records.
2. Discuss the regulations governing patient identification and their practical application.
3. Compare and contrast release of information forms used in an ordinary health care setting with those used in a substance abuse setting.
4. Identify those instances where disclosure of health information of substance abuse treatment may be made without written patient consent.
5. Compare and contrast a court order authorizing disclosure of patient-specific information with a subpoena duces tecum.
6. Discuss procedures for handling a court order authorizing disclosure and a subpoena duces tecum.
7. Explain the difference between the official record and the personal record in the mental health/developmental disability context.
8. Identify the sources of legal requirements in the home health care context.
9. Summarize the benefits and risks associated with genetic information.
10. Explain the similarities and differences between voluntary testing, mandatory testing, and anonymous testing in the HIV setting.
11. Explain the three component steps of the voluntary testing process.
12. Compare and contrast court-ordered HIV/AIDS testing with HIV/AIDS testing pursuant to statutory authority.
13. Describe the situations in which employers may require HIV/AIDS testing of employees.

KEY CONCEPTS

Anonymous testing
Disclosure with patient authorization
Disclosure without patient authorization
Genetic information
Mandatory testing
Official record
Patient identification
Patient notice
Personal record
Preemption
Psychotherapy notes
Release of information
Specialized patient records
Treatment program
Voluntary testing

INTRODUCTION

Although all health information must be treated with care, certain categories of health information demand special treatment. In particular, the health information of those patients undergoing treatment for certain illnesses, such as substance abuse or mental illness, or in nonacute care settings, such as the patient's home, are subject to legal requirements that differ from those of an acute care setting. For purposes of this chapter, health information records for these illnesses or in these settings are referred to as **specialized patient records**.

One distinguishing aspect between specialized patient records and general health records is the nature of the information present in the record. Specialized patient records contain not only truly medical information but also therapeutic mental and emotional information. The volume of this therapeutic mental and emotional information is often greater than that contained in a general health record, as in substance abuse cases in which information may be recorded about the patient's coming to grips with her problem. Such a variety of information, combined with the lengths of stay of many of these patients, creates a voluminous health record, thereby raising storage concerns, which in turn affect record retention policies.

Specialized patient records also differ concerning who makes entries in the record. In a general health record, entries are made by professionals who are licensed and certified, such as the physician who admitted the patient and gave orders directing her care, the nurse who administered medications, and the physical therapist who noted the patient's progress. These health care providers are governed by statutes, rules and regulations, and professional guidelines that address the manner in which they treat a patient and how to document that care properly.

By contrast, a specialized patient record involving substance abuse or mental health will not only include entries by those professionals just listed but also by paraprofessionals, such as teachers, if the patient is a juvenile, or counselors with no license or certification but experience with the illness in question. These paraprofessionals play a role in the treatment of the patient and therefore must document their role in patient care. In many instances, the licensing authority regulating the facility providing the treatment only regulates entries in the record in the context of professionals rendering treatment. In such instances, the question becomes whether the licensing authority permits entries in the record by paraprofessionals and, if so, what rules and regulations govern those entries.

Finally, the health information of those patients who receive treatment for substance abuse or a mental illness are subject to stricter confidentiality requirements than the health information of those patients receiving medical care in an acute care setting. For example, confidentiality requirements in the context of substance abuse often provide that the health care facility cannot confirm that the patient is, has been, or ever was a patient at the facility, absent the patient's permission to do so.

Because of these differences, those who are concerned with protecting health information must be aware of the legal requirements to which specialized patient records are subject. By understanding these requirements, effective policies can be created that manage specialized patient records while addressing legal concerns and issues.

DRUG AND ALCOHOL ABUSE

As a general rule, most legal questions associated with managing health information cannot be answered by looking to federal law. One exception to this rule exists in the context of drug and alcohol abuse treatment. In such a context, federal law speaks directly to the handling of health information.

Two federal laws place restrictions on the disclosure and use of substance abuse patient records: the Drug Abuse Prevention, Treatment, and Rehabilitation Act addressing drug abuse patient records[1] and the Comprehensive Alcohol Abuse and Alcoholism Prevention, Treatment, and Rehabilitation Act of 1970 addressing alcohol abuse patient records.[2] Both laws delegate to the Secretary of Health and Human Services the power to promulgate rules and regulations imposing restrictions on these records.

The rules and regulations[3] that the secretary has promulgated apply to all treatment programs that receive federal assistance.[4] A **treatment program** is defined to include entities whose sole purpose is to provide alcohol or drug abuse diagnosis or treatment. The definition also includes general medical care facilities *if* there is (1) an identified unit for diagnosis, treatment, or referral or (2) medical personnel or other staff whose primary function is to provide such services and who are identified as such providers. Because the federal assistance can be either direct or indirect, virtually every substance abuse program operated in the United States is subject to these laws.[5]

The federal regulations at issue are broad in scope and detail and address many issues central to management of health information. All who work in the substance abuse area must become familiar with these regulations. The theme underlying these regulations is that health information contained in patient records is confidential; therefore, only **disclosure with patient authorization** should be permitted. Thus, this discussion focuses on two main areas, confidentiality and release of information, and only briefly addresses other issues.

Confidentiality

Patient Identification

Under the applicable regulations, confidentiality of health information is much stricter than that in an acute care setting. The regulations restrict identification of a patient who is in a facility or component of a facility publicly identified as providing substance abuse treatment. Acknowledgment of the presence or past presence of a patient can be made only with the patient's written consent or subject to a court order entered in compliance with the regulations.[6]

In practice, the issue of **patient identification** comes into play because of the number of inquiries treatment programs receive concerning their patients. The applicable regulations place an unconditional obligation on the programs not to identify in any way the patients they treat or have treated. These regulations do not, however, prevent a program from disclosing that a person is not and never was a patient with its program. And the regulations do permit acknowledgment of a patient's presence if the facility is not publicly identified as only a substance abuse facility and if acknowledgment would not reveal that the patient is a substance abuser.[7]

The contradiction presented by the regulations raises a practical dilemma: if some inquiries are answered with the response that the law prevents disclosure that a person currently is or previously was a patient, and other inquiries are answered that the person currently is not and previously was not a patient, it will not take much detective work to determine whether a person is or was a patient in the treatment program. The regulations address this dilemma in a backhanded way. They suggest that an inquiring party may be informed of the regulations and advised that disclosure of patient-specific information is restricted by these regulations, without giving away that the restriction applies to any particular patient. As a practical matter, those involved in substance abuse treatment may wish to adopt a uniform method of answering these inquiries, subject to the advice of legal counsel.

Patient Notice

Patients must be given notice of federal confidentiality requirements upon admission to the program or soon after. This **patient notice** must include a written summary of the federal law and regulations.[8] The regulations allow programs to develop their own notices or use a sample notice. This sample notice is illustrated in Figure 11.1. Because the regulations require unconditional compliance, it is important that every treatment program document in each patient's health record that such notice was given and the time frame in which it was given.

Release of Information

Federal regulations governing the disclosure of patient information fall into the following three categories: (1) disclosures made with written patient authorization, (2) those made without written patient authorization but pursuant to federal regulation, and (3) those made subject to a valid court order.

Disclosure with Written Patient Authorization

Release of Information Form Disclosure of patient information in the substance abuse context involves the use of a **release of information** form, a document that permits the dissemination of confidential health information to third parties. To be valid, the completed written authorization form must meet the requirements of the regulations. Similar to the components of a valid general release of information form, a release of information form in the substance abuse context must identify the patient, the program that should release the information, the program or person who should receive the information, what information is to be disclosed, and include the patient's

> The confidentiality of alcohol and drug abuse patient records maintained by this program is protected by Federal law and regulations. Generally, the program may not say to a person outside the program that a patient attends the program, or disclose any information identifying a patient as an alcohol or drug abuser unless:
>
> (1) The patient consents in writing;
> (2) The disclosure is allowed by a court order; or
> (3) The disclosure is made to medical personnel in a medical emergency or to qualified personnel for research, audit, or program evaluation.
>
> Violation of the Federal law and regulations by a program is a crime. Suspected violations may be reported to appropriate authorities in accordance with Federal regulations.
>
> Federal law and regulations do not protect any information about a crime committed by a patient either at the program or against any person who works for the program or about any threat to commit such a crime.
>
> Federal laws and regulations do not protect any information about suspected child abuse or neglect from being reported under State law to appropriate State or local authorities.

Figure 11.1 Sample Notice: Confidentiality of Alcohol and Drug Abuse Patient
Source: 42 C.F.R. § 2.22 (2019).

A written authorization to a disclosure under these regulations must include:

(1) The specific name or general designation of the program or person permitted to make the disclosure.

(2) The name or title of the individual or the name of the organization to which disclosure is to be made.

(3) The name of the patient.

(4) The purpose of the disclosure.

(5) How much and what kind of information is to be disclosed.

(6) The signature of the patient and, when required for a patient who is a minor, the signature of a person authorized to give consent under § 2.14; or, when required for a patient who is incompetent or deceased, the signature of a person authorized to sign under § 2.15 in lieu of the patient.

(7) The date on which the consent is signed.

(8) A statement that the consent is subject to revocation at any time except to the extent that the program or person which is to make the disclosure has already acted in reliance on it. Acting in reliance includes the provision of treatment services in reliance on a valid consent to disclose information to a third party payer.

(9) The date, event, or condition upon which the consent will expire if not revoked before. This date, event, or condition must ensure that the consent will last no longer than reasonably necessary to serve the purpose for which it is given.

Figure 11.2 Components of a Valid Authorization
Source: 42 C.F.R. § 2.31(a) (2019).

signature and date. In addition, the consent must identify the purpose of the disclosure; include a statement indicating that the consent is subject to revocation at any time; and include a date, event, or condition on which the authorization will expire if not revoked before. The components of a valid authorization are illustrated in Figure 11.2.

The regulations allow programs to develop their own forms that comply with the regulations or use a sample form. This sample form, illustrated in Figure 11.3, contains reference to the signature of the parent or guardian where required. The question of whether a minor can authorize disclosure of health information in the substance abuse context is dependent on whether the applicable state law permits the minor to consent for treatment. Where the minor can apply for and obtain substance abuse treatment on her own behalf, she may also authorize disclosure of health information. Conversely, where state law requires parental consent to treatment, the authorization to disclose health information must contain signatures of both the minor patient and the parent or guardian.

A release of information form that does not comply with the regulations is not valid. Examples of invalid release forms include those in which any of the elements are missing, the consent period has expired or is known to have been revoked, or that contain information that is known to be false or reasonably should be known as false. Those involved in the release of health information should develop policies on how to respond to invalid authorization forms after first reviewing the regulations and speaking with legal counsel as necessary.

The following form complies with paragraph (a) of this section, but other elements may be added.

1. I (name of patient) Request Authorize:
2. (name or general designation of program which is to make the disclosure)

   ____

3. To disclose: (kind and amount of information to be disclosed)

   ____

4. To: (name or title of the person or organization to which disclosure is to be made)

   ____

5. For (purpose of the disclosure)

   ____

6. Date (on which this consent is signed)

   ____

7. Signature of patient

   ____

8. Signature of parent or guardian (where required)

   ____

9. Signature of person authorized to sign in lieu of the patient (where required)

   ____

10. This consent is subject to revocation at any time except to the extent that the program, which is to make the disclosure, has already taken action in reliance on it. If not previously revoked, this consent will terminate upon: (specific date, event, or condition).

Figure 11.3 Sample Authorization Form

Notice Accompanying Disclosure Another difference between a general release of information and that used for substance abuse programs is the regulation prohibiting redisclosure. Federal regulations prohibit the person or facility receiving the patient information from further disclosing the information unless the patient has given written consent addressing this redisclosure. A notice prohibiting redisclosure must accompany any disclosure of patient-specific information.

In this situation, the regulations do not give any freedom to the program to develop the notice prohibiting redisclosure. Rather, each program must use the statement listed in the regulation. This statement is illustrated in Figure 11.4.

This information has been disclosed to you from records protected by Federal confidentiality rules (42 CFR part 2). The Federal rules prohibit you from making any further disclosure of this information in this record that identifies a patient as having or having had a substance use disorder either directly, by reference to publicly available information, or through verification of such identification by another person unless further disclosure is expressly permitted by the written consent of the person to whom it pertains or as otherwise permitted by 42 CFR part 2. A general authorization for the release of medical or other information is NOT sufficient for this purpose. The Federal rules restrict any use of the information to investigate or prosecute with regard to a crime any patient with a substance use disorder, except as provided at §§2.12(c)(5) and 2.65.

Figure 11.4 Notice Prohibiting Redisclosure
Source: 42 C.F.R. § 2.32(a) (2019).

In the light of the unconditional compliance required by the regulations, it is important that each treatment program releasing patient information make special efforts to ensure that the receiving party understands that the patient information it receives is confidential and not available for redisclosure. At minimum, the statement prohibiting redisclosure must accompany any disclosure of patient information. Whether additional efforts should be made such as placing a stamp on each page indicating that no further dissemination is allowed is a policy question subject to time and cost constraints and the advice of counsel.

Disclosure Without Written Patient Authorization

As the regulations illustrate, the sensitive nature of patient information in the substance abuse context requires release of patient information by written authorization. The regulations recognize only limited exceptions to the written authorization requirement.

Medical Emergencies The first exception applies to medical emergencies. Patient-identifying information may be released without written consent to medical personnel providing emergency treatment. The emergency treatment is defined as "treating a condition which poses an immediate threat to the health of any individual and which requires immediate medical intervention."[9]

One potential medical emergency may involve an error in manufacturing or packaging of drugs. Such disclosure would be made to Food and Drug Administration (FDA) personnel where there is reason to believe that an individual's health would be threatened because of an error in manufacturing, labeling, or selling a drug under the FDA's jurisdiction. The FDA uses this patient information to notify patients and their physicians of potential dangers.

In every instance where a release is made pursuant to a medical emergency, the treatment program must document the disclosure in the patient record. This documentation must include the name of the medical personnel to whom disclosure was made and their affiliation to any health care facility, the name of the person making the disclosure, the date and time of disclosure, and the nature of emergency or error.[10]

Research Activities The second exception applies to scientific research activities that meet specific requirements. Patient-specific information may be disclosed for research purposes only after the treatment program director determines that the researcher is qualified to conduct the research and has a research protocol that both ensures security of the information disclosed and prohibits redisclosure. The researcher may not identify individual patients in reports and may disclose patient-identifying information only back to the treatment program.[11]

Audit Activities Audits of patient-specific information by qualified organizations and individuals may be conducted without written patient consent if regulatory requirements are met. Access to the information may be provided to persons (1) acting on behalf of a federal, state, or local governmental agency that provides financial assistance to the treatment program or by law regulates the treatment program; (2) acting on behalf of third-party payers, peer review organizations, or private organizations providing financial assistance; or (3) qualified to conduct the audit, as determined by the program director.

After meeting these qualifications, the auditor must agree in writing that the information gathered in the audit will be used only for audit or evaluation purposes or to investigate or prosecute crimes or other activities, as authorized by court order. The auditor must also agree in writing that she will disclose patient-specific information back to the treatment program only. Finally, if copies of records are made or if records are removed from the program's premises, the auditor must agree in writing to maintain the information in accordance with certain security requirements and destroy patient-specific information upon completion of the audit. A peer review organization acting on behalf of Medicare or Medicaid may redisclose patient-identifying information to the Medicare/Medicaid program.[12]

To the Patient Directly The regulations permit patients themselves to access their own records, including inspecting and copying their records.[13] A substance abuse program is not required to obtain the patient's written authorization before providing the patient with access to the patient's record. The provision for direct patient access is similar to HIPAA's provisions on patient access to their own records, only here applied in a substance abuse context.

Disclosures Pursuant to Legal Process

In the course of any given day, a health information manager at a substance abuse treatment program may be presented with a discovery request for production of documents and things, a court order authorizing disclosure of patient-specific information, a subpoena requesting patient-specific information, or a combination of these. Discovery requests, court orders, and subpoenas are issued for a variety of reasons: to investigate or prosecute a crime, to protect against an existing threat or serious bodily injury, or to present evidence of a patient's substance abuse treatment in a legal proceeding where the patient has placed her treatment at issue.

It is important to understand the differences between these three types of legal process. A discovery request to produce a health record seeks disclosure of patient-specific data or records that may be used in litigation. A court order authorizes disclosure of patient-specific information that would otherwise be prohibited by statute and regulation. It does not, however, *require* the disclosure of this information. A subpoena or subpoena duces tecum is a command to appear and/or present certain documents and other things. A subpoena or subpoena duces tecum *alone* does not authorize disclosure of information that would otherwise be prohibited by statute and regulation. In combination, however, these documents *mandate* disclosure of patient-specific information unless a valid legal defense exists against disclosure.[14]

The method used to apply for a court order authorizing disclosure is subject to regulation and is illustrated in Figure 11.5. The components of a valid court order authorizing disclosure are presented in Figure 11.6. Court orders authorizing disclosure will only be issued upon a finding of good cause: there exists no other way to obtain the information and the public interest and need for disclosure outweighs the potential impact on the patient.

How a health information manager handles these discovery requests, court orders, and subpoenas in practice is a matter governed by both federal regulation and common sense. For example, a request by a law enforcement official or related agency for patient information that is not accompanied by a court order authorizing disclosure must be treated under the regulations like requests seeking patient identification addressed previously in this chapter: with a noncommittal response acknowledging the confidentiality restrictions under which the treatment program operates. The mere fact that the request is made by a law enforcement official is not sufficient to overcome the restrictions imposed by the regulations.

Similarly, a discovery request or a subpoena served upon the treatment program by an attorney without a court order does not require under the regulations automatic disclosure of the information sought. That is not to say that the discovery request or the subpoena should be ignored. Rather, health information managers should develop policies, processes, and procedures for handling

(a) Application: An order authorizing the disclosure of patient record for purposes other than criminal investigation or prosecution may be applied for by any person having a legally recognized interest in the disclosure which is sought. The application may be filed separately or as part of a pending civil action in which it appears that the patient records are needed to provide evidence. An application must use a fictitious name, such as John Doe, to refer to any patient and may not contain or otherwise disclose any patient identifying information unless the patient is the applicant or has given a written consent (meeting the requirements of these regulations) to disclosure or the court has ordered the record of the proceeding sealed from public scrutiny.

(b) Notice: The patient and the person holding the records from whom disclosure is sought must be given adequate notice in a manner which will not disclose patient identifying information to other persons and an opportunity to file a written response to the application or appear in person for the limited purpose of providing evidence on the statutory and regulatory criteria for the issuance of a court order.

(c) Review of Evidence: Any oral argument, review of evidence, or hearing on the application must be held in the judge's chambers or in some manner which ensures that patient identifying information is not disclosed to anyone other than a party to the proceeding, the patient, or the person holding the record, unless the patient requests an open hearing in a manner which meets the written consent requirements of these regulations. The proceeding may include an examination by the judge of the patient records referred to in the application.

Figure 11.5 Procedures for Applying for Court Orders Authorizing Disclosure
Source: 42 C.F.R. § 2.64(a-c) (2019).

these situations. Commonly referred to as a litigation response plan, these policies, processes, and procedures may include contacting the attorney upon receipt of the subpoena, informing her of the regulations prohibiting disclosure, and notifying her that a court order is necessary before the health information manager will disclose the information. Other policy considerations may include determining how to handle a court appearance, if one is necessary, and notifying the attending therapist of the subpoena and requesting her review of the record to determine whether disclosure is in the patient's best interest.

An order authorizing disclosure must:

(1) Limit disclosure to those parts of the patient's record which are essential to fulfill the objective of the order;

(2) Limit disclosure to those persons whose need for information is the basis for the order; and

(3) Include such other measures as are necessary to limit disclosure for the protection of the patient, the physician–patient relationship and the treatment services; for example, sealing from public scrutiny the record of any proceedin for which disclosure of a patient's record has been ordered.

Figure 11.6 Components of a Valid Court Order Authorizing Disclosure
Source: 42 C.F.R. § 2.64 (e) (2019).

Miscellaneous Issues

Effect of Other Laws and Regulations

Although federal law directly regulates substance abuse patient records, these regulations expressly recognize that the states will play a role in regulating these types of records. This recognition allows the laws and regulations of the different jurisdictions (state and federal) to coexist, as opposed to excluding the states from any role.

State law and regulation may be equal to, less restrictive than, or more restrictive than federal law. Where a conflict between federal and state law appears, whichever law is stricter will apply.[15] Where a matter is not addressed by federal law, the state law will apply. For example, the federal regulations do not prohibit a patient's access to her own health information.[16] Persons interested in protecting health information must look to the provisions of state law to determine whether the treatment program must provide the patient access to her own health information. For more information regarding access to health information, see Chapter 10, Access to Health Information.

Similarly, there may be a need to reconcile regulations at the federal level with each other. For example, the Health Insurance Portability and Accountability Act (HIPAA) permits disclosure of protected health information to law enforcement officials under certain conditions, for instance, as required by laws that require reporting of certain types of wounds or other physical injuries[17] or to avert a serious and imminent threat to the health or safety of the patient or others.[18] Regulations under federal substance abuse laws, however, permit disclosure to law enforcement officials pursuant to court order, in connection with investigation or prosecution of an extremely serious crime,[19] or to notify the official when a patient is released from a psychiatric hold.[20] While these regulations may have overlapping provisions, they do not match entirely; accordingly, the regulations, which are most strict, will govern disclosure of health information in the substance abuse context.

Disposition of Records

For a variety of reasons, a treatment program may be discontinued or acquired by another program. In those situations, the regulations expressly address the disposition of substance abuse records. Under the regulations, the records must be purged of patient-identifying information or destroyed, including sanitizing any associated hard copy or electronic media, to render patient-identifying information nonretrievable *unless* the patient's written consent is obtained to transfer the record or the applicable statute of limitations requires that the records be maintained for a period beyond the closure or transfer.

If the transfer has not been authorized and the records must be retained for the statute of limitations period, paper-based records must be placed in a sealed envelope or other container and labeled as follows:

> *Record of [insert name of program] required to be maintained under [insert citation to statute, regulation, court order, or other legal authority requiring that records be kept] until a date not later than [insert appropriate date].*[21]

All hard copy media from which the paper records were produced, such as printer and fax ribbons and drums, must be sanitized to render the data nonretrievable. The regulations require that a responsible person hold these sealed and marked records in confidence until the end of the retention period specified on the label. Upon expiration of the retention period, the responsible person must destroy the records.

For electronic records, the regulations address both electronic devices (something that has computing capability, such as a laptop, tablet, etc.) and electronic media (something that can be read on an electronic device, such as a CD/DVD, flash drive, etc.). Electronic patient records transferred to electronic devices and electronic media must be encrypted such that a low probability exists to assigning meaning to the data transferred without the confidential process or key and implemented access controls. Within one year of the discontinuation of the substance abuse program, all electronic media on or in which patient records or patient-identifying information resided before being transferred must be sanitized to render the data nonretrievable. This sanitizing specifically encompasses email and electronic communications about the patient. This change should allow for select patient records to be removed from both the specific site and any operational sources without disrupting other patient records. After transfer of the data is complete, the electronic portable device or media must be placed in a sealed container along with any equipment need to read or access the information. The container must be labeled in the same manner as the sealed envelope containing paper-based records that is shown earlier in this discussion.

The regulations further require a mechanism to decrypt the data previously encrypted. A person must be designated through an access control list with the responsibility to decrypt this data. All tools used to decrypt the data must be stored or located separately from the data previously encrypted and any data decrypted subsequently.

Enforcement and Penalties

Because one of the purposes of the regulations is to ensure that patients who seek treatment for substance abuse are not more vulnerable due to availability of their patient record than those who do not seek treatment, the regulations provide for an enforcement mechanism and criminal penalty for violations. The regulations assume that all federally assisted substance abuse programs will comply with the restrictions that the regulations impose. Any violation of the regulations may be reported to the U.S. attorney for the district in which the violation occurred or to the FDA if a methadone program is involved. Upon conviction, any person who violates the regulations may be fined no more than $500 if a first offense and no more than $5,000 for each subsequent offense.[22]

MENTAL HEALTH AND DEVELOPMENTAL DISABILITY CARE

The treatment of patients with mental illness and/or developmental disabilities[23] takes place in a variety of settings: inpatient psychiatric hospitals, residential treatment facilities, and therapists' offices, to name a few. Although the settings may vary, many of the legal questions concerning mental health and developmental disability information are the same as those involved in health information in general: requirements for accurate and timely documentation, retention of health records, and confidentiality of health information. Although many similarities exist, two main differences separate health information in these contexts from that of a general medical context: (1) additional requirements for record content and (2) more stringent privacy requirements.

Content Requirements

Documentation in the mental health and developmental disability fields often involves situations not present in a general health record. For example, these settings may involve changes in the patient's supervision (from seclusion to use of restraints, privileges, passes, and discharge), significant legal events (commitment orders, interaction with police), and the presence of suicide attempts. Furthermore, restrictions on patient rights may become necessary under certain circumstances. As a matter of both law and good medical practice, each of these situations necessitates proper documentation in the health record.

For any psychiatric facility receiving Medicare funds, the Medicare Conditions of Participation govern. These regulations establish standards for documenting the development of assessment and diagnostic data, psychiatric evaluation, treatment plan, recording patient progress, discharge plan, and summary.[24]

Frequently, state mental health codes specify documentation requirements in these situations. Special attention must be accorded to these codes in order for the health care provider to be in compliance with state law. For example, the applicable state law may specify that a treatment facility devise a written program plan for each patient describing the patient's problems, precise goals of treatment, and the measures to be employed to reach those goals.[25] Where restraints are applied to a patient, the clinical record must reflect each use of restraint and its reason.[26] Similarly, any limitation on the patient's right to correspondence, visitors, phone calls, or access to a spiritual adviser must be documented in the clinical record, along with the reason for the limitation.[27] Any use of special treatment procedures such as electroshock therapy and neuroleptic medication also requires documentation.[28]

In addition to statutory and regulatory requirements, accrediting standards may mandate certain documentation requirements. For example, the Joint Commission (JC), formerly known as the Joint Commission on Accreditation of Healthcare Organizations, promulgates standards for facilities offering mental health, mental retardation, and developmental disability services. In addition to the standard documentation requirements, the JC requires documentation of the patient's legal status and the involvement of family members in the patient's treatment program.[29]

Another significant departure from a general health record involves the existence of two separate records: (1) the official or public record maintained by the treatment facility and (2) the personal record maintained by the clinician. The **official record** contains that information necessary to document the patient's care and treatment: history and mental status exam, consent forms, treatment plans, physician orders, laboratory results, and so forth. This is the record required to be maintained by law.

> **HIPAA/ARRA**
>
> Both the Health Insurance Portability and Accountability Act and the American Recovery and Reinvestment Act address the definition of psychotherapy notes.

By contrast, the **personal record** maintained by the clinician consists of notes in the clinician's sole possession that gives the clinician's viewpoint of the patient and their communications. Often referred to as **psychotherapy notes**, regulations of the Health Insurance Portability and Accountability Act (HIPAA) define these notes as ones recorded by a health care provider who is a mental health professional documenting or analyzing the contents of conversation during a private counseling session or a group, joint, or family counseling session. The definition excludes medication prescription and monitoring, counseling session start and stop times, the modalities and frequencies of treatment furnished, results of clinical tests, and any summary of the following items: diagnosis, functional status, the treatment plan, symptoms, prognosis, and progress to date.[30] The clinician's personal record does not substitute for progress notes in the official record and is kept separate from the official record. There is no legal requirement that a personal record be maintained in addition to the official record. In some jurisdictions, a personal record maintained by a clinician is considered to be the clinician's private property and work product and may not be subject to discovery in a legal or administrative proceeding.[31] The interest in psychotherapy notes has grown enough that the Secretary of Health and Human Services has been ordered to study the use of these notes under the authority of the American Recovery and Reinvestment Act of 2009 (ARRA). The ARRA requirements specify that the Secretary study whether the definition should include test data that is related to direct response, scores, items, forms, protocols, manuals, or other materials that are part of a mental health evaluation.[32]

Privacy Restrictions

As important as confidentiality and release of information are to those who protect health information, they are particularly critical to practice in the mental health and developmental disability fields. This is so because of the additional legal restrictions under which these fields operate.

Patient Identification

As with facilities offering substance abuse treatment, facilities offering mental health and developmental disability treatment are subject to strict confidentiality requirements. The fact that an individual is, was, or will be a patient at the facility may not be disclosed absent patient consent or under limited circumstances.[33] This type of restriction poses the same practical dilemma as in the substance abuse treatment context: how to answer inquiries into patient status. As in that context, those persons protecting health information should develop policies that do not tolerate any disclosure of patient-specific information absent patient consent.

Release of Information

Patient-specific information recorded and communications made in the course of providing mental health or developmental disability services are considered confidential and may not be disclosed except as provided by law. Disclosure may be made pursuant to a patient's written authorization, without a patient's written authorization under limited circumstances, or pursuant to a court order.

At the federal level, the regulations issued pursuant to the HITECH section of the American Recovery and Reinvestment Act address some but not all issues related to release of mental health information. Because federal law is not comprehensive in addressing the disclosure issue, state law must also be reviewed. In some instances, a conflict between federal and state law may appear; whichever law is stricter will apply. For example, HIPAA permits a health care provider to share or discuss a patient's mental health information with family members or other persons involved in the patient's care or payment for care if the patient is notified, is given an opportunity to object, and does not object. The health care provider shall discuss only the information the person involved needs to know.[34] Examples include discussing the patient's medications if a family member is present at a mental health care appointment or discussing with a patient's spouse the warning signs that may signal a developing emergency.[35]

At the same time, state law may limit what information may be disclosed to family members or other persons involved in the patient's care or payment for care. For example, Iowa statutes restrict disclosure of mental health information to the patient's diagnosis and prognosis; current medications and medications received over a past six-month period; and a description of the patient's treatment plan.[36] Further, Iowa law defines which family members the health care providers may disclose information to: the spouse, parent, adult child, or adult sibling of an individual who suffers a chronic mental illness. If the health care provider wishes to disclose matters that are not listed under Iowa law or wishes to disclose matters listed under Iowa law but to a family member who is not also listed in the statute, such as an aunt or uncle, the provider is not permitted to do so under Iowa law, even though HIPAA may permit such disclosure.

Due to the comprehensive nature of the Illinois Mental Health and Developmental Disabilities Confidentiality Act, it will serve as an illustration throughout the remainder of this section. In practice, those interested in protecting mental health information must review the law of the state in which treatment is given to determine the governing requirements.

Disclosure with Written Patient Authorization To be valid, a release of information form must be in writing and meet the specifications of state law. For example, the Illinois act specifically addresses the content of the authorization form. These directives include the person to whom disclosure is to be made, the purpose for disclosure, the nature of the information to be disclosed, the right to inspect and copy the information to be disclosed, the consequences of refusal to authorize, an expiration of authorization date, the right to revoke authorization at any time, and the signatures and date of the patient and of a witness who can attest to the identity of the patient. Any revocation of authorization must be in writing and witnessed. Whatever action taken pursuant to the authorization form and the authorization form itself must then become part of the record.[37]

As in the substance abuse context, any information disclosed pursuant to the patient's written authorization may not be redisclosed to another party, absent patient authorization. The health information manager in practice must determine what steps should be made to notify the recipient of this prohibition on redisclosure. These steps should be made part of written policy and procedure.

Disclosure Without Written Patient Authorization Patient-specific information may be disclosed without patient authorization only where statutory or regulatory authority allows disclosure. Similar to the substance abuse context, state law may allow **disclosure without patient authorization** to health care personnel within the treatment facility or under the treating clinician's supervision.[38] The HIPAA Privacy Rule permits a health care provider to disclose information without patient authorization if the patient is incapacitated or an emergency situation exists as long as the provider determines it is in the patient's best interest to do so. The Privacy Rule permits disclosure only of the protected health information that is directly relevant to another person's involvement in the patient's care or payment for care.[39] If or when the patient regains the capacity to make choices whether to release their information, the patient can choose to agree or object to any future sharing of information. So that disclosure without patient authorization is made only to those health care personnel with a need to know, the health information professional should formulate a release of information policy that specifically lists departments or individuals affiliated with the treatment facility who meet the need-to-know test.

Disclosure without written patient authorization may also be permitted by state law to persons conducting peer review, an attorney defending the treatment facility, and any agency that has custody of the recipient.[40] Further, such disclosure may be made to the parents or legal guardian of the resident, to law enforcement officers, or to the court in a judicial proceeding.[41] Because the authority to disclose without patient authorization is based in most part on state law, the health information professional should become familiar with the applicable state law in addition to the HIPAA Privacy Rule.

Disclosure Pursuant to Court Order Just as in the substance abuse context, the health information professional may be presented with a discovery request, a subpoena, or court order authorizing disclosure of mental health or developmental disability information.[42] How the health information manager responds is a matter governed by state law and policy of the treatment facility. Under no circumstances, however, should any of these documents be ignored.

HOME HEALTH CARE

As in any other portion of the health care delivery system, health information in the home health care setting is subject to legal considerations. Unfortunately, no one comprehensive law exists that addresses the legal requirements for home health care. Rather, the legal requirements arise from a myriad of sources: the Medicare Conditions of Participation, state law and regulation, and accrediting standards. Although each source is separate, they must be reviewed together to obtain an understanding of the legal requirements governing home health care.

For any home health care agency receiving Medicare funds, the Medicare Conditions of Participation govern. These regulations outline the qualifications for home health agency staff and detail the rights of patients treated by that staff. The regulations require that the patient be informed of her rights in advance of or during the initial treatment, both verbally and in writing in the patient's preferred language, and that the agency maintain documentation of that notification. The regulations also require the agency to treat patients with respect and inform the patient of the right to participate in patient care assessments, be informed about rights in the admission, transfer, and discharge processes, and how to make complaints when necessary. The regulations also specify that all clinical records maintained by the home health agency are confidential and that the agency must advise the patient of its policies and procedures regarding the disclosure of clinical records.[43]

In addition to these regulations, home health agencies must meet the requirements of state law. State law may consist of statute, regulation, or both. The applicable state law frequently contains many of the same provisions found in the Medicare regulations. For example, Florida's Home Health Services Act tracks many of the same provisions as the Medicare Conditions of Participation but adds more specificity in certain areas. Under the Florida statute, the contents of the clinical records include:

> *[P]ertinent past and current medical, nursing, social and other therapeutic information, the treatment orders, and other such information as is necessary for the safe and adequate care of the patient.*[44]

The statute also addresses confidentiality and disclosure of information, specifying that the patient's written consent or that of the patient's guardian must be obtained before health information may be disclosed.[45]

Regulations are often found in the context of the state-administered Medicaid program or the licensing requirements for home health care agencies. For example, Tennessee's licensing regulations for home health agencies include details on record content, retention, and security safeguards.[46]

Where state laws or regulations do not specifically address home health care, the health information manager should determine whether county requirements govern. These requirements would typically be issued by the county's department of health or social services.

Although accrediting standards and professional guidelines do not have the force of law, they may be used in establishing the proper standard of care in a negligence action against the home health agency. For that reason, the health information manager should pay close attention to these accrediting standards and professional guidelines. Both the Joint Commission and the Community Health Accreditation Program (CHAP) promulgate standards for community-based and hospital-based organizations offering home health services.[47] And professionals working for home health agencies are guided by the requirements of their respective professional organizations regarding confidentiality of information.

Ethical issues are also interwoven into home health care. For example, the patient's autonomy is respected by seeking informed consent to treatment. Fidelity is shown where the health care provider meets the patient's reasonable expectations of care and confidentiality. Veracity involves the health care provider treating the patient in a truthful manner, without misleading the patient about their care.

CRITICAL THINKING

Technology plays an increasing role in the lives of patients and caregivers. While caregivers may need to spend time on their phones and laptops to document care given, some patients do not understand the use of phones and laptops as relating to their care and see it as a distraction taking time away from delivering patient care. How can a caregiver and a home health patient manage these two positions from an ethical perspective?

Health information managers dealing with home health care agencies and their patient records should become familiar with federal regulations, state licensing laws and regulations, accrediting standards, and professional guidelines. It is particularly important to be aware of the differing legal requirements among states if the home health care agency provides care to patients in more than one state so that the home health care agency is acting in compliance with state law.

GENETIC INFORMATION

Another form of specialized patient record is that involving genetic information. Unlike mental health or substance abuse patient records, genetic information may not exist as a separate and distinct patient record. Rather, this information may be contained in any form or part of a health record. Because it can be found in many different places, the potential exists for many persons to have access to this information. While genetic information may revolutionize health care by predicting diseases and revealing cures, its sensitive nature poses special challenges for protecting the confidentiality of this information and its potential for wrongful use.

Genetic information in the simplest sense means information about an individual or family obtained from a genetic test or an individual's DNA sample.[48] It differs from other health information in that it is not a current or past picture of a person's health; rather, it is a look into the person's health future.

Science has obtained this information in large measure through the work of the Human Genome Project. With funding from the U.S. Congress, the Human Genome Project is a joint effort of the U.S. Department of Energy and the National Institutes of Health. Its mission is to map and characterize each human gene.[49] As discoveries are made, research material is made available to the public on the project's GenBank website.[50]

Health care providers can use these research materials to assist a patient's well-being. Should a genetic test reveal that a patient has a gene for a disease that has not yet manifested itself, the health care provider may increase diagnostic surveillance of the patient, thereby improving the patient's quality of life or chances for survival. A genetic test may also indicate that a patient is merely a carrier of a gene for a specific disease. In this case, the disease will likely not manifest itself in the patient but may manifest itself in the patient's offspring.

Benefits such as these are counterbalanced with concerns about potential misuse. Employers who gain access to their employees' genetic information may reach incorrect and damaging conclusions about the employees and take action accordingly. For more information about this concern, see Chapter 15, Law and Ethics in the Workplace. Health insurers may consider coverage decisions based on the potential for future manifestation of a given disease. Child custody battles could involve consideration of a parent's genetic disposition for future disease. As these concerns illustrate, it is important that genetic information be protected and used wisely.

HIPAA

> Statutory provisions offer protections for the use of genetic information in insurance.

At the federal level, concern over the misuse of genetic information in an insurance coverage decision was so widespread that Congress addressed it by passing the Health Insurance Portability and Accountability Act of 1996 (HIPAA).[51] HIPAA specifically prohibits genetic information, absent a diagnosis of a condition, from being considered a preexisting condition for health insurance purposes. HIPAA also prohibits health insurers from charging an individual a higher premium than others in a group because of the existence of genetic information. In addition to legislation, an executive order at the federal level prohibits departments and agencies of the executive branch from using genetic information in any hiring or promotion action.[52] The order also prohibits the departments and agencies from requesting or requiring genetic test results from applicants or current employees.

Various states have addressed these concerns through legislation prohibiting genetic discrimination and access to genetic information. Missouri law prohibits health insurers from requesting genetic information, inquiring into whether a person has taken or refused a genetic test, and inquiring into the results of any genetic test.[53] California law prohibits health insurers from seeking, using, or maintaining genetic information for any nontherapeutic purposes and from discriminating in the renewal of policies based on genetic characteristics.[54] Arizona law considers the results of genetic testing confidential and protects a person from being compelled to disclose the identity of any person who has taken a genetic test or the results of that test.[55] Maryland law prohibits health insurers from requesting or requiring the results of a genetic test for use in underwriting. It further requires that testing results may be released only on the written authorization of the subject of the genetic test.[56] Wisconsin law prohibits health insurers from conditioning the provision of insurance coverage or benefits or the setting of rates on genetic testing information.[57] As these and other examples illustrate, state legislatures have engaged in a high level of activity dealing with issues surrounding genetic information.[58]

GINA

> The Genetic Information Nondiscrimination Act strengthens efforts at the federal level to protect genetic information from misuse in both the employment and insurance contexts.

This high level of activity by states, combined with increased publicity over the misuse of genetic information by employers and insurers, prompted the U.S. Congress to again address genetic information, passing the Genetic Information Nondiscrimination Act of 2008 (GINA).[59] GINA strengthens the safeguards provided by HIPAA and state laws by including additional protections against misuse of genetic information in insurance and the workplace. Specifically, GINA limits an insurer's ability to use genetic information to raise rates for an entire group

Table 11.1 Protections Afforded Under the Genetic Information Nondiscrimination Act
Prohibits both individual and group health insurers from using an individual's genetic information in determining eligibility or setting premiums.
Prohibits both individual and group health insurers from requiring or requesting an individual undergo a genetic test or collecting genetic information as part of enrollment in a plan.
Prohibits employers or employment agencies from using a person's genetic information in decision making, including decisions involving hiring, firing, job assignments, or other terms and conditions of employment.
Prohibits employers or employment agencies from requesting, requiring, or purchasing genetic information about individuals or their family members.
Prohibits labor unions from excluding or expelling or otherwise adversely affecting the status of a union member because of genetic information with respect to the member.

Source: 42 U.S.C. §§ 2000ff et seq. (2019).

and extends protections to individual health plans. Specific protections afforded by GINA are listed in Table 11.1.

Further, GINA sets a floor of protections, allowing a state to enact more stringent safeguards where appropriate. This approach is the opposite of **preemption**, a doctrine that allows federal laws to take precedence over state laws. By taking such an approach, individual states may offer greater rights or protections to an individual concerning the use of genetic information than those rights and protections provided by GINA.[60]

GINA also offers the potential for clinical research studies to expand further by addressing a major obstacle to patient participation: fear of disclosing genetic information. The medical community has reported that potential research subjects fear discrimination based on how the genetic information they disclose may be used and therefore hesitate to participate.[61] The rights and protections offered by GINA may affect participation positively by increasing the willingness of patients to consider undergoing the genetic tests required as part of a research study protocol. In turn, gene-based research may result in benefits and savings to health care delivery.

ETHICS

The link between patient and family member that arises when genetic testing occurs raises ethical concerns about violating the patient's right to privacy.

The interplay between medical research and genetic information has resulted in a focused application of ethical and legal concepts and principles to emerging areas of medicine. Much of what is occurring in the field of genetic research implicates more than one person, because confirming a genetic basis for a medical condition indicates that at least one of a patient's parents carries the gene in question. As a result, some researchers have faced ethical dilemmas regarding whether they should contact family members of the patient who consented to be part of the research study. Because the parent is not a subject of the study and did not consent to participate in it, the researcher arguably violates the parent's right to privacy if contact is made. However, if contact is not made and the parent is at risk of developing the condition that is the subject of the genetic research study, does the researcher violate ethical principles of doing no harm? Answers to questions such as these are still in the formative stage, resulting in a wide variety of options.

HIPAA/GINA

HIPAA offers protection against genetic discrimination for health insurance purposes; GINA offers protections against genetic discrimination for both employment and insurance purposes.

GINA also specifically addresses the relationship between it and the HIPPA Privacy Rule. A provision in GINA directs inclusion of genetic information as part of the term "health information" and as part of the "use or disclosure" actions of a covered entity.[62] By taking such action, Congress indicated clearly that the protections afforded by GINA are in addition to the safeguards provided by the HIPAA privacy rule concerning the use of genetic information for health insurance purposes.

The responsibility to safeguard patient-specific health information is heightened when genetic information is involved. Anyone dealing with genetic information must remain aware of legislation at both the federal and state levels if they are to protect this information from a breach of confidentiality or improper use.

HIV INFORMATION

Acquired immunodeficiency syndrome (AIDS) is one of the most pressing public health threats. An estimated 1.1 million persons in the United States are infected with the human immunodeficiency virus (HIV), the virus that develops into AIDS.[63] At the present time, no vaccine exists to prevent infection with HIV, nor does a cure exist for AIDS.

As the public health threat posed by AIDS has increased, certain misunderstandings have emerged. Individuals unknowledgeable about the methods of transmission of the disease have created a climate of fear. From this fear has emerged a stigmatization of, and discrimination against, those suffering from AIDS and HIV.

Legislatures across the United States have responded to the stigma and discrimination experiences of AIDS and HIV sufferers, as well as the public health threat, with a complex mix of legislation. This legislation has addressed testing and reporting requirements and confidentiality concerns. The court system has also responded to the AIDS experience, particularly within the context of mandatory testing of health care workers and improper disclosure of HIV status.

Those persons handling patient-specific health information relating to HIV and AIDS must understand the complex legal rules to which this information is subject. By understanding the law applicable to this information, the health information manager is better able to respond to the demands for information made by patients, hospital administrators, researchers, and government agencies.

Background Information About HIV/AIDS

HIV is a retrovirus that attacks and suppresses a person's immune system. It is transmitted in a limited number of ways: through intimate sexual contact, exposure to infected blood or blood components, or passed from mother to child in utero or through breast milk. In the earlier stages of the disease, HIV-infected individuals may experience fever, swollen lymph nodes, weight loss, night sweats, decreased appetite, and diarrhea. As the disease process progresses, the individual is more likely than the average person to experience great difficulty in fighting other infectious diseases, such as Kaposi's sarcoma, *Pneumocystis carinii* pneumonia, and herpes zoster.

It is impossible to know when or if an infected individual will experience the onset of symptoms. Symptoms generally surface on a gradual basis and progress through various stages. Eventually, the individual may fully develop AIDS and die from the disease.

While no one test has been developed that isolates the virus, a variety of tests have been developed to detect the presence of HIV antibody and antigen in blood and body fluids. The most commonly used test, the enzyme-linked immunosorbent assay (ELISA), detects the presence of HIV in serum or plasma. If a positive result arises from the ELISA test, medical protocols generally call for the health care provider to confirm the result by performing a second test on the same specimen. Tests used to confirm positive results include the Western blot assay, the radioimmunoprecipitation assay (RIPA), and the indirect immunofluorescence assay (IFA). If positive results are confirmed by a second test, the individual is considered seropositive for HIV.

An important aspect of any testing for HIV is the concept of confidentiality of test results. Confidentiality in this context can be seen from more than one ethical perspective. Under a utilitarian approach, the idea is that if confidentiality is commonly breached, patients would be deterred from seeking medical assistance for problems of a sensitive nature or involving personal aspects. Under a deontology approach, the right action is one of personal self-determination and control over one's privacy and personal information, including the ability to decide questions involving care. This confidentiality exists in balance with the need to protect those not infected with the virus, thus resulting in development of more than one form of testing.

Testing

Voluntary Testing

The vast majority of HIV testing conducted in the United States involves **voluntary testing**. In the context of managing health information, voluntary testing encompasses three areas: consent for testing, delivery of pretest information, and disclosure of test results.

ETHICS

Voluntary testing for HIV/AIDS is based upon the ethical concept of autonomy.

Voluntary testing necessarily implies that the individual to be tested has consented to the testing. This implication is based upon the ethical concept of autonomy and the individual's self-determination. This implication has been incorporated into state statutes requiring the individual's written informed consent before testing.[64] In addition, states receiving federal funds under the HIV Health Care Services Program must require persons requesting others to be tested for HIV to obtain a written, signed consent from the individuals to be tested.[65]

In addition to written informed consent, most states place a burden on the health care provider ordering the HIV test to deliver certain pretest information to the individual to be tested. Often referred to as pretest counseling or consultation, common requirements include distributing information about the type of tests involved, the testing methodology employed, the meaning of the test results, the methods of transmitting the disease, and the methods of reducing risk of transmission.[66]

Once the test results become available, the health care provider must contact the tested individual with the results. The disclosure of test results is also the subject of state regulation. Commonly referred to as posttest counseling or consultation, the disclosure process generally involves four parts: (1) the test results and the possible need for additional testing; (2) the meaning and importance of the test results; (3) the methods to reduce further transmission, including partner notification programs; and (4) referral to available health care services and support groups.[67] Where the test results are positive for HIV, the health care provider is required to report the identity of the patient to the appropriate public health authorities unless an exception to the reporting requirement applies.

Mandatory Testing

The concept of **mandatory testing** involves a decision by the legislature or a court to force an individual to receive testing for some health reason without granting the individual the right to refuse. In the context of individuals with positive HIV status or AIDS, mandatory testing generally falls into either of two categories: court-ordered testing or testing pursuant to statutory authority.

State law empowers courts to issue orders to protect the public good. AIDS and HIV status are no exception. A court may order testing of an individual if the court has determined by clear and convincing evidence that the individual is reasonably believed to be infected with HIV and is a serious and present health threat to others. Such court-ordered testing does not allow the individual the right to refuse testing.[68]

Statutory authority mandating testing generally targets groups perceived as presenting a public health threat. In some states, prisoners entering or being discharged from correctional facilities must undergo testing without the right to refuse.[69] In addition, some states require sexual offenders who are convicted or have pleaded guilty or nolo contendere and whose crime included sexual intercourse to undergo testing without the right to refuse.[70]

One group that has been targeted for mandatory testing is employees, with mixed results. Some states permit employee testing only on a voluntary basis, with consent and confidentiality issues addressed in the statute.[71] Other states prohibit HIV testing of employees altogether.[72] Some states prohibit HIV testing of employees as a general matter but allow mandatory testing in certain defined situations.

These situations generally involve the employee's ability to perform a particular job in a safe manner. The first situation follows from employment discrimination law and involves a bona-fide occupational qualification to the job in question. To meet the bona-fide occupational qualification, the law places the burden on the employer to demonstrate that the HIV test is job related and necessary to determine an individual's qualifications for a particular job.[73] And in some cases, the law places the burden on the employer to show that no reasonable accommodation short of HIV testing exists.[74]

The second situation follows from disability discrimination law and involves classifying HIV status and AIDS as a disability. For states that classify HIV and AIDS in this manner, testing may be mandated where public health authorities determine that the infected individual would pose a direct threat to the safety or health of others.[75]

After determining that the employer may mandate HIV testing in the employment setting in some states, the next question involves the employer's right to use the HIV test results in making employment decisions. Here, the law is less clear. Only one state, North Carolina, appears to sanction the employer's ability to reject job applicants on the basis of a confirmed HIV-positive test result.[76] Whether other states will grant employers such authority remains to be seen. For further information addressing employment discrimination, see Chapter 15, Law and Ethics in the Workplace.

Anonymous Testing

Many persons in society have elected not to undergo AIDS/HIV testing for fear of learning of a positive result and the possibility of discrimination. In an effort to encourage individuals to submit themselves to HIV testing, some states have passed laws allowing individuals to undergo anonymous testing.[77]

Anonymous testing entails a system that assigns a unique identifier, such as a number or coding system, to the individual. That identifier replaces the individual's signature on the consent form and name on the vial containing the blood sample. It is that identifier, not the individual's name, that is reported to the public health authorities with the test result. Anonymous testing is unavailable in some circumstances, such as testing to determine eligibility to donate blood, plasma, semen, or other human tissue.[78]

CONCLUSION

In order to manage specialized patient records properly, it is critical to understand the different legal requirements that govern these specialized patient records. These legal requirements arise from a myriad of sources: statutes, regulations, accrediting standards, and professional guidelines. All must be reviewed together so that the health information professional can create effective policies that manage specialized patient records while addressing legal concerns and issues.

CASE STUDY

You are the director of health information services in a major medical center that maintains both a psychiatric unit and a substance abuse unit in addition to general medical and surgical units. Your facility plans to join a computer network with fifteen hospitals throughout the state, which will allow online access to laboratory data, regardless of which facility performed the lab work. None of the other fifteen facilities offer psychiatric or substance abuse treatment. Identify and discuss the confidentiality issues present with such a network in the light of the statutory, regulatory, and accrediting requirements governing patients treated in these units.

REVIEW QUESTIONS

1. What are the types of specialized patient records covered in this chapter and their distinguishing characteristics?
2. Explain the contradiction posed by federal regulations concerning patient identification in substance abuse treatment settings.
3. How might a release of information in a substance abuse setting differ from an ordinary health care setting?
4. Why should substance abuse treatment programs comply with the regulations governing release of patient information?
5. What would influence a substance abuse program's decision whether to make additional efforts beyond the governing regulations to safeguard the release of patient information?
6. Name the circumstances where patient information from a substance abuse setting may be disclosed without written patient consent.

7. What effect do court orders and subpoenas duces tecum have, separately and in combination, in a substance abuse setting?
8. How should a subpoena duces tecum be handled in a substance abuse setting if not accompanied by a court order?
9. Documentation of what types of situations may be present in a mental health or developmental disability context that may not be present in a general health record?
10. Name the three ways by which patient information generated from a mental health or developmental disability facility may be released.
11. From what sources do laws and regulations governing home health care arise?
12. Why should genetic information be protected from access by the general public?
13. What is the definition of genetic information?
14. How does the Health Insurance Portability and Accountability Act apply to genetic information?
15. What are the similarities and differences between voluntary testing, mandatory testing, and anonymous testing?
16. Name the three areas that encompass voluntary HIV testing.
17. What must a court determine before ordering testing of an individual for HIV?
18. Name one group that may be mandated to undergo testing for HIV pursuant to a statutory provision.
19. What situations would allow an employer to mandate HIV testing of an employee?
20. What restrictions apply to the disclosure of a patient's identity or test result?

ENRICHMENT ACTIVITY

Tour a substance abuse facility in your local area. Observe the method by which patients receive notice of federal confidentiality requirements, how requests for identification of patients are handled by the facility's staff, and the manner in which the prohibition against redisclosure of patient-specific health information is handled. Compare your observations against the information you learned in this chapter concerning these areas. If a tour of such a facility is unavailable, engage in a group discussion where the group develops the facility's method of patient notification of confidentiality requirements, the method for handling patient identification requests, and the manner in which it handles the redisclosure prohibition.

ENRICHMENT ACTIVITY

Prepare an outline for an inservice education presentation to health care staff describing the special protections granted to substance abuse patient records.

NOTES

1. 21 U.S.C. § 1175, later amended and transferred to 42 U.S.C. § 290ee-3 (2019).

2. 42 U.S.C. § 4582, later amended and transferred to 42 U.S.C. § 290dd-3 (2019).

3. These regulations are titled Confidentiality of Alcohol and Drug Abuse Patient Records and can be found at 42 C.F.R. Ch. 1, Part 2, §§ 2.1-2.67 (2019).

4. Federal assistance means not only direct financial assistance but also includes tax-exempt status, receipt of tax-deductible contributions, authority to dispense controlled substances under the Controlled Substances Act, and licensure or certification by a part of the federal government. 42 C.F.R., Ch. 1, § 2.12(b) (2019).

5. These regulations do not apply to programs maintained by the Veterans Administration because those programs are governed by separate law and regulation. *See* 38 U.S.C. § 7332 (2019).

6. 42 C.F.R. Ch. 1, § 2.13 (2019).

7. 42 C.F.R. Ch. 1, § 2.13(c) (2) (2019).

8. 42 C.F.R. Ch. 1, § 2.22 (2019).

9. 42 C.F.R. § 2.51(a) (2019).

10. 42 C.F.R. § 2.51(a-c) (2019).

11. 42 C.F.R. § 2.52(a-b) (2019).

12. 42 C.F.R. § 2.53(a-d) (2019).

13. 42 C.F.R. § 2.23 (2019).

14. 42 C.F.R. § 2.61(a-b) (2019).

15. 42 C.F.R. § 2.20 (2019).

16. 42 C.F.R. § 2.23(a) (2019).

17. 45 C.F.R. § 164.512(f) (2019).

18. 45 C.F.R. § 164.512 (j) (2019).

19. 42 C.F.R. § 2.63 (2019).

20. 45 C.F.R. § 164.512(f) (2019).

21. 42 C.F.R. § 2.19(b) (2019).

22. 42 C.F.R. § 2.4, 2.5 (2019).

23. Developmental disability commonly refers to a disability attributed to mental retardation, cerebral palsy, epilepsy, autism, or other similar condition.

24. 42 C.F.R. § 482.61(a-e) (2019).

25. Minn. Stat. Ann. § 253B.03.7 (West 2019); Nev. Rev. Stat. § 433.494 (2019).

26. Minn. Stat. Ann. § 253B.03.1 (West 2019).

27. Minn. Stat. Ann. §§ 253B.03.2 (West 2019).

28. Minn. Stat. Ann. §§ 253B.03.6-.6b (West 2019).

29. Joint Commission, Comprehensive Accreditation Manual for Behavioral Health, Management of Information Standard (2007); 45 C.F.R. § 164.501 (2019); see also HIPAA Privacy Rule and Sharing Information Related to Mental Health (2019), available at http://www.hhs.gov/ocr/privacy/hipaa/understanding/special/mhguidance.html.

30. 45 C.F.R. § 164.501 (2019).

31. *See, e.g.*, Ill. Comp. Stat., ch. 740, para. 110/3 (2019).

32. 42 U.S.C. § 13424(f) (2019).

33. *See, e.g.*, N.J. Stat. Ann. § 30:4-24.3 (2019); N.M. Stat. Ann. § 43-1-19 (2019).

34. 45 C.F.R. § 164.510 (2019).

35. Id.; see also HIPAA Privacy Rule and Sharing Information Related to Mental Health (2019), available at http://www.hhs.gov/ocr/privacy/hipaa/understanding/special/mhguidance.html.

36. Iowa Stat. Ann. § 228 (2019).

37. Ill. Comp. Stat. ch. 740, para. 110/5 (2019).

38. *See, e.g.,* Ill. Comp. Stat. ch. 740, para. 110/9 (2019); N.M. Stat. Ann. § 43-1-19 (2019).

39. 45 C.F.R. § 164.510(b)(3) (2019).

40. Ill. Comp. Stat. ch. 740, para. 110/6-/9.1 (2019).

41. N.D. Cent. Code § 25-16-07 (2019).

42. Ill. Comp. Stat. ch. 740, para. 110/10 (2019).

43. 42 C.F.R., Ch. IV, §§ 484.1-.52 (2019).

44. Fla. Stat. Ann. § 400.491 (2019).

45. Fla. Stat. Ann. § 400.494 (2019).

46. Tennessee Comp. R. & Regs. 1200-08-26-.06 (2019).

47. Joint Commission, Accreditation Manual for Home Care, Management of Information (2014); Community Health Accreditation Program, Inc., Standards of Excellence for Home Care Organizations (2019).

48. Or. Rev. Stat. §§ 659A.303 & 659A.300 (2019).

49. Mission Statement of the National Human Genome Research Institute (NHGRI). Available at http://www.genome.gov/10001022.

50. Available at http://www.genome.gov.

51. 42 U.S.C. § 1320d (2019).

52. Exec. Order No. 13145, 65 Fed. Reg. 6877 (2000).

53. Mo. Rev. Stat. § 375.1303 (2019).

54. Cal. Civil Code § 56.17 (West 2019) (nontherapeutic purposes ban) and § Cal. Health & Safety Code § 1374.7 (West 2019) (genetic discrimination ban).

55. Ariz. Stat. § 12-2802 (2019).

56. MD. Code Ann., (Ins.) § 27.909 (2019).

57. Wis. Stat. Ann. § 631.89 (West 2019).

58. Colo. Rev. Stat. § 10-3-1104.7 (2019) (preventing use of genetic information from being used to deny health insurance); Conn. Gen. Stat. § 38a-816 (2019) (defines as an unfair and deceptive business practice for an insurer to refuse to insure, limit insuring, or charge a different rate because of genetic information); 215 Ill. Comp. Stat. Ann. 5/356v (West 2019) (prevents misuse of genetic information by all employers in hiring or firing decisions and by insurance companies in coverage decisions); Kan. Stat. Ann. § 44-1009(9) (2019) (defines as an unlawful practice for an employer to seek to obtain, obtain, or use genetic screening or testing information of an employee or prospective employee or subject an employee or prospective employee to testing); N.M. Stat. Ann. § 24-21-1 to -7 (2019) (prohibits discrimination by an insurer against a person or family member on basis of genetic information); Or. Rev. Stat. § 659A.303 (2019) (prohibits employers from obtaining, seeking to obtain, or using genetic information of an employee or prospective employee); Va. Code Ann. § 40.1-28.7:1 (2019) (prohibits employers from refusing to hire, failing to promote, discharging, or otherwise adversely affecting a condition of employment of an employee or prospective employee).

59. 42 U.S.C. §§ 2000ff et seq. (2019).

60. 42 U.S.C. § 2000ff-8(a) (2019).

61. Hudson, K. L. Prohibiting genetic discrimination, N. Engl. J. Med. 2007 356:2021-3.

62. 42. U.S.C. § 1320d-9 (2019).

63. Centers for Disease Control, U.S. Department of Health & Human Services, HIV Surveillance Reports (2018). Available at https://www.cdc.gov/hiv/pdf/library/reports/surveillance/cdc-hiv-surveillance-supplemental-report-vol-23-4.pdf; https://www.hiv.gov/hiv-basics/overview/data-and-trends/statistics.

64. For example, Illinois' AIDS Confidentiality Act imposes a requirement for written patient consent. 410 ILCS 305/4 (2019). Missouri law requires insurers who mandate HIV testing as a condition of obtaining insurance to obtain the written consent of the applicant to be tested. Mo. Code Regs. tit. 20, § 400.2-100 (2019). Other states requiring written consent include: Ariz. Rev. Stat. Ann. § 20-448.01(B) (2019); Cal. Health & Safety Code § 120990 (West 2019); Conn. Gen. Stat. Ann. § 19a-582(a) (West 2019); La. Rev. Stat. Ann. § 40:1300.13(A) (West 2019); Mont. Code Ann. § 50-16-1007(1) (2019); N.Y. Ins. Law § 2611(a) (McKinney 2019); Ohio Rev. Code Ann. § 3901.46(B)(1) (Baldwin 2019); 35 Pa. Cons. Stat. Ann. § 7605(a) (2019).

65. 42 U.S.C. § 300ff-61(b) (2019).

66. *See, e.g.*, CAL. CODE REGS. tit. 22, § 41149; CONN. GEN. STAT. ANN. § 19a-582(c) (West 2019); FLA. ADMIN. CODE ANN. r. 10D-93-070(4); ILL. ADMIN. CODE tit. 77, §§ 697.110 & .300(d); MO. CODE REGS. tit. 19, § 20-26.040(2) (2019).

67. *See, e.g.*, CAL. CODE REGS. tit. 22, § 41150; CONN. GEN. STAT. ANN. § 19a-582(d) (West 2019); FLA. ADMIN. CODE ANN. r. 10D-93.070(7); ILL. ADMIN. CODE tit. 77, § 697.300(f); MO. CODE REGS. tit. 19, § 20-26.040(2)(D) (2019).

68. See CONN. GEN. STAT. ANN. § 19a-582(e)(8) (West 2019); GA. CODE ANN. § 31-17A-3 (2019); MO. REV. STAT. § 191.674(1) (2019).

69. *See, e.g.*, IDAHO CODE § 39-604 (2019); MICH. COMP. LAWS ANN. § 791.267(2) (West 2019); MO. REV. STAT. § 191.659 (2019).

70. See CONN. GEN. STAT. ANN. § 54-102b (West 2019); FLA. STAT. ANN. § 775.0877(1) (West 2019); ME. REV. STAT. ANN. tit. 5, § 19203-A(5) (West 2019); MO. REV. STAT. § 191.663 (2019); OR. REV. STAT. § 135.139(2) (2019); S.C. CODE ANN. § 16-3-740 (Law. Co-op 2019).

71. These states have passed statutes imposing general restrictions on HIV testing of employees: COLO. REV. STAT. § 25-4-1401 (2019); DEL. CODE ANN. tit. 16 § 1202 (2019); 410 ILCS 305/3 (2019); IOWA CODE § 216.6 (2019); ME. REV. STAT. ANN. tit. 5 § 19204-B.1 (2019); MO. REV. STAT. 191.653 (2019); W. VA. CODE § 16-3C-1 (2019).

72. See CAL. HEALTH & SAFETY CODE § 120975 (West 2019); HAW. REV. STAT. § 325-101(c) (2019); MASS. GEN. LAWS ANN. ch. 111 § 70F (West 2019); N.M. STAT. ANN. § 28-10A-1.A (Michie 2019).

73. See N.M. STAT. ANN. § 28-10A-1.A (Michie 2019); TEX. HEALTH & SAFETY CODE ANN. § 81.102 (West 2019); WASH. REV. CODE § 49.60.172 (West 2019).

74. FLA. STAT. ANN. § 760.50(3)(c) (West 2019); KY. REV. STAT. ANN. § 207.135(2) (b) (Michie/Bobbs-Merrill 2019).

75. See GA. CODE ANN. § 31-17A-2 (2019); N.C. GEN. STAT. § 130a-148(h) (2019); R.I. GEN. LAWS § 23-6.3-4 (2019); WIS. STAT. ANN. § 103.15(2) (West 2019).

76. N.C. GEN. STAT. § 130A-148(i) (1&2) (2019).

77. *See, e.g.*, HAW. REV. STAT. § 325-16 (2) (2019); IOWA CODE ANN. § 141A.7 (West 2019); KAN. STAT. ANN. § 65-6007 (2019); LA. REV. STAT. ANN. § 40:1300.13.E (West 2019); ME. REV. STAT. ANN. tit. 5, § 19203-B (West 2019); MICH. COMP. LAWS ANN. § 333.5133(9) (West 2019); MO. REV. STAT. § 191.686 (2019).

78. *See, e.g.*, 410 ILCS 305/6 (2019); IOWA CODE ANN. § 141.7 (West 2019); LA. REV. STAT. ANN. § 40:1300.13.E.(1) (West 2019).

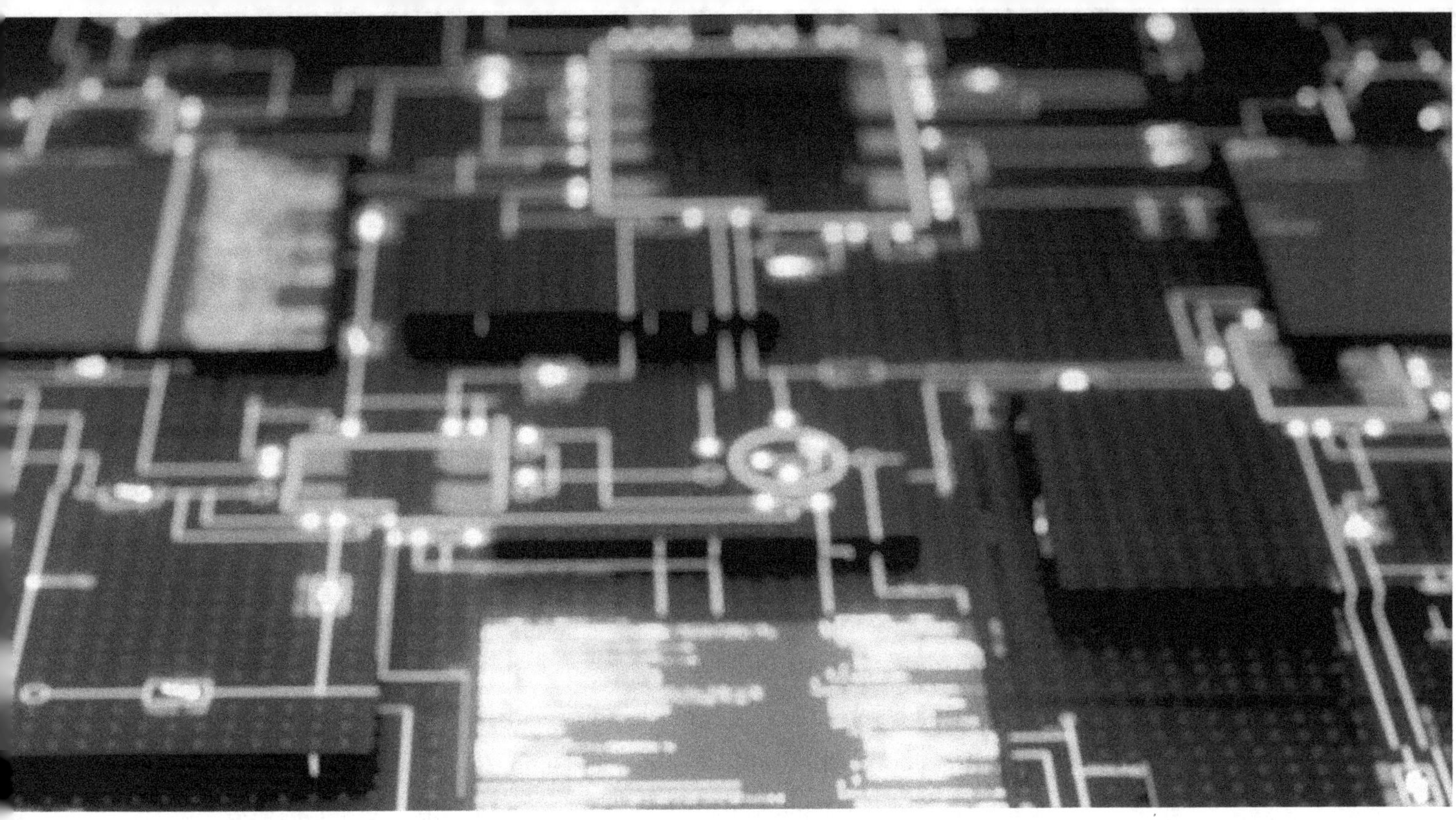

PART

4 SPECIALIZED AREAS OF CONCERN IN HEALTH INFORMATION MANAGEMENT

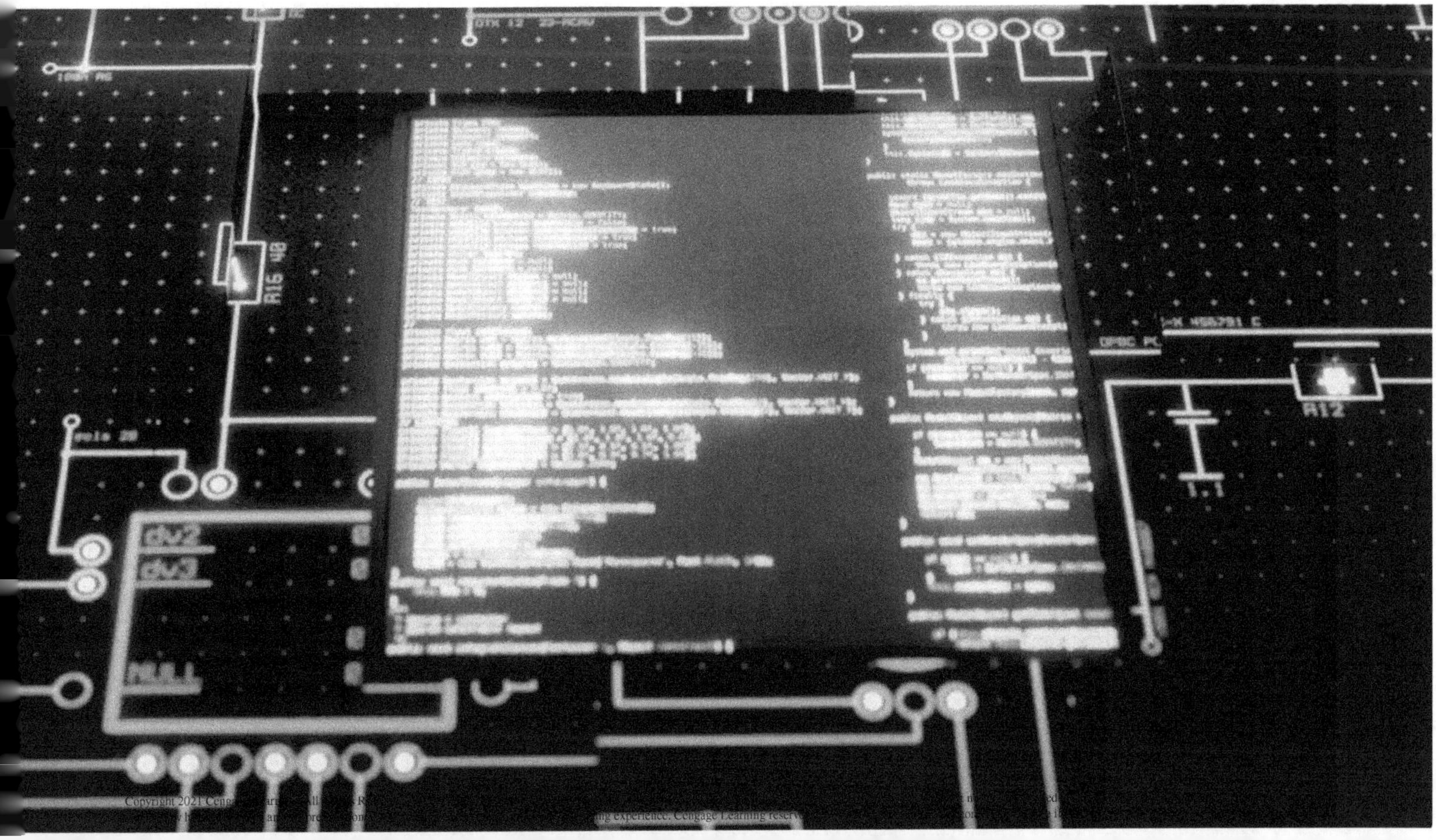

CHAPTER 12

RISK MANAGEMENT, QUALITY MANAGEMENT, AND UTILIZATION MANAGEMENT

LEARNING OBJECTIVES

After reading this chapter, the learner should be able to:

1. Compare and contrast risk management with quality management.
2. Trace the growth and development of risk management.
3. Explain how the three components of patient record requirements relate to risk management.
4. Define an incident report.
5. List the purposes an incident report serves.
6. Differentiate between discovery and admissibility of incident reports.
7. Compose a scenario that illustrates how an incident report may be protected by the attorney–client privilege.
8. Differentiate between the two aims of peer review statutes: privilege and immunity.
9. Analyze the variations of peer review statutes.
10. Identify the reporting requirements of the Health Care Quality Improvement Act.
11. Describe the utilization review process.

KEY CONCEPTS

Admissible
Attorney–client privilege
Case management
Case managers
Confidentiality
Discovery
Database
Electronic protected health information (ePHI)
Enterprise risk management
Hospital incident
Incident report
Peer review committees
Peer review privileges
Professional Standards Review Organizations
Proper documentation
Quality management
Risk
Risk management
Root-cause analysis
Sentinel event
Utilization coordinators
Utilization management
Utilization review

INTRODUCTION

Most legal issues concerning health information management focus on patient-specific health information given and obtained during the course of patient care. Accordingly, the focus of this book has centered on health information contained in patient health records. While the majority of a health information manager's practice focuses on such information, such a practice focus is not exclusive. Health information management practice also addresses nonpatient records.[1]

Two nonpatient record areas in which the health information professionals play a vital role are risk management and quality management. Both are methods of quality control that exist in virtually every hospital and health care facility. Both are distinct improvement techniques; the extent to which they are integrated varies by health care facility. This chapter will not provide an all-encompassing look at risk management and quality management; rather, it will concentrate on the legal bases and requirements for those programs. Further details regarding forms to use and exact methods to employ are left to the broader teaching of quality improvement and management.

Closely related to quality management is utilization management, an activity that requires focus on both the health record and nonpatient records. This chapter provides a description of the evolution of utilization management and the utilization review process.

RISK MANAGEMENT

General Principles

Risk management is a nonclinical function that focuses on how to reduce medical, financial, and legal risk to an organization. This reduction is tied to the definition of **risk**: the estimate of probability of loss from a given event upon the operations or financial performance of an organization. Understanding the universe of probable events, the strategies employed to mitigate and minimize the effects of each of these events, and how to contain negative consequences is central to managing risk.

As a general matter, risk management is designed to achieve two purposes: (1) to identify areas of operational and financial risk or loss to a health care facility and its patients, visitors, and employees; and (2) to implement measures to lessen the effects of unavoidable risks and losses, prevent recurrences of those risks or losses, and cover inevitable losses at the lowest cost.[2] A risk management program is outcome oriented, focusing on the potential risks to the health care facility and the methods used to avoid those risks. In other words, risk management looks at specific incidences to assist in determining what activities should be avoided and how to do so.

The growth and development of risk management in the health care field can be traced to a number of different influences, foremost among them the loss of the doctrine of charitable immunity. For most of this century, health care institutions were shielded from liability for the negligent acts of their employees by the doctrine of charitable immunity. Beginning in the mid-1960s, the doctrine was slowly dismantled through court decisions such as the landmark case of *Darling v. Charleston Community Memorial Hospital*.[3] State legislatures followed the lead set by the court system and abolished the doctrine by statute. Without the protection afforded by the charitable immunity doctrine, health care institutions became exposed to an increasing number of lawsuits brought against them. Details regarding the doctrine of charitable immunity and its relationship with liability principles are addressed in Chapter 4, Principles of Liability.

The growth of risk management was also aided by several other forces. First, the so-called medical malpractice crisis of the 1970s brought to the attention of many health care executives the reality that an increase in the number of medical malpractice lawsuits against their facility could result in not only damage awards but also higher insurance premiums. Second, the Joint Commission (JC), formerly known as the Joint Commission on Accreditation of Healthcare Organizations, began to require hospitals to implement risk management programs in their institutions.[4] Third, state legislatures became involved, establishing by statute minimum requirements for risk management programs in hospitals or delegating that task to administrative agencies.[5] As all of these forces converged on health care institutions, executives realized that the risk management principles already in use in the business community could be applied to the health care community.

Because of its evolution, risk management as a management function necessarily varies by institution. In terms of lines of organizational authority, risk managers may be considered part of the facility's safety department, its finance department, or its operations team. Where a facility operates with in-house counsel, the risk manager may report to that entity. In terms of who serves as a risk manager, the individual may have a background in the legal, nursing, health information management, and/or insurance fields. One constant in risk management, however, is the role of health information managers.

Health information managers play a role in a risk management program in at least two ways: through the traditional method of enforcing patient record requirements and through the use of incident reports.

Patient Record Requirements

Health information professionals have traditionally influenced the risk management process by implementing, enforcing, and educating health care providers about patient record requirements. This education role centers on three areas: documentation, security, and confidentiality.

Documentation

The health information professional cannot stress too heavily the importance of **proper documentation** to reduce risk. Because a health record serves as the legal record of a particular episode of a patient's care, it is the backbone of every professional liability action. As such, it is used to prove what did or did not happen in a particular case and to establish whether the applicable standard of care was met. A properly documented health record benefits a health care provider's defense in a lawsuit; a poorly documented health record hinders the health care provider's defense.

A properly documented health record is both timely and complete, meaning that all entries in the record are authored and authenticated and reflect the total care actually rendered to the patient. In addition, the record meets the appropriate requirements for record content, including the use of approved abbreviations and methods to correct the record where necessary. Further details concerning the requirements of a timely and complete health record are addressed in Chapter 8, Patient Record Requirements.

With proper documentation, the risks to a health care facility may be reduced in a number of ways. For example, complete documentation of a patient's condition, including accurate information about adverse incidents that happened to the patient during treatment (e.g., a medication error), assists the caregiver in rendering appropriate treatment, thereby reducing risk to both the patient and the health care facility. In addition, corrections to the record made according to proper methods reduce risk to the health care facility because it may be concluded that the facility's purpose was to correct a mistake in the documentation of the patient's treatment and not to conceal information. Finally, a complete, timely, and accurate record reduces risk at trial because the health care provider's defense ability is tremendously enhanced.

Security

Security of health information falls within the traditional role of the health information manager. Security issues regarding a risk management program have traditionally centered on the availability of health records for purposes of patient care, access to patient-specific health information by or on behalf of the patient, and the retention of health records. New issues related to database management and electronic health records have emerged, adding more complexity to the security issue.

The ready availability of a health record to health care personnel cannot be understated: various medical disciplines use the health record as a method to communicate about the patient's illness and course of treatment during a particular episode of patient care. And should the patient subsequently require care, health care providers rely on information from prior health records to assist in the diagnosis and treatment of the patient. Failure to make health records available during a current or subsequent episode of patient care may result in harm to the patient and exposure of the health care provider to liability.[6] Such risk can be reduced by actively managing the availability of health records for purposes of patient care.

Availability of health records concomitantly involves the question of access to health information by or on behalf of the patient. Questions of access are governed by a complex web of laws and regulations, addressed in detail in Chapter 10, Access to Health Information. Because of this complexity, requests for access to patient-specific health information should be handled only by those with proper training and supervision. Careful management of these requests reduces risk to the health care facility by ensuring that only those with a right to know have access to patient-specific health information. Careful management also lessens the potential for liability due to improper disclosure of health information.

Availability of health records also involves the question of how long health records should be retained. At minimum, health care facilities reduce the risk of a lawsuit for negligent loss of records by retaining records for the minimum period specified under statute and regulation. Additionally, if records are retained offsite by a commercial contractor due to storage constraints, risk may be reduced by including restrictions in the written contract that address confidentiality safeguards and indemnification in the event of unauthorized disclosure. Finally, when the health care facility can no longer maintain health records beyond the controlling statute and regulation period, it can reduce the risk of civil and criminal liability by ensuring that all record destruction is conducted in the ordinary course of business according to institutional policy. For further information, see Chapter 8, Patient Record Requirements.

> **HIPAA**
>
> The Security Rule requires a risk analysis of electronically protected health information.

Risk management also intersects with database management concerning the clinical data stored in automated systems, such as an electronic health record (EHR). The security management process standards (Security Rule) issued pursuant to the Health Insurance Portability and Accountability Act (HIPAA) require a covered entity to perform a risk analysis to determine security risks and implement standards to reduce risks and vulnerabilities to **electronic protected health information (ePHI)**.[7] Such security risks may include breaches to the confidentiality, integrity, and availability of ePHI. The standards of the Security Rule do not specify the approach for this analysis, nor do they specify what security measures should be implemented, allowing for flexibility by the covered entity. Guidance, however, is provided through papers published on the Centers for Medicare and Medicaid Services (CMS) website. The standards do require, however, that the covered entity document its efforts, maintain this documentation for six years, and provide review and modification of the efforts on a regular basis.[8]

Such documentation is helpful in the event the Centers for Medicare and Medicaid Services (CMS) initiate a risk management review of a covered entity. Such reviews arise from complaints filed against covered entities. Examples of compliance issues and recommended solutions from a recent CMS risk management review of HIPAA security requirements are provided in Table 12.1.

Table 12.1 HIPAA Risk Compliance Issues and Recommendations

Category	Issues	Recommendation
Risk Assessment	• Risk assessment not performed • No formalized, documented risk-assessment process • Outdated risk assessments • All potential risk areas not addressed	• Document supporting procedures for conducting risk assessments • Conduct a formal risk assessment of all systems and applications which store, process, or transmit ePHI • Document completion of periodic risk assessments of all systems and applications that store, process, or transmit ePHI • Identify corrective actions for any weaknesses found • Re-perform the risk assessment every three years or whenever a significant change in the environment occurs
Currency of Policies and Procedures	• No review of policies and procedures within the time frames required • No documented evidence of review and approval of policies and procedures • Documented procedures were inconsistent with procedures followed by CE staff	• Set maximum time frame between reviews and when a significant change in the environment occurs • Document a procedure for conducting periodic reviews • Create standard formats to be used in documenting reviews • Evaluate processes for adopting and distributing updated policies and procedures and determining employee awareness • Conduct periodic assessments of the effectiveness of policies and procedures
Security Awareness and Training	• No documented policies for training • No evidence of training completion • No security awareness training occurring before granting user access • No security refresher training conducted on a regular basis	• Create policies for documenting, administering, and monitoring initial and refresher security awareness training courses • Create procedures verifying that new users have completed initial security awareness training before gaining access to ePHI • Create procedures to monitor course completion and escalate issues related to noncompletion in a timely manner

Table 12.1 *(Continued)*

Category	Issues	Recommendation
Workforce Clearance	• Access to ePHI granted before background investigations complete	• Identify positions that require background checks based on risk level • Develop policies and procedures for completing background investigations • Conduct reinvestigations for positions of high risk • Conduct background investigations of vendors and third parties who have access to ePHI
Workstation Security	• No formalized policy or process for verifying the security of workstations • Noncompliance with policies and procedures for securing workstations • No provisions for staff to employ tools secure their workstations	• Develop policies outlining workstation classifications and types of security controls for each workstation category • Develop procedures to perform security walkthroughs • Perform security walkthroughs • Evaluate the results of security walkthroughs • Address physical security requirements in initial and refresher security awareness training
Encryption	• Not implemented at all workstations or laptops • Not implemented for the transmission of ePHI • Inconsistent encryption employed when implemented	• Create an inventory of laptops, workstations, and any portable devices or media • Create policies for encryption of ePHI, including identification of when encryption is required • Employ an encryption solution on all workstations and laptops that store, process, or transmit ePHI • Identify encryption requirements for portable devices and media as necessary • Implement strong encryption on wireless networks • Communicate encryption requirements to staff through policies and training, both initial and refresher • Update system baselines and build procedures to reflect deployment of encryption solutions

Source: Centers for Medicare and Medicaid Services, Report to Congress on HIPAA Privacy, Security, and Breach Notification Rule Compliance For Calendar Years 2015, 2016, and 2017 (2018), available at https://www.hhs.gov/sites/default/files/compliance-report-to-congress-2015-2016-2017.pdf; HIPAA Compliance Review Analysis and Summary of Results (2009), available at http://clearwatercompliance.com/wp-content/uploads/2008_CMS_HIPAA_ComplRvwAnal.pdf.

EHR

Security risks to electronic health records arise from both technical and nontechnical sources.

Installing security measures such as access and integrity controls are just the beginning of risk management efforts relating to an EHR; nontechnological risks also pose threats. For example, access and security controls installed at the technological level can help prevent unauthorized access to sensitive patient information, and, on a nontechnological level, in-service education programs can raise employee awareness about handling the same information. Similarly, complete and accurate information in the EHR can support the claims management function, serve as the basis of a defense in a lawsuit, and assist in promoting safety education programs—all areas that are central to a successful risk management program. With the use of data mining techniques, the EHR can be searched to assist in analyzing different areas of a health care delivery system, such as obstetrics, psychiatry, anesthesia, and surgery, to determine if they carry higher levels of risk. Finally, the EHR has been helpful in the risk management context through analyzing the occurrence of medication errors, inconsistent data entries, and contradictions in data.

Confidentiality

Long a matter closely associated with health information professionals, confidentiality is central to reducing risk. **Confidentiality** is the obligation of the health care provider to maintain patient information in a manner that will not permit dissemination beyond the health care provider. The health care community has for decades considered the confidentiality of health information a matter of utmost importance. The failure of health care providers to respect confidentiality, combined with greater public awareness of the adverse effects of unauthorized disclosure of health information, may have an impact on risk management programs through an increased number of lawsuits. Such lawsuits generally allege violations of the right to privacy, breach of confidentiality, and/or breach of contract.

One lawsuit illustrating the risks associated with not maintaining confidentiality is *Estate of Behringer v. Medical Center at Princeton.*[9] In *Behringer*, a physician on staff at the hospital was treated at the hospital and diagnosed with acquired immunodeficiency syndrome (AIDS). After news of the doctor's diagnosis was circulated among the hospital staff and his patients, the physician sued the hospital for breach of the duty to maintain the confidentiality of his diagnosis. The court found in his favor, noting that the hospital failed to take reasonable precautions to ensure that his diagnosis and health records were held confidential.

Risks of such lawsuits may be lessened through education of health care professionals concerning the professional and legal obligations to maintain confidentiality. Beyond education, a health care institution may reduce risk by adhering to and enforcing its policies regarding the confidentiality of patient information.

Incident Reports

As discussed previously, proper documentation in the health record includes recording adverse incidents that occur during an episode of patient care. Such documentation in the health record is separate and distinct from an incident report, which is a risk management technique used to describe and manage an adverse incident. Understanding this difference is essential to the proper functioning of a risk management program.

Definition and Purposes

To describe an incident report accurately, the learner must first understand what an incident is. A **hospital incident** is defined as

> *any event or circumstance not consistent with the normal routine operations of the hospital and its staff or the routine care of a patient. It may be an error, an accident, or a situation which could have, or has, resulted in injury to a person or damage to hospital equipment or property.*[10]

Incidents may encompass a variety of events, such as a medication error, a slip and fall, the loss of a patient's belongings, or an equipment malfunction affecting the patient. The incident is not limited to patients alone but may also affect the health care provider, its employees, or a visitor. Because the incident is not routine and could or did result in injury to a person or damage to equipment or property, it is considered adverse.

The **incident report** is the documentation of the adverse incident, whether done on a paper form or through a computerized database with access highly controlled. The report describes the incident itself, including the time, date, and place of occurrence, along with the condition of the subject of the incident (patient, employee, or visitor), statements or observations of witnesses, and any responsive action taken by the health care provider or organization. The report differs from the health record in that if poorly developed, it may also include subjective statements or opinions concerning fault or the circumstances surrounding the incident. By contrast, the health record consists of a basic recounting of facts, devoid of personal opinion or subjective statements. Because the presence of this additional information in the incident report is inconsistent with the purposes of a health record, the health record should not incorporate the incident report. Rather, the incident report should be filed separately from the health record.

An incident report serves multiple purposes: to document fully the circumstances surrounding the incident, to identify situations that may lead to litigation, to educate health care personnel in order to prevent future incidents, and to create a database for monitoring the number and types of incidents. The first two purposes relate to the traditional notion of risk management because they serve to alert the health care provider's attorney and insurance carrier to specific incidences that may lead to a claim against the health care provider. The second two purposes relate not only to risk management but also to quality assurance: in addition to identifying specific incidences of risk, incident reports also permit the health care provider to study patterns of activity to determine which practices should be altered and how to fashion training programs to achieve the optimum result.

These multiple purposes are best served if the incident report is completed as soon as practicable after the incident, when memories are fresh. By completing the report in a timely fashion, the health care provider hastens the availability of the report to its attorney, insurance carrier, and quality assurance department for review and evaluation. And it is the availability of the report to the provider's attorney that will determine whether the report is discoverable and admissible in the event of litigation.

The incident report is an integral component of any loss prevention program. This report can be prepared and submitted electronically in many facilities, although the paper version is usually still available. The data from the paper report may then be abstracted to facilitate data storage and documentation requirements. Once abstracted, the data can be analyzed to determine approaches to reduce risk in the future. An example of this analysis can be seen in Figure 12.1. A trend has emerged toward developing specialized reports, such as medication and surgical occurrence reports.

Discoverability and Admissibility

Because an incident report details the event that caused injury to the patient, employee, or visitor, it is one of the most important sources of information to the parties involved in a lawsuit against the health care provider. Whether the report becomes available to the plaintiff will be determined by the rules of evidence governing discovery and admissibility and the privileges that attach these rules.

Discovery is the process used by parties to obtain information that relates to the subject matter of a lawsuit or an administrative agency proceeding. Discovery occurs before trial and involves identifying and locating books, documents, or other tangible things and persons relating to the subject matter at issue. The information to be discovered may relate to claims or defenses for either side of the lawsuit and is made by a formal request, such as through written interrogatories.[11] Information is considered discoverable if the applicable rules require disclosure of the information upon the formal request of a party. Additional information concerning discovery, including electronic discovery, is addressed in Chapter 2, Court Systems and Legal Procedures; and Chapter 3, Judicial Process of Health Information.

The fact that certain information may be discovered does not automatically mean that the information may be admitted into evidence at trial.[12] Information is considered **admissible** into evidence at trial if the applicable rules establish that the information is both pertinent and proper

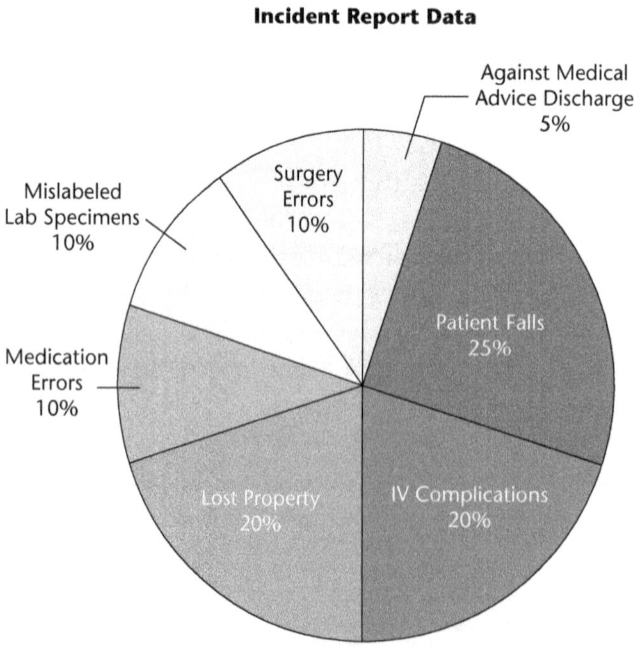

Figure 12.1 Incident Report Data

for the judge and/or jury to consider when deciding the issues involved in the lawsuit. As a general matter, incident reports are governed by the hearsay rule of evidence and its exception covering business records. Detailed material addressing the hearsay rule and business record exception is contained in Chapter 3, Judicial Process of Health Information.

The existence of an incident report does not automatically mean that a party to the lawsuit may either discover or admit the report. In order to discover or admit the report, the party must overcome the application of privileges. A privilege is the legal right to keep certain information confidential and protect it from subpoena, discovery, or introduction into evidence at trial. A privilege will be considered waived if the confidentiality is breached, through either carelessness or deliberate disclosure by the party holding the privilege.[13]

In the context of incident reports, the most frequently used privilege is the attorney–client privilege. Other privileges, such as the attorney work–product privilege, have met with very limited success when applied to incident reports.[14] Because courts have increasingly rejected use of the attorney work–product privilege in this context, the work–product privilege will not be addressed here.

The **attorney–client privilege** protects communications made between attorneys and their clients from disclosure to third parties. It is designed to facilitate full and open communication between attorneys and their clients by assuring clients that the communication will remain confidential. To fall within the privilege, certain criteria must be met: an attorney–client relationship must be established and the client must make the communication in confidence for the purpose of obtaining legal advice from the attorney.[15]

Whether an incident report will be protected by the attorney–client privilege generally centers on the question of whether the report was made for the benefit of the attorney alone or whether dissemination of the report to others, such as the insurance carrier or internal quality assurance department, will defeat the privilege. In some jurisdictions, the report is not protected if disseminated to anyone other than the attorney;[16] in other jurisdictions, as long as the report is not placed in the health record and dissemination is limited to the attorney and the health provider's insurance carrier, the report is protected.[17]

To guarantee protection of the privilege, the health information manager must work to ensure that the incident report is not placed in the health record. This can be accomplished not only through standard health record reviews but also through involvement in developing the provider's written policies and procedures governing incident reports. Such policies and procedures should address (1) the content of the report, including labeling it as confidential and addressing it to the health care provider's attorney; (2) the limited dissemination of the report inside and outside the health care institution; and (3) the training of staff to properly complete the report.

Where incident reports do fall under the category of the attorney–client privilege and are produced by the health care provider as part of the discovery process, the recipient of the incident report will claim that the health care provider has waived any privilege to protect the document. If the disclosure was inadvertent, the health care provider took reasonable steps to prevent disclosure, and the health care provider promptly took reasonable steps to rectify the error, Federal Rule of Evidence 502 would apply to protect the inadvertently disclosed incident report.

In summary, every health information professional must understand the applicable rules of discovery, admission of evidence, and the attorney–client privilege within the health care provider's jurisdiction, whether or not the health information professional is formally involved in the health care provider's risk management program. Without such an understanding, the health information professional may act inadvertently to allow placement of the incident report in the health record, with the result that the attorney–client privilege is lost and the report may be both discovered and admitted into evidence in a particular case. In addition, the health information professional loses the opportunity to educate fellow health care personnel on the proper methods to complete the incident report.

Trends in Risk Management

Traditionally, risk management dealt with assessing patient outcomes and events, writing incident reports, and reviewing past events to determine the need for changes in policy and procedure. Traditional statistical methods were employed to measure risk, and these statistics were reported to higher management levels and boards of directors. Risk management still uses these processes but now includes more focus on database management, primarily in two areas: using data in an automated fashion to measure a health care institution's risk and identifying the risk inherent with databases that contain enormous amounts of sensitive data.

Automated databases can be powerful tools in risk management. Because a **database** is a structured collection of data on multiple entities and their relationships, often arranged for ease and speed of retrieval, it is an ideal method for storing risk management data. The traditional approach of storing paper-based incident reports in a file cabinet did not provide a mechanism for sophisticated information searches, which can be performed in a database format with ease. Using a common and controlled database approach, data can be added and modified over time, thereby providing end users the data needed to perform their jobs as efficiently as possible. With the advent of sophisticated software applications and techniques such as data mining, databases can be searched for risk patterns that may be difficult to detect using traditional statistical methods. Once discovered, these data can be analyzed to predict the probability of future occurrences and to determine how to proceed with action, including mitigation efforts. This effort can lead to more effective loss prevention and reduction programs.

Risk management has grown to include areas not traditionally considered within its scope. Occurrences that organizations often require to be reported to the risk manager are falls, lost property, IV complications, mislabeled lab specimens, and against-medical-advice discharges. Management of these types of occurrences is integral to an effective loss prevention program. In addition, risk managers are involved in investigations coordinated with clinical engineering to comply with the federal Safe Medical Devices Act, safety inspections mandated by the Joint Commission, and COBRA investigations.

Risk management also involves claims management; risk managers often act as liaison to a health care organization's attorneys. This may include conducting record reviews, arranging depositions, and providing the necessary documentation for claims investigations. The risk manager may also participate in interviews with professional and other staff related to adverse occurrences.

Another part of an effective risk management program is Sentinel Event Review, a requirement of the Joint Commission since 1998. A **sentinel event** is an unexpected occurrence involving death or serious physical or psychological injury, or other risks thereof; serious injury includes loss of limb or limb function. The standards that relate specifically to the management of sentinel events are found in the Improving Organization Performance section of the JC accreditation manual. Organizations are required to establish mechanisms to identify, report, and manage these events. Organizations are also required to conduct a **root-cause analysis** to identify the cause of the event and should include a clinical as well as an administrative review. Examples of sentinel events that must be reviewed include significant medication errors, significant adverse drug reactions, confirmed transfusion reactions, and surgery on the wrong patient or wrong body part. Infant abduction and the discharge of an infant to the wrong family are also considered sentinel events.

Facilities are encouraged but not required to report sentinel events to the JC within forty-five days of the event. If a facility chooses not to report the event and a family member makes the JC aware, or the JC becomes aware by other means, the JC will communicate to the facility the requirement to submit the findings of the root-cause analysis and action plans. Failure to do so within the specified time frame could result in placing the organization on Accreditation Watch status until the response is received and the protocol approved. An on-site review will not occur unless the JC deems it necessary due to a potential threat to patient health or safety or if there appears to be significant noncompliance with the Joint Commission standards.

Although risk management has already moved from a traditional focus to one that includes database management, it is evolving even further in this century. In view of the many external factors that influence health care organizations, particularly those beyond the organization's control, a new concept has been applied to risk management: enterprise risk management. **Enterprise risk management (ERM)** refers to the function of analyzing and evaluating all of the risks that confront an organization, not just the legal, financial, and medical risks that are traditionally considered. These risks are listed in Table 12.2. ERM considers these risks, and others not listed here, in combination and determines how they affect the health care organization's strategic plan and overall health. ERM also considers risks in the context of the opportunities they may present, with the goal of exploring how those risks may be exploited to gain a competitive advantage.

A feature central to ERM is the focus on interrelationships and interdependencies. Instead of viewing risks in isolation and organizational departments as separate entities, ERM examines risks together across departmental lines. ERM also examines risks across activities and functions, factoring in how they interplay. Furthermore, ERM examines the health care organization's relationship with external entities, sometimes resulting in a collaborative regional effort to mitigate and control loss. Such an approach is particularly applicable to emergency preparedness planning, because it permits the risk manager to examine the organization's infrastructure and estimate how it will be affected by a catastrophic event. Such a proactive approach may well reduce costs to the health care organization, in both financial terms and how well the organization accomplishes its mission. As ERM increases in acceptance, its use in the health care industry should also increase.

When risks are identified that impact the organization's business model and competitive advantage, ERM intersects with strategy. These risks can arise in multiple ways, such as a shift in consumer sentiment favoring outpatient care over inpatient hospitalization or the occurrence of an economic event, like a recession or financial crisis. It is incumbent upon risk managers to spot such

Table 12.2 Enterprise Risk Management Concerns
Traditional legal, financial, and medical risks
The threat of terrorism and its impact on professionals, patients, and the community
The heightened emphasis on corporate governance and compliance with statutes, regulations, and ethical standards
The increased presence of oversight authorities that monitor business practices
The expanded awareness of patients and the public in general of medical and medication errors
The shortage of qualified staff in certain health care professions or in certain geographic regions
The effect of the economy in general and in specific local regions upon the demand for unreimbursed health care

risks, analyze them in the context of strategy, and contribute towards the development of strategies that will lessen the risks identified.

One additional way in which risk management is addressing the twenty-first century is in its relationship with social media. Given that patient use of social media is becoming more common, health care providers have identified instances where their reputations were called into question publicly by patients complaining about the quality of care they received. Those statements that place the health care provider in a negative light pose risk to the health care provider's reputation, not only with that patient but also with all who may encounter the negative statements in social media. Left unchecked, these statements not only harm reputations but also may influence potential patients to avoid using the health care provider for any future care. A reduction in potential patient load may have serious financial consequences for the health care provider. For these reasons, some risk managers now include social media as part of their responsibilities.

CRITICAL THINKING

In addition to risks to a health care provider's reputation, social media posts of a negative nature may pose legal risks. What types of social media posts could pose legal risks to a health care provider?

QUALITY MANAGEMENT

The second area in which the health information professional plays a vital role concerning non-patient records is **quality management**. Quality management has long been a part of the health information professional's role in the health care delivery system. Over the past decade, various terms and methods have been applied to describe quality management, including *performance improvement, continuous quality improvement, total quality management, quality control, quality review*, and *problem detection*. While each of these terms or methods differs from the one preceding it, all fall within the umbrella of quality management.

As with risk management, quality management is an improvement technique that health care providers use. Although similar databases may be involved, quality management significantly differs from risk management. Quality management is a clinical function, focusing on how to improve patient care. It looks at patterns of activity to define optimum performance and determine how to achieve it. As such, quality management is primarily process oriented rather than outcome oriented. By contrast, risk management looks at specific incidences of risk or loss to determine which activities to avoid. Risk management focuses primarily on the outcome, not the process.

Quality management activities in health care institutions are conducted under the control and direction of **peer review committees**. A peer review committee is composed of health care professionals who are charged with the responsibility for evaluating, maintaining, and/or monitoring the quality and utilization of health care services.[18] Peer review committees typically discharge this responsibility through audit and review of patient information against established guidelines. Where a pattern emerges indicating that the established guidelines were not met, the peer review committee determines what further action should be taken, including education and training of staff.

Peer Review Privileges

An effective quality management program benefits a health care institution by allowing neutral evaluators the opportunity to provide useful feedback and recommendations designed to improve patient care. To achieve this benefit, the committee members must fully participate and offer candid criticism of the information they review. Yet health care institutions cannot force health care professionals such as physicians to participate in peer review activities when the institution's medical staff acts as a semi-autonomous body. Furthermore, health care professionals may hesitate to honestly analyze or criticize a colleague if the analysis or criticism they make will be published or otherwise disclosed. Finally, participation and candor may be inhibited by the fear of lawsuits charging defamation, violations of antitrust laws, or the loss of patient referrals.

To address these concerns, state legislatures have passed peer review statutes. The aims of these statutes are twofold: (1) to protect the deliberations and records of peer review committees from access by nonparticipants and (2) to protect participants in peer review activities from civil liability. Not all statutes address both aims; however, most statutes address the first aim.[19] Under the first aim, peer review deliberations and records are considered "privileged," that is, protected from subpoena, discovery, or introduction into evidence. Under the second aim, participants are considered "immune" from monetary liability in the event of a lawsuit or other legal proceeding.

Because **peer review privileges** are a matter of state statute, the protections they afford necessarily vary from state to state.[20] For example, many of the statutes passed in the 1970s protected only peer review activity that took place in hospitals. As new entities such as health maintenance organizations became involved in health care, peer review statutes were revised to afford these entities the same protections afforded hospitals.[21] Nonetheless, some states have failed to revise their statutes to include these new entities, making it likely that peer review activities conducted by these entities fall outside the scope of the statute's protections.

State statutes also vary regarding the definition of peer review activity. Some statutes do not define the term beyond general language such as records and proceedings; other statutes explicitly state which documents and materials fall within their protections.[22] As a general rule, a statute's failure to include an explicit definition of what peer review activity is protected will result in excluding some activities from that protection. Certain activities commonly associated with peer review activity, such as the credentialing process, could therefore fall outside the scope of the statute's protection.

The statutes further vary by the nature of civil immunity afforded to participants. Some statutes provide absolute immunity from all suits,[23] while others provide only qualified immunity if a defamation action is brought.[24] Where immunity is granted, the law assumes that the participant acted in good faith. If a plaintiff can demonstrate that the participant acted with malice, the participant is no longer shielded from liability.

In addition to statutory variations, the peer review privilege may vary by the way in which courts have interpreted it. Many statutes give courts the authority to require disclosure under certain exceptional circumstances, such as a criminal action brought against a health care provider accused of a felony. Each situation varies, but courts generally order disclosure in those cases where the information sought is essential to protect the public interest and the information cannot be obtained from another source.[25]

Every health information professional involved in quality management activities should understand the statutory peer review privilege as it applies in his jurisdiction. Such an understanding will assist the health information professional in ensuring that the health care provider's quality management policies and procedures conform to the law and preserve the confidentiality of peer review materials.

Medical Staff Disciplinary Process

Closely interwoven with any quality management program is the physician disciplinary process. Conclusions reached during peer review activities may directly bear on a health care institution's decision to limit or discontinue a physician's practice in the institution or otherwise discipline a physician. And in some health care institutions, the peer review committee is charged with direct responsibility over the professional disciplinary process. For those persons involved with decisions concerning staff privileges and disciplinary actions, it is necessary to understand the requirements of the Health Care Quality Improvement Act.

Passed in 1986, the Health Care Quality Improvement Act is designed to improve the exchange of information about decisions relating to the professional competence and conduct of physicians, dentists, and other health care practitioners.[26] The desired result of such an exchange of information is an improvement in the quality of medical care through restrictions on the ability of certain physicians and dentists to change locations without disclosing previous incompetent performance or misconduct. The act accomplishes this result through the use of the National Practitioner Data Bank and complex reporting and query requirements. The U.S. Department of Health and Human Services has published regulations further defining the reporting and query requirements.[27]

Information concerning professional competence and conduct is reported to the National Practitioner Data Bank by hospitals, medical societies, licensing boards, prepaid medical practices, and other health care entities involved in peer review activities. Specific information contained in the Data Bank includes data concerning malpractice payments, licensure actions, and adverse actions such as the loss of staff privileges of physicians and dentists in all fifty states. Figures 12.2 through 12.6 illustrate the types of information that must be reported to the Data Bank.

With these data available in the Data Bank, health care entities such as hospitals are required to query the Data Bank whenever receiving an application for a position on the medical staff. Once admitted to the medical staff, the health care entity must continue to query the Data Bank every two years concerning each staff member. The act presumes that receipt of information concerning incompetence or misconduct will result in the denial, restriction, or termination of staff privileges.

In coordination with the Data Bank, Congress has created a national health care fraud and abuse database named the Healthcare Integrity and Protection Data Bank (HIPDB).

1. The physician's or licensed health care practitioner's name, date of birth, work address and, if known, home address and Social Security number
2. The name of each professional school attended and the year of graduation
3. For each professional license, the license number, the field of licensure, and the name of the state or territory in which the license is held
4. The physician's or licensed health care provider's Drug Enforcement Administration registration number, if known
5. The payment amount, date of payment, and whether the payment is for a judgment or a settlement
6. The name, if known, of any hospital with which the physician or licensed health care practitioner is associated
7. A description of the acts or omissions and injuries or illnesses upon which the action or claim was based
8. Other information as required by the secretary of health and human services from time to time after publication in the *Federal Register* and an opportunity for public comment

Figure 12.2 Requirements for the Reporting of Medical Malpractice Payments

1. The physician's or dentist's name, date of birth, work address and, if known, home address and Social Security number
2. Name of each professional school attended and the year of graduation
3. For each professional license, the physician's or dentist's license number, the field of licensure, and the name of the state or territory in which the license is held
4. The physician's or dentist's Drug Enforcement Administration registration number, if known
5. A description of the acts or omissions or other reasons for the action taken
6. A description of the board action, the date the action was taken, and its effective date
7. Classification of the action in accordance with a reporting code adopted by the Secretary of Health and Human Services
8. Other information as required by the Secretary from time to time after publication in the *Federal Register* and an opportunity for public comment

Figure 12.3 Requirements for the Reporting of Sanctions Taken by Boards of Medical Examiners

Actions based on professional competence or professional conduct:

1. which revoke or suspend or otherwise restrict a physician's or dentist's license;
2. which censure, reprimand, or place on probation a physician or dentist; or
3. under which a physician's or dentist's license is surrendered

Figure 12.4 Reportable Actions Taken by the Boards of Medical Examiners

Actions taken by health care entities:

1. which adversely affect the clinical privileges of a physician or dentist for a period longer than thirty days; or
2. which involve the acceptance of the surrender of clinical privileges or other restriction by a physician or dentist

Figure 12.5 Reportable Actions Taken by Health Care Entities: Clinical Privileges

Part of the Health Insurance Portability and Accountability Act, the HIPDB contains reports of final adverse actions taken against health care providers, suppliers, or practitioners when liability is admitted or found. The information to be reported includes the name and tax identification number of the provider, supplier, or practitioner who is subject to the adverse action; the name of any health care entity with which the provider, supplier, or practitioner is associated; the nature of the adverse action and whether such action is on appeal; and a description of the acts, omissions, or injuries that form the basis for adverse action. Examples of adverse actions include improper payments, medically unnecessary services, delays in diagnosis or treatment, and adverse patient outcomes. Access to the HIPDB is limited to federal and state governmental agencies and health plans that are required to report adverse actions and to individual providers, suppliers, and practitioners who query about themselves.

1. The physician's or dentist's name, date of birth, work address and, if known, home address and Social Security number
2. Name of each professional school attended and the year of graduation
3. For each professional license, the license number, the field of licensure, and the name of the state or territory in which the license is held
4. The physician's or dentist's Drug Enforcement Administration registration number, if known
5. A description of the acts or omissions or other reasons for privilege loss or surrender
6. A description of the entity's action, the date the action was taken, and its effective date
7. Other information as required by the secretary of health and human services from time to time after publication in the *Federal Register* and an opportunity for public comment

Figure 12.6 Requirements for the Reporting of Adverse Actions Taken by Health Care Entities

Health care institutions that have taken steps to restrict a physician's privileges or otherwise discipline a physician through peer review activities have been subject to lawsuits. Health care institutions faced with these lawsuits have found protection through the act's grant of qualified immunity.

Actions taken by health care institutions to restrict staff privileges, when those actions are the result of peer review activities, may be protected by the act from liability. Under the act, those who participate in peer review activities are immune from civil damage actions if the statute's fairness and reporting requirements are met.

Health information professionals involved in questions of physician staff privileges and disciplinary actions face the challenge of understanding the complex reporting and query requirements of the act and its implementing regulations. The health information professional's successful integration of the reporting and query requirements into the credentialing and disciplinary process will result not only in compliance with the law but also in improvement in the quality of patient care.

UTILIZATION MANAGEMENT

Utilization management refers to a combination of planned functions directed to patients in a health care facility or setting that includes prudent use of resources, appropriate treatment management, and early comprehensive discharge planning for continuation of care. The process uses established criteria as specified in the organization's utilization review plan. **Utilization review** is the clinical review of the appropriateness of admission and planned use of resources that can be and often is initiated prior to admission and conducted at specific time frames as defined in an organization's utilization review plan. This review involves the process of comparing preestablished criteria against the health care services to be provided to the patient to determine whether the care is necessary. To understand how utilization management differs from quality management and risk management, see Table 12.3.

Table 12.3 Contrasts between Quality Management, Risk Management, and Utilization Review

	Quality Management	Risk Management	Utilization Management
Focus	Improve quality of patient care (clinical)	Reduce risk and liability (nonclinical)	Use resources wisely (clinical)
Approach	Review of a process Audit and review against preestablished guidelines	Review of an adverse event	Compare patient data against preestablished criteria
Methods Used	Peer review committees National Practitioner Data Bank HIPDB	Incident report analysis Sentinel event review	Evidence-based guidelines Medical necessity review
Driver	Accrediting bodies Regulatory bodies	Liability insurers	Third-party payers, QIOs

Historical Development

Efforts at utilization management began in the 1950s and were employed at facilities that had frequent bed shortages as a way to allocate space to patients who demonstrated the greatest need. Utilization management first became mandatory in 1965 with the passage of the federal law establishing the Medicare program. The focus of the legislation at that time was on reducing the patient's length of stay (LOS) in an effort to control the rising costs of health care. Medical evaluation studies were also part of the review process that focused on improving the quality of patient care. Physician involvement was central to the process and continues to this day, although many changes in the procedures employed have taken place through the years.

During the 1970s, utilization management became a required component of JC accreditation standards as well as a requirement for participation in the Medicaid reimbursement program. Further legislation in 1972 led to the formation of **Professional Standards Review Organizations** (PSROs), groups tasked with monitoring the appropriateness and quality of outcomes. In 1977, new legislation known as the Utilization Review Act defined the review process by requiring hospitals to conduct continued-stay reviews for medical necessity and the appropriateness of Medicare and Medicaid inpatient hospitalizations. The Health Care Financing Administration (HCFA), now called Centers for Medicare and Medicaid Services (CMS), began operation, charged with managing the Medicare and Medicaid programs that had previously been the responsibility of the Social Security Administration. Simultaneously, Congress passed fraud and abuse legislation to enable enforcement of the provisions of the act.

With enactment of the Tax Equity and Fiscal Responsibility Act (TEFRA) of 1982, the titles of these PSROs changed to Peer Review Organizations (PROs). TEFRA also established the first Medicare prospective payment system (PPS), which was implemented the following year. Using PPS, reimbursement was no longer based on a per diem rate but on a predetermined rate based on the discharge diagnosis in relation to diagnosis-related groups (DRGs). TEFRA's changes placed additional focus on managing the length of stay through early and effective discharge planning. While these changes in the reporting and scope of utilization management occurred, the focus continued to be directed toward managing the cost of health care and assuring the best level of quality health care possible. CMS recently changed the PRO designation to Quality Improvement Organization (QIO) as part of the "8th Scope of Work" (SOW), a document that updates the direction and focus of the organization.[28]

By the 1990s, the process of determining medical necessity expanded beyond the beneficiaries of Medicare and Medicaid to include the efforts of many managed care and group health insurance plans. Precertification for hospital admissions and surgical procedures became requirements of many of these private entities. In addition, some plans required authorization from primary care physicians before treatment in emergency care centers in nonemergency circumstances would be reimbursed as well as preauthorization for diagnostic radiological procedures.

A further redesign in the twenty-first century has led to a redesign of QIOs with one component focusing on quality of care concerns and appeals (BFCC-QIOs) and another focusing on improving the quality of health care for targeted conditions (QIN-QIOs). This change in focus has entailed separating the process of case review from quality improvement.[29]

Utilization review has evolved in the twenty-first century to incorporate evidence-based guidelines as part of the screening process. Several private companies, such as Milliman and McKesson (InterQual), have published evidence-based guidelines that are widely used at the time of preadmission, admission, and continued stay or concurrent review as well as during discharge planning. Some are based on the level of illness and the patient services required, whereas others focus on ambulatory care, observation status, inpatient and surgical care, general recovery, home care, and chronic care.

Utilization Review

Complying with the changing aspects of utilization review has been a challenge for many health care professionals. **Case management** refers to the ongoing review of patient care in various health care settings related to assuring the medical necessity of the encounter and the appropriateness of the clinical services provided. **Case managers**, also known as **utilization coordinators**, are frequently nurses or health information managers with responsibility for managing the review process and coordinating the patient's care with physicians, nurses, and other allied health professionals. In many settings, the case management function is organized into a department and may also include social workers and clerical assistants to help with communication and coordination of the review activities. Utilization management continues to be a physician-centered function, though it is coordinated by case managers. In large facilities, case managers may specialize in specific areas, such as cardiology, orthopedics, or pediatrics; in smaller facilities, case managers must be trained to facilitate the variety of cases that the organization treats. Long-term care facilities and home health services are also required to have an established utilization management plan, although their requirements differ. In all settings, the focus rests on medical necessity and appropriate management of health care resources.

The utilization review process consists of several steps of review; these are listed in Figure 12.7. Each step plays a role in determining medical necessity. During the preadmission and admission review steps, the case manager uses criteria and screening software, and in some cases may contact the patient's third-party payer, to confirm that the admission is approved. Concurrent review, sometimes referred to as continued-stay review, assures the continued medical necessity and appropriateness of care being delivered to the patient, along with appropriate documentation to support the decisions made concerning necessity and appropriateness. Discharge planning involves coordinating activities for the patient's release from the health care facility, along with appropriate documentation of the discharge status in the patient's health record. Case managers

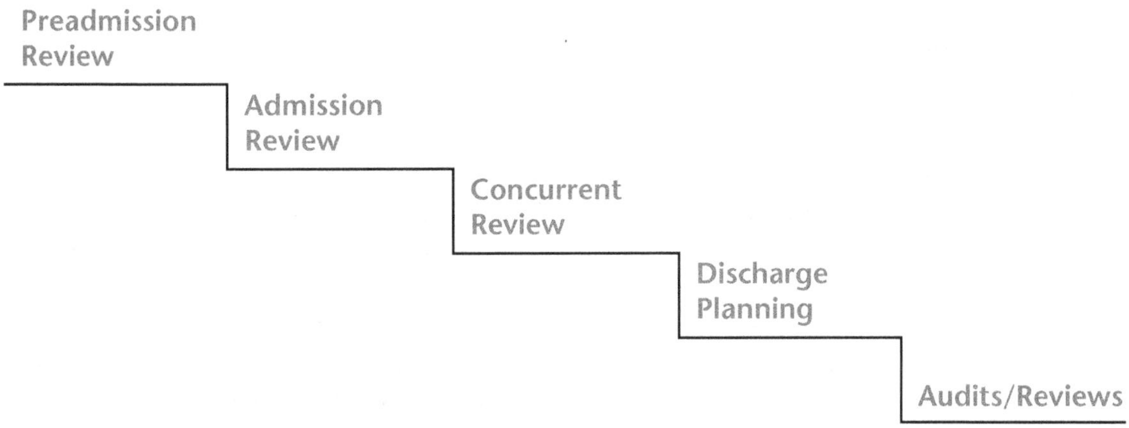

Figure 12.7 Steps in the Utilization Review Process

work closely with health information managers to conduct various audits and reviews for compliance with the Work Plan of the Office of Inspector General of the Department of Health and Human Services.

Although this discussion of the steps in the utilization review process has focused on the acute care setting, utilization review may vary in other settings. For example, utilization review in home care and skilled nursing facilities is similar to the acute care setting in design and process, but uses criteria that are more specific to the scope of the facility. Medical necessity and appropriateness of the plan of care are central to utilization review. Coordinators who work with the discharge planners or case managers at acute care facilities usually conduct preadmission reviews before the patient receives this new form of treatment. The type and amount of service provided are determined using specific criteria or in consultation with the patient's third-party payer.

Utilization management remains central to the delivery of patient care in the twenty-first century. Both accrediting and licensing standards contain elements of utilization management with which health care organizations must comply. For example, the current JC standards specify that the provisions of ongoing care are based on patient needs even when denial of payment has been determined. The standard also includes provisions for the patient's family to be involved in the decision-making process. Similar requirements are present in the Condition for Participation in the Medicare and Medicaid reimbursement programs.[30] Utilization management will continue to evolve as health care in the United States adapts to new changes.

CONCLUSION

As this chapter demonstrates, complex legal requirements govern a health care provider's risk management and quality management programs and utilization review processes. The health information professional's knowledge of these requirements will influence the success of the health care provider's programs. Key to that influence is the ability to apply that knowledge to a particular situation. Health information professionals face that challenge by educating the health care provider's staff concerning patient record requirements, protecting incident reports from discovery, and reporting adverse actions regarding clinical privileges. In each example, the health information professional applies legal principles to real-life situations. For these reasons, health information professionals must understand the legal bases and requirements of risk management, quality management, and utilization review.

CASE STUDY

You are a health information professional closely involved with risk management at General Hospital, a teaching institution. Beginning this July, the hospital will incorporate presentations by hospital employees into its Grand Rounds series of lectures. You have been asked to present the lecture covering risk management. Compose a presentation addressing the legal aspects of risk management, particularly concentrating on patient record requirements and incident reports.

REVIEW QUESTIONS

1. What are the general principles of risk management?
2. What events influenced the development of risk management?
3. How does a properly documented health record reduce the risk of a health care facility?
4. Compare and contrast the ready availability of a health record in the risk management context.
5. How does the concept of patient confidentiality relate to the concept of reducing risk?
6. What is an incident report?
7. What purposes are served by an incident report?
8. What are the advantages of completing an incident report as soon as practicable after an incident?
9. How does discovery differ from admissibility in the context of incident reports?
10. What is a privilege, and how can it be waived?
11. How does quality management differ from risk management?
12. What are the aims of peer review statutes?
13. Explain the concept of a peer review committee and its duties.
14. How do peer review statutes differ?
15. What is the National Practitioner Data Bank, and how does a health care institution use the data it contains?
16. What is the focus of utilization management?

ENRICHMENT ACTIVITY

Interview the official responsible for processing applications to join the medical staff at a local health care facility. Discuss what consideration is given to the information held by the National Practitioner Data Bank in processing those applications. Examine whether the steps followed by the facility are consistent with the requirements of the Health Care Quality Improvement Act and its implementing regulations.

ENRICHMENT ACTIVITY

Review articles in health care journals concerning risk management. How do the discussions address incident reports and discoverability and admissibility issues? Compare the information in these articles with the concepts covered in this chapter, and discuss these with your instructor.

NOTES

1. By nonpatient records, I refer to those records addressing the issues of quality control in a health care setting, such as incident reports and peer review documents.

2. Barry R. Furrow et al., Health Law, Ch. § III at 49 (1987).

3. 211 N.E.2d 253 (Ill. 1965), *cert. denied*, 383 U.S. 946 (1966).

4. Joint Commission, Comprehensive Accreditation Manual for Hospitals, Performance Improvement, PI.3.10 (2004).

5. *See, e.g.*, Alaska Stat. § 18.20.075 (2019); Fla. Stat. Ann. § 395.0197 (West 2019); Md. Health-Gen. Code Ann. § 19-319(g) (2019); N.C. Gen. Stat. § 131E-96 (2019); R.I. Gen. Laws § 23-17-24 (2019).

6. *See, e.g.*, *Butterfield v. Okubo*, 831 P.2d 97 (Utah 1992) (unavailability to emergency room physician of infant's past medical records concerning breathing difficulties resulted in liability for failing to prescribe appropriate treatment).

7. 45 C.F.R. § 164.306 (2019).

8. 45 C.F.R. § 164.306(e) (2019).

9. 592 A.2d 1251 (N.J. Super. Ct. 1991).

10. John F. Monagle, Risk Management: A Guide for Health Care Professionals 29 (1985).

11. Fed. R. Evid. 26(b) (1).

12. *See, e.g.*, Fla. Stat. Ann. § 395.0197(4) (West 2019) (incident reports shall be "subject to discovery, but are admissible as evidence in court").

13. 23 Charles A. Wright & Kenneth W. Graham, Jr., Federal Practice and Procedure: Evidence § 93 (1980).

14. *See, e.g.*, *Kay Laboratories, Inc. v. District Court*, 653 P.2d 721 (Colo. 1982) (rejecting attorney work-product privilege); *Weiner v. Memorial Hosp.*, 453 N.Y.S.2d 142 (1982) (rejecting attorney work-product privilege).

15. McCormick on Evidence (Thomson Reuters, 7th ed. 2013).

16. *See Kay Laboratories, Inc. v. District Court*, 653 P.2d 721 (Colo. 1982); *Bernardi v. Community Hosp. Ass'n.*, 443 P.2d 708 (Colo. 1968).

17. *See, e.g.*, *Sierra Vista Hosp. v. Shaffer*, 56 Cal. Rptr. 387 (1967); *Sligar v. Tucker*, 267 So.2d 54 (Fla. Dist. Ct. App. 1972); *Community Hosps. of Indianapolis, Inc. v. Medtronic*, 594 N.E.2d 448 (Ind. Ct. App. 1992); *Enke v. Anderson*, 733 S.W.2d 462 (Mo. Ct. App. 1987); *Clark v. Norris*, 734 P.2d 182 (Mont. 1986).

18. The composition and responsibilities of peer review committees are defined by both statute and accrediting agencies, such as the Joint Commission on Accreditation of Healthcare Organizations. *See, e.g.*, Conn. Gen. Stat. Ann. § 19a-17b (West 2019); Haw. Rev. Stat. Ann. § 624-25.5 (2019); Kan. Stat. Ann. § 65-4915 (2019); Mo. Rev. Stat. § 537.035(2) (2019); Joint Commission, Comprehensive Accreditation Manual for Hospitals, Medical Staff, MS.4.90 (2004).

19. In fact, some statutes expressly deny immunity to peer review participants while simultaneously affording protection to peer review materials. *See, e.g.*, Cal. Health & Safety Code § 1370 (West 2019).

20. This portion of the text draws heavily on Robert W. McCann, Protecting the Confidentiality of Peer Review Information, JOURNAL OF THE AM. HEALTH INFO. MGMT. ASS'N., Dec. 1993, at 52–56, and is cited with permission of the American Health Information Management Association.

21. *See, e.g.*, ARIZ. REV. STAT. ANN. § 36-445-01 (2019) (hospitals and outpatient surgical centers); DEL. CODE ANN. § 1768 (2019) (hospitals, medical societies, health maintenance organizations); OHIO REV. CODE ANN. § 4731.224 (Baldwin 2019) (hospitals and ambulatory surgical centers); TENN. CODE ANN. § 63-6-219 (2019) (malpractice support groups, health care institutions, health maintenance organizations, preferred provider organizations).

22. *Compare* ARIZ. REV. STAT. ANN. § 36-445.01 (West 2019) ("all proceedings, records and materials prepared in connection with the reviews"); CONN. GEN. STAT. ANN. § 19a-17b (West 2019) ("the proceedings of a medical review committee conducting a peer review"); R.I. GEN. LAWS § 5-37.3-7 (2019) ("the proceedings and records of medical peer review boards"); with D.C. CODE ANN. § 44-805 (2019) ("the files, records, findings, opinions, recommendations, evaluations, and reports of a peer review body"); IOWA CODE ANN. § 147.135 (West 2019) ("all complaint files, investigation files, reports, and other investigative information relating to licensee discipline or professional competence in the possession of a peer review committee"); KAN. STAT. ANN. § 65-4915 (2019) ("the reports, statements, memoranda, proceedings, findings and other records submitted to or generated by peer review committees").

23. *See, e.g.*, CONN. GEN. STAT. ANN. § 19a-17b (West 2019); DEL. CODE ANN. § 1768 (2019); IOWA CODE ANN. § 147.135 (West 2019); MO. REV. STAT. § 537.035 (2019); OR. REV. STAT. § 41.675 (2019).

24. *See, e.g.*, ALA. CODE § 6-5-333 (2019); ARIZ. REV. STAT. ANN. §§ 36-2401(3) & 2402(b) (2019); FLA. STAT. ANN. § 766.101(4) (West 2019); TENN. CODE ANN. § 63-6-219(c) (2019); W. VA. CODE § 30-3C-2 (2019).

25. *See, e.g.*, D.C. CODE § 32-505(a) (3) (2019).

26. 42 U.S.C. §§ 11101-11152 (2019).

27. 45 C.F.R. §§ 60.1-.14 (2019).

28. The 8th Scope of Work (SOW), Title XI of the Social Security Act, Part B, as amended by the Peer Review Act of 1982. Details about the Centers for Medicare and Medicaid Services' Quality Improvement Organizations Program are available at https://www.cms.gov/Medicare/Quality-Initiatives-Patient-Assessment-Instruments/QualityImprovementOrgs/index.html?redirect=/qualityimprovementorgs/.

29. Id.

30. 42 C.F.R. Part 456. Utilization Control, Subparts B and C (2019).

CHAPTER 13

INFORMATION SYSTEMS

LEARNING OBJECTIVES

After reading this chapter, the learner should be able to:

1. Identify the reasons supporting the transformation to an electronic health record.
2. Compare and contrast the three broad categories of laws and regulations governing the creation and storage of an electronic record.
3. Discuss the business record exception to the hearsay rule and its application to an electronic health record.
4. Evaluate the role of the health information professional in meeting the requirements of the business record exception.
5. List the types of lawsuits that may arise from a breach of confidentiality of an electronic health record.
6. Compare and contrast physical security, personnel security, and risk prevention techniques.
7. Evaluate risk prevention techniques associated with electronic health record systems.
8. Identify the electronic tools that have transformed the health care field's business processes.
9. Compare and contrast the security issues associated with the use of the Internet and e-mail.
10. Explain why the field of telemedicine has not advanced more rapidly.
11. Discuss future legal trends in information technology affecting health care.
12. Discuss future ethical trends in information technology affecting health care.

KEY CONCEPTS

Administrative safeguards
Admissibility
Authentication
Authorship
Blockchain
Breach
Business record exception
CRISPR
Digital divide
Digital imaging
E-health organizations
Electronic health record (EHR)
Electronic mail
Information security policies
Internet
Legal health record
Nanobot
Nanomedicine
Personnel security
Physical safeguards
Physical security
Risk assessment
Risk prevention techniques
Security
Technical safeguards
Telemedicine
Text messaging

INTRODUCTION

The interrelationship between health information management and information technology has grown steadily over the recent decades. With the advent of the enterprise master patient index, automated transcription systems, clinical data repositories, computer-assisted coding, federal regulations relating to electronic transmission of billing data, integrated patient care information systems, optical disk technology, electronic data interchanges, and the electronic health record, today's health information manager must become intimately aware of information technology and all that it offers to the health information management field. This awareness serves to assist the practitioner in protecting the health information housed in information technology.

This chapter provides a basis for the health information professional to gain an understanding of the legal issues present in information technology, particularly those associated with the electronic health record as it relates to accreditation, licensure, and liability. This chapter also identifies emerging legal issues associated with information technology trends affecting the health care environment. By understanding the legal issues, the health information professional is one step closer to properly evaluating, selecting, and implementing an information system that not only satisfies the needs of the health care organization but also sufficiently addresses legal issues and concerns.

ELECTRONIC HEALTH RECORDS

Over the last thirty years, the health care industry has transformed from using a traditional paper-based patient record into an **electronic health record (EHR)**. The vision of a completely electronic health record has become real and commonplace in multiple health care settings. It is the exception to the rule to find a paper-based health record in a health care setting any longer.

Multiple reasons explain this transformation. First and foremost among these reasons is the ever-increasing demands for more detailed and sophisticated patient data, which has highlighted the need for quick access to a wide variety of clinical data. These demands emerged not only from within the health care facility but also from outside the facility: external forces such as regulatory agencies, accrediting organizations, and insurance companies requested increasingly detailed patient data over the last few decades. The traditional paper health record simply could not keep pace with these demands.

Forces external to health care providers have also placed the issue of electronic health records at center stage. For example, the federal government's efforts in health care reform have centered on improving health care delivery through the use of electronic health records.[1] The Institute of Medicine recommended that all health care providers adopt an electronic health record as their standard health record,[2] as did the president of the United States through his State of the Union Address.[3] In 2009, Congress passed the American Recovery and Reinvestment Act (ARRA), which set the goal of creating electronic health records for Americans by the year 2014. Requirements of ARRA led establishment of standards, implementation specifications, and certification criteria for the electronic exchange and use of health information.

EHR	Over several administrations, the U.S. government has recommended and incentivized the adoption of electronic health records.

Additionally, electronic health records offer physical space savings. In most facilities, the health information manager's role has shifted from paper management to information management. Some facilities have seen operating costs for storage of records reduced as a result. This format difference translates into possible cost savings because of the potential for reduction in administrative costs.

Fortunately, advancements in technology have made automation of health information possible. This development should contribute toward the interoperability of various forms of electronic health records.

> **ARRA**
>
> The American Recovery and Reinvestment Act establishes a process for adoption and endorsement of standards, implementation specifications, and certification criteria for electronic health records.

Additionally, electronic tools have influenced the manner in which the health care industry has conducted itself from a business perspective. An extensive body of literature currently exists addressing the technological aspects of an electronic health record and its impact on the health information profession. Therefore, this discussion concentrates on the legal issues involved in the automation of patient-specific data, beginning with an explanation of what constitutes a legal health record and progressing to details concerning accreditation, licensure, and liability issues.

Legal Health Record

Sometimes things that seem obvious are not so evident upon close inspection. Such is the case with the concept of the legal health record in the electronic context. The definition of a **legal health record** provides guidance for health care settings maintaining paper-based, electronic, and hybrid (both paper and electronic) health records:

the legal business record generated at or for a health care organization, which is produced upon request.

In a paper-based setting, one might assume that the legal health record consists of those documents found within the patient's file. The patient's file, however, has always contained documents that were never considered part of the legal health record—for example, correspondence or requests for release of information. Because they were not considered part of the legal health record but merely resided in the patient's file, documents such as correspondence were never produced when a request was made to produce the legal health record.

This is also the case when the electronic environment is involved. Electronic systems operated by health care providers contain more than the patient's health record. For example, the master patient index may be a component of such a system, as may be practice guidelines and prompts to be followed by clinicians delivering patient care. While part of the health care provider's electronic system, these items do not constitute a portion of the patient's health record. Accordingly, the focus rests on what is considered the organization's business record: the documentation of the delivery of health care services to a patient during the patient's stay or episode of care by a health care provider or organization.

Because of this focus, it is incumbent upon each health care provider to define that subset of the electronic system that can be called the patient's legal health record. Such subsets may vary by practice setting because what is memorialized or captured in one health care setting may not be memorialized or captured in another setting. As a general rule, data and documentation that are patient-specific, created or generated by the health care provider, and memorialize the patient care delivered are considered the patient's legal health record in an electronic context. Data that serve as the source of the memorialization (e.g., the audio file of dictation later memorialized in the electronic system) are generally not considered part of the legal health record, though it may be retrieved upon request. Similarly, administrative data, such as audit trails, and derived data, such as aggregate data used to create accreditation or statistical reports, are not considered part of the legal health record. Any decisions reached initially should be reviewed by the health care provider's legal counsel for concurrence and revision if required. Once the definition is reached, the health care provider or organization should educate those persons delivering care to the patient so that all will share a common definition concerning entries they make in the patient's electronic health record.

Accreditation and Licensure Issues

Licensing authorities and accrediting organizations play a major role in the life of a health care provider: the state licensing authority authorizes the provider to practice in a particular state, and the accrediting organization sets standards for each provider's compliance. For this reason, it is important to understand the impact these bodies have on health care providers employing an electronic health record.

ARRA

The American Recovery and Reinvestment Act of 2009 redefines the electronic health record.

The basis of any discussion of an electronic health record involves accurate definitions of the terms. While definitions have varied over time, electronic health records are generally considered to be records created, authenticated, stored, and retrieved by computers. The American Recovery and Reinvestment Act of 2009 (ARRA) defines the electronic health record as:

> *[A]n electronic record of health-related information on an individual that is created, gathered, managed, and consulted by authorized health care clinicians and staff.*[4]
>
> *The term "qualified electronic health record" means an electronic record of health-related information on an individual that—:*
>
> *(A) includes patient demographic and clinical health information, such as medical history and problem lists; and*
>
> *(B) has the capacity—*
>
> *(i) to provide clinical decision support;*
>
> *(ii) to support physician order entry;*
>
> *(iii) to capture and query information relevant to health care quality; and*
>
> *(iv) to exchange electronic health information with, and integrate such information from other sources.*[5]

What exactly is meant by the term *capacity* in this definition is not certain. Further regulations interpreting this provision may address this question. For learning purposes, this chapter addresses the patient record in an electronic form as an electronic health record or EHR.

Many views have developed over time to describe the functionality of an EHR. These views range from how much data to include (e.g., all patient data vs. limited patient data); whether to offer decision support capabilities (e.g., clinical-guideline-driven prompts); whether the EHR should be enterprise specific or community specific; and whether the EHR should differ based on practice settings (e.g., hospital, ambulatory care, or nursing home). Only recently has the Institute of Medicine identified the core functionalities that constitute an electronic health record.[6] These functionalities are listed in Table 13.1.

Any health information professional evaluating and selecting an EHR must closely examine the requirements and limits that licensing authorities and accrediting bodies place on an electronic health record. This section examines those requirements and limits in the context of the creation, storage, and authentication of electronic health information.

Creation and storage of patient-specific information in an electronic medium is an accepted activity authorized by federal law, state law, and appropriate licensing authorities. The variation among states arises from whether a statute or administrative regulation authorizes this activity and whether certain media is specified for storage purposes. Accordingly, the health information professional must know and understand the respective state's definition of the phrase "electronic health record" and the relationship of ARRA provisions to the phrase.

Authentication

As discussed in Chapter 8, Patient Record Requirements, all entries recorded in the patient record must be authored and authenticated. **Authorship** identifies the health care provider who

Table 13.1 Functionalities of an Electronic Health Record

Health Information and Data	Found in the defined data set to include medical and nursing diagnoses, medication lists, allergies, demographics, clinical narratives, and laboratory results
Results Management	Results of all types available in electronic form reduces the lag time between when results are created and when they are available to the clinician
Electronic Communications and Connectivity	Electronic communication facilitates dialogue between health care providers and with patients, including the delivery of education to the patient in a home setting
Decision Support Management	Features such as preventive service reminders, alerts concerning possible drug interactions, and clinical-guideline-driven prompts
Order Entry and Management	E-prescribing allows for checks of proper dosage amounts and drug–allergy and drug–drug interactions, thereby reducing medication errors
Patient Support	Immediate access to real-time information available to multiple caregivers at multiple locations simultaneously improves coordination and continuity of patient care
Reporting and Population Health Management	Data necessary to meet the reporting requirements of public health agencies, accrediting organizations, and quality/safety oversight boards
Administrative Processes	Activities such as scheduling of hospital admissions and procedures and the validation of insurance eligibility via electronic means

has made an entry in the record, in writing, by dictation, by keyboard, or by keyless data entry. **Authentication** confirms the entry, by written signature, initials, or computer-generated signature code. This confirmation implies that the entry as recorded is accurate. Such entries in the record must have been made contemporaneously with the occurrence of the event. Because of the nature of an EHR, the timeliness of the entry can be established automatically, as can the timeliness of any corrections or updates. Moreover, the EHR can establish the identity of the person making or correcting an entry, assuming that computer passwords are not shared and biometric identification techniques are used. Corrections to entries made in the EHR are addressed in detail in Chapter 8, Patient Record Requirements.

EHR	The technology present in an EHR aids in authorship and authentication of entries in the record.

For an electronic health record, such authentication is represented by an electronic signature, sometimes referred to as a computer-generated signature code. Any statute or regulation that expressly authorizes the use of an electronic health record would permit authentication by electronic signature. Conversely, a state's statute or regulation requiring a physician's signature to authenticate a health record, without expressly authorizing use of a computer key or code as an electronic signature, leaves the question open to speculation. Where the statute or regulation is not clear, the licensing authority's interpretation of the statute or regulation will serve as the guide to proper authentication.

Electronic signatures are also addressed by the Electronic Signatures in Global and National Commerce Act of 2001 (E-SIGN).[7] This act applies to the use of electronic signatures in international and national commerce. It states that electronic signatures may not serve as a legal bar to contracts or other records involved in interstate and foreign commerce. This act would support authentication of entries made in the record by computer key.

Accrediting bodies, by contrast, expressly recognize authentication by computer methods. The Medicare Conditions of Participation, the Joint Commission, and Det Norske Veritas (DNV) Healthcare permit authentication of entries made in the record by computer key.[8] It then rests with the health care organization to utilize a software program that establishes the electronic signature as unique to the author and to represent the authentication of that author in order to meet the accrediting standards.

Liability Issues

Any discussion of liability issues in the context of an electronic health record can be broken down into two subcategories: (1) liability issues for which the patient record serves as proof in a lawsuit involving the quality of patient care and (2) liability issues that arise from unauthorized access to, or careless handling of, patient information (see Figure 13.1). For liability issues involving the patient record as proof in a lawsuit, the focus rests on whether the EHR may properly be admitted as evidence. For liability issues involving access or handling of patient information, the focus rests on the legal requirement to keep the EHR safe and secure. The following discussion addresses each of these focuses and offers practical advice to the health information manager who may face these issues in practice.

Admissible Evidence

As discussed in Chapter 8, Patient Record Requirements, and Chapter 3, Judicial Process of Health Information, health records serve as the backbone of virtually every professional liability action.

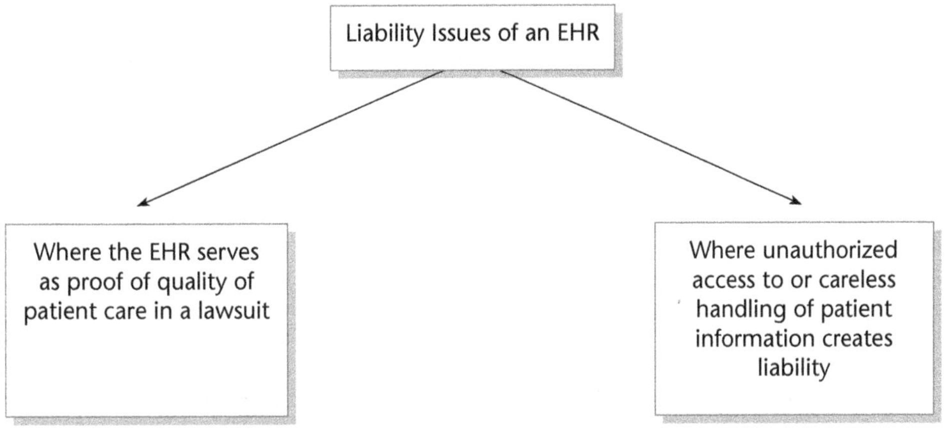

Figure 13.1 Categories of Liability Issues of an EHR

They are used to reconstruct an episode of patient care and establish whether the applicable standard of care was met. Other civil actions require the admissibility of health records, including credentialing and disciplinary proceedings of physicians and other health professionals. Additionally, health records may be used in criminal matters to establish the cause of the victim's death or an insanity defense.

In each lawsuit in which the health record will be used to prove or disprove a fact, the issue of admissibility of the health record will be present. **Admissibility** concerns pertinent and proper evidence that may be considered by the judge and/or jury when deciding the issues in a lawsuit. As a general matter, health records are not admitted into evidence unless they overcome the hearsay rule. This rule prohibits the introduction into evidence of out-of-court statements that are offered to prove the truth of the matter asserted. This introduction into evidence is accomplished through the use of the business record exception to the hearsay rule or through a subset to that exception specifically governing health records.[9] For more general information concerning the hearsay rule and the business record exception, see Chapter 3, Judicial Process of Health Information.

Under the **business record exception**, the party seeking to admit the health record must first meet the foundation requirements of the exception. A foundation is made by establishing that the record was (1) made and kept in the ordinary course of business, (2) at or near the time the event was recorded, and (3) by a person with knowledge of the acts, events, conditions, opinions, and diagnoses appearing in it.[10] After meeting these requirements, the party seeking to introduce the record must demonstrate the accuracy and trustworthiness of it. The party accomplishes these tasks by presenting the custodian of records as a witness to explain record-keeping procedures.

Just as with traditional paper-based records, health information professionals must be able to testify as to both the foundation and trustworthiness and accuracy requirements of the business record exception. In addition to the knowledge that the health information professional possesses as to the paper-based system, the health information professional must possess knowledge of those aspects unique to an electronic system. First, the health information professional should be familiar with the manner in which the data are recorded—for example, who makes the entry, whether the entry is made by someone using a computer key or biometric identification,[11] what data entry procedures are routine, and so forth. This knowledge will be useful in meeting the foundation requirement. Second, the health information professional should be familiar with both the hardware and software used in the system, the quality control measures used to ensure the reliability and validity of the data, and the policies and rules governing access to the system and how to make corrections to the record. This knowledge will apply to meeting the accuracy and trustworthiness requirements.

Finally, the health information professional must possess knowledge of the end product that the party is trying to admit into evidence. Instead of admitting into evidence the paper record used by the health care professional to record patient data, the party is admitting into evidence a computer printout of the data that the health care professional recorded directly into the computer. This computer printout may serve either as the original record of care or its equivalent, depending on what that jurisdiction's statutes, rules, and regulations allow.[12] The health information professional should be familiar with the equipment used to produce the printout, the reliability of the software used to process the data, and the actual creation of the printout.

The use of a computer printout of an electronic health record as evidence of patient care in court has been widely accepted. Federal courts have allowed the computer printout into evidence in instances where the foundation and trustworthiness and accuracy requirements have been met. One example is *United States v. Sanders.*[13] In *Sanders*, the government prosecuted a pharmacist for Medicaid fraud, relying in large measure on computer printouts kept by the state agency involved in administering Medicaid funds. The printout showed the number and type of reimbursement claims made by the pharmacist and paid by the state. The court admitted the printouts into evidence pursuant to Federal Rule of Evidence 803(6) after the custodian of records' testimony established the foundation and trustworthiness and accuracy requirements.

Security Issues

Within an electronic context, **security** refers to the means to regulate access to and ensure preservation of data. Within the health information context, security is implicated through a disruption of the health care facility's computer system, an interruption or discontinuation of a telemedicine session, unauthorized access to patient health records, or the destruction of patient information, among other examples. Such unauthorized access, destruction, or modification leads to privacy violations, particularly a breach of confidentiality. The security of computer systems is only as good as the measures taken to safeguard the system. Some measures often taken in the context of computer systems are listed in Table 13.2.

Table 13.2 Information Technology Security Measures	
Authentication	The process of ensuring that people are who they say they are
Permission	The level of access to an operating system or application given to a person or group of persons
Encryption	The mechanism to prevent third parties from eavesdropping on a communication
Damage Prevention	Preventing malicious attempts to damage data or bring down a computer
Disaster Recovery	The plans used to resume immediate computer operations in the event of a problem

Just as in a paper-based record system, the security of the patient record in an electronic system is of immense importance. Health care providers are charged under the Medicare Conditions of Participation, the standards of the Joint Commission and DNV Healthcare, and most state licensing laws with the responsibility to safeguard patient information.[14] Health care providers are also charged under the Health Insurance Portability and Accountability Act and the American Recovery and Reinvestment Act of 2009 with following security and privacy regulations issued by the Department of Health and Human Services.[15] The codes of ethics of virtually all health care professions address the requirements to safeguard patient information. The breach of any of these responsibilities may result in legal liability: claims of breach of confidentiality, invasion of privacy, defamation, or negligence may result from unauthorized access to or careless handling of patient information, or a health care provider may be sanctioned by her professional association for not adhering to the code of ethics.

ARRA/HIPAA/ETHICS

The security of health information is governed by federal statutes and regulations such as the American Recovery and Reinvestment Act, the Health Insurance Portability and Accountability Act, and the ethical codes of professional associations.

Safeguarding access to the health record is essential to maintaining the record's integrity and the confidentiality of the data contained in it. Electronic health records pose many of the same security issues as paper-based patient records. Who has access to the record? How does that person use the data contained in the record? With a paper-based record, patient information is contained in a single physical file folder and access to this folder can be monitored and controlled. No matter how stringent security arrangements are, however, it is not always possible to know who has had access to a paper-based health record. The same concerns are present in an electronic system. The tracking capabilities available with computers offer the advantage of knowing who has had access to the patient record and when. Nonetheless, the presence of computer terminals throughout a health care facility, combined with participation in computer networks, raises the possibility of larger numbers of individuals gaining unauthorized access to confidential patient information.

Whether the health care provider chooses a traditional paper-based patient record, an electronic health record, or a hybrid record, the same legal requirements apply: the record must be kept secure and guarded from unauthorized access. Special security issues are present with an electronic health record, however, and these security issues may be subdivided into the following categories: physical security, personnel security, and risk prevention techniques.[16] The interrelationship of these categories is illustrated in Figure 13.2.

CRITICAL THINKING

A tenet of autonomy is that the patient decides with whom they will share and will not share their personal health information. What happens to the patient's autonomy when the patient's health data are shared or linked without the patient's knowledge?

Physical Security As the health information manager may imagine, **physical security** concerns the physical protection of the nuts and bolts of the computer system and the health record. Physical security is best illustrated by a series of questions. What protections from the physical environment

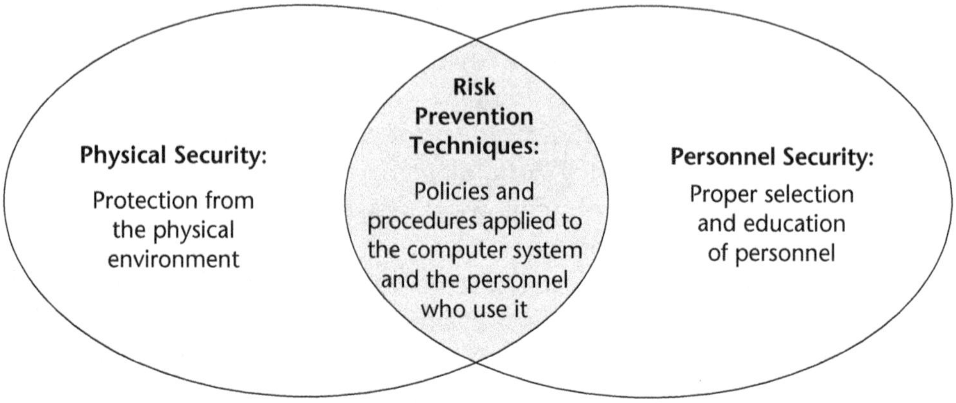

Figure 13.2 Interrelationship of Categories of Security Issues

are in place? Do the protections include temperature and humidity controls, power surge and failure protection devices, and the like? Are fire alarms installed and magnetic media used for storage secured in a fireproof location? Are there rules limiting access to computer terminals and storage areas? Are terminals bolted to desks and disks stored in locked cabinets to prevent theft? Are maintenance requirements documented and maintenance logs maintained? These questions must be addressed to ensure physical security of the electronic health record.

Personnel Security **Personnel security** focuses on the human aspect of security. In addition to the normal reference checks associated with hiring of personnel, the health care provider may wish to consider the following for personnel hired to work with the EHR: screening for past criminal history, work-related security problems, or a high school or college record of computer hacking. Once hired, the health care provider should educate the employee about the provider's confidentiality policy and the employee's responsibility to keep data confidential. Further education should address how to access the computer system properly, the limits on access to information, and the consequences for violating the provider's policy. Furthermore, health care providers should document this education of employees. For example, the health care provider may require employees to sign a statement acknowledging that they understand and will abide by the provider's confidentiality policy and procedures. This statement should also address the consequences for violating the provider's confidentiality policy. The employer should maintain a record of employees' attendance at inservice sessions and the viewing of online tutorials that are specifically designed to address the security, privacy, and confidentiality of health data.

Risk Prevention Techniques Risk prevention techniques merge physical and personnel security concepts. **Risk prevention techniques** serve to protect the integrity and confidentiality of the data at issue. In practice, these techniques translate into policies and procedures to be applied to the computer system and the personnel who use it. The following discussion of risk prevention techniques, although not exhaustive, should serve health information professionals evaluating an electronic health record system. These risk prevention techniques are listed in Table 13.3.

One basic risk prevention technique involves determining who has access to what information for what purpose at which times. Different levels of access apply to different personnel and should be maintained by the system administrator. The highest level of health information manager in an organization should participate in assigning levels of access to various groups of personnel. Some need read-only access, whereas others will need to also copy and/or edit data. Editing capabilities

Table 13.3 Risk Prevention Techniques of an EHR

1. Restrict access.
2. Determine who has access, and for what purpose.
3. Use computer passwords, key cards, or biometric ID.
4. Restrict copying functions.
5. Place security mechanisms in contracts with outside computer service bureaus.
6. Establish confidentiality agreements among network participants.
7. Address the potential for computer sabotage.
8. Safeguard the use of laptop computers and personal digital assistants.

can range from adding data to the system to deleting data. Editing capabilities in an electronic health record are similar to corrections being made to a paper-based health record. Any policy that involves editing capabilities must address (1) how corrections to the record are made so that it is possible to compare the original data to the corrected data; (2) who is authorized to make corrections; and (3) what restrictions exist on editing another person's entry. The health care provider should then create an audit trail to determine if the policy is being followed.

Another risk prevention technique involves the use of unique computer passwords, key cards, or biometric identification. Because computer passwords are widely used to access health information, this section focuses on them. The health care provider should control issuing these passwords. Requiring the use of longer rather than shorter passwords or combinations of alpha and numeric characters are simple security efforts that can be used. The health care provider should require employees not to disclose or share their password with others and should strictly enforce this requirement. Further, employees should be required to log off the system immediately after finishing a session so that no other person can access data using another's password. Failure to log off the system after use leaves confidential information unprotected. And when an employee ends employment with the health care provider, the provider should expeditiously cancel that employee's access to the systems housing electronic health records.

Risk prevention techniques must also address the risk associated with one of the best benefits of an electronic health record system: storage savings. As noted earlier in this chapter, electronic health record systems permit the storage of a tremendous amount of patient data. The converse to this benefit is the risk that data stored electronically may also be copied electronically, and the more data stored electronically, the more data that can be copied electronically without proper authority to do so. To decrease risk, the health care provider should consider restricting the copying function to no more than one patient record at a time and should run periodic security checks to determine who is copying what data, how often, and for what purpose.

> **HIPAA/ARRA**
>
> Both the Health Insurance Portability and Accountability Act and the American Recovery and Reinvestment Act address the obligation of a third party to safeguard protected health information.

One additional risk posed by computer storage involves the use of an outside computer service bureau to store patient data. Laws, regulations, and standards governing health information not only address the health care provider's obligation to safeguard confidential patient data but also address the obligations of a third party, such as a computer service bureau, to safeguard these data. Because the business associate rule is incorporated into the Privacy Rule issued pursuant to the Health Insurance Portability and Accountability Act (HIPAA) and the provisions of the American Recovery and Reinvestment Act of 2009, computer service bureaus are required to safeguard these data.[17] To minimize the risk of unauthorized access to or mishandling of confidential patient information by a computer service bureau, a health care provider should include the HIPAA provisions in the service contract. Such provisions cover the confidential nature of the data, the use to which the data will be put, the security mechanisms to be used to safeguard these data, and indemnification in the event data are improperly disclosed by the service bureau. Additional information about the HIPAA provisions governing business associates can be found in Chapter 10, Access to Health Information.

One often overlooked risk prevention technique involves the safeguarding of electronic protected health information (ePHI) accessed, stored, and/or transmitted (1) using portable media and devices, such as flash or jump drives, and (2) through offsite means such as laptop computers, tablet PCs, mobile devices, and home computers or noncorporate equipment. As portable media/devices and offsite access become more common in the health care environment, they are being used to facilitate the collection of more complete and accurate information from the patient. Because of the nature of portable media/devices, the use of wireless technology, and increased offsite access to ePHI, the risks for breach of patient confidentiality are increased for these means and devices as compared to networked desktop computers.

To minimize these risks, the health care provider should establish or improve control over portable media/devices and offsite access, provide employees with theft awareness instructions, and invest in certain computer accessories designed to make theft less profitable. The health care provider should consider improved controls, including the establishment of written policies and procedures covering the loan and use of portable media/devices and whether ePHI should even be maintained on these media/devices at all. If this information is to be maintained on portable media/devices, the health care provider should institute standard practices for backing up the information on a secure computer network or disk stored separately from these portable media/devices. In addition, the health care provider should instruct employees to avoid leaving a portable media/device unattended for any length of time and to carry the media/device in something other than a readily identifiable computer carrying case. Furthermore, the health care provider may wish to add an antitheft plaque or engraving on the portable media/device to identify the health care provider as owner. Many antitheft plaques contain a metallic bar code and registration number that, when removed, show the imprint of the words *stolen property*. Removal of these plaques may damage the computer casing, resulting in a lower retail value for the portable media/device by the thief. The Centers for Medicare and Medicaid Services (CMS) has issued guidance to covered entities to address risks associated with portable media/devices and offsite access to ePHI. Those risks are addressed in Table 13.4.

Risk prevention techniques should also address communications that are external to the provider. If health care providers agree to network their computer systems with those of other providers, they risk the confidentiality of patient data because more users have access to those patient data. This risk can be minimized by establishing confidentiality agreements among the network participants. If the network involves public channels of communication such as wireless technology, telephone lines, radio waves, and microwaves, the health care provider may consider encrypting patient data communicated over these public channels.

Furthermore, risk prevention techniques should address computer sabotage. Computer sabotage often arises as the act of a disgruntled employee or an outside user, such as those who participate with the health care provider in a computer network. A common form of computer sabotage is the

Table 13.4 Risks Associated with Accessing, Storing, and Transmitting ePHI		
Activity	**Risk**	**Strategies**
Accessing ePHI	Log-on/Password information lost or stolen	• Implement two-factor authentication for granting remote access to systems contain ePHI • Implement technical process for creating unique user names and performing authentication
	Employees access ePHI offsite when not authorized to do so	• Develop and employ proper clearance procedures and verify training of workforce prior to granting remote access • Establish remote access roles specific to applications and business requirements • Address unauthorized access of ePHI in required sanction policy
	Home or offsite workstations left unattended	• Establish appropriate procedures for session termination (time-out) on inactive portable or remote devices
	Contamination of systems by a virus introduced from an infected external device used to gain remote access to ePHI	• Install personal firewall software on all laptops that store or access ePHI or connect to networks containing ePHI • Install, use, and regularly update virus-protection software on all portable and remote devices
Storing ePHI	Portable media/device is lost or stolen	• Identify types of hardware and electronic media that must be tracked and develop inventory control system • Implement process for maintaining records of movements of, and persons responsible for, or permitted to use hardware and electronic media containing ePHI • Require use of lock-down or other locking mechanisms for unattended laptops • Password protect files • Password protect all portable or remote devices • Require all portable or remote device to employ encryption technologies of appropriate strength • Deploy security updates to portable devices • Consider use of biometrics on portable devices

Continued

Table 13.4 *(Continued)*

Activity	Risk	Strategies
Storing ePHI *(Continued)*	Use of external device to access corporate data resulting in loss of operationally critical ePHI on the remote device	• Develop processes to ensure backup of all ePHI entered into remote systems • Encrypt backup and archival media at appropriate strength
	Loss or theft of ePHI left on devices after inappropriate disposal by the organization	• Establish ePHI deletion policies and media disposal procedures
	Data left on an external device accidentally or intentionally	• Prohibit or prevent download of ePHI onto remote systems or devices without operational justification • Train workforce on policies requiring deletion of files intentionally or unintentionally saved to an external device • Minimize use of browser-cached data in Web-based application which manage ePHI
	Contamination of systems by virus from a portable storage device	• Install virus-protection software on all portable or remote devices that store ePHI
Transmitting ePHI	Data intercepted or modified during transmission	• Prohibit transmission of ePHI via open networks where appropriate • Prohibit use of offsite devices or wireless access points for nonsecure access to e-mail • Use more secure connections for e-mail via SSL and the use of message-level standards • Implement and mandate strong encryption solutions for transmission of ePHI
	Contamination of systems by a virus introduced from an external device used to transmit ePHI	• Install virus-protection software on portable devices that are used to transmit ePHI

Source: HIPAA Security Guidance for Remote Use of and Access to Electronic Protected Health Information. Available at https://www.hhs.gov/sites/default/files/ocr/privacy/hipaa/administrative/securityrule/remoteuse.pdf?language=es.

introduction of a computer virus into a computer system. Such viruses may destroy or alter data or cause a computer system to slow or crash. Health care providers should recognize the potential for computer sabotage when considering whether to participate in a computer network and should consider the use of antivirus software and firewalls to combat this problem. Further, health care providers can discourage the possibility of hackers' scanning for passwords by limiting the number of access attempts. For example, the user can be allowed three log-on attempts. Attempts to log on that exceed the maximum number of permitted log-ons can result in long delays that discourage hackers.

As this discussion indicates, the security issues involved with an electronic health record are complex and multifaceted. This section has focused on identifying the risks that automation poses to confidential patient data and the safeguards that can be crafted to minimize these risks. By addressing these issues, the health information manager lessens the possibility of legal liability for unauthorized access to or careless handling of patient information.

HIPAA SECURITY RULE

Layered above all of these levels of security are the security control provisions found in HIPAA's Security Rule. This rule establishes security safeguards that (1) protect the confidentiality of data so that only those persons authorized may see the data; (2) ensure data integrity by protecting it from unauthorized creation, modification, or deletion; and (3) allow data to be available when needed. Table 13.5 compares these three categories.

> The Security Rule establishes security safeguards for protected health information that a covered entity creates, receives, maintains, or transmits in an electronic format.
>
> HIPAA

Seventeen different security standards exist. These standards specify the use of integrity controls and encryption technology when transmitting electronic protected health information; information access management techniques such as authorization, establishment, and modification of access privileges (permission levels); workforce security standards such as clearance checks of personnel and termination procedures; and access controls such as automatic log-off and emergency access procedures.

These security standards in turn create thirty-five implementation specifications, which fall within two categories: required and addressable. Required specifications mean that a covered entity must implement the standard, allowing no flexibility for the covered entity to determine what is reasonable in the implementation process. Addressable specifications mean that the covered entity is not bound to implement the specification as identified by the Department of Health and Human Services (DHHS) but has some flexibility to determine reasonableness in implementation. This additional flexibility does not mean that the covered entity can ignore the specification if it decides it is unreasonable. Rather, the addressability component is designed such that a covered entity that finds a specification unreasonable must document that unreasonableness and identify what other steps it has taken to protect personally identifiable health information that it considers reasonable.

Table 13.5 HIPAA Security Safeguards

	Administrative Safeguards	Physical Safeguards	Technical Safeguards
Number of Standards	Eight	Four	Five
Specifications	Nine required and eleven addressable implementation specifications	Two required and six addressable implementation specifications	Two required and five addressable implementation specifications
Regulatory Provision	Section 164.308	Section 164.310	Section 164.312

The essence of **administrative safeguards** under HIPAA is to help covered entities take actions and create policies and procedures to manage the development, implementation, and maintenance of security measures to protect personally identifiable health information. These actions, policies, and procedures should be designed to assist the covered entity in preventing, detecting, containing, and correcting security violations. Each covered entity is required to perform a **risk assessment** of its security practices, which should identify the way protected health information in an electronic format is accessed and any potential vulnerabilities of that information. Examples of activities a covered entity may engage in to comply with the administrative safeguards include monitoring computer access activity by end users (e.g., log-in access attempts), protecting PHI from viruses and software attacks, changing passwords on a periodic basis, and creating contingency plans for continuing operations in the event of a disaster, emergency situation, or loss of data. The essence of **physical safeguards** under HIPAA is to help covered entities protect their electronic information systems and related building and equipment from unauthorized intrusions and natural and environmental hazards. This focus on systems, facilities, and equipment addresses security from a macro level and differs from administrative safeguards, which addresses security from a micro level. For example, the physical safeguards would restrict an individual's access to facilities housing electronic information systems, whereas the administrative safeguards would restrict an individual's access to the data residing in a database. Examples of activities a covered entity may engage in to comply with the physical safeguards include establishing access levels to physical space based on a person's role or function; ensuring that workstations are properly secure (including portable devices); establishing disposal policies and procedures for disks, tapes, storage devices, and other equipment; and establishing regular backup routines.

The essence of **technical safeguards** under HIPAA is to help covered entities employ technological solutions to secure ePHI. This focus on technology should assist the covered entity in limiting unauthorized access and ensuring data integrity. Examples of activities a covered entity may engage in to comply with the technical safeguards include employing encryption technology with its electronic mail (e-mail) system, examining activity occurring on its computer networks, assigning unique identifiers to end users as a way to identify and track their use of electronic information systems, and employing account validation or password identification schemes to authenticate a user's identity. Encryption that is employed to protect ePHI should be of a sufficient strength algorithm so that ePHI is unusable, unreadable, or indecipherable to unauthorized persons.

In addition, the Security Rule addresses training requirements for staff concerning the vulnerability of protected health information in a covered entity's possession and the procedures to be followed to protect such information. While the rule itself does not specify what training should be provided to which employee, a training program on computer security basics is necessary for all staff, including managers, agents, contractors, and maintenance personnel. This training could address such topics as virus protection, password management, physical/workstation security, mechanisms to report known or suspected breaches, monitoring procedures, and sanctions, both at the individual and organizational levels. Once training has been delivered, the covered entity must document that it was provided as well as document how it will periodically review, validate, and update the training program.

Woven throughout, the Security Rule is the requirement that a covered entity establish effective information security policies. **Information security policies** are those policies that define the framework around which an information security program is managed.[18] These policies answer the "who, what, where, when, why, and how" questions of information security. Information security policies may have common elements, such as specification of roles and responsibilities, standards to which employees must adhere, and the level of compliance that is expected with those standards. These policies may be applied at different levels, such as organization, system specific, or issue specific.

> **HIPAA**
> While proceeding from different angles, both the Privacy and Security Rules serve to protect data from unauthorized uses and disclosures.

The relationship between the HIPAA Security and Privacy Rules is symbiotic in their protection of personally identifiable health information. Both rules employ similar terminology, the parallel treatment of business associates, and three major safeguards. The HIPAA Privacy Rule serves to protect health information by providing patients with more control over their own health information through safeguards and limitations imposed upon covered entities. These safeguards and limitations specify the actions covered entities may engage in or are prohibited from engaging in while protecting the information, particularly with regard to the use and release of information. The HIPAA Security Rule serves to protect this same information by specifying the technical requirements, policies, and procedures that covered entities can use to protect data from known threats and vulnerabilities. Although both rules proceed from different angles, they both serve the ultimate goal of protecting data from unauthorized uses and disclosures.

The Security Rule also mirrors the Privacy Rule in the way that it assigns responsibility for compliance with HIPAA's mandated security directives to an individual within the covered entity. This Security Officer is tasked with the responsibility of developing and implementing information security policies, procedures, and technology systems required under the rule to maintain the confidentiality, integrity, and availability of both protected health information and the organization's health care information systems. The Security Officer accomplishes this through a variety of actions, many of which are listed in Table 13.6.

Breaches

The HITECH-HIPAA Omnibus Final Rule modifies HIPAA to address concerns of covered entities on how they should handle breaches of protected health information in the event these breaches occur. The Omnibus Final Rule clarifies the definition of a breach of protected health information and the risk assessment approach a covered entity must follow after discovering a breach has occurred. Under the Omnibus Final Rule, a **breach** is defined as "the acquisition, access, use, or disclosure of protected health information in a manner ... which compromises the security or privacy of protected health information."[19] This definition applies to all breaches, whether occurring with a covered entity or a business associate. More information about the manner in which the Rule applies to business associates can be found in Chapter 10, Access to Health Information.

Table 13.6 HIPAA Security Officer Actions
Design, implement, manage, and enforce HIPAA security directives
Address organization's needs for access controls, disaster recovery, business continuity, and information risk management
Perform risk assessments and audits
Lead incident response team to security breach
Lead awareness and training efforts for workforce
Improve IT security within the organization and with vendors, consultants, and other third parties

In the event a covered entity learns of a breach or repeated breaches, the Rule requires the provider to engage in a risk assessment of the situation(s). The risk assessment focuses on the probability of whether protected health information has been compromised. Four factors are considered in this assessment and are listed in Table 13.7. Where the probability that PHI has been compromised through the risk assessment is low, a notification of the breach will not be necessary. Where the probability is higher than low, notification of the breach is required under the Rule.[20]

The Omnibus Final Rule provides specifics concerning when and how notification should take place. The provider should notify those patients affected by the breach of security within sixty days of the date of the breach, using the content of Table 13.8 in the notice, unless a low probability exists that PHI has been compromised. The notice must be written in plain language, be written at an appropriate reading level, and should be easily read by the individual recipient. Notification may be delayed if the notification would impede a criminal investigation or damage national security. If law enforcement notifies the covered entity in writing of this possibility, the covered entity must comply for the time period specified by law enforcement. Where the breach affects more than 500 residents of a state or jurisdiction, notice must also be sent to prominent media outlets and the Secretary of Health & Human Services.[21]

Table 13.7 Breach Risk Assessment Factors
The nature and extent of the protected health information (PHI) involved, including the types of identifiers and the likelihood of re-identification.
The unauthorized person who used the PHI or to whom the disclosure was made. Whether the PHI was actually acquired or viewed.
The extent to which the risk to PHI has been mitigated.

Source: 45 C.F.R. §164.402 (2019).

Table 13.8 Content of Notice of Breach of Confidentiality

CONTENT OF NOTIFICATION—Regardless of the method by which notice is provided to individuals under this section, notice of a breach shall include, to the extent possible, the following:

- A brief description of what happened, including the date of the breach and the date of the discovery of the breach, if known.
- A description of the types of unsecured protected health information that were involved in the breach (such as full name, Social Security number, date of birth, home address, account number, or disability code).
- The steps individuals should take to protect themselves from potential harm resulting from the breach.
- A brief description of what the covered entity involved is doing to investigate the breach, to mitigate losses, and to protect against any further breaches.
- Contact procedures for individuals to ask questions or learn additional information, which shall include a toll-free telephone number, e-mail address, Web site, or postal address.

Source: 42 U.S.C. § 17932(f) (2019); 45 C.F.R. §164.404(c) (2019).

In addition to notifying individual patients, the media, and the Secretary, covered entities possess an obligation to document their breach investigation and notification activities. The burden of proof of doing so rests on the covered entity who must be able to demonstrate that all notifications were made or that an impermissible use or disclosure did not constitute a breach, meaning no notification was required.[22]

ELECTRONIC HEALTH ISSUES

Electronic tools such as the Internet, electronic mail, text messaging, digital imaging, and telemedicine are now indispensable tools for conducting business in the health care field. While these tools open up a myriad of opportunities, they also raise legal concerns relating to privacy and security of patient-specific health information.

Internet

The use of the **Internet** in the health care field can be viewed from more than one perspective. The health care provider may visit sites on the World Wide Web to obtain information to deliver better patient care by reviewing the latest health care news, accessing libraries of medical data and clinical alerts, scheduling continuing education, and researching poison center databases and the results of clinical studies. At the same time, patients may visit Web sites to seek answers to their health care needs by researching their conditions, registering for clinical trials, learning about their prescriptions, scheduling participation in screening programs, and purchasing durable medical equipment.

In addition, some organizations actively engage in electronic health practice, known as e-health, to exchange health information between the patient and the health care provider. These entities are known as **e-health organizations**, defined as organizations that collect and display individually identifiable health information over the Internet.[23] Patients who participate in e-health are known as e-health consumers, defined as individuals whose individually identifiable health information is collected, maintained, or displayed over the Internet.[24]

Certain security issues are associated with use of the Internet for e-health. Patient-specific health information may be obtained or used inappropriately by unauthorized persons or organizations. This information may be copied or altered without detection, resulting in financial or health-related harm to the consumer. Or the patient-specific health information may be incorrect, incomplete, or merely out of date.

Health care providers who engage in e-health practice should remain aware that the same requirements for safeguarding the confidentiality of patient-specific health information in a traditional setting also apply to an e-health practice. Although the method of delivering care is different, the application of statutes, rules, and regulations to the provision of care has not changed. For example, e-health organizations that treat Medicare patients are subject to the Medicare Conditions of Participation, just as they would be if they were treating the patient in a face-to-face setting.[25] Those that operate federally assisted alcohol and substance abuse programs are also subject to federal regulations governing the confidentiality of alcohol and substance abuse information.[26] And those that submit billing electronically to insurers for reimbursement are held to the privacy guidelines of the Health Insurance Portability and Accountability Act (HIPAA).[27] Finally, accrediting standards such as those issued by the Joint Commission and ethical tenets such as those issued by the American Health Information Management Association also apply to providers in an e-health setting.[28] Health information professionals involved in an e-health practice should assist in the design and monitoring of technology safeguards in order to ensure that the use of new information technologies is not at the expense of consumers' privacy.

Health care providers who render care beyond the reach of the United States must be aware of the data privacy and security provisions of other countries. For example, the European Union has promulgated the General Data Protection Regulation, providing data and privacy protections for individuals within the European Union.[29] The regulation addresses data protection principles, including technical and organizational safeguards to be used by individuals, organizations, and businesses that handle personal data. The regulation establishes rights for individuals involving who may access personal data, imposing restrictions on access to personal data, how inaccurate personal data may be corrected, and when personal data may be erased.

Electronic Mail and Text Messaging

Over the past two decades, **electronic mail** (e-mail) has become one of the most popular modes of communication in the United States. E-mail is a form of communication between parties or individuals using only electronic means, such as across the Internet or computer networks. As with private industry, the health care field has incorporated e-mail into its business methods. Health care organizations using e-mail that contains patient-specific health information should carefully consider security precautions as part of their business practice.

Although seemingly private when created, e-mail should never be considered a private form of communication. Once sent, e-mail may be collected, stored, and reviewed by people other than the intended recipient if that recipient forward the e-mail on to others. Further, many organizations maintain a policy of the right to review any e-mail sent or received by any member of the organization. And with the use of daily backups to networked computer systems, e-mail may be stored even after the recipient or sender has deleted the e-mail from her personal computer.

Similar to e-mail, the use of text messaging in the health care environment has exploded in the first part of the twenty-first century. **Text messaging** refers to short electronic messages sent over a cellular network from one cell phone to another or by fixed or portable devices over a telephone network. It is often used as a substitute for voice calls, either for convenience or because voice communication may be impossible or undesirable.

Both law and regulation attempt to address the pace of technology by specifically protecting online privacy. It is important to note that the laws and regulations that apply to patient-specific health information stored in a paper-based health record logically extend to the health information contained in an e-mail or text message. The Medicare Conditions of Participation, federal regulations issued pursuant to HIPAA and those governing alcohol and substance abuse, and the accrediting standards of the Joint Commission, formerly known as the Joint Commission on the Accreditation of Healthcare Organizations, all apply to patient-specific health information contained in an e-mail or text message. In particular, the Joint Commission (JC) has specifically addressed text messaging in two contexts: (1) communicating with patients, and (2) orders in a hospital or other health care setting. The JC states it is acceptable for a health care provider to text patient (except for patient care orders) as long as a secure text-messaging platform is used. The JC states it is not acceptable for physicians or other health care providers to text orders for patients, even if the method employed is a secured text-messaging platform. The JC concludes the method provides no ability to verify the identity of the person sending the text or a way to keep the original message as validation of what is entered into the medical record.[30] The Centers for Medicare and Medicaid Services allows for the use of text messaging between members of the health care team if accomplished through a secure platform but does not permit texting of orders, determining that the texting of orders violates the Conditions of Participation and Conditions of Coverage.[31] Further security regulations issued pursuant to HIPAA address the use of e-mail, as do

HIPAA's privacy regulations in the context of notifying the patient of the health care organization's information privacy practices.[32]

It is important to note who initiates and responds to e-mail and text messages when determining compliance with law and regulation. The patient may send health information to the provider via e-mail or text messaging that is not encrypted or otherwise protected. Doing so does not violate the HIPAA Security Rule because the HIPAA Security Rule does not apply to the patient but applies to the health care provider. Once the health care provider receives the patient's health information, the HIPAA Security Rule comes into play. It is the storage of this health information and responses to the patient's communication that will require application of the HIPAA Security Rule.[33]

In addition to legal requirements, prudent business practice dictates that health care organizations develop an action plan concerning the use of e-mail and text messaging as forms of clinical documentation. Of foremost concern is to address patient confidentiality and informed consent policies along with the instructions to patients on the proper structure, permissible content, and sensitivity needs of e-mail and text messaging as forms of clinical communication. Technical security measures should also be taken to ensure the safe use of e-mail and text messaging. For example, the use of encryption algorithms may protect the content of the e-mail or text message while in transit and prevent unauthorized users from reading the e-mail or text message.[34] Similarly, disclosure and redisclosure policies should define the circumstances under which e-mail and text messages should be forwarded and distributed to multiple recipients. Finally, organizations should establish processes to incorporate e-mail and text messages into the existing health record, whether paper based or electronic in format, so that the record is a true and correct reflection of the patient's care.[35] In creating this action plan, health care organizations may look to industry guidelines addressing each of these issues.[36]

Digital Imaging

One technology with the potential to save money for health care organizations is digital imaging. **Digital imaging** permits a paper document to be scanned on a device that works similarly to a photocopier. The image is saved to an optical disc, a compact disc (CD), or magnetic tape, and after electronic indexing can be viewed through a server or Web browser. The image is then available to multiple users who need access to the data contained in the image. Advantages of a digital imaging system are listed in Table 13.9.

Unlike e-health and e-mail, some states have enacted laws and regulations dealing directly with digital imaging.[37] These laws and regulations generally address digital imaging in the context of storage media for health information. Medical images most often exist in a Digital Imaging and Communications in Medicine (DICOM) format, which combines sets or series of images with a

Table 13.9 Advantages of a Digital Imaging System
1. Simultaneous access by multiple users to the same medical record
2. Easy accessibility compared to locating a paper-based medical record
3. Data integrity (the image cannot be altered)
4. Protection against disaster
5. Savings on storage space
6. Audit trail capabilities

description of the patient and the modality. Together they are considered protected health information (PHI). Under federal law, HIPAA-covered entities must implement procedures to protect and secure access to this type of data and address record retention issues.

Telemedicine

One area of technology that has expanded the means of medical practice is the use of telemedicine. **Telemedicine** is defined as:

> *the use of electronic communications and information technologies to provide or support clinical care at a distance.*[38]

Often used in remote areas where access to health care professionals may be limited, telemedicine serves to connect patients with a health care professional through the use of multimedia communications and information systems. This connection allows the health care professionals to diagnose, treat, and monitor patients. Examples of use include the transfer of diagnostic images such as CAT scans, MRIs, and x-rays to a specialist for a second opinion; the use of video visits for home-bound patients; and videoconferencing between a counselor and a patient located some distance apart.

Telemedicine technologies can include facsimile, audio capabilities including radio and telephone, still images, full-motion video, and color screens to facilitate face-to-face contact. Application packages can include image capture, blood pressure and pulse meters, analog-based audio stethoscopes, and digital dermascopes built into the video system. These technologies can be used as permanent features of the health care facility or could be located on a rollabout system.

Telemedicine offers the opportunity for tremendous benefits to both patients and health care professionals. A listing of such benefits is shown in Table 13.10.

Table 13.10 Benefits of Telemedicine

1. Improved access to health care, such as obtaining second opinions
2. Improved continuity of care, patient education, and timely treatment (including monitoring the condition of chronically ill patients; reduced travel time for physicians, other health care providers, and patients; and better access for patients in underserved areas)
3. Improved access to health records and information (including promoting self-help by increasing the online availability of health information, knowledge-based self-diagnosis programs, and distance learning programs, online discussion groups for peer support, and research data/information)
4. Improved continuing medical education
5. Improved delivery of health care by bringing a wider range of services such as radiology, mental health services, and dermatology to underserved communities and individuals in urban and rural areas
6. Increased recruitment and retention of health professionals in rural areas by providing ongoing training and collaboration with other health professionals
7. The potential for improved control of health care costs by helping to avoid unnecessary patient trips and allocation of resources to outlying areas

Source: Adapted from Telemedicine Report to Congress by the Joint Working Group on Telemedicine (1997); American Health Information Management Association, Practice Brief-Telemedicine Services and the Health Record (Updated) (2013); J. Welch, *The Technology of Medicine*, 70 AM. HEALTH INFOR. MGMT. ASS'N. Vol. 2 (1999).

One of the reasons the field of telemedicine has not advanced more rapidly is the unresolved question of which state's laws apply to such issues as privacy, licensing, and medical reimbursement. The following examples illustrate how complicated the questions concerning telemedicine have become:

- Is the patient receiving care in the state in which she resides or the state in which the health care professional is present?
- Has the physician created a physician–patient relationship through the use of telemedicine, thereby subjecting the physician to claims of medical malpractice?
- Does the physician's malpractice insurance provide coverage for services provided in another state or is a rider for out-of-state services required?
- Is the physician practicing medicine in the state in which the patient resides or where the physician is present, thereby raising licensing and reimbursement concerns?
- In the event of technical failures, is there liability for injuries caused by the disconnection of the signal between the patient and the physician?
- In the event health information is lost while being transported across state lines, has there been a wrongful disclosure of a health record? Complicating this situation, the law of which state would apply: the one from which the records were sent, the one to which the records were sent, the one in which the transmission became disconnected, or the one in which the company operating the transmission medium resides?

Settling these types of questions would lead to a determination of which state's law applies to any given situation, providing a more stable environment in which telemedicine could expand.

Very limited guidance concerning telemedicine is provided on the federal level. The Telecommunications Act of 1996 provides the general public with access to modern communication media, such as the Internet, but addresses telemedicine in only two sections.[39] While promoting telemedicine, the act does not address any standards by which telemedicine should be governed. The Comprehensive Telehealth Act of 1996 addresses Medicare reimbursement payments but little else.[40] The CHRONIC Care Act of 2018 expands provisions for reimbursement of telemedicine services through certain Medicare plans. [41]

CRITICAL THINKING

The same ethical issues present in traditional forms used to care for patients apply in the telemedicine context. Might patients be concerned whether their information will be held in confidence and secured appropriately if telemedicine is the means by which care is delivered? Why or why not?

Provisions of HIPAA that address privacy and security of health records apply in the telemedicine context just as they do in the traditional health care context. The patient data gathered as part of a telemedicine encounter should be incorporated into the patient's health record and be made available as part of the patient's longitudinal record over time. Providers must safeguard privacy and confidentiality of electronic protected health information (ePHI) and use precautions and care in storing images, electronic files, audio/video tapes. Providers can reduce risks by encrypting data and ensuring controls on the collection, use, and disclosure of ePHI.

It has therefore been up to the states to provide guidance through legislation and regulation. In most instances, states have defined telemedicine and allowed for its practice in the state, sometimes modifying licensure statutes to permit out-of-state physicians to treat patients within the state borders.[42] Some states have taken a more expansive approach to telemedicine regulation, imposing requirements for informed consent from the patient before treatment.[43] California has taken the lead in creating more comprehensive legislation governing consent requirements for consultation, physician licensure, unprofessional physician conduct, and payment for services.[44] In addition to these statutes, the American Health Information Management Association has developed recommended guidelines for health information practitioners to follow concerning the content of and security measures to be used in a telehealth record.[45] Although much work has been performed by state legislatures, much work remains to be done in order to answer the many questions discussed earlier.

FUTURE LEGAL AND ETHICAL TRENDS IN INFORMATION TECHNOLOGY

Much legal attention has focused on the electronic health record and on traditional means of caring for patients using technology. With the advent of new technologies that are separate from patient care, legal impacts may arise in the health care arena that have not yet been considered. Some of those issues are outlined here.

Data and Privacy

Of particular concern is the safeguarding of protected health information and privacy rights of patients when new technologies are employed to store and transmit data.

One example is the need to transfer patient health data seamlessly across health care systems and governmental entities. For example, health departments at the federal, state, and local levels work in collaboration to control the spread of infectious diseases. A key component of this collaboration is the sharing of data across and between these many entities. Legal issues associated with sharing of data arise in the context of privacy and security laws and regulations, making the use of cloud technology to store protected health information problematic.

Blockchain technology, a resource used in the financial arena, offers promise in the health care sphere. **Blockchain** is the technology that creates a digital database containing information that can be simultaneously used and shared within a large decentralized, publicly accessible network. The technology verifies each transaction and records it in a virtually incorruptible, encrypted ledger shared by all the computers in the network. Advantages to blockchain technology include the ability to access data without using an intermediary and the barriers it poses to those who try to hack the technology. The technology, particularly the use of encryption, presents the potential for complying with privacy and security laws and regulations when transmitting and storing protected health information. Employing blockchain in any particular situation involves consideration of proper controls, such as determining which computers should maintain the ledger, who should have permission to read or modify the data, and how identification of patients and health care organizations should be managed. These types of questions fall squarely within the realm of both compliance and information technology.

A second example involving data and patient privacy rights involves the use of nanobots in medicine. A **nanobot** is a microscopically small robot, about the size of a blood cell. Nanobots have been used in medicine with enough frequency that a new term has been coined, **nanomedicine**, to describe that domain of medicine that uses nanotechnology to prevent and treat severe diseases such as cancer and heart disease. Examples include using nanobots to travel through capillaries of the brain to communicate with biological neurons or as part of a drug targeting a specific cancer cell.

The question becomes how should data transmitted from the nanobot to the physician be protected and what levels of informed consent should be considered? The data being transmitted is identifiable to the patient and presumably falls within the definition of protected health information, making it subject to privacy and security laws. In terms of informed consent, the health care provider must ensure the patient knows and understands what exactly he is consenting to, including the means by which the data will be transmitted.

> **ETHICS**
> Both legal questions and ethical issues are present with CRISPR technology.

A third example involves genetic material. Numerous questions about privacy rights surround genetic material, including who may have access to the information the genetic material conveys. Similarly, **CRISPR** technology, a genetic engineering technique, allows for the snipping and editing of genes. This technology allows for the altering of the genome composition of whole organisms, with the potential that any alterations will be passed to future generations. The ability to take such expansive action raises not only legal questions but ethical issues. There are currently no laws regulating attempts to alter or edit human genomes and efforts to create ethical guidelines on the subject are in the formative stages. Materials discussing the handling of genetic information in health records is found in Chapter 11, Specialized Patient Records.

Digital Access

One ethical issue interwoven with the Internet and the availability of information in health care is the digital divide. The **digital divide** describes the gulf between those who have access to and those who do not have access to modern information and technology, such as smartphones, personal computers, and the Internet. Access to money and tools can impact individuals, communities, and countries. A similar divide exists in the health care context in the sense that some entities can afford to make investments in health IT while others cannot.

Investing in information technology in the health care setting can be a costly endeavor for a health care provider, setting up the possibility of disparity between the capabilities available to health care providers. There can be a significant financial hardship on small and/or rural physician practices and nonprofit organizations as they often do not have the means to absorb the costs of information technology purchases and reimbursement policies vary widely among insurers regarding the use of information technology.

The divide is also present on the patient side of the equation. Not all patients have ready and affordable access to the Internet, whether through personal computers or smartphones. The capabilities of personal computers and smartphones have increased through the development of health care–related applications. If the costs of these devices decrease steadily, the potential may arise to close this gap, allowing many more people access to health care through the Internet.

> **ETHICS**
> The presence of a digital divide in health care is an ethical dilemma capable of resolution.

Addressing the digital divide from an ethical perspective is aided by review of the ethical theories and concepts discussed in Chapter 5, Ethical Standards. Both the theories of utilitarianism, which promotes the concept of the common good, and deontology, which looks to universal values, could be used to support the idea of bridging the digital divide. Similarly, the concept of justice, involving treating all people fairly, would seem to support bridging the digital divide. Making health care information technology available to everyone, providers and patients alike, can enhance not only the delivery of patient care but the sharing of ideas and knowledge.

CONCLUSION

The transformation from a paper-based health record to an electronic health record has progressed across the nation. To aid this transformation, the health information professional must be able to identify the legal issues that an electronic health record presents that may affect accreditation, licensure, and liability. Knowledge of these legal requirements is essential to a proper evaluation, selection, and implementation of an information system that safeguards health information from unauthorized access or careless handling.

Health information professionals owe to their employers, patients, and the public at large an obligation to understand the legal issues present in information technology and to prevent improper use of confidential data maintained in an electronic health record. This chapter assists in providing a basis for the development of such understanding and the application of confidentiality standards for the electronic health record. This chapter also identifies emerging legal issues associated with information technology trends affecting the health care environment.

CASE STUDY

General Hospital has determined that within three years, the paper-based health record it currently uses will be replaced with an electronic health record. General Hospital prefers to have a vendor install a computer system that allows for some tailoring to its institutional needs. You are a member of a committee that will evaluate and select the computer system. What legal issues should you raise to the committee and hospital about possible barriers and problems to implementing an electronic health record? Assuming those barriers and problems are resolved, what legal issues should you address with the committee and hospital in the evaluation and selection process?

REVIEW QUESTIONS

1. What impact do licensing authorities and accrediting organizations have on a health care provider's decision to adopt an electronic health record system?
2. Define an electronic health record.
3. How is authentication represented in an electronic health record?
4. What is admissibility, and how does it apply to the electronic health record?

5. How is the health information manager affected by the foundation and trustworthiness requirements?
6. What legal theories would support a lawsuit arising from a breach of confidentiality of the electronic health record?
7. What protections from the physical environment should be in place to protect an electronic health record?
8. What steps should be taken to ensure personnel security in an electronic health record environment?
9. Name at least three risk prevention techniques used to evaluate an electronic health record system.
10. How does the business associate rule apply to the electronic health record?
11. What efforts should the health information professional take to safeguard portable computers and mobile devices?
12. Discuss the concept of computer sabotage and how the dangers it poses can be minimized.
13. Do federal regulations and accrediting standards apply to the use of e-mail and text messaging?
14. Would a physician be in compliance with Joint Commission accrediting standards to text orders for patients?
15. Name barriers faced in the effort to expand telemedicine.
16. What advantages are offered with the use of blockchain technology to transmit personally identifiable health information?
17. Name an ethical issue associated with nanobots.
18. Do laws currently exist regulating the altering and editing of human genomes through CRISPR technology?
19. Name ethical theories and concepts that could be used to bridge the digital divide.

ENRICHMENT ACTIVITY

Obtain several examples of policies governing the security of electronic health information from local health care facilities. For each policy, examine its strengths and weaknesses. For example, were the categories of physical security, personnel security, and risk prevention techniques addressed? Are there any flaws in the policies?

ENRICHMENT ACTIVITY

Review articles in health care journals concerning electronic health (e-health) information. Are the discussions comprehensive? Should additional analysis have been provided concerning legal issues associated with e-health?

NOTES

1. In 1996, Congress passed the Health Insurance Portability and Accountability Act (HIPAA), Pub. L. 104-191, addressing the electronic transmission of patient-specific health information. 42 U.S.C. § 1320d (2019). Subsequent regulations issued pursuant to HIPAA address both security and privacy of health information. In 2009, Congress passed the American Recovery and Reinvestment Act, which addressed the use of electronic health records. 42 U.S.C. §§ 201, 300jj, 17901-17954. (2019).

2. Institute of Medicine. (1991). *The Computer-Based Patient Record: An Essential Technology for Health Care.* Washington, DC: National Academies Press.

3. January 10, 2004. Wkly. Compilation Presidential Documents 94, 2004 WLNR 11425351.

4. 42 U.S.C.§ 17921 (5) (2019).

5. Id. § 300jj (13) (2019).

6. Institute of Medicine. (2003). *Key capabilities of an electronic health record system: Letter report.* Washington, DC: National Academies Press. Available at http://www.nap.edu.

7. §15 U.S.C. § 7001-7031 (2019).

8. 42 C.F.R. § 482.24(c) (2019); Joint Commission on Accreditation of Healthcare Organizations, Comprehensive Accreditation Manual for Hospitals, Management of Information, IM 6.10 (2004); DNV Healthcare's NIAHO Accreditation Requirements, Medical Record Services §26, MR 5 (2014).

9. Federal Business Records Act, 28 U.S.C. § 1732(a) (2014) (general business record exception); Fed. R. Evid. 803(6) (general business record exception); Ga. Code Ann. § 24-7-8 (Michie 2014) (subset of the general business record exception applicable to medical records).

10. Fed. R. Evid. 803(6).

11. Examples of biometric identification include voiceprint, thumbprint, and retinal scan.

12. For example, Indiana law requires its courts to treat printouts of electronically recorded hospital medical records as originals for purposes of admissibility into evidence. Ind. Code § 34-43-1-1 (Burns 2019).

13. 749 F.2d 195 (5th Cir. 1984).

14. *See, e.g.*, Medicare Conditions of Participation, 42 C.F.R. § 405.1722(a) (2019); Joint Commission, Accreditation Manual for Hospitals, Management of Information IM 6.10 (2004); DNV Healthcare's NIAHO Accreditation Requirements, Medical Record Services §26, MR 4 (2014).

15. 45 C.F.R. §§ 164.502-.528 (2019); 42 U.S.C. § 17931(a) (2019).

16. Jonathan P. Tomes, JD, *Compliance Guide to Electronic Health Records*, Chap. 10 (Faulkner & Gray 1994).

17. 45 C.F.R. § 164.506 (2019); 42 U.S.C. § 17931(a) (2019).

18. BEAVER, K., & HEROLD, R. *The practical guide to HIPAA privacy and security compliance.* (Boca Raton, FL: Auerbach 2004).

19. 45 C.F.R. §164.402 (2019).

20. 45 C.F.R. §164.402 (2019).

21. 45 C.F.R. §§ 164.404(b); .406, .408, & .412 (2019).

22. 45 C.F.R. §164.4.14 (2019).

23. AHIMA Releases E-Health Tenets, *Journal of AHIMA* 71, no. 10 (2000): 94–99. Available at http://www.ahima.org.

24. Ibid.

25. 42 C.F.R. §§ 483-484 (2019).

26. 42 C.F.R. Part 2 (2019).

27. 45 C.F.R. §§ 164.502-.528 (2019).

28. AHIMA Releases E-Health Tenets, *Journal of AHIMA* 71, no. 10 (2000): 94–99. Available at http://www.ahima.org.

29. European Commission of the European Union. (2018). Available at https://eur-lex.europa.eu/legal-content/EN/TXT/?qid=1528874672298&uri=CELEX%3A32016R0679.

30. Joint Commission on Accreditation of Healthcare Organizations, Comprehensive Accreditation Manual for Hospitals, Management of Information FAQs (2017). Available at https://www.jointcommission.org/mobile/standards_information/jcfaqdetails.aspx?StandardsFAQId=1615&StandardsFAQChapterId=79&ProgramId=5&ChapterId=0&IsFeatured=False&IsNew=False&Keyword=tex; and https://www.jointcommission.org/mobile/standards_information/jcfaqdetails.aspx?StandardsFAQId=1616&StandardsFAQChapterId=79&ProgramId=5&ChapterId=0&IsFeatured=False&IsNew=False&Keyword=tex.

31. Centers for Medicare & Medicaid Services. (2017). Available at https://www.cms.gov/Medicare/Provider-Enrollment-and-Certification/SurveyCertificationGenInfo/Downloads/Survey-and-Cert-Letter-18-10.pdf.

32. 45 C.F.R. §§ 164.502 -.528 (privacy) (2019); 45 C.F.R. §§ 164.302-.318 (security) (2019).

33. Guide to Privacy and Security of Electronic Health Information, Chapter 4 Understanding Electronic Health Records, the HIPAA Security Rule, and Cybersecurity, Office of the National Coordinator for Health Information Technology. Available at https://www.cms.gov/Medicare/Provider-Enrollment-and-Certification/SurveyCertEmergPrep/Downloads/Chapter-4-Health-Information-Technology.pdf.

34. *E.g.*, Standard E2473-05 (2011) of the American Society for Testing and Materials addresses encryption of electronic mail. Standard Practice for the Occupational/Environmental Health View of the Electronic Health Record, ASTM standard E2473-05.

35. American Health Information Management Association, Practice Brief: Information Security—An Overview (Updated) (2010).

36. Storck, L. (Feb. 2017). Policy Statement: Texting in Health Care. *Online Journal of Nursing Informatics (OJNI)*, 21(1). Available at http://www.himss.org/ojni; American Academy of Dermatology Association and the American Osteopathic Association (2013). Healthcare Insurance Portability and Accountability Act (HIPAA) Security Standards. Available at https://osteopathic.org/wp-content/uploads/2018/02/AOA-HIPAA-Security-Manual.pdf.

37. Miss. Code Ann. § 41-9-77 (2019); Tenn. Code Ann. § 68-11-302 (2019); Wash. Rev. Code § 5.46.010 (2019).

38. Telemedicine Report to Congress by the Joint Working Group on Telemedicine (1997). Available at https://www.ntia.doc.gov/legacy/reports/telemed/cover.htm.

39. Telecommunications Act of 1996, 47 U.S.C. §§ 254(b) & (h) (2019).

40. 42 U.S.C. § 1395i, mm (2019).

41. Creating High-Quality Results and Outcomes Necessary to Improve Chronic (CHRONIC) Care Act of 2018, S. 870, 115th Cong. (2018) (enacted).

42. See Ark. Code Ann. § 10-3-1702 (2019); Cal. Bus. & Prof. Code § 2290.5 (West 2019); Colo. Rev. Stat. § 12-36-106 (2019); Haw. Rev. Stat. § 453-2 (2019); 225 Ill. Comp. Stat. 60/49.5 (West 2019); Miss. Code Ann. § 73-25-34 (2019); MONT. Code Ann. §§ 37-3-301 & -342 (2019); Ohio Rev. Code Ann. § 4731-296 (2019); Okla. Stat. tit. 36 § 6802 (2019); Tenn. Code Ann. § 63-6-209 (2019); W. Va. Code § 30-3-13 (2019).

43. *See, e.g.*, Ariz. Rev. Stat. § 36-3602 (2019); Cal. Bus. & Prof. Code § 2290.5 (West 2019).

44. California Telehealth Advancement Act of 2011, A.B. 415(codified in scattered sections of the Health & Safety Code and the Business & Professions Code).

45. American Health Information Management Association, Practice Brief—Telemedicine Services and the Health Record (Updated) (2013); Kadlec, Lesley; Buttner, Patty. "HIM's Role in Telemedicine and Telehealth Technology." *Journal of AHIMA* 88, no.11 (November 2017): 48–49.

CHAPTER 14

HEALTH CARE FRAUD AND ABUSE

LEARNING OBJECTIVES

After reading this chapter, the learner should be able to:

1. Explain the meaning of fraud and abuse.
2. Compare and contrast the major laws supporting a prosecution for health care fraud and abuse.
3. Describe the roles of various law enforcement agencies in the prosecution of health care fraud and abuse.
4. Explain the meaning of compliance and compliance programs.
5. List the components of a compliance program.

KEY CONCEPTS

Administrative simplification
Anti-kickback statute
Civil money penalty
Compliance
Compliance program
Corporate integrity agreements
Fraud and abuse
Mail and wire fraud
National health information infrastructure
Permissive and mandatory exclusion
Physician self-referral prohibitions
Qui tam actions
Reasonable cause
Reasonable diligence
Relators
Remedy
Unbundling
Upcoding
Whistle-blowers
Willful neglect

INTRODUCTION

During the past thirty years, health care fraud and abuse has become a front-burner issue. Federally funded health care programs such as Medicare and Medicaid have lost of billions of dollars through fraud and abuse, as have private insurance companies. In response, Congress and state legislatures have passed laws to address this problem, federal and state governments have increased their enforcement efforts of existing regulations and laws, and private insurance companies have escalated their efforts to expose fraudulent claims. Newspaper and journal articles are often filled with allegations in this area, and continuing education programs that provide updates on this topic are well attended.

The increase in scrutiny has caused health care providers and organizations to change their methods of operation and created new jobs that did not exist a decade ago. Because health information professionals manage many risk areas open to health care fraud and abuse, such as accurate documentation, coding, and billing, it is important for these professionals to know and understand this area of law. This understanding can assist the organization in preventing the submission of false or inaccurate claims to the government or private payers.

FRAUD AND ABUSE

Fraud and abuse is defined as a false misrepresentation of fact that is relied on by another to that person's detriment and is a departure from reasonable use. This false misrepresentation of fact may take the form of words or conduct, including false or misleading allegations or concealment of facts that should have been disclosed. This misrepresentation is done knowingly and is not the result of negligence. The departure from reasonable use means that the misrepresentation is contrary to the proper order established by usage in the industry.

In the health care context, fraud and abuse refers to the efforts of a health care provider or organization to misrepresent facts to a government entity or third-party payer so that those facts appear legal and customary in the industry and result in some form of benefit, monetary or otherwise, to the health care provider or organization. This misrepresentation is not a matter of mistake but rather a willful act or omission. In other words, fraud and abuse requires a willful and knowing action on behalf of the health care provider or organization to misrepresent a fact, to the government's or third-party payer's detriment.

The most common forms of health care fraud and abuse relate to the areas of false claims and billing practices—for example, billing for services not rendered, such as submitting bills for physician examinations, x-rays, and laboratory tests that were never delivered. Other examples are upcoding and unbundling. **Upcoding** involves submitting a bill for a higher level of reimbursement than actually rendered in order to receive a higher reimbursement rate. **Unbundling** involves submitting separate bills for each component of a procedure instead of using the proper procedural code for the entire procedure, resulting in a higher reimbursement rate to the health care provider—for example, billing separately for groups of laboratory tests performed together in order to receive a higher reimbursement.

Other common forms of health care fraud and abuse include a health care provider's referral of a patient to a facility in which the provider holds a financial interest (commonly referred to as a Stark violation)[1] or a provider's referral of a patient to another provider in exchange for compensation (commonly referred to as a kickback violation).[2] Additionally, the health care provider may bill for services not considered medically necessary, double-bill for a service rendered, or bill for a covered service when the service provided was not in fact covered.

Major Laws Addressing Fraud and Abuse

The federal government has responded to the economic threat posed by health care fraud and abuse by passing legislation specifically addressing the issue and by focusing prosecution efforts by using existing legislation originally intended for different purposes. A list of the major laws addressing health care fraud and abuse is contained in Table 14.1.

Table 14.1 Major Laws Addressing Fraud and Abuse

1. False Claims Act
2. Qui tam actions
3. Anti-kickback statutes
4. Physician self-referral prohibitions (Stark I and II)
5. Mail and wire fraud statutes
6. Health Insurance Portability and Accountability Act (HIPAA)
7. Deficit Reduction Act of 2005

The linchpin for the prosecution of health care fraud and abuse is the False Claims Act (FCA).[3] Originally used during the Civil War to prosecute individuals and organizations that supplied the Union with inferior products or cheated the government outright, the FCA has taken on a new use over the past two decades. It is used to protect the government against those who charge for services not rendered and is often used in the Medicare and Medicaid context. Typically, a health care provider or organization violates the FCA by knowingly submitting a false or fraudulent claim to the government or by making a false statement in order to get the claim approved or paid.[4] This knowing submission may be proven by showing that the provider or organization (1) actually intended to commit fraud, or (2) knew the statement was false and was either deliberately ignorant of the truth or acted with reckless disregard of the truth when submitting the false statement.

FCA claims are typically brought as **qui tam actions**,[5] which allow private plaintiffs (technically referred to as **relators**) to sue on behalf of the U.S. government and receive a portion of the recovered funds, if successful. The relator begins the lawsuit on his own initiative; however, the government may decide to intervene in the case and take over prosecution or may join in the prosecution with the relator. The government may decide to allow the relator to proceed with the case on his own without any form of government intervention.

Typically, a relator is a current or former employee of the health care provider or organization who has learned of the fraud and abuse and wishes to expose the activity. These relators are called **whistle-blowers**. Whistle-blowers have included physicians who supervised laboratories and supervisors responsible for billing, coding, and claims processing procedures.[6] Relators have even included persons whose insurance benefits were the subject of coverage and payment disputes between Medicare and third-party payers.[7]

ETHICS

The act of whistle-blowing is supported by the ethical values of beneficence, nonmaleficence, fidelity, and veracity.

The concept of whistle-blowing relates to several ethical values, including beneficence, nonmaleficence, fidelity, and veracity, all discussed in detail in Chapter 5, Ethical Standards. The whistle-blower adheres to the values of doing good (beneficence), preventing harm (nonmaleficence), devotion to one's duties (fidelity), and telling the truth (veracity). Deciding whether to act as a whistle-blower in a given situation is fraught with difficulty. Table 14.2 provides a listing of considerations used to determine whether to act as a whistle-blower.

Table 14.2 Justification of Whistle-Blowing

1. The wrongdoing in question is grave and has created, or is likely to create, serious harm.
2. The professional who is contemplating blowing the whistle has appropriate information and is competent to make a judgment about the wrongdoing.
3. The professional has consulted others to confirm his information and judgment.
4. All other internal resources to resolve the problem have been exhausted.
5. There is a good likelihood that the whistle-blowing will serve a useful purpose.
6. The harm created by the whistle-blowing is less than the harm done by a continuation of the wrongdoing.

Source: Edge, R. & Groves, J. (2006). *Ethics of Health Care*. Albany, NY: Cengage.

CRITICAL THINKING

Health care professionals sometimes experience conflicts because they are often responsible to many masters: their patients, their employers, their professional associations, and state licensing boards. Such conflicts can make it difficult to decide how to proceed on the correct path when one suspects fraud and abuse. Consider whether any of the following pose constraints on health care professionals who might consider acting to expose fraud and abuse:

1. Habits of professional socialization requiring the following of orders;
2. Fear of loss of job/security;
3. Institutional policies;
4. Fear of lawsuits.

Another potent weapon in the fight against health care fraud and abuse is the federal **anti-kickback statute**.[8] This statute prohibits the offer or solicitation of remuneration, including kickbacks and rebates, in exchange for referrals of federally payable services, including Medicare services. Many states have followed Congress's lead, passing their own legislation prohibiting payment for referrals for services offered by managed care companies and private insurance companies. In the strictest sense, an instance where a physician is paid for referrals would be prohibited under anti-kickback statutes at both the federal and state levels. Health care organizations have been prosecuted under this statute for, among other things, acting pursuant to the terms of a partnership agreement that allowed for profit sharing and below-cost testing in exchange for test referrals that could be billed at full rates.[9] Because the anti-kickback statutes examine the relationships between health care providers closely, it has become customary to formalize business relationships through the use of written agreements. This formalization process has resulted in providers' engaging in more arm's-length transactions for goods and services, allowing for the avoidance of impropriety.

Several exceptions to the anti-kickback statutes exist—called "safe harbors"—so that those activities listed in the exceptions will be considered legitimate practices. Those health care providers who question whether any individual transaction falls within a safe harbor may seek an advisory opinion from the Office of Inspector General of the U.S. Department of Health and Human Services.

Physician self-referral prohibitions[10] have also been the subject of much litigation. In response to concerns that physicians were abusing the system by referring patients to their own services, Congress passed laws that prohibit self-referral for a number of services. Under the first law (commonly referred to as Stark I), a physician is barred from referring Medicare patients to a clinical laboratory in which the physician or an immediate family member possesses a financial interest. Congress later extended the prohibition to other services so that a physician is barred from referring Medicare patients to a designated health service in which the physician or immediate family member possesses a financial interest (commonly referred to as Stark II). The term *designated health service* is broad enough to include durable medical equipment, clinical laboratories, occupational therapy, physical therapy, hospital services, orthotics and prosthetics, radiology, parenteral and enteral nutrition services and supplies, home health services, and outpatient prescription drugs. Under Stark II, a physician violates the law by referring a Medicare patient to any entity just listed if the physician or immediate family member holds any financial interest in the entity. By making such a referral, the physician taints the claim for reimbursement made by the referred entity. Very limited ownership and compensation exceptions are available, and the criteria to qualify under them are very specific. Requests for an advisory opinion concerning these exceptions are directed to the Centers for Medicare and Medicaid Services.

Several other statutes sometimes form the basis of fraud and abuse lawsuits or serve as an adjunct to a claim filed under one of the statutes previously addressed. The prosecution of a fraud and abuse case may involve the use of federal **mail and wire fraud** statutes.[11] These statutes prohibit the use of the U.S. Postal Service or commercial wire services for the advancement of a scheme relating to fraud. Because modern business practices routinely involve the use of the mail system or wire services, it would be fairly easy for a health care provider or organization involved with fraud to violate these statutes. A violation of these statutes is a felony, punishable by a fine of $1,000, a five-year term of imprisonment, or both. Other charges brought as part of a prosecution may include false statements made pursuant to obtaining a benefit or payment under the Social Security Act, conspiracy to defraud, money laundering, or Racketeer Influenced and Corrupt Organizations (RICO). State laws may also apply, allowing state attorneys general to charge wrongdoers with claims of kickbacks, self-referrals, improper fee-splitting, bribery, and deceptive trade practices.

Because of the significance of the remedies the federal government may wield in a fraud and abuse case, health care providers and organizations have two additional incentives to obey the law. First, the federal government may apply the **civil money penalty** law to a violation.[12] Under this statute, the Department of Health and Human Services (HHS) is permitted to recover money damages for false or fraudulent claims. The health care provider would be responsible to make restitution to the government for the fraud at issue and could also be fined up to three times the amount of damages plus an additional fine not to exceed $10,000. An even more significant deterrent to health care providers and organizations is the statute providing for **permissive and mandatory exclusion** from participation in Medicare and all other federally financed health care programs.[13] This statute provides for the exclusion of a health care provider or organization due to criminal or other program violations. For instance, a five-year-to-permanent mandatory exclusion applies to health care providers and organizations that have received felony criminal convictions. For misdemeanor actions, debarment from participation for a minimum of one year may apply. Because it is not economically feasible for a health care provider or organization to forgo service to Medicare beneficiaries, the exclusion provision is a powerful weapon for the government to exercise.

HIPAA

Increased penalties and new enforcement mechanisms are part of HIPAA's focus on fraud and abuse.

Another development in the prosecution of health care fraud and abuse is the Health Insurance Portability and Accountability Act (HIPAA).[14] HIPAA both modifies the civil money penalty law and provides enhanced resources for the federal government to combat health care fraud. The civil money penalty law is modified to include penalties for actions specifically related to health care fraud and abuse, such as unbundling, upcoding, and seeking reimbursement for services rendered after being excluded from participation in Medicare or Medicaid. A list of these actions is provided in Table 14.3. HIPAA also has established or strengthened four programs to assist with fraud enforcement (see Table 14.4).

Additional laws in the form of regulations address the escalating levels of culpability for which increasing civil money penalties may be imposed. Provisions of the HITECH-HIPAA Omnibus Final Rule define the terms that are used to make this assessment. The term **reasonable cause** refers to an act or omission in which a covered entity or business associate knew, or by exercising reasonable

Table 14.3 HIPAA Enhancements

1. Engaging in upcoding.
2. Engaging in patterns of claiming medically unnecessary items of service.
3. Transferring remuneration to a Medicare beneficiary that may influence the beneficiary to order or receive items or services, to include the waiver of coinsurance and deductibles for service.
4. Submitting a claim when the provider has been excluded from the Medicare and Medicaid programs while retaining ownership or a controlling interest in an entity that still participates in Medicare or Medicaid.

Table 14.4 Fraud Enforcement Programs

1. Fraud and Abuse Control Program—operated jointly by the Department of Justice and the Office of Inspector General to control health care fraud and abuse and conduct investigations relating to the delivery of health care services.
2. Medicare Integrity Program—directs the Department of Health and Human Services to enter into agreements with private companies to carry out fraud and abuse protections.
3. Beneficiary Incentive Program—encourages Medicare beneficiaries to report suspected cases of fraud and abuse.
4. Health Care Fraud and Abuse Data Collection Program—designed to create a national health care fraud and abuse database in coordination with the National Practitioner Data Bank.

diligence would have known, that the act or omission violated an **administrative simplification** provision, but in which the covered entity or business associate did not act with willful neglect. The term **reasonable diligence** refers to the business care and prudence expected from a person seeking to satisfy a legal requirement under similar circumstances. The term **willful neglect** refers to conscious, intentional failure or reckless indifference to the obligation to comply with the administrative simplification provision violated.[15] The lowest penalty applies to covered entities who did not know nor could have known of a violation. The amount increases for circumstances where the covered entity knew or by exercising due diligence should have known of the violation. The highest penalty applies to covered entities who demonstrate willful neglect and fail to correct the violation within thirty days of discovery.[16]

HIPAA also criminalizes the disclosures of individually identifiable health information with the intent to use that information for personal gain and malicious harm.[17] The case of *United States v. Smith*[18] illustrates the use of HIPAA in this manner. In *Smith*, a licensed practical nurse employed by a nursing home accessed a patient's protected health information (PHI), including the patient's name and details of the patient's diagnosis, and disclosed the PHI to her husband. In turn, the husband threatened the patient with using the PHI against the patient in an upcoming legal proceeding. In lieu of proceeding to trial, the nurse pled guilty to one count of wrongful disclosure of PHI for personal gain and malicious harm and was sentenced to two years of probation and one hundred hours of community service. Her nursing license expired before the state board of nursing took action against her.

Additionally, the Deficit Reduction Act of 2005[19] provided additional strength to combat fraud and abuse in the Medicaid program. This law changed the nature of compliance programs for some institutions from voluntary to mandatory, required employers to educate staff concerning administrative remedies to violations of the False Claims Act, added more resources at the federal level for combating fraud and abuse, and provided a financial incentive to states to adopt laws similar to the federal False Claims Act. Furthermore, the language of this act allowed states to make their laws even more stringent or broad than the federal False Claims Act.

ARRA	The American Recovery and Reinvestment Act strengthens enforcement of HIPAA regulations in several ways.

Finally, the American Recovery and Reinvestment Act of 2009 (ARRA) strengthens the HIPAA regulations in four ways. First, ARRA specifically states that business associates are covered by the HIPAA Security Rule, including the administrative, technical, and physical safeguard requirements, making them subject to civil and criminal penalties for not complying with the terms of the Security Rule. Second, it clarifies who can be held accountable for wrongful disclosure of protected health information. Under ARRA, both individuals and health care entities may be prosecuted for wrongful disclosure of protected health information. ARRA also addresses noncompliance due to willful neglect. Finally, ARRA addresses the civil money penalty provisions of HIPAA, specifying that restitution provided to the government due to health care fraud and abuse may be used to fund HHS's enforcement activity.[20]

Law Enforcement Agencies

Several law enforcement agencies share responsibility to prosecute health care fraud and abuse. One of the most prominent agencies is the Office of Inspector General (OIG) of the Department of Health and Human Services. The OIG is authorized to conduct civil, administrative, and criminal investigations of fraud associated with the federal Medicare and Medicaid programs. In keeping with its responsibilities, the OIG provides guidance to health care providers on how to comply with applicable local, state, and federal laws and regulations. OIG has experienced considerable success during the last two decades by launching several initiatives aimed at recovering alleged overpayments made in connection with specific types of improper claims. Examples of these initiatives are listed in Table 14.5.

Table 14.5 OIG Fraud and Abuse Initiatives

Physicians at Teaching Hospitals (PATH)	Focused on the billing of services rendered by residents and teaching physicians; differentiating between services already paid under Medicare Part A's graduate medical education and indirect medical education programs from those services that could be billed properly under Medicare Part B.
72-Hour Rule Project Hospital Outpatient Laboratory Project	Focused on the payments made to hospitals for services provided to patients within a 72-hour window of the patient's admission; collecting overpayments made due to double billing. Focused on unbundling practices for claims dealing with hematology and automated blood chemistry tests.
PPS Patient Transfer Project	Focused on payments made through the prospective payment system (PPS) that did not follow the practice of paying the transferring hospital according to the applicable diagnosis-related group (DRG) code and the transferee hospital according to the per diem allowances and applicable DRG code.

Although each of these initiatives has resulted in recoupment of funds to the government, OIG's strong emphasis on this approach has not been without criticism. Some have claimed that the subjects of these initiatives committed honest mistakes or, at most, negligence and should not have been prosecuted but educated concerning the proper manner in which to submit claims for payment. DHHS has responded by instituting and emphasizing preventive programs to be operated by the CMS (Centers for Medicare and Medicaid Services). Examples include the Correct Coding Initiative (CCI), designed to promote national correct coding methodologies, and the Payment Error and Prevention Program (PEPP), designed to reduce the Medicare payment error rate. CMS also coordinates with OIG to publish numerous guidance materials, available on the CMS Web site, to explain and clarify its regulations. These materials identify risk areas and offer suggestions on proper billing practices and internal controls.

The law enforcement agency with the widest responsibility to investigate health care fraud is the Federal Bureau of Investigation (FBI). In contrast to the agencies listed previously, the FBI possesses authority that extends beyond the jurisdiction of a particular governmental program. The FBI may work jointly with the OIG, the DCIS, the Postal Inspection Service, or the Centers for Medicare and Medicaid Services (CMS), or it may act on its own based on complaints received through calls, letters, or visits from members of the public. Additionally, the FBI may investigate due to the efforts of a whistle-blower acting pursuant to the False Claims Act.

Other law enforcement agencies and their areas of responsibility include the Postal Inspection Service, responsible for investigating fraud schemes involving the U.S. mail system, and the Defense Criminal Investigative Service (DCIS), responsible for investigating fraud schemes committed against the military's health insurance programs. At the state level, attorneys general may bring civil actions related to health care fraud and abuse. Typically filed in state court, these civil actions may be filed in federal court if the charge is a violation the American Recovery and Reinvestment Act of 2009.[21] Virtually all states have a Medicaid Fraud Control unit (MFCU). These MFCUs concentrate on investigating and prosecuting providers that defraud the Medicaid program.

Investigations of health care fraud typically extend over several years and may involve interviews with the whistle-blower, members of the public, and possibly the health care provider or organization itself. Documentation may be obtained through the use of subpoenas and search warrants. Institutions other than the health care provider, such as CMS and billing services, may be asked to supply further documentation.

In the event that the health information professional is confronted by a law enforcement agent with a search warrant, the professional should remember that he has a duty to cooperate with the agent but at the same time has the obligation to notify the provider's or organization's legal counsel of the request presented by the agent. Although it may appear difficult to balance the duty and obligation, it is imperative that the professional do so. Upon notice, legal counsel will assist the professional in determining how to respond cooperatively to the agent's request, including what to say and what not to say. Until legal counsel has provided advice or has arrived on the premises, the health information professional should cooperate with the agent's request to gather specific records and information while not answering any additional questions.

Upon completion of the investigative process, the law enforcement agency works with the local U.S. attorney's office to pursue prosecution of health care providers or organizations suspected of wrongdoing. Both government offices will determine whether to proceed with a lawsuit, including which statute forms the basis of the claim against the health care provider or organization. To avoid going to trial, those same government agencies may craft a financial settlement agreement with those suspected of wrongdoing.

COMPLIANCE PROGRAMS

Compliance has been a part of health information management since the beginning of the profession. For decades, health information professionals have worked to comply with voluntary accreditation standards, federal and state laws and regulations, institutional bylaws and rules, and professional codes of ethics. The effort to comply with these external forces became even more complex with the advent of third-party payment systems and government reimbursement programs. With the focus on health care fraud and abuse intensifying and the advent of implementing rules addressing privacy and security under the Health Insurance Portability and Accountability Act, compliance is now a formalized part of health information management.

Compliance is defined as the efforts to establish a culture that promotes prevention, detection, and resolution of instances of conduct that do not conform to applicable local, state, and federal laws and regulations. A **compliance program** ensures the establishment of effective internal controls that promote adherence to the applicable local, state, and federal laws and regulations and the program requirements of federal, state, and private health plans.

ETHICS

Compliance programs may be grounded in an ethics-based approach.

The establishment of compliance programs can be performed from an ethics-based or minimum legal requirements approach. Under the ethics-based approach, a health care organization decides that it wishes to conform to local, state, and federal laws and regulations because it is the right thing to do or because a cost–benefit analysis reveals it would be a sound business practice. The ethics-based approach encourages good behavior and is in essence a voluntary form of improvement. This approach demonstrates to employees and the community at large that the health care organization is committed to responsible corporate conduct. Under the minimum legal requirements approach, a health care organization decides it will conform to local, state, and federal laws and regulations because of the fear of punishment in the event of nonconformance—the so-called fear of getting caught. Because the conformance standards are externally imposed, the motivation under this approach is to avoid or minimize penalties or punishment.

Under either approach, the result is that health care providers that implement effective compliance programs reduce their exposure to civil damages and penalties, criminal sanctions, and administrative remedies. The provider also benefits through a greater ability to assess and improve the efficiency, effectiveness, and quality of patient services. The health care provider develops a centralized internal mechanism for distributing information on health care statutes, regulations, and other program directives. HIM professionals can assist the health care provider's efforts to ensure compliance by focusing on strengthening the documentation processes for patient care, by ensuring that diagnostic and procedure codes are assigned appropriately, and by managing health information responsibly.

ETHICS

HIM professionals play a role in a health care provider's compliance program.

> **CRITICAL THINKING**
>
> Suppose a health care organization develops a compliance program and names a compliance officer. What other actions could the health care organization take to show responsible conduct or has the health care organization done enough by taking these steps?

Compliance programs take all shapes and sizes, mostly dependent on the type of health care provider or organization. The Office of the Inspector General (OIG) of the Department of Health and Human Services has released compliance program guidelines for hospitals, clinical laboratories, long-term care facilities, hospices, home care organizations, ambulance suppliers, clinical laboratories, pharmaceutical manufacturers, and physician offices.[22] These guidelines are not actually compliance programs; rather, they provide basic procedural and structural information for health care providers and organizations to use in tailoring a compliance program to fit their own culture, structure, and processes. These compliance program guidelines share the key elements listed in Table 14.6.

With the passage of the Deficit Reduction Act of 2005, those entities who receive $5 million or more in annual Medicaid reimbursement must educate their employees using handbooks and written policies about the administrative remedies available for violations of the False Claims Act and any corresponding state laws. This requirement alone changes the practice of corporate compliance from one of a voluntary nature to one of a mandatory nature. It is unknown how soon this requirement may be applied to entities receiving lesser amounts of Medicaid reimbursement.

In addition to voluntary processes, compliance can also take the form of a mandatory process. The Red Flag Rules issued by the Federal Trade Commission (FTC) are an example of a mandatory compliance process. The term "Red Flag" refers to the warning signs of identity theft. The Red Flag Rules govern most health care providers and institutions and require those providers and institutions to create prevention programs to identify, detect, and respond to patterns, practices, and activities that could indicate identity theft.[23]

In the context of medical identity theft, numerous examples exist. Health records may indicate medical treatment that is inconsistent with a patient's physical exam or medical history. Health records may show a discrepancy in blood type, age, race, or other physical descriptions. A patient

Table 14.6 Compliance Program Guidelines

1. Written standards of conduct and policies and procedures.
2. Designation of a chief compliance officer to oversee the compliance program.
3. Regular, effective education and training programs for all affected employees.
4. A process for receiving complaints of possible violations.
5. Development of a system to respond to allegations of improper or illegal activities and enforcement of appropriate disciplinary actions through well-publicized disciplinary directives.
6. Audits and other evaluation techniques to monitor compliance.
7. Investigation and corrective action of identified problems.

Source: Office of Inspector General, U.S. Department of Health and Human Services, https://oig.hhs.gov/compliance/compliance-guidance/index.asp.

may contact the health care provider questioning an explanation of benefits from his insurance company or a bill from the health care provider for treatment or care that he never received. A patient's credit report may indicate collection efforts for health care services rendered to someone impersonating the patient. Any of these examples, and others not mentioned, can cause considerable problems for the victim to rectify.

Health care providers and institutions demonstrate compliance with the Red Flag Rules by creating a written program to identify the warning signs of identity theft and applying it to day-to-day operations. The written program must be appropriate to the size and complexity of the organization creating it. This application to day-to-day operations involves training all levels of management and staff and mitigating the effects of identity theft whenever found by the health care provider or institution. Further, compliance is demonstrated through appropriate and effective oversight of service provider/business associate arrangements and through revisions to the written program on a periodic basis to incorporate new risks and trends. Failure to comply with the requirements of the Red Flag Rules subjects a health care provider or institution to civil monetary penalties, regulatory enforcement action, and negative publicity. Further information about the components of an identity theft prevention and detection program can be found in Chapter 10, Access to Health Information.

Compliance programs have also been imposed on health care providers through financial settlement agreements. These agreements settle litigation brought by the government in the battle against fraud and abuse.[24] In some instances, the government has reduced the fines of those accused of fraud and abuse where an effective compliance program was in place. In other instances, the government has required the establishment of compliance programs as part of the financial settlement agreement.

Commonly referred to as **corporate integrity agreements** (CIAs), these financial settlements are written agreements that specify the rules of conduct to be followed to **remedy** the fraud and abuse found, plus any monitoring and reporting requirements. These agreements differ from a corporate compliance program in that the compliance program is an internal, not external, document that is adopted by the health care entity voluntarily as opposed to under the direction of the government. Further, a CIA can be more stringent and expensive to implement than a compliance program. For these reasons, many health care entities place great emphasis on compliance programs, because the risk of being subject to a CIA outweighs the risks associated with adopting and operating a compliance program.

One example of a CIA involved the case of *CVS Pharmacies*. In *CVS*, pharmacy employees in several different locations disposed of old prescription data, including prescription bottles with labels, by tossing them in the dumpster. After media reports surfaced that protected health information (PHI) subject to HIPAA protection was easily available to any person willing to dive into a trash dumpster to retrieve the information, the Office of Civil Rights of the U.S. Department of Health and Human Services joined forces with the Federal Trade Commission to investigate. The investigation determined that CVS had failed to implement adequate policies and procedures governing disposal of PHI, had failed to adequately train its staff on proper disposal methods, and had failed to maintain and implement a sanctions policy for staff who failed to dispose of PHI properly. In addition to a multimillion-dollar fine, CVS was directed to correct its failings, institute internal monitoring, engage a third-party assessor to conduct compliance assessments, and submit compliance reports for a three-year period.[25]

In addition, health information professionals may be guided by the U.S. Sentencing Guidelines for Organizations. These guidelines, listed in Table 14.7, form the basis for the compliance program guidelines and financial settlement agreements instituted by the federal government.[26]

Table 14.7 U.S. Sentencing Guidelines for Organizations

1. Establish compliance standards and procedures for all employees to follow to prevent and detect criminal conduct.
2. The organization's governing body shall exert reasonable oversight in implementation of a compliance program; high-level executives shall ensure an effective compliance program; and specific individuals shall be assigned overall responsibility to oversee compliance with Step 1.
3. Use due diligence not to delegate substantial discretionary authority to individuals the organization knows or should have known to engage in illegal activities or other conduct inconsistent with and effective compliance or ethics program.
4. Take steps to communicate effectively to all employees and other agents the standards and procedures by conducting effective training programs and otherwise disseminating information appropriate to such individuals' respective roles and responsibilities.
5. Take reasonable steps to ensure compliance with the standards, evaluate the program's effectiveness periodically, and employ mechanisms to report or seek guidance anonymously or confidentially.
6. Use consistent promotion and enforcement of the standards to include appropriate incentives and appropriate disciplinary action.
7. If criminal conduct has been detected, take all reasonable steps to respond to the criminal conduct and prevent further criminal conduct, including making any necessary modifications to the organization's compliance and ethics program.

Source: U.S. Sentencing Guideline 8B2.1 (2018).

Whether part of a compliance program or operating outside the program, some health care entities have employed technology as a means to combat fraud. Most of this technology exists in two forms: advanced analytics software for use in the **national health information infrastructure** and automated coding software. The advanced analytics software allows multiple parties who operate within the infrastructure (an interoperable electronic exchange between health care providers, government, and third-party payers) to examine data to detect fraud. For example, a third-party payer may be able to review electronically stored clinical encounter data to validate claims submitted by the health care provider for payment. By validating the clinical encounter before making payment, the third-party payer reduces the opportunity for financial loss in the first place, as opposed to discovering the invalidity of the claim after payment has been made.

Automated coding software assigns the correct code based on official guidelines and reporting rules programmed into the software. These codes are assigned after evaluation of the patient's clinical data that is stored electronically. A coding professional or clinician reviews the automated assignments and edits as necessary, with more editing needed in instances where the clinical encounter is complex or the coding software is not highly sophisticated. By validating or editing the automated assignments, the health care provider is in a position to prevent submission of fraudulent codes to a third-party payer. Some coding software programs allow a review of all codes assigned over a period of time, allowing the health care provider to detect patterns that may indicate instances of manipulation of the computer program or other forms of fraud. As technology develops further, both advanced analytics software and automated coding software should grow more sophisticated in preventing, detecting, and prosecuting fraud.

CONCLUSION

In the face of increased scrutiny, health care providers and organizations have responded to questions of health care fraud and abuse by developing compliance programs to document that they are adhering to the rule of law. These compliance programs make good business sense and will likely not disappear in the future. Because health information professionals manage risk areas critical to an allegation of health care fraud and abuse, they owe to their employers, third-party payers, and the government at large an obligation to assist in preventing the submission of false or inaccurate claims.

CASE STUDY A

You are in charge of Anywhere Hospital's compliance program. As part of the hospital's orientation program, you provide an overview of the compliance program to new employees. Outline what information you will include in your presentation.

CASE STUDY B

You are the head of the health information management department at General Hospital. An FBI agent has arrived at your office with a search warrant in hand. He asks to speak with you about the hospital's health records. How should you respond?

REVIEW QUESTIONS

1. What forms of fraud and abuse may be present in a health care setting?
2. What do the terms *upcoding* and *unbundling* mean?
3. What is the False Claims Act, and how does it apply to the health care setting?
4. What statute permits criminal prosecution of improper disclosure of individually identifiable health information?
5. Name two remedies the federal government may use in a fraud and abuse case, and explain their application.
6. Name the federal law enforcement agencies that share responsibility for prosecuting health care fraud and abuse and explain their role.
7. Compare and contrast the approaches to the establishment of a compliance program.
8. What are the benefits to a health care provider that develops an effective compliance program?
9. How does a corporate compliance program differ from a corporate integrity agreement?

ENRICHMENT ACTIVITY

Imagine you have just been promoted to the position of chief compliance officer at a health care facility. Based on the contents of this chapter, draft an outline of the elements of your organization's compliance program. Make sure to address compliance standards, procedures, and policies. If your instructor has a current compliance program document from an existing health care facility, compare your draft to the health care facility's compliance program and edit accordingly.

NOTES

1. 42 U.S.C. § 1395nn(b) (2019).
2. 42 U.S.C. § 1320a-7b(b) (2019).
3. 31 U.S.C. § 3729-33 (civil) and 42 U.S.C. § 1320a-7b(a) (criminal) (2019).
4. An example of a criminal prosecution of Medicare fraud is *United States v. Gieger*, 190 F.3d 661 (5th Cir. 1999) (conspiracy to submit false claims to Medicare concerning ambulance services).
5. Qui tam is part of the longer Latin phrase: *qui tam pro domino rege quam pro se ipso in hac parte sequitur*, meaning he "who brings the action for the king as well as himself." *See United States ex rel. Stinson v. Prudential Ins.*, 944 F.2d 1149, 1152 n.2 (3d. Cir. 1991).
6. *United States ex rel. Merena v. Smithkline Beecham Clinical Laboratories*, 114 F. Supp. 352 (E.D. Pa. 2000).
7. *United States ex rel. Cooper v. Blue Cross & Blue Shield of Florida*, 19 F.3d 562 (11th Cir. 1994).
8. 42 U.S.C. § 1320a-7b(b) (2019).
9. *United States ex rel. Kneepkins v. Gambro Healthcare Inc., et al.* 115 F. Supp. 2d 35 (D. Mass. 2000).
10. 42 U.S.C. § 1395nn; see *also, United States ex rel. Thompson v. Columbia/HCA Healthcare Corp.*, 125 F.3d 251 (5th Cir. 1997).
11. 18 U.S.C. § 1341, 1343 (2019).
12. 42 U.S.C. § 1320a-7a (2019).
13. 42 U.S.C. § 1320a-7 (2019).
14. 42 U.S.C. § 1320d (2019).
15. 45 C.F.R. §160.401 (2019).
16. 45 C.F.R. §160.404 (2019).
17. 42 U.S.C. §§ 1320d-6(a)(3) & (b)(3); 18 U.S.C. § 2 (2019).
18. 4:07-cr-00378 (Eastern District of Arkansas 2008).
19. 42 U.S.C. §§ 1396, 10701-1, 1092e (2019).
20. 42 U.S.C. §§ 17931(a-b); 17934(c); 17938; 17939 (2019).
21. Id. at 17939(d) (2019).
22. For example, individual guidance per health care provider is found on the OIG Web site: https://oig.hhs.gov/compliance/compliance-guidance/index.asp.
23. Identity Theft Flags and Address Discrepancies under Fair and Accurate Credit Transactions Act of 2003, Final Rule, 16 C.F.R. Part 681 (2019) (requiring hospitals to create a plan to identify "red flags" that signal potential identity theft).
24. Examples of cases involving settlement agreements include: *Merena*, supra n. 6; *Assoc. Mutual Hosp. Serv. of Michigan v. Health Care Service Corp. of Illinois*, 71 F. Supp. 2d 750 (W.D. MI. 1999).
25. http://hhs.gov/ocr/privacy/hipaa/enforcement/examples/cvsresolutionagreement.html. (Last accessed February 10, 2019.)
26. U.S. Sentencing Guideline 8B2.1 (2018).

CHAPTER 15

LAW AND ETHICS IN THE WORKPLACE

LEARNING OBJECTIVES

After reading this chapter, the learner should be able to:

1. Define the concept of employment.
2. Differentiate between the various types of employees.
3. Explain the concept of the at-will employment doctrine.
4. Describe the interplay between ethics and law in the context of employment.
5. Trace the development of employee rights.
6. Describe the various civil rights and workplace protection laws that relate to human resource management.

KEY CONCEPTS

At-will employment
Codes of conduct
Collective bargaining
Disability
Employee
Employer
Employment
Exempt employees
Full-time employees
Functional limitation
Hostile work environment
Independent contractor
Labor unions
Leased employees
Living wage laws
Part-time employees
Physical examination
Qualification
Quid pro quo
Reasonable accommodation
Regular employee
Salary
Serious health condition
Sexual harassment
Statutory employee
Substantially equal
Undue hardship
Unemployment insurance
Utilitarianism
Wages
Workers' compensation
Workplace barrier

INTRODUCTION

Much of the study of the workplace, including personnel and human resource management, is intertwined with laws and ethics. At every turn, a manager or an organization considering whether to take action or refrain from taking action concerning an employee must consider the legal protections afforded to employees under federal, state, and local laws. Further, employees must be well versed in their rights concerning employment if they are to fully participate in the workplace. At the same time, both managers and employees must be versed in the role that ethics plays in employment. This chapter addresses employment law and ethics, beginning with an overview of the types of employees present in today's workplace. The chapter continues with a discussion of employee rights and how they are applied in the workplace, with a discussion of the relationship between ethics and law provided as appropriate.[1]

EMPLOYMENT

At the heart of human resource management is the concept of employment. **Employment** is the process of providing work, engaging services or labor, and paying for the work performed. Those persons, businesses, or organizations that provide the work, engage the services or labor, and pay for the work performed are **employers**. The vast majority of individuals who are engaged in these services or labor are employees. As a generality, an **employee** is an individual hired by another, such as a business firm, to work for **wages** or a **salary**. Wages refers to an hourly rate of pay; salary refers to a rate of pay given on a weekly, monthly, or yearly schedule.[2] Employees are covered by a host of laws at the federal, state, and local levels, ranging from insurance and pension benefits to workplace safety requirements and protections from discrimination. Employee rights derived from these laws are addressed later in this chapter.

Many types of employees exist, and the meaning of each employee type carries with it certain benefits and protections under federal and state laws. A **regular employee**, sometimes referred to as a common law employee, is one who has a continuing relationship with the employer. To create a continuing relationship, it is not necessary for the work to be performed on a daily basis; rather, the work must be performed according to some frequency—for example, several days per month. Employees are generally classified as **full-time employees** if they work thirty hours per week or more, and **part-time employees** if they work less than thirty hours per week. Many part-time employees are paid on an hourly basis, and under some state laws may receive different benefits than fulltime employees. At one time, employers used the term *permanent employee* interchangeably with *regular employee*; however, *permanent employee* has since lost favor, because it implies that an employee has some right to stay with the business or organization indefinitely without change. Absent the protections brought by unions, employees are generally considered employed at will, a concept addressed in more detail later in this chapter.

Leased employees, sometimes referred to as temporary employees, are employed by a service firm and are assigned to work at a business or an organization. Both the work product and the manner in which the work is performed by the leased employee are subject to the control of the business or organization. While leased employees may work at the premises and under the direction of a business or organization, they receive their paychecks and benefits from the service firm. Leased employees often perform work for a fixed period, typically on a specific project. Once the project is completed or the fixed period ends, the leased employee is assigned to work at another business or organization. Leased employees are expected to abide by the rules and regulations of the business or organization where they are assigned to work. But under many state laws, the employees must look to the service firm and not to the client business or organization for benefits such as unemployment insurance compensation.

Not all individuals who work with businesses and organizations can be classified as employees. Many businesses and organizations use independent contractors to complete work. An **independent contractor** is an individual who agrees to perform certain work according to her own means, manner, and methods of performance. This personal control over means, manner, and methods does not mean that the business or organization does not exercise any form of control—merely that the amount of control is limited. In the employer–independent contractor relationship, the level of control exercised by a business or organization is limited to the results or products of the independent contractor's work. By contrast, in the employer–employee relationship, the employer has control over the means, manner, and methods of completing work, along with the end result or product of that work. Many independent contractors offer their services to multiple businesses and organizations, thereby solidifying their independence from any one employer.

A classification of work that does not fall into the category of employee or independent contractor is a statutory employee. A **statutory employee** is one who has been designated by specific laws as subject to the tax-withholding requirements imposed upon employers but who might not otherwise be considered an employee. The issue of control has no relevance to this definition, since those groups of workers who have been designated as statutory employees under these laws include delivery drivers, life insurance agents, and traveling salespeople who sell business-to-business.

Many legal consequences result from the classification of workers as employees, independent contractors, or statutory employees. Whether a given worker receives certain benefits and protections rests largely on her classification. If individuals are classified as employees, the law imposes certain obligations upon employers to verify the identity and employment authorization of every employee hired. Such obligations arise pursuant to the Immigration Reform and Control Act[3] and are met through the use of the federal Employment Eligibility Verification form, commonly known as the I-9 form. An example of the I-9 form is illustrated in Figure 15.1.

In addition to using the I-9 form, employers may participate in the federal government's E-Verify program. This program is operated jointly by the Department of Homeland Security and the Social Security Administration (SSA). Participating employers can check the work status of new hires online by comparing information from an employee's I-9 form against SSA and Department of Homeland Security databases. This comparison allows the employer to determine the employment eligibility of new hires and the validity of their Social Security numbers.

While some consistency exists within federal law, contrasts with state law concerning classifications are not unusual. For example, a worker may be properly classified as not an employee pursuant to the tax requirements of federal law but be classified as an employee under state law for workers' compensation or unemployment insurance purposes. As a general rule, the strictest law is the law that takes precedence over the other laws in any given situation. Accordingly, it is important that each employer becomes familiar with the variations among federal, state, and local laws when classifying workers and providing benefits and protections.

EMPLOYEE RIGHTS

Important to any discussion involving management is the issue of employee rights. Legislation that affects the working relationship between employers and employees has a great impact on human resource management. A comprehensive list of the federal laws regulating the workforce is contained in Table 15.1. Several of the most significant laws affecting the employer–employee relationship are discussed in this section.

Overview

Traditionally, all employees were considered at-will employees. **At-will employment** is an employment arrangement that allows the employer to terminate the employee at any time and allows the employee to leave the employer at any time.

Under this arrangement, the employer may hire, fire, promote, and demote any employee it chooses as long as there is no employment contract (such as a labor agreement) or federal, state, or local law to the contrary. This means that employers may have a good reason, a bad reason, or no reason to hire, fire, promote, or demote an employee, as long as such action does not violate the law. Some states have placed restrictions on the employment-at-will doctrine, asserting that

Employment Eligibility Verification
Department of Homeland Security
U.S. Citizenship and Immigration Services

USCIS
Form I-9
OMB No. 1615-0047
Expires 08/31/2019

▶ **START HERE: Read instructions carefully before completing this form. The instructions must be available, either in paper or electronically, during completion of this form. Employers are liable for errors in the completion of this form.**

ANTI-DISCRIMINATION NOTICE: It is illegal to discriminate against work-authorized individuals. Employers **CANNOT** specify which document(s) an employee may present to establish employment authorization and identity. The refusal to hire or continue to employ an individual because the documentation presented has a future expiration date may also constitute illegal discrimination.

Section 1. Employee Information and Attestation *(Employees must complete and sign Section 1 of Form I-9 no later than the **first day of employment**, but not before accepting a job offer.)*

Last Name *(Family Name)*	First Name *(Given Name)*	Middle Initial	Other Last Names Used *(if any)*

Address *(Street Number and Name)*	Apt. Number	City or Town	State	ZIP Code

Date of Birth *(mm/dd/yyyy)*	U.S. Social Security Number	Employee's E-mail Address	Employee's Telephone Number
	☐☐☐ - ☐☐ - ☐☐☐☐		

I am aware that federal law provides for imprisonment and/or fines for false statements or use of false documents in connection with the completion of this form.

I attest, under penalty of perjury, that I am (check one of the following boxes):

☐ 1. A citizen of the United States

☐ 2. A noncitizen national of the United States *(See instructions)*

☐ 3. A lawful permanent resident (Alien Registration Number/USCIS Number): ____________

☐ 4. An alien authorized to work until (expiration date, if applicable, mm/dd/yyyy): ____________
Some aliens may write "N/A" in the expiration date field. *(See instructions)*

Aliens authorized to work must provide only one of the following document numbers to complete Form I-9:
An Alien Registration Number/USCIS Number OR Form I-94 Admission Number OR Foreign Passport Number.

1. Alien Registration Number/USCIS Number: ____________
OR
2. Form I-94 Admission Number: ____________
OR
3. Foreign Passport Number: ____________
Country of Issuance: ____________

QR Code - Section 1
Do Not Write In This Space

Signature of Employee	Today's Date *(mm/dd/yyyy)*

Preparer and/or Translator Certification (check one):
☐ I did not use a preparer or translator. ☐ A preparer(s) and/or translator(s) assisted the employee in completing Section 1.
(Fields below must be completed and signed when preparers and/or translators assist an employee in completing Section 1.)

I attest, under penalty of perjury, that I have assisted in the completion of Section 1 of this form and that to the best of my knowledge the information is true and correct.

Signature of Preparer or Translator	Today's Date *(mm/dd/yyyy)*

Last Name *(Family Name)*	First Name *(Given Name)*

Address *(Street Number and Name)*	City or Town	State	ZIP Code

STOP *Employer Completes Next Page* STOP

Form I-9 07/17/17 N Page 1 of 3

Source: Courtesy of the US Citizenship & Immigration Services, www.uscis.gov.

Figure 15.1 Federal Employment Eligibility Verification (Form I-9)

Employment Eligibility Verification
Department of Homeland Security
U.S. Citizenship and Immigration Services

USCIS
Form I-9
OMB No. 1615-0047
Expires 08/31/2019

Section 2. Employer or Authorized Representative Review and Verification

(Employers or their authorized representative must complete and sign Section 2 within 3 business days of the employee's first day of employment. You must physically examine one document from List A OR a combination of one document from List B and one document from List C as listed on the "Lists of Acceptable Documents.")

Employee Info from Section 1	Last Name *(Family Name)*	First Name *(Given Name)*	M.I.	Citizenship/Immigration Status

List A Identity and Employment Authorization	OR	**List B** Identity	AND	**List C** Employment Authorization
Document Title		Document Title		Document Title
Issuing Authority		Issuing Authority		Issuing Authority
Document Number		Document Number		Document Number
Expiration Date *(if any)(mm/dd/yyyy)*		Expiration Date *(if any)(mm/dd/yyyy)*		Expiration Date *(if any)(mm/dd/yyyy)*
Document Title		Additional Information		QR Code - Sections 2 & 3 Do Not Write In This Space
Issuing Authority				
Document Number				
Expiration Date *(if any)(mm/dd/yyyy)*				
Document Title				
Issuing Authority				
Document Number				
Expiration Date *(if any)(mm/dd/yyyy)*				

Certification: I attest, under penalty of perjury, that (1) I have examined the document(s) presented by the above-named employee, (2) the above-listed document(s) appear to be genuine and to relate to the employee named, and (3) to the best of my knowledge the employee is authorized to work in the United States.

The employee's first day of employment *(mm/dd/yyyy)*: ______________ ***(See instructions for exemptions)***

Signature of Employer or Authorized Representative	Today's Date *(mm/dd/yyyy)*	Title of Employer or Authorized Representative

Last Name of Employer or Authorized Representative	First Name of Employer or Authorized Representative	Employer's Business or Organization Name

Employer's Business or Organization Address (Street Number and Name)	City or Town	State	ZIP Code

Section 3. Reverification and Rehires *(To be completed and signed by employer or authorized representative.)*

A. New Name *(if applicable)*			**B.** Date of Rehire *(if applicable)*
Last Name *(Family Name)*	First Name *(Given Name)*	Middle Initial	Date *(mm/dd/yyyy)*

C. If the employee's previous grant of employment authorization has expired, provide the information for the document or receipt that establishes continuing employment authorization in the space provided below.

Document Title	Document Number	Expiration Date *(if any) (mm/dd/yyyy)*

I attest, under penalty of perjury, that to the best of my knowledge, this employee is authorized to work in the United States, and if the employee presented document(s), the document(s) I have examined appear to be genuine and to relate to the individual.

Signature of Employer or Authorized Representative	Today's Date *(mm/dd/yyyy)*	Name of Employer or Authorized Representative

Form I-9 07/17/17 N — Page 2 of 3

Figure 15.1 *(Continued)*

LISTS OF ACCEPTABLE DOCUMENTS
All documents must be UNEXPIRED

Employees may present one selection from List A
or a combination of one selection from List B and one selection from List C.

LIST A **Documents that Establish Both Identity and Employment Authorization**	OR	LIST B **Documents that Establish Identity**	AND	LIST C **Documents that Establish Employment Authorization**
1. U.S. Passport or U.S. Passport Card		**1.** Driver's license or ID card issued by a State or outlying possession of the United States provided it contains a photograph or information such as name, date of birth, gender, height, eye color, and address		**1.** A Social Security Account Number card, unless the card includes one of the following restrictions: (1) NOT VALID FOR EMPLOYMENT (2) VALID FOR WORK ONLY WITH INS AUTHORIZATION (3) VALID FOR WORK ONLY WITH DHS AUTHORIZATION
2. Permanent Resident Card or Alien Registration Receipt Card (Form I-551)		**2.** ID card issued by federal, state or local government agencies or entities, provided it contains a photograph or information such as name, date of birth, gender, height, eye color, and address		**2.** Certification of report of birth issued by the Department of State (Forms DS-1350, FS-545, FS-240)
3. Foreign passport that contains a temporary I-551 stamp or temporary I-551 printed notation on a machine-readable immigrant visa		**3.** School ID card with a photograph		**3.** Original or certified copy of birth certificate issued by a State, county, municipal authority, or territory of the United States bearing an official seal
4. Employment Authorization Document that contains a photograph (Form I-766)		**4.** Voter's registration card		**4.** Native American tribal document
5. For a nonimmigrant alien authorized to work for a specific employer because of his or her status: **a.** Foreign passport; and **b.** Form I-94 or Form I-94A that has the following: (1) The same name as the passport; and (2) An endorsement of the alien's nonimmigrant status as long as that period of endorsement has not yet expired and the proposed employment is not in conflict with any restrictions or limitations identified on the form.		**5.** U.S. Military card or draft record		**5.** U.S. Citizen ID Card (Form I-197)
6. Passport from the Federated States of Micronesia (FSM) or the Republic of the Marshall Islands (RMI) with Form I-94 or Form I-94A indicating nonimmigrant admission under the Compact of Free Association Between the United States and the FSM or RMI		**6.** Military dependent's ID card		**6.** Identification Card for Use of Resident Citizen in the United States (Form I-179)
		7. U.S. Coast Guard Merchant Mariner Card		**7.** Employment authorization document issued by the Department of Homeland Security
		8. Native American tribal document		
		9. Driver's license issued by a Canadian government authority		
		For persons under age 18 who are unable to present a document listed above:		
		10. School record or report card		
		11. Clinic, doctor, or hospital record		
		12. Day-care or nursery school record		

Examples of many of these documents appear in Part 13 of the Handbook for Employers (M-274).

Refer to the instructions for more information about acceptable receipts.

Form I-9 07/17/17 N Page 3 of 3

Figure 15.1 *(Continued)*

Table 15.1 Federal Employment Laws

Age Discrimination in Employment Act (ADEA)
Americans with Disabilities Act (ADA)
Civil Rights Act of 1964
Davis-Bacon Act
Drug-Free Workplace Act
Employee Polygraph Protection Act
Employment Retirement Income Security Act (ERISA)
Equal Employment Opportunity (EEO) Act and implementing guidelines concerning sexual harassment and employee selection practices
Equal Pay Act
Fair Credit Reporting Act
Fair Labor Standards Act
Family Medical Leave Act (FMLA)
Genetic Information Non-Discrimination Act (GINA)
Immigration Reform and Control Act (IRCA)
Lilly Ledbetter Fair Pay Act
Medical and Health Care Continuation Act
National Labor Relations Act
Newborns' and Mothers' Health Protection Act
Occupational Safety and Health (OSH) Act
Older Workers' Benefit Protection Act
Pregnancy Discrimination Act
Privacy Act
Rehabilitation Act of 1973
Uniformed Services Employment and Reemployment Rights Act (USERRA)
Vietnam-Era Veterans Readjustment Assistance Act (VEVRAA)
Worker Adjustment and Retraining Notification (WARN) Act

Source: Adapted from Mattingly, R. (1997). *Management of Health Information: Functions and Applications*. Albany, NY: Delmar.

phrases contained in an employer's handbook may create an implied contract or employment, thereby limiting the employer's rights to hire, fire, promote, and demote.

Placed in historical perspective, this doctrine resulted in an arrangement that was terribly lopsided at the beginning of the last century because control rested with employers to treat employees in virtually any fashion the employer wished. As a result, numerous abuses occurred. For example, many children in America routinely worked sixteen-hour days, employees injured and/or disabled as a result of their job were left to fend for themselves, employees were harassed and intimidated at will, and employees could be fired for reasons related to their religion, race, gender, national origin, and even personality. On a larger scale, employers could combine forces (so-called trusts) to fix prices and cripple normal market forces, destroying competitors, both large and small. All of these actions and more could be taken by the employer without the employee or the public possessing any real avenue through which to seek redress.

Over the last one hundred years, the at-will employment doctrine has undergone a dramatic change. Early in the last century, crusading journalists wrote articles and books detailing many of the business practices listed earlier, shocking the general public. American society responded to these types of abuses by demanding improvements in employer actions. This demand began in the context of ethics, with many in society becoming skeptical with the principle of paternalism as the basis for employer actions and embracing concepts such as autonomy, fairness, and justice as the bases for action that would benefit the employee. These demands spurred the growth of **labor unions**, groups of employees joined together to protect their jobs, seek improvements in working conditions, and create a formal method to communicate with the employer as a group that had not been accomplished individually. These demands further manifested in calls for the trusts to be dissolved (busted) and the need for government to play a role in regulating business. Society demanded that employers place value upon the ethical concepts they championed, and when many employers did not react in the manner in which society demanded, society turned to the law to accomplish its goals.

> ETHICS
>
> Ethics and law often intersect, as many ethical principles form the basis for many employment laws.

Following the advent of labor unions, Congress passed the National Labor Relations Act, one of the earliest examples of using the ethical concept of rights as the basis for an employment protection law. Also known as the Wagner Act, this law guarantees workers broad rights to organize and bargain collectively with their employer. It also provides workers with rights to engage in concerted efforts and activities such as strikes and picket lines. The Act bans employment discrimination to discourage unionization, employer domination of unions, and an employer's refusal to bargain in good faith with a union.

Once considered unusual in this area, the health care field has seen an increasing development in union activity. Some commentators directly relate this rise in union activity to a combination of the cost containment measures employed by hospitals and the decrease in reimbursement brought about by various prospective payment systems. In dealing with both issues, many hospitals have reduced the number of staff they employ and have correspondingly increased their patient-to-staff ratio. Others have focused on the lack of open communication by hospital management about noneconomic matters (e.g., an institution's goals or plans for change). In those instances where hospital management has not responded to staff complaints about dissatisfaction in the quality of work life, or has failed to communicate widely with staff, unions have filled the void.

> ETHICS
>
> A logical extension of the ethical concept of "rights" are laws that broaden protections afforded employees through the granting of legal rights.

Following the ethical concept of rights even further, Congress has enacted several civil rights laws that have broadened the protections afforded employees. For example, Title VII of the Civil Rights Act of 1964 bans discrimination in compensation, terms, and conditions of employment based on race, religion, color, sex, or national origin. The Equal Pay Act prohibits an employer from paying the workers of one sex less than the rate paid to the opposite sex for jobs substantially similar or identical in skill, effort, and responsibility and performed under similar working conditions. The Sexual Harassment Guidelines issued pursuant to Title VII require the employer to maintain a sexual-harassment-free work environment. Under the Family and Medical Leave Act (FMLA), employers must offer their employees up to a total of twelve weeks of leave during a twelve-month period for the birth of a child or the placement of a child through adoption or foster care; a serious health condition of the employee; or to care for a spouse, child, or parent with a serious health condition. The Age Discrimination in Employment Act (ADEA) bars employment discrimination against persons aged forty or older with respect to hiring, promotion, demotion, compensation, transfer, and other terms and conditions of employment. The Americans with

Disabilities Act (ADA) bars employment discrimination against qualified individuals with a disability and requires employers to provide qualified individuals with reasonable accommodations to assist them in performing the essential functions of the job, absent a financial hardship to the employer. The Worker Adjustment and Retraining Notification (WARN) Act requires employers to provide sixty days of warning before closing offices or beginning a massive layoff. Finally, the Employee Retirement Income Security Act (ERISA) prevents an employer from discharging an employee who would otherwise attain immediate vested pension rights or who exercised her rights under ERISA.

Employment protections are also provided under the Occupational Safety and Health (OSH) Act. This federal act sets mandatory standards for safety and health for all employees in general industry, maritime operations, construction, and agriculture. It requires employers to operate a place of employment that is free from recognized hazards that are likely to cause serious injury or a fatality.

Employment protections may also be provided under federal laws not traditionally targeted toward employment. For example, the Consumer Credit Protection Act protects workers whose earnings have been subjected to a wage garnishment from being fired. Similarly, an employee who exercises a public duty, such as attending federal jury duty, is protected from firing by the Jury System Improvement Act. Both the Federal Railroad Safety Act and the Federal Employer's Liability Act prohibit employers from firing an employee who files a complaint, furnishes facts, or testifies about a railroad accident. Finally, the Uniformed Services Employment and Reemployment Rights Act (USERRA) and the Military Selective Service Act offer protections to veterans and military personnel who are called up for short-term emergency duty or extended reserve duty.

Employee protections may also arise as a result of actions by the head of the executive branch. The president is the head of the executive branch in the federal system, while the governor is the head of the executive branch in the state system. Executive orders interpret, implement, or provide administrative effect to a provision of the U.S. Constitution or law. Executive orders gain the effect of law after they are published in the *Federal Register*, in the case of the federal system, or in a comparable publication on the state level. At the federal level, Executive Order 11246 bars discrimination in federal government employment and mandates each executive department and agency to maintain equal employment opportunity programs.[4]

A broad range of laws and regulations also exists at the state and local levels. Laws and regulations govern wage and hour issues, workers' compensation, and unemployment insurance. These laws and regulations also commonly influence policy decisions within an organization. Some states have chosen to create their own civil rights and occupational safety and health enforcement operations to supplement federal coverage. For instance, some states protect workers from discharge for refusing to violate criminal laws—such as participating in illegal schemes—or for observing the general public policy of a state—such as refusing to perform unethical research. Last, local governments may pass ordinances influencing the work environment, such as **living wage laws** that require employers to pay employees more than the federal minimum wage.

As made clear by the previous discussion, no one law encompasses all of the rights afforded to an employee. In many instances, multiple laws may offer protection on the same subject matter. For example, laws at the federal, state, and local levels may all offer civil rights protections to employees in a given locality. Or several laws at one level of government may cover the same subject matter—for example, multiple federal laws that provide protections to veterans. As a general rule, the strictest law is the law that takes precedence over the other laws. Accordingly, managers and supervisors must be mindful of employment laws at the federal and state levels as well as those in the local business community.

Employment Law Application

Employers who are committed to complying fully with employment laws ensure equal opportunity and safe workplace conditions for both job applicants and current employees. Applying these laws in the work context requires an understanding of the doctrines and principles involved. The following paragraphs address the major employee protection laws found in the modern work context.

Discrimination

Virtually all private employers, employment agencies, and labor organizations in the United States are affected by Title VII of the Civil Rights Act and its subsequent amendments, the Equal Employment Opportunity (EEO) Act and the Civil Rights Act of 1991. These acts protect current and potential employees from discrimination throughout all stages of employment: recruiting, selecting, compensating, orienting, training, disciplining, and discharging. Such discrimination may be based on gender or marital status, race or color, religion or national origin, age, disability or physical handicap, or genetic information. The principles of nondiscrimination were codified into law so that people would be considered on the basis of individual capacities and not on the basis of any characteristics generally attributable to a group.

Antidiscrimination laws also serve to promote the ethical concepts of justice and rights. Justice requires treating all people with fairness, while the concept of rights addresses a just claim or entitlement that others are obliged to respect. Antidiscrimination laws build on both of these concepts by creating standards that require applying fair treatment to all employees plus providing a basis upon which an employee may seek redress in a court of law.

ETHICS

Antidiscrimination laws serve to promote the ethical concepts of justice and rights.

Sex Discrimination Discrimination based on gender or marital status is commonly referred to as sex discrimination. Sex discrimination may take the form of unequal pay for equal work, sexual harassment, or discrimination with regard to childbirth leave or pregnancy-related conditions, as shown in Table 15.2. Prohibitions against sex discrimination are meant to stop hiring, promotion, and work practices that are based on gender stereotypes. Wage inequities between the genders for equal work are prohibited by Title VII, the Equal Pay Act, and the Fair Labor Standards Act. All three laws apply to jobs that are considered **substantially equal**, meaning they are performed under similar working conditions and require equal skill, effort, and responsibility. Wage differences are allowed where they reflect a legitimate, preestablished seniority system, merit system, or system that measures earning by quantity or quality of production. For example, a health care organization hired six male lab technicians in year one and four female lab technicians in year five. Although all ten lab technicians currently perform the same job, the six male lab technicians

Table 15.2 Forms of Sex Discrimination
Unequal pay for equal work
Sexual harassment
Discrimination in childbirth leave
Discrimination in pregnancy-related conditions

receive greater hourly pay rates than the four female lab technicians because of their seniority and number of years with the organization.

Sexual discrimination also encompasses sexual harassment. **Sexual harassment** refers to unwelcome sexual advances, requests for sexual favors, and verbal or physical conduct of a sexual nature made in return for job benefits, promotions, or continued employment. This type of sexual harassment is considered ***quid pro quo*** sexual harassment or "this for that." Sexual harassment may also arise in a hostile working environment. In a **hostile work environment**, the unwelcome sexual conduct must be sufficiently pervasive or severe enough to alter the terms or conditions of employment. Examples of a hostile work environment include sharing sexually explicit photos, making sex-related or gender-demeaning jokes, or repeatedly requesting dates from a person who clearly is not interested. One instance of these examples is generally not enough to be considered a hostile work environment; rather, a combination or repetition of these and other examples may bring a workplace to the level of a hostile work environment. Claims of sexual harassment may be based on either the quid pro quo or hostile work environment, or both. Furthermore, sexual harassment can occur between people of different or the same genders.

Employers seeking to prevent and eliminate sexual harassment can do so by developing a comprehensive policy, publicizing that policy, investigating any complaints promptly and adequately, and taking action appropriate to the situation. Practical actions—which include disseminating written materials indicating that sexual harassment of any kind is not tolerated; training managers, supervisors, and employees in identifying sexual harassment; and providing mechanisms to address complaints in confidence and without reprisals—offer support to the premise that an employer or organization is complying with the law.

Another form of sexual discrimination involves childbirth leave or pregnancy-related conditions. The Pregnancy Discrimination Act bars discrimination based on pregnancy, childbirth, and related medical conditions. The Family Medical Leave Act (FMLA) allows an employee to take up to twelve weeks of unpaid leave in any twelve-month period for the birth, adoption, of foster care of a child; to care for a child, spouse, or parent with a serious health condition; or to recuperate from a serious health condition that makes it impossible to work. A **serious health condition** is any injury, illness, impairment, or physical or mental condition requiring either inpatient care at a hospital, hospice, or residential medical care facility, or continuing treatment by a health care provider. Employers are permitted under the FMLA to seek medical certification concerning the need for leave when the leave request involves a serious health condition. Whereas the Pregnancy Discrimination Act applies only to women, the FMLA applies to both women and men.

Racial, Religious, and National Origin Discrimination Discrimination based on race or color constitutes unlawful discrimination under Title VII of the Civil Rights Act. Immutable characteristics of race, such as skin color, hair texture, or certain facial features, cannot be used by an employer to consider job applicants or current employees in any stage, term, condition, or privilege of employment. Such discrimination may take many forms, including harassment. Examples of harassment include the use of ethnic slurs, racial jokes, offensive or derogatory comments, or other verbal or physical conduct based on an individual's race or color. Title VII also bars discrimination based on a condition that predominantly affects one race, absent a showing of a business necessity and a relationship to a job. For example, sickle cell anemia is a condition that occurs predominantly in African Americans. Without a business necessity and a relationship to the job, an employer's policy excluding individuals with sickle cell anemia from the workplace would violate Title VII.

Religious discrimination in employment is barred pursuant to the provisions of Title VII, making it illegal to consider adherence to a particular faith the basis on which to deny an applicant a job.

Furthermore, Title VII requires employers to reasonably accommodate the religious practices of employees and job applicants unless doing so causes an undue hardship. Religious practices or beliefs include moral or ethical beliefs concerning what is right or wrong that are sincerely held with the strength of traditional religious views. The employer may not require the individual employee or applicant to establish or prove the truth, validity, or reasonableness of her religious beliefs; rather, the employer must attempt to provide reasonable accommodation if the beliefs are sincerely held by the employee or applicant. The burden of identifying that a conflict exists between the employee's or applicant's religious beliefs and a job requirement rests on the employee or applicant. For example, an employer who is notified by an employee that her religion requires worship on workdays must make reasonable accommodation for the employee's religious belief unless to do so would impose an undue hardship.

Title VII of the Civil Rights Act bars discrimination based on national origin, including birthplace, ancestry, culture, or linguistic characteristics common to a specific ethnic group. Such discrimination may include denying employment based on an individual's accent or manner of speaking or harassment through the use of ethnic slurs and other verbal or physical conduct relating to an individual's national origin. Furthermore, the Immigration Reform and Control Act prohibits discrimination based on whether the person is or is not a U.S. citizen. Together, these two laws serve as the basis for protecting workers from discrimination based on national origin. For example, a rule requiring that employees speak only English on the job may violate Title VII unless the employer shows that the requirement is necessary for conducting business. An employer who conducts business with the public may, however, require employees to be fluent in English so that they can interact with customers. The difference is that English is not mandated as the *only* language an employee may speak on the job.

Age Discrimination As with the examples of discrimination previously addressed, federal law offers protections to workers who are forty years of age or older. The Age Discrimination in Employment Act (ADEA) bars discrimination because of a person's age and applies during both the employment and preemployment stages, making it unlawful to include age preferences, limitations, or specifications in job notices or advertisements. As a general premise, an employer may not make employment decisions in which the employee's age is a substantial factor. This prohibition is qualified, however, since the ADEA allows employers to consider age if they can show that age is a bona fide occupational **qualification** reasonably necessary to the normal operation of the particular business.

The Older Works Benefit Protection Act (OWBPA) bars discrimination in benefits because of a person's age. The OWBPA requires employers who request employees to sign releases or waivers in connection with an offer of early retirement to do so in writing, to provide the employee with sufficient time to consider the offer, and to provide the employee with the opportunity to seek advice from a lawyer. Further, the OWBPA provides the employee a time window in which to repudiate an offer of early retirement to which the employee previously agreed. Large-scale early retirement programs and mass termination programs that involve releases or waivers require even more from employers; the employer must provide a longer time frame for employees to consider the agreement and provide those employees with data concerning the ages of all individuals in the same job classification who are not eligible for these programs.

Disability Discrimination Disability discrimination is covered under both the Rehabilitation Act and the Americans with Disabilities Act (ADA). Both acts apply to employees, job applicants, customers, and other visitors to an organization, as well as to a wide range of businesses that serve the public. Within the employment context, these acts operate to protect employees and job applicants from discrimination based on a disability, the perception of a disability, or a past record of impairment, such as an illness that has been cured, controlled, or is in remission.

Evaluating the applicability of the ADA to a given situation is a three-step process: determining qualifications, disability, and reasonable accommodation. This process is illustrated in Table 15.3. Initially, the employer must determine that the individual in question is qualified for a position. To meet the definition of qualifications, an individual must possess the requisite skills, education, experience, and licensure requirements for the job. This means that the individual can perform the essential functions of the job with or without reasonable accommodation. Essential functions are those duties that are so fundamental to the position that the job cannot be performed adequately without them. Being qualified also means that the individual possess the required education, degrees, certificates, professional licenses, and any other qualifications, along with the knowledge, skills, and abilities to perform the job. The burden rests on the individual to demonstrate that she possesses the requisite job qualifications and can perform the essential functions. If the individual cannot perform the essential functions or show that she possesses the requisite job qualifications, she is not considered qualified for the job and the ADA evaluation process ends.

It is not always apparent whether an individual will be able to perform the essential functions of the job. In those instances, medical information will be necessary. When requesting medical information, the employer should identify the essential functions of the job and provide a written list of those functions to the individual's health care provider. The individual's health care provider should respond with advice concerning whether the individual can perform the essential functions with or without reasonable accommodation. If the health care provider recommends reasonable accommodation, the health care provider should address specific suggestions for reasonable accommodation in response.

After determining that the individual is qualified, the employer must decide whether the individual possesses a disability. **Disability** refers to a physical or mental impairment that substantially limits one or more of the major life activities of an employee, a record of such an impairment, or being regarded as having such an impairment. Guidance for this determination can be obtained from the regulations of the Equal Employment Opportunity Commission (EEOC), which indicate that the issue turns on (1) the nature and severity of the impairment, (2) the duration or expected duration of the impairment, and (3) the permanent or long-term impact of the impairment.[5] The EEOC has already established certain impairments as constituting disabilities, such as cerebral palsy, epilepsy, muscular dystrophy, mental retardation, and HIV/AIDS infection, to name only a few. The burden rests on the individual to show that her impairment is a disability. Not all impairments constitute disabilities since they may not substantially limit one or more major life activities. The employer may also consider corrective or mitigating measures when determining the existence of a disability. If there is no disability, the ADA evaluation process ends.

The most challenging aspect for an employer complying with the ADA is determining the reasonable accommodations for qualified individuals with disabilities without incurring undue hardship to the employer. A **reasonable accommodation** is any change in the work environment or in the manner in which things are customarily done that enables a qualified person with a disability to have equal employment opportunities. As with the question of disability, medical documentation may be

Table 15.3 Application of the ADA

1. Determining Qualification	Does the person possess the requisite qualifications for the job? Can the person do the job?
2. Determining Disability	Is a disability present? If so, what is the disability?
3. Determining Reasonable Accommodation	What accommodations are workable and affordable for the employer to make?

necessary to determine the individual's functional limitations. A **functional limitation** is a physical or mental limitation of a major life activity caused by a disability. An analysis of a functional limitation is important to the extent it bears a relationship with a workplace barrier. A **workplace barrier** is any workplace obstacle, whether physical or procedural, that prevents an employee from performing the duties of the job, whether those duties are considered essential or marginal. Work areas where the duties of the job are performed, such as an office or cubicle, should be examined for potential barriers. Nonwork areas frequented by the employee, such as conference rooms, entryways, and lounges, should also be considered. If a workplace barrier exists that limits the individual's ability to perform the job, and a reasonable accommodation would overcome that barrier, the employer should provide the reasonable accommodation, absent undue hardship to the employer. **Undue hardship** refers to a specific accommodation that creates significant difficulty or expense for the employer. The employer may consider the nature and cost of the requested accommodation plus its impact on the employer's operations when considering the issue of undue hardship.

Under the ADA, an employer is not required to propose reasonable accommodations but only provide them, making the employee or job applicant bear the burden of suggesting workable and affordable changes to the workplace or hiring process. If it appears that the individual needs an accommodation, the employer may initiate the process by asking whether the individual wants an accommodation. After receiving such a request, the employer should confirm the request in writing and make a determination of whether the individual is both qualified and disabled before addressing the question of reasonable accommodation. The steps of the reasonable accommodation process are listed in Table 15.4.

The search for potential reasonable accommodations will vary based on the circumstances of the situation. In an ideal situation, the employer and the requesting individual work together to identify the potential reasonable accommodations. Reasonable accommodations generally do not include personal-use items since they are also required for the individual's use in a nonemployment setting. Examples of personal-use items usually not considered as a reasonable accommodation to be supplied by the employer include eyeglasses, hearing aids, wheelchairs, and crutches. Examples of reasonable accommodations that an employer may provide are listed in Table 15.5.

Table 15.4 Reasonable Accommodation Process

Submission of Request	From employee or job applicant identifying the disability and seeking an accommodation; employer confirms the request in writing.
Determining an Individual's Qualification	Does the individual possess the requisite qualifications for the job? Can the individual perform the essential functions of the job?
Substantiating the Disability and Need for Accommodation	Does the individual have a physical or mental impairment that substantially limits a major life activity? Do the individual's functional limitations due to disability relate to a workplace barrier?
Potential Reasonable Accommodations	Employer and individual search for and evaluate potential reasonable accommodations.
Select and Provide Reasonable Accommodations	Employer selects, funds, and provides reasonable accommodation; employer and individual monitor effectiveness of reasonable accommodation.

Table 15.5 Examples of Reasonable Accommodations
Supplying and/or altering office equipment or devices, including automation and information technology
Altering or modifying the workplace, including lights and chairs
Relocating a job within the office
Telecommuting, provided that the employer has adopted a formal written telecommuting policy
Obtaining a reader or interpreter services
Changing the means by which instructions are provided
Restructuring the job
Relocating the individual to another existing vacant position for which the individual is qualified and can perform the essential functions

Once potential reasonable accommodations are identified, the employer should evaluate them to determine whether they will overcome the workplace barrier and also whether the costs constitute an undue hardship. An employee's preference for a particular reasonable accommodation may be considered, but an employer is not bound to provide a preferred reasonable accommodation if the one provided is effective. Ultimately, it is the employer's right and responsibility to choose the accommodations it determines are the most appropriate in the given situation. If no potential reasonable accommodations exist that address the issues of workplace barrier and undue hardship, the ADA evaluation process ends.

Once a decision on reasonable accommodations is reached, the employer should notify the individual or her designee in writing. This writing should address whether or not a reasonable accommodation will be provided, what the reasonable accommodation will be, and when the reasonable accommodation will be available. If the employer decides to deny the request for reasonable accommodation, the writing should provide the reasoning for the decision. Once a reasonable accommodation is implemented, the employer should test the effectiveness of the accommodation, assess whether it meets expectations, and make any adjustments as needed. Continued monitoring is necessary, because some individuals may no longer need an accommodation if their circumstances change.

In summary, accommodations assist qualified disabled employees and job applicants by allowing them to remain functional and independent in the workplace. Absent undue hardship, the employer should try to provide accommodation, within reason and within a specified time period, for a qualified disabled employee to perform essential functions of the job or for a qualified disabled job applicant to complete the application and interview process.

Genetic Discrimination Discrimination based on genetic information is a development that straddled the end of the last quarter of the twentieth century and the beginning of the twenty-first century. That discrimination arose because of the virtual explosion of information gained through medical research, particularly information arising from the sequencing of the human genome as part of the Human Genome Project. This new information greatly accelerated the development of genetic tests that could identify the role of genes involved in both common and uncommon diseases. As tests became more sophisticated, they could be used to identify the specific gene involved in a disease already contracted by a patient and to predict the onset or likelihood of a future disease occurring in an individual patient.

It is the use of the information provided by these tests that resulted in the need for laws to address misuse of genetic information. For some employers, the onset or even likelihood of an employee contracting a particular disease was cause for concern, not only with regard to the effect the disease would have on the employee, and potentially her coworkers, but also on the potential cost increases to employer-provided insurance coverage. Such concerns sometimes resulted in employers reviewing family medical history or genetic tests of employees who participated in an employer-sponsored wellness program. Depending on the information learned, the employer may have discriminated against the employee by changing the employee's work status, terms, or conditions of employment, or even fired the employee.

Over time, such concerns gradually moved beyond employees to include potential employees, resulting in some employers requiring job applicants to provide samples of bodily fluids as part of a preemployment **physical examination** so that the fluids could be subject to genetic testing. Where genetic tests revealed the presence or even likelihood of a job applicant contracting a genetic-based disease, some of these employers considered that information when determining whether to offer employment to the applicant. In some instances, the employer refused to hire a job applicant otherwise qualified for the open position.

In sporadic instances, employees have sued employers for requiring preemployment genetic screening. In *Norman-Bloodsaw v. Lawrence Berkeley Laboratory*,[6] employees of a research facility sued, claiming that nonconsensual testing for medical and genetic information violated their civil rights. The laboratory had tested each employee for syphilis, sickle cell trait, and pregnancy without the employee's knowledge or consent as part of an employer-sponsored health exam. The court ruled in favor of the employees, allowing them to proceed with their case alleging Title VII and privacy violations.

HIPAA

The Health Insurance Portability and Accountability Act was the first effort at the national level to address the misuse of genetic information by insurance companies.

It was these actions and others that resulted in the growing recognition for law to play a role in eliminating discrimination based on genetic information. Efforts began at the state level, resulting in laws that varied widely in their scope and degree of protection.[7] The U.S. Congress addressed the issue in a narrow manner in the Health Insurance Portability and Accountability Act of 1996 (HIPAA), imposing restrictions on insurers who had previously used genetic information to set premiums and determine eligibility for benefits in group health plans.[8] At the federal level, an executive order prohibits departments and agencies of the executive branch from using genetic information in any hiring or promotion action.[9] The order also prohibits the departments and agencies from requesting or requiring genetic test results from applicants or current employees. Not until twelve years later did Congress again address the issue, enacting the Genetic Information Nondiscrimination Act of 2008 (GINA).[10] GINA provides protections against misuse of genetic information in insurance and the workplace. Specific protections provided by GINA are included in Table 15.6.

GINA

The Genetic Information Nondiscrimination Act strengthens efforts at the federal level to protect genetic information from misuse in both the employment and insurance contexts.

The U.S. Congress has authorized the Equal Employment Opportunity Commission (EEOC) to create regulations implementing GINA. The EEOC is further authorized to consider discrimination due to genetic information as an unlawful employment practice in violation of federal law.

Table 15.6 Protections Afforded under the Genetic Information Nondiscrimination
Prohibits both individual and group health insurers from using an individual's genetic information in determining eligibility or setting premiums.
Prohibits both individual and group health insurers from requiring or requesting that an individual undergo a genetic test or collecting genetic information as part of enrollment in a plan.
Prohibits employers or employment agencies from using a person's genetic information in decision making, including decisions involving hiring, firing, job assignments, or other terms and conditions of employment.
Prohibits employers or employment agencies from requesting, requiring, or purchasing genetic information about individuals or their family members.
Prohibits labor unions from excluding or expelling or otherwise adversely affecting the status of a union member because of genetic information with respect to the member.
Source: 42 U.S.C. §§ 2000ff et seq. (2019).

Remedies currently available to victims of discrimination under other antidiscrimination laws are also available under GINA. Additional information concerning GINA can be found in Chapter 7, Bioethics Issues, and Chapter 11, Specialized Patient Records.

Workplace Protections

In addition to the workplace protections offered by antidiscrimination laws, employee rights are provided under laws and regulations governing health, safety, pay, hours, and conditions of the workplace. These laws and regulations offer protections to employees in the form of both prohibitions on certain practices and entitlement to certain conditions or treatment in the workplace.

Many of the laws addressing workplace protections find their basis in the ethical theory of utilitarianism. **Utilitarianism** proposes that everyone, including persons, organizations, and society in general, should make choices promoting conditions that would allow an individual to seek the greatest amount of happiness or benefits. Laws offering workplace protections are consistent with utilitarianism because these laws promote conditions that are desirable and bring about good ends for the largest amount of people.

ETHICS

Utilitarianism is consistent with many workplace protection laws because both seek to promote desirable conditions that benefit the greatest number of people.

Health and Safety Workplace health and safety issues are governed primarily by the Occupational Safety and Health Act. This Act created the Occupational Safety and Health Administration (OSHA) under the U.S. Department of Labor as the central agency charged with enforcing safety precautions in the workplace. OSHA covers virtually every private employer in the United States and issues regulations governing workplace safety. In general, these regulations guide employers in providing a workplace free of dangers that may cause physical harm to those who work there.

Many states also address workplace safety issues through their own OSHA laws and regulations, some of which may be more stringent than the federal OSHA requirements. In addition, a large number of states have laws addressing the use, storage, and handling of hazardous substances in the workplace. Many state and local government workers are governed by OSHA laws and regulations issued at the state level rather than the federal level.

To comply with federal and state OSHA requirements, an employer must develop and implement a health and safety program to achieve employee protections. Recommended components of a health and safety program are listed in Table 15.7. Within the health care environment, some employees engaged in direct patient care may encounter hazardous work conditions, particularly in the context of exposure to communicable diseases. Health care providers can minimize risks to employees by operating effective infection control practices, forming effective infection control committees, and applying safety precautions such as those involving the handling of bodily fluids. The workplace is primarily an office environment in the health information management field. Typically, an office environment does not pose the same hazardous work conditions as those present in a direct patient care environment. Nonetheless, efforts should be made toward an ergonomics education program that addresses both workstation design and employee work habits. Such efforts may alleviate repetitive stress disorders such as carpal tunnel syndrome and tendonitis. Health and safety checklists and report forms provide the means to identify and correct problems. Specific hazardous conditions, such as those created by secondhand smoke, can be addressed by policies that prohibit introduction of the hazard into the workplace (e.g., smoking prohibition in all interior spaces and any outdoor area located in front of air-intake ducts).

Certain record-keeping and reporting requirements are borne by employers as a result of OSHA regulations. These include keeping injury and illness logs, safety training records, and medical records of employees who have been exposed to hazardous substances or harmful physical agents.

Hours, Pay, and Conditions of Employment Several federal statutes address the hours, pay, and conditions under which employees work. The Federal Labor Standards Act (FLSA) offers workers specific protections against excessive work hours and substandard wages. Often referred to as the "minimum wage law," the FLSA establishes the minimum wage that must be paid to employees. The FLSA also establishes the maximum number of hours that an employee may work in a given time frame. For example, the FLSA mandates a forty-hour workweek and includes overtime pay provisions for those employees who work in excess of forty hours. The FLSA contains a specific exception to the general forty-hour requirement where health care workers are concerned. Under this exception, an eighty-hour pay period over two weeks may be used, with overtime pay applicable to hours worked in excess of eighty hours and in excess of eight hours per day. Overtime pay is generally calculated at one and a half times the regular rate at which an employee is normally compensated.

Table 15.7 Recommended Components of a Health and Safety Program
Clear designation of responsibilities of management and line staff
Provisions for conducting inspections and abating hazards, including health and safety checklists
Establishment of a safety committee, designation of a safety manager, or identification of a safety liaison with the building landlord
Training of all management and line staff, including health and safety education
Record keeping and reporting
Self-evaluation of the health and safety program

Some employees are considered exempt from the minimum wage/maximum hour provisions of the FLSA and are referred to as **exempt employees**. Although the subject of much litigation, employees fall under the exempt category if they are paid a salary as opposed to wages, exercise discretion in performing their work, are primarily responsible for managing a business or department, routinely manage others, and possess the authority to hire and fire other employees. Conversely, employees who are paid wages as opposed to salary; do not exercise discretion in performing their work; are not responsible for managing a business, department, or other employees; and do not possess the authority to hire and fire other employees do not fall under the exempt category. Many positions that are classified as executive, administrative, or professional are considered exempt under the FLSA.

The FLSA's overtime provisions place an obligation upon the employer to exercise control over the workplace in terms of the total number of hours an employee works. In a traditional work environment where employees work face-to-face with supervisors, management can exercise this control more easily. Exercising this control in nontraditional work environments, however, such as ones involving telecommuting, is far more difficult; the supervisor may be unaware of any additional hours the employee is working at home beyond the scheduled hourly total. Nonetheless, the same principle applies to telecommuting contexts as to the traditional work environment: if the employer knows or has reason to believe that the employee is continuing to work beyond the amount requested by the employer, those additional hours must be counted as overtime and are subject to overtime pay. This principle applies because the law places the burden upon the employer to exercise control over the work environment, whether that environment is a traditional one or not.

Equality of pay is the subject of two federal laws. The Equal Pay Act (EPA) also provides wage protections, specifically for workers who perform the same or substantially similar jobs. Subsumed within the definition of wages are fringe benefits such as bonuses, expense accounts, profit-sharing plans, and leave benefits. Assuming that jobs are substantially similar or identical in terms of skill, effort, and responsibility, the EPA requires equal pay between the sexes. Not all pay differences are attributable to matters other than sex—such as seniority or merit pay systems—or are based on quantity or quality of production. The Lilly Ledbetter Fair Pay Act of 2009 addresses when discrimination in compensation begins to be considered a wrong that can be addressed under federal law. This Act allows a person who was compensated in a discriminatory fashion to bring a lawsuit when the discriminatory practice first begins or whenever the employee's compensation is affected by the employer's discriminatory compensation decision. This last phrase is important because each paycheck received by the employee could be affected by the discriminatory compensation decision of the employer, meaning that an employee could be discriminated against in pay for years before discovering the problem and still be able to sue based on the last paycheck where evidence of discriminatory compensation is present.

Conditions of employment are addressed by the FMLA, the Employee Retirement Income Security Act (ERISA), and federal laws governing unionization of the workforce. The FMLA allows eligible employees to take up to twelve weeks of unpaid leave during any twelve-month period for the birth or adoption of a child, placement of a child in foster care, or for a serious health condition of the employee or the employee's spouse, child, or parent. Additionally, the FMLA provides that the employer must allow the employee to return to the same or a similar position as held before taking leave. The employer must also continue to make the same benefit contributions during the leave period as were required before the employee took leave. Many states have laws similar in scope to the FMLA, as do local municipalities in the form of leave ordinances.

ERISA addresses employee pensions and other benefit programs. ERISA offers protections by establishing minimum standards for pension and welfare plans and barring discriminatory treatment of persons with regard to their entitlement and use of benefits. For ERISA purpose, welfare plans include health and the life insurance plans. ERISA does not require employers to establish pension and welfare plans; it merely regulates those employers who do establish them.

Federal law governing unionization of the workforce was designed initially to protect employees from abuses by their employers. Additional federal laws granted protections to employers from the excesses of unions and to union members from unions themselves. These protections were addressed through the creation of the National Labor Relations Board (NLRB). The NLRB establishes fair **collective bargaining** procedures and identifies unfair labor practices. The NLRB also oversees labor union representation elections and hears disputes related to labor law. Many unions work to negotiate better working conditions, benefits, and employment contracts for their members. Unions also work to resolve workplace disputes through structured grievance procedures.

While federal law addresses many conditions of employment, state law addresses others, including workers' compensation and unemployment compensation programs. Both programs are intricate and complex, making an extensive discussion of them beyond the scope of this chapter. An overview of each program follows.

Workers' compensation is a program designed to replace income and provide medical expense to employees who are injured, become ill, or die as a result of their jobs. This program not only benefits employees and their dependents but also offers protection to employers from being sued for those injuries, illnesses, or deaths that occur on the job and are covered by the workers' compensation program. The benefits paid to employees are financed by employer contributions. Although national in scope, most employees are governed by workers' compensation programs that arise from state law and are administered by individual states. If a federal civilian employee is involved, work injury benefits are governed by the Federal Employees Compensation Act. Accordingly, great variations exist with regard to who is eligible for benefits, what conditions are covered, and the proper process for filing claims. General guidelines addressing how to handle an employee injury in the workplace are provided in Table 15.8.

Unemployment insurance is a program designed to provide regular income to those who have lost their jobs. Funding for this program comes from a tax on employers; unlike workers' compensation, this tax is paid by the employer to both state and federal governmental entities who jointly run the program. Unemployment insurance covers a broad spectrum of the workforce, as long as minimum requirements are met. Some employees are disqualified from receiving benefits due to their behavior on the job or because of the time they left employment. Many states have strict rules with regard to filing a claim, the time periods before receiving unemployment income, or appealing a benefit decision.

Conditions of employment also encompass the concept of employee privacy. This concept is broad based and includes such issues as the use of drug and lie detector tests and the surveillance and monitoring techniques available for use with telephone calls, voice mail, computer files, and electronic mail. The perspective on employee privacy is, in essence, a contrast between two opposing interests. While employees may expect to possess as many rights to privacy in the

Table 15.8 Workplace Injury Guidelines
Report the accident to a supervisor immediately.
Document the circumstances surrounding the accident and provide a copy of the document to the supervisor.
Obtain a written account of the accident from eyewitnesses, if any.
Obtain medical attention if the situation warrants.
Complete any paperwork requirements of the organization's human resources department.

workplace as they do outside of the workplace, many employers believe that they themselves possess legitimate interests in using these tests and techniques as a way to maintain a safe, harassment-free work environment. Federal and state laws generally fall somewhere in the middle of these two views, offering limited protections to employees while granting employers some authority to engage in these activities.

> **HIPAA**
>
> Some employers are considered covered entities under HIPAA, subjecting them to the provisions of the Privacy Rule.

Employee privacy is also implicated by the regulations of the Health Insurance Portability and Accountability Act (HIPAA). Some employers are considered covered entities under HIPAA, making them subject to virtually all provisions of the Privacy Rule. Other employers are not considered covered entities per se but fall within protections of the Privacy Rule because they offer some form of a health plan or group health plan as a benefit to their employees. Unless the plan is self-administered, with less than fifty participants, the HIPAA Privacy Rule will apply to the health information received by those employers pursuant to such a plan. Accordingly, issues related to marketing restrictions and the use and disclosure of protected health information become concerns for employers who are not considered covered entities per se. In both of these situations, the Privacy Rule requires employers to establish firewalls or procedural and operational separations between health-related functions and general employment-related functions. Failure to protect such information may result in sanctions or other penalties. Additional information concerning the HIPAA Privacy Rule can be found in Chapter 8, Patient Record Requirements; Chapter 10, Access to Health Information; and Chapter 13, Information Systems.

Social Media

One emerging issue in employment law is the role of social media and the duties employers have to address issues raised by employee postings in social media. As a generality, employee postings are protected forms of free speech. This allows employees to post to a vast audience their views and feelings about a multitude of issues, including their employer. Employers vary in the manner in which they monitor employee postings, with some employers actively monitoring social media sites as part of their risk management program and others not monitoring at all unless a matter is brought to their attention by a third party. As a general rule, employers monitor employee social media postings to determine if the employer's positive online image is maintained and to comply with antidiscrimination laws.

A health care provider's positive online image contributes to the health care provider's reputation in the community. Negative statements in social media by the health care provider's own employees may not only cause reputational harm but may influence patients not to use the health care provider for any future care. A reduction in patient load may have serious financial consequences for the health care provider.

Similarly, employers have a duty to address discriminatory and harassing conduct that has a bearing on the workplace, even if that conduct occurs outside the workplace setting. Where that discriminatory or harassing conduct involves postings on social media by the health care provider's employees, many employers would consider these postings as contributing to a hostile work environment. Once aware of this conduct, employers have a duty to respond to it.

The responses employed should be those which are contained in the health care provider's policies and procedures concerning social media. These policies and procedures should outline what conduct is prohibited, such as disclosing protected health information or posting photographs of patients without their consent, and what conduct is discouraged, such as disparaging comments about the employer. These policies and procedures should outline the consequences to the employee in the event that the employee engages in prohibited actions, including whether disciplinary action will be considered. Disciplinary action can range from verbal warning to termination to reporting of misconduct to a professional licensing authority or association.

CRITICAL THINKING

When an individual accepts employment with an organization, consider whether the individual voluntarily agrees to any restrictions on social media use imposed by the employer such as the ones discussed in this chapter. Even if the individual knows what the restrictions may entail, is the individual in a position to negotiate the terms of any such restrictions?

Ethics Application

While ethics may serve as the basis for many of the laws governing employment, a portion of the application of ethics in the workplace takes the form of codes of conduct and programs that incorporate the values found within these codes into policies and procedures. **Codes of conduct**, sometimes referred to as codes of ethics, are written lists of a profession's values and standards of conduct. Extensive materials concerning codes of conduct are contained in Chapter 6, Ethical Decisions and Challenges. The importance of ethics and codes of conduct to the workplace is in their application, as opposed to their existence as documents in a manual.

ETHICS

Multiple ways exist to apply ethics to the workplace, and an organization can choose any combination of ways as a means to emphasize the role of ethics in the workplace.

The application of ethics/codes of conduct in the workplace is seen in the policies and procedures of the organization and the actions that are taken based on them. For example, an organization may value diversity in the workforce and align its policies and procedures to match this value. This may require the employer to recruit from a wide applicant pool and reach out to communities who are currently underrepresented in the organization. After hiring a more diverse workforce, the organization may create workgroups that reflect diversity and delegate decision-making authority to them, reaching farther down the organizational hierarchy than in the past. Research has shown that "the more varied the group, the better the decision-making capability and the more solid and reliable the results."[11] By following such an approach, the organization tasks the workgroup to take initiative, assume risks, and be accountable and responsible for work performed and products produced. Solid and reliable decisions that result from this approach in turn benefit the organization.

The application of ethics in the workplace can also be seen by the training offered to an organization's staff on the subject of ethics. This training may focus on the organization's code of conduct, on the policies and procedures that incorporate the code, or on both. This training can be a formal program focused on ethics/codes of conduct that is offered as part of new employee orientation and as a refresher at different times throughout an employee's tenure with the organization. Alternatively, ethics/codes of conduct may be presented as an element of each training session offered by the organization, regardless of the topic of the training session. In that manner, the employee learns that the organization has considered the ethical aspects of each policy or procedure it issues and has incorporated it into the behaviors expected of employees. Under either approach, the organization stresses the value it places on ethics/codes of conduct, sending the message to employees that it values ethics/codes of conduct.

Application of ethics in the workplace may be present as a dimension in performance appraisals. Whether falling within the category of judgment or business ethics, a portion of an appraisal can address whether and how the employee applies ethical standards to the workplace. Elements addressing ethics can be taken directly from the organization's code of conduct, its values statement, or can be defined in advance of an appraisal by working with the organization's human resource department. Examples of elements that may be used in performance appraisals are listed in Table 15.9. Each of these elements can be rated and explained to the employee as part of the performance appraisal. Specific deviations from the organization's ethical expectations can be addressed, with goals set for future performance.

Each of these three areas, incorporating ethics into policies and procedures, training staff on the role of ethics in the workplace, and including ethical issues into performance appraisals, is an example of applying ethics in the workplace. Organizations need not stop at these three examples but may combine these and other examples together to form a comprehensive ethics and compliance program for application in the workplace. According to the Federal Sentencing Guidelines for Organizations, a comprehensive ethics and compliance program incorporates six components, all of which are listed in Table 15.10.

For those organizations that can demonstrate a clear effort to operate ethically, but nonetheless violated the law in some way, the Sentencing Guidelines indicate the potential for lower penalties to the organization.

Table 15.9 Ethics Elements in a Performance Appraisal
Does the employee treat others with respect?
Does the employee keep commitments?
Does the employee inspire the trust of others?
Does the employee work with integrity?
Does the employee model ethical behavior?
Does the employee uphold the values of the organization?

Table 15.10 Components of a Comprehensive Ethics and Compliance Program
Written standards of ethical workplace conduct
Means for an employee to anonymously report violations of ethics standards
Orientation or training on ethical workplace conduct
A specific office, telephone line, e-mail address, or website where employees can get advice about ethics-related issues
Evaluation of ethical conduct as part of regular performance appraisals
Discipline for employees who commit ethics violations
Source: Federal Sentencing Guidelines for Organizations § 8B2.1 (2019).

CONCLUSION

Many of the protections afforded employees in the modern workplace had their beginnings in ethics, particularly the values held by society. As society's demands became more sophisticated, a more formal approach evolved: the creation of laws granting legal rights in the employment setting. Many of the protections offered in employment law address issues of discrimination. Further protections are offered in the areas of health, safety, pay, hours, and conditions of employment. In combination, these many protections have changed how both employers and employees view their respective roles in the employment context.

CASE STUDY

Anywhere Hospital recently experienced negative publicity in the local community because of some unethical actions taken by a few of its employees concerning protected health information. The hospital subsequently took disciplinary action against those employees. Hospital administration has asked you to serve as part of a task group to address ethical issues in the workplace. The work product your task force produces will be used to prevent recurrence of these unethical actions. What areas will you recommend the task force to focus upon?

REVIEW QUESTIONS

1. What is employment?
2. How does the employer–employee relationship differ from the employer–independent contractor relationship?
3. What does the at-will employment doctrine allow employers and employees to do?
4. How can the content of an employer's handbook affect the employment-at-will doctrine?
5. What is a labor union and what does it do?
6. How do antidiscrimination laws apply to ethics?
7. What is the most challenging aspect of the ADA for an employer to comply with? Why?
8. What legal protections are afforded at the federal level to protect genetic information?
9. Why would an employer consider it appropriate to monitor an employee's social media postings?
10. What role do ethics play in workplace protections?
11. What is a workers' compensation program and who is benefited by it?

ENRICHMENT ACTIVITY

Search the Internet for information about union participation in the health care field. Note the other types of employees who share the same union as health care workers. Determine from the websites the types of workplace issues the unions are addressing in the health care field. Report this information to your instructor, making sure to provide the appropriate Web address for each site.

NOTES

1. This chapter is based in large measure upon a portion of Chapter 12, Human Resource Management, in my text *Today's Health Information Management: An Integrated Approach*, 2nd ed. (Delmar Cengage Learning, 2014).

2. Many of the definitions addressed in this section may be found in *Webster's New World College Dictionary* (4th ed.) (2001). Foster City, CA: IDG Books Worldwide, Inc. Because the Internal Revenue Service (IRS) is the governmental agency responsible for determining whether monies should be routinely withheld from employee paychecks, its classification of the different types of employees is also used in this discussion; see http://www.irs.ustreas.gov.

3. The Immigration Reform and Control Act (IRCA) of 1986 obligates every employer to verify, within three days of hire, the identity and employment authorization of every employee hired. 8 U.S.C. § 1324–1365 (2019).

4. Exec. Order No. 11246, 30 Fed. Reg. 12319 (1965).

5. 42 C.F.R. § 1630 (2019).

6. 135 F.3d 1260 (9th Cir. 1998).

7. ARIZ. STAT. § 12-2802 (2019) (treats genetic testing results as confidential); CAL. CIVIL CODE § 56.17 (West 2019) (nontherapeutic purposes ban); CAL. HEALTH & SAFETY CODE § 1374.7 (West 2019) (genetic discrimination ban); COLO. REV. STAT. § 10-3-1104.7 (2019) (preventing use of genetic information from being used to deny health insurance); CONN. GEN. STAT. § 38a-816 (2019) (defines as an unfair and deceptive business practice for an insurer to refuse to insure, limit insuring, or charge a different rate because of genetic information); 215 ILL. COMP. STAT. ANN. 5/356v (West 2019) (prevents misuse of genetic information by all employers in hiring or firing decisions and by insurance companies in coverage decisions); KAN. STAT. ANN. § 44-1009(9) (2019) (defines as an unlawful practice for an employer to seek to obtain, obtain, or use genetic screening or testing information of an employee or prospective employee or subject an employee or prospective employee to testing); MD. CODE ANN., INS. § 27-909 (2019) (prohibits use of genetic test results in insurance underwriting); MO. REV. STAT. § 375.1303 (2019) (prohibits insurers from requesting genetic information, inquiring into whether a person has taken or refused a genetic test, and inquiring into the results of any genetic test); N.M. STAT. ANN. § 24-21-1 to -7 (2019) (prohibits discrimination by an insurer against a person or family member on basis of genetic information); OR. REV. STAT. § 659A.303 (2019) (prohibits employers from obtaining, seeking to obtain, or using genetic information of an employee or prospective employee); VA. CODE ANN. § 40.1-28.7:1 (2019) (prohibits employers from refusing to hire, failing to promote, discharging, or otherwise adversely affecting a condition of employment of an employee or prospective employee); WIS. STAT. ANN. § 631.89 (West 2019) (prohibits insurers from using genetic test information to set rates or condition coverage or benefits).

8. 42 U.S.C. § 1320d (2019).

9. Exec. Order No. 13145, 65 Fed. Reg. 6877 (2000).

10. 42 U.S.C. §§ 2000ff et seq. (2019).

11. Lebo, F. (1996). *Mastering the Diversity Challenge* (p. 3). Delray Beach, FL: St. Lucie Press.

APPENDICES

APPENDIX A TABLE OF CASES

Chapter 1:

Chapter 2:

Chapter 3:

Chapter 4:

Chapter 7:

Chapter 8:

Chapter 9:

Chapter 10:

Chapter 12:

Chapter 13:

Chapter 14:

Chapter 15:

Case Name	Chapter
Adkins v. Sarah Bush Lincoln Health Ctr., 20	1
Ahrens v. Katz, 147	8
Apple, Inc. v. Samsung Electronics Co. Ltd., 36	2
Assoc. Mutual Hosp. Serv. of Michigan v. Health Care Service Corp. of Illinois, 309	14
Babcock v. Saint Francis Med. Ctr., 20	1
Balkissoon v. Capitol Hill Hosp., 20	1
Baltzwell v. Baptist Med. Ctr., 180	9
Baptist Health v. Murphy, 20	1
Bartley v. E. Maine Med. Ctr., 20	1
Bartling v. Superior Court, 20	1
Bernardi v. Community Hosp. Ass'n., 265	12
Bernardi v. Community Hospital Association, 71	4
Biddle v. Warren Gen. Hosp., 85	4
Biddle v. Warren General Hospital, 74	4

Case Name	Chapter
Bing v. Thunig, 80	4
Bly v. Rhoads, 180	9
Bock v. John C. Lincoln Hosp., 20	1
Bondu v. Gurvich, 149	8
Bouquett v. St. Elizabeth Corp., 20	1
Brannon v. Wood, 85	4
Bricker v. Sceva Speare Mem'l Hosp., 20	1
Brinton v. IHC Hosps., Inc., 20	1
Brooks v. Robinson, 77	4
Buckelew v. Grossbard, 85	4
Burditt v. U.S. Department of Health and Human Services, 65	4
Butterfield v. Okubo, 265	12
Campbell v. St. Mary's Hosp., 20	1
Cangelosi v. Our Lady of the Lake Reg'l Med. Ctr., 85	4
Cannell v. Medical & Surgical Clinic, S.C., 214	10
Canterbury v. Spence, 180	9
Carr v. St. Paul Fire & Marine Insurance, 154	8
Clark v. Columbia/HCA Info. Servs., Inc., 20	1
Clark v. Norris, 265	12
Clemens v. Fairview Med. Ctr. Inc., 20	1
Clough v. Adventist Health Sys., Inc., 20	1
Cobbs v. Grant, 180	9
Collins v. Itoh, 180	9
Collins v. Westlake Community Hospital, 145	8
Community Hosps. of Indianapolis, Inc. v. Medtronic, 265	12
Connors v. Univ. Assoc. in Obstetrics & Gynecology, Inc., 85	4
Conrad v. Imatani, 180	9
Corn v. French, 85	4
Crocker v. Synpol, Inc., 85	4
Cross v. Trapp, 180	9
Cruzan v. Director, Missouri Department of Health, 174	9
CVS Pharmacy, 153	8
CVS Pharmacy, 306	14
Darling v. Charleston Community Memorial Hospital, 72	4
Darling v. Charleston Community Memorial Hospital, 245	12
Dashiell v. Griffith, 85	4
Dutta v. St. Francis Reg'l Med. Ctr. Inc., 20	1
Dworkin v. St. Francis Hosp., Inc., 20	1
E. Tex. Med. Ctr., Cancer Inst. v. Anderson, 20	1
Egan v. St. Anthony's Med. Ctr., 20	1

Case Name	*Chapter*
Enke v. Anderson, 265	12
Enrich v. Windmere Corp., 85	4
Estate of Behringer v. Medical Center at Princeton, 170	9
Estate of Behringer v. Medical Center at Princeton, 250	12
Feyz v. Mercy Mem'l Hosp., 20	1
Foran v. Carangelo, 78	4
Garrison v. Bd. of Trs. of Mem'l Hosp. of Laramie County, 20	1
Gianetti v. Norwalk Hosp., 20	1
Gilliam v. Thomas, 85	4
Golan v. Louise Wise Services, 215	10
Green v. Owensboro Med. Health Sys. Inc., 85	4
Greisman v. Newcomb Hosp., 20	1
Hagan v. Osteopathic Gen. Hosp., 20	1
Hageman v. Southwest Gen. Health Ctr., 56	3
Hagenbuch v. 3B6 Sistemi Elettronici Industriali S.R.L., 33	2
Halley v. Birbiglia, 180	9
Harris v. Cafritz Mem'l Hosp., 85	4
Hawkins v. Kinsie, 20	1
Henry by Henry v. St. John's Hospital, 147	8
Henry v. Lewis, 61	3
Holmes v. Gamble, 85	4
Hook v. Rothstein, 180	9
Horne v. Patton, 85	4
Horowitz v. Bogart, 78	4
Hoven v. Kelble, 85	4
Hurlock v. Park Lane Medical Center, 145	8
In re: Milton Hershey Medical Center, 171	9
John Doe v. Mary Smith, 42	2
John Roe v. Jane Doe, 170	9
John Roe v. Jane Doe, 5	1
John Roe v. Jane Doe, 57	3
Johnson v. Misericordia Community Hospital, 72	4
Johnson v. Misericordia Community Hospital, 85	4
Johnson v. Vaughn, 85	4
Jones v. Harrisburg Polyclinic Hosp., 85	4
Jones v. Porretta, 85	4
Katsetos v. Nolan, 85	4
Kay Laboratories, Inc. v. District Court, 265	12
Kennis v. Mercy Hosp. Med. Ctr., 85	4
Kerr v. Bock, 85	4

Case Name	*Chapter*
Keys v. Guthmann, 85	4
Kiester v. Humana Hops. Alaska, Inc., 20	1
King v. Searle Pharm., 85	4
Kohoutek v. Hafner, 180	9
Lake Hosp. & Clinic, Inc. v. Silversmith, 20	1
Larrimore v. Homeopathic Hospital Association, 69	4
Lewisburg Cmty. Hosp. v. Alfredson, 20	1
Lohrmann v. Iredell Mem'l Hosp., Inc., 20	1
Lyons v. St. Vincent Health Ctr., 20	1
Mahan v. Avera St. Luke's, 20	1
Mahmoodian v. United Hosp. Ctr. Inc., 20	1
Marbury v. Madison, 17	1
Mary Smith v. John Doe, 41	2
Mason v. Cent. Suffolk Hosp., 20	1
McDonald v. Massachusetts General Hosp., 85	4
McElhinney v. William Booth Mem'l Hosp., 20	1
McGlone v. Landreth, 77	4
McWain v. Tucson Gen. Hosp., 85	4
Med. Ctr., Hosps., v. Terzis, 20	1
Metcalf v. Coleman, 20	1
Miller v. Eisenhower Med. Ctr., 20	1
Miller v. Sauberman, 35	2
Miller v. St. Alphonsus Reg'l Med. Ctr., Inc., 20	1
Mireles v. Broderick, 85	4
Mohr v. Williams, 85	4
Mordecai v. Blue Cross/Blue Shield of Alabama, 4	1
Morgan v. Children's Hosp., 85	4
Mrozinski v. Pogue, 85	4
Mucci v. Houghton, 85	4
N. Valley Hosp., Inc. v. Kauffman, 20	1
Natale v. Sisters of Mercy, 20	1
Natanson v. Kline, 180	9
Norman-Bloodsaw v. Lawrence Berkeley Laboratory, 325	15
Pacheco v. Ortiz, 61	3
Parker v. Washington, 85	4
Pederson v. Dumouchel, 85	4
People v. Bickham, 61	3
Pepple v. Parkview Mem'l Hosp., Inc., 20	1
Pratt v. Davis, 179	9
Prevost v. Coffee County Hospital Authority, 4	1

Case Name	Chapter
Pyramid Life Ins. Co. v. Masonic Hosp. Assoc., 213	10
Rabens v. Jackson Park Hosp. Found., 213	10
Rao v. Auburn Gen. Hosp., 20	1
Ravenis v. Detroit General Hospital, 145	8
Rice v. Jaskolski, 180	9
Robles v. Humana Hosp. of Cartersville, 20	1
Roe v. Wade, 124	7
Rolater v. Strain, 179	9
Rooney v. National Super Markets, Inc., 85	4
Rowe Entertainment, Inc. v. William Morris Agency, Inc., 39	2
Sadler v. Dimensions Healthcare Corp., 20	1
Sard v. Hardy, 180	9
Satilla Health Servs. Inc. v. Bell, 20	1
Saur v. Probes, 85	4
Schloendorff v. Society of New York Hosp., 179	9
Schmidt v. Gibbs, 85	4
Scott v. Bradford, 180	9
Seavers v. Methodist Med. Center of Oak Ridge, 85	4
Seitzinger v. Cmty. Health Network, 20	1
Seymour v. Victory Memorial Hospital, 82	4
Sides v. St. Anthony's Medical Center, 71	4
Sierra Vista Hosp. v. Shaffer, 265	12
Silver v. Castle Mem'l Hosp., 20	1
Sisson v. Elkins, 85	4
Skripek v. Bergamo, 180	9
Sligar v. Tucker, 265	12
Smith v. Our Lady of the Lake Hosp., Inc., 20	1
St. Louis v. Bay State Med. Ctr., Inc., 20	1
States v. Lourdes Hosp., 85	4
Stempler v. Speidell, 85	4
Straube v. Emanuel Lutheran Charity Bd., 20	1
Tarasoff v. Regents of University of California, 72	4
United States ex rel. Cooper v. Blue Cross & Blue Shield of Florida, 309	14
United States ex rel. Kneepkins v. Gambro Healthcare Inc., et al., 309	14
United States ex rel. Merena v. SmithKline Beecham Clinical Laboratories, 309	14
United States ex rel. Stinson v. Prudential Ins., 309	14
United States ex rel. Thompson v. Columbia/HCA Healthcare Corp., 309	14
United States v. Gieger, 309	14
United States v. Sanders, 274	13
United States v. Smith, 301	14

Case Name	*Chapter*
Van Valkenburg v. Paracelsus Healthcare Corp., 20	1
Van Zee v. Sioux Valley Hosp., 85	4
Vann v. Harden, 85	4
Vogler v. Dominguez, 85	4
Walker v. Rumer, 85	4
Warwick v. Bliss, 85	4
Weekly v. Solomon, 180	9
Weiner v. Memorial Hosp., 265	12
Whalen v. Roe, 163	9
White v. Monsanto Co., 85	4
Wilkinson v. Vesey, 180	9
Wilkinson v. Vesey, 85	4
Williams v. Sprint/United Management Co., 33	2
Wong v. Garden Park Cmty. Hosp., Inc., 20	1
Wood v. Hilton Head Hosp., Inc., 20	1
Woodard v. Porter Hosp., Inc., 20	1
Ybarra v. Spangard, 71	4
Zubulake v. UBS Warburg, LLC, 36	2
Zubulake v. UBS Warburg LLC, 39	2
Zubulake v. UBS Warburg, LLC, 36	2

APPENDIX B
LIST OF COMMON ACRONYMS

Many of these acronyms may also be found in the text.

AAPC	American Academy of Professional Coders
ACP	American College of Physicians
ACS	American College of Surgeons
ADA	American Dental Association; American Dietetic Association; American Diabetes Association; Americans with Disabilities Act
ADEA	Age Discrimination in Employment Act
ADR	Alternative Dispute Resolution
AHA	American Hospital Association
AHIMA	American Health Information Management Association
AIDS	Acquired Immunodeficiency Syndrome
AJPH	*American Journal of Public Health*
AMA	American Medical Association
ANA	American Nurses Association
AOA	American Osteopathic Association
APHA	American Public Health Association
ARRA	American Recovery and Reinvestment Act
ART	Accredited Record Technician
BAPCPA	Bankruptcy Abuse Prevention and Consumer Protection Act
BC	Blue Cross
BS	Blue Shield
BSN	Bachelor of Science in Nursing
CAHEA	Committee on Allied Health Education and Accreditation
CAT	Computerized Axial Tomography
CBO	Congressional Budget Office
CCI	Correct Coding Initiative
CCS	Clinical Coding Specialist
CDC	Centers for Disease Control (formerly, Communicable Disease Center)
CFR	Code of Federal Regulations
CHAMPUS	Civilian Health and Medical Program of the Uniformed Services
CHAMPVA	Civilian Health and Medical Program of the Veterans Administration
CHAP	Community Health Accreditation Program
CIA	Corporate Integrity Agreements
CLIA	Clinical Laboratory Improvement Amendments
CME	Council on Medical Education; Continuing Medical Education
CMS	Center for Medicare and Medicaid Services
COBRA	Consolidated Omnibus Budget Reconciliation Act
COD	Certificate of Destruction
CON	Certificate of Need
CPR	Computerized Patient Record
CPT	Current Procedural Terminology
CRISPR	Clustered Regularly Interspaced Short Palindromic Repeats

CSR	Code of State Regulations
CT	Computed Tomography
CVS	Chronic Villus Sampling
DC	Doctor of Chiropractic
DCIS	Defense Criminal Investigative Services
DDS	Doctor of Dental Surgery
DHEW	Department of Health, Education and Welfare; succeeded by the DHHS
DHHS	Department of Health and Human Services
DICOM	Digital Imaging and Communications in Medicine
DMD	Doctor of Dental Medicine
DNR	Do Not Resuscitate
DNV	Det Norske Veritas
DO	Doctor of Osteopathy
DPM	Doctor of Podiatric Medicine
DRG	Diagnostic-Related Group(s)
ECRM	Enterprise Content Record Management
EENT	Eye, Ear, Nose, and Throat
EEO	Equal Employment Opportunity
EEOC	Equal Employment Opportunity Commission
EHR	Electronic Health Record
ELISA	Enzyme-linked Immunosorbent Assay
EMS	Emergency Medical Services
EMTALA	Emergency Medical Treatment and Active Labor Act
ENT	Ear, Nose, and Throat
EPA	Environmental Protection Agency; Equal Pay Act
ePHI	Electronic Protected Health Information
ERISA	Employment Retirement Income Security Act
ERM	Enterprise Risk Management
ESI	Electronically Stored Information
E-SIGN	Electronic Signatures in Global and National Commerce Act
FBI	Federal Bureau of Investigation
FCA	False Claims Act
FCRA	Fair Credit Reporting Act
FDA	Food and Drug Administration
FOIA	Freedom of Information Act
FLSA	Fair Labor Standards Act
FMLA	Family Medical Leave Act
FTC	Federal Trade Commission
FTCA	Federal Tort Claims Act
FY	Fiscal Year
GAO	General Accounting Office
GDP	Gross Domestic Product
GINA	Genetic Information Nondiscrimination Act
GNP	Gross National Product
GP	General Practitioner
GYN	Gynecology
H-B	Hill-Burton Act
HCFA	Health Care Financing Administration

HCPCS	Health Care Financing Administration Common Procedure Coding System
HEW	Health, Education, and Welfare; succeeded by HHS
HFAP	Health Facilities Accreditation Program
HFMA	Healthcare Financial Management Association
HGP	Human Genome Project
HHA	Home Health Agency
HHS	Health and Human Services
HIAA	Health Insurance Association of America
HIM	Health Information Management
HIPAA	Health Insurance Portability and Accountability Act
HIPDB	Healthcare Integrity and Protection Data Bank
HITECH	Health Information Technology for Economic and Clinical Health Act
HIV	Human Immunodeficiency Virus
HMO	Health Maintenance Organization
HAS	Health Services Administration
ICD-9-CM	International Classification of Diseases 9th Revision Clinical Modification
ICF	Intermediate Care Facility
ICRA	Immigration Control and Reform Act
IFA	Indirect Immunofluorescence Assay
HIS	Indian Health Service
IOM	Institute of Medicine
IPA	Individual Practice Association
IRB	Institutional Review Board
JAHIMA	*Journal of the American Health Information Management Association*
JAMA	*Journal of the American Medical Association*
JC	Joint Commission
JCAH	Joint Commission on Accreditation of Hospitals; succeeded by JCAHO
JCAHO	Joint Commission on Accreditation of Healthcare Organizations
JME	*Journal of Medical Education*
LOS	Length of Stay
LPN	Licensed Practical Nurse
LVN	Licensed Vocational Nurse
MCAT	Medical College Admission Test
MCFU	Medicaid Fraud Control Unit
MCH	Maternal and Child Health
MD	Doctor of Medicine
Med	Medicine
MEDLARS	Medical Literature and Analysis Retrieval System
MH	Mental Health; Mental Hygiene
MHCCA	Medical and Health Care Continuation Act
MPP	Medicare Participating Physician
MR	Mental Retardation
MRA	Medical Record Administration
MRI	Magnetic Resonance Imaging
MRT	Medical Record Technology
NBME	National Board of Medical Examiners
NCHS	National Center for Health Statistics
NCI	National Cancer Institute

NEI	National Eye Institute
NEJM	*New England Journal of Medicine*
NHII	National Health Information Infrastructure
NIH	National Institutes of Health
NIMH	National Institutes of Mental Health
NLM	National Library of Medicine
NLN	National League of Nursing
NLRB	National Labor Relations Board
NMR	Nuclear Magnetic Resonance
OB	Obstetrics
OD	Doctor of Optometry
OIG	Office of Inspector General
OMB	Office of Management and Budget
OR	Operating Room
OSHA	Occupational Safety and Health Administration
OTA	Office of Technology Assessment
OWBPA	Older Workers Benefit Protection Act
PA	Physical Assistant
PATH	Physicians at Teaching Hospitals
PDA	Personal Digital Assistant
PDF	Portable Document Format
PEPP	Payment Error and Prevention Program
PHI	Protected Health Information
PHR	Personal Health Record
PL	Public Law
PPO	Preferred Provider Organization
PPS	Prospective Payment or Pricing System
PRO	Professional Review Organization
PRRB	Provider Reimbursement Review Board
PSDA	Patient Self-Determination Act
PSRO	Professional Standards Review Organization
QA	Quality Assurance
QIO	Quality Improvement Organization
RFP	Request for Proposal
RHIA	Registered Health Information Administrator
RHIT	Registered Health Information Technician
RICO	Racketeer Influenced and Corrupt Organizations
RM	Risk Management
RN	Registered Nurse
RRA	Registered Record Administrator
SNF	Skilled Nursing Facility
SOW	Scope of Work
SSA	Social Security Administration
SSI	Supplementary Security Income
STD	Sexually Transmitted Disease
TB	Tuberculosis
TEFRA	Tax Equity and Fiscal Responsibility Act
TIFF	Tagged Image File Format

UCR	Usual, Customary, and Reasonable
UR	Utilization Review
USERRA	Uniformed Services Employment and Reemployment Rights Act
VA	Veterans Affairs
VD	Venereal Disease
VEVRAA	Vietnam Era Veterans' Readjustment Assistance Act
VNA	Visiting Nurse Association
WARN	Worker Adjustment and Retraining Notification Act
WHO	World Health Organization
WIC	Women, Infants and Children

(Adapted in part from Raffel and Barsukiewicz, *The U.S. Health System: Origins and Functions, 5th edition.* Clifton Park, NY: Delmar Learning, 2002).

APPENDIX C SELECTED LAWS AFFECTING HIM

This sample listing includes federal statutes and regulations that directly govern the collection, use, and dissemination of health information, plus those applicable to the subareas of health care fraud and abuse, health care technology, and personnel management. Although an attempt is made to be inclusive, the nature of changes in the law makes this listing by definition comprehensive only to an extent.

21st Century Cures Act	21 U.S.C.§ 355 42 U.S.C.§ 17935
Age Discrimination in Employment Act	29 U.S.C. §§ 621–634
Agency for Health Care Policy and Research Reauthorization Act	42 U.S.C. § 201
American Recovery and Reinvestment Act	42 U.S.C. § 201 et seq.
Americans with Disabilities Act	42 U.S.C. §§ 12101–12213
Bankruptcy Abuse Prevention and Consumer Protection Act	11 U.S.C. § 351
Cancer Registries Amendment Act	42 U.S.C. § 280e
Chronic Care Act	S. 870, 115th Cong. (2018)(enacted)
Civil Rights Act (Title VII)	42 U.S.C. § 2000
Clinical Laboratory Improvement Amendments	42 C.F.R. § 493.1291 45 C.F.R. § 164.524
Comprehensive Alcohol Abuse and Alcoholism	42 U.S.C. § 290ee–3
Prevention, Treatment, and Rehabilitation Act	42 C.F.R. Ch.1, Part 2, §§ 2.1–2.67
Comprehensive Telehealth Act	42 U.S.C. § 1395i, mm
Deficit Reduction Act	42 U.S.C. §§ 1396, 10701–1, 1092e
Drug Abuse Prevention, Treatment, and Rehabilitation Act	42 U.S.C. § 290dd–3
Electronic Signatures in Global and National Commerce Act	15 U.S.C. §§ 7001–7031
Emergency Medical Treatment and Active Labor Act	42 U.S.C. §§ 1395 et seq.
Employee Retirement Income Security Act	29 U.S.C. §§ 1001–1191, 1201–1242, 1301–1461
Equal Employment Opportunity Act	42 U.S.C. § 2000a
Equal Pay Act	29 U.S.C. § 201
Fair and Accurate Credit Transactions Act (Red Flag requirements)	16 C.F.R. Part 681
Fair Credit Reporting Act	15 U.S.C. § 1681
Fair Labor Standards Act	29 U.S.C. § 201 et seq.
Family Medical Leave Act	29 U.S.C. §§ 2601 et seq., 6381 et seq.
Federal Business Records Act	28 U.S.C. § 1732
Federal Employees' Compensation Act	5 U.S.C. § 8101 et seq.
Federal Employers Liability Act	45 U.S.C. § 51 et seq.
Federal Railroad Safety Act	49 U.S.C. § 20101 et seq.
Food and Drug Act	21 U.S.C. §§ 301–360bb
Genetic Information Nondiscrimination Act	42 U.S.C. § 2000ff et seq.
Health Care Fraud and Abuse Statutes Anti-kickback statutes (Stark I and II)	42 U.S.C. § 1395nn(b) 42 U.S.C. § 1320a–7b(b)
False Claims Act	31 U.S.C. § 3729–33 (civil) 31 U.S.C. § 3729–3731 (criminal)

Mail fraud	18 U.S.C. §§ 1341, 1342
HealthCare Quality Improvement Act	42 U.S.C. §§ 11101–11152 42 C.F.R. §§ 60.1–.14
Health Information for Economic and Clinical Health Act (HITECH)	42 U.S.C. § 300jj, 17921–17954
Healthcare Research and Quality Act	42 U.S.C. § 29 et seq.
Health Insurance Portability and Accountability Act	42 U.S.C. § 1320d
General Administrative Requirements	45 C.F.R. § 160.101–.552
Administrative Requirements	45 C.F.R. § 162.100–.1802
Security and Privacy Requirements	45 C.F.R. § 164.102–.534
HIV Health Services Program	42 U.S.C. § 300(ff)
Health Maintenance Organizations Act	42 U.S.C. § 300e et seq.
Health Professions Education Extension Act	42 U.S.C. § 799
Identity Theft and Assumption Deterrence Act	18 U.S.C. § 1028
Immigration Reform and Control Act	8 U.S.C. § 1324–1365
Institutional Review Boards FDA	42 C.F.R. § 50.1 et seq.
DHHS	42 C.F.R. § 46.101 et seq.
Lilly Ledbetter Fair Pay Act	42 U.S.C. § 2000e–5
Malcolm Baldridge National Quality Improvement Act	15 U.S.C. § 3711a
Medicaid Program	42 U.S.C. § 1396
Medicare Conditions of Participation	42 U.S.C. § 1395(e) et seq.
General health	42 C.F.R. § 482.1–.66.
Mental health	42 C.F.R. § 483.100–138
Long-term care facilities	42 C.F.R. § 483.100–.75
Home health	42 C.F.R. Ch. IV, §§ 484.1–.265
Specialized providers	42 C.F.R. § 485.50–.729
Medicare Prescription Drug, Improvement and Modernization Act	42 U.S.C. § 1395w
Military Selective Service Act	50 U.S.C. §§ 451–471a
National Bureau of Standards Act	15 U.S.C. § 271 et seq.
National Labor Relations Act	29 U.S.C. §§ 151–169
National Library of Medicine Act	42 U.S.C. § 201
National Research Act	42 U.S.C. § 201
Occupational Safety and Health Act	29 U.S.C. §§ 651–678
Older Workers Benefit Protection Act	29 U.S.C. § 621
Patient Self-Determination Act (governing living wills and advance directives)	42 U.S.C. § 1396 et seq. 42 C.F.R. §§ 417.436 42 C.F.R. §§ 431.20 42 C.F.R. §§ 434.28
Pregnancy Discrimination Act	42 U.S.C. § 2000e
Privacy Act	5 U.S.C. § 552a
Safe Medical Devices Act	21 U.S.C. §§ 3601, 383
Social Security Act	42 U.S.C. § 301 et seq.
Tax Equity and Fiscal Responsibility Act	26 U.S.C. §§ 291, 6700 et seq.
Telecommunications Act (governing telemedicine)	47 U.S.C. §§ 254(b) & (h)
Uniformed Services Employment and Reemployment Rights Act	38 U.S.C. §§ 4301–4333
Utilization Review Act	42 C.F.R. Part 456, Subparts B & C

APPENDIX D THE PATIENT CARE PARTNERSHIP

The Patient Care Partnership can be found by accessing the Student Online Companion Site for Legal & Ethical Aspects of Health Information Management 5th edition at login.cengage.com.

GLOSSARY

A

Abortion The termination of pregnancy before the viability of the fetus.

Accounting of disclosures A list of all disclosures made of a patient's health information.

Action A judicial or administrative proceeding for the enforcement or protection of a right; a lawsuit.

Active euthanasia The practice of actions that speed the process of dying; also called positive euthanasia.

Actual damages Those damages awarded to make the plaintiff whole and restore him or her to the position in existence before the injury; sometimes referred to as compensatory damages.

Adjudication The final decision of a court, usually made after the trial of the case; the court's final judgment.

Administrative safeguards A set of standards under the HIPAA Security Rule designed to help covered entities take actions and create policies and procedures to manage the development, implementation, and maintenance of security measures to protect personally identifiable health information.

Administrative simplification The streamlining and standardization of seemingly inefficient and non-uniform practices in the health care industry; a goal of the Health Insurance Portability and Accountability Act (HIPAA).

Admissibility Information is considered admissible into evidence at trial if the applicable rules establish that the information is both pertinent and proper for the judge and/or jury to consider when deciding the issues involved in the lawsuit.

Admissible Pertinent and proper evidence. Rules of evidence determine if evidence is pertinent and proper. For example, in the context of medical records, the applicable rule of evidence is the hearsay rule.

Adoption records Records of the individual placed for adoption. Access to adoption records is controversial. The competing issues involved in access are the interests of the biological parent(s) in placing the child up for adoption, often with the promise of confidentiality, and the interests of the adoptee for genetic information and information about his or her natural identity.

Advance directive Written instructions recognized under state law, such as living wills or durable powers of attorney for health care, that relate to the kind of health care the patient wishes to have or not have if he or she becomes incapacitated.

Allografts Transplants using a donor's body part; sometimes referred to as homografts.

Alternative dispute resolution A practice involving several methods of resolving conflicts and disagreements to the satisfaction of all parties without using the court system.

Anonymous testing A system that assigns a unique identifier to the individual tested, thereby protecting his or her identity.

Anti-kickback statute A law prohibiting the offer or solicitation of remuneration, including kickbacks and rebates, in exchange for referrals of Medicare-payable services.

Appeal The process by which a higher court is requested by a party to a lawsuit to review the decision of a lower court. Such reconsideration is normally confined to a review of the record from the lower court, with no new testimony taken and no new issues raised. Review by the higher court may result in affirmation, reversal, or modification of the lower court's decision.

Appellant A party who appeals from a lower court to a higher court.

Appellee A party against whom a case is appealed from a lower court to a higher court.

Arbitration The use of a neutral third party to hear both sides of a dispute and render a written decision, called an award. The award is imposed on the parties following consideration of each side's position.

Artificial insemination The planting of sperm into a woman's body to facilitate conception.

Assault An act of force or threat of force intended to inflict harm upon a person or to put the person in fear that such harm is imminent; an attempt to commit a battery. The perpetrator must have or appear to have the present ability to carry out the act.

Assumption of risk A doctrine stating that a plaintiff who voluntarily exposes himself or herself to a known and appreciated danger may not recover damages caused by incurring that risk.

Attorney–client privilege The legal protection of communications between a client and his or her attorney, made in confidence for the purpose of obtaining legal advice.

At-will employment An employment arrangement that allows the employer to terminate the employee at any time and allows the employee to leave the employer at any time.

Audit trail A record or catalog showing a sequence of user activity of a computer system, including who accessed what data, when such access occurred, and whether and what changes were made.

Authentication Confirms the content and accuracy of an entry into the medical record by written signature, initials, or computer-generated signature code.

Authorization Permission given to the health care provider by the patient allowing the provider to disclose patient-specific health information.

Authorship Identifies the health care provider who has made an entry in the patient record, in writing or by dictation, keyboard, or keyless data entry.

Autografts Transplants using one's own body parts.

Autonomy The ethical concept of independence, self-determination, or freedom; derives from two Greek words: *autos*, meaning self, and *nomos*, meaning governance.

B

Battery The unconsented to touching or striking of one person by another or by an object put in motion by him or her, with the intention of doing harm or giving offense. Battery is both a crime and a tort.

Belmont Report A document which identifies the ethical principles to be used to prevent unethical use of human subjects in research.

Beneficence The ethical concept meaning the qualities of kindness, mercy, and charity; refers to the obligation to do good in all circumstances.

Best-interest standard The standard used to determine the best interest of an individual when the individual cannot make such a decision alone.

Bioethics The study of ethical issues that result from technologic and scientific advances, especially in biology and medicine.

Blockchain The technology that creates a digital database containing information that can be simultaneously used and shared within a large decentralized, publicly accessible network.

Breach The acquisition, access, use, or disclosure of protected health information in a manner that compromises the security or privacy of protected health information.

Breach of confidentiality The unauthorized, unprivileged disclosure to a third party of nonpublic medical information that a physician or hospital has learned within a physician–patient or hospital–patient relationship.

Breach of contract The failure to perform according to the terms of the parties' agreement.

Breach of duty of care The failure to conform to a particular standard of care toward another. Such failure to conform will result in liability for harm sustained by another person.

Business associate One who performs or assists in performing a function or activity involving the use or disclosure of individually identifiable health information on behalf of a health care provider.

Business record exception An exception to the hearsay rule that permits business records to be admitted into evidence even though they are hearsay. Medical records admitted as evidence under this exception must first meet the foundation requirements of the exception.

Business records rule An exception to the hearsay rule that permits business records to be admitted into evidence even though they are hearsay.

C

Case management The ongoing review of patient care in various health care settings related to assuring the medical necessity of the encounter and the appropriateness of the clinical services provided.

Case managers Those persons with responsibility for managing the utilization review process and coordinating the patient's care with physicians, nurses, and other allied health professionals.

Categorical imperative A principle of deontology that means a command derived from a principle that does not allow exceptions.

Causation A causing; the producing of a result.

Cause of action An action; a lawsuit; a case.

Certificate of destruction A document that shows what data and records were destroyed, who destroyed those data and records, and the method used for that destruction.

Certification Recognition by a professional association that an individual possesses the knowledge, experience, and expertise of the standards set by the professional association.

Certification process The process by which the health information manager verifies that the copy of the health record provided in response to legal request is an exact duplicate of the original health record.

Certiorari A writ issued by a higher court to a lower court requiring the certification of the record in a particular case so that the higher court can review the record and correct any actions taken in the case that are not in accordance with the law. The Supreme Court of the United States uses the writ of certiorari to select the lower federal court and the state court cases it is willing to review.

Charitable immunity A defense that shields a charitable institution from liability for any torts committed on its property or by its employees.

Civil law Noncriminal law.

Civil money penalty A fine imposed on a health care provider who files false or fraudulent claims.

Clerks of court A government official responsible for maintaining the official record of all court actions within a court system.

Clinical information system System with a central focus of clinical data, not financial or billing information.

Code of Federal Regulations A publication of the U.S. government that contains regulations issued by administrative agencies.

Codes of conduct Written lists of a profession's values and standards of conduct; sometimes referred to as codes of ethics.

Codes of ethics Written lists of a profession's values and standards of conduct; sometimes referred to as codes of conduct.

Collective bargaining The process by which a contract is negotiated between a union and employer setting forth the relationship between the two.

Common law (1) A law found in the decisions of the courts rather than in statutes; judge-made law. (2)English law adopted by the early American colonists, which is part of the U.S. judicial heritage and forms the basis of much of U.S. law today.

Comparative justice The concept referring to balancing the competing interests of individuals and groups against one another, with no independent standard used to make this comparison.

Comparative negligence The doctrine adopted by most states that requires a comparison of the negligence of the defendant with the negligence of the plaintiff; the greater the negligence of the defendant, the lesser the level of care required of the plaintiff to permit him or her to recover. In other words, the plaintiff's negligence does not defeat his or her cause of action, but it does reduce the damages he or she is entitled to recover.

Compensatory damages Those damages awarded to make the plaintiff whole and restore him or her to the position in existence before the injury; sometimes referred to as actual damages.

Complaint (1) The initial pleading in a civil action, in which the plaintiff alleges a cause of action and asks that the wrong done to him or her be remedied by the court. (2) A formal charge of a crime.

Compliance The efforts to establish a culture that promotes prevention, detection, and resolution of instances of conduct that do not conform to applicable local, state, and federal laws and regulations.

Compliance program A program ensuring the use of effective internal controls that promote adherence to the applicable local, state, and federal laws and regulations and the program requirements of federal, state, and private health plans.

Compound authorization An authorization for use or disclosure of patient-specific health information that has been combined with another document.

Computerized patient record Records created, authenticated, stored, and retrieved by computers.

Confidentiality The obligation of the health care provider to maintain patient information in a manner that will not permit dissemination beyond the health care provider. The origin of confidentiality is found in the Hippocratic Oath.

Conflict of interest The clash between an individual's selfish interests and his or her obligation to an organization or group.

Conflict of laws An inconsistency between different jurisdictions over the same issue in a legal action.

Consent A concurrence of wills. An agreement by a person in the possession and exercise of sufficient mental capacity to make an intelligent choice to do something proposed by another.

Constitution (1) The system of fundamental principles by which a nation, state, or corporation is governed. A nation's constitution may be written (example: the U.S. Constitution) or unwritten (example: the British Constitution). A nation's laws must conform to its constitution. A law that violates a nation's constitution is unconstitutional and therefore unenforceable. (2) The document setting forth the fundamental principles of governance. (3) The Constitution of the United States.

Continuum of ownership Questions of ownership of health information range from the traditional view of the health care provider having sole ownership of the medical record, to a joint patient–health care provider ownership of the medical record, toward a trend placing health information in a trust capacity.

Contraception The efforts to prevent or interfere with conception or impregnation through voluntary or artificial means; sometimes referred to as birth control.

Contract An agreement entered into, for adequate consideration, to do, or refrain from doing, a particular thing. The Uniform Commercial Code defines a contract as the total legal obligation resulting from the parties' agreement. In addition to adequate consideration, the transaction must involve an undertaking that is legal to perform, and there must be mutuality of agreement and obligation between at least two competent parties.

Contract law The branch of law concerned with agreements between two or more parties that creates some type of obligation to act (do something) or refrain from acting (not do something).

Contributory negligence In the law of negligence, a failure by the plaintiff to exercise reasonable care that, in part at least, is the cause of an injury. Contributory negligence defeats a plaintiff's cause of action for negligence in states that have not adopted the doctrine of comparative negligence.

Copy and paste The practice of duplicating information within the same patient record or moving it across multiple records.

Corporate integrity agreements Financial settlements involving written agreements that specify the rules of conduct to be followed to remedy health care fraud and abuse, plus any monitoring and reporting requirements.

Corporate negligence A doctrine defined as the failure of a hospital, entrusted with the task of providing the accommodations necessary to carry out its purpose, to follow the established standard of conduct to which it should conform.

Corrections to the record A method by which a mistake contained in a patient's health record is altered or modified according to standard practices.

Cost–benefit analysis All possible options are considered, the utility or value of each option is determined, and the option that poses the highest total utility is chosen. Net benefits are compared against costs to reach a decision. The option that offers society the best benefits at the least cost or offers businesses the greatest return for the lowest costs is seen as the logical choice.

Counterclaim A claim in a lawsuit brought by the defendant against the plaintiff.

Court order (1) An adjudication by a court. (2) The ruling by a court with respect to a motion or any other question before it for determination during the course of a proceeding.

Court structure A multitiered structure consisting of trial courts, intermediate courts of appeal, and supreme courts. The multitiered structure is the same at both state and federal levels.

Credentialing process The examination by the hospital's governing board of the physician's background, experience, and licensure against established criteria.

Criminal law The branch of law that declares certain conduct injurious to the public order and provides specified punishment for those found to have engaged in such conduct.

CRISPR A genetic engineering technique that allows for the snipping and editing of genes. The acronym stands for Clustered Regularly Interspaced Short Palindromic Repeat.

D

Damages The sum of money that may be recovered in the courts as financial reparation for an injury or wrong suffered as a result of breach of contract or tort. Divided into three types: nominal, actual, punitive.

Database A structured collection of data on multiple entities and their relationships, often arranged for ease and speed of retrieval.

Deeming authority The substitution of complying with the requirements and standards of an accrediting organization in lieu of complying with the Medicare Conditions of Participation issued by the Centers for Medicare and Medicaid Services.

Defamation Libel or slander; the written or oral publication, false or intentional, of anything that is injurious to the good name or reputation of another person.

Defendant The person against whom an action is brought.

De-identified data or health information Health information that is stripped of all identifiers.

Deontology The ethical theory that asserts that ethical decision making is based on moral rules and unchanging principles that are derived from reason and can be applied universally; sometimes referred to as formalism or duty orientation.

Deponent The person answering the questions in a deposition.

Depositions A discovery device in which one party subpoenas a witness to appear at a given time and place to testify under oath to uncover details of a case.

Digital divide The gulf between those who have access to and those who do not have access to modern information and technology, such as smartphones, personal computers, and the Internet.

Digital imaging A system by which paper documents are scanned on devices that work similar to a photocopier, allowing the image to be saved and viewed through a server or web browser.

Disability A physical or mental impairment that substantially limits one or more of the major life activities of an employee; a record of such impairment; or being regarded as having such an impairment.

Disclosure of information Disclosure of health information is governed by two principles: (1) medical records remain within the provider's control and safekeeping and may be removed only in accordance with a court order or subpoena; (2) the health care provider may not disclose or withhold health information at will.

Disclosure with patient authorization Health information may be disclosed to third parties on written authorization of the patient. Certain components must be present for the written authorization form to be valid.

Disclosure without patient authorization Health information may be disclosed to third parties without written patient authorization in limited circumstances, such as medical emergencies, scientific research activities, and audits.

Discoverability Information is considered discoverable if the applicable rules require disclosure of the information upon the formal request of a party.

Discovery A means for providing a party, in advance of trial, with devices or tools used to obtain facts and information about the case from the other side in order to prepare for trial. Examples include depositions, written interrogatories, production of documents or things, physical and mental examinations, and requests for admission.

Disparagement The belittling or criticizing of the skills, knowledge, or qualifications of another professional.

Distributive justice The ethical concept of fair distribution of burdens and benefits using an independent standard.

Diversity jurisdiction The jurisdiction of a federal court arising from diversity of citizenship when the jurisdictional amount has been met.

Double-effect principle The principle that recognizes that ethical choices may result in untoward outcomes.

Durable power of attorney for health care Allows a competent individual to name someone else to exercise health care-related decisions on his or her behalf, in the event the individual becomes incapacitated or unable to make personal decisions. This term is sometimes referred to in a shorten fashion as durable power of attorney.

Duty of care An obligation, enforced by law, to conform to a particular standard of care toward another. Failure to conform to this standard will result in liability for any harm sustained by another person.

E

E-discovery A form of discovery that focuses on information stored electronically, such as that contained in electronic health records, and requires collecting, preparing, reviewing, and producing electronic documents in a variety of criminal and civil actions and proceedings.

E-health organizations Organizations that collect and display individually identifiable health information over the Internet.

Electronic case filing systems Electronic record systems used in various court systems consisting of a component for case management (example: a database of cases and parties), plus electronic creation and storage of pleadings and testimony (example: digital images and audio recordings).

Electronic health record A record of health-related information on an individual that is created, gathered, managed, and consulted by authorized health care clinicians and staff.

Electronic mail A form of communication between parties or individuals using only electronic means.

Electronic protected health information (ePHI) Individually identifiable health information that is transmitted by electronic media, maintained in electronic medium, or transmitted or maintained in any other form or medium.

Electronic signature A type of signature that uses software applications to bind a signature or other distinguishable mark to a specific electronic document.

Electronically stored information A distinct category of information that includes e-mails, Web pages, word processing files, and databases stored in the memory of computers, magnetic discs (such as computer hard drives and floppy disk), optical discs (such as DVDs and CDs), and flash memory (such as thumb or flash drives).

Emancipation The legal ability of a minor to act as an adult when he or she has moved away from home and receives no support from his or her parents.

Employee An individual hired by another, such as a business firm, to work for wages or a salary.

Employers Those persons, businesses, or organizations that provide the work, engage the services or labor, and pay for the work performed.

Employment The process of providing work, engaging services or labor, and paying for the work performed.

Employment challenges Lawsuits brought by employees of health care providers asserting the employee's legal right to refuse to undertake or undergo certain actions required by the employer.

Encryption A form of technical security used to ensure that data transferred from one network location to another is secure from eavesdropping or interception.

Enterprise content and record management Those electronic records management principles (all of the digital and analog records) and enterprise content management principles (the technology, tools, and methods) to capture, store, deliver, and preserve content across an enterprise.

Enterprise risk management The function of analyzing and evaluating all of the risks that confront an organization, not just the legal, financial, and medical risks that are traditionally considered.

Equitable relief A remedy available in equity rather than at law; generally relief other than money damages.

Ethical challenges Situations in which no clear cut "right" answer exists, and an individual is required to make a choice between two or more equally unfavorable alternatives or between a neutral alternative and a tempting but unfavorable alternative.

Ethical concepts Abstract ideas or thoughts that deal with ethics.

Ethical guidelines Standards of conduct issued by professional organizations to guide their members' future course of action. These standards are sometimes used to establish the standard of care in a negligence action.

Ethical theories The systematic statements or plans of principles used to deal with ethical dilemmas.

Ethics The formal study of moral choices that conform to standards of conduct; derived from the Greek word *ethos*.

Ethics committees Groups formed within an organization to establish new and evaluate existing ethics codes and corporate polices and to address ethical issues that arise in the workplace.

Etiquette An area of study focusing on how human beings relate to one another under certain circumstances; a social code of customs and rituals.

Eugenics The effort to improve the human species through control of hereditary factors in mating.

Euthanasia The act or practice of causing death painlessly, with the aim to end suffering.

Evidence The means by which any matter of fact may be established or disproved. Such means may include testimony, documents, and physical objects. The law of evidence is made up of rules that determine what evidence is to be admitted or rejected in the trial of a civil action or a criminal prosecution and what weight is to be given to admitted evidence. Medical records may be used as evidence in civil or criminal court actions or in administrative agency proceedings.

Executive branch The branch of government responsible for enforcing and administering the laws.

Exemplary damages Those damages awarded above and beyond actual damages, often in instances where there is proof of outrageous, malicious, or intentional conduct; sometimes referred to as punitive damages.

Exempt employees A category under the Fair Labor Standards Act for an employee who is paid a salary as opposed to wages, exercises discretion in performing his work, is primarily responsible for managing a business or department, routinely manages others, and possesses the authority to hire and fire other employees.

Exigent circumstances Generally a time-sensitive or emergency situation that allows a search to proceed without a warrant.

Expert witness A person who is permitted to testify at trial because of special knowledge or proficiency in a particular field relevant to the case.

Express consent The verbal or written consent of a patient to receive diagnostic or therapeutic treatment or procedures.

F

Failure to warn A negligence theory that applies to a psychotherapist's failure to take steps to protect an innocent third party from a dangerous patient. Also known as failure to protect.

False arrest The intentional detention or restraint of someone against his or her will with the intent to make an arrest or actually make the arrest.

False imprisonment The intentional detention or restraint of someone against his or her will without legal justification. Such detention or restraint must be intentional, meaning that the person imposing confinement does so willfully.

Family planning The behavior associated with controlling the size of one's family or spacing the births within that family.

Federal question jurisdiction Refers to cases that question or involve a U.S. constitutional principle, treaty, federal statute, or federal rule or regulation. It also includes cases that would normally proceed in state court but did not because they occurred on federal land.

Felony A crime of a grave or serious nature punishable by a term of imprisonment exceeding one year.

Fidelity The ethical concept of faithfulness, loyalty, and devotion to one's obligations or duties.

Foundation One of the requirements of the business record exception to the hearsay rule. The preliminary evidence must show the relevance and authenticity of the material to be introduced into evidence.

Foundation requirements Foundation requirements of the business record exception must be established during testimony by the health information manager. The manager must possess knowledge of the requirements to create and maintain a medical record issued by governmental entities, accrediting agencies, and internal policies and procedures of the health care provider, along with knowledge of the manner in which data are recorded.

Fraud and abuse A false misrepresentation of fact that is relied on by another to that person's detriment and is a departure from reasonable use. This false misrepresentation of fact may take the form of words or conduct.

Full-time employees An employee who works thirty hours per week or more.

Functional limitation A physical or mental limitation of a major life activity caused by a disability.

G

Garnishment A proceeding by a creditor to obtain satisfaction of a debt from money or property of the debtor that is in the possession of a third person or is owed by such a person to the debtor.

Gene therapy The genetic altering of organisms for various purposes; sometimes referred to as genetic engineering.

Genetic information Information about an individual or family obtained from a genetic test or an individual's DNA sample. Genetic information relates to a person's future, not past, health.

Genetic screening A form of testing where a person's genetic makeup is tested to reveal a predisposition to certain diseases or other abnormalities.

Good Samaritan statutes Statutes that protect physicians and other rescuers from civil liability as a result of their actions or omissions in rendering emergency care, unless their actions or omissions were grossly negligent or intentionally injuring to the patient.

Governmental immunity A doctrine that precludes a plaintiff from asserting a meritorious lawsuit against a governmental entity unless the governmental entity consents to the lawsuit.

H

Health care relationship A connection between a health care provider, patient, and/or hospital that serves as the basis of a lawsuit.

Health information The data generated and collected as a result of delivering care to a patient.

Health record A document that contains a complete and accurate description of a patient's history, condition, diagnostic and therapeutic treatment, and the results of treatment.

Health record banks Repositories of personal health records in electronic form operated by governmental or commercial entities who serve as trusted custodians of the data contained in the health record bank.

Health record content The characteristics essential to constitute an adequate health record.

Hearsay Out-of-court statements that are offered to prove the truth of the matter asserted.

Hearsay rule The rule that hearsay testimony is not admissible unless it falls within an exception to the hearsay rule.

Heterografts Transplants involving animal tissue, cells, or organs into human bodies; sometimes referred to as xenografts.

Homografts Transplants using a donor's body part; sometimes referred to as allografts.

Hospital incident Any event or circumstance not consistent with the normal routine operations of the hospital and its staff or the routine care of a patient. It may be an error, an accident, or a situation that could have, or has, resulted in injury to a person or damage to hospital equipment or property.

Hospital–patient relationship Begins when the patient is voluntarily admitted to the hospital and agrees to pay for the treatment to be rendered. The relationship ends when the patient leaves the hospital through discharge or against medical advice.

Hospital–physician relationship A contractual agreement between the physician and the hospital allowing the physician to bring patients to the hospital to receive treatment.

Hostile work environment A form of sexual harassment involving unwelcome sexual conduct that is sufficiently pervasive or severe enough to alter the terms or conditions of employment.

Human Genome Project An enterprise designed to map the genes found in human DNA and determine the sequences of the chemical base pairs that make up human DNA.

Hybrid records Health records that are based partially in paper form and partially in electronic form.

I

Identifiable biospecimen A biospecimen for which the identity of the human subject is or may be readily ascertained by the investigator or associated with the biospecimen.

Identifiable private information The private information for which the identity of the human subject is or may readily be ascertained by the investigator or associated with the information.

Identity theft The knowing transfer or use, without lawful authority, of the identity of another person with the intent to commit, aid, or abet any unlawful activity that constitutes a violation of federal, state, or local law.

Impaired colleagues Those colleagues who can no longer function appropriately in the workplace due to substance abuse, such as use of alcohol or drugs.

Implied consent The patient's consent to receive diagnostic or therapeutic treatment or procedures without expressing verbal or written action by the patient; often existing in situations in which a patient voluntarily submits to a procedure with apparent knowledge of that procedure and the procedure present slight or no apparent risk, such as taking the patient's pulse or temperature.

Improper disclosure The disclosure of test results or other health information to a third party without the consent of the individual treated.

In vitro fertilization The fertilization of human gametes outside the human body in a test tube or other artificial environment.

Incident report The documentation of an adverse incident, whether done on a paper form or through a computerized database with access controls. It describes the incident itself, including the time, date, and place of occurrence, along with the condition of the subject of the incident, statements or observations of witnesses, and any responsive action taken.

Incompetent A person who is unable or unfit to make decisions.

Independent contractor An individual who agrees to perform certain work according to his or her own means, manner, and methods of performance.

Information security policies Those policies that define the framework around which an information security program is managed; policies that answer the who, where, what, when, and how questions of information security.

Informed consent The legal doctrine that requires the health care provider to disclose information to the patient about treatment options and risks so that the patient may knowledgeably consent to treatment.

Injunction A court order that commands or prohibits some act or course of conduct. It is preventive in nature and designed to protect a plaintiff from irreparable injury to his or her property or property rights by prohibiting or commanding the doing of certain acts. An injunction is a form of equitable relief.

Institutional review board A group formally designated by an institution to safeguard the rights and welfare of human subjects by reviewing, approving, and monitoring medical research.

Intellectual property Property (examples: copyrights, patents, trade secrets) that is the physical or tangible result of original thought. Modern technology has brought about widespread infringement of intellectual property rights (examples: the unauthorized reproduction and sale of videotapes, audiotapes, and computer software).

Intentional infliction of emotional distress Conduct by the defendant that is so extreme and outrageous that it causes the plaintiff to suffer severe emotional distress.

Intentional torts Torts committed by persons with the intent to do something wrong.

Internet An electronic communications network that connects computer networks and organizational computer facilities around the world.

Interrogatories A discovery device consisting of one party submitting written questions about a lawsuit to another party or witness.

Invasion of privacy The dissemination of information about another person's private, personal matters.

J

Judicial branch The branch of government responsible for interpreting the law through adjudication and resolution of disputes.

Jurisdiction (1) In a general sense, the right of a court to adjudicate lawsuits of a certain kind. (2) In a specific sense, the right of a court to determine a particular case; in other words, the power of the court over the subject matter of, or property involved in, the case at bar. (3) In a geographical sense, the power of a court to hear cases only within a specific territorial area. (4) Authority; control; power. (5) District; area; locality. The term also applies to the authority of an administrative agency to hear and determine a case brought before it.

Jury instructions Directions given to the jury by the judge before he or she sends the jurors out to deliberate and return a verdict, explaining the law that applies in the case and spelling out what must be proven and by whom.

Justice The ethical concept referring to the obligation to be fair to all people; encompasses the ideas of fairness, honesty, and impartiality.

L

Labor unions Groups of employees joined together to protect their jobs, seek improvements in working conditions, and create a formal method to communicate with the employer as a group.

Laches The equitable doctrine that a plaintiff's neglect or failure to assert a right may cause the court to deny him or her relief if, as a result, the defendant has changed position so that the defendant's rights are at risk.

Law A body of rules of action or conduct prescribed by a controlling authority that has binding legal force.

Leased employees Employees who are employed by a service firm and are assigned to work at a business or an organization; sometimes referred to as temporary employees.

Legal health record The legal business record generated at or for a health care organization that is produced upon request.

Legal process Stages through which a lawsuit passes.

Legal remedy A remedy available through legal action.

Legislative branch The branch of government responsible for enacting laws.

Libel Defamation expressed in print, writing, pictures, or signs and made available to a third party.

Licensure The process by which an authorized authority, often at the state level, grants permission to a qualified individual to perform certain activities that would otherwise be considered illegal absent a license.

Limited data set A form of data in which direct identifiers have been removed.

Litigation hold The actions of a party who possesses electronically stored information (ESI) to make efforts to prevent routine destruction and preserve ESI that may be discoverable, even before the time when a lawsuit is filed.

Litigation response plan A tool consisting of policies and procedures that address how to respond to legal process requests.

Living wage laws Ordinances passed by local governments that require employers to pay employees more than the federal minimum wage.

Living will A document, executed while a patient is competent, that provides direction as to medical care in the event the patient is incapacitated or unable to make personal decisions. A form of advance directive; each state must determine the legal rights of the patient to use a living will.

M

Mail and wire fraud The use of the U.S. Postal Service or commercial wire services for the advancement of a scheme relating to fraud.

Malpractice Misconduct involving a professional who fails to follow a standard of care prevalent for his or her profession that results in harm to another person.

Mandatory testing A decision by the legislature or court that forces an individual to receive testing for some health reason, without granting the individual the right to refuse.

Mediation The use of a neutral third party to assist both sides of a dispute in resolving their differences and reducing their resolution to writing. The resolution is based on the parties' agreement.

Medical abandonment The unilateral severing, by the physician, of the physician–patient relationship without providing the patient with reasonable notice at a time when there is a necessity for continuing care.

Medical advice The provision of a professional's opinion about what action an individual should or should not take with regard to their health.

Medical identity theft The knowing transfer or use, without lawful authority, of health information and the identity of another person with the intent to commit, aid, or abet any unlawful activity that constitutes a violation of federal, state, or local law.

Medical malpractice The failure of a medical professional to follow a standard of care prevalent for his or her profession that results in harm to the patient. Legal theories supporting a medical malpractice lawsuit include negligence, *res ipsa loquitur*, failure to warn, vicarious liability, and corporate negligence.

Medical record content The characteristics that are essential to constitute an adequate medical record.

Medical staff privileges The scope and limit of a physician's practice in a medical institution as defined by the institution's governing board.

Mental examination A discovery device used to evaluate the mental condition of a plaintiff in a lawsuit when such condition is in question.

Metadata Unseen or hidden information in common computer files, which can indicate when a document was created or revised and can contain edits, notes, or other private data.

Minimum necessary standard This standard requires the health care provider to make reasonable efforts to limit the patient-specific health information to the minimum necessary to accomplish the intended purpose of the use, disclosure, or request.

Misdemeanor A crime of a less serious nature punishable by a fine or a term of imprisonment of less than a year.

Morals The principles or fundamental standards of "right" conduct that an individual internalizes; derived from the Latin word *mores*.

Motion to quash An approved method to challenge a subpoena duces tecum in which a court determines whether documents and things must be produced pursuant to the subpoena.

N

Nanobot A microscopically small robot, about the size of a blood cell.

Nanomedicine A domain of medicine that uses nanotechnology to prevent and treat severe diseases such as cancer and heart disease.

National Health Information Infrastructure An interoperable electronic exchange of data between health care providers, government, and third-party payers.

Negligence The failure to do something that a reasonable person would do in the same circumstances, or the doing of something a reasonable person would not do. Negligence is a wrong generally characterized by carelessness, inattentiveness, and neglectfulness rather than by positive intent to cause injury.

Negotiation and settlement The parties to a dispute work without the help of a neutral third party to reach resolution of a dispute and memorialize the resolution.

No-knock warrant A warrant that allows the police to enter without announcing their presence in advance.

Nominal damages Those damages awarded for the vindication of a right in which minimal injury can be proved or in recognition of a technical invasion of a person's rights.

Nonintentional torts Torts committed by persons who lack the intent to do something wrong.

Nonmaleficence The ethical concept meaning the prohibition against doing harm; refers to the obligation to prevent evil or harm.

Notice of preservation A letter notifying an adversary of the need to preserve relevant electronic evidence, even if paper copies are available.

Notice of privacy practices A notice required by law that requires the health care provider to notify the patient of the uses of patient-specific health information and provide an opportunity to consent, reject, or request restriction of the information for any of the uses contained in the notice.

O

Official record A record containing that information necessary to document the patient's care and treatment: history and mental status exam, consent forms, treatment plans, physician orders, laboratory results, etc. This record is required to be maintained by law.

Open record statutes Statutory provisions that address confidentiality requirements using a presumption of disclosure of information upon request, absent statutory exemption.

Order of garnishment A written order directed to a third person to whom the losing party in a lawsuit is indebted that orders payment of the debt directly to the winning party.

Order of preservation A court order requiring a party to preserve electronic and other evidence, regardless of the party's need to engage in routine deletion or destruction practices and procedures.

Ordinances Laws passed at the local level by legislative bodies such as city councils or boards of aldermen.

Organ transplantation A form of surgery wherein one body part (tissue or organ) is transferred from one site to another or from one individual to another.

P

Part-time employees Employees who work less than thirty hours per week.

Passive euthanasia The practice in which no heroic measures are taken to preserve life; also called negative euthanasia.

Paternalism An outdated principle in which the health care professional acts in the role of a father to his children, deciding what is best for the patient's welfare without first being required to consult with the patient.

Patient identification Federal regulations restrict identification of a patient who is in a facility publicly identified as providing substance abuse treatment. Written consent of the patient or a court order is required for disclosure.

Patient notice Patients must be given notice of federal confidentiality requirements upon admission to a substance abuse treatment program or soon thereafter.

Patient record system Set of components that form the mechanism by which patient records are created, used, stored, and retrieved.

Patient rights The recognition that the patient is entitled to determine for him- or herself the extent to which he or she will receive or forego care and treatment.

Peer review committee A group of health care professionals who are charged with the responsibility for evaluating, maintaining, and/or monitoring the quality and utilization of health care services.

Peer review privileges State statutes that protect peer review deliberations and records from subpoena, discovery, or introduction into evidence. These statutes may also protect participants in peer review deliberations from civil liability.

Perinatal ethics The ethical questions involved in or occurring during the period closely surrounding birth.

Permissive and mandatory exclusion A deterrent to fraud and abuse where the health care provider is barred from participation in the Medicare program and all other federally financed health care programs.

Personal health record A collection of a patient's important health information that can be drawn from multiple sources and that is managed, shared, and controlled by or primarily for the individual patient.

Personal jurisdiction The authority of a court over the parties to a lawsuit.

Personal record A record, separate from the official medical record, maintained by the clinician in the mental health or developmental disability context that gives the clinician's viewpoint of the patient and their communications.

Personnel security In addition to standard considerations involved in employee hiring, personnel security as related to the computerized patient record also involves comprehensive knowledge of the computer system and a continual, documented updating of education relating to it.

Physical examination A discovery device used to evaluate the physical condition of a plaintiff in a lawsuit when such condition is in question.

Physical safeguards A set of standards under the HIPAA Security Rule designed to help covered entities protect their electronic information systems and related building and equipment from unauthorized intrusions and natural and environmental hazards.

Physical security The physical protection of the medical record.

Physician–patient privilege The legal doctrine that prevents forced disclosure of, or testimony about, information obtained by the health care provider during the course of treatment.

Physician–patient relationship Traditionally, the cornerstone of U.S. health care. Begins when the patient requests treatment and the physician agrees to render the treatment. Exists as an express or implied contract.

Physician self-referral prohibitions Laws that prohibit physicians from referring patients to services when the physician possesses a financial interest in or will receive payment in return for the referral.

Placebos Medically inert substances that are used as a control in testing the effectiveness of another medicated substance.

Plaintiff A person who brings a lawsuit.

Plain view doctrine A policy that allows police to seize contraband or evidence that is openly visible in an area where the police are authorized to be.

Pleadings Formal statements by the parties setting forth their claims or defenses (examples: a complaint, a cross-complaint, an answer, a counterclaim). The various kinds of pleadings in civil cases, and the rules governing them, are set forth in detail in the Federal Rules of Civil Procedure and, with respect to pleading in state courts, by the rules of civil procedure of several states. These rules of procedure abolished common law pleading.

Preemption A doctrine adopted by the U.S. Supreme Court that certain matters are of such a national, as opposed to local, character that federal laws preempt or take precedence over state laws. As such, a state law inconsistent with that of the federal law will be held invalid.

Prenatal surgery Surgery conducted upon the fetus prior to birth.

Prenatal testing The tests performed after conception but before birth that are designed to detect fetal abnormalities.

Pretrial conference A stage in a lawsuit prior to trial in which the status and issues of the case are discussed between the parties and the judge on a formal basis.

Privacy The right to be left alone or the right to control personal information. The patient's right to privacy is the underpinning to legal protections for patient-specific health information.

Privacy statutes Laws that generally correspond with the principles found in the federal Privacy Act: a presumption of confidentiality that may be rebutted with evidence of patient authorization to disclose information.

Private law A law that regulates conflicts between private parties (examples: contract law, tort law).

Privilege A concept protecting the statements made by persons within a specific relationship, such as attorney–client, from forced disclosure.

Probable cause A belief based on specific facts that a crime has been or is about to be committed.

Procedural law That portion of law that focuses on the steps through which a case passes. Criminal procedural law ranges from the initial investigation of a crime through trial, sentencing, and the eventual release of the criminal offender.

Production of documents and things A discovery device that permits one side of a lawsuit to inspect and copy documents and things that are not already in that side's physical possession.

Professional disclosure standard A standard used in the negligence context to determine liability. It is measured according to the level of information a reasonable health care provider would disclose under the same or similar circumstances.

Professional Standards Review Organizations (PSROs) Groups tasked with monitoring the appropriateness and quality of outcomes in health care facilities.

Proper documentation Timely and complete, meaning that all entries in the record are authored and authenticated and reflect the total care actually rendered to the patient.

Protected health information (PHI) Individually identifiable health information that is transmitted by electronic media, maintained in electronic medium, or transmitted or maintained in any other form or medium.

Psychiatric advance directive A legal document expressing a person's preference for future mental health treatment, which may include appointment of another person to interpret those preferences during a crisis.

Psychotherapy notes Notes recorded by a health care provider who is a mental health professional documenting or analyzing the contents of conversation during a private counseling session or group, joint, or family counseling session.

Public health threat A wide variety of health care problems that potentially endanger the public health and must be reported to a public health agency. Common public health threats include communicable diseases, child abuse, fetal deaths, and cancer.

Public law The body of rules and principles governing the rights and duties between government and a private party, or between two parts or agencies of government. It defines appropriate behavior between citizens, organizations, and government. Examples include criminal law, constitutional law, substantive law, and procedural law.

Punitive damages Those damages awarded above and beyond actual damages, often in instances where there is proof of outrageous, malicious, or intentional conduct; sometimes referred to as exemplary damages.

Q

Qualifications The required education, degrees, certificates, and professional licenses along with the knowledge, skills, and ability to perform the essential functions of the job.

Quality management An improvement technique that examines patterns of activity to define optimum performance and determine how to achieve that performance. It is a clinical function that is process oriented and focuses on the improvement of patient care.

Quid pro quo A Latin phrase meaning "this for that"; a type of sexual harassment.

Qui tam actions Lawsuits that allow private plaintiffs to sue on behalf of the U.S. government and receive a portion of the recovered funds if successful.

R

Reasonable accommodation Any change in the work environment or in the manner in which things are customarily done that enables a qualified person with a disability to have equal employment opportunities.

Reasonable cause An act or omission in which a covered entity or business associate knew, or by exercising reasonable diligence would have known, that the act or omission violated an administrative simplification provision, but in which the covered entity or business associate did not act with willful neglect.

Reasonable diligence The business care and prudence expected from a person seeking to satisfy a legal requirement under similar circumstances.

Reasonable fees A fee charged by the health care provider for the reproduction of the medical record. Individual facilities have policies determining what a reasonable fee should be. The amount of the fee is a controversial national issue.

Reasonable patient standard A standard used in the negligence context to determine liability. It is measured as the level of care that would be exercised by a reasonably prudent person under the same or similar circumstances.

Record destruction policy The general principles determining the length of time medical records must be maintained before being destroyed. The length of time is determined by state statutes and state and federal regulations.

Record retention policy The general principles determining the length of time medical records must be maintained by the health care provider. The length of time is influenced by the needs of continuing patient care, education, research, and the law, to name a few.

Record retention schedule A document that details what data will be retained, the retention period, and the manner in which the data will be stored.

Regular employee One who has a continuing relationship with an employer; sometimes referred to as a common law employee.

Relators The technical term used to describe the private plaintiffs who bring qui tam actions.

Release of information The written consent form that permits the dissemination of confidential health information to third parties. The components of a valid release of information are determined by state law and federal and state regulation.

Remedy The means by which a right is enforced, an injury is redressed, and relief is obtained. Examples: damages; an injunction. (1) To redress; to make right; to correct; to rectify. (2) To compensate; to indemnify; to make whole.

Remittitur A reduction by the judge of the amount of a verdict because of the excessiveness of the award.

Request for admission A discovery device involving written questions submitted to another party or witness designed to obtain an admission of certain facts.

Res ipsa loquitur Means "the thing speaks for itself." Used only when a plaintiff cannot prove negligence with the direct evidence available to him or her.

Res judicata Means "the thing [i.e., the matter] has been adjudicated"; the thing has been decided. The principle that a final judgment rendered on the merits by a court of competent jurisdiction is conclusive of the rights of the parties and is an absolute bar in other actions based on the same claim, demand, or cause of action.

Respondeat superior Means "let the master respond." The doctrine under which liability is imposed on an employer for the acts of its employees committed in the course and scope of their employment.

Reversed and remanded An expression used in appellate court opinions to indicate that the court has reversed the judgment of the trial court and that the case has been returned to the trial court for a new trial.

Rights The concept of a just claim or entitlement, whether based on law, ethics, or morality, that others are obliged to respect.

Risk The estimate of probability of loss from a given event upon the operational or financial performance of an organization.

Risk assessment An analysis of security practices that identifies the way protected health information in an electronic format is accessed and any potential vulnerabilities of that information.

Risk management A nonclinical function that focuses on how to reduce medical, financial, and legal risk to an organization. It is a management function that is outcome oriented.

Risk prevention techniques Policies and procedures that serve to protect the integrity and confidentiality of the data at issue. These policies and procedures merge physical and personnel security concepts and apply to the computer system and the personnel who use it.

Root-cause analysis An activity used to identify the cause of an event, including a clinical as well as an administrative review.

Rules The principles established by authorities that prescribe or direct certain action or forbearance from action.

S

Salary A rate of pay given on a weekly, monthly, or yearly schedule.

Satisfying the judgment A method used by the winning party in a lawsuit to collect the amount of judgment awarded (in cases involving money or property).

Security The means to regulate access to, and ensure preservation of, data.

Sentinel event An unexpected occurrence involving death or serious physical or psychological injury, or other risks thereof; serious injury includes loss of limb or limb function.

Separation of powers The division of powers between the three distinct branches of government— legislative, executive, and judicial— and the system of checks and balances that supports that division.

Serious health condition Any injury, illness, impairment, or physical or mental condition requiring either inpatient care at a hospital, hospice, or residential medical care facility or continuing treatment by a health care provider.

Service of process A stage in a lawsuit involving the delivery of the summons and complaint.

Sexual harassment The unwelcome sexual advances, requests for sexual favors, and verbal or physical conduct of a sexual nature made in return for job benefits, promotions, or continued employment.

Show cause order A court decree directing a person or organization to appear in court and explain why the court should not take a proposed action. If the person or organization fails to appear or sufficiently persuade the court to take no action, the court will take the action originally proposed.

Slander Defamation expressed by oral expressions or transitory gestures made to a third party.

Specialized patient records Health records of patients undergoing treatment for certain illnesses, such as substance abuse or mental illness, or in nonacute care settings, such as the patient's home. These records are subject to different legal requirements from those in an acute care setting.

Spoliation The wrongful destruction or material alteration of evidence or the failure to preserve property or data for another's use as evidence when litigation is pending or reasonably foreseeable.

Standard of care The level of care a reasonably prudent professional would have rendered in the same or similar circumstances.

Stare decisis Means "standing by the decision." *Stare decisis* is the doctrine that judicial decisions stand as precedent for cases arising in the future. It is a fundamental policy of our law that, except in unusual circumstances, a court's determination on a point of law will be followed by courts of the same or lower rank in later cases presenting the same legal issue, even though different parties are involved and many years have elapsed.

Statutes Laws written by federal and state legislatures. They become effective upon signature of the president (federal) or governor (state).

Statutes of limitations Federal and state laws prescribing the maximum period of time during which various types of civil actions and criminal prosecutions can be brought after the occurrence of the injury or offense.

Statutory employee One who has been designated by specific laws as subject to the tax-withholding requirements imposed upon employers but who might not otherwise be considered an employee.

Stem cell research The careful, systematic study and investigation of a special kind of cell not committed to conduct a specific function that has the capability to renew itself and differentiate into specialized cells.

Sterilization The actions taken to make an individual incapable of reproducing, whether by removing the reproductive organs or by preventing them from functioning effectively.

Subject matter jurisdiction The authority of a court over the questions at issue in a lawsuit.

Subpoena A command in the form of written process requiring a witness to come to court to testify; short for *subpoena ad testificandum.*

Subpoena ad testificandum *Ad testificandum* means "testify under penalty." A subpoena ad testificandum is a subpoena to testify.

Subpoena duces tecum *Duces tecum* means "bring with you under penalty." A subpoena duces tecum is a written command requiring a witness to come to court to testify and at that time to produce for use as evidence the papers, documents, books, or records listed in the subpoena. It is often used in the context of health information management to command the custodian of the records to produce a particular record at trial or deposition and provide testimony to the authenticity of the record produced.

Substantially equal Jobs or work performed under similar working conditions and requiring equal skill, effort, and responsibility.

Substantive law That portion of law that creates, defines, and regulates rights and duties. Criminal substantive law defines specific offenses, the general principles of liability, and the specific punishment.

Substituted consent The legal doctrine that allows an authorized person to consent to or forgo treatment on the patient's behalf when the patient is not legally competent to provide consent.

Summons (1) In a civil case, the process by which an action is commenced and the defendant is brought within the jurisdiction of the court. (2) In a criminal case involving a petty offense or infraction, process issued for the purpose of compelling the defendant to appear in court. In such a case, a summons is used as an alternative to arrest.

Surrogate mother One who agrees to bear a child conceived through artificial means and relinquishes it upon its birth to others for rearing.

T

Tacit consent The patient's consent to receive diagnostic or therapeutic treatment or procedures without expressing verbal or written action by the patient; often existing in situations in which a patient voluntarily submits to a procedure with apparent knowledge of that procedure and the procedure presents slight or no apparent risk, such as taking the patient's pulse or temperature.

Technical safeguards A set of standards under the HIPAA Security Rule designed to help covered entities employ technological solutions to secure electronic protected health information (ePHI).

Telemedicine The delivery of health care services over a distance with the use of interactive telecommunications and computer technology.

Text messaging Short electronic messages sent over a cellular network from one cell phone to another or by fixed or portable devices over a telephone network.

Tort A wrong involving a breach of duty and resulting in an injury to the person or property of another. A tort is distinguished from a breach of contract in that a tort is a violation of a duty established by law, whereas a breach of contract results from a failure to meet an obligation created by the agreement of the parties. Examples of activities considered a tort include medical malpractice, defamation, and invasion of privacy.

Tort law The rights and duties that exist between parties who are independent of a contract. When one party claims that the wrongful conduct of the other party has caused harm, the aggrieved party may seek compensation.

Treatment program Entities whose sole purpose is to provide alcohol or drug abuse diagnosis and treatment.

Trial A hearing or determination by a court of the issues existing between parties to an action; an examination by a court of competent jurisdiction, according to the law of the land, of the facts or law at issue in either a civil case or a criminal prosecution, for the purpose of adjudicating the matters in controversy.

Trustworthiness requirements One of the requirements of the business record exception to the hearsay rule. It must be established through testimony of the health information manager. To assist in establishing trustworthiness, the manager must possess knowledge of internal policies and procedures governing access to the medical record and quality control techniques, such as approved methods to make corrections to and use abbreviations in the record.

U

Unbundling Submitting separate bills for each component of a procedure instead of using the proper procedural code for the entire procedure, resulting in a higher reimbursement rate to the health care provider.

Undue hardship A specific accommodation that creates significant difficulty or expense for the employer.

Unemployment insurance A program designed to provide regular income to those who have lost their jobs.

Upcoding Submitting a bill for a higher level of reimbursement than actually rendered in order to receive a higher reimbursement.

Utilitarianism The theory that proposes that everyone, including persons, organizations, and society in general, should make choices that promote the greatest balance of good over harm for everyone; sometimes referred to as consequentialism.

Utilization coordinators Those persons with responsibility for managing the utilization review process and coordinating the patient's care with physicians, nurses, and other allied health professionals.

Utilization management A combination of planned functions directed to patients in a health care facility or setting that includes prudent use of resources, appropriate treatment management, and early comprehensive discharge planning for continuation of care.

Utilization review The clinical review of the appropriateness of admission and planned use of resources that can be and often is initiated prior to admission and conducted at specific time frames as defined in an organization's utilization review plan.

V

Values The concepts that give meaning to an individual's life and serve as the framework for decision making.

Veracity Habitual truthfulness and honesty; the opposite of the practice of intentionally deceiving or misleading.

Verdict The final decision of a jury concerning questions of fact submitted to it by the court for determination in the trial of a case.

Vicarious liability A doctrine that makes a health care organization responsible for the negligent acts of its employees committed within the course and scope of their employment. Also known as *respondeat superior.*

Vital records Those records concerned with vital events, such as births, deaths, marriages, divorces, abortions, and late fetal deaths.

Voluntary testing Testing with patient consent. Voluntary testing for HIV encompasses three areas: consent for testing, delivery of pretest information, and disclosure of test results.

W

Wages An hourly rate of pay.

Warrant A court's prior permission for the police to search and seize.

Whistle-blower Generally, a current or former employee of a health care provider or organization who has learned of fraud and abuse and wishes to expose the activity.

Willful neglect The conscious, intentional failure or reckless indifference to the obligation to comply with the administrative simplification provisions.

Withdrawing treatment The decision of the patient, his or her family, or his or her legal guardian to discontinue activities or remove forms of patient care.

Withholding treatment The decision of the patient, his or her family, or his or her legal guardian to discontinue activities or remove forms of patient care.

Words of authority Verbs found in statutes, ordinances, rules, and regulations that set forth duties, rights, prohibitions, and responsibilities under law.

Workers' compensation A program designed to replace income and provide medical expenses to employees who are injured, become ill, or die as a result of their jobs.

Workplace barrier Any workplace obstacle, whether physical or procedural, that prevents an employee from performing the duties of the job, whether those duties are considered essential or marginal.

Work–product privilege The materials prepared in anticipation of litigation that may be shielded from discovery; sometimes referred to as the work-product doctrine.

Writ of execution A written document that orders the sheriff or other local official to take property of the losing party of a lawsuit and sell it to satisfy the judgment.

X

Xenografts Transplants involving animal tissue, cells, or organs into human bodies; sometimes referred to as heterografts.

INDEX

www.ingramcontent.com/pod-product-compliance
Lightning Source LLC
Chambersburg PA
CBHW080506140525
26586CB00004B/19